Ring of Fire

Ring of Fire

An Encyclopedia of the Pacific Rim's Earthquakes, Tsunamis, and Volcanoes

Bethany D. Rinard Hinga

 ABC-CLIO

Santa Barbara, California • Denver, Colorado • Oxford, England

The following entries in this volume were written by Angus M. Gunn: Chilean Earthquake and Tsunami (1960); Kobe Earthquake, Japan (1995); Mexico City Earthquake, Mexico (1985); Sanriku Earthquake and Tsunami, Japan (1896).

Library of Congress Cataloging-in-Publication Data
Rinard Hinga, Bethany D.
   Ring of fire : an encyclopedia of the Pacific Rim's earthquakes, tsunamis, and volcanoes / Bethany D. Rinard Hinga.
      pages cm
   Includes bibliographical references and index.
ISBN 978-1-61069-296-0 (alk. paper)–ISBN 978-1-61069-297-7 (ebook)
1. Earthquakes–Pacific Area–Encyclopedias.   2. Volcanoes–Pacific Area–Encyclopedias.
3. Tsunamis–Pacific Area–Encyclopedias.   I. Title.   II. Title: Encyclopedia of the Pacific Rim's earthquakes, tsunamis, and volcanoes.
QE537.5.R56 2015
551.209182'303–dc23   2014037773

ISBN: 978-1-61069-296-0
EISBN: 978-1-61069-297-7

19 18 17 16 15   1 2 3 4 5

This book is also available on the World Wide Web as an eBook.
Visit www.abc-clio.com for details.

ABC-CLIO, LLC
130 Cremona Drive, P.O. Box 1911
Santa Barbara, California 93116-1911

This book is printed on acid-free paper ∞
Manufactured in the United States of America

Contents

List of Entries

List of Entries by Earthquake, Tsunami, and Volcano

Earthquake-Related Entries

Anchorage Earthquake (also known as the Prince William Sound Earthquake), Alaska, United States (1964)

Arica Earthquake and Tsunami, Chile (1868)

Cascadia Subduction Zone

Chilean Earthquake and Tsunami (1960)

Chimbote Earthquake, Peru (1970)

Collision Zone

Concepción Earthquake, Chile (1835)

Divergent Boundary

Earthquake

Earthquake Hazards

Earthquake Magnitude

Earthquake Prediction

Elastic Rebound Theory

Great Kanto Earthquake, Japan (1923)

Guatemala Earthquake (1976)

Gutenberg, Beno

Indian Ocean Earthquake and Tsunami (2004)

Jiji Earthquake, Taiwan (1999)

Kalapana Earthquake, Hawaii, United States (1975)

Kobe Earthquake, Japan (1995)

Lehmann, Inge

Loma Prieta Earthquake, California, United States (1989)

Mexico City Earthquake, Mexico (1985)

Mitigation

Modified Mercalli Intensity Scale

New Zealand Earthquake (2011)

Northridge Earthquake, California, United States (1994)

Okushiri Island Earthquake and Tsunami, Japan (1993)

Orphan Tsunami

Papua New Guinea Earthquake and Tsunami (1998)

Pisco Earthquake (2007)

Plate Tectonics

Richter, Charles

San Andreas Fault

San Francisco Earthquake, California, United States (1906)

Sanriku Earthquake and Tsunami, Japan (1896)

Seiche

Seismology

Seismometer

Sendai Earthquake and Tsunami, Japan (2011)

Subduction Zone

Tangshan Earthquake, China (1976)

Transform Boundary

Tsunami

Tsunami Warning Centers

Unimak Island Earthquake and Tsunami, Alaska, United States (1946)

Volcanoes and Earthquakes, Mythology of

Preface

The Pacific Rim is one of the most geologically active regions of the planet. Here, it is possible to observe the raw power of planet Earth through unexpected and often violent events, such as volcanic eruptions, earthquakes, and tsunamis. This book examines the specific interactions of tectonic plates in and around the Pacific Ocean. The region of interest extends from the west coasts of North America and South America to the Aleutian Islands of Alaska. It extends from the Aleutian Islands southward through the Kamchatka Peninsula of Russia; through the Kuril Islands, Japan, and the Philippines; to Indonesia and southward to New Zealand. The Pacific Rim includes incredibly diverse geographic regions created by immense tectonic forces.

This encyclopedia explores the vast Pacific region of the earth from historical, geographical, and geological perspectives. All entries pertain to some aspect of Pacific Rim volcanic, earthquake, or tsunami activity or the study of such events. It is thoroughly cross-referenced, which enables readers to further explore a topic simply by following suggestions about which other related entries might be of interest or provide further clarification on a subject.

The scope of this book is quite broad, ranging from the configuration of and interaction between the tectonic plates that comprise the Pacific region to descriptions of specific disastrous events—including features found on individual volcanoes. The book includes information about topics at both ends of this scale and from every point in between. I tried to tell important stories as was appropriate, rather than simply conveying facts. It has been my experience that often it is from the narrative that scholars learn most effectively.

I was approached in the spring of 2012 about writing this book. It has been an ever-present part of my life since that time—through two career changes, one cross-country move, and one new child. Through the experience of writing I have had a chance to relive some of my youth and many of my travels, as well as to learn more about distant lands I have yet to visit. I have been fascinated by the natural world, and specifically by volcanoes, since I was a child. When Mount St. Helens erupted in 1980, I was eight years old and living on a farm in central Iowa. I had family members who lived near Mount St. Helens. They sent me newspaper articles and photos, and brought me volcanic ash when they came to visit. From that time onward, I became obsessed by all things volcanic.

I entered college as the rare student—one who knew exactly what I wanted to do with my life . . . study volcanoes. I had some wonderful experiences as an undergraduate, when studying older volcanoes in Colorado and New Mexico. After graduation, I secured a coveted summer internship at the Hawaiian Volcano Observatory. Through the summer, I spent a great deal of time both in the laboratory and the field learning about Hawaiian volcanism by studying the ongoing eruption of the Kilauea volcano with my mentors, the first all-female Geology Group in the observatory's history. I was fortunate to reconnect with my friends at the Hawaiian Volcano Observatory when I began work on my dissertation a few years later. I worked with seismologist Dr. Paul Okubo, and used volcanic earthquakes within the western half of Kilauea to map its subsurface structure. To Dr. Okubo and the rest of the staff at the observatory who graciously assisted me in one major way or another as I learned the ins and outs of Hawaiian seismology and observatory databases, I will always be grateful.

I was fortunate to spend the first 17 years of my career in the classroom at Tarleton State University. I taught courses in geology—including natural disasters—to a generation of students. Most of this book, however, was written while I was employed at the University of Nebraska at Kearney. I wish to thank Dr. Kenya Taylor for her personal example, showing that it is possible—and, in fact, enjoyable—to engage in research even after leaving the classroom. Dr. Taylor encouraged me to keep my interests in geology alive as I moved from teaching in my academic field to an administrative role in higher education. This book serves as my bridge from one world to the other. I hope it serves as a bridge for you, as well, to an understanding of natural events that all too often turn into natural disasters.

Introduction

Geologists often speak of the earth as a dynamic planet—a world that constantly is in a state of dramatic change. Across much of the earth, however, it is difficult to see direct evidence of these rapid changes because most geologic processes are achingly slow. Even in the best of circumstances, it takes hundreds to thousands of years for sediment to be buried and turned into rock. Rocks are weathered into sand, but the weathering process can take thousands or even millions of years. Mountains can rise from the plains, but this often takes tens of millions of years. Why then is Earth considered such a dynamic planet? The answer lies in the relentless movement of the earth's tectonic plates.

The earth's plates are in constant motion because of the circulation of the upper mantle beneath them. At places where plates come into contact with each other, the earth changes rapidly and dramatically. It is at these places that earthquakes disrupt people's daily lives. It is at these places that volcanoes destroy landscapes, only to rebuild them in a new image. It is along shorelines with such plate contact that tsunamis can sweep in and carry away communities in a tragic few minutes. In very few places are these types of events seen more frequently than in the region called the "Ring of Fire."

The Ring of Fire is a name given most deservedly to the Pacific Rim. The Ring of Fire extends from New Zealand clockwise in an almost circular arc through the Tonga and Kermadec Arcs; then westward to Indonesia; northward through the Philippines, Japan, and the Kamchatka Peninsula of Russia; eastward through the Aleutian Islands; and then southward along the western coasts of North America and South America. The Ring of Fire also contains active regions within its interior, including the Galapagos Islands and Hawaiian Islands.

Throughout this book there are many recurring themes, including hazard (the likelihood that a natural event will occur) and risk (the ways that a population might be adversely affected by that event). The book includes references to the process of scientific discovery and (it is hoped) will provide an understanding of just how recently science became aware of the full range of possibilities within events such as volcanic eruptions. The strongest theme presented herein is plate tectonics. Without the tectonic setting found around the rim of the Pacific, there would be no Ring of Fire. Plate tectonics cause the dramatic events covered in this text . . . volcanoes, earthquakes, and tsunamis, and related events such as landslides and wildfires.

The specific tectonic setting that causes most events is called a subduction zone. A subduction zone is a type of plate boundary found where two plates meet and are moving toward each other. At these locations, one plate is forced downward and underneath another. Although it happens slowly—usually no faster than an inch or two per year—subduction is an extremely violent process. Beneath the solid tectonic plates found at the earth's surface is the upper mantle, which is another solid layer of the earth. One solid is being thrust downward into another solid material, resulting in a great deal of friction causing the plates to "stick" to each other. When strain builds to a critical level within the rocks at the plate boundary, the rocks break and slip, causing an earthquake.

The most violent earthquakes on the planet occur in subduction zones. In the history of recorded earthquakes, no greater earthquakes have occurred than those that happen within the Ring of Fire. The most significant earthquake ever recorded occurred just off the coast of Chile in 1960. It was a magnitude 9.5 earthquake that shook the earth for several minutes near the earthquake's epicenter, and caused the entire planet to vibrate for days afterward. The earthquake generated a tsunami that crossed the Pacific Ocean. It caused deaths in Hawaii and significant damage in Japan.

Another effect of subduction is the heating of the plate that has been thrust into the mantle. Although the upper mantle is not quite hot enough to melt the subducted plate at the types of pressures found at that depth in the earth, it certainly is hot enough to drive water from the subducted slab into the surrounding mantle. This process has an odd effect on the solid mantle above this plate: It lowers its melting temperature. The reduced melting temperature enables a small percentage of the mantle rock in that region to melt.

Molten rock is less dense than the surrounding solid rock, thus the molten rock rises. It can rise all the way to the surface where it feeds volcanic eruptions. Anywhere a subduction zone is found, there is a chain of volcanoes that marks the location in the mantle where melting is occurring. Entire island nations have been formed from hardened molten rock. One of the largest and most geographically diverse island nations on Earth is Indonesia. All of the islands within Indonesia were formed by a subduction zone. Whether the island was formed as a volcano rose from the sea or by immense forces pushing the sea floor up above sea level, tectonic forces birthed these islands. The same is true of Japan, the Philippines, and the Aleutian Islands.

Volcanoes formed at subduction zone sites are a type called a "composite volcano." This type of volcano often is tall and steep-sided, and produces great volumes of lava, volcanic ash, and other debris. The volcanic eruptions can be extremely violent, sending plumes of volcanic ash tens of thousands of feet in the air, turning daylight into instant darkness—sometimes for days at a time. Eruptions can issue forth pyroclastic flows—fast-moving torrents of hot ash and deadly gases—and send pieces of rock tumbling downhill at speeds approaching 100 miles per hour. Such an eruption incinerates, topples, or otherwise destroys everything in its path. If enough volcanic ash and microscopic droplets of sulfuric acid are sent high enough into the atmosphere, then a single eruption has the ability to cool the atmosphere and change weather patterns for more than a year.

The 1815 eruption of Tambora in Indonesia resulted in the year from 1815 to 1816 being dubbed "the year without a summer" in the northeastern United States and Europe. Because of the eruption, temperatures in those regions never reached typical summertime levels, and in some places snow fell in June. Crops failed. Skies glowed an eerie red. It even is suggested that the abysmal weather conditions inspired a young Mary Shelley—sequestered with friends in a castle that year—to write her masterpiece, *Frankenstein*. Although it is difficult to believe that a single eruption of a single volcano can have such far-reaching consequences, it is something that has happened time and again within the Ring of Fire.

Within the center of the Ring of Fire, in the vast blue waters of the Pacific, are two island chains that owe their existence to tectonic forces that have nothing to do with plate boundaries, but rather to a hot spot. A "hot spot" is an area of the mantle that, for reasons not yet fully understood by scientists, is unusually hot. Heat rises from as deep in the earth as (at least) the top of the lower mantle (and possibly deeper) to the upper mantle. The excess heat in the upper mantle causes melting to occur. Volcanoes form above the hot spot and then erupt frequently. Hot spots remain fixed in place, rooted to the location deep in the earth where they originate. Over time the plate above a hot spot moves. At the surface, a chain of volcanoes often is formed over a hot spot. This can be demonstrated with a simple thought experiment. Imagine a candle sitting stationary on a table. This represents a hot spot. If you take a piece of paper—representing a tectonic plate—and pass it slowly above the candle, you will find a scorched area in the paper that traces a line. That line represents a chain of volcanoes formed by the hot spot. The orientation of the line on the paper indicates the direction of movement of the paper as it was passed over the candle, and represents the direction of movement of the plate.

The Hawaiian Islands are an excellent example of a volcanic mountain chain created by a hot spot. The Hawaiian Islands have been intensely studied by geologists for more than 100 years. The volcanoes Kilauea and Mauna Loa make excellent natural laboratories for studying volcanism because they erupt frequently. These volcanoes also are much more approachable than those found at subduction zones, so it is relatively easy to design repeatable experiments to gather valuable longitudinal data sets. The Hawaiian hot spot has been active for at least 80 million years. This can be determined because it is possible to trace a single long chain of volcanoes from the current location of the hot spot—just off the southeast coast of the island of Hawaii—all the way north and west to the Aleutian Islands, where the northernmost underwater mountain in the chain (called a "seamount") is poised to be subducted beneath the Aleutians. This mountain chain is known as the Hawaii-Emperor Seamount Chain, and is composed of thousands of volcanoes. In its geology, the chain holds a history of the movement of the Pacific Plate. Measuring a distance between two islands in the chain that are of known age enables researchers to determine how fast the Pacific Plate moved during the time interval measured. The seamount chain makes a sharp bend in the north-central Pacific, which can be unequivocally tied to a change in the direction of movement of the Pacific Plate. Without seamounts, a great deal of information about the Pacific Plate and its history would remain unknown.

The Pacific Rim is one of the earth's most geographically diverse and geologically dynamic areas. Throughout this book readers will discover many places that tell the fascinating story of the Ring of Fire. I hope you enjoy reading about these places and these events as much as I enjoyed writing about them.

Timeline of Disasters in the Pacific Rim Region in the Modern Era

1815:	Tambora Eruption, Indonesia	Largest eruption of Nineteenth Century. The climate cooled by more than a degree. Event caused "year without a summer" in Europe and northern North America.
1835:	Concepción Earthquake, Chile	Witnessed by Charles Darwin. Earthquake and resulting tsunami caused considerable damage in Concepción, Chile.
1868:	Arica Earthquake and Tsunami, Chile	Death toll of 25,000 due to earthquake and tsunami.
1883:	Krakatau Eruption (also known as "Krakatou" Eruption), Indonesia	Eruption produced ash clouds that darkened the skies for two days. Pyroclastic flows reached shorelines of Java and Sumatra. Caldera collapse generated a tsunami that was responsible for most of the 36,000 deaths associated with the eruption.
1896:	Sanriku Earthquake and Tsunami, Japan	More than 26,000 people died. The tsunami coincided with high tide; wave reached up to 125 feet (38 meters) high. The event occurred when a fishing fleet was at sea. The fishermen returned to discover their homes destroyed and their families gone.
1906:	San Francisco Earthquake, California, United States	Estimated to be a magnitude 8 earthquake and caused moderate damage. The resulting fire destroyed much of San Francisco. As many as 4,000 people were killed.
1912:	Katmai Eruption, Alaska, United States	This was the greatest eruption of the Twentieth Century, and occurred in a remote area of Alaska. Pyroclastic flows created the "Valley of Ten Thousand Smokes."
1923:	Great Kanto Earthquake, Japan	This earthquake destroyed much of the Tokyo-Yokohama metropolitan area. Approximately 143,000 people were killed, and 71% of Tokyo residents and 85% of Yokohama residents lost their homes.

1946:	Unimak Island Earthquake and Tsunami, Alaska, United States	The magnitude 8.1 earthquake generated a Pacific-wide tsunami. At Unimak Island, wave height was estimated to be more than 100 feet (30 meters). Scotch Cap Lighthouse on Unimak Island was destroyed and 159 deaths occurred in the Hawaiian Islands, where waves reached more than 30 feet (9 meters) in height. This disaster prompted formation of the Pacific Tsunami Warning System.
1951:	Lamington, Mount, Eruption, Papua New Guinea	Pyroclastic flows killed more than 3,000 people.
1960:	Chilean Earthquake and Tsunami	The greatest earthquake recorded to date, the magnitude 9.5 earthquake killed 5,000 people and generated a Pacific-wide tsunami. Waves were up to 75 feet (23 meters) high along the Chilean coast and 30 feet (9 meters) high in Hawaii. There were 61 tsunami deaths in Hilo, Hawaii, alone.
1964:	Anchorage Earthquake, Alaska	Second largest earthquake of the Twentieth Century (a magnitude 9.2), occurred in 1964 on Good Friday. The earthquake triggered landslides, including one that destroyed the Turnagain Heights neighborhood near Anchorage. A local tsunami was generated at Prince William Sound. Of 125 deaths attributed to the earthquake, 110 died as a result of the tsunami.
1970:	Chimbote Earthquake, Peru	Until the 2010 Haiti earthquake, the 1970 Chimbote earthquake was the deadliest disaster in the western hemisphere. In 2010, 76,000 people lost their lives in the magnitude 7.9 earthquake and the resulting landslides occurring near the base of the Andes.
1975:	Kalapana Earthquake, Hawaii, United States	The 1975 magnitude 7.2 earthquake damaged many buildings on the island of Hawaii. A local tsunami with wave heights up to 46.6 feet (14 meters) high caused two deaths and caused additional damage.
1976:	Guatemala Earthquake	The magnitude 7.5 earthquake occurred on the boundary between the Caribbean and the North American plates and caused 23,700 deaths.
1976:	Tangshan Earthquake, China	Deadliest earthquake of the Twentieth Century, it killed more than 200,000 people. Some estimates place death toll at more than 500,000. Most deaths were due to building collapses.
1980:	St. Helens, Mount, Eruption, Washington, United States	A catastrophic eruption triggered by a magnitude 5.0 earthquake and a massive landslide that decapitated the volcano. Fifty-seven people were killed. The volcano now has a 1.8-mile wide horseshoe-shaped crater. Later eruptions created a large lava dome in the crater.

1982:   El Chichón Volcano, Mexico   A large eruption that killed about 2,000 people and sent greater than expected amounts of sulfur dioxide aerosols into the atmosphere. The earth's atmosphere cooled by an average of 0.72° F (.04° C) for one year.

1985:   Mexico City Earthquake, Mexico   The epicenter of this earthquake was some distance from Mexico City, but silt and clay beneath the city amplified seismic waves and caused liquefaction. More than 400 buildings collapsed, including hospitals. The death toll was at least 9,500 people.

1985:   Nevado del Ruiz, Colombia   A relatively small eruption that generated a lahar which swept down the Lagunillas River and overtook the city of Armero. More than 22,000 people died.

1989:   Loma Prieta Earthquake, California, United States   Most of 63 deaths were caused by the collapse of elevated roadways, including the Cypress Freeway, Embarcadero, and Bay Bridge. This earthquake also is well-known because it interrupted the 1989 World Series.

1991:   Pinatubo, Mount, Eruption, Philippines   The second largest eruption of the Twentieth Century. The incident is considered to be a successful case of forecasting a volcanic eruption. Tens of thousands of people were evacuated from the immediate area before the volcano erupted, keeping the death toll down to about 300 people. Global temperatures dropped 0.72° F (.04° C) from sulfur dioxide aerosols injected into the atmosphere from this eruption.

1991–1995:   Unzen Eruption, Japan   The Mount Unzen Volcano is known for lava domes. A dome-building eruption in 1991 generated pyroclastic flows that killed volcanologists Katia and Maurice Krafft and Harry Glicken, as well as the 40 journalists accompanying them. The Kraffts and Glicken were filming pyroclastic flows for a film about volcanic hazards targeting public officials and those at risk from volcanic eruptions.

1993:   Galeras Volcano, Colombia   The small eruption of Galeras occurred while a group of volcanologists was inside the crater. Nine people died and many were severely injured.

1993:   Okushiri Island Earthquake and Tsunami, Japan   The magnitude 7.8 earthquake generated a local tsunami that killed 198 people. Japanese officials rebuilt the devastated areas and built a tsunami wall for protection.

1994:	Northridge Earthquake, California, United States	The 1994 Northridge earthquake killed 57 people and injured 9,000. Twenty thousand people were left homeless. The earthquake occurred along a fault that previously was unknown.
1995:	Kobe Earthquake, Japan	The earthquake killed more than 5,400 people and left 300,000 people homeless. The event also is known as the "Great Hanshin Disaster."
1998:	Papua New Guinea Earthquake and Tsunami	A magnitude 7.0 earthquake caused an underwater landslide that generated a devastating local tsunami. The tsunami washed completely over small communities and killed approximately 3,000 people.
1999:	Jiji Earthquake, Taiwan	The Jiji earthquake caused the death of 2,416 people. Despite strictly enforced building codes, more than 100,000 buildings were damaged or destroyed because ground shaking exceeded the design code for buildings in Taiwan.
2004:	Indian Ocean Earthquake and Tsunami	A magnitude 9.0 earthquake off the coast of Sumatra triggered an ocean-wide tsunami that killed nearly 250,000 people in 12 countries. No tsunami warning system existed in the Indian Ocean region which contributed to the death toll.
2007:	Peru	An earthquake near Pisco killed more than 500 people and left thousands homeless for years. A local tsunami was generated and it had wave heights of up to 33 feet (10 meters).
2011:	New Zealand Earthquake	The earthquake near Christchurch, New Zealand, killed 185 people, most of whom died in the collapse of two multi-story office buildings in the city's business district.
2011:	Sendai Earthquake and Tsunami, Japan	A magnitude 9.0 earthquake occurring off the coast of Honshu generated a tsunami that killed more than 20,000 people. Tsunami damage to the Fukushima Daiichi nuclear power plant caused a partial meltdown. High levels of radioactivity were observed around the plant and in water leaking from the plant for years after the earthquake happened.
2014:	Mount Ontake Eruption, Japan	An eruption of Mount Ontake occurred while several hundred hikers were on its upper slopes. The eruption killed 57 people. An additional six people are missing and presumed dead.

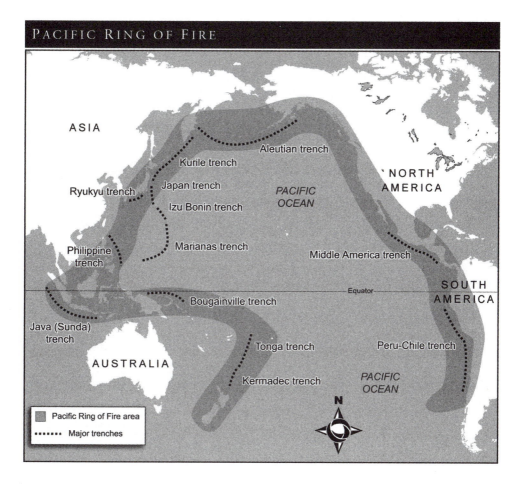

PACIFIC RING OF FIRE

ASIA

NORTH
AMERICA

Aleutian trench

Kurile trench

Japan trench

Ryukyu trench

Izu Bonin trench

PACIFIC
OCEAN

Philippine
trench

Marianas trench

Middle America trench

SOUTH
AMERICA

Equator

Bougainville trench

Java (Sunda)
trench

Tonga trench

Peru-Chile trench

AUSTRALIA

Kermadec trench

PACIFIC
OCEAN

N

Pacific Ring of Fire area

Major trenches

A

Aa

The term "aa" is used for active or cooled lava flows that have a rough, jagged surface. The top surface of this type of lava flow often is composed of sharp fist-sized rock rubble. A cross-section—or profile—of an aa flow reveals that the bottom of the flow also is composed of fist-sized rock rubble. Rubble on the flow bottom is created when pieces of aa tumble off the front of a moving lava flow and the lava then flows over it. When moving, an aa flow sounds like hundreds of glasses breaking because of the semi-molten lava breaking into pieces that then fall to the ground. Although the surface of an aa flow is distinctive, if the surface is scraped or worn away then the interior of the lava flow is no different than its counterpart, "pahoehoe." Both types of flow are composed of the rock basalt. The interior of both pahoehoe and aa flows tends to be dense, solid black rock.

Although made of the same rock, aa and pahoehoe are formed under slightly different circumstances. If erupted in a quiet, flowing eruption, most lava emerges as pahoehoe. In two circumstances, however, pahoehoe can change into aa. In the first case, the flowing lava at the surface vents most of its dissolved gases into the atmosphere as the flow moves downhill. As it loses its dissolved gases, the lava becomes more viscous, or pasty and sticky. At this point, it breaks into small, jagged pieces as it flows, thus becoming aa. In the second circumstance, lava flowing quickly down a steep hill can break into jagged pieces as it moves. This happens because basalt lava, though liquid, is very viscous. If forced to move too fast, then lava breaks rather than flows; fast-moving lava flows tend to become aa flows. Notably, pahoehoe can turn into aa, but aa cannot turn into pahoehoe.

A fast-moving aa flow commonly forms accretionary lava balls, which are large, nearly spherical accumulations of rock. Accretionary lava balls are formed in a manner similar to making large snowballs. A small piece of hardened lava is carried on top of a moving lava flow. As it tumbles around on top of the still-liquid lava, the small hardened piece gathers more lava and becomes larger; this continues for as long as the flow remains molten. A typical size for an accretionary lava ball is about one meter in diameter, but in some cases they can reach ten feet (more than three meters) in diameter.

Cooled, hardened aa flows are difficult to walk on because the flow surface is uneven, and because the surface easily can cut clothing and skin, and quickly wears out shoes or boots. "Aa" is a Hawaiian word that has been adopted in many languages as the scientific term for this form of lava. In the Hawaiian language, it is spelled "ʻaʻa."

See Also: Basalt; Pahoehoe.

Further Reading

U.S. Geological Survey. Volcano Hazards Program. (2012, July 26). *Lava, Lava Flows, Lava Lakes, Magma.* Retrieved from http://vulcan.wr.usgs.gov/Glossary
U.S. Geological Survey. Volcano Hazards Program. (2012, July 26). *Volcano hazards program photo glossary: Aa.* Retrieved from http://volcanoes.usgs.gov/images/pglossary/aa.php

Aleutian Islands

The name "Aleutian Islands" comes from the Aleut people who have inhabited the chain's eastern islands since before the end of the last ice age. "Aleutian" is derived from the Aleut word "allithuh," which means "community" or "host." The islands occupy the northernmost Pacific Ocean, and form a barrier between the Pacific Ocean and the Bering Sea to its north. The islands were formed as a result of subduction of the Pacific Plate beneath the North American Plate. The U.S. portion of the islands extends from just beyond the tip of the Alaska Peninsula at Unimak Island nearly 1,200 miles (1,900 kilometers) westward to Attu Island. The islands west of Attu Island belong to Russia. The Aleutian Islands largely are uninhabited, with just a few isolated fishing villages, lighthouse crews, U.S. military, U.S. National Park Service, U.S. Coast Guard, National Weather Service (United States), and U.S. Fish and Wildlife Service outposts. On and around these islands, weather is inhospitable, terrain is rugged, and seas are rough.

The islands have been the site of many violent earthquakes. Several of these earthquakes have caused deaths and damage near the epicenters. The earthquakes also have generated Pacific-wide tsunamis—caused the loss of life in the entire Pacific Rim. One example is the 1946 earthquake at Unimak Island, Alaska. This earthquake was felt strongly on Unimak and neighboring islands, but did not cause any severe damage. It generated a tsunami, however, that grew to enormous proportions at Unimak. The tsunami swept away the Scotch Cap Lighthouse—a structure that rose five stories high above its base, which was 40 feet (12 meters) above sea level. Five people were in the lighthouse when the tsunami hit, and all five were killed. The tsunami then sped southward. It caused 159 deaths in the Hawaiian Islands and 1 death in California, and damaged fishing boats in Chile.

Each island in the Aleutians was formed by volcanic eruptions, thus the entire chain is composed of active, dormant, and extinct volcanoes. Since the start of recording volcanic events, approximately 40 volcanoes within the Aleutians have been active. Most recently, Pavlof Volcano erupted in 2014. The Aleutian volcanoes do not pose a direct threat to any large population centers, but they are extremely hazardous to aircraft. For that reason the volcanoes are watched very closely via satellite for any activity that involves volcanic ash.

When jet engines encounter volcanic ash it clogs the engines and abrades the precisely machined aircraft parts—often resulting in engine failure. There have been multiple instances when airliners that have encountered volcanic ash clouds have experienced engine failure and fallen several thousand feet before pilots were able to restart the engines and land the planes safely. The Aleutians lie beneath one of the busiest air cargo corridors in the world—the flight path between Asia and the United States and Europe—therefore volcanic ash is monitored very carefully in the Aleutian Islands area.

See Also: Cleveland Volcano, Alaska, United States; Pavlof Volcano, Alaska, United States; Shishaldin, Volcano, Alaska, United States; Subduction Zone; Unimak Island Earthquake and Tsunami, Alaska, United States (1946).

Further Reading

The Aleuts. (1998). In *Red book of the peoples of the Russian Empire.* Retrieved from http://www.eki.ee/books/redbook/aleuts.shtml
USC Tsunami Research Group. (2014, June 9). *1946 Aleutian tsunami.* Retrieved from http://www.usc.edu/dept/tsunamis/alaska/1946/webpages/

Anchorage Earthquake (also known as the Prince William Sound Earthquake), Alaska, United States (1964)

At 5:36 p.m. local time on Good Friday, March 27, 1964, the area around Anchorage, Alaska, was shaken by one of the most powerful earthquakes in history. The earthquake's focus (the location where the earthquake begins) was reported to be 61.04°N, 147.73°W, with a depth of about 15 miles (25 kilometers). Its epicenter (the point on the earth's surface located directly above the focus of an earthquake) was a sparsely populated area at the northern extent of Prince William Sound in south-central Alaska. The aftershock zone revealed that the segment of fault that broke and moved during the earthquake—known as the rupture area—was approximately 500 miles (800 kilometers) long and 155 miles (250 kilometers) wide. The Anchorage earthquake occurred before plate tectonics theory was widely accepted. Although contemporary scientific reports do not name the Alaska-Aleutian subduction zone as the source of the Anchorage earthquake, individuals involved in the investigation gathered and reported data that lead to that unmistakable conclusion.

The Anchorage Earthquake was the second largest of the Twentieth Century, surpassed only by the Chilean earthquake of 1960. In a 1966 report published by the United States Geological Survey (Hansen et al., 1966) and a multi-volume report published by the United States Coast and Geodetic Survey (Wood et al., 1969), the surface wave magnitude (M_s) of the earthquake was reported to be 8.3 to 8.4. Surface wave magnitudes are extremely difficult to calculate for earthquakes with large rupture areas, however, such as the Anchorage Earthquake. In 1977, a new magnitude calculation referred to as "moment magnitude" (M*w*) was proposed for large earthquakes having fault rupture lengths of more than 62 miles (100 kilometers). As a result of this revolutionary study and new magnitude calculation, the magnitude of the Anchorage earthquake of 1964 was revised upward to 9.2, which is the magnitude officially recognized today.

The Anchorage earthquake was studied in great detail by geologists, seismologists, geographers, surveyors, oceanographers, and engineers using the best technology of the time. Thousands of individuals felt the earthquake, and many of them also recorded their experiences using still photography and video, on voice recordings, and on official questionnaires designed by scientists to determine the severity of ground shaking and damage throughout the affected area. Shaking from the earthquake was felt over a 700,000 square mile (1.8 million square kilometer) area that included most of Alaska and Canada's Yukon Territory, as well as parts of the Northwest Territories and British Columbia. Severe damage to buildings directly attributed to ground shaking was confined to about 80,000 square miles (207,000 square kilometers) of south-central Alaska in the communities of Anchorage, Valdez, Seward, Kodiak, Cordova, and smaller settlements nearby.

Structures destroyed by ground shaking included the control tower at the Anchorage Airport; buildings constructed with prefabricated concrete slabs, such as the J.C. Penney Building in downtown Anchorage; buildings having unreinforced masonry walls or veneers; and structures that did not have all elements of the building—from the foundation to the frame and the roof—tied together firmly. In general, tall buildings fared much worse than buildings having one to three stories.

The Anchorage earthquake also triggered landslides. A study of aerial photographs taken shortly after the earthquake indicate 1,958 avalanches and snow slides, 58 combined snow and rock slides, and 20 rock slides in the unpopulated mountains near the epicenter. Although most landslides happened in unpopulated areas, those that occurred in Anchorage and surrounding communities were enormously destructive. They were characterized by the opening of enormous ground cracks, and both lateral and vertical movement of soil and rocks. The result was the destruction of several homes and businesses, and the disruption of local infrastructure such as railways, streets, and utility lines.

Five major landslides occurred in the Anchorage metropolitan area. They were named for their locations: Fourth Avenue Slide; L Street Slide; First Avenue Slide; Government Hill Slide; and Turnagain Slide. The landslides varied widely in the volume of earth involved and damage sustained as a result of the landslide. The smallest landslide was the First Avenue Slide, which resulted in very little damage. The Fourth Avenue Slide occurred on relatively flat ground, but nonetheless caused several buildings on the north side of Fourth Avenue to collapse. The L Street Slide displaced railroad tracks and caused damage to apartment buildings, residences, and utility lines.

What Do I Do in an Earthquake?

For people who are unaccustomed to feeling the earth move, even a relatively small earthquake can be an unsettling experience. The largest earthquakes, however, leave almost everyone feeling scared and anxious. It's important to realize that there are things you can do that can help you stay as safe as possible. If you're outside and away from tall buildings, you're probably in the best spot possible. Stay put. If you're outside and near tall buildings, it is best to stand either in a doorway or far away from buildings so you don't get hurt by falling glass and other debris that might be falling from the buildings. If you're indoors, find a table or other object you can get under that will protect you from falling debris. Notice the theme here . . . you want to protect yourself from falling debris in any way you can. Most deaths in earthquakes come from being hit by falling debris, or from collapse of buildings. Building collapse is rare in the United States, thanks to enforced building codes in areas prone to earthquake activity. If you can protect yourself from falling debris whether you are inside or outside of a building, you should be in good shape.

The most severe and spectacular damage occurred as a result of the two remaining landslides, the Government Hill and Turnagain slides. The Government Hill Slide destroyed the Government Hill Elementary School as well as two homes and a railroad building. Dramatic photos of the school in ruins are among the iconic images from this earthquake. Though the damage from the earthquake was severe and there was loss of life, photos of the school underscored that had the earthquake happened on a different day, the results could have been much worse. The earthquake and related phenomena caused 125 deaths. The low death toll is a result of the earthquake striking in an area of low population density, the fact that it occurred on a holiday and after the business day was over, and because many buildings are engineered to withstand a large earthquake.

The Turnagain Slide produced some of the most remarkable landslide damage of this earthquake. The slide involved an area adjacent to Cook Inlet that measured nearly 8202 feet (2,500) meters along the shoreline, and extended 656 feet (200 meters) inland on the east end to about 1,312 feet (400 meters) inland on the west end. The Turnagain Heights Subdivision largely was destroyed by the Turnagain Slide. Seventy-five homes were lost; large cracks opened and blocks of earth subsided. Some portions of the shoreline were moved more than 656 feet (200 meters) seaward, and many houses in the subdivision moved as much as 574 feet (175 meters) laterally. Troughs that were 31- to 49-feet (10- to 15-meters) deep engulfed homes. The eyewitness account of Robert B. Atwood, editor and publisher of the "Anchorage Daily Times," illustrates the dramatic and confusing scene in the Turnagain Heights area.

I had just started to practice playing the trumpet when the earthquake occurred. In a few short moments it was obvious that this earthquake was no minor one: [T]he chandelier made from a ship's wheel swayed too much. Things were falling that had never fallen before. I headed for the door. At the door I saw walls weaving. On the driveway I turned and watched my house squirm and

> groan. Tall trees were falling in our yard. I moved to a spot where I thought it would be safe, but, as I moved, I saw cracks appear in the earth. Pieces of ground in jigsaw-puzzle shapes moved up and down, tilted at all angles. I tried to move away, but more appeared in every direction (Cloud & Scott, 1969).

Atwood's experience was far from uncommon within his neighborhood. As he continues, Atwood describes the scene he found as he scrambled toward safety.

> I noticed that my house was moving away from me, fast. As I started to climb the fence to my neighbor's yard, the fence disappeared. Trees were falling in crazy patterns. Deep chasms opened up. Table-top pieces of earth moved upward, standing like toadstools with great overhangs, some were turned at crazy angles. A chasm opened beneath me. I tumbled down. I was quickly on the verge of being buried. I ducked pieces of trees, fence posts, mailboxes, and other odds and ends. Then my neighbor's house collapsed and slid into the chasm. For a time it threatened to come down on top of me, but the earth was still moving, and the chasm opened to receive the house. When the earth movement stopped, I climbed to the top of the chasm. I found angular landscape in every direction (Cloud & Scott, 1969).

The entire subdivision and, in fact most, of Anchorage were underlain by a rock unit known as the Bootlegger Cove Clay. Clays are notorious for becoming slippery when they are shaken or become wet. During the earthquake, the unstable clay became an efficient sliding surface that caused the seemingly solid ground to disintegrate into the topsy-turvy landscape described by Mr. Atwood.

Dramatic changes also occurred along the shoreline of southern Alaska. The coastal area near the epicenter was studied in detail by Plafker (1965). Plafker used post-earthquake elevation of barnacles—which are known to live in a narrow vertical range—to determine the amount of vertical uplift that occurred during the earthquake. He found that the maximum amount of uplift on land was approximately 33 feet (10 meters) on Montague Island. Off the coast of Montague Island, vertical displacements of nearly 50 feet (15 meters) were measured. Inland the land subsided up to 7.5 feet (2.3 meters). A large block of southern Alaska was tilted toward the north. The uplifted area was roughly 35,000 square miles (90,000 square kilometers) in size, and the subsided area was approximately 42,500 square miles (110,000 square kilometers).

The most deadly hazard for this earthquake proved to be the tsunamis it generated. Tsunamis are generated when there is a significant vertical disturbance of the ocean floor. The two primary causes of this disturbance are earthquakes and landslides. Both of these events occurred in the case of the Anchorage earthquake. Of the 125 people who lost their lives as a result of this earthquake, 110 were victims of tsunamis and 15 lives were lost as a result of landslides and building collapse. Many of the casualties of the tsunamis in Alaska were victims of local waves generated by submarine landslides due to severe ground shaking.

Although the most damaging and deadly waves were confined to Alaska, tsunami waves were large enough in Oregon and California to cause 15 deaths and millions of dollars in damage. The tsunami was detected at tide stations as far away as Chile and the Philippines, though wave heights were less than one meter at these distant locations.

One of the first communities to be struck by the tsunami was Valdez, Alaska, approximately 47 miles (75 kilometers) east of the epicenter. Valdez first was struck by landslides during the earthquake. The landslides carried away docks and waterfront buildings, and generated a local tsunami that deposited driftwood at an elevation of more than 165 feet (50 meters) above low-tide level. Additional waves generated at the epicenter entered the area and destroyed the few remaining water-front buildings and the fishing fleet which was anchored there. Thirty-one people died in Valdez.

Seward, Alaska, located approximately 95 miles (150 kilometers) southwest of the epicenter, also was hit hard by landslides and tsunami. Like Valdez, a long, nar-row piece of land that housed waterfront buildings and dock facilities—including those use by the Standard Oil Company—slid into the water during the earthquake. Oil spilled from ruptured storage tanks and ignited. Waves spread the burning oil along the waterfront, igniting additional fires in debris and the remaining buildings. About 30 minutes later, waves generated at the epicenter struck the remains of Seward, destroying railroad and highway bridges and the docks belonging to the Alaska Railroad. Burning oil continued to set additional fires further inland. Twelve deaths were reported in Seward, and the economy of the area was nearly destroyed.

Whittier, Alaska, suffered much the same fate as Seward. Landslides occurred during the earthquake, and witnesses reported that three waves struck the town. One wave reached a height of 115 feet (35 meters). Among the structures destroyed were numerous docks, two saw mills, and the Union Oil Company tank farm. As in Seward, a fire began at the oil company facility and caused additional damage. Thirteen deaths occurred at Whittier.

Of the 110 deaths attributed to the tsunami, fifteen occurred outside of Alaska. Four children were killed in Newport, Oregon, while camping on the beach with their parents. Although Newport had no tidal gauge, wave heights in local rivers reached 11.5 to 13 feet high (3.5 to 4 meters). The remaining 11 deaths occurred in Crescent City, California. California residents had ample warning of the tsunami's arrival, and investigators cite several factors that caused the death toll to be greater than expected. One factor is that the underwater topography of the area serves to concentrate wave energy in the area of Crescent City, therefore the waves there were higher than waves in surrounding areas. Another is that, although the city was evacuated, the evacuation orders were incomplete. People in the area had experi-enced tsunamis before, and their past experiences led them to believe that the first and second waves were the worst that could be expected. In this case, however, the third and fourth waves were much larger than the first and second. As a result, the people who had returned to homes and businesses to begin the cleanup process were caught unaware. Most of the damage and deaths occurred as a result of these third and fourth waves.

Another testament to the power of this earthquake was the occurrence of seiches (a "standing" wave oscillating in a body of water; the sloshing of water in confined basins) in the Gulf of Mexico, specifically in bays along the Texas and Louisiana coasts. Flooding occurred at Bayou Lafourche, Louisiana, and several boats in that area broke loose from their moorings and either sank or washed ashore. The Eighth Naval District Headquarters in New Orleans noted a sudden rise of 1.6 feet (0.5 meter) in the water level of the Mississippi River. Several boats, including a Coast Guard cutter and a barge, broke or came loose from their moorings and caused minor damage to the wharf. Near Denham Springs, Louisiana, a 5-foot (1.5 meter) seiche damaged boat houses, docks, and boats. Three commercial vessels broke loose from moorings in Houston, Texas. Similar reports of boats breaking loose were reported along the Texas coast.

Earthquakes of this magnitude (9.2) are rare. When they occur, scientists, engineers, and public officials have an exceptional opportunity to learn from them. Following the Anchorage earthquake, structural engineers thoroughly studied the ways in which buildings failed. From their studies, the engineers found weaknesses in contemporary designs and developed ways to build safer homes and businesses. The studies provided data to support the rewriting of building codes for earthquake-prone regions. Geologists and construction engineers gained a fuller understanding of how the various rocks and soil types in this region behave in earthquakes of this magnitude, and can more confidently identify sites that are suitable for building, or those which are at too great a risk for habitation. This is reflected in new city zoning.

A greater awareness of tsunami hazards led to the formation of the Alaska Tsunami Warning System, part of a Pacific-wide network of monitoring stations that keep constant watch on the coastlines around the Pacific Rim so they can provide the people in danger with the most accurate and timely tsunami warnings possible. The general public also is more aware of tsunami hazards. It is a common site in towns such as Crescent City, California, to see references to past tsunamis. West coast states also have posted signs warning visitors that they are entering or exiting a tsunami inundation zone, and other nearby signs direct people to higher ground in the event of a tsunami evacuation. Thus, even events that cause widespread destruction—such as this earthquake—can be studied and produce positive outcomes.

See Also: Earthquake; Earthquake Hazards; Seiche; Subduction Zone; Tsunami.

Further Reading

Alaska Earthquake Information Center. (2014). *The great Alaska earthquake of 1964.* Retrieved from http://www.aeic.alaska.edu/quakes/Alaska_1964_earthquake.html

Cloud, W. K., & Scott, N. H. (1969). Distribution of intensity, Prince William Sound earthquake of 1964. In L. E. Liepold (Ed.), *The Prince William Sound, Alaska, earthquake of 1964 and aftershocks, volume IIB and C* (pp. 5–48). United States Coast and Geodetic Survey: Washington, DC: Government Printing Office.

Hansen, W. R., Eckel, E. B., Schaem, W. E., Lyle, R. E., George, W., & Chance, G. (1966). *The Alaska earthquake March 27, 1964: Field investigations and reconstruction effort*

(U.S. Geological Survey Professional Paper 541). Washington, DC: United States Government Printing Office.

Kanamori, H. (1970). The Alaska Earthquake of 1964: Radiation of long-period surface waves and source mechanism. *Journal of Geophysical Research 27*(26), 5029–5040.

Kanamori, H. (1977). The energy release in great earthquakes. *Journal of Geophysical Research 82*(20): 2981–2987.

Malloy, R. J., & Merrill, G.F. (1969). Vertical crustal movement of the sea floor associated with the Prince William Sound, Alaska, earthquake. In L. E. Liepold (Ed.), *The Prince William Sound, Alaska, earthquake of 1964 and aftershocks, volume IIB and C* (pp. 327–338). United States Coast and Geodetic Survey: United States Government Printing Office.

National Information Service for Earthquake Engineering (NISEE). Pacific Earthquake Engineering Research Center (EERC). University of California, Berkeley. (2012, August 1). *The earthquake engineering online archive*. Retrieved from http://nisee .berkeley.edu/elibrary/

Plafker, G. (1965). Tectonic deformation associated with the 1964 Alaska earthquake. *Science 148*(3678), 1675–1687.

Spaeth, M. G., & Berkman, S. C. (1965). The tsunami of March 28, 1964, as recorded at tide stations. United States Coast and Geodetic Survey: United States Government Printing Office.

Steinbrugge, K. V. (1967). Introduction to the earthquake engineering of the Prince William Sound, Alaska, earthquake. In F. J. Wood (Ed.), *The Prince William Sound, Alaska, earthquake of 1964 and aftershocks, volume IIA* (pp. 1–6). United States Coast and Geodetic Survey: United States Government Printing Office.

Steinbrugge, K. V. (2012, July 27). *Catalog of earthquake related sounds*. 1985 update, Record 1. Retrieved from http://webshaker.ucsd.edu/soundRecords.html

Steinbrugge, K. V., Manning, J. H., & Degenkolb, H. J. (1967). Building damage in Anchorage. In F. J. Wood (Ed.), *The Prince William Sound, Alaska, earthquake of 1964 and aftershocks, volume IIA* (pp. 7–217). United States Coast and Geodetic Survey: United States Government Printing Office.

Tilgner, E. E., & Peterson, J. R. (1969). The Alaska tsunami warning system. In L. E. Liepold (Ed.), *The Prince William Sound, Alaska, earthquake of 1964 and aftershocks, volume IIB and C* (pp. 309–324). United States Coast and Geodetic Survey: United States Government Printing Office.

Wilson, S. D. (1967). Landslides in the City of Anchorage. In F. J. Wood (Ed.), *The Prince William Sound, Alaska, earthquake of 1964 and aftershocks, volume IIA* (pp.253–297). United States Coast and Geodetic Survey: United States Government Printing Office.

Andesite

Andesite is a type of extrusive igneous rock, or rock that forms at the surface when magma cools. Its name is derived from the name "Andes," which is a volcanic mountain range in South America where the rock is prevalent. Andesite must be formed at the surface of the earth as a lava flow, making it an extrusive igneous rock. It must also contain between 52% and 63% silica (SiO_2 or silicon dioxide) by weight. Andesite typically consists mostly of microscopic minerals that indicate rapid cooling, as occurs at the earth's surface. Only fairly coherent solid lava flows with this composition are accurately called andesite. Rocks with the same andesitic composition, however, can be formed in numerous other ways.

A rock formed beneath the earth's surface—an intrusive igneous rock—can have the same andesitic composition, but the correct name of this type of rock is "diorite." The name is different because the rock was formed in a different environment and therefore has different characteristics. Diorite is formed in the earth's subsurface, therefore it cools very slowly. Slow cooling results in a rock composed entirely of interlocking minerals that are visible to the naked eye.

Pumice, a rock that is so lightweight that it is able to float on water, also can have an andesitic composition. Pumice is formed when gases in the liquid magma come out of solution as the magma rises toward the surface. The gases form frothy foam at the top of the magma chamber. When magma is close enough to the surface of the earth to force gases out of solution, the gas exerts rapidly increasing pressure within the volcano. Often, this eventually causes an explosive eruption that expels large volumes of pumice and volcanic ash. Volcanic ash also can have an andesitic composition. Ash particles range from sand-sized to flour-sized. Under a microscope, ash particles reveal a shape that indicates the ash once was a mixture of the froth that forms pumice, the solid rock that was broken into tiny pieces by the force of the eruption, and the small bits of magma that were erupted in a semi-liquid state, but which again were broken into tiny pieces by the force of the eruption.

Rocks and ash with andesitic composition typically are gray or brown in color. In some instances, diorite can be composed of a roughly equal mixture of very dark-colored and very light-colored minerals. Andesitic magmas typically are between 1,700 and 2,200 degrees Fahrenheit (950 and 1,200 degrees Celsius) at the time of eruption. In magma form, andesite is relatively viscous. Viscosity of andesite magma varies widely depending on a number of factors, such as the volume of dissolved gases, percentage of the magma that is solid crystals, and temperature. Even at its least viscous, however, an andesitic lava flow has much the same consistency as tar. At its most viscous, andesitic magma is nearly solid when it is erupted. In this case, it creates a lava dome that does not travel far from the vent.

Andesite typically is erupted from composite volcanoes. Composite volcanoes usually have a tall, steep-sided cone shape, and are composed of a combination of various types of volcanic rock (basalt, andesite, and sometimes rhyolite) as well as other types of volcanic deposits, such as pumice and volcanic ash. This type of volcano is found near subduction zones. At a subduction zone, a tectonic plate consisting of oceanic lithosphere is forced downward into the mantle, beneath another plate. As the downgoing plate is heated, water is driven out of it and that water invades the surrounding mantle. Water reduces the melting temperature of the mantle, which allows small pockets of mantle rock to melt. Those small pockets of molten rock, or magma, have the composition of the part of the mantle that has melted. It is close in composition to basalt, with less than 50% SiO_2. This magma is less dense than the solid rocks surrounding it, so it begins to rise toward the surface. Often, magma collects temporarily at the base of the more dense lithosphere above it. There, and as the magma rises through the lithosphere, the high temperature of the magma causes partial melting of the more silica-rich lithosphere. The molten lithosphere is incorporated into the magma body, changing its composition from basalt to andesite. Thus, at subduction zones, the most common type of magma erupted is andesitic in composition. If the magma sits underground for any length of time, its composition can change even more drastically, creating rhyolitic magma.

See Also: Basalt; Composite Volcano; Dacite; Earth Structure; Lava Dome; Plate Tectonics; Rhyolite.

Further Reading

Bardintzeff, J. M., & McBirney, A. R. (2000). *Volcanology* (2nd ed.). Boston: Jones and Bartlett.

Cas, R. A. F., & Wright, J. V. (1988). *Volcanic successions: Modern and ancient.* London: Chapman & Hall.

Fisher, R. V., Heiken, G., & Hulen, J. B. (1997). *Volcanoes, crucibles of change.* Princeton, NJ: Princeton University Press.

Francis, P., & Oppenheimer, C. (2004). *Volcanoes* (2nd ed.). Oxford: Oxford University Press.

U.S. Geological Survey. (2012, August 3). *Volcano hazards program photo glossary: Andesite.* Retrieved from http://volcanoes.usgs.gov/images/pglossary/andesite.php

Arenal Volcano, Costa Rica

Arenal is a composite volcano located in the northern lowlands of Costa Rica. It is part of a chain of volcanoes in Central America formed as a result of subduction of the Cocos Plate beneath the Caribbean Plate to its east. The volcano's summit is 5,478 feet (1,670 meters) above sea level. The volcano was one of the most active in Costa Rica during its most recent eruption, from 1968 until 2010. Prior to that, the volcano had experienced 400 years of dormancy. The 1968 eruption began with a violent explosion that threw large blocks up to 3.1 miles (5 kilometers) from the vent. This was followed by pyroclastic flows that killed 89 people. Most of the remainder of the eruption was characterized by relatively harmless small-scale eruptions that tossed lava bombs (any viscous—partially molten—lava fragment larger than 2.5 inches (65 millimeters) in diameter and ejected from a volcano is called a "volcanic bomb" or "lava bomb") from the crater and sent large slow-moving lava flows down its slopes. However, at least six more hazardous eruptions occurred between 1968 and 2010.

Arenal has long been a tourist attraction. Hot springs dot the area surrounding the volcano. There is a large lake at the base of the volcano. The region is a popular site for many types of recreational activities including hiking, swimming, fishing, and whitewater rafting. The volcano itself is located within Arenal National Park. In May of 2010, the park had to be closed temporarily when an eruption sent eight streams of lava down the volcano's flanks. Gases and ash accompanied the eruption, creating a hazard for park visitors. The volcano is monitored by the Arenal Miravalles Seismological and Volcanological Observatory in cooperation with the Costa Rican Institute of Electricity.

The Institute of Electricity has developed a large hydroelectric project a short distance from Arenal. The project at Arenal Lake generates more than 40% of Costa Rica's power. The Institute of Electricity therefore has a vested interest in monitoring all activity around Arenal to effectively manage the dam and hydroelectric plant. The mountain is instrumented with six seismometers and three strong motion accelerometers. There also is a network of tilt meters designed to measure inflation and deflation of the volcano by measuring the tilt of its slopes. Sporadic gas monitoring also has been undertaken. Since the end of Arenal's most recent eruption in 2010, only minor amounts of steam and volcanic gases have been detected, which is to be expected for a volcano that has just ended a decades-long eruptive cycle. The gases are expected to remain at low levels until the next eruptive cycle occurs, which could be decades or centuries in the future.

See Also: Cocos Plate; Subduction Zone.

Further Reading

Arenal.net. (2011). Arenal Volcano overview. Retrieved June 3, 2014, from http://www .arenal.net/arenal-volcano-overview.htm

San Jose AFP Staff. (2010, May 24). Costa Rica volcano erupts, national park evacuated. *Terra Daily.* Retrieved from http://www.terradaily.com/reports/Costa_Rica_volcano _erupts_national_park_evacuated_999.html

Smithsonian Institution. National Museum of Natural History. Global Volcanism Program. (2014, October 9). *Arenal.* Retrieved from http://www.volcano.si.edu/volcano .cfm?vn=345033

Arica Earthquake and Tsunami, Chile (1868)

On August 13, 1868, a strong earthquake struck the coastal border between Peru and Chile. The epicenter was presumed to have been located near the city of Arica. At that time, Arica was part of Peru; however, the border between Chile and Peru was in dispute. The border dispute was settled and the area now falls within Chile. The earthquake occurred at approximately 4:30 p.m. local time. It occurred after a series of foreshocks that had alerted the population and sent many people outside.

As a result, many people in inland communities escaped death and injury because they had already fled structures that later collapsed. Those in coastal communities however, were not as fortunate. The earthquake spawned a Pacific-wide tsunami that caused immense loss of life in the region of the epicenter. The approximate death toll of this earthquake and resulting tsunami was 25,000, and damage estimates approach $300 million. The earthquake was felt from the Pacific coast in the west to the Andes in the east, and from the equator to southern Chile.

The Arica earthquake of 1868 was one of a series of natural disasters that occurred in South America that year. For much of 1868, an outbreak of yellow fever had plagued Lima and the surrounding towns, and more than 10,000 people died. Some people felt that this was a harbinger of other disasters to come. Coincidentally, the presentiment happened to be correct. Many residents of Lima, Callao, and other towns affected by yellow fever fled to other cities such as Tacna, Arequipa, and Arica to escape the outbreak. Even a United States store ship, the *Fredonia*, was towed to Arica in an effort to isolate its crew from the deadly sickness. For many people, the flight from yellow fever actually led to death due to the earthquake and tsunami of August 13, 1868. Although Lima largely was unaffected by the earthquake, Arica was devastated—first by the earthquake and later by a series of tsunami waves that reached 60 feet (18 meters) in height. Just a few days after the Arica earthquake, on August 16, 1868, another large earthquake struck Ecuador causing significant damage in and around the capital city of Quito. This followed a month-long outbreak of catarrhal fever, which killed thousands of Quito's citizens.

The city of Arequipa was affected more adversely than any other inland city. At the time of the earthquake, Arequipa was recognized as the second city of Peru. It had a population of about 50,000, and in size; population; and social, financial, and political importance was second only to the capital city of Lima. Arequipa was founded in 1540 by Spanish conquistador Pizarro. The city had experienced a devastating earthquake in 1821, and had been rebuilt with massive one-story dwellings made of light but strong volcanic rock. Citizens of Arequipa believed that buildings of this architectural style would withstand future earthquakes. Masonry structures, however, are notoriously unstable and prone to collapse in earthquakes as large as the August 1868 temblor. An eyewitness in Arequipa reported the following on August 16, 1868, just three days after the earthquake.

> . . . The houses being solidly built and of one story resisted for about one minute, which gave time for the people to rush into the middle of the streets; so the mortality, although considerable, is not so great as might have been expected. If the earthquake had taken place at night, few indeed would have been left to tell the story. As it is, the prisoners in the Careel (public prison) and the sick in the hospital have perished (Squier, 1869).

Although there is some confusion on the issue, Volcano Misti, which stood above the city of Arequipa, could have had a small eruption, a landslide, or a flare in hot spring activity. After the earthquake, some in the city noticed that rivers flowing from El Misti turned various colors and smelled of sulfur. Flooding on these same rivers also occurred, presumably as a result of snow and ice melt (again, either from melting avalanches or volcanic activity). Several small towns along these rivers were flooded . . . sweeping people and debris further down the valley of Arequipa. In all, Arequipa suffered the loss of 4,000 to 5,000 homes and all 22 churches, all occupants of the hospital and jail, and an additional 300 individuals who were crushed by falling debris.

As horrifying as the damage was in Arequipa, other areas fared much worse. The coastal cities of the region sustained significant damage from both the earthquake and its resulting tsunami. Hardest hit was the city of Arica. Vivid accounts of the events during and immediately after the earthquake were recorded by numerous individuals, including an officer of the United States warship *Wateree*, which was in port in Arica the day of the earthquake. According to the officer, as the crew was finishing dinner large clouds of dust were seen in the distance, about 10 miles (16 kilometers) from Arica. The dust cloud approached Arica over the next few minutes, and the crew had the presence of mind to calculate its speed at roughly 600 miles per hour (1,000 kilometers per hour). The sailors began to see the mountains in the distance begin to shudder, and then observed numerous landslides in the same area of the mountains. Soon crew members noticed the city shaking and crumbling into ruins. The noise was deafening. The people on land ran into any open space they could find, and their screams could be heard from the ship. The water that surrounded the ship, however, seemed undisturbed.

As soon as the earthquake was over the *Wateree* and the *Fredonia* (another American ship in port) sent their surgeons ashore to help the wounded who were gathering portside seeking refuge and rescue from the ships. As soon as the surgeons reached shore, however, the sea retreated to low-tide level then rushed back ashore to a height of 40 feet (12 meters) above the high-tide mark. By all accounts, this took only five minutes. The tsunami, however, was not over. The officer's account continues.

> The water rushed back into the ocean more suddenly than it had advanced upon the land, and carried with it the Custom-House and the residence of the English Consul. This awful spectacle of destruction by the receding flood had hardly been realized when the sea rose again, and now the vessels in port began dragging. The water rose to the same height before, and on rushing back it brought not only the debris of a ruined city with it, but even a locomotive and tender and a train of four cars were seen carried away by the fearful force of the waves. During this advance of the sea inland another traffic shock, lasting about eight minutes, was felt. . . . It was then that the thundering approach of a heavy sea-wave was noticed, and a minute afterward a sea-wall of perpendicular height to the extent of from forty-two to forty-five feet, capped with a fringe of bright, glistening foam, swept over the land, stranding far in-shore the United States steamer *Wateree*, the *America*, a Peruvian frigate, and the *Chanarcillo*, an English merchant vessel (Squier, 1869).

In all, witnesses reported 11 separate waves during the tsunami. The largest wave measured at Arica came about four hours after the earthquake. Maximum wave height was 59 feet (18 meters). Waves reached 40 feet (12 meters) in Iquique, Chile; 50 feet (15 meters) at Chala, Peru; 40 feet (12 meters) in Islay, Peru; and 25 feet (7.5 meters) in Coquimbo, Chile. The tsunami was detected across the Pacific, and lasted at least two to three days. Wave heights were recorded of up to 16 feet (5 meters) on the east coast of New Zealand; 15 feet (4.5 meters) in Hilo, Hawaii; 10 feet (3 meters) on Hokkaido, Japan; 8 feet (2.4 meters) on Kodiak Island, Alaska; and 4 feet (1.2 meters) in Sydney, Australia.

Captain J. H. Gillis of the *Wateree* sent a report to the commander of the United States squadron in the South Pacific with an accounting of the events of that day, and its results. The *Wateree* came to rest about 3 miles (4.8 kilometers) north of the city of Arica and 1,500 feet (450 meters) inland. Only one of its crew members was lost to the tsunami, and the ship was upright and largely undamaged. It was too far from the ocean, however, to be refloated and put into service. The other U.S. ship, the *Fredonia*, was destroyed when it was smashed on the rocks of El Morro de Arica, a rocky headland. All of those on board were lost, but five members of the crew were onshore at the time of the tsunami, and four of them survived. The crew of the *Wateree* rendered what aid was possible, and then abandoned the ship.

Those who escaped the tsunami did so by fleeing into the hills. They were greeted by a gruesome sight of a different sort. The desert hills above Arica hold burial sites of the ancient Aymara people. Ground shaking during the earthquake caused hundreds of the buried bodies to come to the surface in what Squier (1869) described as an "appalling spectacle of the grave literally giving up its dead." This offended the proper Victorian senses of Squier, and presumably his English and American readers as well.

See Also: Chile; Chilean Earthquake and Tsunami (1960); Earthquake; Subduction Zone; Tsunami.

Further Reading

National Oceanic and Atmospheric Administration (NOAA). National Geophysical Data Center. Arica, Chile, earthquake. Retrieved August 5, 2012, from http://www.ngdc.noaa.gov/nndc/struts/results?EQ_0=983&t=101650&s=8&d=22,26,13,12&nd=display

Squier, E. G. (1869). The great South American earthquakes of 1868. *Harper's New Monthly Magazine 38* (227), 603–623.

U.S. Geological Survey. Earthquake Hazards Program. (2012, August 5). Retrieved from http://earthquake.usgs.gov/earthquakes/world/events/1868_08_13.php

Augustine Volcano, Alaska, United States

Mount St. Augustine is a 4,100-foot (1,260-meter) tall volcanic island in the western part of Cook Inlet. It is located approximately 180 miles (290 kilometers) southwest of Anchorage in southern Alaska, and is part of the eastern Aleutian

Island chain. In 1778, British explorer Captain James Cook named the island for Saint Augustine.

Augustine is a composite volcano, which is a type of volcano composed of layers of lava flows and pyroclastic material. In the case of Augustine, the composition of those rocks primarily is andesite with minor amounts of dacite and basalt. It is built on a base of rocks dating from the Jurassic age through the Tertiary age (200 million years to 2 million years old) that have been uplifted due to tectonic activity at this very active boundary between the North American Plate and Pacific Plate. Uplift at Augustine continues in modern times. Between 11 and 13 inches (30 and 33 centimeters) of uplift was measured on the northwest side of Augustine Island after the 1964 Alaska Earthquake.

Augustine erupts fairly frequently, with nine confirmed eruptions since its discovery by Cook in 1778, and five additional reports of eruptions that cannot be confirmed. Each known eruption has been characterized by explosive activity that produced pyroclastic flows, volcanic ash, and pumice; debris avalanches; short, steep lava flows; and lava domes. Augustine is located far from major population centers but still is a dangerous volcano. The major hazards associated with Augustine are ash plumes and the catastrophic collapse of lava domes.

Ash plumes can be ejected to heights of more than 18 miles (30 kilometers) in the atmosphere, and are capable of spreading around the globe. Many properties of volcanic ash make it harmful to people, animals, plants, and machinery. Volcanic ash particles are very small (7/100 inch; < 2 millimeters), hard, and abrasive. They have the ability to hold an electrostatic charge and to hold onto water and acid aerosol droplets. Although Augustine Island is uninhabited, the residents of southern Alaska and beyond have encountered ash from eruptions of Augustine, and are sure to have the same experiences in the future. People who encounter ash might develop eye and respiratory problems or skin irritation from the abrasive, often acid-coated ash particles. Long-term exposure can lead to chronic lung problems including lung cancer. In the environment, volcanic ash can reduce visibility, create slippery driving conditions, contaminate water supplies and clog water-supply equipment, affect animal health, strip or burn crops, and—if left to accumulate on roofs—cause roof collapse and the deaths of building occupants.

In southern Alaska, Augustine and other volcanoes are particularly problematic because they are located in a busy flight path between North America and Asia. Aviation is a dangerous undertaking when volcanic ash is in the atmosphere because the ash can abrade and clog a plane's engines, leading to complete engine failure. No fatal crashes have yet occurred as a result of volcanic ash clouds, but there have been several frightening incidents in which both commercial passenger jets and cargo planes have lost all engine power. In each case the pilots were able to restart engines, but only after falling several thousand feet.

Catastrophic lava dome collapse is a hazard of the Augustine Volcano because such collapses on the steep-sided mountain generate debris avalanches. When a debris avalanche is fast and voluminous enough, it has the ability to churn into the ocean and create a localized tsunami. One such local tsunami was generated as the result of a debris avalanche from the north flank of the Augustine Volcano on

October 6, 1883. There were many eyewitnesses to the event, but none close to Augustine at the time. Field evidence indicates that the wave height must have been at least 65 feet (20 meters) on the shores of Augustine Island. Elsewhere in the Cook Inlet, waves reached 20 to 26 feet (6 to 8 meters) in height.

The most recent eruption of Augustine occurred in 2005–2006. There were four distinct phases to this eruption. First was precursory activity, which lasted from May 2005 until December 2005. The initial sign of impending volcanic activity was an increase in small earthquakes beneath the volcano. Two months later deformation of the volcano occurred, indicating pressurization of the magma chamber below. The initial phase culminated in small steam explosions in December 2005, leading to the opening of vents and eventually the emission of small amounts of ash.

The second phase of the eruption was the explosive phase, which began in January 2006 and lasted for slightly more than two weeks. A swarm of earthquakes beneath the volcano on January 11, 2006, warned of an impending eruption. Later that day, instruments recorded explosive eruptions occurring an hour apart. Ash plumes rose more than 5.6 miles (9 kilometers) above sea level. Additional explosive eruptions with ash emissions occurred from January 13 to January 17, 2006.

The third phase—one of more or less continuous eruption—began on January 28, 2006, and ended on February 2, 2006. Volcanic ash plumes drifted south, and pyroclastic flows destroyed monitoring stations on the west and north sides of the volcano. The fourth phase, during which effusive eruption was the norm, lasted from early February until March 31, 2006. During this phase, the volcano produced lava flows that moved down the north and northeastern flanks of the volcano, as well as ash and pyroclastic flows. The 2005–2006 eruption of Augustine stopped on March 31, 2006.

See Also: Andesite; Composite Volcano; Lava Dome; Subduction Zone; Tsunami.

Further Reading

Alaska Volcano Observatory. (2012, August 5). *Augustine volcano description and information.* Retrieved from http://www.avo.alaska.edu/volcanoes/volcinfo.php?volcname=Augustine

Beget, J. E., & Kowalik, Z. (2006). Confirmation and calibration of computer modeling of tsunamis produced by Augustine Volcano, Alaska. *Science of Tsunami Hazards 24* (4), 257–266.

Casadevall, T. J. (1993). *Discussions and recommendations from the Workshop on the Impacts of Volcanic Ash on Airport Facilities, Seattle, Washington, April 26–28, 1993.* United States Geological Survey (Open-File Report 93-518).

International Volcanic Health Hazard Network. (2012, August 5). *The health hazards of volcanic ash: A guide for the public.* Retrieved from http://www.ivhhn.org/images/pamphlets/Health_Guidelines_English_WEB.pdf

Neal, C.T., Casadevall, T. J., Miller, T. P., Hendley II, J. W., & Stauffer, P. H. (2004). *Volcanic ash—Danger to aircraft in the North Pacific.* (U.S. Geological Survey Fact

Sheet 030-97. Online Version 1.0). Retrieved August 5, 2012, from http://pubs.usgs
.gov/fs/fs030-97/

Wood, C. A., & Kienle, J. (1992). *Volcanoes of North America: United States and Canada.*
Cambridge: Cambridge University Press.

Australian Plate

The Australian Plate plays a major role in the geology of the southern Pacific. The plate obviously contains the continent of Australia, but also interacts with the Pacific and Eurasian plates that surround it to the east and north. On the southeastern margin of the Australian Plate is the island nation of New Zealand. New Zealand straddles the boundary between the Pacific Plate and the Australian Plate. A small transform section of the plate boundary makes up the Alpine Fault that cuts across New Zealand's South Island. The North Island's volcanic activity is due to subduction of the Pacific Plate beneath the Australian Plate. North of New Zealand, the Tonga Arc is caused by subduction of the Pacific Plate beneath the Australian Plate. The islands of Tonga owe their existence to volcanic activity resulting from the subduction but they also experience many large earthquakes every year. North of Tonga, the subduction zone makes an abrupt turn to the west. It extends through Vanuatu and the Solomon Islands to Papua New Guinea, and changes subduction direction. Along this boundary, the Australian Plate is subducting beneath the Pacific Plate. From the western tip of the island of New Guinea westward throughout the Indonesian archipelago, the Australian Plate is subducting beneath the Eurasian Plate. This subduction has created the Indonesian islands, and is responsible for the volcanic and earthquake activity seen throughout the country.

The nation of Tonga is found on the Australian Plate. Tonga is the site of nearly 50 volcanoes, several of which have been active in the last 200 years. One of the most intriguing eruptions within the Tonga Arc was that of Home Reef, a submarine volcano. When it erupted in August 2006, it produced a large pumice raft that was photographed by yachtsmen. The photographs were widely distributed and represented a coveted glimpse of this rare phenomenon.

The island of New Guinea also lies on the Australian Plate. The island is divided almost precisely in half; the eastern portion is the nation of Papua New Guinea (a former British possession), and the western half belongs to Indonesia. Strong earthquakes occur in all of these areas. The tectonic situation around the eastern portion of Papua New Guinea is extremely complex. Six microplates in this area interact to form a diffuse boundary between the Pacific Plate and Australian Plate. The North and South Bismarck, Manus, Solomon Sea, Woodlark, and Caroline plates create a situation in which a series of small subduction zones and transform boundaries create the small islands to the northeast of Papua New Guinea. Although large earthquakes are common throughout the nations on the edges of the Australian Plate, deaths caused by those earthquakes are relatively rare. The deadliest of these earthquakes occurred in New Zealand when 256 people lost their lives in an earthquake at Hawke's Bay in 1931. Tsunamis tend to be more destructive and deadly than the earthquakes themselves. Major loss of life has occurred throughout Oceania as a result of both locally generated tsunamis and those arriving from distant shores.

See Also: New Zealand; Papua New Guinea; Rabaul, Papua, New Guinea; Ruapehu, Mount, New Zealand; Subduction Zone; Taupo Volcano, New Zealand; Tonga.

Further Reading

Fransson, F. (2006). *Fredrik and crew on Maiken*. Retrieved June 16, 2014, from http://yacht-maiken.blogspot.com/2006/08/stone-sea-and-volcano.html

Smithsonian Institution. National Museum of Natural History. Global Volcanism Program. (2014, June 16). Retrieved from http://www.volcano.si.edu/search_volcano_results.cfm

U.S. Geological Survey. (2013). *Historic world earthquakes*. Retrieved from http://earthquake.usgs.gov/earthquakes/world/historical_country.php

B

Ballard, Dr. Robert D.

Dr. Robert Ballard is best known for discovering the wreckage of the *Titanic* in 1985. But before he turned his attention to marine archaeology and finding shipwrecks, he had a distinguished career in marine geology and geophysics. Ballard holds bachelor's degrees in chemistry and geology from the University of California at Santa Barbara, and a doctorate in geology and geophysics from Woods Hole Oceanographic Institution. He served in the United States Navy on active duty during the Vietnam War, and as a commander in the United States Naval Reserves for an additional 30 years. One of Ballard's earliest jobs as a young adult was with the Ocean Systems Group of North American Aviation. This was Ballard's first exposure to deep ocean submersibles. He has spent most of his career working with and designing such submersibles.

Dr. Ballard was instrumental in a number of landmark discoveries on the ocean floor. In 1973, he was a member of Project FAMOUS (French-American Mid-Ocean Undersea Study). This pioneering project was responsible for mapping large sections of the Mid-Atlantic Ridge, and helped confirm the new theory of plate tectonics. In 1975, Ballard and his team descended into the Cayman Trough in the Caribbean. There, they collected rocks that helped unlock secrets of the composition of the earth's crust.

Perhaps Ballard's most exciting scientific discovery occurred in 1977. Ballard was co-chief scientist on an expedition to the Galapagos Rift in the eastern Pacific Ocean. It was on that expedition that Dr. Ballard and his colleagues made the first discovery of an entirely new type of ecosystem in the ocean depths. The food chain in this ecosystem has as its base microorganisms that perform chemosynthesis (manufacture of food from heat energy and sulfur compounds) rather than photosynthesis (manufacture of food from sunlight and carbon compounds). This discovery was completely new to science and has tremendous implications for the possibility of life in other inhospitable places on Earth and on other planets. Two years later, in 1979, as chief scientist of a new exploration mission, Dr. Ballard returned to the eastern Pacific and discovered the first "black smokers"—hydrothermal vents that continually spew super-heated water and sulfur compounds. Black smokers form tall chimney-like structures on the ocean floor at some locations on mid-ocean ridges. A sample of these chimneys showed them to be almost pure crystalline zinc sulfide. Discovery of these hydrothermal vents solved the question of how heat and water were cycled through the oceanic crust, a query which had plagued

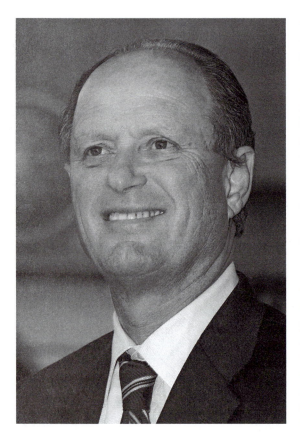

Geologist and ocean explorer Dr. Robert Ballard. (SHI WENN Photos/Newscom)

scientists since the proposal of sea-floor spreading and plate tectonics.

As a frequent user of deep submersibles, it is not surprising that Dr. Ballard became interested in designing new submersibles that would better suit exploration, scientific sampling, and underwater photography. He developed ANGUS (Acoustically Navigated Geological Underwater Survey), a submersible camera that could take up to 16,000 photographs in a single 12- to 14-hour dive. Although ANGUS was a valuable tool, it required development of film and viewing on a reel-to-reel projector several hours after the dive. Recognizing this shortcoming of ANGUS, Ballard employed new technology and designed an automated remote-controlled photographic robot that could broadcast live images to a monitor on the host ship. This advance enabled scientists to take a more active role in remote exploration by being able to steer the robotic submersible to locations of interest during the dive.

In 1982, Dr. Ballard organized the Deep Submergence Laboratory at Woods Hole Oceanographic Institute and began developing a remotely operated submersible. Funded by the United States Navy, this submersible was more sophisticated than anything that had come before, transmitting broadcast-quality color images via fiber optic cable from the ocean depths to the ship on the surface. Ballard named the submersible "Argo-Jason." Ballard was using this submersible when he and his team found the wreckage of the *Titanic* on September 1, 1985.

Since 1985, Ballard has spent much of his time searching for sunken ships. His finds include numerous ships from World War II, including the German ship *Bismarck*, several Japanese warships off Guadalcanal, the USS *Yorktown*, and *PT-109*, a boat commanded by John F. Kennedy. Dr. Ballard also found the *Lusitania* and confirmed the somewhat controversial assertion that it was sunk by a German torpedo that struck and ignited its coal bunker. Other significant finds include Phoenician ships off the coast of Israel, and four 1,500-year-old wooden ships in the Black Sea.

Dr. Ballard has done a great deal to give back to the scientific community and educate the public throughout his career. National Geographic cameras were along on the 1977 expedition in which the chemosynthetic ecosystems were discovered. Ballard served as a National Geographic Explorer-in-Residence for many years. He frequently speaks to audiences across the world about his work. In 1989, Dr. Ballard founded the JASON Project, a program to bring his brand of science to classrooms around the world. Students are able to view live transmissions from JASON submersibles as they explore the undersea world, as well as learn about other natural phenomena such as volcanoes and storms via interactive video feeds. Ballard currently is the director of the Institute for Archaeological Oceanography at the University of Rhode Island's Graduate School of Oceanography.

Dr. Ballard has received a number of honors and awards for his pioneering work. He has 13 honorary degrees and six military awards. He also received the Hubbard Medal, Lindbergh Award, and Explorers Medal from the National Geographic Society. In 2003, the National Endowment for the Humanities awarded Ballard the National Humanities Medal, which was presented by President George W. Bush. Dr. Ballard continues his scientific work as president of the Institute for Exploration in Mystic, Connecticut, as Scientist Emeritus at Woods Hole Oceanographic Institute, and as Scientist Emeritus at the Graduate School of Oceanography at the University of Rhode Island. Ballard is a member of the National Oceanic and Atmospheric Association's Science Advisory Board, and serves as one of 16 commissioners on the President's Commission on Ocean Policy.

See Also: Divergent Boundary; Hydrothermal Vent; Plate Tectonics.

Further Reading

Academy of Achievement, a Museum of Living History. (2010). *Robert D. Ballard, Ph.D.* Retrieved from http://www.achievement.org/autodoc/page/bal0bio-1
Premiere Motivational Speakers Bureau. (2012, August 7). *Robert Ballard, oceanic researcher who discovered the wreckage of the* Titanic. Retrieved from http://premiere-speakers.com/robert_ballard/bio
United States Navy Museum. (2012, August 7). *Biography: Dr. Robert Ballard 1942–.* http://www.history.navy.mil/branches/teach/ends/ballard.htm

Basalt

Basalt is the most common rock in the earth's crust. It covers the entire ocean floor—which constitutes nearly 70% of the earth's surface. Basalt also is the primary product of shield volcanoes and cinder cones. The Hawaiian Islands, Galapagos Islands, and Iceland are examples of ocean islands composed primarily of basalt. Capulin Mountain in northern New Mexico, SP Crater near Flagstaff, Arizona, and Parícutin in southern Mexico are examples of cinder cones with basaltic compositions. There also are immense areas of the continents covered by vast volumes of basalt erupted over geologically short periods of time. These are termed "flood basalts."

The largest of the flood basalts is the Siberian Traps, erupted roughly 250 million years ago in Siberia. (The term "trap" comes from the Swedish word for "staircase," a description of the landscape formed by these lava flows.) The Siberian Traps alone have an estimated volume of 475,000 cubic miles (2 million cubic kilometers). Other flood basalts exist in India (Deccan Traps), southern Africa (Karoo flood basalt province), Iceland, the southern Pacific Ocean (Ontong-Java Plateau), and the northwestern United States (Columbia River Basalts).

Basalt is an extrusive igneous rock, which means that it is cooled and hardened at the surface of the earth, often in the form of a lava flow. At the time of eruption, the temperature of basalt typically is between 2,000 and 2,300 degrees Fahrenheit (1,100 and 1,250 degrees Celsius). Dark in color, basalt is composed primarily of microscopic minerals and is fairly dense in relation to other igneous rocks. Basalt samples can have small visible crystals of the green mineral olivine, the light-colored mineral plagioclase, and the dark green to black mineral pyroxene. Basalts also have a small percentage of iron-oxide minerals, giving them weak magnetic properties. Basalts are classified based on their chemistry, however, rather than their visible mineral content.

The most widely accepted classification of igneous rocks uses the weight percent of silica (SiO_2) in a rock to determine the rock's identity. Basalts have between 38% and 53% silica by weight. The low silica percentage means basalt has fairly low viscosity. As a result, it is able to flow long distances. Basalt lava flows have been known to flow more than 12 miles (20 kilometers) from a vent, and form a wide variety of features such as aa and pahoehoe textures, lava tubes, accretionary lava balls, and lava molds. Aa is a surface texture of basalt lava flows that consists of sharp, irregularly shaped blocks. Accretionary lava balls are large accumulations of aa that can reach up to 10 feet (3 meters) in diameter. Pahoehoe surface texture is smooth or rope-like. Lava tubes are formed when a crust forms on top of an open lava channel. Lava molds are formed when a lava flow engulfs an object, such as a tree. It sets the tree on fire so it is destroyed, but the lava retains the shape of the outside of the tree.

Although the term "basalt" refers to a specific extrusive igneous rock, the term "basaltic" is used to describe the chemical composition of other rocks, formed in ways other than via lava flows. Other basaltic igneous rocks include the intrusive rock gabbro, which forms the oceanic crust, and the pyroclastic material scoria, which is the "lava rock" often seen in gas barbecue grills and landscaping stores.

The composition of basalt is most similar (of the common magma types) to the primary magma created when a small percentage of the mantle melts. Because of this, it is considered to be the parent magma to all other common types of magma seen on Earth, and has been studied in great detail for clues about the earth's interior. Slight variations in the chemistry of basalts indicate variations in the chemistry of the mantle beneath a region, and therefore are important for use in determining the physical and chemical properties of parts of the earth that are inaccessible to humans directly. These chemical variations also illuminate the processes that change magma's composition as it rises through the crust.

Basalt is present on the moon and in meteorites as well as on Earth. The areas of the moon that appear smooth and dark are called "mare" (pronounced mahr'-ay), a term that means "sea" or "ocean," and they are vast basalt lava flows. Meteorites with basaltic composition have been collected on Earth and analyzed for clues about the formation of planets and moons in our solar system.

See Also: Aa; Cinder Cone; Pahoehoe; Pyroclastic Materials; Shield Volcano.

Further Reading

Basaltic Volcanism Study Project. (1981). *Basaltic volcanism of the terrestrial planets.* New York: Pergamon Press.

Francis, P., & Oppenheimer, C. (2004). *Volcanoes* (2nd ed.). Oxford: Oxford University Press.

Tarbuck, E. J., Lutgens, F. K., & Tasa, D. (2011). *Earth: An introduction to physical geology* (10th ed.). Upper Saddle River, NJ: Pearson Prentice Hall/Pearson Education, Inc.

U.S. Geological Survey. (2102, August 17). *Volcano hazards program photo glossary: Basalt.* Retrieved from http://volcanoes.usgs.gov/images/pglossary/basalt.php

C

Caldera

A caldera is a volcanic collapse feature that is roughly circular or oval in shape. Calderas are formed when an eruption or a series of eruptions drains much of the magma chamber beneath the summit of a volcano. The partially vacated chamber leaves the top of the volcano unsupported, and the volcano's top ultimately collapses under its own weight. Calderas can form during the course of a single voluminous eruption, or form in stages over hundreds of years. Calderas are associated with both shield volcanoes and composite volcanoes, although calderas in these settings can look vastly different from each other. The structure of most calderas includes a depression measuring from less than 300 feet (100 meters) deep to more than 3,000 feet (1,000 meters) deep, and bounded by faults that drop the floor downward. These faults are appropriately termed "ring faults" because they are found in concentric rings around the edge of the caldera. Ring faults often correspond with ring dikes, which are conduits arranged in concentric rings around the caldera that carry magma to the surface during eruptions.

Unlike craters—which are formed from explosive activity—calderas are formed by a collapse. On shield volcanoes and smaller composite volcanoes, calderas can be quite small, measuring less than 3 miles (5 kilometers) in diameter. Rhyolitic composite volcanoes, however, can grow to enormous proportions, and form the largest of the calderas, reaching 45 miles (75 kilometers) or more in diameter.

The smallest of calderas arguably are those that form on the flanks of shield volcanoes, such as those in the Hawaiian Islands. On Kilauea Volcano, dozens of small calderas—termed "pit craters"—have formed throughout its eruptive history. One of the smallest of these craters is Devil's Throat, found on the east rift zone of Kilauea. This pit crater is only 165 feet by 138 feet (50 meters by 42 meters) at the rim, and 165 feet (50 meters) deep.

Kilauea Volcano also has a caldera at its summit. The depression is 2 miles wide by 3 miles (3 kilometers by 5 kilometers) long, and it is 540 feet (165 meters) deep at its deepest point. The caldera has a series of ring faults associated with it, which extend the structural dimensions to 3.7 miles by 3.7 miles (6 kilometers by 6 kilometers), a size more typical for "small" calderas. One example of a small caldera on a composite volcano was created during the 1991 eruptions of Mount Pinatubo in the Philippines. In a single nine-hour eruption, the volcano erupted between 1.2 and 2 cubic miles (5 to 8 cubic kilometers) of

Caldera in the Andes Mountains, Chile. (Colin Monteath/Hedgehog House/Minden Pictures/ Newscom)

pumice and ash. The summit of the volcano collapsed, forming a circular caldera 1.5 miles (2.5 kilometers) in diameter (Francis & Oppenheimer, 2004). This was one of the largest volcanic eruptions in the Twentieth Century. Other, much larger eruptions, however, dwarfed this event and formed much larger calderas.

Silicic or rhyolitic calderas have recently gained a great deal of attention because of the proliferation of articles, television documentaries, and press accounts of "supervolcanoes." This term was coined by the media, and only recently has been reluctantly recognized by scientists. It is reserved for eruptions having a Volcanic Explosivity Index (VEI) of 8 or greater. Eruptions of this scale are exceedingly rare. The last eruption of VEI 8 or greater occurred about 74,000 years ago. Estimated at VEI 8.8, the eruption of Toba, Indonesia, is estimated to have discharged 670 cubic miles (2,800 cubic kilometers) of magma. Population studies of our human ancestors indicate that, at about the same time as the eruption occurred, there was a population crash. Some scientists hypothesize that this eruption discharged so much material into the atmosphere that it caused climate change that was rapid enough and sufficiently drastic to cause the near extinction of humans.

Eruptions of VEI 6 have produced respectable-sized calderas that have caused unimaginable suffering and loss of life. The 1883 eruption of Krakatau in Indonesia is an example of this size eruption. Krakatau was an island composed of three separate peaks. In its August 26–27, 1883 eruption, the volcano discharged approximately 4 cubic miles (16 cubic kilometers) of pumice and ash. Two thirds of the island collapsed into the sea, creating a caldera that was 4.5 miles (7 kilometers) wide. A tsunami was created by the caldera collapse, and more than 165 coastal villages on the islands of Sumatra and Java were swept away. This resulted in the death of 36,000 people. Beginning in 1927, a new volcanic island began forming within the caldera. Called Anak Krakatau ("child of Krakatau,") the new island continues to erupt frequently.

In the United States, scientists have recognized a number of calderas of various ages and sizes. Howel Williams of the University of Oregon conducted pioneering work on calderas, using Crater Lake, Oregon, as his example. Native Americans witnessed the eruption, so an oral history of the event existed. Prior to the eruption that created the caldera, the mountain that today is called Crater Lake was called Mount Mazama. Between 6,600 and 7,000 years ago, a great eruption raged for several days and deposited thick blankets of pumice on the volcano's slopes. Pyroclastic flows roared down its slopes and deposited even more ash and pumice in the valleys leading away from the peak. Finally, when the magma chamber had been sufficiently depleted to leave the cone unsupported, the top of the volcano collapsed and formed a caldera. In the early 1980s, Charles Bacon calculated that between 12 and 14 cubic miles (51 to 59 cubic kilometers) of magma were erupted by Mount Mazama, and between 10 and 12.5 cubic miles (40 to 52 cubic kilometers) of the mountain were lost when the caldera formed. Today, the caldera at the mountain's summit is approximately 4,000 feet (1,200 meters) deep and contains a lake that is 2,000 feet (600 meters) deep in places. Less than 1,000 years ago, renewed volcanic activity resulted in the formation of Wizard Island, a cinder cone within the lake.

The Valles Caldera in northern New Mexico is a "resurgent caldera," which is characterized by slow uplift of the caldera floor. This uplift often exceeds 3,200 feet (1 kilometer), which makes these calderas look like a broad depression with a raised center. The Valles Caldera is typical of many resurgent calderas in its geometry and volcanic features. Inside the caldera, there not only is a raised area in the center, but a ring of lava domes also marks the location of a prominent ring dike beneath the caldera floor. These lava domes are the result of small, low-volume eruptions occurring long after the large caldera-forming eruption. Other resurgent calderas in the United States include the Yellowstone Caldera in Wyoming, and the Long Valley Caldera in California. Toba in Indonesia also is a resurgent caldera.

Resurgent calderas also can occur in clusters, although scientists still do not understand why. The San Juan Mountains of south-central Colorado contain a cluster of at least 18 individual calderas that range in age from 22 million to 30 million years old. The largest of these is the La Garita Caldera. La Garita Caldera is 21 miles (35 kilometers) wide and 46 miles (75 kilometers) long. It appears to be the source of a rock unit that indicates an eruption volume of 1,200 cubic miles (5,000 cubic kilometers). Perhaps the best known of the calderas is the Creede Caldera, which is home to the Creede mining district. Minerals deposited along ring dikes and ring faults have provided prospectors with ample opportunities to mine both rare and valuable minerals from this volcanic region. Other regions with caldera clusters include the Altiplano-Puna Volcanic Complex in South America and the Sierra Madre Occidental Volcanic Field in western Mexico.

See Also: Composite Volcano; Crater Lake, Oregon, United States; Krakatau Eruption (also known as "Krakatoa" Eruption), Indonesia (1883); Pinatubo, Mount, Eruption, Philippines (1991); Rhyolite; Shield Volcano; Toba Eruption, Indonesia; Volcanic Explosivity Index (VEI).

Further Reading

Francis, P., & Oppenheimer, C. (2004). *Volcanoes* (2nd ed.). Oxford: Oxford University Press.

Lipman, P. W. (2000). Calderas. In H. Sigurdsson, B. Houghton, H. Rymer, J. Stix, & S. McNutt (Eds.), *Encyclopedia of volcanoes*. San Diego, CA: Academic Press.

Swanson, E. R., & McDowell, F. W. (1984). *Calderas of the Sierra Madre Occidental Volcanic Field Western Mexico (Abstract)*. Retrieved August 20, 2012, from http://www.agu.org/pubs/crossref/1984/JB089iB10p08787.shtml

U.S. Geological Survey. Cascades Volcano Observatory. *Description: 1883 eruption of Krakatau*. (United States Geological Survey, Krakatau, 2012). Retrieved August 20, 2012, from http://vulcan.wr.usgs.gov/Volcanoes/Indonesia/description_krakatau_1883_eruption.html

U.S. Geological Survey. Cascades Volcano Observatory. *Report: Eruptive history of Mount Mazama and Crater Lake Caldera, Cascade Range, U.S.A.* (United States Geological Survey, Mount Mazama, 2012). Retrieved August 20, 2012, from http://vulcan.wr.usgs.gov/Volcanoes/CraterLake/Publications/BaconJVGR83/abstract.html

U.S. Geological Survey. Hawaiian Volcano Observatory. (2006, October 12). Devil's Throat has evolved into a shadow of its former self. *Volcano Watch*. (U.S. Geological Survey, Devil's Throat, 2006). http://hvo.wr.usgs.gov/volcanowatch/archive/2006/06_10_12.html

U.S. Geological Survey. Hawaiian Volcano Observatory. *Kilauea—Perhaps the world's most active volcano*. (United States Geological Survey, Kilauea, 2012). Retrieved August 20, 2012, from http://hvo.wr.usgs.gov/kilauea/

Williams, H. (1976). *The ancient volcanoes of Oregon*. First Condon Lecture, delivered 1948. Oregon State System of Higher Education.

Canada

Canada is the northernmost of three countries that comprise the continent of North America, and occupies the northern portion of the North American Plate. Eastern Canada is composed of very old, very stable rocks. The western part of Canada, however, is geologically dynamic. Western Canada faces hazards from large earthquakes, volcanic eruptions, and tsunamis. Luckily, however, this portion of Canada is sparsely populated, with the exception of Vancouver Island and the surrounding areas. The Rocky Mountains extend northward from Canada's border with the United States of America, into the provinces of Alberta, British Columbia, the Yukon, and the Northwest Territories. Of particular interest is the Cascadia

Subduction Zone which lies just off the Pacific Northwest Coast. At this plate boundary, the small Juan de Fuca Plate to the west is being subducted beneath the North American Plate to the east.

The Cascadia Subduction Zone is a site of frequent earthquakes, including a magnitude 6.8 event that occurred near Seattle, Washington, in 2001. Scientists believe that the Cascadia Subduction Zone is capable of producing magnitude 8.0 and larger earthquakes, and associated tsunamis. An orphan tsunami in the year 1700 recently was identified as being associated with a massive magnitude 9.0 earthquake at the Cascadia Subduction Zone, likely in southern Canada. Other notable earthquakes include a magnitude 8.0 earthquake on the border between the Yukon Territory and Alaska in 1899; a magnitude 7.0 earthquake on Vancouver Island, British Columbia, in 1918; a magnitude 7.3 earthquake at Vancouver Island, British Columbia, in 1946; and a magnitude 8.1 earthquake just off Haida Gwaii (formerly the Queen Charlotte Islands), British Columbia, in 1949. The most recent significant earthquake in the region was a magnitude 7.7 just off Haida Gwaii in October 2012.

The subduction zone also has produced a chain of volcanoes which includes the Cascade Range. The Cascades extend from northern California northward to southern British Columbia. Mount Garibaldi often is cited as the northernmost of the Cascade volcanoes. However, this is not the northernmost extent of volcanoes in Canada. Both dormant and extinct volcanoes associated with subduction of the Juan de Fuca Plate are present throughout the western part of British Columbia, northward into the western portion of the Yukon Territory. The northernmost volcanoes in this line, however, have not been active in more than 10,000 years. Canada's most recent eruption—in 1800—was that of the Iskut-Unuk River Cones, a young basaltic volcanic center in western British Columbia.

See Also: Basalt; Cascadia Subduction Zone; Juan de Fuca Plate; North American Plate; Orphan Tsunami; Pacific Plate; Tsunami.

Further Reading

Smithsonian Institution. National Museum of Natural History. Global Volcanism Program. (2014, June 4). Retrieved from http://www.volcano.si.edu/

U.S. Geological Survey. Earthquake Hazards Program. (2014, June 4). *Canada earthquake information.* Retrieved from http://earthquake.usgs.gov/earthquakes/world/?region =Canada

Caribbean Plate

The Caribbean Plate is located adjacent to the eastern Pacific Ocean in Central America. The plate has a long and interesting tectonic history. At its eastern edge, the Caribbean Plate overrides the North American and South American plates as they subduct beneath it. This has created the Lesser Antilles, an island arc that contains a number of dangerous volcanoes. The deadly and disastrous 1902 eruption of Mont Pelée on Martinique is one example of the possible behavior of these volcanoes. A large pyroclastic flow emerged from the summit crater of Pelée, and less than a minute later it engulfed the city of Saint-Pierre. Almost all of the 28,000 residents in the city were killed, and not a single building was left intact. An ongoing eruption on the British possession of Montserrat has also experienced multiple pyroclastic flows. The capital city of Plymouth and much of the surrounding countryside have been completely consumed by them over a nearly twenty-year period, leaving nearly half of the island uninhabitable.

The western edge of the Caribbean Plate forms part of the Pacific Rim. Here, both the Cocos and Nazca plates are subducting beneath the Caribbean Plate. The Central American countries of Guatemala, El Salvador, Honduras, Nicaragua, Costa Rica, and Panama are located on the Caribbean Plate. All of those countries are prone to powerful earthquakes, and all have at least a few volcanoes that have erupted in the last few thousand years. The country of Guatemala contains not only the western edge of the Caribbean Plate, but also part of its northern extent.

The northern boundary of the Caribbean Plate is a transform boundary. In 1976, a deadly earthquake on this boundary killed approximately 23,000 people. In El Salvador, twin events in January and February of 2001 triggered landslides that killed several hundred people dead. A 1972 earthquake beneath the capital city of Managua, Nicaragua, left approximately 5,000 people dead; most were killed by building collapse. Panama and Honduras largely have been spared these types of events.

A number of volcanoes in Central America exist as a result of the subduction zone along the Middle America Trench. In Guatemala, more than 1 million people live within close proximity to both the Fuego and Santa María volcanoes. The Costa Rican volcanoes Poás and Arenal are popular tourist destinations; both volcanoes are centerpieces of national parks that bear their names. Although the volcanoes are almost continuously active, they rarely behave in dangerous manners and are relatively safe for tourists to approach. Nicaragua also has its share of active volcanoes, including Telica, San Cristóbal, and Concepción. None has erupted violently in the recent past.

See Also: Arenal Volcano, Costa Rica; Cocos Plate; Costa Rica; El Salvador; Guatemala; Guatemala Earthquake (1976); Nazca Plate; Nicaragua; Poás Volcano, Costa Rica; Santa María, Guatemala; Subduction Zone; Transform Boundary.

Further Reading

Smithsonian Institution. National Museum of Natural History. Global Volcanism Program. (2014, June 16). http://www.volcano.si.edu/

U.S. Geological Survey. (2014, June 16). *Historic world earthquakes*. Retrieved from http://earthquake.usgs.gov/earthquakes/region.php

Cascadia Subduction Zone

The Cascadia Subduction Zone is located off the coast of the northwestern United States and southern Canada. It is approximately 620 miles (1,000 kilometers) long, extending from northern Vancouver Island (Canada) to Cape Mendocino, California. It separates the North American plate from the adjacent Explorer, Juan de Fuca, and Gorda plates. Subduction is occurring along this boundary at a rate of approximately 1.6 inches (40 millimeters) per year.

Subduction is a violent process in which solid oceanic lithosphere is forced downward into the solid, yet flexible, mantle beneath the neighboring lithospheric plate. Although each subduction zone is different they all share certain characteristics. At all subduction zones, the rocks in the region are subjected to a great deal of strain (deformation). This leads to the formation of a wide variety of landforms created by the compression of rocks occurring as the two plates move toward each other. In the case of the Cascadia Subduction Zone, the Coast Ranges and Olympic Mountains on the Olympic Peninsula of Washington are mountains that were—and continue to be—formed as a result of this compression. The Coast Ranges and Olympic Mountains contain rocks formed at the bottom of the ocean that were squeezed, uplifted, and crumpled or folded into mountains. Another component of the Coast Ranges is a package of rocks formed when ocean-floor sediment is scraped from the downgoing plate and sticks to the edge of the continent where it is compressed and folded. The process of sticking ocean-floor sediment onto the edge of a continent at a subduction zone is called "accretion," and the landform created in this way is called an "accretionary wedge" or "accretionary prism."

Subduction also is responsible for creating a chain of volcanoes that appears on the overriding plate. This is the case for the volcanoes forming the Cascade Range in western North America. The Cascade Range extends from Mount Meager in southern British Columbia, Canada, southward to Lassen Peak in northern California. The Cascades contain such notable mountains as Mount Rainier, Mount Hood, Mount St. Helens, Mount Shasta, and Crater Lake. Subduction of the small plates beneath the west coast of North America has fueled volcanic eruptions in the Cascades for at least 40,000 years and possibly longer.

Subduction zones also are sites of frequent earthquakes, a small percentage of which could be large and damaging. Notable recent earthquakes on the Cascadia Subduction Zone include the magnitude 6.8 Nisqually earthquake, which occurred west of Olympia, Washington, on February 28, 2001; and the magnitude 7.7 Masset earthquake, which occurred in the Queen Charlotte Islands off the coast of British Columbia, Canada, on October 28, 2012. The Nisqually earthquake occurred in the middle of the work day. Buildings swayed and the ground rolled, but residents saw very little actual damage from that earthquake. It occurred at a depth of 32 miles (52 kilometers) beneath the earth's surface, so the epicenter was 32 miles from the earthquake's most severe effects. The Masset earthquake occurred at a much shallower depth (10.5 miles, or 17 kilometers) but in a sparsely populated area, so no major damage resulted. The earthquake, however, did generate a small tsunami that warranted issuance of a tsunami warning for the Hawaiian Islands. The largest waves that struck Hawaii were measured on Maui at only 2.5 meters above average sea level, so residents of both Canada and Hawaii were spared the worst effects of the Masset earthquake as well.

The Nisqually and Masset earthquakes are typical of the large earthquakes on the Cascadia Subduction Zone occurring since European settlement in the early 1800s. Consequently, many scientists questioned whether this particular subduction zone was capable of producing large, damaging earthquakes or Pacific-wide tsunamis. This is not purely an academic or theoretical question; it has serious implications for many aspects of modern life. The answer determines which building codes should be adopted to give buildings and their occupants the best chance of surviving an earthquake, and what information local residents need about earthquake and tsunami hazards.

The question, "Is the Cascadia Subduction Zone capable of large, damaging earthquakes?" was answered in the 1990s by a number of scientists in Canada, the United States, and Japan, as well as by Native American leaders in the region of the Cascadia Subduction zone. Two American scientists determined that groves of trees along the Washington coastline had been inundated with seawater during ground subsidence resulting from large earthquakes 300 years ago, 1,700 years ago, and 3,100 years ago. They found not only that the ground had subsided, but that tsunami deposits buried the lower parts of the trees. These two findings led to the conclusion that earthquakes and locally generated tsunamis did occur on the Cascadia Subduction Zone, and are likely to occur again.

Native American leaders of the region provided additional evidence of these events in the form of legends and oral traditions dating back to the period before European settlement of the area. The traditions of Nuu-chah-nulth people include stories of earthquakes. Nuu-chah-nulth legends speak of dwarves who "had houses inside of mountains, where they enticed the unwary [visitors] to dance with them around and around a great wooden drum. Sooner or later [the visitor] stumbled against the drum, and became afflicted with a peculiar disease called 'earthquake foot'—every time he took a step the ground shook" (Hutchinson & McMillan, 1997). The Nuu-chah-nulth people also tell of the destruction of a village on Pachena Bay, located near what is today Bamfield, British Columbia. According to oral history,

> They had practically no way or time to try to save themselves. I think it was at nighttime that the land shook . . . I think a big wave smashed into the beach. The Pachena Bay people were lost . . . But they . . . who lived at[the] 'House-Up-Against-Hill,' the wave did not reach because they were on high ground . . . Because of that they came out alive. They did not drift out to sea with the others (Hutchinson & McMillan, 1997).

The Cowichan people of southeastern Vancouver Island speak of an earthquake that occurred before European settlement. The earthquake shook houses apart and caused rockslides. One village was completely destroyed. These stories clearly indicate that strong earthquakes and locally generated tsunamis became part of the Native American consciousness and history long before any European contact.

In addition to oral tradition and legend, archaeological studies undertaken since the 1990s prove that during the last 3,000 years multiple coastal villages were occupied for long periods of time, and then were abandoned around the time of major geologic events. When villages were actively occupied, scientists found cultural materials and food waste, which includes discarded oyster and clam shells. When villages were abandoned, there is a sharp boundary between cultural and food materials and geologic materials such as clay and sand, which are typical of tsunami deposits. One study that examined archaeological sites along the coasts of Vancouver Island and Washington State indicates that six major earthquakes that were significant enough to cause abandonment of coastal villages took place within the last 3,000 years. The last of these occurred roughly 300 years ago, around the year 1700. This correlates well with another study of sunken forests and wetlands, which found evidence for the same six earthquakes and a resulting tsunami. Tsunami generation requires that a relatively shallow earthquake of magnitude 7 or greater occurs in a coastal region, and that the earthquake displaces the ocean floor vertically. These studies prove that the Cascadia Subduction Zone indeed is capable of experiencing damaging earthquakes that are large enough to produce tsunamis.

The discovery of an abundance of evidence for a great earthquake in 1700 CE solved a mystery that had puzzled the people of Japan for more than 300 years. In the year 1700 CE, a great wave struck the Japanese islands without warning. There was no local earthquake or large storm, yet the wave struck the coastline with enormous force, and reached heights of 16 feet (5 meters). Records from Japan indicate that no earthquake occurred in January of 1700 CE. Computer modeling, archaeological studies, tree-ring studies, and geologic studies confirm that an earthquake with a magnitude between 8.7 and 9.2 occurred at that time in the Cascadia Subduction Zone. It ruptured the entire 620-mile (1,000-kilometer) length of the subduction zone and would have been strong enough to generate a tsunami the size of the one observed in Japan. Although the Cascadia Subduction Zone has not produced a great earthquake (one with a magnitude greater than 8) in 300 years, there is no reason to believe it will not do so in the future.

See Also: Canada; Japan; Subduction Zone; Tsunami; United States of America.

Further Reading

Atwater, B. F., & Yamaguchi, D. K. (1991). Sudden, probably coseismic submergence of Holocene trees and grass in coastal Washington State. *Geology 19*(7), 706–709.

Clague, J. J. (1997). Evidence for large earthquakes at the Cascadia Subduction Zone. *Reviews of Geophysics 35*(4), 439–460.

CNN. (2012, October 29). *Canada quake triggers Hawaii tsunami scare.* Retrieved from http://www.cnn.com/2012/10/28/world/americas/canada-earthquake/index.html?iref=allsearch

Hutchinson, I., & McMillan, A. D. (1997). Archaeological evidence for village abandonment associated with late Holocene earthquakes at the northern Cascadia Subduction Zone, *Quaternary Research* 48 pp.79–87.

Ludwin, R. S., Dennis, R., Carver, D., McMillan, A. D., Losey, R., Clague, J., Jonientz-Trisler, C., Bowechop, J., Wray, J., & James, K. (2005). Dating the 1700 Cascadia Earthquake: Great coastal earthquakes in native stories. *Seismological Research Letters* *76*(2).

U.S. Geological Survey. (2013). *Canada volcanoes and volcanics.* Retrieved May 23, 2013, from http://vulcan.wr.usgs.gov/Volcanoes/Canada/description_canadian_volcanics.html

U.S. Geological Survey. (2013, May 23). *The orphan tsunami of 1700—Japanese clues to a parent earthquake in North America.* (Professional Paper 1707). Retrieved from http://pubs.usgs.gov/pp/pp1707/pp1707.pdf

U.S. Geological Survey. Earthquake Hazards Program. (2012, October 29). *Masset. M7.7– 139 km S of Masset, Canada.* Retrieved from http://earthquake.usgs.gov/earthquakes/eventpage/usb000df7n#summary

U.S. Geological Survey. Earthquake Hazards Program. (2012, October 29). *Nisqually.* Retrieved from http://earthquake.usgs.gov/earthquakes/eqarchives/year/2001/2001_02_28.php

Chaitén Volcano, Chile

Chaitén is a relatively small, inconspicuous volcano located on the Gulf of Corcovado on the Chilean coast, and approximately 6 miles (10 kilometers) northeast of the town of Chaitén. Its summit rises to an elevation of 3,681 feet (1,122 meters) above sea level. It is a somewhat unique volcano in that its primary eruptive product is rhyolite. Rhyolite magma is prone to both extremely violent gas-driven eruptions as well as quiet extrusion of lava that often forms domes on the floors of craters and calderas. Its last explosive eruption is thought to have occurred about 9,400 years ago. That eruption created a caldera approximately 1.8 miles (3 kilometers) in diameter. The caldera-forming eruption produced great volumes of rhyolite ash and pumice, and was capped by basalt scoria. This indicates that shortly before the eruption basalt was injected into the magma chamber from below, likely providing the new gas-rich magma necessary to trigger the eruption. Rhyolite magma from the top of the magma chamber first was erupted, and then basalt from the bottom of the magma chamber erupted. Based on estimates of the volume of the mountain that collapsed as the caldera formed, the eruption 9,400 years ago warrants a Volcanic Explosivity Index (VEI) of 5. Sometime after the explosive eruption, an obsidian lava dome was emplaced on the caldera floor. The obsidian dome had a volume of nearly 0.12 cubic mile (0.5 cubic kilometer).

On May 2, 2008, Chaitén began an eruption that took both scientists and area residents by surprise. It is not known precisely whether the volcano truly provided little precursory activity, or if the activity simply was not detected. The volcano was not considered to be a threat to the region, so there was no monitoring network in place prior to the 2008 eruption. The closest instruments were more than 185 miles (300 kilometers) to the north, so they only detected a few large earthquakes in the week leading up to the eruption. The earthquakes detected did not raise any alarms at the time because they were located up to 12 miles (20 kilometers) away from the volcano. Late on April 30, just 27 hours before the first large eruption, local residents felt a series of earthquakes that provided the first warning of the onset of volcanic activity. Late on May 1, a magnitude 3.5 earthquake was detected approximately 8 miles (15 kilometers) north of the town of Chaitén. A few hours later, ash began falling in town, signifying that a small eruption had occurred at approximately the same time as the earthquake. On May 2, at 3:30 a.m. local

Steam, ash, and gases rise above Chaitén Volcano. (Chine Nouvelle/SIPA/Newscom)

time, the distant seismometers detected a large swarm of earthquakes, occurring at a rate of up to 20 per hour, which coincided with a Plinian eruption that lasted six hours. The eruption column reached a height of 12 miles (20 kilometers), well into the stratosphere. Around noon local time on May 2, pyroclastic flows were observed on the north and northeast sides of the volcano. Heavy ash fall blanketed the town of Chaitén, and over the next several days was blown eastward over Argentina and the southern Atlantic Ocean. All 4,625 residents of Chaitén were forced to evacuate, most by sea. Though seismic activity decreased dramatically by May 3, ash emission continued until May 6, when another Plinian eruption began. Again, the eruption column reached into the stratosphere. The same event occurred a third time on May 8. By that date, it was clear that Chile and the scientists at Servicio Nacional de Geología y Minería (SERNAGEOMIN) (National Service of Geology and Mining) had a major volcanic crisis on their hands. The United States offered to send a team of scientists from the Volcano Disaster Assistance Program (VDAP) to help. The government of Chile sent a formal request for its services, and one week later VDAP scientists were on the ground in Chile, helping local scientists install a seismic monitoring system on the volcano's flanks.

The eruption of Chaitén went through two distinct phases. Throughout the first half of May 2008, the volcano was in an explosive phase. During this time, most of its activity was explosive in nature, lofting ash columns up to 12 miles (20 kilometers) into the atmosphere, and creating pyroclastic flows. Major Plinian eruptions occurred on May 2, May 6, and May 8, and less vigorous eruptions occurred through May 12. Following the explosive phase was an effusive phase in which lava was erupted somewhat quietly from the vent in the old lava dome located on the caldera floor. The result was enlargement of the existing dome. From late May through September 2008, dome growth primarily was exogenous in nature—meaning that new lava was erupted onto the surface of the existing dome. From October 2008 through mid-February 2009, the eruption switched to one of spine formation. Nearly solid magma was erupted to the surface, forming tall, narrow spines of new rock. Between late February 2009 and the end of the eruption in late 2009 or early 2010, the eruption was almost entirely endogenous. Endogenous dome growth occurs beneath the surface of the dome. No new lava is visible at the surface, but additional rock volume is added to the interior of the dome.

The eruption was notable to both the public and the scientific community for a number of reasons. Heavy ash fall to the east of the volcano affected daily life in communities downwind of the volcano. Near the volcano, 298 square miles (480 square kilometers) of forest were damaged by tephra fall and pyroclastic flows. Livestock and crops were lost, electrical distribution networks were damaged, surface-water supplies were fouled, and there was minor disruption of telecommunications. The ash clouds from the volcano also caught pilots and air traffic control by surprise in the early hours of the eruption on May 1–2, 2008. Five aircraft flying near Argentina's Bariloche Airport were damaged as they flew through volcanic ash clouds at an unusually low altitude of less than 6,500 feet (2,000 meters). Although all flights landed safely, the planes suffered turbine and engine damage. This is notable not only because hundreds of passengers and crew members above those five flights were in danger but also because, in theory, this situation should not have happened. The hazards of aviation around ash clouds have been known for decades.

Between 1973 and 2000, more than 100 commercial aircraft had encounters with volcanic ash clouds. One of the most dramatic involved a British Airways 747-200 that flew through an ash cloud from the volcano Galunggung while over Indonesia, en route from Kuala Lampur to Perth, Australia. The plane lost power to all four of its engines, as well as all of its electrical systems. The plane fell for nearly 30 minutes before the crew was able to restart the engines and land safely in Jakarta. In the 1980s, the International Civil Aviation Organization, a United Nations program, set up a worldwide volcanic ash monitoring system. Nine Volcanic Ash Advisory Centers (VAACs) were established around the world. The VAAC nearest Chaitén is located in Buenos Aires. Chaitén, which had not had an explosive eruption in more than 9,000 years, was not considered a major threat. The lack of monitoring of the volcano and the surprising nature of the volcano meant that volcanic ash plume data from satellite monitoring was somewhat delayed in getting to the VAAC and pilots. Additional problems resulted from discrepancies between observers and incoming data, and problems with the VAAC modeling software that did not accurately predict the path of the ash clouds.

The composition of the eruptive products from Chaitén also was of interest to the scientific community. Rhyolite eruptions are relatively rare phenomena. This was the first major rhyolite eruption since Novarupta (Alaska) in 1912. It was something of a geological oddity, and attracted scientists from around the world to study the volcano and its deposits.

The rhyolite magma also provided additional challenges to the VAAC in Buenos Aires. Satellites have instruments that detect sulfur dioxide (SO_2), which is present in volcanic ash clouds but not in normal clouds. Rhyolite ash is low in sulfur dioxide, making it difficult for satellites to detect this type of volcanic ash clouds. When the VAACs realized the nature of the ash they were monitoring, they adjusted as best they could to provide accurate and timely advisories.

The surprise eruption of Chaitén prompted action within the Chilean government to plan, fund, and implement a national volcano monitoring program (Red Nacional de Vigilancia Volcánica), modeled after a strategy proposed by the U.S. Geological Survey for monitoring volcanoes in the United States. The program has as its backbone a plan to build real-time monitoring networks for Chile's highest risk volcanoes. Additional necessary measures include hazard mapping, continued international monitoring collaborations, and refinement of eruptive and ash-distribution models.

See Also: Caldera; Chile; Lava Dome; Rhyolite.

Further Reading

Carn, S. A., Pallister, J. S., Lara, L., Ewert, J. W., Watt, S., Prata, A. J., Thomas, R. J., & Villarosa, G. (2009). The unexpected awakening of Chaitén Volcano, Chile. *EOS 90*(24), 205–212.

Grambling, C. (2010). Tracking volcanic ash: Helping airplanes avoid catastrophe. *Earth Magazine* (digital ed.). Retrieved from http://www.earthmagazine.org/tags /april-2010

Lara, L. E. (2009). The 2008 eruption of the Chaitén Volcano, Chile: A preliminary report. *Andean Geology 36*(1), 125–129.

Major, J. J., & Lara, L. E. (2013). Overview of the Chaitén Volcano, Chile, and its 2008–2009 eruption. *Andean Geology 40*(2), 196–215.

Smithsonian Institution. (2014). National Museum of Natural History. Global Volcanism Program. *Chaitén summary*. Retrieved from http://www.volcano.si.edu/volcano .cfm?vnum=1508-041

U.S. Geological Survey. Volcano Disaster Assistance Program. (2011, February 14). *VDAP responses at Chaitén in Chile*. Retrieved from http://volcanoes.usgs.gov/vdap /activities/responses/chaiten.php

Chile

The country of Chile is located along the west coast of southern South America. It is a long and narrow country bordered by the Pacific Ocean to the west and to the east the Andes Mountains—many of which are volcanoes. Chile has an extraordinarily high number of active volcanoes, including seven that have erupted since the year 2000. Chile also has been the site of many extremely strong earthquakes, including the largest earthquake of the Twentieth Century which occurred on May 22, 1960. The magnitude 9.5 event also is the largest instrumentally recorded earthquake to date. Many of Chile's large coastal earthquakes tend to generate tsunamis. Fault motion almost always involves some vertical movement, which is a requirement for generating a large Pacific-wide tsunami. Volcano and earthquake activity in Chile is caused by subduction of either the Nazca Plate or Antarctic Plate (depending on location) beneath the South American Plate.

Chile contains active volcanoes of all types but, by far, the most common type of volcano within the country is the composite volcano. Six of the world's tallest volcanoes are located within Chile, including the tallest volcano in the world, Ojos del Salado, which is a towering 22,595 feet (6,887 meters) tall. Ojos del Salado has not erupted in historic times, but the tallest volcano that has erupted in recorded history also is in Chile. It is the Llullaillaco Volcano, which has an elevation of 22,109 feet (6,739 meters). Llullaillaco last erupted in 1877. The mountain also is famous because of the frozen mummified human remains found on its slopes between 1983 and 1985. The mummies were buried with textiles, gold and silver

Copahue Volcano in the Chilean Andes. (JORGE VILLEGAS Xinhua News Agency/Newscom)

statues, and pottery. They are some of the best preserved mummified bodies ever found, largely because of the extreme cold and arid environment. Llullaillaco is located within the Atacama Desert—the driest place on Earth.

Several volcanoes in Chile have erupted since the year 2000. The Chaitén Volcano erupted fairly violently in 2008, and disrupted air travel in the region for several days. The Cerro Hudson Volcano is the southernmost volcano in Chile related to subduction of the Nazca Plate. South of this volcano, any eruptive activity is associated with subduction of the Antarctic Plate beneath South America. Cerro Hudson, a broad composite volcano buried beneath ice sheets, last erupted in 2011. The Láscar Volcano is a large stratovolcano—or composite volcano—located on the border of Chile, Bolivia, and Argentina. In April of 2013, a short-lived eruption sent small amounts of ash into the atmosphere. The Llaima Volcano, one of Chile's largest and most active volcanoes, last erupted in 2008–2009. The Peteroa vent within the Planchón-Peteroa volcanic center had its last eruption in 2011. A small ash cloud issued from the Puyehue-Cordón Caulle volcanic complex in February 2014. The Villarrica volcano last erupted in 2013.

Although a great number of major earthquakes have occurred in Chile, only a few have resulted in more than 1,000 fatalities. This is due in large part to the fact that earthquakes are such a common occurrence in Chile that buildings have been engineered to withstand significant shaking. People also are wary of earthquakes, therefore when a cluster of strong earthquakes occurs, they respond immediately to keep their families safe. Clusters of strong earthquakes in some cases have turned out to be foreshocks to a much larger earthquake, so wariness serves the population well in those circumstances. The estimated magnitude 9.0 Arica earthquake that occurred in 1868 is believed to have killed 25,000 people, and produced a tsunami that produced damage in New Zealand, Hawaii, and Japan. A 1906 magnitude 8.2 earthquake near Valparaiso killed 3,882 people. A magnitude 7.8 earthquake in January of 1939 resulted in 28,000 fatalities near Chillán. The 1960 earthquake and the tsunami it generated killed more than 1,000 people in Chile, more than 60 people in the Hawaiian Islands, 32 people in the Philippines, and 138 people in Japan.

See Also: Arica Earthquake and Tsunami, Chile (1868); Chaitén Volcano, Chile; Chilean Earthquake and Tsunami (1960); Nazca Plate; South American Plate; Subduction Zone.

Further Reading

Smithsonian Institution. National Museum of Natural History. Global Volcanism Program. (2014, June 11). Retrieved from http://www.volcano.si.edu/volcano.cfm?vn=357120

U.S. Geological Survey. (2014, June 11). *Historic world earthquakes. Chile.* Retrieved from http://earthquake.usgs.gov/earthquakes/world/historical_country.php#chile

Volcano Discovery. (2014, June 11). *Llullaillaco volcano.* Retrieved from http://www.volcanodiscovery.com/llullaillaco.html

Volcano Discovery. (2014, June 11). *Which is the world's highest volcano?* Retrieved from http://www.volcanodiscovery.com/volcanology/worlds-highest-volcano.html

Chilean Earthquake and Tsunami (1960)

On May 22, 1960, an earthquake with magnitude of 9.6—the largest earthquake ever instrumentally recorded and the Twentieth Century's most powerful quake—shook southern Chile near Concepción, 200 miles (322 kilometers) south of the capital, Santiago. A 750-mile (1,207-kilometer) stretch of the fault line involved was ruptured, and extensive destruction followed to both human life and property. There were aftershocks—as many as a dozen of magnitude 6.0 or greater. The earthquake also caused a tsunami, which was most destructive along the coast of Chile and also caused numerous casualties and property damage in other places around the Pacific Ocean. It was estimated that more than 5,000 people lost their lives and some 3,000 were injured.

The Pacific Rim often is known as the Ring of Fire due to its frequent and often severe seismic and volcanic events. This area experienced the most powerful earthquakes ever recorded, those of magnitude 9.0 or greater, between 1950 and 2011: The 9.0 Kamchatka earthquake in 1952, the 9.5 Chile earthquake in 1960, the 9.2 Alaska earthquake in 1964, the 9.1 Indian Ocean earthquake in 2004, and the 9.0 Sendai, Japan earthquake in 2011. The places where all of these huge quakes struck were subduction zones; that is, places where tectonic plates are constantly moving beneath other tectonic plates. From time to time, as they move, an obstruction of some sort stops plate movement and strain (deformation) builds up. When the plates snap free of the obstruction, the release of energy causes an earthquake.

The location where the oceanic plate subducts beneath the continental plate in Chile is some distance offshore; hence, the epicenter of the quake also was offshore. The land area north of Concepción rose three feet as a result of the Chile earthquake in 1960, and land to the south was pushed upward by five feet. These were indications of the dislocations that occurred in the ocean depth at the epicenter—dislocations that created a tsunami. Concepción soon discovered the power of that tsunami when a 20-foot (6-meter) wave swept ashore, damaging or destroying half a million homes.

Along the Chilean coast, the tsunami brought 40-foot (12-meter) waves that, in some places, rose as high as 75 feet (24 meters). Dunes were washed away and sand was transported inland as far as 1,500 feet (457 meters). In one location where the tsunami reached 45 feet (14 meters), a thin layer of sand was found 6 miles (9.7 kilometers) inland. Over the 24 hours that followed the earthquake, places all around the Pacific Rim felt the tsunami. It reached Alaska after 18 hours, Japan after 22 hours, and hit Hawaii after 15 hours with a wave height of 10 feet, rising at times to 30 feet. This tsunami traveled at speeds of 400–500 miles per hour (mph) (644–805 kilometers per hour (kph)) depending on the amount of friction experienced below sea level.

There were three waves in the tsunami, each separated by substantial amounts of time. The third wave did most of the damage to Hawaii, even though the state was well prepared. Two years after a 1946 tsunami, an elaborate warning system was installed. The system included observation posts throughout the

Pacific Ocean that could relay information from tidal gauges to Hawaii or any other island nation affected. Unfortunately, a change in the way the Hawaiian warning signal was broadcast by radio left islanders puzzled. A decision had been made to move from a three-stage signal to a single-stage signal, but many people had forgotten about the change and waited for a second and third siren before acting. This led to far fewer people evacuating dangerous shore areas than was typical.

As in 1946, in 1960 the town of Hilo on the island of Hawaii suffered most severely. The other Hawaiian Islands experienced only moderate damage. At Hilo Bay, the highest wave towered more than 30 feet (9 meters) above normal sea level and raced inland at 30 mph (42 kph). Boulders as heavy as 20 tons (18 metric tonnes) were picked up from the bayfront seawall and carried 500 feet (152 meters) across a park without leaving a mark on the grass. Two-inch (51-millimeter) diameter pipes supporting parking meters were bent parallel to the ground. Entire city blocks were swept clean as buildings were wrenched from their foundations and deposited as piles of debris 300 feet (91 meters) away. More than 500 buildings were destroyed. At Hilo alone 61 people were crushed or drowned by the waves and an additional 43 required hospitalization.

See Also: Arica Earthquake and Tsunami, Chile (1868); Chile; Conception, Earthquake Chile, (1835); Sendai, Japan, Earthquake (2011).

Further Reading

Prager, E. J. (1999). *Furious earth: The science and nature of earthquakes, volcanoes, and tsunamis.* New York: McGraw-Hill.

Chimbote Earthquake, Peru (1970)

On May 31, 1970, a magnitude 7.9 earthquake occurred 22 miles (35 kilometers) west of the Peruvian fishing port of Chimbote, approximately 35 miles (56 kilometers) beneath the continental shelf. In that location, the Nazca Plate is subducting beneath the South American Plate. It is not unusual for Peru to experience large earthquakes, but this was by far the most damaging and deadly it had experienced to that time. In fact, until a magnitude 7.0 earthquake struck Haiti in January 2010, this event held the grim distinction of being the most deadly disaster in the western hemisphere. As many as 76,000 people lost their lives as a direct result of the earthquake and its associated phenomena. Additionally, 140,000 people were injured, and another 800,000 were left homeless. This was a disaster that overwhelmed Peru's resources and left people disenfranchised for years. Most of the damage and loss of life occurred within the department of Ancash.

The earthquake struck at 3:23 p.m. local time. Witnesses describe a few seconds of almost gentle ground motion at first, followed by severe shaking that lasted

Campo Santo, a park in Yungay, Peru, memorializes the 20,000 people who died here from landslides triggered by an earthquake in 1970. (Howie Garber / DanitaDelimont.com Danita Delimont Photography/ Newscom)

for approximately 45 seconds. When the earthquake was over, damage was significant along a 160-mile (260-kilometer) long stretch of the Peruvian coastline, from the town of Chiclayo in the north to Lima in the south. The city of Casma had a population of 13,000 people. Although there were relatively few deaths in the city, about 90% of its structures were severely damaged. Chimbote, the city nearest the epicenter, suffered 3,000 deaths and about 80% of its structures sustained severe damage or completely collapsed. Water, sewer, phone, and power lines were severed. Roads, railroads, and bridges also were damaged or destroyed. The widespread damage to buildings in cities along the coast largely was due to poor construction practices. Any buildings made of adobe crumbled and collapsed. Other buildings constructed of poor-quality concrete collapsed as well. Buildings composed of reinforced concrete with adequate bracing, or of wood frame, fared well in the earthquake.

Although damage in the coastal areas was severe, the area that suffered the greatest losses was located 50 miles (80 kilometers) inland, in the Callejón de Huaylas. The Callejón de Huaylas, also known as the Santa Valley for the Río Santa that runs through it, is a richly fertile valley where farmers grow wheat, barley, and corn. Before the earthquake, wealthy land owners held the majority of the fertile land on the valley floor, which was worked by laborers who lived on the sides of the valley in small towns or on very small plots of land. Because the valley floor is composed of loose, unconsolidated material, the surface waves from the earthquake were amplified. Many buildings in the valley were built of adobe, and those buildings—houses, businesses, churches, schools, and government buildings—collapsed into clouds of dust. In the city of Huaraz alone, more than 20,000 people were killed, most by the collapsing buildings. Especially difficult for people to comprehend was the death of 400 children in the Santa Elena Convent. They were attending a celebration of the school's director when the earthquake began. The building collapsed on top of them.

The Callejón de Huaylas is bordered to the west by the Cordillera Negra (Black Mountains) and to the east by the Cordillera Blanca (White Mountains). The Cordillera Negra consist of rounded mountains that rise 7,500 feet (2,300 meters) above the valley floor. The valley floor has an average elevation of 9,100 feet (2,770 meters) above sea level. The Cordillera Blanca are even more impressive. They rise an average of 12,000 feet (4,000 meters) above the Santa Valley. The two highest peaks are Huascarán Norte at 21,873 feet (6,667 meters) and Huascarán Sud, at 22,211 feet (6,770 meters). The mountains of the Cordillera Blanca are steep-sided and covered in snow and ice. Because of their steep terrain, these mountains are prone to deadly ice falls and frequent landslides.

May 31, 1970 was a Sunday. Families were out and about, visiting relatives, shopping, or otherwise enjoying the day with family and friends. A group of Czech climbers were ascending Huascarán Norte, and a separate group of Japanese climbers were on a nearby peak. As the earth began to shake, the Japanese climbers saw an enormous mass of ice and rock break free from Huascarán Norte. They estimated it to be nearly 3,000 feet (1 kilometer) wide. They watched in horror as it fell to the unstable glacier below. It continued downward, engulfing the Czech team. The avalanche gained speed and is estimated to have been traveling at 155 miles per hour (250 kilometers per hour) down the steepest face of Huascarán Norte. It rode on a cushion of air, which allowed it to travel at tremendous speeds. Friction apparently caused the ice and snow within the avalanche to melt, turning the ice, snow, and rock into a muddy debris flow. Before the avalanche reached the Río Santa, about 2,000 people had been swept up and killed.

As the avalanche neared the base of the mountain, it struck a high hill called Shacsha and split into two lobes. One lobe covered the town of Yangay, which had served as the provincial capital. An estimated 18,000 people were buried beneath debris in the city. Only about 300 residents survived. A group of children had been attending a circus on the outside of town, and a clown led them to higher ground when he saw the avalanche bearing down on them. Most of the children became orphans that day. Another 92 people escaped the avalanche by climbing the city's cemetery hill. A few others evaded the debris because they were located on unusually high hills. The other lobe of the avalanche buried the town of Ranrahirca. Ranrahirca had been hit just eight years earlier by a debris avalanche that killed most of the town's residents. This avalanche killed almost all of the remaining people in town.

Debris from the avalanche continued across the valley and ascended more than 246 feet (75 meters) up the base of the Cordillera Negra before settling back down into the valley the Río Santa. Mud, boulders weighing up to 14,000 tons, trees, corpses, and other materials were swept down the Río Santa at approximately 20 miles per hour (35 kilometers per hour). As it plunged down the river valley and eventually into a steep-walled canyon, the debris flow continued to take lives. It dammed the Río Santa for a short time, and then surged downstream. It choked the canyon and overwhelmed the rail line that provided the only escape route from that end of the valley—it killed all of the passengers aboard the train that was in the canyon.

Recovery was painfully slow. All land routes into and out of Callejón de Huaylas were destroyed or blocked. Telephone lines were severed. The first word of the destruction in the valley came from a shortwave radio operator. Despite his efforts to summon help, Peruvian government officials were skeptical that such severe damage could have resulted from the earthquake. It took four days for the first outside help to arrive, and six days before temporary shelter and small amounts of food and water were brought to the survivors. Government officials realized they had a bigger disaster than they could handle on their own, so they reached out for international aid. The Peruvian government recently had changed hands, however, and the leaders wanted to change the culture of life in the valley. While the government conducted studies, it prevented people from staking out their property lines or beginning rebuilding efforts. As a result, most families were left languishing in temporary shelters, completely dependent on aid for more than two years.

When the government finally started the rebuilding process, it brought in prefabricated concrete housing. The Peruvian government then dictated that all property belonged to the government and was for sale in small 3,230 square foot, or 0.07 acre (300 square meter) parcels. Because residents had lost everything in the earthquake and landslides, most could not afford even these modestly priced parcels of land. People also were encouraged to take out loans from the government to build their new homes on their parcels of land, which many were opposed to doing. The government's aim was to eliminate the social and socioeconomic classes that had developed in the valley, but it instead succeeded in demoralizing the entire population. Many years passed before the government changed hands again and people were allowed to do as they wished with their land, their homes, and even with regard to their religious customs.

See Also: Earthquake; Earthquake Hazards; Nazca Plate; Peru; South American Plate; Subduction Zone.

Further Reading

Erickson, G. E., Plafker, G., & Concha, J. F. (1970). *Preliminary report on the geologic events associated with the May 31, 1970, Peru earthquake* (U.S. Geological Survey Circular 639).

Zeilinga de Boer, J., & Sanders, D. T. (2005). *Earthquakes in human history.* Princeton, NJ: Princeton University Press.

Cinder Cone

A cinder cone (also known as a scoria cone) is a relatively small volcanic cone built of cinder-like scoria. Scoria is a rock that typically is red or black in color, and is basaltic to andesitic in composition. It contains many holes, or vesicles, formed by expanding gas bubbles that do not have a chance to pop before the magma cools and hardens around them. Scoria is usually erupted as a pyroclastic material; tossed into the air during an eruption and cooling enough to harden before it reaches the ground. In addition to scoria, cinder cones also commonly produce lava bombs, volcanic ash, and lava flows.

Cinder cones are among the smallest of volcano types, rarely reaching heights of more than 1,000 feet (300 meters) or diameters of 5,500 feet (1,700 meters). They are classified as monogenetic volcanoes, meaning that they are the product of a single volcanic eruption. The eruption that forms a cinder cone can last just a few hours or continue for many years. When the eruption is over, however, that particular cone never erupts again. There are very few exceptions to this general rule, but one such exception is Cerro Negro in Guatemala. Cerro Negro has erupted 24 times since 1850.

Cinder cones most commonly are found in one of two settings, one of which is a volcanic field. A volcanic field is a collection of a large number of cinder cones in the same region. Examples of volcanic fields include the Raton-Clayton Volcanic Field in the northeastern corner of New Mexico, the Trans-Mexican Volcanic Belt in the southwestern Mexican state of Michoacán (which includes the famous volcano Paricutín), the San Francisco Peaks Volcanic Field north of Flagstaff, Arizona, and Craters of the Moon National Monument and Preserve in Idaho. In each of these locations, dozens to hundreds of cinder cones of varying ages dot the landscape, often surrounded by lava flows that issued from these cones. These volcanic fields often are long-lived, remaining active for tens of thousands of years.

Wizard Island, a nearly symmetrical cinder cone located inside the caldera of Crater Lake, Oregon. (Greg Vaughn / VWPics/Newscom)

The second setting in which a cinder cone can be found is as a parasitic cone on another type of volcano. Contrary to images conjured up by its name, a parasitic cone does not have the same detrimental effect on the host volcano that a parasitic organism has on its host. It simply is a vent through which an eruption on that particular volcano occurs. Mount Etna, a complex composite volcano on the Italian island of Sicily, has dozens of cinder cones on its flanks, each a vent site from a single eruptive episode. The shield volcanoes of Hawaii and the Galapagos Islands also are host to a large number of cinder cones.

See Also: Andesite; Basalt; Parícutin Volcano, Mexico; Pyroclastic Materials.

Further Reading

Francis, P., & Oppenheimer, C. (2004). *Volcanoes* (2nd ed.). Oxford: Oxford University Press.

Tarbuck, E. J., Lutgens, F. K., & Tasa, D. (2011). *Earth: An introduction to physical geology* (10th ed.). Upper Saddle River, NJ: Pearson Prentice Hall.

Vespermann, D., & Schmincke, H.-U. (2000). Scoria cones and tuff rings. In H. Sugurdsson, B. Jouhgton, H. Rymer, J. Stix, & S. McNutt (Eds.), *Encyclopedia of Volcanoes*. San Diego, CA: Academic Press.

Cleveland Volcano, Alaska, United States

The Mount Cleveland Volcano is located in the central Aleutian Islands in Alaska. It comprises the western half of Chuginadak Island. Cleveland is attached to the eastern half of the island, which houses Chuginadak Volcano, by a narrow and low-lying isthmus. The lower flanks of Cleveland have been extensively eroded, but the upper portion of the volcano is steep-sided, conical, and symmetrical. The elevation at the summit of Cleveland is 4,675 feet (1,730 meters) above sea level. The volcano is consistently relatively active, emitting small amounts of volcanic ash through minor explosions from its summit crater periodically. The volcano has been observed to lose snow more quickly than other volcanoes of the same height. This is perhaps because of consistent volcanic activity at its summit. At the time of this writing, the volcano is considered to be experiencing activity above background levels, but it is not in current eruption; however, it has erupted sporadically for years.

The Cleveland Volcano holds the distinction of being the only Aleutian volcano to claim a human life. The island was the site of an outpost for a small detachment of soldiers from the 11th Army Air Force during World War II. The volcano erupted in 1944 with moderate amounts of explosive activity and a relatively high volume of ash. A soldier on a reconnaissance mission ventured too close to the volcano and was killed, possibly by a lahar (a moving fluid mass consisting of water and volcanic debris). Military personnel were evacuated and the base was abandoned for the duration of the war. Military observation flights eventually resumed, however, and in 1953 an observer noted dark ash on the snow around Cleveland's vent.

Today, the volcano is monitored by the Alaskan Volcano Observatory. Scientists have outfitted the volcano with seismometers and with an infrasound network to detect disturbances in the atmosphere even in the long, dark winters or in inclement weather. The area also is monitored by satellites capable of detecting thermal anomalies in the volcano's crater as well as volcanic ash plumes. Chuginadak Island is uninhabited, therefore the greatest hazard posed by Cleveland Volcano is from airborne volcanic ash that can intersect flight paths between North America and Asia.

See Also: Aleutian Islands; Lahar.

Further Reading

Miller, T. P., McGimsey, R. G., Richter, D. H., Riehle, J. R., Nye, C. J., Yount, M. E., & Dumoulin, J. A. (1998). *Catalog of the historically active volcanoes of Alaska.* United States Geological Survey (Open-File Report OF 98-05282).

U.S. Geological Survey. (2014, May 28). *Cleveland activity.* Retrieved from http://www.avo.alaska.edu/activity/Cleveland.php

Wood, C. A., & Kienle, J. (1992). *Volcanoes of North America, United States and Canada.* Cambridge: Cambridge University Press.

Cocos Plate

The Cocos Plate is a relatively small oceanic plate located just south of Mexico and Central America. Its southern margin is a spreading center called the Galapagos Ridge. At its northern margin it is being subducted beneath both the North American Plate and the Caribbean Plate. The boundary between the Caribbean and North American plates is a transform boundary that runs through the country of Guatemala. The western margin of the plate is a spreading center called the East Pacific Rise. The eastern margin of the Cocos Plate is an oblique (diagonal) transform boundary between the Cocos and Nazca plates.

The Cocos Plate has a long and interesting history. The plate originally was part of a much larger tectonic plate called the Farallon Plate. The Farallon Plate was a large oceanic plate that made up the eastern part of the Pacific Ocean. The Farallon Plate, however, was being consumed at a subduction zone to its east faster than it could be created at the spreading center to its west. The result was complete subduction of part of the larger Farallon Plate. Where the Farallon Plate was subducted completely, the Pacific Plate came into contact with the North American Plate. It was through this action that the San Andreas Fault—the boundary between the Pacific and North American plates—was born. The Pacific Plate is moving northwestward, so the sense of motion between the North American

Plate and its neighbor to the west changed dramatically from what it had been before the disappearance of the Farallon Plate that was in that area. The San Andreas is a transform boundary rather than a subduction zone. As current plate motions persist, the San Andreas Fault will continue to lengthen as more of the old Farallon Plate is subducted. The Cocos Plate also will get smaller as it continues to be destroyed faster than it can be created at the East Pacific Rise or Galapagos Ridge.

The current plates seen in the eastern Pacific are the remnants of the old Farallon Plate. These remnants—from north to south—are the Juan de Fuca Plate adjacent to the Pacific Northwest of the United States, and southern British Columbia. The tiny Rivera Plate is adjacent to southern Mexico. The Cocos Plate, as described here is the third remnant, and the Nazca Plate to its south is the fourth remnant of the Farallon Plate. All of these remnant plates continue to move eastward, as did the larger Farallon Plate. Subduction of portions of the Farallon Plate does not appear to have caused any serious reorganization in mantle convection currents that determine the rate and direction of plate motion.

Subduction of the Cocos Plate beneath Mexico and Central America has created a volcanic belt that stretches the entire length of the northern plate boundary. All volcanoes in southern Mexico and Central America are related to this subduction. The plate boundary also is the site of many earthquakes. Occasionally, those earthquakes are large and dangerous. The Mexico City earthquake of 1985 and the Guatemalan earthquake of 1976 are examples of major earthquakes that caused tremendous damage and tragic loss of life.

See Also: Guatemala Earthquake (1976); Juan de Fuca Plate; Mexico City Earthquake, Mexico (1985); Nazca Plate; San Andreas Fault.

Further Reading

Tarbuck, E. J., Lutgens, F. K., & Tasa, D. (2011). *Earth: An introduction to physical geology* (10th ed.). Upper Saddle River, NJ: Pearson Prentice Hall.

Colima Volcano, Mexico

Colima is a composite volcano located about 75 miles (125 kilometers) south of Guadalajara within the Mexican Volcanic Belt. It is an extremely active volcano, experiencing more than 30 eruptive periods since 1585, when eruptions were observed by Spanish settlers. Known locally as "Volcán de Fuego" (Volcano of Fire), Colima is monitored using seismometers and webcams by scientists at the Observatorio Vulcanológico at the Universidad de Colima. Occasional overflights of the volcano by various Civil Defense agencies provide additional information about the volcano's activity. Colima Volcano formed as a result of subduction of the Cocos Plate beneath the Caribbean Plate to its east.

Volcán Colima is a prominent volcanic complex that includes two large peaks and many smaller cinder cones at the base of the larger peaks. Nevado de Colima is the highest peak in the complex, at an elevation of 14,173 feet (4,320 meters). It has not been active in historic times. Volcán Colima, the second highest peak, rises to an elevation of 12,628 feet (3,850 meters). It sits within a larger caldera that has a breach in its south rim. Both the caldera and the individual peaks within the area have been sources of large debris avalanches. One such debris avalanche that occurred approximately 18,000 years ago traveled more than 75 miles (120 kilometers) from its source on the mountainside. Debris covered at least 849 square miles (2,200 square kilometers).

Typical of many composite volcanoes, eruptions at Colima can consist of explosive outbursts that launch volcanic ash several miles upward into the atmosphere, pyroclastic flows, lahars, and lava flows, including the growth of multiple lava domes. An explosive eruption in 1991 generated a tall eruption column, pyroclastic flows produced by collapse of a lava dome, and later lava flows. The current eruptive cycle began in January of 2013 and continues as of this writing. In March 2014, a thick lava flow began moving down the western and southern slopes of Colima's upper cone. Throughout April of 2014, rock falls from a growing lava dome in the volcano's crater generated small pyroclastic flows that reached 0.6 to 1.2 miles (1 to 2 kilometers) downslope. An eruption column in May 2014 sent ash to an altitude of 20,000 feet (6.1 kilometers) above the earth. These periodic outbursts are completely within the typical range of behavior for Colima observed over the last few hundred years.

See Also: Cocos Plate; Lahar; Pyroclastic Flow; Subduction Zone.

Further Reading

Francis, P., & Oppenheimer, C. (2004). *Volcanoes* (2nd ed.). Oxford: Oxford University Press.
Smithsonian Institution. National Museum of Natural History. Global Volcanism Program. (2014, June 4). *Colima*. Retrieved from http://www.volcano.si.edu/volcano.cfm?vn =341040
Volcano Discovery. (2014, June 4). *Volcano news: Colima Volcano (Mexico)*. Retrieved from http://www.volcanodiscovery.com/colima/news.html
Volcano World. (2014, June 4). *Colima*. Retrieved from http://volcano.oregonstate.edu/colima

Collision Zone

A collision zone is a feature recognized in plate tectonic theory. It is one member of a class of plate boundaries called convergent boundaries. At convergent boundaries, two lithospheric plates move toward each other. A collision zone is defined as an area where two pieces of continental lithosphere collide with each other. This type of interaction between plates also is known as continental-continental convergence.

Both pieces of continental lithosphere are thick and relatively buoyant, therefore neither plate yields to the other. Instead, these plates are intensely deformed due to extremely high pressure at the boundary. In the short term, residents of these areas can expect numerous earthquakes that occasionally can be large and damaging. In the long term, rocks are folded into mountains and high plateaus. The continental plates also are sutured together, meaning that they no longer behave as two separate and independent entities. Mountains and earthquakes might be present far from the actual point of contact between the two plates.

One of the best-known and most often cited examples of a modern collision zone is the boundary between India, which is on the Indian-Australian Plate, and mainland Asia, which is the Eurasian Plate. In the distant past when Pangaea was assembled, India was located in the southern Hemisphere, tucked between Australia and Antarctica. When Pangaea began to break apart—roughly 200 million years ago—India moved northward at a relatively fast rate. The oceanic lithosphere between Asia and India subducted beneath Asia. Volcanic activity occurred on the southern boundary of mainland Asia. Eventually, the ocean closed and, about 50 million years ago, the two landmasses made initial contact. At this point, the plate boundary transitioned from a subduction zone to a collision zone. Volcanic activity ceased. Rocks on both continental blocks came under enormous pressure and began to deform. A high plateau—now known as the Tibetan Plateau—formed, and tall peaks rose even higher to become the Himalaya Mountains. The Himalayas have been in existence for about 20 million years. Today the Himalayas are the highest mountain range on the planet. The mountain range gets taller every year because of continued collision between India and mainland Asia.

Deformation of the Eurasian Plate is far-reaching. The entire region of southern and eastern Asia is affected by this plate boundary. As for all collision zones, earthquakes are commonplace here, as are hills and mountains caused by the immense pressure between the two plates. China has seen more than a million deaths in the last 1,000 years from collision zone earthquakes. The most deadly earthquake in recorded history occurred in Shensi, China, in 1556. An estimated 830,000 people died in that earthquake alone. An earthquake in Tangshan, China, in 1976 killed between 255,000 and 600,000. An earthquake in Bhuj, India, in 2001 killed more than 25,000 people. A 2005 earthquake in the Pakistan/Kashmir area killed 86,000, and a 2008 earthquake in Sichuan, China, killed more than 70,000 people.

See Also: Australian Plate; Plate Tectonics.

Further Reading

Kearey, P., Klepeis, K. A., & Vine, F. J. (2009). *Global tectonics.* (3rd ed.). Hoboken, NJ: Wiley-Blackwell.

Tarbuck, E. J., Lutgens, F. K., & Tasa, D. (2011). *Earth: An introduction to physical geology* (10th ed.). Upper Saddle River, NJ: Pearson/Prentice Hall.

Colombia

Colombia is the country located furthest northwest on the continent of South America and on the South American Plate. Columbians face hazards from earthquakes, volcanic eruptions, and tsunamis—much of which is the result of the subduction of the Nazca Plate beneath the South American Plate in this area. Tsunamis from distant earthquakes have hit the shores of Colombia as well. Western Colombia is dominated by mountainous terrain created both through faulting and folding of rocks, and via volcanic activity. Volcanoes exist in both the Cordillera Occidental range near the coast and the Cordillera Oriental range, which is further inland. These two ranges of the Andes Mountains merge in southwestern Columbia to become a single mountain range as it enters Ecuador to the south. The main government organization in Colombia responsible for monitoring geologic hazards is the Colombian Institute of Geology and Mines (Instituto Colombiano de Geología y Minería), or INGEOMINAS. Scientists at INGEOMINAS monitor the country's volcanoes and seismic activity, prepare the population for the eventuality of earthquakes by educating them about geologic hazards, and issue warnings when volcanic activity threatens population centers.

In Colombia, millions of people live within 18.6 miles (30 kilometers) of at least one historically active volcano. All of Colombia's major cities, including the capital city of Bogotá, and the cities of Cali and Medellín, are located in mountainous areas near volcanic centers. At least 12 volcanoes within Colombia have erupted in historic times—which in this location stretch back to the mid-1500s. The most recent eruptions within Colombia occurred at Galeras and Nevado del Ruiz in 2013. These two volcanoes are well-known in the volcanological community for tragedies that the volcanoes caused. In 1985, a lahar generated by Nevado del Ruiz struck the city of Armero, burying the town and killing more than 22,000 people in a single night. This event was galvanizing for volcano scientists around the world. Efforts were redoubled to educate communities about the volcanic hazards they face, and to put in place warning systems that would enable people to evacuate in time to avoid volcanic disasters. Galeras was the site of an eruption in 1993 that killed six volcanologists and wounded several others as they visited the volcano's crater during a field workshop. There remains a great deal of controversy over whether that tragedy could have been avoided if expedition leaders had heeded warnings that the volcano was producing seismic signals that had in the past preceded small eruptions.

Columbia also experiences large and damaging earthquakes. Colombia's most deadly earthquake was an estimated magnitude 7.3 earthquake that occurred on May 18, 1875. The earthquake occurred in northern Colombia and caused 16,000 fatalities. Since that time, much of the construction in Colombia's cities has been undertaken with proper earthquake engineering in mind. Major earthquakes in 1987 and 1999 killed 1,000 and 1,185 respectively, but other than these events there have been relatively few deaths from large earthquakes. A magnitude 8.0 earthquake in 1970 produced only a single fatality.

See Also: Galeras Volcano, Colombia (1993); Nazca Plate; Nevado del Ruiz, Colombia; South American Plate; Subduction Zone.

Further Reading

Smithsonian Institution. National Museum of Natural History. Global Volcanism Program. (2014). Retrieved from http://www.volcano.si.edu/

U.S. Geological Survey. (2014, June 5). *Historic world earthquakes. Columbia.* Retrieved from http://earthquake.usgs.gov/earthquakes/world/historical_country.php#colombia

Composite Volcano

A composite volcano is a volcanic cone that has a rather complex history. Although the volcano itself always has tapped the same magma chamber, the composition and nature of its products might have changed greatly over time, as has its eruptive style. Composite volcanoes go by many names, including composite cone, stratocone, and stratovolcano. All of these terms describe the same type of volcano. Composite volcanoes are composed of layers of lava flows and pyroclastic materials. They can have cinder cones or lava domes on their flanks. They might or might not have craters or calderas at their summits. They can start as shield volcanoes or cinder cones and develop into a composite volcano after hundreds of eruptions over thousands of years of activity. Because this type of volcano is complex by nature, there is no "typical" way in which one develops.

Mount St. Helens in Washington is an example of a composite volcano. Early in its history, Mount St. Helens erupted a great deal of basalt, which still can be found around the base of the volcano. In fact, a set of lava tubes in these basalt flows—called the Ape Caves—is a popular destination within the Mount St. Helens National Volcanic Monument. After the basalt phase, the volcano began erupting andesite and built up an impressive symmetrical cone composed of andesite lava flows and pyroclastic material. Within the last few thousand years, the main eruptive material has been dacite. This is the material that makes up the many lava domes found on the flanks and within the current crater of the volcano. The eruptive style has changed from gentle to explosive, the magma type has changed, and the materials erupted from the volcano have varied throughout its long history. If there is a typical history for a composite volcano, then Mount St. Helens has that history; it is one of variety and change. Most volcanoes around the edge of the Pacific Rim are composite volcanoes.

See Also: Andesite; Basalt; Caldera; Crater; Dacite; Pyroclastic Materials.

Further Reading

Francis, P., & Oppenheimer, C. (2004). *Volcanoes* (2nd ed). Oxford: Oxford University Press.

Concepción Earthquake, Chile (1835)

On February 20, 1835, a major earthquake struck the area near Concepción and Valdavia, Chile. This earthquake occurred decades before the first seismograph was invented, so there is no way to calculate an exact magnitude. The earthquake occurred in the afternoon and shook the ground for many miles around the epicenter for a period of two minutes. The earthquake's epicenter has not been pinpointed due to the lack of instrumental seismic data, but there is a great deal about the earthquake that can be inferred from contemporary descriptions of the earthquake itself and the damage it left behind. First, the epicenter was likely near the city of Concepción. Towns around Concepción Bay were nearly leveled by the earthquake, and then debris was swept away by a tsunami. Second, the magnitude of the earthquake can be roughly figured with information about the duration of ground shaking. An earthquake duration of two minutes is consistent with an earthquake of magnitude 8 or greater, although the duration of ground shaking is not a reliable measure of earthquake size. Third, the fact that a tsunami was generated puts some constraints on the size, location, and fault motion of the earthquake. The earthquake had to be at least a magnitude 7 because only earthquakes of this size or greater typically produce tsunamis. The quake had to have had an epicenter near the shoreline and at a relatively shallow depth to convey enough energy into the ocean to cause a tsunami. Finally, movement along the fault had to have some component of vertical motion. Current estimates place the earthquake near the shore at Concepción with an estimated magnitude of 8.2.

The earthquake is notable on its face because of the destruction seen throughout the Concepción region. However, it has become a well-known earthquake because of one of its famous observers. The earthquake was experienced near Valdavia by British naturalist and father of the theory of evolution, Charles Darwin. In 1835, Darwin was three years into his famous voyage on the British exploration ship the *Beagle*. The ship had pulled into port in Valdavia, and Darwin went ashore to make observations, take measurements, and collect samples. He describes his earthquake experience in almost underwhelming terms. He had lain on the ground in the woods to rest, and felt the earth begin to tremble. Darwin compared the feeling to that of skating on thin ice that bends under the body. He called the sensation almost a giddy feeling. He was not terribly alarmed and had no trouble standing up, but acknowledged that it was a strange sensation to feel that which we take for granted as being solid moving under his feet. Darwin was calm enough throughout the experience to time the earthquake.

The *Beagle*'s captain, Captain FitzRoy, and some of the ship's officers were in Valdavia during the earthquake, and their experience was quite different. They witnessed violent shaking of the city's buildings and terrified residents running outside in fear for their lives as the boards of their wooden homes creaked and rattled. No buildings were destroyed, however, and there was no loss of life in Valdavia due to this earthquake.

Two days later, the ship left Valdavia and traveled to Concepción. Immediately upon their arrival on March 4, Darwin and the ship's crew knew that the cities in this area had a vastly different experience. Very few buildings in Concepción or the port of Talcahuano were left standing, and more than 500 people were dead. The earthquake had caused nearly every home, business, church, and public building to disintegrate into a rubble heap. Other horrors followed. The earthquake generated a tsunami that struck the area with great force. Much of the rubble in the port of Talcahuano was swept clean by tsunami waves that attacked the shoreline. Darwin took great care in describing the effects of the earthquake on the area, and took great pains to make sense of what the earthquake meant for civilization. He discussed the economic and health impacts he imagined from such a disaster and understood in a way that many Europeans were unable just how devastating such an event could be to a population.

See Also: Earthquake; Earthquake Hazards; Earthquake Magnitude; Tsunami.

Further Reading

Darwin, C. (1839). *Journal of researches into the geology and natural history of the various countries visited by the HMS Beagle under the command of Captain Fitzroy, RN, from 1832 to 1836.* London: H. Colburn.
Lee, R.V. (2010). Darwin's earthquake. *Revista Médica de Chile 138*(7), 897–901.
White, P. (2012). Darwin, Concepción, and the geological sublime. *Science in Context 25*(1), 49–71.

Costa Rica

Costa Rica is located in Central America, between the countries of Nicaragua and Panama. It is located on the Caribbean Plate. Costa Rica formed in part because of volcanic activity resulting from subduction of the Cocos Plate beneath the Caribbean Plate. The country has a continuous mountain range that runs from northwest to southeast, nearly through the center of the country. It is home to many volcanoes. Six of these volcanoes have erupted in historical times: Arenal, Irazú, Miravalles, Poás, Rincón de la Vieja, and Turrialba. A seventh, Barva, erupted about 6,050 years ago and no written records exist of its last eruption. Costa Rica is one of the few locations in the world that is known for volcano tourism. The most active volcanoes in Costa Rica are Arenal and Poás. Both of these volcanoes are located within national parks that bear their names. The parks include not only the volcanoes and their summits, but also lush tropical rainforests and other ecosystems that are hosts to exotic animal and plant species. The parks are visited by thousands of tourists each year, and the volcanoes usually are fairly approachable. It is rare that volcanic unrest causes one of these parks to be closed to the public. The last time this occurred was at Arenal National Park in 2010. The volcano had a more active eruption than usual, and small pyroclastic flows descended the mountain's flanks. Arenal has been the most deadly of the Costa Rican volcanoes. A violent eruption in 1968 killed 89 people.

Costa Rica has also been the site of a number of major earthquakes. A magnitude 6.4 earthquake near Cartago killed 700 people in 1910, a magnitude 7.6 earthquake killed 47 people in 1991, and a magnitude 6.1 earthquake in 2009 caused 40 fatalities. The country's shorelines are at risk from both locally generated tsunamis and those generated elsewhere in the Pacific; however, historically, few large and damaging tsunamis have occurred in Costa Rica.

See Also: Arenal Volcano, Costa Rica; Cocos Plate; Poás Volcano, Costa Rica; Pyroclastic Flow; Subduction Zone.

Further Reading

San Jose AFP Staff. (2010, May 24). Costa Rica volcano erupts, national park evacuated. *Terra Daily.* Retrieved from http://www.terradaily.com/reports/Costa_Rica_volcano _erupts_national_park_evacuated_999.html

Smithsonian Institution. National Museum of Natural History. Global Volcanism Program. (2014, June 10). Retrieved from http://www.volcano.si.edu/volcano.cfm?vn=345033

U.S. Geological Survey. (2014, June 10). *Historic world earthquakes. Costa Rica.* http://earthquake.usgs.gov/earthquakes/world/historical_country.php#costa_rica

Crater

The term crater is used to describe a bowl- or funnel-shaped depression that generally is found at or near the summit of a volcano. It often houses the primary vent for that volcano and its eruptions. Craters usually are formed in one of two ways. In the case of a cinder cone or other cone built primarily by pyroclastic material (such as a tuff ring), a cone is built around the volcano's vent. As pyroclastic material is erupted skyward, then falls back to earth near the vent, a funnel-shaped depression is created with the vent in the center. This becomes the crater. Other craters are formed when a volcano blasts rock away as it forms a new vent, or clears a vent sealed by solidified magma from the volcano's previous eruption. This type of crater can occur on any type of volcano.

Craters are similar in appearance to calderas. Calderas are created when a magma chamber below the surface is emptied, leaving the ground surface unsupported. The earth's surface collapses, leaving a circular or oval-shaped depression. Because the edges of craters also can be eroded due to collapse during or after an eruption, there is no sharp line of distinction between the two types of features. The primary method of formation is typically used to describe the feature.

In many settings, calderas erroneously are referred to as craters, especially when they are small and clearly the site of a past or present eruption. One famous

Aerial view of volcanic craters on Isabela Island, Galapagos Islands, Ecuador. (Frans Lanting Mint Images/Newscom)

example is Crater Lake, Oregon. Crater Lake actually is a lake formed in a caldera rather than a crater. In the case of Hawaiian volcanoes, many of the small calderas found on the flanks of Kilauea and Mauna Loa are referred to as "pit craters." Several of these pit craters, however, never have been eruption sites and were formed purely by collapse.

See Also: Caldera; Crater Lake, Oregon, United States; Pyroclastic Materials; Vent.

Further Reading

Lipman, P. W. (2000). Calderas. In H. Sigurdsson, B. Houghton, H. Rymer, J. Stix, & S. McNutt (Eds.), *Encyclopedia of Volcanoes.* San Diego, CA: Academic Press.

Tarbuck, E. J., Lutgens, F. K., & Tasa, D. (2011). *Earth: An introduction to physical geology* (10th ed.). Upper Saddle River, NJ: Pearson Prentice Hall.

Crater Lake, Oregon, United States

Crater Lake represents the remains of an ancient peak that erupted violently approximately 7,700 years ago. This happened recently enough that Native American populations most certainly witnessed the eruption, although there are no written records describing what they saw. This eruption was a classic caldera-forming eruption in which an immense volume of magma was erupted, leaving the summit of the volcano unsupported. The summit collapsed, leaving it several thousand feet lower than it was prior to the paroxysmal eruption. Crater Lake likely got its name before caldera formation was understood—otherwise it might have been called "Caldera Lake."

Crater Lake is one of many volcanoes formed above the Cascadia Subduction Zone, where the Juan de Fuca Plate is being subducted beneath the western edge of

Partial view of Crater Lake, Oregon. Crater Lake is a composite volcano whose summit collapsed in an eruption several thousand years ago, creating a massive caldera. The caldera is now home to an extremely deep lake. (julius fekete/Photoshot/Newscom)

the North American Plate. Volcanism due to the subduction process has built the Cascade Mountains, a chain of volcanoes that stretches from Lassen Peak in northern California to Glacier Peak in southern British Columbia. Crater Lake is one of the largest mountains in the chain. It is located in a remote area of southern Oregon.

The first geologist to research Crater Lake and its formation was a Welsh scientist named Howel Williams. He studied the volcanoes throughout Oregon, but is best known for his classic study of caldera formation at Crater Lake. Williams referred to the pre-caldera mountain as Mount Mazama. Prior to the caldera-forming eruption 7,700 years ago, Mount Mazama was a massive cone with an elevation of more than 12,000 feet (3,600 meters) at its summit. It towered above the landscape. During the last ice age, Mazama had a number of glaciers that started at its summit and descended the flanks of the mountain. One glacier extended 17 miles (27 kilometers) down today's Rogue River valley. Even after the vast ice sheets melted, two glaciers on Mazama's southern flank extended 4 miles (6 kilometers) from its summit. It must have been a beautiful, peaceful landscape.

The caldera-forming eruption appears to have had two major phases. The first phase of the eruption likely occurred at a central summit vent. A single large column of steam, gases, ash, and other pyroclastic material was ejected from the vent and traveled several miles upward into the atmosphere. Approximately 19 cubic miles (30 cubic kilometers) of material were erupted during this phase of the eruption. This phase likely emptied much of the top of the rhyolite-rich magma chamber, and weakened the rocks at around the volcano's summit.

Volcano Tourism

Every year, millions of people visit volcanoes while on vacation. The geothermal fields of Mount Fuji in Japan are a popular tourist destination. Burial in warm volcanically heated sand eases the pain of arthritis and other chronic medical conditions. Kilauea Volcano is located in Hawaii Volcanoes National Park. This volcano draws hundreds of thousands of visitors per year to view flowing lava, steam vents, and volcanic craters. Yellowstone National Park in Wyoming is another volcanic destination in the United States that draws thousands of visitors each year, mostly in the summer months when roads are passable. The park's volcanic landscape, hot springs, and geysers are mesmerizing to behold. Many of these places also are beautiful and remote—appealing to people who enjoy getting away from heavily populated areas and experiencing the power of nature. Volcanoes hold an eerie fascination for much of the public, so it should be no surprise that they are top tourist destinations. Every country that has volcanoes has tourist destinations centered on those volcanoes.

In the second phase of the eruption, concentric rings of cracks formed around the summit of the volcano and material erupted from these rings. Eruption columns collapsed, and the debris came raining back down onto the slopes of the volcano. Material rushed into the old glacial valleys carved into the volcano's flanks and pyroclastic flows spread out in all directions away from the summit. The rhyolite that had been at the top of the magma chamber was completely drained, and the volcano began tapping deeper portions of the magma reservoir. Those deeper portions included crystal-rich dacite and andesite. Today, the light-colored deposits of rhyolite are topped by darker deposits of dacite blocks and andesite scoria, which is a medium-gray rock riddled with holes. At this stage of the eruption, the magma chamber was nearly empty and the top of the volcano was left unsupported. The summit of the volcano collapsed and a caldera was formed. It is estimated that Mount Mazama lost approximately 5,000 feet (1,500 meters) in height. Where the summit once stood, there was a gaping hole 4,000 feet (1,200 meters) deep. A lake eventually filled about half the depth of the caldera. Today, the average elevation around the rim of the caldera is about 8,000 feet (2,440 meters) above sea level, and the elevation of the lake's surface is 6,173 feet (1,182 meters). The caldera is home to the deepest lake in the United States. At its deepest, it is 1,943 feet (592 meters) deep. The water is a deep sapphire blue, and the slopes of the volcano are a mixture of sheer rock cliffs and forested slopes. Crater Lake truly is a majestic sight.

When the caldera-forming eruption was over, the volcano was quiet for a period; however, two later eruptions of the mountain occurred. One subsequent eruption created a cone on the bottom of the lake that rises nearly 1,500 feet (457 meters) above the floor of the caldera. The summit of this cone is nearly 500 feet (150 meters) beneath the surface of the lake, and has been imaged with radar. A second eruption created Wizard Island, located in the western part of the lake. Wizard Island is a cinder cone that rises 800 feet (244 meters) above the surface of the lake. Crater

Lake is contained within Crater Lake National Park, which is open to visitors year-round.

See Also: Andesite; Caldera; Cascadia Subduction Zone; Crater; Dacite; Juan de Fuca Plate; North American Plate; Pyroclastic Materials; Rhyolite.

Further Reading

Francis, P., & Oppenheimer, C. (2004). *Volcanoes* (2nd ed). Oxford: Oxford University Press.

National Park Service. (2014, May 12). Crater Lake National Park, Oregon. Retrieved from http://www.nps.gov/crla/index.htm

Williams, H. (1976). *The ancient volcanoes of Oregon.* Eugene, OR: University of Oregon Press.

D

Dacite

"Dacite" is a term used to describe both a type of magma and an extrusive igneous rock (one that has been erupted to the earth's surface) that has between 62% and 70% weight percent silicon dioxide (SiO_2). When dacitic magma cools beneath the ground surface, it forms the intrusive igneous rock granodiorite. Dacite is typically medium to light gray in color, and often a small percentage of the rock is composed of visible crystals. As magma, it is extremely viscous despite the fact that in its liquid state it is usually 6% to 7% water. Dacite is practically solid as it emerges from a vent.

The high water content and silica contents of dacitic magma have implications for eruptive behavior. All magma contains dissolved water and gases, known as volatiles. At mantle depths where magma is generated, all of these volatiles are dissolved in the liquid magma. The closer the magma gets to the surface of the earth, however, the lower the ambient pressure becomes. Lower pressure forces water and gases to come out of solution. Water is converted to steam, which is a gas as well. At a depth of 0.6 mile (1 kilometer) in a magma chamber, gases make up approximately 1% of the magma volume. As magma rises through the volcano's plumbing system toward the surface and encounters ever-lower amounts of pressure, the gas expands significantly. At the same time, the extremely high viscosity of dacitic magma means that gas bubbles have little chance to rise through the magma because it is much more like a solid than a liquid. Gas bubbles cannot rise through the magma and pop to release the gases into the atmosphere, and instead they are trapped within the magma. At the earth's surface, the same gases that occupied only 1% of the magma volume at a depth of 0.6 mile (1 kilometer) have expanded to occupy 91% of the magma volume. Once the magma nears the surface, the internal gas pressure within the magma is greater than the strength of the rocks containing the magma. The confining rocks break and gases expand at an incredibly fast rate. This causes an explosive eruption that fragments the magma into small pieces and creates large amounts of pyroclastic material, most of which is volcanic ash. This is typical behavior at the onset of eruption of a composite volcano with dacitic magma.

Once the violent, explosive eruption is over, much of the gas pressure has been released. If there is sufficient magma left in the volcano's plumbing system, dacite can flow to the surface of the earth relatively quietly, forming a short but thick lava flow that covers the vent. This is known as a volcanic dome. Most composite volcanoes have multiple domes. They can occur in the crater of the volcano or cover a vent on one of the volcano's flanks. Mount St. Helens in Washington State has a dome covering the vent from its 1980–1986 eruption, but it also has a number of domes on its flanks.

See Also: Andesite; Basalt; Lava Dome; Pyroclastic Materials; Rhyolite.

Further Reading

Decker, R., & Decker, B. (1998). *Volcanoes* (3rd ed., Academic Version). New York: W.H. Freeman Press.

Wallace, P., & Anderson, Jr., A. T. (2000). Volatiles in magmas. In H. Sigurdsson, B. Houghton, H. Rymer, J. Stix, & S. McNutt (Eds.), *Encyclopedia of volcanoes.* San Diego, CA: Academic Press.

Dike

A dike is a vertically or semi-vertically oriented crack in the earth's crust that has been injected with magma. It is a magma pathway that forms beneath and within a volcano. It can carry magma from a magma chamber upward toward the surface. When a dike propagates (expands and advances) and encounters the surface, it becomes a site of a fissure eruption, or "curtain of fire." A fissure eruption is a spectacular but usually short-lived occurrence. After several hours, eruption along the length of the fissure typically narrows to a single site, which becomes the central vent for an ongoing eruption.

Dikes usually are hidden from view beneath active volcanoes, but they are prominent features of ancient, eroded volcanic landscapes. In many instances they form striking features that cut across other rock units. In one manifestation, dikes can form wall- or pillar-like structures on the landscape. This occurs when a dike is emplaced within relatively soft rock, and it cools and hardens into very hard rock. Because of the difference in rock hardness, erosion preferentially removes the softer rock leaving the dikes exposed in spectacular landforms. One of the most remarkable examples of a dike system is Ship Rock, also known in Navajo as "Tse Bitai," which is located in northwestern New Mexico. This dike system was created about 30 million years ago, about 2,500 to 3,300 feet (750 to 1,000 meters) beneath the surface of the ground. It served as the plumbing system beneath a large volcano. When the volcano's eruptions ceased, the magma in the dikes cooled and hardened. In the intervening 30 million years, erosion removed the volcano above this dike system, leaving only the solidified magma held within the dikes. Now, Ship Rock rises 2,000 feet (600 meters) above the surrounding landscape and is a major landmark in the region.

See Also: Magma.

Further Reading

Carrigan, C. R. (2000). Plumbing systems. In H. Sigurdsson, B. Houghton, H. Rymer, J. Stix, & S. McNutt (Eds.), *Encyclopedia of volcanoes.* San Diego, CA: Academic Press.
New Mexico Bureau of Geology and Mineral Resources. (2013, June 17). The Ship Rock landform. Retrieved from http://geoinfo.nmt.edu/tour/landmarks/shiprock/

Divergent Boundary

A divergent boundary is one of three major types of plate boundaries defined in plate tectonic theory. It is a location where two lithospheric plates move away from each other. Divergent boundaries go by a variety of names, somewhat dependent on their location on the earth. In ocean settings, divergent boundaries also are called "spreading centers," "mid-ocean ridges," or simply "ridges." On continents, divergent boundaries often are called "rift zones." Regardless of the specific name given the effect is the same. In the area adjacent to the boundary itself the lithosphere is stretched and thinned. This brings hot asthenospheric material closer to the surface of the earth. At the actual plate boundary new oceanic lithosphere is created.

The process that begins seafloor spreading is somewhat of a mystery. Scientists theorize that some reorganization of circulation within the asthenosphere could be to blame. As hot material rises in the upgoing arms of neighboring convection cells, extra heat from deep in the asthenosphere causes rocks to expand and the earth's surface to become elevated. The area near the plate boundary often causes a topographic high point, such as a mountain range. In the centers of oceans this creates the mid-ocean ridge. On land, an elevated plateau or mountain range can be created on the continent. At the actual plate boundary where the lithosphere is thinnest, the elevation drops significantly and becomes a valley, often called a "rift valley." Here and in the

The Mygrata Grotogya rift fissure along a divergent plate boundary with geothermal steam in North East Iceland. (Tony Waltham/Robert Harding/Newscom)

margins of the valley, volcanic activity is common. In the ocean, fluid basalt lava is erupted onto the ocean floor.

Activity is more varied in continental rifts. Typically, cinder cones and shield volcanoes occupy the rift valley and the mountainous areas to either side of the valley might experience more violent eruptions from composite volcanoes. New magma and intrusive igneous rocks create new lithosphere of basaltic composition at the plate boundary. In oceanic settings this widens the existing ocean. In continental settings this forms the beginnings of what could become a new ocean floor. If there is a connection made between the rift valley and the shoreline, seawater invades the valley. At this point, a new ocean is born.

Eastern Africa is one location where a continental rift system is in place and is well on its way to becoming the world's newest ocean basin. Rift valleys begin in the north in Eritrea and Ethiopia, and continue southward through Kenya and Tanzania. Volcanic activity is common within and adjacent to the rift valley, as are earthquakes. Saltwater already is invading the rift valley's hot springs in the northern part of the rift valley, but it will be another million years before seawater consistently is found standing throughout even those northernmost reaches of the valley.

The waterways that separate the horn of Africa from the Arabian Peninsula are examples of relatively newly formed ocean basins. The Gulf of Aden and the Red Sea are both rift valleys that developed fairly recently in geologic history. Once the rift valleys expanded and dropped in elevation enough to make a connection with the ocean, narrow seaways formed. They continue to expand at an extremely slow rate. In all of these areas earthquakes are common phenomena.

The more typical presentation of a divergent boundary is in a well-developed ocean. In the Atlantic Ocean, for example, a mature spreading center exists in the Mid-Atlantic Ridge. This mountain range extends the full length of the Atlantic Ocean, from north of Iceland southward to near Antarctica. It parallels the coastlines of Africa and South America on either side, so it clearly is related to the continents that separated to form the ocean more than 150 million years ago. The Mid-Atlantic Ridge is the site of frequent volcanic eruptions, hydrothermal vents, and relatively minor earthquakes. The two sides of the Atlantic are pulling apart at a rate of approximately 0.12 inches (3.2 millimeters) per year (a half-spreading rate of 0.06 inches (1.6 millimeters) per year). This is an extremely slow spreading rate as compared to other mid-ocean ridges. An example of a fast-spreading mid-ocean ridge is the East Pacific Rise, which experiences approximately 5.9 inches (150 millimeters) of spreading per year.

On a map, it is clear that divergent boundaries are broken into segments. This happens because of the curvature of the earth. The segments are connected by a type of plate boundary called a "transform boundary." Transform boundaries earned their name through their function. These boundaries transfer movement from one segment of a plate boundary to another. They terminate at both ends in another type of plate boundary. Anywhere these segments are present, the transform boundaries terminate at a segment of a mid-ocean ridge or rift zone.

See Also: Basalt; Cinder Cone; Composite Volcano; Earth Structure; Plate Tectonics; Shield Volcano; Transform Boundary.

Further Reading

Kearey, P., Klepeis, K. A., & Vine, F. J. (2009). *Global tectonics* (3rd ed.). Hoboken, NJ: Wiley-Blackwell.

Tarbuck, E. J., Lutgens, F. K., & Tasa, D. (2011). *Earth: An introduction to physical geology* (10th ed.). Upper Saddle River, NJ: Pearson/Prentice Hall.

E

Earth Structure

Earth formed roughly 4.6 billion years ago when a massive cloud of gas and dust in interstellar space—called a "nebula"—began to condense. Most matter went to the mass in the center of this cloud, which became the sun. Debris that was not incorporated into the sun became the planets, comets, meteors, asteroids, and cosmic dust that comprise our solar system today. As Earth formed, dense elements and compounds fell toward the center of the planet and lighter materials migrated upward toward the surface. This differentiation of the planet based on densities of materials is the origin of the layers recognized today.

Earth can be divided into layers in two different ways, based on two different sets of criteria. The first property used for this division is composition. The uppermost layer of the earth is called the crust. The crust is the earth's thin, rocky outermost layer and mostly is composed of light elements and compounds. It is the only layer of the earth ever seen directly. Crust comes in two varieties. Crust found beneath continents is called "continental crust," and that found beneath the oceans is "oceanic crust." Beneath the continents the crust on average is 25 miles (40 kilometers) thick. This type of crust can be as thin as 12.5 miles (20 kilometers) near the continental margins, or as thick as 43.5 miles (70 kilometers) beneath the planet's tallest mountain ranges. Continental crust has an average composition of granodiorite or its extrusive equivalent, dacite. Oceanic crust is thinner and denser than continental crust. Oceanic crust is a fairly uniform 5 miles (7 kilometers) thick beneath the world's oceans, regardless of how deep the water is above the ocean floor. The average density of oceanic crust is similar to that of basalt.

Beneath the crust is the earth's mantle. The mantle comprises 82% of the earth's volume. It extends from the base of the crust to a depth of 1,800 miles (2,900 kilometers) beneath the surface. The earth's mantle is composed of peridotite—a rock that contains more iron and magnesium than basalt—and therefore is more dense than basalt. Because it is rock, the mantle of the earth is solid; however, evidence exists of the deformation of the rocks and even circulation of these rocks throughout the mantle. The rocks therefore are solid but deformable.

Humans never have visited the earth's mantle, but there are samples of peridotite from two main sources. One source of peridotites is a volcanic structure called a "diatreme." Diatremes are carrot-shaped volcanic conduits that bring rocks from the mantle directly up to the earth's surface in violent eruptions. A number of diatremes exist on each and every continent. Some are economically important because they contain not only peridotite and related rocks, but diamonds as well. Not all diatremes are diamond-bearing, however. Another setting in which mantle rocks can be found is a structure known as an "ophiolite." Ophiolites are sections of oceanic crust and upper mantle that have been shoved up onto a continent as a result of tectonic activity. Ophiolites exist in many current and former convergent plate boundaries, but one of the best preserved is the Semail Ophiolite in the Sultanate of Oman. At this site a complete section of oceanic crust exists—from the pillow lavas erupted directly onto the ocean floor to the upper part of the mantle.

The core begins at a depth of 1,800 miles (2,900 kilometers) and extends to the earth's center, located at a depth of 3,958 miles (6,371 kilometers). The earth's core is composed of a nickel-iron alloy with trace amounts of oxygen, silicon, and sulfur. Humans have not visited the core and likely never will. The composition of the core is known because of its density, and the composition of meteorites in our solar system.

It is a relatively simple exercise to calculate the mass of the earth, and the volume of the earth also is known. To determine density, mass is divided by volume. The average density of the earth is 0.199 pounds per cubic inch (5.52 grams per cubic centimeter). The density of the earth's crust is roughly 0.100 pounds per cubic inch (2.77 grams per cubic centimeter), and the core's density is about 0.130 pounds per cubic inch (3.6 grams per cubic centimeter). Therefore, the core must be much denser than the rest of the planet. The density of an iron-nickel alloy fits the supposed density of the core—0.397 pounds per cubic inch (11 grams per cubic centimeter)—quite well. The composition of meteors in the solar system also provides a clue to the composition of the earth's core. Meteors are rocks left over from the formation of the sun and planets of our solar system. The four terrestrial planets closest to the sun were formed by such rocks colliding with each other and accreting to form the bodies seen today. Many meteorites collected on the earth contain a great deal of iron and nickel. Because there is not a great deal of iron and nickel found at the earth's surface, the only logical conclusion is that it is contained in the earth's interior.

The core is divided into two parts. The outer core is liquid and has a thickness of 1,410 miles (2,270 kilometers). The inner core is solid and has a thickness of 754 miles (1,216 kilometers). Both portions of the core are thought to have the same composition, but the change in state of matter from liquid in the outer core to solid in the inner core likely is due to greater pressure. The boundary between the solid mantle and liquid outer core is a mysterious zone known as the D" layer (pronounced "D double-prime"). It is a transition zone between the solid mantle and the earth's core, where the two layers are interacting thermally and probably chemically as well.

Another method that enables researchers to determine the presence and location of layers throughout the earth is careful study of seismograms. Energy from earthquakes provides a great deal of information about the earth's interior, because the energy acts somewhat like an x-ray. Although seismograms do not give an image as would an x-ray, they do provide information about how quickly seismic energy travels through various materials inside the earth. One of the first boundaries within the earth found with seismology was the boundary between the crust and mantle. It was discovered in 1909 by Andrija Mohorovičić, who studied records of an earthquake occurring in Croatia in 1909. This boundary between the crust and mantle today is referred to as the "Mohorovičić Boundary," or the "Moho." Velocities of seismic waves increase significantly at the Moho.

Another distinct boundary exists at an average depth of 62 miles (100 kilometers). This is a boundary within the upper mantle, and it marks a zone where the velocity of seismic waves drops precipitously. Known as the "Low Velocity Zone" (LVZ), this is an area of weakness within the solid upper mantle. It marks the boundary between the lithosphere above and the asthenosphere below. The lithosphere consists of the crust and uppermost mantle. The tectonic plates are plates of lithosphere, and not simply plates composed of crust. The crust and uppermost mantle move together. The asthenosphere is a layer within the mantle within which circulation—or convection—is known to occur. Convection that either occurs wholly within the asthenosphere or that at least involves the asthenosphere is what drives plate motion.

An additional boundary exists at the base of the asthenosphere at a depth of 410 miles (660 kilometers). This is an interesting boundary for three reasons. First, researchers do not think that it marks a boundary between rocks of different compositions, but rather of different densities. When the minerals in peridotite are exposed to the kind of pressures found at that depth, the minerals change their arrangement of atoms to one that is more compact, making the minerals denser. This would certainly affect the velocity of seismic waves, as they travel faster in denser material. Another reason that this is an interesting boundary is because it is the greatest depth at which earthquakes occur on the earth. When subduction occurs, slabs of oceanic lithosphere descend into the mantle. Earthquakes continue to occur in the downgoing slab until the slab reaches the boundary between the asthenosphere and the lower mantle. At that depth all earthquake activity stops. It is thought that the slabs become too hot and perhaps too pliable to break when they reach that depth in the earth. Lastly, it is possible to map these downgoing slabs in the earth by using seismic waves. Waves travel at a different speed through the cold descending slabs than they do through the hot mantle. When the slabs reach the boundary between the asthenosphere and lower mantle, the slabs either bend and deform or they slide along the boundary. They do not penetrate any deeper into the earth. This is an interesting observation, and indicates that the slabs' deformation and sliding likely are related to the density difference between the asthenosphere and lower mantle.

The boundary between the lower mantle and the outer core was discovered by Beno Gutenburg in 1913, and is referred to as the "Gutenburg Discontinuity." This discontinuity is marked by an instant decrease in the velocity of P waves (the fastest of all seismic waves, able to travel through solids, liquids, and gases) to that found in the uppermost mantle, and a complete disappearance of S waves (seismic waves that can only travel through solids). The effect is to be expected when a liquid layer is present. P waves are slowed considerably as they move from solids into liquids, but S waves are stopped completely because they cannot travel through any medium other than a solid. In 1936, a Danish seismologist named Inge Lehmann proposed the presence of a solid inner core, based on information gathered from studying large earthquakes and the paths taken by waves through the core. By tracing the path of P waves through the core, Lehmann found that they had to speed up considerably in the innermost part of the core for the waves to fit the observations.

See Also: Lehmann, Inge; Plate Tectonics; Seismology; Subduction Zone.

Further Reading

Kearey, P., Klepeis, K. A., & Vine, F. J. (2009). *Global tectonics* (3rd ed.). Hoboken, NJ: Wiley-Blackwell.
Richter, C. F. (1958). *Elementary seismology*. San Francisco: W.H. Freeman and Company.
Tarbuck, E. J., Lutgens, F. K., & Tasa, D. (2011). *Earth: An introduction to physical geology* (10th ed.). Upper Saddle River, NJ: Pearson Prentice Hall.

Earthquake

The term "earthquake" has several recognized and related definitions. It can be used to describe the sudden slip on a fault, and to describe the ground shaking resulting from sudden slip on a fault. Additionally, it can describe the seismic energy that moves through the earth following the sudden slip on a fault. These three definitions describe the same rapid and complex sequence of events that surround the occurrence of rapid movement of the earth's lithosphere along a fault. When the word "earthquake" is mentioned, most people immediately think of the ground shaking that occurs. Seismologists often think of the seismic energy that moves through the earth and can be detected using a seismograph. Geologists—who often look at the entirety of earth history—might think of how this particular event fits into the bigger picture of fault motions and plate tectonics. All of these views are correct and contribute to an understanding of the phenomenon known as earthquakes.

Careful observation of rocks on the planet indicates that earthquakes have been occurring since the earliest days of the earth. Rocks have been broken and moved several miles from their original starting points. Earthquakes are partially responsible for the creation of the continents and oceans on Earth today. Over millions of years, the relatively small incremental movements along faults can build impressive mountain ranges. The Rocky Mountains in North America, the Alps in Europe, and the Himalayas in Asia all were created by earthquakes. People often think of earthquakes' destructive power—but they also have the ability to

The magnitude 8.9 earthquake that struck Sendai, Japan in 2011 as seen on a drum at St. Louis University, USA. (Bill Greenblatt/UPI/Newscom)

construct majestic mountains and deep valleys. Earthquakes provide a window into the interior of the planet. Humans are unable to visit the deep interior of the earth, but seismic waves from large earthquakes can travel through the entire earth. It is because of the careful study of earthquake records that we know the structure of the earth.

Earthquakes are common occurrences, happening thousands of times each and every day. Most of these earthquakes receive little attention because they are too small to be felt or to inflict any damage, or because they occur in remote regions of the earth. The earthquakes generally publicized are those that strike populated regions, causing fatalities and damage, or those that occur in areas that rarely experience earthquakes. Although the vast majority of earthquakes occur at plate boundaries and volcanoes, every year a small percentage of earthquakes happens in other locations. A magnitude 5.8 earthquake that occurred in central Virginia in 2011 is an example of one of these rare earthquakes occurring in an area that is not presently a plate boundary.

The most common way earthquake size is measured is using a magnitude scale. The first magnitude scale was devised by Charles Richter and Beno Gutenburg in the early 1930s. Magnitude scales have been refined and redefined many times since then, therefore seismologists no longer use the term "Richter scale," and instead refer to the magnitude scale. The magnitude scale is a logarithmic scale—which means that for every increase of 1 on the scale, there is a 10-fold increase in the amplitude (height) of ground shaking. For every increase of 2 on the scale, there is a 10 times 10, or 100-fold increase in the amplitude of ground shaking. Energy release also is related to earthquake magnitude. For every increase of 1 on the magnitude scale, there is a 30-fold increase in energy output. For every increase of 2 on the magnitude scale, there is a 30 times 30, or 900-fold increase in the energy release due to the earthquake. Because the scale is logarithmic, the scale can accommodate the very tiny, unfelt earthquakes as well as those that are so powerful that they can destroy entire cities.

Large earthquakes pose many hazards to nearby populations. Ground shaking can cause buildings, bridges, overpasses, communications towers, and other manmade structures to crumble. It can snap utility lines, leaving cities without water, electrical power, natural gas, Internet access, or phone service for days or even weeks. Fires can start for a number of reasons—candles that tip over, sparks igniting natural gas, electrical lines igniting flammable material—and without intact water lines, firefighters are hampered in their efforts to put them out. Under specific conditions, liquefaction can occur. In this phenomenon, soft, water-saturated material such as soil, sand, or mud begins to act more like a liquid than a solid. It no longer can support heavy structures, and those structures become partially buried. In the case of a large coastal earthquake that causes vertical displacement of the ocean floor, a tsunami can result. Despite these hazards, many of the world's most populous cities are located in earthquake-prone regions.

See Also: Earth Structure; Earthquake Hazards; Earthquake Magnitude; Plate Tectonics; Richter, Charles; Seismology.

Further Reading

Bolt, B. A. (2004). *Earthquakes* (5th ed.). New York: W.H. Freeman and Company.
Richter, C. F. (1935). An instrumental earthquake magnitude scale. *Bulletin of the Seismological Society of America 25*(1), 1–32.
U.S. Geological Survey. Earthquake Hazards Program. (2013, June 17). *Earthquake Glossary—earthquake*. Retrieved from http://earthquake.usgs.gov/learn/glossary/?term=earthquake
U.S. Geological Survey. Earthquake Hazards Program. (2013, June 17). *Magnitude 5.8—VIRGINIA*. Retrieved from http://earthquake.usgs.gov/earthquakes/eqinthenews/2011/se082311a/#summary

Earthquake Hazards

Each year millions of earthquakes occur. Most are too small to feel, some are large enough to feel but do little or no damage, and a very small number are large enough to cause damage and loss of life. Although it is impossible to predict earthquakes, the type of damage likely to occur in a large earthquake is completely predictable. Earthquake hazards are well-known.

The most fundamental and immediate of earthquake hazards is ground shaking. The ground can move quickly back and forth, up and down, and in lurching motions. The ground can be displaced by several feet within a few seconds. This ground motion can cause a number of other events to occur during and after an earthquake, including avalanches, landslides, tsunamis, seiches, dam or levee failures, fires, structure collapse, soil liquefaction, and amplifica-

Only a few sturdy buildings survived the 1923 Great Kanto Earthquake. The earthquake and subsequent fires destroyed much of Yokohama. (Josef Kraus/ picture alliance / Peter Kraus/Newscom)

tion of ground motion. Ground shaking also can cause objects to fall from shelves, out of cabinets, and off of building facades, and can make glass break and shower down onto people in streets or on sidewalks.

Avalanches, landslides, and mudslides fall into the broader category of "mass wasting," or downslope movement of material under the influence of gravity. Even though gravity is the force that brings the material down a slope, earthquakes often shake enough material loose to allow mass wasting to take place. Although mass wasting does not require an earthquake to occur, earthquakes are known and frequent culprits in causing both large and small mass wasting events. One such tragic event occurred in the mountainous region near Chimbote, Peru in 1970. In the late afternoon of May 31, 1970, a magnitude 7.9 earthquake occurred. Landslides rushed down the mountains at speeds nearing 200 miles per hour (320 kilometers per hour) and buried two villages. Approximately 70,000 people lost their lives, and most deaths were due to the landslides.

Tsunamis are sea waves caused by a disturbance of the ocean floor. Scientists become concerned about tsunamis forming when a shallow earthquake of magnitude 7.0 or greater occurs in a coastal region, or an area just offshore. Tsunamis travel at speeds of several hundred miles per hour across the open ocean and can affect regions thousands of miles from where they are generated. Tsunamis can be just a few inches to nearly 2,000 feet tall, but most damaging tsunamis fall within the 20- to 30-foot (6- to 9-meter) range. Waves taller than this only are found closest to the area in which the tsunami was formed.

A seiche is also a type of water motion but is not related to a tsunami. A seiche is rhythmic sloshing of water in any enclosed body such as a lake, reservoir, bay, or larger basin, such as the Gulf of Mexico. Seiches can occur far from the earthquakes that cause them. For example, a major earthquake in Alaska in 1964 caused seiches in the Gulf of Mexico that were up to six-feet (two-meters) tall. Boats, boat houses, and small piers were damaged.

The collapse of man-made structures is all too common in large earthquakes that strike populated regions. Without safeguards such as reinforced and braced

How Can We Engineer Buildings to Withstand Earthquakes?

As long as there have been earthquakes occurring near human populations, people have been concerned about how to protect themselves from the buildings in which they live when earthquakes strike. First through observation, and later through experimentation and computer modeling, scientists and engineers have worked together to determine building strategies that minimize the risk of building collapse and severe structural damage when used in earthquake-prone regions. Some types of building materials fare better in earthquakes than others. Adobe and masonry, for example, fare poorly in strong earthquakes. Adobe crumbles from ground shaking, and masonry breaks apart as the mortar between bricks or rocks fails. Steel- and wood-framed structures fare the best in strong earthquakes.

In addition to building materials, there are certain elements that can be built into a man-made structure to make it more stable in an earthquake. X-shaped braces used within the walls of a building strengthen the entire structure. Tying together all elements of a building using heavy bolts keeps the building intact. Filling the areas between studs in a wall helps the wall resist shear (sideways) forces. Buttresses—or exterior supports—can force walls to stay intact. An even more ingenious (and fairly recent) development involves isolating the building from the ground. This type of structure, called a "base isolator," insulates the building from ground shaking by damping (lessening) the ground shaking that reaches the building. Base isolators have many forms, but the two most common are alternating stacks of rubber and steel plates built around a lead core, and those that look like casters inside of large, slightly convex bowls. The entire weight of a building sits on the base isolators.

Although there are many ways to engineer buildings to withstand earthquakes, this engineering has significant financial costs; therefore, worldwide, many people are unable to afford this type of construction. As a result, many millions of people are at risk from building collapse during earthquakes. This is one reason that the death toll in the 2010 Haiti earthquake was so high. Buildings there were constructed of unreinforced masonry, and most collapsed when the earthquake struck. More than 200,000 people were crushed by buildings that simply disintegrated into rubble.

walls, structural ties between all elements of a building or bridge, and flexible building materials, man-made structures are destined to fail. In seismology, there is a saying: "Earthquakes don't kill people. Buildings do." In the United States, Japan, and other industrialized countries, many if not most buildings and bridges have been engineered to withstand shaking from even very powerful earthquakes. In Alaska, the Alaskan Pipeline was designed to withstand several feet of horizontal ground motion by placing the pipeline on slider beams. By allowing the pipeline to move during an earthquake, it has withstood several earthquakes without spilling a drop of oil as a result of ground shaking. In 2002, a magnitude 7.9 earthquake occurred on the Denali Fault. Even this large earthquake left the pipeline undamaged. Earthquake engineering works—but it is a Twentieth Century invention. Many civilizations around the world have existed for hundreds or even thousands of years, therefore buildings and other structures built by such civilizations were not built with the benefit of this knowledge. In 2003, an earthquake struck the ancient city of Bam, Iran. The city was home to a citadel built 2,000 years ago. Unfortunately, the citadel Arg-e-Bam—a UNESCO World Heritage Site—was constructed of mud brick, and when the magnitude 6.7 earthquake hit the citadel crumbled. Local hospitals and many homes also collapsed, killing more than 26,000 people.

Historically, fire has been a tremendous hazard in the aftermath of major earthquakes in populated regions. In 1906, San Francisco experienced a tremendous earthquake. As damaging as the earthquake was, the fires that followed were the true disaster. Gas mains ruptured, as did gas lines into individual homes. Fires were ignited rapidly. Unfortunately, the city's water mains broke as well, leaving firefighters with no water with which to fight the fires. Most of the city burned in the three days following the earthquake. Fires were only extinguished by using dynamite to create large fire breaks.

Liquefaction is a phenomenon in which soil, sand, or other loose material either emits water or begins to act like liquid. When loose material is shaken it begins to compact (occupy less space). The compaction of sediment into less physical space means there is less space between the individual particles to hold air or water. Water and air are forced upward and out of the sediment. This can cause an occurrence known as a "sand blow." Sand, water, and air are erupted out of the ground like a miniature geyser. Mud volcanoes can form in this way as well. The other form of liquefaction, in which loose material begins to act like liquid, occurs for the same reason—compaction. The only difference is that the material does not shoot forcefully out of the ground. Instead, the density of the soil is reduced. This can become quite dangerous because the material no longer can support heavy loads, and objects such as buildings and vehicles can start sinking into the ground. Well-known cases of liquefaction in which major portions of buildings sank into the ground occurred in Mexico City in 1985, and in Niigata, Japan in 1964. In both cases apartment buildings were partially toppled and partially buried.

Loose, unconsolidated material also can be deadly for other reasons. During a shallow earthquake, most of the energy is released into the earth's crust. When this happens, powerful surface seismic waves are generated. Those surface waves are the most damaging of the seismic waves in a shallow earthquake. Surface waves become amplified—and thus more damaging and deadly—in loose material. This phenomenon is well-known and understood, and is the primary reason intensity is not a reliable method for determining an earthquake's epicenter. The Mexico City earthquake of 1985 is a striking example of this. The epicenter of what is referred to as the "Mexico City Earthquake" actually occurred just off the coast of Mexico near the town of Zihuatanejo. There was some serious damage near the epicenter, but damage 220 miles (350 kilometers) to the east in Mexico City was catastrophic. Many multistory buildings collapsed and between 9,500 and 35,000 people lost their lives. The extent of damage in Mexico City can be blamed on the material that underlies the city buildings. Mexico City was built on a dry lake bed, and the entire city is underlain by sand, silt, and mud. Surface waves were amplified in these materials and the city suffered horrific losses.

See Also: Chimbote Earthquake, Peru (1970); Earthquake; Indonesia; Krakatau Eruption (also known as "Krakatoa" Eruption), Indonesia (1883); Mexico City Earthquake, Mexico (1985); San Francisco Earthquake, California, United States (1906); Seismology.

Further Reading

BBC News. (2003). *Iran earthquake kills thousands.* Retrieved from http://news.bbc .co.uk/2/hi/3348613.stm.

Romero, F. (2010, January 13). Top 10 deadliest earthquakes. *Time Magazine.* Retrieved from http://content.time.com/time/specials/packages/article/0,28804,1953425_1953424 _1953359,00.html

Tarbuck, E. J., Lutgens, F. K., & Tasa, D. (2011). *Earth: An introduction to physical geology* (10th ed.). Upper Saddle River, NJ: Pearson Prentice Hall.

University of California Berkeley Seismological Laboratory. (2008). *Today in earthquake history: Mexico City 1985.* Retrieved from http://seismo.berkeley.edu/blog/seismoblog .php/2008/09/19/title

Yousafzai, G. (2013). Iran earthquake news: Tehran lowers death toll, Pakistan bears brunt. *Huffington Post.* Retrieved from http://www.huffingtonpost.com/2013/04/16/iran -earthquake-news-pakistan-death-toll_n_3092563.html

Earthquake Magnitude

"Magnitude" is a term coined in 1935 by Charles Richter. Today, it is the most common measure of earthquake size used. Each earthquake has a single magnitude, calculated using equations that incorporate measurements taken directly from seismograms. Prior to the early 1930s, the only measure for earthquake size that existed was "intensity," a somewhat subjective description of the amount of damage caused by an earthquake in numerous locations in the area affected by ground shaking. The area of maximum damage was assumed to be the epicenter. Earthquakes could only be compared in severity based on the maximum damage recorded at each.

Although it certainly is helpful for homeowners, insurance companies, and city planners to know how severe shaking is likely to be in future earthquakes, intensity is neither a mathematical nor an objective measure of earthquake size. Intensity is strongly affected by surface geology, earthquake depth, and local construction practices, and to some extent the observational skills of an observer. An intensity study is time consuming, and is designed to end in production of a map illustrating the severity of ground shaking across an entire region. Richter was interested in inventing a scale of earthquake size that was independent of all of these effects.

What Richter designed was a mathematical calculation that used the maximum amplitude (height) of a seismic wave on a seismogram recorded with a Wood-Anderson torsion seismometer. The amplitude was measured in microns, and then a formula was applied that corrected the measurement to what it would be at a distance of 62 miles (100 kilometers) from the earthquake's epicenter. The earthquake's magnitude as calculated by Richter is the logarithm of this corrected amplitude. Richter found that he had to use a logarithmic scale (where each increase of 1 on the magnitude scale signified an increase of 10 times the corrected amplitude of ground motion) because earthquakes span an incredible size range. Tiny micro-earthquakes are not felt—even at the epicenter—under the most favorable of circumstances. In this case, perhaps less than a single micron of movement might occur at a distance of 62 miles (100 kilometers) from the epicenter. Extremely large earthquakes, however, might have several centimeters of ground motion recorded at a distance of 62 miles (100 kilometers). A linear scale that used these direct measurements of amplitude is impractical. The use of a logarithmic scale, however, compacts the size of earthquakes to a reasonable scale for which people have a more inherent understanding.

Contrary to popular belief, the magnitude scale does not go from 0 to 10. It can have negative values and has no theoretical upper limit. The largest earthquake recorded, however, from the invention of the modern seismometer to the date of this writing is an earthquake that occurred in Chile in 1960. It was calculated to have a magnitude of 9.6.

Richter's magnitude formulas revolutionized seismology studies. Scientists finally had a standard and objective method to compare one earthquake to another. The size of an earthquake no longer had to be determined by damage done during the event. Scientists could determine the size of an earthquake even if it did not occur near a major population center and, in fact, even if the earthquake was not felt. The invention of the modern seismometer in the early 1900s paved the way for such innovations. Seismologists can detect an earthquake on a seismometer, and then use measurements and calculations to determine how far away the earthquake occurred from the location where it was detected, and the earthquake's location.

As groundbreaking as Richter's work was, it was not without flaws. Richter did his work using the seismometers that belonged to his place of employment, the California Institute of Technology in Pasadena, California. He spent painstaking hours determining just the right factors for correction using earthquakes recorded on that network of instruments. For southern California, his equations worked beautifully. When researchers tried to apply Richter's method and equations to earthquakes that occurred farther away or in other regions of the world, however, they found that they did not work quite as well. Other scientists found more universally acceptable equations and local correction factors, and these moved the science of seismology forward. Today, magnitudes calculated by Richter's methodology and formulas are called "local magnitudes," and designated "M_L."

Other magnitude formulas exist and are based on a multitude of different measurements. Local magnitudes are best calculated at distances of less than 62 miles (100 kilometers) from the epicenters of earthquakes. Local magnitudes also are most accurate for relatively small-magnitude earthquakes (less than M_L of 5.0).

Body wave magnitude (m_b) is one alternative to local magnitude that is routinely calculated. Calculating a body wave magnitude requires measuring the maximum amplitude of the P wave in the calculations. It seems to work well for deep earthquakes up to an approximate m_b of 7.0. For shallow earthquakes, surface wave magnitude (M_S) often is calculated. Because a great deal of energy is sent into the near-surface rocks, it provides a better estimate of earthquake size than body wave magnitude, particularly if the earthquake is large (greater than $M_S = 7.0$). Surface wave magnitudes are calculated using the maximum amplitude of the surface waves on a seismogram.

The ultimate goal of many seismologists is to determine how much energy was released in an earthquake, therefore an additional scale has been formulated that links energy released with magnitude. This is called the moment magnitude scale (M_W). It seems to be the most accurate scale for determining magnitudes of extremely large earthquakes. Using a seismogram, it is possible to calculate any of the many varieties of magnitude. When there is a discrepancy between two types of magnitudes for the same earthquake, knowing which measurement is most correct often is a matter of experience. The only major limitation to the use of magnitude scales is that they cannot be applied to any earthquakes that occurred before the invention of the modern seismometer.

See Also: Earthquake; Gutenberg, Beno; Modified Mercalli Intensity Scale; Richter, Charles F.; Seismology.

Further Reading

Bolt, B. A. (2004). *Earthquakes* (5th ed.). New York: W.H. Freeman and Company.
Gutenberg, B. and Richter, C. F. (1956). Earthquake magnitude, intensity, energy, and acceleration. *Bulletin of the Seismological Society of America*, *46*(2), 105–145.
Hanks, T. C., and Kanamori, H. (1979). A moment magnitude scale. *Journal of Geophysical Research*, *84*(B5), 2348–2350.
Kanamori, K. (1978). Quantification of earthquakes. *Nature*, *271*(5644), 411–414.
Richter, C. F. (1935). An instrumental earthquake magnitude scale. *Bulletin of the Seismological Society of America 25*(1), 1–32.

Earthquake Prediction

Earthquakes are one of the most destructive and deadly events in the natural world. Because of the large potential for loss of life and property in the active seismic zones of the world, people have long dreamed of the day when earthquakes become predictable, forecasted events. Scientists and the general public have studied many aspects of the earth and atmosphere looking for patterns that foretell the occurrence of a large and damaging earthquake. Unfortunately, despite these efforts, few earthquakes have been forecast with any accuracy.

In many studies and tales of earthquake prediction, the term "prediction" and "forecast" have been used interchangeably. The term "prediction" implies an uneducated guess based on non-scientific information, whereas the term "forecast" implies a data-derived decision. Even scientific literature—which typically is fanatically precise in the use of all technical terms—leans decidedly toward "earthquake prediction" as the name of the topic in question. Although all efforts discussed here fall under the "forecast" model, the terms inevitably will continue to be used interchangeably. In the cases noted below, scientists collected data in an effort to determine a pattern that could be used to forecast an impending major earthquake.

In the 1960s and 1970s, much of the scientific community thought that earthquake prediction was an attainable goal. In those decades, giant strides were made in the understanding of plate tectonics and fault mechanics. There was great optimism about the potential ability to forecast earthquakes by the end of the 1970s.

Japan and China were the first two countries to start organized earthquake-prediction study programs in the 1960s. Not long after, similar programs were begun in the Soviet Union and United States. Research was focused on monitoring the earth and atmosphere for possible precursors of major earthquakes in hopes of finding definitive patterns signaling an imminent large earthquake. Measurements were taken of velocities of seismic waves through the earth to determine whether they were anomalous in the region of interest. The levels of groundwater in wells were monitored to see if any changes occurred that were not explained by precipitation. The earth's magnetic field, electrical properties, and microgravity were measured. The number of small earthquakes in the area was monitored. The skies were monitored for the appearance of "earthquake lights," strange phenomena believed to be releases of electromagnetic energy stored in stressed rocks. The ground was monitored for tilt and uplift. Radon emissions were monitored. Even animal behavior was observed. In very few cases were patterns found. When patterns were found they rarely were so recognizable that they could be used to predict an earthquake.

1975 was an interesting year in earthquake-prediction studies. That year, several seismologists in the state of California were asked to serve on a panel that would advise the state government about the validity of earthquake prediction as a science. The first order of business was to determine what constituted a valid prediction. A valid forecast must have four essential elements: (1) a defined period in which the event will occur; (2) the location of the forecast event; (3) the magnitude of the forecast event; and (4) a statement of the odds that an earthquake of this type would occur by chance.

Halfway across the globe, scientists in China were observing an area adjacent to the last set of large earthquakes that had occurred in northern China. Seismologists concluded that the area was ripe for a large earthquake, and issued a long-range forecast stating that an earthquake was likely in that region. Near the city of Haicheng, a citizen's army of observers measured well-water levels; conducted surveys to determine whether the elevation of the land had changed; and monitored animal behavior, noting any anomalies such as restless horses and snakes emerging early from hibernation burrows. On February 4, 1975, a swarm of earthquakes began near Haicheng. At that point, county officials alerted citizens, and scattered evacuations were ordered. A magnitude 7.3 earthquake occurred that evening. The city of Haicheng itself was not evacuated. Because of sturdy construction in town, the fact that many people already were sleeping outdoors because of the nearly constant tremors of the earthquake swarm, and the time of day in which the earthquake occurred (the evening), the number of deaths due to the earthquake was relatively small as compared to the population of the region. About 2,000 people lost their lives.

Although Chinese officials touted the success of the year-long monitoring effort in successfully predicting an earthquake, the real trigger for the limited evacuations that occurred was an earthquake swarm that occurred in the 24 hours prior to the large earthquake occurring. The following year, an earthquake in Tangshan, China, was not predicted, and at least 240,000 people died. China largely abandoned its expensive earthquake prediction program after the Tangshan quake. Other countries followed suit shortly thereafter. To date, it is difficult to say with any certainty that any earthquakes successfully have been forecast as imminent and with forecasts including an accurate time, date, location, and magnitude.

See Also: Earthquake; Seismology.

Further Reading

Bolt, B. A. (2004). *Earthquakes* (5th ed.). New York: W.H. Freeman and Company.

Tarbuck, E. J., Lutgens, F. K., & Tasa, D. (2011). *Earth: An introduction to physical geology* (10th ed.). Upper Saddle River, NJ: Pearson Prentice Hall.

Wang, K., Chen, Q.-F., Sun, S., & Wang, A. (2006). Predicting the 1975 Haicheng earthquake. *Bulletin of the Seismological Society of America, 96*(3), 757–795.

Ecuador

The country of Ecuador is located in northwestern South America. The equator passes through Ecuador near the capital city of Quito. Ecuador's residents are no strangers to both volcanic and earthquake activity. Tsunamis also have hit the country's shores many times. The volcanoes primarily are located in one of two locations—within the Andes Mountains of mainland Ecuador, and within the Galapagos Islands, which belong to Ecuador.

The Galapagos Islands also are located on the equator, but are approximately 370 miles (600 kilometers) off the coast of mainland Ecuador in the Pacific Ocean. Volcanoes within the Galapagos Islands are shield volcanoes with basaltic composition. The islands were formed as a result of activity at the Galapagos Hot

The Andean composite volcano Cotopaxi in Ecuador. (Loren McIntyre Stock Connection Worldwide/Newscom)

Spot—which has remained relatively fixed in location while tectonic plates have moved over the mantle plume. This activity resulted in a chain of islands and a number of seamounts (submerged volcanoes). Eruptions within the islands are fairly frequent occurrences. Darwin Volcano erupted in 1813, Santiago erupted in 1906, Pinta was active in 1928, Marchena erupted in 1991, Wolf was active in 1982, Alcedo erupted in 1993, Sierra Negra was active in 2005, and Fernandina erupted in 2009.

Many parallels have been drawn between the Hawaiian Islands and the Galapagos Islands, because both are island chains in the Pacific created by hot spots. Both chains also are home to many unique plants and animals. Of course the finches and tortoises of the Galapagos are famous because they are two of the many animals from the islands that Charles Darwin cited in his book, *On the Origin of Species,* when describing his breakthrough theory of evolution by means of natural selection. Although there certainly are geologic and biological similarities in the two island chains, the Galapagos Islands formed in a more complex tectonic environment. They are found on a boundary between the Nazca and Cocos plates. For this reason, there is a less obvious linear progression of islands and ages of volcanoes within the chain. This also could explain why so many volcanoes historically have been more active in the Galapagos Islands versus in the Hawaiian Islands.

Most volcanoes within the Andes Mountains are composite volcanoes with andesitic to dacitic composition (Andesite's name is derived from the word Andes). A great deal of variation in composition exists within single volcanoes, however, and along the chain as well. The Andes exist because the Nazca Plate is subducting beneath the South American Plate, creating both earthquake activity along the plate boundary and the Andes Mountains, which run the length of the west coast of South America. The tallest volcanoes in the world are found in the Andes, and most of the 10 tallest volcanoes are found in Chile.

The seventh tallest volcano, however, is Chimborazo in Ecuador. Chimborazo stands at an elevation of 20,702 feet (6310 meters). It last erupted about 1,500 years ago. Many of Ecuador's mainland volcanoes are extremely active. Guagua Pichincha is a volcano immediately adjacent to the capital city of Quito. It has been active more than 20 times since the mid-1500s. The last eruption occurred in 2002, and dusted Quito with a small amount of ash. Cotopaxi, the centerpiece of Cotopaxi National Park, was last active in 1940. El Reventador is active quite frequently. As of this writing (2014) it has been active for six years, since July of 2008. It frequently emits ash plumes and steam, and has been known to produce small pyroclastic flows even during low-level activity. The volcano's current cone is built within an older breached cone with a deep cleft in one side, so pyroclastic flows and lahars often are directed to an uninhabited region, causing less risk to nearby populations than might otherwise be the case. Sangay also remains active as of this writing. It began this current eruptive cycle in 1934. Tungurahua also is active at present. It began its current eruptive period in November of 2010. Tungurahua is producing blocks, bombs, and incandescence within its crater as well as sporadic ash plumes.

Both the Galapagos Islands and mainland Ecuador experience earthquakes. Few major earthquakes have occurred in the Galapagos Islands, but mainland Ecuador has experienced quite a few large, damaging earthquakes. In January of 1906, an earthquake with an estimated magnitude of 8.8 struck just off the coast of Esmeraldas, Ecuador. It generated a tsunami that killed between 500 and 1,500 people where it came ashore in Ecuador. The tsunami was detected as far away as Japan. It caused damage in Hawaii, where the maximum runup was 11.8 feet (3.6 meters) near Hilo on the island of Hawaii. It also was detected on Maui and Oahu. Maximum run-up near Kahului, Maui, was 1 foot (0.3 meter), and in Honolulu (Oahu) it was 0.8 feet (0.25 meters). A magnitude 6.8 earthquake occurred in August of 1949, and killed 5,050 people near Ambato. A magnitude 7.2 earthquake in August 1998 caused damage in coastal cities such as Guayaquil, but no fatalities. Another magnitude 6.8 earthquake occurred in November of 2007 on the border between Peru and Ecuador. Although it was felt throughout the country it did not cause any deaths.

See Also: Andesite; Basalt; Cocos Plate; Dacite; Galapagos Islands; Guagua Pichincha, Ecuador; Nazca Plate; Pacific Plate; Subduction Zone.

Further Reading

Smithsonian Institution. National Museum of Natural History. Global Volcanism Program. (2014, June 11). Retrieved from http://www.volcano.si.edu/search_volcano_results.cfm

U.S. Geological Survey. Hawaiian Volcano Observatory. (2014, June 11). *On the trail of hotspots: The Galapagos and Hawaiian Islands*. Retrieved from http://hvo.wr.usgs.gov /volcanowatch/archive/2006/06_03_30.html

U.S. Geological Survey. (2014, June 11). *Historic world earthquakes. Ecuador*. Retrieved from http://earthquake.usgs.gov/earthquakes/world/historical_country.php#ecuador

Volcano Discovery. (2014, June 11). *Which is the world's highest volcano?* Retrieved from http://www.volcanodiscovery.com/volcanology/worlds-highest-volcano.html

El Chichón Volcano, Mexico

El Chichón is a relatively small volcano located in the state of Chiapas, Mexico. It is composed of a lava dome complex surrounded by a cone of pyroclastic material called a "tuff cone." Although the volcano is small in size as compared with many others throughout Mexico, it proved itself capable of producing large, damaging eruptions. A series of major eruptions occurred in March and April of 1982. The eruptions consisted of ash clouds, pyroclastic flows, and larger than expected quantities of sulfur dioxide. The eruption itself is believed to be responsible for about 2,000 deaths and represents Mexico's largest volcanic disaster in modern history, but the eruption will be remembered more for its climatic effects than the destruction it caused locally.

Prior to 1982, there was very little concern about El Chichón. The mountain was "discovered" and determined to be a volcano in 1928 by German scientist Frederick Müllerreid. Local folklore told of a small eruption in the 1850s, but larger eruptions occurred more than 1,200 years prior. No one spent much time worrying about El Chichón, and the Mexican government did not spend resources monitoring the volcano on an ongoing basis. During the winter of 1980–1981, René Canul, a geologist at the Comisión Federal de Electricidad (CFE), however, heard rumbling and reported earthquakes. In late 1981, Zoque Indians and ranchers who lived in the area began complaining of earthquakes. Water around the mountain began to warm and gave off the smell of sulfur. A steam cloud also hung over the summit of the mountain. Officials, however, were not terribly alarmed. The rumbling, the steam, and the earthquakes seemed to be nothing new. But as the earthquake activity increased in early 1982, the government decided to send scientists to the mountain to investigate. The team was delayed and scientists did not arrive until after the volcano's initial eruption on March 28, 1982.

The eruption of March 28 sent a cloud of ash and gases 10.5 miles (17 kilometers) high above the mountain, and showered hot rocks on the communities closest to the volcano. A number of deaths occurred, and people around the mountain realized that they were in grave danger. Many struggled with the decision of whether to stay or leave. They did not want to leave their homes and land, but recognized that the volcano might not be finished erupting.

Scientists arrived on March 30 and set up multiple seismic stations to monitor earthquake activity. They found that the number of earthquakes was increasing daily, and that they were occurring at deep levels beneath the volcano—signaling additional magma movement. Scientists from CFE, headed by Federico Mooser, flew over the volcano. The volcano still was seething with activity, and was emitting fine ash that was hazardous to air traffic. The scientists reported this information to the governor. The government was ready to forcibly evacuate people as far as 14 miles (23 kilometers) from the volcano's summit, but Mooser urged a calm wait-and-see approach. Unfortunately, many lost their lives as a result of this decision.

On April 3, 1982, seismographs near El Chichón recorded more than 500 earthquakes. A major eruption began at 7:32 p.m. It waned after a few hours, only to begin again with the paroxysmal eruption at 5:20 a.m. on April 4, which was Palm Sunday. A priest in a nearby town referred to the day as "Ash Sunday," because the sky remained dark in that area for 44 hours. When the eruption was over, it was clear that the entire landscape had changed. Many villages, ranches, and farms were buried. Pyroclastic flows had destroyed nearly every building in the village of Francisco León.

The villages of Nicapa, Chapultenango, Esquipula Guayabal, and El Naranjo fared little better. A former resident of Nicapa who had evacuated before the final and largest eruption lamented the loss of 20 head of cattle, a few horses, plus his crops of beans, corn, and coffee. Everything had been leveled. All of the man's friends and family who stayed near Nicapa had died in the eruption. An unknown number of people died in the eruptions of 1982. Census figures are not terribly reliable in the rural regions of Mexico, and many people left the area permanently when they evacuated before the eruptions of April 3–4. Numerous villages were buried or incinerated entirely by the ash fall and pyroclastic flows, therefore many bodies never will be found. The best estimate of the death toll is likely slightly more than 2,000 people.

As tragic as the eruption was, the entire scientific community took note of the eruption of El Chichón because of its short-term effect on the climate. Scientists estimate that over the following year, the northern hemisphere was cooled by an average of 0.72° F (0.4° C). This was an unexpected result due to the size of the eruption. The eruption of El Chichón released approximately the same amount of material into the atmosphere as Mount St. Helens did in 1980, but El Chichón produced cooling comparable to that of the much larger 1991 eruption of Mount Pinatubo (Philippines). Cooling is caused by the blasting of large amounts of dust and sulfuric acid aerosols into the stratosphere. The aerosols and dust block sunlight from reaching the earth's surface and cool the lower atmosphere. The eruption of El Chichón produced higher than normal amounts of sulfuric-acid aerosols, causing greater than expected cooling.

See Also: Lava Dome; Mexico; Pyroclastic Materials.

Further Reading

Livescience.com. (2012). 30 years later: Eruption of Mexico's El Chichón. Retrieved March 24, 2014, from http://www.livescience.com/31299-el-chichon-eruption-anniversary.html

Smithsonian Institution Global. National Museum of Natural History. Volcanism Program. (2014, March 14). *El Chichón.* Retrieved from http://www.volcano.si.edu/volcano .cfm?vn=341120

Weintraub, B. (1982). Fire and ash, darkness at noon. *National Geographic Magazine 162*(5), 660–678.

El Salvador

El Salvador's volcanic and earthquake activity is the result of subduction of the Cocos Plate beneath the Caribbean Plate. El Salvador is one of the smallest countries in Central America, yet it has experienced on average one destructive earthquake per decade for the last 100 years. One of the most deadly was a sequence of two earthquakes that occurred near San Miguel one month apart, on January 13 and February 13, 2001. In these events, which had magnitudes of 7.7 and 6.6 respectively, earthquakes damaged thousands of homes and triggered hundreds of landslides. Landslides were the main cause of fatalities. Combined, these earthquakes and related phenomena killed more than 1,200 people. Other deadly earthquakes occurred in 1986, when a magnitude 5.5 earthquake near San Salvador killed approximately 1,000 people; in 1965, when a magnitude 6.3 earthquake near La Libertad caused 125 fatalities; and in 1951, when a magnitude 6.2 earthquake near Jucuapa caused 400 casualties.

El Salvador also has more than its share of volcanoes. Most of the several dozen volcanoes within the borders of El Salvador have not been active in historic times. Those which have been active within historic times, however, are located near large population centers. Many of these volcanoes also are extremely dangerous, not only because of their potential for large, destructive eruptions but also because of the resident populations in close proximity to the mountains. Ilopango is a 5 mile by 7 mile (8 kilometer by 11 kilometer) caldera, and has a population of nearly 3 million people living within 18.5 miles (30 kilometers) of it. The caldera has the potential to erupt quite violently. Its last eruption was in 1879–1880 and was relatively minor, but its previous eruption—which had occurred near the year 450 C.E.—had an estimated Volcanic Explosivity Index of 6, comparable to the 1991 eruption of Mount Pinatubo. If such an eruption were to happen today, the nearby cities would be largely destroyed by ash fall.

Izalco Volcano has a population of more than 1 million living in close proximity, so this volcano has the potential to create a crisis situation as well. Izalco's last eruption in 1966 luckily was very minor. Sal Salvador Volcano dominates the skyline west of El Salvador's capital city of San Salvador. Nearly 3 million people live in the shadow of this volcano. Its last eruption was in 1917. Santa Ana, which last erupted in 2005, has more than 1.2 million people living near its slopes.

See Also: Cocos Plate; Subduction Zone.

Further Reading

Bommer, J. J., Benito, B., Ciudad-Real, M., Lemoine, A., Lopez-Menjivar, M., Madariaga, R., Mankelow, J., Mendez de Hasbun, P., Murphy, W., Nieto-Lovo, M., Rodriguez-Pineda, C., & Rosa, H. (2002). The El Salvador earthquakes of January and February 2001: Context, characteristics and implications for seismic risk. *Soil Dynamics and Earthquake Engineering 22*(5), 389–418.

Smithsonian Institution. National Museum of Natural History. Global Volcanism Program. (2014, June 11). Retrieved from http://www.volcano.si.edu/search_volcano_results.cfm

U.S. Geological Survey. (2014, June 11). *Historic world earthquakes. El Salvador.* Retrieved from http://earthquake.usgs.gov/earthquakes/world/historical_country.php#el_salvador

Elastic Rebound Theory

Following the 1906 earthquake near San Francisco, California, a great deal of research into the nature of the earthquake was conducted. Relatively little was known about the mechanisms within the earth that created earthquakes. Plate tectonics was a construction of the 1960s, so nothing was known about plate boundaries or the interactions between plates that science now accepts as fact. In the Nineteenth Century, a great many ideas about earthquakes existed and, one at a time, were proven false. Many scientists were unaware that there was a relationship between faulting and earthquakes. Early in the Nineteenth Century, some geologists thought that volcanoes alone were responsible for earthquakes. Later in the 1800s, people began to recognize relationships between mountainous terrain and earthquakes, although the exact nature of that relationship remained unknown for another hundred years. Yet another group thought that gravity and earthquakes must be related, even in the largest of earthquakes.

It wasn't until the 1906 earthquake that a scientific examination of the fault plane, exposed near the town of Olema, north of San Francisco, and offsets of objects such as fence lines along the fault led to a clear understanding that the earthquake and movement along faults were related to each other. Additionally, scientist H. F. Reid correctly inferred that movement along the fault actually caused the earthquake. Upon further investigation, Reid came up with an idea he called "Elastic Rebound."

For years—perhaps decades—the San Andreas Fault had been deforming the rocks in the area. Although the rocks next to the fault were locked in place by friction, the rocks just a few inches to a few miles away from the fault had been in motion and slowly deforming as a result of the buildup of strain. Energy was stored in these rocks. At a critical point, the potential energy stored in the rocks overcame the strength of the rocks, and the fault broke. The potential energy was turned into kinetic energy (movement). When that occurred, the distorted rocks snapped back into some form of equilibrium with their surroundings, and the stresses in the area were reset. The rocks at the fault broke and behaved in a brittle manner, but those just a short distance from the fault behaved in an elastic manner—much like the movement of a rubber band. When a rubber band is stretched between two fingers, it is being deformed and potential energy is being stored within the band. If one finger is removed quickly, potential energy in the rubber band is converted into kinetic energy as it snaps the finger left holding it. But after the rubber band expends its kinetic energy, it returns to an undeformed state with no stored potential energy.

See Also: Earthquake; San Andreas Fault; San Francisco Earthquake, California, United States (1906).

Further Reading

Reid, H. F. (1910). *The California earthquake of April 18, 1906: Report of the State Earthquake Investigation Commission in two volumes and atlas. Volume II: The mechanics of the earthquake.* Washington, DC: Carnegie Institution of Washington.
Richter, C. F. (1958). *Elementary seismology.* San Francisco: W.H. Freeman and Company.

Eurasian Plate

The Eurasian Plate contains the continents of Europe and Asia, exclusive of the Indian subcontinent. It is primarily a continental plate, although it does contain a significant amount of oceanic lithosphere. In addition to the land areas, the plate also includes the South China Sea and Sea of Japan to the east and Iceland to the west, as well as half of the northern Atlantic Ocean. This is a very large plate that contains a host of mountain chains such as the Alps and the Urals, as well as the northern Himalayas and the Zagros Mountains. All of these mountain chains were created as a result of continental collision. As important as these features are to the history, geography, and culture of these regions, they are not related to the Pacific Rim or the geologic hazards seen there. The Eurasian plate's interactions with the Pacific, Australian, and Philippine plates are quite substantial, however, and it is these interactions that generate a great many of the western Pacific's major island chains, major volcanic eruptions, and destructive earthquakes.

The Eurasian Plate joins with the North American Plate in eastern Siberia at an ambiguous boundary. The boundary is not marked so much by earthquakes or volcanic eruptions as are many boundaries. Instead, the boundary largely is defined based on the ages and "fabrics" of rocks found in the subsurface there. The two plates have been joined for a very long time.

The next plate to the south that interacts with the Eurasian Plate is the Philippine Plate. The Philippine Plate is a mostly oceanic plate that lies in the westernmost Pacific between the Mariana Islands and the Philippines. Interaction between the Eurasian Plate and Philippine Plate produced the islands of the Philippines, as well as the southern islands of Japan, such as Kyushu and Shikoku. A great deal of volcanic activity is associated with both of these island nations. A major eruption at Pinatubo (Philippines) in 1991 left central Luzon vulnerable to lahars for more than a decade after the eruption, and lowered global temperatures for a full year. At most of the western margin of the Philippine Plate, it is subducting beneath the Eurasian plate. In one small stretch between Taiwan and the northernmost tip of the Philippines, however, the South China Sea is subducting beneath the Philippine Plate. For this reason, Taiwan has a number of volcanoes, three of which have been active in the last 5,000 years. It also has a fair amount of earthquake activity, as evidenced by the 1999 Jiji, Taiwan, earthquake.

The southeastern portion of the Eurasian Plate interacts with the Australian Plate as well. Here, the Australian Plate is subducting beneath the Eurasian Plate, creating the Indonesian archipelago. Indonesia extends from the Andaman Islands in the west to Irian Jaya in the east, a distance of more than 3,200 miles (5,000 kilometers). The island nation is comprised of more than 15,000 individual islands that range broadly in size. The two things all of these islands have in common are volcanic origin and high levels of earthquake activity—both of which are the result of subduction. The world's largest eruption since the evolution of modern humans occurred in Indonesia at the volcano Toba. The volcano Krakatau also is located in Indonesia, between the two major islands of Java and Sumatra. The greatest death toll in modern times from a single earthquake and tsunami also occurred as a result of an earthquake along this plate boundary. In December 2004, a massive magnitude 9.1 earthquake off the west coast of Sumatra generated a tsunami that spanned the entire Indian Ocean and killed nearly a quarter million people. Large earthquakes are extremely common in this area of the world.

See Also: Indian Ocean Earthquake and Tsunami (2004); Indonesia; Japan; Jiji Earthquake, Taiwan (1999); Krakatau Eruption (also known as "Krakatoa" Eruption), Indonesia (1883); Mariana Trench; Philippines; Subduction Zone; Toba Eruptron, Indonesia.

Further Reading

Smithsonian Institution. National Museum of Natural History. Global Volcanism Program. (2014, June 12). Retrieved from http://www.volcano.si.edu/search_volcano_results.cfm
Tarbuck, E. J., Lutgens, F. K., & Tasa, D. (2011). *Earth: An introduction to physical geology* (10th ed.). Upper Saddle River, NJ: Pearson Prentice Hall.

Ewing, William Maurice

William Maurice Ewing was born on May 12, 1906 in Lockney, Texas. Ewing showed an interest in and affinity for math and science in high school, and was awarded the Hohenthal Scholarship to the Rice Institute (now Rice University) in Houston, Texas. He earned a bachelor's degree in mathematics and physics with honors in 1926. Ewing continued his education at Rice, earning a master's degree in 1927 and a Ph.D. in 1930. His Ph.D. thesis was entitled, "Calculation of Ray Paths from Seismic Travel-Time Curves." This was to be an interesting prelude to Ewing's career of seismic studies. His understanding of ray theory was critical to many of his fundamental discoveries of the structure of the ocean floor.

Ewing began his career as an instructor of physics at the University of Pittsburgh, but a year later moved to Lehigh University, where he taught until 1940. As a young faculty member at Lehigh, Ewing was approached by geologists William Bowie and Dick Field about conducting experiments on the continental shelf, the shallowest parts of the oceans. Ewing was extremely interested and made use of the limited amount of ship time he was able to get to test the design of research instruments in the oceans. He demonstrated that measurements could be made successfully in the ocean, and worked for the next several years to find enough time on research vessels to continue his work.

In 1940, Ewing successfully lobbied for a leave of absence from Lehigh and moved to Woods Hole Oceanographic Institution in Massachusetts with his research group. There, he continued his seismic work at sea, and expanded his interests to include gravity measurements at sea using a research submarine. Ewing and his colleagues found that there was a gravity low along the Puerto Rican Trench, just as there was near Indonesia. This later became one of many lines of evidence that helped scientists piece together clues that led to plate tectonic theory and, more specifically, what happens at subduction zones.

Another of Ewing's accomplishments from this period at Woods Hole was inventing a number of water-tight instruments, including the first waterproof camera. He also wrote a manual for the Navy just before World War II entitled, *Sound Transmission in Sea Water*. This publication caught the attention of those in charge of naval research, and suddenly Ewing had a great deal of money and ship time he could dedicate to his studies of the ocean floor. During World War II, he was instrumental in the discovery and exploitation of a low-velocity sound channel in the ocean, called the SOFAR (Sound Fixing and Ranging) Channel. The SOFAR Channel acts as a wave guide that traps sounds in this layer in the ocean. If an explosion is made near or within the SOFAR Channel, the sound travels incredible distances before becoming too quiet to hear, or to detect with instruments. In one of his experiments, Ewing dropped a small charge off the west coast of Africa, and the explosion was heard off the Bahamas. The navy has made great use of the SOFAR channel in the decades since its discovery.

In 1944, Ewing was offered a faculty position at Columbia University. He brought several members of his research group with him from Woods Hole, and together they continued to work on research in marine geology. In 1948, the widow of banker Thomas Lamont offered to donate their estate at Palisades to Columbia University, and the university in turn offered the estate and a sizable cash donation from Mrs. Lamont to Ewing. Ewing and his group took possession as soon as possible, and the facility was christened the Lamont Geological Observatory. Ewing continued to raise funds to support his new Geological Observatory. In 1968, Ewing visited a representative of the Doherty Foundation which offered him $7 million. The gift was accepted and the observatory was renamed the Lamont-Doherty Geological Observatory. It was initially part of Columbia University's geology department, but later became its own entity within the university.

In 1953, Ewing rented an old schooner called the *Vema* for his work at sea, and negotiated an option to purchase the ship. University officials relented and purchased the vessel for the Geological Observatory, which gave Ewing a ship at his disposal. Years later a second ship, the *Robert D. Conrad*, built by the Office for Naval Research, joined the fleet. Ewing and his research group made full use of the ships. In the years that followed, he and his research associates—including graduate students—discovered the depth of the crust-mantle boundary beneath the oceans, determined the thickness of sediment overlying the ocean floor in several locations, and proved that the Atlantic and Pacific Ocean floors were very similar in structure. Ewing also did a fair amount of echo-sounding research that disclosed the shape of the ocean floor. These fundamental discoveries were built upon, and eventually Ewing's discoveries led to greater understanding of the role of the ocean in plate tectonics. It is for his role in developing Plate Tectonic Theory that Ewing perhaps is best known. In later years, he dabbled in a number of other interests, one of which was lunar seismology.

In 1972, after disputes with university administration, Ewing retired abruptly from Columbia University and resigned his position at Lamont-Doherty Geological Observatory. He moved back to his home state of Texas, and accepted a position at the Marine Biomedical Institute of the University of Texas at Galveston. Ewing hoped to build a marine geophysics institute there, and set about designing instruments for the ship *Ida Green*. Ewing lived only long enough to see the first results from experiments conducted on the ship. He suffered a cerebral hemorrhage on April 28, 1974, and died on May 4 without regaining consciousness. Ewing was just one day shy of his 68th birthday.

See Also: Plate Tectonics.

Further Reading

Bullard, E. C. (2014, June 9). William Maurice Ewing, 1906–1974. National Academy of Sciences. Retrieved from http://www.nasonline.org/publications/biographical-memoirs/memoir-pdfs/ewing-william.pdf

Dunn, D. A. (2014, June 9). William Maurice Ewing (1906–1974). American Geophysical Union. Retrieved from http://honors.agu.org/william-maurice-ewing-1906%e2%80%931974/

Extrusive

The term "extrusive" is used to describe an igneous (magma-derived) rock that is formed at or above the earth's surface. All pyroclastic material could be considered extrusive, as is basalt, andesite, dacite, and rhyolite. Obsidian is a natural volcanic glass which also is extrusive. The main hallmark of extrusive volcanic rocks is that they form quickly. As a result, they either have no mineral crystals, as is the case with obsidian; or the vast majority of their crystals are small to microscopic, as is the case with basalt, andesite, dacite, and rhyolite. They also can have an abundance of gas bubbles in them, as is the case with the pyroclastic material pumice. The gas bubbles cool and harden into solid rock very soon after eruption, leaving holes in the rock called vesicles. Some basalts and andesites have abundant vesicles in them as well. The pyroclastic material scoria is full of vesicles, and volcanic ash can be formed when a rock full of vesicles is pulverized during the eruption process. A microscopic view of some volcanic ash samples shows broken bubbles.

See Also: Andesite; Basalt; Dacite; Intrusive; Pyroclastic Materials; Rhyolite.

Further Reading

Tarbuck, E. J., Lutgens, F. K., & Tasa, D. (2011). *Earth: An introduction to physical geology* (10th ed.). Upper Saddle River, NJ: Pearson Prentice Hall.

F

Farallon Plate

The Farallon Plate was a large oceanic plate that used to lie just east of the Pacific Plate, on the eastern side of what today is the East Pacific Rise. The Pacific Plate was moving northwest, as it continues to do today. The Farallon Plate was moving eastward. About 180 million years ago, North and South America began moving westward as a result of spreading at the Mid-Atlantic Ridge. This caused the Farallon Plate to be subducted beneath those two plates. In fact, it was subducted faster than it could be formed at its spreading center (the East Pacific Rise). As a result, the Farallon Plate began to shrink. The East Pacific Rise inched closer to the coast of North America every year. About 28 million years ago, a segment of the East Pacific Rise made contact with the subduction zone off the west coast of North America, and the Pacific Plate came into direct contact with the North American Plate. This contact created the San Andreas Fault. Motion along the Pacific-North American plate boundary is such that the Pacific Plate is moving northwest relative to the North American plate. Thus, movement on the San Andreas Fault, which also is the plate boundary between the Pacific and North American plates, is the same. The western side of the fault is moving northwest relative to the eastern side of the fault.

Subduction of the Farallon Plate off the coast of North America divided the large plate into smaller plates separated by the Pacific Plate. To the north sits the Juan de Fuca Plate. It meets the North American Plate at the northernmost extent of the San Andreas Fault and its northernmost associated transform boundary, the Mendocino Fracture Zone. North of here, the Juan de Fuca Plate continues to move eastward and be subducted beneath the North American Plate. The result is the Cascade Range—a chain of volcanoes that begins in northern California and continues northward to southern British Columbia—as well as the Cascadia Subduction Zone. The Juan de Fuca Plate is shrinking in size, and someday will disappear completely beneath North America.

To the south of the San Andreas, there is a long series of very young spreading centers throughout the Gulf of California, between the Baja Peninsula of Mexico and mainland Mexico. In this area, the Gulf of California is expanding very slowly through the production of new oceanic lithosphere at these spreading centers. South of the Gulf of California is a very small plate, called a microplate, that represents a tiny remnant of the Farallon Plate. It is called the Rivera Plate. The Rivera Plate is subducting beneath Mexico's west coast. Just southeast of the Rivera Plate is the Cocos Plate. The Cocos Plate is subducting beneath southern Mexico and much of Central America. It has produced a chain of volcanoes and is the site of occasional large and damaging earthquakes. The plate south of the Cocos Plate is the Nazca Plate. It is being subducted beneath South America. This subduction zone has created the Andes Mountains, a continuous mountain range that runs the length of western South America. As a result of this subduction, the Andes range is partially volcanic in origin. The west coast of South America also is the site of some of the most powerful earthquakes recorded in the last 100 years, as well as large Pacific-wide tsunamis. The Peru-Chile Trench marks the location where the Nazca Plate dives beneath the South American Plate.

In the future, it is expected that these pieces of the former Farallon Plate will continue their eastward motion, and will continue to be destroyed at a faster rate than they are replenished at their spreading centers. Eventually, all remnants of the Farallon Plate will be gone from the surface of the earth and it will be nearly impossible to tell that the large plate ever existed. It gives one pause to realize that this process might have repeated itself many times in the earth's long history.

See Also: Cascadia Subduction Zone; Cocos Plate; Chilean Earthquake and Tsunami (1960); Juan de Fuca Plate; North American Plate; South American Plate; Subduction Zone.

Further Reading

Pacific Northwest Seismic Network. (2014, June 12). *Plate tectonics.* Retrieved from http://www.pnsn.org/outreach/about-earthquakes/plate-tectonics

Tarbuck, E. J., Lutgens, F. K., & Tasa, D. (2011). *Earth: An introduction to physical geology* (10th ed.). Upper Saddle River, NJ: Pearson Prentice Hall/Pearson Education, Inc.

U.S. Geological Survey. (2014, June 12). *Shrinking Farallon Plate.* Retrieved from http://pubs.usgs.gov/gip/dynamic/Farallon.html

Fiji

Fiji is an island nation located approximately 3,400 miles (5,470 kilometers) east of Australia in the southern Pacific Ocean. Fiji lies on a subduction zone between the Australian Plate to the south and the Pacific Plate to the north. Subduction is occurring here at a rate of about 3.4 inches (8.6 centimeters) per year, which is relatively fast. As a result of the subduction, Fiji is both a volcanic island nation and one that regularly experiences earthquakes. It contains only 19 known volcanoes, and only two of those have been active in historic times. Nabukelevu Volcano is located on the southwest end of Kadavu Island in the southern end of the Fiji island chain. It last erupted in the year 1660, resulting in pyroclastic flows and dome growth. Taveuni is a shield volcano, and is the third largest of the Fiji Islands.

The last known eruption of Taveuni Volcano was around the year 1550. The eruption produced a basalt lava flow near the southern tip of the island.

Fiji also has a number of earthquakes every year but, in general, they are not overly large or damaging. In November 2009, a magnitude 7.3 earthquake occurred near the village of Rakiraki on the north coast of the island of Viti Levu. This location is approximately 65 miles (100 kilometers) north of Suva, the capital city of Fiji. The earthquake caused no damage, however, because it was a fairly deep earthquake, occurring 364 miles (585 kilometers) beneath the surface. Due to its location on a subduction zone, Fiji experiences both shallow and deep earthquakes. Earthquakes at subduction zones occur within the subducted lithosphere, so they can occur at very shallow depths or as deep as 416 miles (670 kilometers) beneath the surface.

See Also: Australian Plate; Pacific Plate; Subduction Zone.

Further Reading

Smithsonian Institution. National Museum of Natural History. Global Volcanism Program. (2014, June 13). *Taveuni.* Retrieved from http://www.volcano.si.edu/volcano.cfm?vn=245010

U.S. Geological Survey. (2014, June 13). *Historic world earthquakes. Fiji.* Retrieved from http://earthquake.usgs.gov/earthquakes/world/historical_country.php#fiji

G

Galapagos Islands

The Galapagos Islands are located on the equator about 600 miles (1,000 kilometers) west of Ecuador in the Pacific Ocean. These islands were formed by hot spot activity in this location over the last several million years. The oldest of the Galapagos Islands are a few million years old, but geologists have evidence that the hot spot itself has been active for about 90 million years. The Galapagos Islands are located on the Nazca Plate, and on the Galapagos Platform, which is an anomalously shallow part of the sea floor. The platform continues to the east of the islands, beneath a chain of seamounts (submerged volcanoes) known as the Carnegie Ridge. The Galapagos Hot Spot produced these seamounts in addition to the islands. The volcanoes of the Carnegie Ridge area are much older than the current Galapagos Islands. The Carnegie Ridge volcanoes were formed over the hot spot then were eroded from above and lowered with the oceanic crust as it moved away from the hot spot and cooled. The tops of multiple seamounts on the Carnegie Ridge have been found to be flat-topped with rounded cobbles, which are clear indications of wave erosion.

In addition to the seamounts of the Carnegie Ridge—which make sense in terms of existing plate motions—there is another chain of seamounts associated with the Galapagos Hot Spot. The Cocos Ridge extends to the northeast from the islands and also is a chain of seamounts. These were formed due to a migration of the Galapagos Ridge, a spreading center between the Cocos and Nazca plates, away from the hot spot. The hot spot used to sit directly underneath the ridge, but the ridge has since moved. That movement created a chain of volcanoes that lead directly to the islands seen today.

The existing islands of the Galapagos generally are younger to the southeast, in the direction of plate motion. The youngest and most active parts of the Galapagos Archipelago generally are found toward the west. The Galapagos Islands, however, do not show a clear progression of oldest to youngest as do those in the Hawaiian Islands. In Hawaii, the volcanoes follow a very clear linear progression from oldest to youngest, and very few volcanoes are active at any given time. In the Galapagos, nine volcanoes have been active in the last 200 years or so. Geologists at Cornell, however, are quick to point out that the magma output of just one of the Hawaiian volcanoes, Mauna Loa, is likely equal to the output of all Galapagos volcanoes within the last 200 years; perhaps these two hot spots are not so different from each other after all.

Pahoehoe lava flow with a large shield volcano in the background, Fernandina Island, Galapagos Islands, Ecuador. This shield volcano is typical of those seen in the Galapagos Islands. It is an inverted soup bowl shape. (Patrick Endres/Newscom)

The primary type of volcano in the Galapagos Islands is a shield volcano, but tuff cones and other related features also are present—as they are in other settings of oceanic hot spot volcanoes such as the Hawaiian Islands. The shapes of the shield volcanoes in the Galapagos are distinctive as compared to other shield volcanoes around the world. The Galapagos volcanoes have an "inverted soup bowl" shape to them, meaning that they have relatively steep sides that give way to relatively flat tops. Summit calderas are much larger than those seen at other active shield volcanoes, and in some cases they also are much deeper. The reason that these volcanoes look so different from their counterparts around the world is because they tend to erupt along ring fractures that are concentric to the summit caldera, rather than along rift zones on their flanks. Because of this mechanism of eruption, the volcanoes form a well-developed center and less well-developed flanks. The reason why Galapagos volcanoes erupt in this way is unknown.

Five separate islands within the Galapagos have experienced eruptions since the year 1813. As of this writing, the most recent eruption in the Galapagos was Fernandina in 2009. It was a fairly short-lived eruption lasting only about 27 days, and produced lava flows on the volcano's southwest flank. Cerro Azul is located at the southwest tip of Isabela Island. In May and June of 2008, it erupted from its summit and southeast flank. Sierra Negra, also located on Isabela Island, erupted from the northern rim of its caldera for eight days in 2005. Alcedo, on Isabela Island, erupted from its south caldera wall in 1993. The start and finish of the eruption were not observed, so an exact duration of the Alcedo eruption is unknown. Marchena, on an island that shares its name, erupted for about two months in 1991. Lava flows occurred on the west and southwest parts of the caldera rim. Wolf on Isabela Island erupted for approximately a week and a half in 1982. Other notable eruptions include Santiago in 1906, Pinta in 1928, and Darwin in 1813.

Darwin's Galapagos Islands

Part of the reason that the Galapagos Islands are so famous stems from the fact that they were visited in the 1830s by a young Charles Darwin. Darwin spent time on a number of the islands in the chain, and collected many animal and plant specimens. He noted that tortoises on various islands had different shells. He also recognized finches that looked somewhat like those on the continent of South America, but not exactly. Darwin mulled over these differences for decades, and eventually cited these as some of his prime examples of evolution by means of natural selection.

A population of finches made its way to the islands. Because food stores on the islands were much different from those on the mainland of South America, birds having tiny variations in their beak shapes had greater ease in eating certain types of food. Those birds became more comfortable in their environment because they had plenty to eat, thus they also were more successful at reproduction, and more offspring had the traits that made the birds more successful in their particular environment. Eventually—after many hundreds of generations—the original population of finches evolved into several new species.

Although eruptions are quite commonplace in the Galapagos Islands, large and damaging earthquakes are not. Occasional earthquakes are to be expected because the islands are part of an active chain of volcanoes. Nearly constant earthquakes accompany any volcanic eruption, but in this location simply are too small to feel. The islands are not very close to a plate boundary, therefore large earthquakes are rare.

See Also: Ecuador; Hawaiian Islands; Mauna Loa, Hawaii, United States; Shield Volcano.

Further Reading

Cornell University. (2014, June 13). *Galapagos geology on the Web*. Retrieved from http://www.geo.cornell.edu/geology/GalapagosWWW/GalapagosGeology.html

Smithsonian Institution. National Museum of Natural History. Global Volcanism Program. (2014, June 13). Retrieved from http://www.volcano.si.edu/search_volcano_results.cfm

Galeras Volcano, Colombia (1993)

Galeras is a composite volcano located in southwestern Colombia near the city of Pasto. It is frequently active, usually producing relatively small eruptions from a cone in its summit caldera. The presence of the caldera, however, is one indicator that this volcano is not always so tame. Galeras is capable of producing large and damaging eruptions. A major eruption in 1936 sent pyroclastic flows down the northeast flank of the volcano. The caldera-forming eruptions and at least one major landslide episode likely occurred several thousand years ago to give the volcano the general shape it has today.

In many ways, Galeras is a fairly unremarkable volcano, if there is such a thing. It erupts often, but usually not very violently. The city of Pasto is near its base, but since the amphitheater of the caldera opens away from the city, most of Galeras' eruptions pose little risk to the population. Prevailing winds usually carry volcanic ash away from Pasto, as well. Galeras is neither particularly dangerous nor particularly deadly. A small eruption that occurred in January of 1993, however, makes this volcano noteworthy.

In the scientific community—and particularly in a community as small as that composed of people who study active volcanoes—few things are as valuable as collaboration and the exchange of ideas with colleagues. In January 1993, gas geochemist Dr. Stanley Williams of Arizona State University convened a conference on Volcán Galeras, complete with a workshop that promised a visit to the summit caldera of Galeras. The subject of the conference was Volcán Galeras. Most of the more than 100 attendees were experts in some field of volcanology, some even are quite well-known. There were representatives from many countries, including the United States, Russia, Ecuador, Guatemala, the United Kingdom, and Switzerland. The meeting went well, and January 14 was set aside for an optional field trip into the caldera of Galeras. More than 20 people descended into the Galeras caldera that morning. Some were anxious to collect gas samples near the cone in the caldera. Another group was there to take gravity measurements. Yet another group planned to collect temperature data at some of the steam and gas vents in the crater. Galeras also was a tourist destination, and permits were issued for members of the general public to hike to the summit of the volcano. On this particular day, three such hikers descended to the caldera floor with Williams and his group, along with a small group of reporters.

Shortly after 1:30 p.m. that afternoon, the volcano exploded. There was a loud noise similar to a terrible clap of thunder and then black ash rose from the throat of the volcano. Glowing rocks were thrown high into the sky. Within seconds, hot boulders were raining down on the group, with some breaking apart on impact. In all, six scientists and three hikers died in the eruption. The expedition leader, Stanley Williams, was critically injured after sustaining at least one major blow to the head and a shattered lower leg. One police officer from a police station on the rim of Galeras was severely injured. The rest of the scientists in the caldera that day survived with minor injuries.

Stanley Williams received a great deal of criticism in the years following that ill-fated expedition. Although he insisted that there was no reason to believe that they were in any danger, and volcanic eruptions cannot be predictably forecast, he was contradicted by a preponderance of evidence. In studies conducted at other volcanoes—and also at Galeras—strange seismic signals dubbed "tornillos" (which is Spanish for "screw") were observed shortly before minor eruptions occurred. A scientist manning Galeras' seismic station noted the presence of tornillos on the seismic station in the few hours preceding the eruption. He radioed this information to the leaders of the group in the caldera, but no evacuation order was given. Many people believe that it was reckless for the leaders to not evacuate upon learning of the tornillos, and that the deaths could have been prevented if

Williams and the other leaders had been more cautious in their approach to the volcano.

Conflicting accounts of the tragedy were published in 2001. Geologist and journalist Victoria Bruce wrote a book entitled *No Apparent Danger* and championed the side that blamed Williams' recklessness for the deaths that day. Williams co-wrote a book entitled *Surviving Galeras* that detailed the precautions taken and unpredictable nature of active volcanoes. Regardless, the event will be remembered for the tragic deaths of six volcanologists and three family members who were out for a pleasant day enjoying the wonders of nature.

See Also: Caldera; Colombia.

Further Reading

Bruce, V. (2001). *No apparent danger: The true story of volcanic disaster at Galeras and Nevado Del Ruiz.* New York: HarperCollins Publishers.

Smithsonian Institution. National Museum of Natural History. Global Volcanism Program. (2014, May 9). *Galeras.* Retrieved from http://www.volcano.si.edu/volcano.cfm?vn =351080#

Williams, S., & Montaigne, F. (2001). *Surviving Galeras.* Boston: Houghton Mifflin Company.

Geodesy

Geodesy is a field of geophysics that studies the geometrical, structural, and gravitational properties of the earth (and other planets), and how those properties change through time. Changes in these properties of the earth can happen for a number of reasons. For example, the extra weight of glaciers on a landscape depresses the solid earth and lowers its elevation. When the glaciers melt, the solid earth rebounds and the elevation of the region increases.

As a volcano builds toward eruption, magma fills the magma chamber beneath. The extra magma causes the volcano to inflate—or rise slightly in elevation—before erupting. As an eruption begins the volcano often deflates. Earthquakes also have the ability to move sections of the earth up to several feet, both vertically and horizontally. These changes are monitored by scientists called "geodesists"; the science of measuring the changes and determining their cause is "geodesy."

Geodesy is one of the oldest of the earth sciences. People have been measuring the earth and trying to understand the size and shape of the planet for millennia. In roughly 250 BCE, Eratosthenes, a Greek mathematician, used his knowledge of geometry to calculate the circumference of the earth. Surveying has been in use since Roman times, although its practitioners have employed increasingly sophisticated methods through the centuries.

Today, sophisticated tools and methods exist that have advanced the study of geodesy. These tools also are helpful in the study of geologic hazards because they enable scientists to determine how the earth responds to stresses and how it changes shape before and after earthquakes, landslides, and volcanic eruptions. Laser sighting now regularly is used in conjunction with traditional survey methods to determine distances between two points. Tilt meters—simple instruments that determine minute amounts of tilt in a landscape—are particularly helpful when placed on the flanks of a volcano because they are sensitive enough to detect miniscule changes in the angle of the volcano's slopes, which can indicate a magma chamber filling with magma. Three of the most commonly used modern geodetic tools in geologic hazard studies are GPS (Global Positioning System), LIDAR (light detecting and ranging), and InSAR (interferometric synthetic aperture radar).

The Global Positioning System (GPS) is a creation of the United States military. A system of satellites orbits the earth twice each day, continuously broadcasting radio signals providing location and precise time from onboard atomic clocks. The radio signals travel at the speed of light to GPS devices (receivers) here on earth. The GPS device records exact arrival times of radio signals from multiple satellites and calculates travel times from each satellite within its direct line of sight. After the GPS device calculates the exact distance from each satellite, it can triangulate the position of the device on earth. At least four satellites must be visible to the GPS device for this to work. In general, the more satellites a GPS receiver can "see," the more accurate the location it can calculate. This accuracy, however, also depends on the device itself as well as data-processing methods.

GPS units used in vehicles to provide directions to drivers, as well as handheld units used for recreational purposes such as geocaching, boating, and hiking, are accurate to within 10 feet (3 meters). Surveying companies, utility companies, and others requiring improved accuracy can use "differential GPS" systems which are accurate to within 4 to 6 inches (10 to 15 centimeters). Systems which are even more precise are used by government agencies and earth scientists around the world. These systems have real-time positioning capability to within an inch or two, and post-survey accuracy after processing to less than 1/10 inch. It is this last category of GPS monitoring that is most helpful in the study of geologic hazards. Scientists are able to track movement of tectonic plates, detect inflation and deflation of volcanoes, and see small slope movements that might indicate a landslide hazard. Both LIDAR and InSAR are dependent on GPS technology.

A light detecting and ranging (LIDAR) instrument consists of a laser, a scanner, and a specialized GPS receiver that are mounted on an airplane or helicopter. As the aircraft flies over the landscape, the laser is pointed at the ground below. As the specialized GPS receiver records the aircraft's position, the laser emits pulsed bursts. The distance to the earth's surface is calculated by measuring the time it takes a laser pulse, traveling at the speed of light, to be reflected from the ground surface back to the aircraft. Data then are downloaded and plotted, providing a three-dimensional image of the earth's surface. LIDAR is especially helpful because different types of lasers have the ability to penetrate various types of ground cover, such as vegetation and water. Therefore LIDAR also is used to measure seafloor and riverbed elevations. When an area is surveyed with LIDAR multiple times—such as before and after a lahar, pyroclastic flow, flood, lava flow, ash fall, or other event—scientists can compare the images and determine how much change has occurred in the landscape. These types of surveys help scientists understand how geologic and weather events change the landscape, the volume of material moved by a stream, or even the volume of material erupted by a volcano.

Interferometric Synthetic Aperture Radar (InSAR) is used for studying deformation of the ground, most often caused by earthquakes and volcanoes. A satellite is used to map a region in three dimensions using radar waves. Sometime (days to years) later, a satellite maps the same area again. Data from the two satellite maps are processed to calculate the differences in elevation between the first and second maps. A third map, indicating the calculated values of elevation change, is color-coded to indicate the magnitude of elevation difference detected between the two passes of the satellite. This third map is called an interferogram. Using this technique, scientists are able to study ground deformation in remote regions, or determine the amount of movement that occurred as a result of an earthquake rather quickly and without a great deal of field work. One example of how InSAR alerted scientists to a potentially dangerous situation was in the study of the Three Sisters volcanoes in central Oregon. Two satellite passes in 1997 and 2001 were compared using the InSAR method, and the resulting interferogram showed with absolute clarity a bull's-eye pattern centered just to the south of the southernmost volcano. At the center of the bull's eye 6 inches (15 centimeters) of uplift had occurred, indicating that the magma chamber beneath this volcano could be filling with new magma. Although no other signs of activity were noted at the time and the volcano was not heavily monitored, scientists had proof that magma was being emplaced about 4 miles (6 kilometers) beneath the surface. In other cases, InSAR studies of faults in which satellite maps are constructed before and after a major earthquake enable scientists to determine how far—and in which direction—the earthquake moved one side of the fault relative to the other.

See Also: Seismology; Volcano Monitoring Techniques.

Further Reading

American Geophysical Union. (2013, June 13). *Welcome to the geodesy section of the American Geophysical Union.* Retrieved from http://www.agu.org/sections/geodesy/

Diggins, J. E., & Bell, C. (1965). *String, straightedge, and shadow: The story of geometry.* New York: The Viking Press.

GPS.gov. (2013, June 14). *Official U.S. Government information about the Global Positioning System (GPS) and related topics.* Retrieved from http://www.gps.gov/

Helz, R. L. (2013, June 14). *Monitoring ground deformation from space.* (U.S. Geological Survey. Fact Sheet 2005-3025). Retrieved from http://volcanoes.usgs.gov/activity/methods/insar//public_files/InSAR_Fact_Sheet/2005-3025.pdf

National Oceanic and Atmospheric Administration. (2013, June 13). *LIDAR—Light detection and ranging—is a remote sensing method used to examine the surface of the earth.* Retrieved from http://oceanservice.noaa.gov/facts/lidar.html

GeoNet

GeoNet is New Zealand's official government agency responsible for research on and response to the country's geologic hazards. GeoNet's scientists are responsible for gathering and distributing information about the many seismic and volcanic hazards of the island nation, and for providing emergency response. The GeoNet scientists also conduct scientific research to better understand geologic hazards, including not only earthquakes and volcanoes, but also tsunamis and landslides. Research also extends to hazard mitigation, including the production of seismic and volcanic hazard assessments as well as earthquake engineering. When volcanoes become active, GeoNet scientists provide round-the-clock monitoring and are responsible for advising public officials of the probability of an eruption. Scientists also monitor the oceans and earthquake activity worldwide, and are able to provide timely warnings of tsunamis.

See Also: New Zealand.

Further Reading

GeoNet. (2014, October 16). Retrieved from http://info.geonet.org.nz/display/geonet/About+GeoNet

Great Kanto Earthquake, Japan (1923)

On September 1, 1923, one of the deadliest and most destructive earthquakes of the Twentieth Century devastated Japan's populous Kanto plain. The Great Kanto Earthquake destroyed much of Japan's industrial heartland, killed more than 100,000, slowed the Japanese economy for years, and revealed tensions among sectors of Japan's population as well as between the Japanese and their Korean colonial subjects.

The Great Kanto Earthquake, an estimated 8.3 magnitude quake, lasted for at least 4 and perhaps as many as 10 minutes. The initial quake struck at lunchtime, and there were more than 800 aftershocks in the hours and days that followed. The fires that resulted spread from wood and charcoal cooking stoves in Japanese houses and proved to be as destructive as the powerful quake itself. High winds fanned the flames that often trapped groups of refugees even after they had managed to escape from their shattered homes and businesses. Ultimately, as many as 143,000 people lost their lives, and another 50,000 were injured. Some 71% of the population of Tokyo and 85% of Yokohama's residents lost their homes.

The Kanto region was Japan's industrial core. The damage caused by the quake and its aftermath seriously disrupted Japan's industrial and commercial infrastructure by placing huge burdens on an already strained economy. A short-lived

Crown Prince Hirohito inspects fire damage following the Great Kanto Earthquake of 1923. (Kyodo/Newscom)

reconstruction boom did little to lift the general economic gloom, and recovery was slow to come to the region.

The earthquake was taken by many rural Japanese as a judgment on the nature of modern civilization; that the fruits of modernity could so easily be reduced to rubble prompted many farmers to redouble their efforts to eschew modern urban values in favor of local rural ones. Additionally, rumors that Korean residents of the Kanto area planned to use the chaos that followed the earthquake to loot, riot, or otherwise threaten the Japanese led to the widespread abuse of Koreans by groups of Japanese vigilantes. Government pleas to recognize the official imperial policy of assimilation and declarations that "Japanese and Koreans are one people" fell largely on deaf ears, as an estimated 6,000 to 10,000 Koreans were killed in the aftermath of the quake.

See Also: Japan.

Further Reading

Allen, J. M. (1996). The price of identity: The 1923 Kanto Earthquake and its aftermath. *Korean Studies 29*, 64–93.

Duus, P. (1998). *Modern Japan*. Boston: Houghton Mifflin.

Guagua Pichincha, Ecuador

Guagua Pichincha is a large composite volcano located immediately adjacent to Quito, the capital city of Ecuador. The volcano is part of the Andes Mountains, created as a result of the Nazca Plate being subducted beneath the South American Plate. Guagua Pichincha sits within the caldera of an extinct volcano, "Rucu Pichincha." Rucu Pichincha's caldera is breached on the west side of the volcano, away from Quito, so most pyroclastic flows and lahars are directed away from the metropolis. The summit of the volcano is located 15,692 feet (4,784 meters) above sea level. The city of Quito is creeping up the slopes of the mountain. A popular theme park on its eastern slope includes a cable car that ferries visitors to the volcano's summit where, on a clear day, passengers can view the crater of the volcano several hundred feet below.

Guagua Pichincha has been fairly active in the time since Spanish explorers arrived, with dozens of eruptions occurring since the mid-1500s. The largest historical eruption occurred in the year 1660. A plinian eruption column rose to an altitude of about 15.5 miles (25 kilometers). It deposited volcanic ash and pumice in Quito to a depth of 1 foot (30 centimeters). Nearly constant earthquakes threw residents of Quito into a panic, but there were no reports of casualties. Pyroclastic flows and ash fall to the west of the volcano, however, had a disastrous effect on agriculture, causing a dire economic downturn.

Modern eruptions at Guagua Pichincha have been fairly small, limited to phreatic and minor ash eruptions, as well as dome growth. Two young volcanologists, however, were killed while on the volcano in 1993. The researchers were on the lava dome in the crater and a phreatic eruption occurred. These are the only two deaths reported in all of the volcano's recorded history. The most recently reported activity at Guagua Pichincha is an instrumentally recorded burst of activity that was never observed. It occurred in February of 2009.

A minor eruption of the volcano Guagua Pichincha, located adjacent to the capital city of Quito, Ecuador. (Notimex/Newscom)

See Also: Lava Dome; Nazca Plate; Pyroclastic Flow; South American Plate; Subduction Zone.

Why Do People Live on Volcanoes?

Volcanoes can be violent and deadly, therefore asking why humans would choose to live on them is a legitimate question. The same question, however, could be asked about almost any part of the world. San Francisco has earthquakes, so why would anyone live there? The Midwest has tornadoes, the areas surrounding the Gulf of Mexico and along the Atlantic Ocean have hurricanes, and Hawaii has tsunamis. Why would anyone live in these places?

There are several reasons for people to choose to live on volcanoes. One is that volcanoes often are beautiful and picturesque places. Another is that the eruptive products of volcanoes produce rich, fertile soil that is excellent for agriculture. A third reason is that many volcanoes only rarely are active, therefore many generations of families can live in this type of area and never experience an eruption. In other words, it is a calculated risk that people choose to take.

In general, people learn to live with the hazards they face. Those in the Midwest live with the hazard of severe weather. They know how to keep their families as safe as possible, and they accept the risk of living in that location. The same is true of those who live in earthquake-prone areas; they know how to deal with the hazard and they accept the risk. Volcanic regions are no different. People generally are aware of the risks associated with living in the shadow of a volcano, and accept the risks as part of the decision to live there. Scientists work hard to understand the possible hazards posed by specific volcanoes so that they can help people make intelligent decisions about specific building locations, and give instructions about what to do in an emergency. Living on or near a volcano carries with it the responsibility of learning about the surroundings and how to stay safe.

Further Reading

Smithsonian Institution. National Museum of Natural History. Global Volcanism Program. (2014, June 4). *Guagua Pichincha*. Retrieved from http://www.volcano.si.edu/volcano.cfm?vn=352020

Volcano Discovery. (2014, June 4). *Guagua Pichincha Volcano*. Retrieved from http://www.volcanodiscovery.com/guagua_pichincha.html

Guatemala

Guatemala is the northernmost of the Central American countries. It is bordered to the north by Mexico, to the northeast by Belize, and to the south by Honduras and El Salvador. Just off the southwest coast of Guatemala is a subduction zone, where the Cocos Plate is subducting beneath both the Caribbean Plate and the North American Plate. The result is that the southern part of Guatemala is mountainous, with many volcanic peaks. Although Guatemala is not a particularly large country it has 175 known volcanoes—6 of which have erupted in historic times. Guatemala also has been known to experience large and damaging earthquakes. The most deadly of these occurred in 1976.

Guatemala lies at the boundary of three tectonic plates. The southern edge of the North American Plate contains the northern half of Guatemala. The southern half of Guatemala lies on the northern edge of the Caribbean Plate. The boundary between the two is a transform boundary, with motion in a left-lateral or sinistral motion. This means that if a person were to straddle the plate boundary, the left side would be moving toward that person. Thus, the northern part of the country is moving west relative to the southern part of the country. Along this plate boundary, earthquakes are quite common.

The country's most deadly earthquake—which occurred in February 1976—was located on this transform boundary. The earthquake killed more than 23,000 people. Many died as a result of the collapse of their adobe homes and businesses. Others died as a result of landslides in outlying areas. Some aftershocks caused additional loss of property and deaths. Most plate movement was on the Motagua Fault Zone, although minor amounts of motion occurred on the Mixco fault as well. Other deadly earthquakes occurred in 1902 and 1942. The 1902 earthquake resulted in 2,000 fatalities, and the 1942 earthquake killed 38 people.

Guatemala's volcanoes overwhelmingly are composite volcanoes, although the country is home to a large volcanic field full of cinder cones as well. The volcano "Fuego" is one of Central America's most active volcanoes. It looms above the city of Antigua. Eruptions have been frequent since the Spanish first settled the area in the early 1500s. Fuego tends to erupt vigorously, producing major ash-fall deposits and occasional pyroclastic flows and lava flows. Its last eruption began in 2013. "Santa Maria" is another frequently active volcano in Guatemala. It is a composite volcano with a large crater on its southwest flank that was formed during a catastrophic eruption in 1902. The volcano has been building lava domes since 1922. Dome growth often is accompanied by lava flows, explosions, pyroclastic flows, and lahars. Its most recent eruption also began in 2013. "Pacaya" is a volcanic center near the nation's capital of Guatemala City. Like Fuego, it is extremely active and has frequent eruptions. Unlike Fuego and Santa Maria, it is a complex volcano consisting of multiple peaks and a cluster of volcanic domes within a caldera. Eruptions often are mildly explosive, hurling red-hot bombs out of the crater. Occasional lava flows also are seen. Other historically active volcanoes in Guatemala are Acatenango, Almolonga, and Atitlán.

See Also: Caribbean Plate; Cocos Plate; Lahar; North American Plate; Pyroclastic Flow; Subduction Zone.

Further Reading

Smithsonian Institution. National Museum of Natural History. Global Volcanism Program. (2014, June 13). Retrieved from http://www.volcano.si.edu/search_volcano_results.cfm

U.S. Geological Survey. (2014, June 13). *Historic world earthquakes. Guatemala.* Retrieved from http://earthquake.usgs.gov/earthquakes/world/historical_country .php#guatemala

Guatemala Earthquake (1976)

At 3:03 a.m. on February 4, 1976, a magnitude 7.5 earthquake shook a wide swath of Guatemala. The earthquake occurred on the Motagua Fault, which traverses the country in a broad arc from west to east just north of the capital, Guatemala City. The earthquake caused an estimated 23,700 deaths and left more than 76,000 people injured. Property losses totaled more than US$1 billion, and nearly 1 million people were homeless after the earthquake. This earthquake was damaging not only to buildings, roads, and railways, but to the nation's economy as well.

The epicenter of the February 4, 1976, earthquake was located approximately 120 miles (193 kilometers) east-northeast of Guatemala City. Guatemala sits within a complex plate boundary region in which three plates interact. Most of Guatemala lies on the western part of the Caribbean Plate, although the northernmost section of the country lies on the North American Plate. The Cocos Plate is subducting northeastward beneath the Caribbean Plate at a velocity of 2.95 inches (7.5 centimeters) per year. This causes a great deal of earthquake activity along a zone parallel to the shoreline, as well as the occurrence of a chain of volcanoes located an average of 45 miles (75 kilometers) from the country's west coast. Within Guatemala, the Caribbean Plate also is sliding eastward past the southern extent of the North American Plate at a rate of approximately 0.83 inches (2.1 centimeters) per year. This particular earthquake occurred on the transform boundary between the North American Plate to the north and Caribbean Plate to the south. Maximum slippage on the fault was about 10.7 feet (3.25 meters), measured about 15.5 miles (25 kilometers) north of Guatemala City. Average slippage was approximately 3.3 feet (1 meter).

The February 4, 1976, earthquake caused extensive damage within Guatemala City and in many outlying villages. The most significant damage appears to have occurred near the western end of the ruptured fault segment, within the state of Chimaltenango. All structures within the towns of San Pedro Sacatepéquez, El Jicaro, Sumpango, Tecpan, and Gualán (all in the state of Chimaltenango) were destroyed or so heavily damaged that they had to be torn down. Damage was unpredictable in many ways. In some areas nearer the fault, adobe structures—which typically crumble in large earthquakes—were left relatively undamaged. Other adobe structures further from the fault—especially those in the highlands—were destroyed. Many modern buildings and other structures in Guatemala City were severely damaged, including hospitals, schools, bridges, the airport, grain silos, and parapets on older buildings and churches. Landslides also were common occurrences during the February 4 earthquake and the larger aftershocks that followed. Major landslides blocked the main highway leading east and west from Guatemala City toward the coasts on either side of the country. Slides also blocked railways and destroyed communication routes, interrupting commerce within the country.

Large, damaging earthquakes unfortunately are a somewhat frequent occurrence in Guatemala. Destructive earthquakes have been recorded since the time of the earliest Spanish settlements in the country. In 1541, an earthquake near the first important Spanish settlement of Ciudad Vieja killed about 150 Spaniards and at least 600 local residents. The administrative offices of the province were moved to Antigua after the earthquake, and this city became Guatemala's original capital. Antigua suffered damaging earthquakes at least 11 times between 1565 and 1773. Following the earthquake of 1773, the country's capital was moved to Guatemala City. Prior to the 1976 earthquake, Guatemala City had experienced a number of damaging earthquakes. The most deadly of these was a series of earthquakes that began on December 29, 1917. Two more earthquakes, on January 3 and January 24 of 1918, destroyed or seriously damaged roughly 40% of the homes in the city.

See Also: Cocos Plate; Earthquake Hazards; Guatemala.

Further Reading

Espinosa, A. F. (Ed.). (1976). *The Guatemalan earthquake of February 4, 1976, A preliminary report.* (U.S. Geological Survey Professional Paper 1002). Washington, DC: U.S. GPO.
Plafker, G. (1976). Tectonic aspects of the Guatemala earthquake of 4 February 1976. *Science 193* (4259), 1201–1208.

Gutenberg, Beno

Beno Gutenberg was a brilliant and enormously influential seismologist. His contributions to the science are as numerous as they are important. He is credited with discovering the earth's core, as well as the depth of its outer surface. He also calculated travel times for seismic waves throughout the earth. Additionally, Gutenberg found the low-velocity zone in the upper mantle that today is known as the top of the earth's asthenosphere; correctly associated tiny vibrations found on seismograms with disturbances of the ocean floor due to storms; worked with Richter to define magnitude scales for both local and distant earthquakes; mapped locations of earthquakes around the globe used in later studies of plate tectonics; and championed mantle convection as a valid mechanism in the earth. After Gutenberg's death, convection was cited as the force within the earth that drives plate motion.

Beno Gutenberg was born in Darmstadt, Germany, in 1889. His father owned a small soap factory. Although Beno's father wanted him to eventually take over the family business, Beno was interested in studying natural sciences. He enrolled in the University of Göttingen in 1908 to study under Emil Wiechert at the newly opened Institute of Geophysics. Gutenberg studied seismology, meteorology, and other forms of geophysics. He was especially interested in seismology. In 1910, Gutenberg was told that he had reached the limit of knowledge in the field of seismology, and that he should begin working on a thesis project. He chose to research microseisms—tiny vibrations found on seismograms, and usually referred to as "background noise." Gutenberg related these microseisms to movements of the ocean and published his first scientific paper on the subject in 1910. He received his Ph.D. in geophysics in 1911. Dr. Gutenberg continued work at the University of Göttingen as a post-doctoral researcher for one year; during that time he published work on the structure of the earth.

Gutenberg spent a year in the military from October 1912 to October 1913. After leaving the military in 1913, he found work as a seismologist at the Central Bureau of the International Association of Seismology in Strassbourg. Only 10 months later, however, World War I broke out and Gutenberg again entered the military. He worked as a meteorologist and, among other duties, also used sound waves to determine the locations of cannons. The work was similar to locating earthquakes in seismology. Even after the war, Gutenberg performed meteorological research because he liked the topic.

Following World War I, Gutenberg found it impossible to locate a scientific position, so he worked in his father's soap factory. He did not find academic work until 1924, when he was hired as a lecturer at the University of Frankfurt. The lecturer's salary was so small that Gutenberg continued to work full-time at his father's soap factory, but he still managed to remain an active researcher and publish groundbreaking work. In 1929, Gutenberg was invited to attend a meeting at the Seismology Lab at Caltech in Pasadena, California. He attended and impressed the members of the meeting immensely. Within a few months, he was offered a position as a seismologist at the lab, and professor at the university. Gutenberg accepted the position and moved his family to California soon after. He worked at the "Seismo Lab" for the rest of his productive career. Dr. Gutenberg worked with many other giants in the field of seismology, including Charles Richter and Hugo Benioff. Gutenberg and his wife Hertha socialized with many of the other professors at Caltech, including Albert Einstein. Einstein played violin and Gutenberg was a pianist, and they played in the same chamber music orchestra.

Gutenberg served as president of the Seismological Society of America from 1945 to 1947, was head of the Seismology Lab at Caltech from 1947 to 1957, was named a fellow of the American Academy of Arts and Sciences in 1950, served as president of the International Association of Seismology and the Physics of the Earth's Interior (IASPEI) from 1951 to 1954, and received the Bowie Medal from the American Geophysical Union in 1953. Gutenberg retired in 1958, but remained active in some organizations and research. In January 1960, Dr. Gutenberg contracted pneumonia; he died on January 25, 1960.

See Also: Earth Structure; Richter, Charles; Seismology.

Further Reading

American Geophysical Union. (2014, May 9). *Beno Gutenberg (1889–1960)*. Retrieved from http://honors.agu.org/bowie-lectures/beno-gutenberg-1889-1960/
Office of the Home Secretary. National Academy of Sciences. (1999). *Biographical memoirs* (Vol. 76). Washington, DC: National Academies Press.

H

Haleakala, Maui, Hawaii, United States

"Haleakala" translates to "house of the sun." This name was given to the summit area of the East Maui Volcano on the island of Maui in the Hawaiian Islands. Haleakala is the location where the demigod Maui is said to have stood when he captured the sun to slow its flight through the sky so his mother's kapa (cloth made from pounded bark) could dry properly. Today, the name Haleakala is synonymous with the name of the volcano.

Haleakala is the oldest volcano in the Hawaiian Islands that is thought to still be active, although the date of its last eruption is somewhat in question. In 1841, people who lived on Maui were asked about the most recent eruption of the volcano, and they stated that their grandparents had seen the mountain erupt. These reports led researchers to believe the most recent lava flow could have occurred around the year 1750. Discrepancies in maps drawn by explorers La Perouse (in 1786) and Vancouver (in 1793), however, led others to believe that Haleakala was active around 1790, but neither of the maps is sufficiently accurate to draw any precise conclusions. Radiocarbon dating yielded a much older date for Haleakala's most recent lava flows. Results indicate that the last eruption of Haleakala occurred between the years 1480 and 1600. Scientists believe that Haleakala is likely to erupt again, although the next eruption might not occur for hundreds of years.

Haleakala has three rift zones. Two of these, the Southwest Rift Zone and East Rift Zone, are well defined and appear to be the location of most flank eruptions. A third, less well-developed rift zone extends from the summit to the north. Haleakala shows characteristics of being in both the post-caldera phase of its life cycle, and the post-erosional phase. It is not uncommon for volcanoes to skip or combine stages in their life cycles, so this is not a complete surprise. Haleakala's rift zones are marked by large cinder cones, as might be expected in a post-caldera phase. The volcano has undergone extensive erosion, however, and the chemistry of some of its rocks is similar to what might be expected in the post-erosional phase. The largest erosional feature on Haleakala is the summit crater. Unlike the summit calderas on the large, young volcanoes of Kilauea and Mauna Loa on the island of Hawaii, this summit crater was not formed by volcanic processes—it was formed by intense erosion of the summit of the volcano by streams. This erosion took thousands of years, and has created spectacular valleys on Haleakala; waterfalls are common sights within these valleys. Haleakala also

A cinder cone near the summit of Haleakala on the island of Maui. (Design Pics / Rita Ariyoshi/Rita Ariyoshi/Newscom)

has post-erosional volcanic features. Like Oahu, there are tuff cones and other features common to post-erosional phase volcanoes. One large tuff cone, Molokini, sits just off the west coast of southwest Maui. It is a popular site for scuba diving and snorkeling and is teeming with marine life. Molokini lies along Haleakala's Southwest Rift Zone.

See Also: Hawaiian Islands; Kilauea Volcano, Hawaii, United States, Hawaii; Maui, Legend of; Mauna Loa, Hawaii, United States.

Further Reading

McDonald, G. A., Abbott, A. T., & Peterson, F. L. (1983). *Volcanoes in the sea: The geology of Hawaii* (2nd ed.). Honolulu: University of Hawaii Press.

U.S. Geological Survey. Hawaiian Volcano Observatory. (2014, May 20). *East Maui, or Haleakala—A potentially hazardous volcano.* Retrieved from http://hvo.wr.usgs.gov/volcanoes/haleakala/main.html

U.S. Geological Survey. Hawaiian Volcano Observatory. (2014, May 20). *Youngest lava flows on East Maui probably older than A.D. 1790.* Retrieved from http://hvo.wr.usgs.gov/volcanowatch/archive/1999/99_09_09.html

Hawaiian Islands

The Hawaiian Islands are located in the north-central Pacific Ocean, well within the boundaries of the Pacific Plate. The island chain was created by the Hawaiian Hot Spot, which has been active for at least 70 million years. Although most people think only of the eight inhabited islands of the state of Hawaii, there actually are dozens of islands that comprise the Hawaiian archipelago. The Hawaiian Islands simply are the southernmost part of what is known as the Hawaiian Ridge-Emperor Seamounts chain. The islands extend from Hawaii in the southeast to Kure Atoll in the northwest. Beyond Kure, all islands created by the hot spot have subsided so they are far beneath the waves. Imaging of the ocean floor, however, shows that seamounts (submerged mountains) continue well beyond Kure Atoll.

The Hawaiian-Emperor chain has an interesting geometry. The islands and seamounts trend northwest from Hawaii for a distance of about 2,200 miles. At that point, the chain makes a bend and the seamounts trend north. Rocks collected from the location of the bend are 43 to 45 million years old. Which means that—at about that time—the Pacific Plate experienced an abrupt change in its direction of motion. Eventually, the Hawaiian-Emperor chain intersects the Aleutian Trench. It is only reasonable to assume that some seamounts have been subducted beneath the North American Plate at the trench.

The Hawaiian Islands were created as the Pacific Plate moved over the Hawaiian Hot Spot. Above the hot spot, nearly continuous volcanism has the ability to create some of the largest volcanoes on the planet. As a particular spot on the plate moves away from the hot spot, however, volcanic activity wanes and volcanoes become extinct. The heat emanating from the hot spot plays an important role not only in building the volcanoes by volcanic processes, but also in buoying the islands. As a volcano becomes extinct and moves away from the hot spot, it begins to subside as the lithosphere cools. Volcanoes then lose elevation and begin sinking into the ocean depths. This is the process that has created the Northwest Hawaiian Islands, those islands beyond the 8 traditionally thought of as the State of Hawaii.

Many of the northwestern islands in the chain really are just atolls—which are coral reefs that fringe a submerged island. Volcanic activity ceased millions of years ago in these areas, and the ocean took over. Atolls usually are circular or horseshoe-shaped, and often have a shallow area in the center. Because they are lonely outposts of land in a vast sea, they are unique habitats for sea birds, nesting grounds for sea turtles, and resting places for marine mammals (such as the endangered Hawaiian Monk Seal). The shallow water also provides habitat for corals, invertebrate animals, and reef creatures. In recognition of the unique habitat provided by these islands, and of the cultural and ecological significance of this area of the Pacific Ocean, President George Bush signed a presidential proclamation in 2006 that designated the Northwest Hawaiian Islands and surrounding waters as the Papahanaumokuakea Marine National Monument. In 2010, the monument also was designated as a mixed (natural and cultural) World Heritage Site. It is the first such mixed World Heritage Site in the United States, and the second World Heritage Site in Hawaii.

At the other end of the Hawaiian archipelago, the southeastern part of the island of Hawaii sits above the hot spot. The island of Hawaii is comprised of five volcanoes, three of which have been active in historic times. The volcano Kilauea is the most frequently active, and at the time of this writing it has been in nearly continuous eruption since January of 1983. Second most active is the volcano Mauna Loa, which is the most massive volcano on the planet. Mauna Loa tends to erupt every 10 to 20 years. It makes up almost half of the island of Hawaii by itself. Third most active is the volcano Hualalai, found in the western portion of the island. It sits above the resorts and fine sand beaches of the Kona coast, and threatens those areas with its next eruption. The Kona airport is built on fairly recent lava flows from Hualalai. The other two volcanoes on the island of Hawaii are Mauna Kea, upon which 13 of the world's best astronomical telescopes are built, and Kohala, a highly dissected and likely extinct volcano.

The island of Maui is next up the chain to the northwest. The volcano Haleakala was likely active sometime around 1600, but there exist no reliable accounts of the eruption from which to pinpoint a date. The island also contains an older volcano in its western extent, but that volcano has not erupted in historic times. The same is true of the remaining islands, although the island of Oahu has several relatively recent (geologically speaking) tuff cones that might be only a few thousand years old. Kauai is highly eroded and has a number of deep gorges and beautiful valleys. Advancing toward the northwest, the northernmost island within the traditional boundaries of the state of Hawaii is Niihau, a small island just west of Kauai. Niihau also has been severely eroded.

Earthquakes are relatively common occurrences in the Hawaiian Islands—particularly within and beneath the youngest of the volcanoes on the islands of Hawaii and Maui—and tend to occur in one of three settings. Perhaps the least common setting is within the mantle beneath the islands. Earthquakes in the mantle are likely caused by adjustments of the mantle to the great weights of the islands above. The second setting is within the volcanic pile. The sheer mass of the lava flows that comprise these islands is enough to make the slopes unstable. There are several sliding zones within each of the large active volcanoes, and "tectonic" (or non-volcanic) earthquakes occur in these areas with great regularity. The third setting is within the volcanic plumbing systems of the active volcanoes.

Although the vast majority of earthquakes are too small to feel, they are recorded by the extensive seismic networks of the Hawaiian Volcano Observatory. The observatory records and documents thousands of earthquakes every year. Many of the small volcanic earthquakes provide insight into the volcano's behavior. Every once in a while, an earthquake occurs that is large enough for island residents to feel. Most of these are too small to cause any real damage, but occasional large and damaging earthquakes do occur. These rarely are related directly to the magma plumbing system, and instead are "tectonic" or mantle earthquakes.

The most recent large, damaging earthquake within the Hawaiian Islands was a magnitude 7.2 earthquake in 1975 that occurred beneath the south flank of Kilauea Volcano, near the town of Kalapana. The earthquake caused island-wide damage, and generated a local tsunami that killed two Boy Scout leaders who were camping with their troop in a coastal area of Hawaii Volcanoes National Park. In 2006, a less damaging magnitude 6.7 earthquake occurred in the mantle deep below the northwestern portion of the island of Hawaii. It caused damage and power outages as far away as Oahu, about 150 miles (240 kilometers) north of the quake's epicenter. Related to earthquakes, tsunamis are relatively common occurrences in the Hawaiian Islands. Because the islands are located in the center of the Pacific Ocean, they are vulnerable to tsunamis generated anywhere around the ocean's periphery. Deaths have occurred in Hawaii due to tsunamis generated in Chile, Alaska, Japan, and, of course, locally as in the case of the 1975 Kalapana earthquake.

The old religion of the Hawaiian people was populated with gods who controlled the natural world. Two gods within the Hawaiian pantheon who controlled volcanic behavior and island formation were Maui and Pele. Maui is said to have fished in the ocean using a magic hook and pulled up the islands. Pele is the goddess of the volcano. She is portrayed as a beautiful, lusty woman with a fiery temper. Her many attempts to seduce unsuspecting gods and mortals have led to violent firefights with them or their lovers in an attempt to either seek revenge for their rejection or battle for their affections. Pele still is revered and worshiped today.

See Also: Chilean Earthquake and Tsunami (1960); Haleakala, Maui, Hawaii, United States; Hawaiian Volcano Observatory; Hot Spot; Hualalai, Hawaii, United States; Kalapana Earthquake, Hawaii, United States (1975); Kilauea Volcano, Hawaii, United States; Maui, Legend of; Mauna Kea, Hawaii, United States; Mauna Loa, Hawaii, United States; Pele, Legend of.

Further Reading

Geology.com. (2014, October 16). *Plate tectonics and the Hawaiian Hot Spot*. Retrieved from http://geology.com/usgs/hawaiian-hot-spot/

National Ocean Service. Office of National Marine Sanctuaries. National Oceanic and Atmospheric Administration. (2014, June 16). *Papahanaumokuakea Marine National Monument*. Retrieved from http://www.papahanaumokuakea.gov/about/

Welch, W. M. (2006, October 16). Buildings shake, power fails in Hawaii earthquake. *USA Today*.

Hawaiian Volcano Observatory

The Hawaiian Volcano Observatory was founded in 1912. It is the oldest volcano observatory in the United States, and is second in age only to the Vesuvius Observatory on Mount Vesuvius in Italy. The idea for the Hawaiian Volcano Observatory was born out of a series of devastating events which occurred in the late 1800s and early 1900s. In 1883, the volcano Krakatau in Indonesia erupted and killed an estimated 36,000 people. Most of those people were killed by a tsunami that the volcano caused when it collapsed into the ocean. The tsunami engulfed the coastlines surrounding the island that was Krakatau.

Several people, however, were killed or injured by what appears to have been a pyroclastic flow. Pyroclastic flows were unknown to science at the time, and the small number of deaths and injuries from them in the 1883 eruption were dwarfed by the horror of the tens of thousands killed by the tsunami. The death and injury several people described as coming from searing heat that overtook them in an instant never was fully investigated. In 1902, a pyroclastic flow from the volcano Mont Pelée on the Caribbean island of Martinique swept through the city of Saint-Pierre, killing approximately 28,000 people within a few minutes. News of this event spread rapidly around the world, and scientists were baffled by reports of an entire city's population being annihilated by a single event.

In 1902, Dr. Thomas A. Jaggar, Jr. was employed as a geology professor at Harvard University. He was selected to be one of five scientists representing the United States in a scientific mission to investigate the eruption on Martinique. Jaggar was strongly affected by what he found, as were the other scientists from around the world who had been sent to Martinique to piece together the story of Saint-Pierre. Jaggar later described seeing bodies everywhere—men, women, and children who appeared to be caught largely by surprise while going about their daily lives. Dr. Jaggar and his colleagues documented what they could, and then Jaggar spent time traveling throughout the Caribbean. He found two of the very few survivors of the Martinique eruption in a hospital on the island of Barbados. He interviewed them to gain a better understanding of what happened the morning of the eruption. It did not take Jaggar long to realize that the scientific community had little practical knowledge of how volcanoes work, how they behave, and what warning signs they might give before they erupt.

In April of 1906, Mount Vesuvius began erupting. Dr. Jaggar left immediately in hopes of watching the volcano erupt. Unfortunately, he arrived after the eruption ended. Jaggar did, however, make an incredibly important discovery while he was there: Mount Vesuvius was home to a volcano observatory—Italy's Vesuvius Observatory. Jaggar immediately saw the genius in the idea of a volcano observatory. If a volcano can be kept under constant surveillance, then a great deal can be learned about its behavior. Perhaps other cities could be spared the fate of Saint-Pierre.

Jaggar considered a site in the Aleutian Islands for his volcano observatory, but his wife talked him out of the idea. In 1909, the Jaggars traveled to Japan, making a fateful stop in the Hawaiian Islands. They spent three days on the volcano Kilauea. Dr. Jaggar spent hours each day in the volcano's caldera observing a lava lake in the pit crater, "Halema'uma'u." He knew he had found the right site for his volcano observatory, but there were a number of hurdles to overcome. One was that the site was incredibly remote. It was a three-day voyage from Honolulu to Kilauea's summit—by ship, then rail, then buckboard wagons pulled by horses. There was a hotel at the summit of Kilauea but little else. It was, however, a perfect natural laboratory. Kilauea erupted frequently and Mauna Loa just to the north also had fairly frequent eruptions. The climate in Hawaii was much preferable to that of the Aleutian Islands, providing a nearly constant length of day and comfortable year-round temperatures.

When the Jaggars returned to Honolulu to await their ship to Japan, Jaggar was invited to speak at the University Club of Honolulu. He spoke about his experiences in Martinique, Alaska, and Italy. He then told the audience of his idea to build a series of earth observatories, which he called "geonomic" observatories. A reporter for the *Pacific Commercial Advertiser* newspaper asked him some probing questions, and then requested a meeting with Jaggar when he returned from Japan. The reporter was the owner of the newspaper and an influential businessman in Honolulu, Mr. Lorrin Thurston. As planned, on his return trip Jaggar met with Thurston and the territorial governor. They assured Jaggar that he would have support for any work he might wish to do on Kilauea.

After a great deal of planning and persuasion, Jaggar was able to obtain a short leave of absence from his teaching position to do research on Kilauea beginning in January 1912. He also obtained an agreement to redirect a substantial gift from donor Caroline Whitney to support the work on Kilauea. The instrument vault (cement basement) built to house the seismometers and other equipment he purchased was named the "Whitney Seismological Observatory." Although the instruments themselves were decommissioned decades ago, the vault is preserved intact at its original site near the modern Volcano House Hotel in Hawaii Volcanoes National Park. Unfortunately, this site rarely is open to the public.

Jaggar's old friend Frank Perret helped design instruments and perform experiments. Thurston, himself, and several other businessmen who had an interest in the volcano, also helped with field work. By mid-1912, Thurston had raised enough money to pay Jaggar's salary, and that of his staff, for five years. He negotiated with the Massachusetts Institute of Technology (MIT), Jaggar's new employer, to obtain a five-year leave of absence for Jaggar so that Jaggar could run the observatory. Thurston, in turn, agreed to turn over control of the observatory to MIT. Thurston did indeed support the observatory for five years. Yale University then made a bid for a hostile takeover—which resulted in Jaggar working without pay for two years. In 1919, the United States Weather Bureau took over the observatory. In 1924, the observatory became part of the United States Geological Survey. In 1935, ownership was transferred to the National Park Service for 12 years, and then in 1947 was transferred back to the United States Geological Survey. It remains part of the United States Geological Survey today.

The work Jaggar did during his time at the observatory was ground-breaking, as was his collaboration with other scientists. With encouragement, funding, and design ideas from Jaggar, his friend Arthur Day designed a probe that could be used to measure the temperature of lava. Aided by a custom-designed pulley system, Jaggar's friends Frank Perret and Lorrin Thurston performed the first measurement of lava temperature in the lava lake at Halema'uma'u in 1911—while Jaggar was at home with his pregnant wife.

In early 1912, Jaggar was able to travel to the island, and intensive work began. Jaggar enlisted help from a number of well-known scientists of the time. Harry O. Wood assisted with seismologic monitoring. Perret and Day designed instruments. Jaggar bought a Ford Model T and drove it across lava fields to visit observation posts, and used it to haul water to drilling sites on the island.

Jaggar even helped design various amphibious vehicles which he used to get around the island. He was a hardy soul who dedicated his life to study of the Hawaiian volcanoes. Jaggar wrote weekly reports of volcanic activity that were published in Thurston's newspaper, kept meticulous records, and was methodical in his monitoring practices.

Jaggar's methods and constant monitoring paid off soon after he began his full-time work at the observatory. He had noticed through the study of tilt records that the Hawaiian volcanoes almost seemed to breathe—they would inflate and deflate periodically. During an ongoing eruption, Jaggar noticed that periods of inflation often accompanied less vigorous activity, and deflation was associated with more voluminous eruptions. In 1914, Jaggar observed that Mauna Loa was inflating, and there was a sharp increase in the number of earthquakes occurring beneath the volcano. He forecast an eruption of the mountain within the following few days. His forecast proved correct, and a new era of volcano monitoring began. Jaggar became more confident and more precise in his forecasts, and was able to tell people with a high degree of accuracy not only *when* a volcano was building toward eruption, but also *where* the eruption was most likely to break out.

Jaggar also was a pioneer in tsunami forecasting. In 1933, after noting a record from a distant earthquake on his seismograph, he determined that the earthquake occurred in Japan, and that it was large enough to have spawned a tsunami. In addition, Jaggar calculated its likely arrival time in the Hawaiian Islands. He issued a tsunami warning. He urged companies to send their ships out to sea, and warned people to stay away from the shoreline. The first wave arrived within 10 minutes of his predicted arrival time.

Jaggar retired from his position at the volcano observatory in 1940, but the staff of the volcano observatory continues to perform groundbreaking work. The full-time staff monitors Kilauea and Mauna Loa as closely as any hospital would monitor a patient in its intensive care unit. The volcanoes are monitored instrumentally for earthquakes, ground tilt, and gas emissions. They are visually monitored using webcams, and by geologists both on the ground and in helicopters. Seismic data gathered at the volcano observatory is shared with the Pacific Tsunami Warning Center in Honolulu. The scientific staff also continues to write weekly summaries of the volcano's behavior that are published in newspapers throughout the islands.

The observatory is a world-class facility that attracts and welcomes scientists at all levels to train on-site. University students from around the world can be found working as interns or gathering data for thesis projects. Professional scientists often test new equipment they have designed to monitor volcanoes, and techniques to forecast eruptions at Hawaii's volcanoes. The volcanoes are relatively easy to approach and eruptions are generally fairly benign, making Kilauea in particular an excellent proving ground for instrumentation before it is sent to more formidable volcanoes elsewhere. Scientists from NASA have used lava fields on the Hawaiian volcanoes for comparison with landscapes found on other planets. The observatory has become a prototype for numerous others, both within the United States and around the world.

See Also: Hawaiian Islands; Jaggar, Jr., Thomas Augustus; Kilauea Volcano, Hawaii, United States; Mauna Loa, Hawaii, United States.

Further Reading

Apple, R. A. (1987). Thomas A. Jaggar, Jr., and the Hawaiian Volcano Observatory. In R. W. Decker, T. L. Wright, & P. H. Stauffer (Eds.), *Volcanism in Hawaii.* (U.S. Geological Survey Professional Paper 1350). Washington, DC: U.S. GPO.

Dvorak, J. (2012). The origin of the Hawaiian Volcano Observatory. *Physics Today 64* (5).

Jaggar, T. A. (1956). *My experiments with volcanoes.* Honolulu: Hawaiian Volcano Research Association.

McNarie, A. D. (2012). The watchmen. *Hana Hou: The Magazine of Hawaiian Airlines 15* (2).

Hazard and Risk

The words "hazard" and "risk" often are used interchangeably. In the everyday colloquial use of those words, they are suitable synonyms. Each word evokes images of an event that could cause harm. Scientists, however, often have much more precise definitions for words than does the general public. The terms "hazard" and "risk," for example, have different meanings in the scientific community. A hazard is a destructive event that can occur in a given area or location, along with the probability of the event's occurrence. Risk is defined as the hazard, multiplied by vulnerability, multiplied by value. Vulnerability is the proportion of a resource such as people or land likely to be affected if the event occurs. Value is the amount or type of property threatened, or the number of lives threatened. It is possible to mitigate risk, but not hazard.

The San Andreas Fault in California is an excellent place in which to illustrate the difference between hazard and risk. All areas adjacent to the San Andreas Fault are places where an earthquake hazard exists. In other words, the probability is rather high that an earthquake will occur along the San Andreas Fault. Risk, however, varies immensely along the length of the fault. The city of San Francisco has considerable risk related to the San Andreas Fault. The fault runs through the city where there is a great deal of infrastructure—homes, businesses, roads, bridges, and dams; and electric, sewer, water, telephone, and fiber optic lines exist within the city and its suburbs. Should an earthquake occur, there is a good chance that many of these features will be damaged or destroyed—which makes the vulnerability level high. The city and its surrounding suburbs also are home to roughly one million people—which makes the value high. Because both vulnerability and value are high, risk also is extremely high. Some areas along the fault, however, are unpopulated desert regions. There is no infrastructure to be disrupted, no home or business to be destroyed, and no people whose lives can be lost. In those areas, there is little to no risk.

See Also: Mitigation.

Further Reading

U.S. Geological Survey. Hawaiian Volcano Observatory. (2014, March 24). *Lava-flow hazard zones, Island of Hawai'i.* Retrieved from http://hvo.wr.usgs.gov/hazards/FAQ_LavaFlowHazardZone/P2.html

Hess, Harry

Rear Admiral Dr. Harry Hammond Hess was born in New York City on May 24, 1906. He attended Yale University, where he began his education majoring in electrical engineering. Hess changed his major to geology after two years and graduated with a bachelor's degree in 1927. He worked for two years as an exploration geologist, and then began work on a graduate degree at Princeton University. After earning his Ph.D., Hess taught at Rutgers University for one year (1932–1933), and then worked for a year as a research associate at the Geophysical Laboratory of Washington, DC. Hess spent the remainder of his career as a faculty member at Princeton University. He served as department chair from 1950 to 1966. Hess spent time as visiting professor at the University of Cape Town, South Africa, from 1949–1950, and at the University of Cambridge, England, in 1965.

Hess joined the United States Navy during World War II. He became Captain of the U.S.S. *Cape Johnson*, which was a transport ship equipped with sonar—a relatively new technology at the time. Hess saw combat in the Marianas, Leyte, Linguayan, and Iwo Jima. While he was en route to various destinations across the Pacific, Hess also took sonar soundings of the ocean floor. Data he collected became critical in his later work.

Hess was a believer in Alfred Wegener's idea of Continental Drift. Although he thought that the continents had in fact moved, he disagreed wholeheartedly with Wegener's ideas about how that had happened. Wegener had a vague notion about continents plowing their way through the sea bed, which was implausible at best. Data that Hess collected during the war enabled him to formulate an entirely new concept of how continents have moved across the face of the earth. He called his idea "seafloor spreading."

Hess formulated a hypothesis that he circulated in the Office of Naval Research. In the manuscript, he answered some of the basic questions Wegener had been unable to address during his brief life. Hess had collected data that told him there were mountain ranges in the centers of the oceans, called "mid-ocean ridges." These ridges marked the place where the sea floor split and magma oozed up between the two sides. This created new sea floor, which moved like a conveyor belt away from the mid-ocean ridge. It cooled and sank into the deep ocean plains, and eventually made its way to deep ocean trenches, where it was recycled back into the earth. Although his hypothesis was met with a great deal of resistance at the time he initially circulated it, the resulting paper, "History of the Ocean Basins," published in 1962, now is regarded as one of the must-read classic papers in geology, and a crucial contribution to plate tectonic theory. For a time, it was the most-referenced paper in the field of geophysics.

Hess remained active in public service throughout his career. He remained in the Naval Reserve after World War II and eventually rose to the rank of rear admiral. He was called on for advice during the Cuban Missile Crisis in 1962. That year he also was appointed by President John F. Kennedy to chair the Space Science Board of the National Academy of Sciences. Not only was he a major force in geology because of his role in the development of plate tectonics, he also played a vital role in designing America's space science program. Hess died on August 25, 1969, while he was chairing a meeting of the Space Science Board. He is buried at Arlington National Cemetery.

See Also: Divergent Boundary; Plate Tectonics.

Further Reading

Arlington National Cemetery. (2014, May 12). Harry Hammond Hess, Rear Admiral, United States Navy. Retrieved from http://www.arlingtoncemetery.net/hhhess.htm

PBS People and Discoveries. (2014, May 12). *Harry Hess 1906–1969*. Retrieved from http://www.pbs.org/wgbh/aso/databank/entries/bohess.html

U.S. Geological Survey. (2014, May 12). *Harry Hammond Hess: Spreading the seafloor.* Retrieved from http://pubs.usgs.gov/gip/dynamic/HHH.html

Hood, Mount, Oregon, United States

Mount Hood is a composite volcano located approximately 40 miles (64 kilometers) east of Portland in northern Oregon. Its summit is 11,240 feet (3,426 meters) above sea level. Mount Hood is a prominent peak within the Cascade Mountains of the Pacific Northwest. Like the other mountains in the Cascades, Mount Hood was formed as a result of subduction of the Juan de Fuca Plate beneath the North American Plate. Mount Hood's cone is composed mostly of andesite, but the volcano has erupted a great deal of dacite within the last 15,000 years. Pyroclastic flows and lahar deposits dominate this most recent time period. Lava domes that dot the upper reaches of the volcano are prominent landmarks.

The vicinity of Mount Hood has been an active volcanic center for approximately 17 million years. The Colombia River Basalts, a flood basalt erupted between 17 million and 12 million years ago, were erupted from many areas near Mount Hood. These are overlain by basaltic and andesitic lavas from an earlier mountain, the "Sandy Glacier Volcano." Today's Mount Hood was formed on top of this ancestral volcano. The cone itself is composed of a combination of andesite lava flows, pyroclastic deposits, and lahars. The summit of Mount Hood is

Mount Hood and the Hood River Valley, Oregon.
(Greg Vaughn / VWPics/Newscom)

composed of andesite and dacite lava domes. The rocks near the summit have been weakened and altered by acidic hydrothermal activity. This has created a large volume of water-saturated clays that are prone to catastrophic failure, creating landslides and lahars even in the absence of volcanic activity.

On December 25, 1980, unusually intense rainfall triggered a landslide on the east flank of Mount Hood, at the head of Polallie Creek. The landslide quickly transformed into a debris flow, which mixed with water. As it moved into the East Fork of the Hood River, it was a raging lahar with a volume twenty times greater than that of the original landslide. The lahar created a temporary dam in the river. When the dam was breached just a few short minutes later, the resulting flood destroyed about 6 miles (10 kilometers) of highway and killed one person. A total of $13 million in damage was reported. Such events can be expected in the future.

Mount Hood's deposits tell of a history that includes decades to centuries of frequent eruptions separated by periods of quiescence that can last from a few hundred years to more than 10,000 years. In the volcano's fairly recent past, only two eruptive cycles are noted; one occurred approximately 1,500 years ago, and another occurred during the late 1700s. The eruptive period in the 1700s was witnessed by Native Americans living in the area, by explorers, and by early settlers. The landmark known as Crater Rock—high on the volcano's cone near the summit—was erupted around 1780. The Lewis and Clark expedition passed very near Mount Hood in November 1805 and April 1806. The explorers wrote of their visit to the mouth of the Sandy River. They named it the Quicksand River because they said it had a bottom made of quicksand. It also was choked with sediment and very shallow. This bears no resemblance to the usual state of the river, which has a steep, narrow boulder-strewn channel. Settlers reported activity in 1859 and 1865 as well in the form of flying rocks, voluminous steaming, fire, and smoke from the area of Crater Rock. It is entirely possible that they were witnessing small phreatic eruptions triggered by water seeping into the cooling dome. No deposits from this later activity ever have been found.

Although Mount Hood is quiet for now it remains a hazard to thousands of residents, as well as to the local economy. Mount Hood is a year-round heavy-use recreational area. In the summer, families go hiking, fishing, and swimming near the volcano. In the winter it is a popular ski destination. The mountain is monitored continuously for seismic activity by the Cascades Volcano Observatory, part of the U.S. Geological Survey. The Observatory also monitors gases emitted by the volcano on a yearly basis, and has Global Positioning System receivers on the mountain to help measure possible ground deformation.

See Also: Andesite; Basalt; Dacite; Lahar; Pyroclastic Flow.

Further Reading

Sherrod, D. R. (1992). Hood, Oregon. In C. A. Wood, & J. Kienle, *Volcanoes of North America, United States and Canada.* Cambridge: Cambridge University Press.
U.S. Geological Survey. (2014, May 23). *Mount Hood.* Retrieved from http://volcanoes .usgs.gov/volcanoes/mount_hood/

Hot Spot

In modern plate tectonic theory, a hot spot is defined as a place where anomalously hot material streams upward through the mantle toward the earth's surface. Hot spots are responsible for volcanic activity, which brings earthquake activity with it. Well-known examples of features formed by hot spot activity are the Hawaiian Island chain, Iceland, Yellowstone Volcano, Reunion Island, and the Galapagos Islands.

In oceanic settings, hot spots have been responsible for the formation of both island chains, such as the Galapagos and Hawaiian Islands, and large igneous provinces such as the Ontong-Java Plateau in the southwestern Pacific. In continental settings volcanic activity is more varied. The Siberian Traps in northern Russia, Columbia River Basalts in the United States, and the Karoo Basalts in South Africa are examples of large igneous provinces composed almost exclusively of basalt. The same hot spot that produced the Columbia River Basalts, however, also is thought to be responsible for the Yellowstone volcano—a massive and highly explosive composite supervolcano located primarily in the state of Wyoming. As basalt magma from the mantle hot spot mixes with melted continental lithosphere, the magma changes composition and becomes andesitic or rhyolitic. This change in magma composition causes a change in eruptive behavior of resulting volcanoes such as Yellowstone.

There still is much debate in the scientific community about what, exactly, a hot spot is, and where it originates. The general consensus is that a hot spot is a plume of hot material that originates at the core-mantle boundary. Some research, however, conflicts with this view. Sound evidence suggests that some hot spots originate much shallower than the core-mantle boundary. From its place of origin, the hot material—which is perhaps 360° F to 540° F (200° C to 300° C) warmer than the surrounding mantle—streams upward. As it gets close to the base of the lithosphere it spreads out into a mushroom-like shape. In the upper mantle, the higher temperature of the plume melts surrounding mantle and produces magma. Magma finds its way to the surface and erupts, forming volcanoes.

Scientists also think that hot spots are fixed in place over their sites of origin. The lithospheric plates move over these hot spots, often creating a chain of volcanoes in the ocean or a wide swath of volcanic activity on a continent. Hot spots can remain active for as long as 140 million years. Evidence for the life span of a hot spot comes from the geologic record. The Siberian Traps and Karoo Basalts were emplaced much more than 140 million years ago, and there is no geophysical trace of an active hot spot beneath these locations today. Hot spots that are between 100 million and 140 million years old, including that of Tristan de Cunha in the south Atlantic, are failing. Those which are less than 100 million years old—such as the Hawaiian and Galapagos hot spots—are active and continuing to produce large amounts of magma.

See Also: Andesite; Basalt; Galapagos Islands; Hawaiian Islands; Plate Tectonics; Rhyolite; Supervolcano.

Further Reading

Bressan, D. (2011, September 16). Large igneous provinces and mass extinctions. *Scientific American Blog*. Retrieved from http://blogs.scientificamerican.com/history-of-geology/2011/09/16/large-igneous-provinces-and-mass-extinctions/

Kearey, P., Klepeis, K. A., & Vine, F. J. (2009). *Global tectonics* (3rd ed.). Hoboken, NJ: Wiley-Blackwell.

Tarbuck, E. J., Lutgens, F. K., & Tasa, D. (2011). *Earth: An introduction to physical geology* (10th ed.). Upper Saddle River, NJ: Pearson Prentice Hall/Pearson Education, Inc.

Hualalai, Hawaii, United States

Hualalai is the third youngest of five volcanoes that comprise the island of Hawaii. Its last eruption occurred in the late 1700s and lasted until 1801. Six different vents were active during that time. Hualalai towers above many of the island's tourist hotels and beautiful beaches, as well as the Keahole Airport just north of Kailua-Kona. The airport is built on a lava flow from Hualalai. Although it has been more than 200 years since its last eruption, there is absolutely no reason to believe that the volcano is extinct. In fact, 80% of the surface of the volcano has been covered with lava flows in the last 5,000 years. Scientists think that Hualalai has just entered the post-caldera phase of its life cycle, so it is easing toward old age. For this reason, the composition of its lava is changing from what is expected in the earlier, shield-building stage. It also is steeper and is experiencing more explosive eruptions than younger volcanoes on the island. Evidence for greater explosive activity of Hualalai than of the younger volcanoes—Mauna Loa and Kilauea—is the larger size of Hualalai's cinder cones. Another indicator of its more explosive eruptions is the greater abundance of volcanic ash found on Hualalai versus that found on younger volcanoes. Additionally, the time between eruptions is expanding. Eruptions are expected from Hualalai only once every few hundred years.

Like other shield volcanoes in the Hawaiian Islands, Hualalai has two well-developed rift zones. One extends northwest from the summit area, and the other extends southeast from the summit. Hualalai also has a third, weakly developed rift zone that extends north from a point a few kilometers east of the summit. A number of vents, many marked by large cinder cones, line the rift zones and make them obvious features on the volcano, even when examining it from far below at sea level. The summit of Hualalai is 8,271 feet (2,521 meters) above sea level. There is no evidence of an existing caldera at the summit, but it is possible that any caldera that did exist was filled with lava at the beginning of the post-caldera stage of volcanism.

Hualalai's most recent lava flows contain nodules of rock brought to the surface from deep inside the volcano. Some rocks appear to be pieces of the mantle that were brought to the surface through the magma plumbing system, then coated with a bit of black lava and carried along by lava flows. The rocks range in size from a fraction of an inch to about 1 foot (0.3 meter) across. They number in the thousands, and are famous among geologists. It is rare to find these pieces of mantle rock at the surface, therefore the rocks are much sought-after. They are found in greatest abundance in road cuts on the main highway in western Hawaii, and near a telephone relay station just off the highway in the same flow.

See Also: Hawaiian Islands; Kilauea Volcano, Hawaii, United States; Mauna Loa, Hawaii, United States.

Further Reading

McDonald, G. A., Abbott, A. T., & Peterson, F. L. (1983). *Volcanoes in the sea: The geology of Hawaii* (2nd ed.). Honolulu: University of Hawaii Press.

U.S. Geological Survey. Hawaiian Volcano Observatory. (2014, May 19). *Hualalai, Hawaii's third active volcano*. Retrieved from http://hvo.wr.usgs.gov/volcanoes/hualalai/main.html

Hydrothermal Vent

The mid-ocean ridges and submerged volcanoes, known as "seamounts," are home to hot water springs called hydrothermal vents. In 1977, scientists with the Scripps Institution of Oceanography, Oregon State University, and Woods Hole Oceanographic Institution explored an area on the Galapagos Ridge west of

Ecuador that had, in prior expeditions, tantalized them with brief spikes of anomalously warm water. They sent a remotely operated vehicle to the site to take thousands of photographs and continuous temperature readings. What the researchers found was completely new to science. Hydrothermal vent fields along the mid-ocean ridges were a new discovery, as were the animal and microbe communities found there. These communities of life survived not on sunlight and photosynthesis, but on chemical and thermal energy and sulfur compounds. Bacteria that form the basis of this food chain went through the process of chemosynthesis rather than photosynthesis. They supported large communities of clams, mussels, crabs, shrimp, fish, sea cucumbers, and other organisms. Extensive research on these hydrothermal vent communities has led biologists to believe that they can stay active for decades, until hydrothermal activity wanes and the temperature and mineral output are insufficient to sustain life. Still other communities could die as a result of disruption by volcanic activity.

The initial hydrothermal vents discovered on the Galapagos Ridge expel water at approximately 65° F (18° C). These vents emit both water and sulfur gases from the ocean floor. Bacteria metabolize the sulfur compounds into simple sugars. Some animals graze on these bacteria and others host them in their bodies in symbiotic relationships. Hydrothermal vent communities teem with life. Mineral-laden water deposited coatings on rocks, and in some cases create gleaming chimneys of sulfur compounds, manganese, and other metals. These vents are like oases on the desert-like deep ocean floor.

In the decades since this important discovery was made, hydrothermal vent communities have been found in many other locations around the world. They appear to be a common feature on mid-ocean ridges, seamounts, and in some back-arc basins (areas between land areas and adjacent subduction zones). Some hydrothermal vents are much more energetic than others, as one might expect when comparing volcanic areas anywhere else in the world. In the most extreme cases, large chimneys several feet tall spew superheated water as hot as 750° F (400° C). The chimneys are massive sulfide deposits and include additional materials such as manganese, gold, and copper. Hydrothermal vent fields usually are several hundred yards long and nearly as wide. They occur at the very centers of mid-ocean ridges, within depressions known as axial valleys that mark the actual boundary between diverging plates.

See Also: Divergent Boundary.

Further Reading

Corliss, J. B., & Ballard, R. D. (1977). Oases of life in the cold abyss. *National Geographic 152* (4), 441–453.

Corliss, J. B., Dymond, J., Gordon, L. I., Edmond, J. M., von Herzen, R. P., Ballard, R. D., Green, K., Williams, D., Bainbridge, A., Crane, K., & van Andel, T. H. (1979). Submarine thermal springs on the Galapagos Rift. *Science 203* (4385), 1073–1083.

Vrijenhoek, R. C. (2009). Hydrothermal vents. In R. G. Gillespie, & D. A. Clague (Eds.), *Encyclopedia of islands*. Berkeley: University of California Press.

Indian Ocean Earthquake and Tsunami (2004)

The Indian Ocean tsunami of December 2004 was one of the worst natural disasters in modern history. Triggered by a magnitude 9.0 earthquake off the west coast of the Indonesian island of Sumatra, the tsunami's massive waves impacted a dozen countries from Indonesia to Africa, killing nearly 250,000 people and leaving millions homeless. The event brought forth an unprecedented international aid campaign and plans for a tsunami-warning system in the Indian Ocean.

The earthquake that set off the disaster hit at 8 a.m. local time on December 26, 2004. Caused by the buildup of pressure over hundreds of years as the India tectonic plate slipped below the Burma tectonic plate, the quake struck along a 620-mile (998-kilometer) fault line and caused parts of the ocean floor to rise by more than 30 feet (9 meters). Considered a megathrust earthquake, it was the fourth-largest since 1900. Only the Chilean earthquake of 1960 (magnitude 9.5) and the Alaskan earthquakes in 1957 and 1964 (magnitudes 9.1 and 9.2, respectively) were larger. A 1952 earthquake off Russia's Kamchatka Peninsula was equal in strength, and also was a magnitude 9.0.

This violent release of energy below the Indian Ocean's surface displaced hundreds of cubic miles of seawater, sending waves across the ocean at hundreds of miles per hour—the speed of a jet plane. Waves up to 65 feet (20 meters) high pummeled shorelines directly facing the quake's epicenter, and many nations' coastlines were inundated by waves 30 to 50 feet (9 to 15 meters) high.

Lacking a tsunami-detection or early-warning system, the region was almost completely unprepared for such a catastrophic disaster. Tsunamis are relatively rare occurrences in the Indian Ocean, therefore few people knew the early warning signs or how to react. In some areas, the ocean actually receded rapidly, to several feet beyond the low-tide point, several minutes before the first waves hit—a classic tsunami warning sign. Few people knew what this meant, however, and many actually walked out to the beach out of curiosity. Tsunami warning systems exist throughout the Pacific Ocean—which is far more prone to such natural disasters—but none monitored the Indian Ocean tsunami in 2004. When the tsunami hit, Indian Ocean nations were blindsided.

The hardest hit by far was Indonesia, where an estimated 167,000 people died. The western tip of the island of Sumatra was devastated, with the city of Banda Aceh virtually destroyed and many coastal villages losing more than 70% of their

Tsunami damage near Aceh, Indonesia. The mosque in the center of the photo is the only building left standing following the 2004 earthquake and tsunami. (UPI Photo/Jacob Kirk/Navy)

residents. About 500,000 people were left homeless.

Sri Lanka also suffered the deaths of about 35,000 people and the destruction of its southern and eastern coastlines; more than a half-million Sri Lankans lost their homes. In India, more than 16,000 people died and tens of thousands more were made homeless. The most devastated areas were the southeastern coast and the remote Andaman and Nicobar islands, which lie just north of the earthquake's epicenter. Thailand's west coast was severely damaged, with more than 8,000 people killed. In the Maldives, 20 of the nation's 200 inhabited islands were wiped off the map, permanently submerged underwater.

Myanmar, Bangladesh, Malaysia, and the Seychelles also sustained hundreds of deaths and varying degrees of damage, and even the East African nations of Somalia, Kenya, and Tanzania felt the tsunami's effects. In Somalia, more than 2,000 miles from the quake's epicenter, about 200 people died and tens of thousands lost their homes. The total regional death toll is unknown, as countless thousands were swept out to sea and never seen again.

In addition to the loss of life and private homes, the tsunami's impact on health, jobs, and economies in Indian Ocean nations was immense. Hundreds of thousands of workers lost their jobs. Fishing industries vital to virtually all the affected coastal areas were devastated. Tourism infrastructure, especially in Thailand, Sri Lanka, and the Maldives, also sustained major damage. Agricultural lands were consumed by the ocean waves or rendered unfit for cultivation due to salinization. Drinking-water supplies also were salinized and sewage systems were destroyed. Many people became sick and died in the tsunami's aftermath, due to contaminated water and the lack of available health care.

The international community responded to the crisis with an unprecedented outpouring of support, including aid, money, and volunteer efforts. Nonprofit agencies, foreign governments, and individual citizens helped with rescue and recovery efforts, donating money, medicine, technical expertise, and general labor. The International Red Cross alone received more than $2.5 billion earmarked for tsunami recovery—much of it from individuals.

Surviving a Tsunami

Tsunamis can travel across entire oceans, but they usually prove to be deadliest nearest their sources. Near the source is where a tsunami usually is largest, and people there have the least amount of warning. It is possible for a tsunami to come ashore just a few short minutes after the earthquake that generated it. The primary rule for surviving a tsunami is to get to higher ground. If you are at the beach in an earthquake-prone area and you feel a strong earthquake, then it is best to be safe and head inland and uphill as quickly as possible. For those closest to earthquakes, there likely is not enough time for officials to sound an alarm because the tsunami moves so quickly—it is onshore before the warning can be sounded. If you hear a tsunami warning siren, however, the same rule applies. Move uphill quickly. If there are no hills in the area, then climb a palm tree or move to the uppermost story of a sturdy building. Many shorelines around the Pacific now have signs posted that warn people that they are in a tsunami hazard zone, and show which direction to go to find safe ground. It is a good precaution to look for these signs and be aware of the potential danger.

Rebuilding efforts took years due to the sheer scale of the destruction, as well as government and aid agency bureaucracy. Although much progress was made, nonprofit groups criticized many countries for withholding aid from the neediest citizens. Reconstruction often focused on rebuilding business and tourism infrastructure rather than on building homes for individuals. A survey by relief agency Oxfam found that aid mainly was directed to landowners and businesses rather than to the poorest citizens who were most affected by the disaster. Poor people spent the longest amount of time in temporary shelters, particularly in the hardest hit countries of Indonesia, Sri Lanka, India, the Maldives, and Thailand.

In Sri Lanka, conflicts between the government and the separatist Liberation Tigers of Tamil Eelam slowed rebuilding efforts. In India, aid groups found that money was directed away from dalits—India's lowest-caste group. A United Nations-sponsored report found that, in some cases, coastal residents were prevented from returning to their lands while governments allowed new businesses to locate there instead. Several years after the tsunami, tens of thousands of people remained homeless, even as economies and tourism enterprises rebounded.

Another result of the tsunami disaster was the establishment of an earthquake early-warning system in the Indian Ocean. The first of several tsunami buoys was placed in the ocean between Sri Lanka and Thailand in December 2006. Public awareness campaigns and tsunami drills also aimed at preparing Indian Ocean communities. These efforts, however, are hindered by a lack of warning sirens in small coastal communities throughout the region. In July 2006, a minor tsunami off the Indonesian island of Java killed more than 600 people—even though monitors in the Pacific Ocean alerted the Indonesian government—because the government had no way of communicating with village residents.

See Also: Indonesia; Tsunami Warning Centers.

Further Reading

Indian Ocean Tsunami (2004). (2014, August 12). In *World geography: Understanding a changing world*. Santa Barbara, CA: ABC-CLIO.

Indonesia

Indonesia is an island nation located along an arc northwest of Australia. It stretches from Irian Jaya on the island of Papua in the east to the Andaman Islands in the west. The island arc stretches more than 3,200 miles (5,000 kilometers) from one end to the other. The islands were created by interaction between the Eurasian and Australian plates, as well as the Burma and Sunda microplates (which are slivers of lithosphere between the two major plates). Subduction created this volcanic island arc, and it continues to cause major earthquakes with great regularity.

Indonesia occupies an important place in the natural history of the world. It is home not only to great displays of the earth's raw tectonic power, but also is home to many endemic species, and is where Alfred Wallace, a contemporary of Charles Darwin's, independently formulated a theory of evolution that agreed with Darwin's. Throughout the Indonesian islands, Wallace saw much of the same evidence supporting evolution that Darwin noted in his observations at the Galapagos Islands.

Indonesia owes its entire existence to volcanic activity. All of the more than 15,000 islands within the chain were built by volcanoes in some form or fashion. At any given time, a handful of Indonesian volcanoes are active in one way or another. Most volcanoes in Indonesia are of the composite type, although volcanoes of all types occur within the country. At least 78 volcanoes are known to have erupted in historic times, and most of those have erupted multiple times. Some, such as Anak Krakatau, seem to be in a nearly constant state of unrest; others awake only after decades or centuries of dormancy. Many of Indonesia's volcanoes are located near large population centers. More than one million people live within 18.5 miles (30 kilometers) of 24 historically active volcanoes, including Agung, Arjuno-Welirang, Batur, Cereme, the Dieng Volcanic Complex, Galunggung, Gede, Guntur, Kelut, Lamongan, Lawu, Merapi, Merbabu, Muria, Papandayan, Perbakti-Gagak, Rinjani, Salak, Semeru, Slamet, Sumbing, Sundoro, Tangkubanparahu, and Tengger Caldera. Even larger populations reside in close proximity to volcanoes that have not been active in historic times, but which are not definitively extinct.

One of Indonesia's most famous eruptions was that of Krakatau in August 1883. Krakatau is located in the Sunda Strait, between the islands of Java and Sumatra. Both islands experienced the full fury of the 1883 eruption. It also was one of the first major volcanic eruptions that the world quickly learned of via relatively modern communication methods—in this case, the mode of communication was telegraph. Prior to the time of the Krakatau eruption, fast worldwide communication methods did not exist; it often took months for news of a major event such as this to reach distant shores. In this instance, however, the world knew of the disaster in almost real time. The eruption generated an enormous ash column that darkened skies for two days. Pyroclastic flows stripped shorelines of vegetation and killed unwitting victims. Most deaths from the eruption, however, were due to the tsunami generated. The summit of the volcano collapsed in on itself after the magma chamber beneath was mostly emptied by the violent eruption, and water rushed into the void. This created a local tsunami that killed most of the 36,000 victims of the 1883 disaster. Deaths occurred on both Java and Sumatra. Less than 40 years after the 1883 eruption a new volcano began growing in Krakatau's place. The new volcano, called "Anak Krakatau" ("Child of Krakatau"), has been in nearly constant low-level eruption since 1927.

Toba is another volcano within Indonesia that has received a great deal of attention in the media. Toba is classified by many as a "super volcano"; a volcano that, in the past, has erupted with such violence as to cause worldwide disruption in climate and local devastation on a scale that approaches apocalyptic. The last super eruption of Toba occurred about 74,000 years ago. The eruption is believed to have laid waste to the region around the volcano, created a large caldera (now filled with water and dubbed "Lake Toba"), and depressed worldwide temperatures such that ecosystems worldwide suffered for years. Geneticists have identified a "bottleneck" in the human population that corresponds to roughly the same time as the Toba eruption. This has raised concern that the eruption reduced the worldwide human population to just a few thousand individuals. Although this certainly paints a frightening scenario, not all eruptions—even those of super volcanoes—are super eruptions. Most eruptions at super volcanoes are of the same scale as those of any other volcano, therefore the odds are good that the next eruption of Toba will not be as devastating as the one occurring 74,000 years ago.

In addition to major volcanic eruptions, Indonesia is well-known for its powerful earthquakes. The largest Indonesian earthquake of the last 100 years occurred on December 26, 2004, off the west coast of northern Sumatra. This earthquake was a magnitude 9.1 event, the third largest in the world since instrumental recording of earthquakes began. Not only did the quake level buildings in the vicinity of the epicenter, but it was felt as far away as Bangladesh and India. This earthquake generated a tsunami that caused more than 225,000 deaths across Indonesia and in many other countries in Southeast Asia and eastern Africa. Hardest hit was Banda Aceh, where the tsunami swept over the entire island, stripping the island not only of buildings, but also of much of its soil and vegetation. Very few of Banda Aceh's residents survived the tsunami.

The lack of a tsunami warning system in the Indian Ocean meant there were no formal lines of communication between governments in the region. As a result, no prior warning was given to other countries about the approaching tsunami. This led to tens of thousands of deaths in low-lying coastal areas in countries such as Thailand and Sri Lanka. Had a tsunami alert been raised, many people might have been saved by timely evacuations. Following the 2004 earthquake, many after-shocks as large as magnitude 8.6 occurred for several months. Although no major tsunamis were generated from these aftershocks, area residents were on edge and readily evacuated after feeling strong tremors.

The normal earthquake pattern within the Indonesian archipelago is such that magnitude 6 or greater earthquakes occur somewhere in the country more than once per month, and magnitude 7 or greater earthquakes occur every few months. At least one magnitude 8 earthquake generally is expected to occur about every year and a half. The December 2004 magnitude 9.1 earthquake was the only one of that size to occur in the last 100 years, but that is the approximate extent of existing earthquake records. This means there is no way to determine whether that rate of occurrence is "normal" or unusual. Only time will tell.

See Also: Australian Plate; Eurasian Plate; Indian Ocean Earthquake and Tsunami (2004); Krakatau Eruption (also known as "Krakatoa" Eruption), Indonesia (1883); Subduction Zone; Toba Eruption, Indonesia.

Further Reading

Smithsonian Institution. National Museum of Natural History. Global Volcanism Program. (2014, June 13). Retrieved from http://www.volcano.si.edu/search_volcano_results.cfm
Tarbuck, E. J., Lutgens, F. K., & Tasa, D. (2011). *Earth: An introduction to physical geology* (10th ed.). Upper Saddle River, NJ: Pearson Prentice Hall/Pearson Education, Inc.
U.S. Geological Survey. (2014, June 13). *Historic world earthquakes. Indonesia.* Retrieved from http://earthquake.usgs.gov/earthquakes/world/historical_country.php#indonesia

Institute of Geological and Nuclear Sciences, New Zealand

The Institute of Geological and Nuclear Science is a research organization in New Zealand that is a limited liability company operated by the New Zealand government. It provides vital services to the people of New Zealand, including earthquake and other natural hazard monitoring, research from the microscopic to the national scale, and consulting services for the general public. The Institute provides expertise to the private sector as well, including for a number of energy industries, agriculture, insurance, and engineering companies. It advises international development agencies and provides services to governments, museums, and research organizations in New Zealand and abroad. The Institute operates as a company rather than a government agency, therefore it is responsible for generating income. Income is derived from research contracts, consulting, laboratory services, monitoring geological hazards for the New Zealand Earthquake Commission, serving as an advisor to public officials, sales of products such as maps and reports, and from a few government grants.

See Also: Hazard and Risk; New Zealand.

Further Reading

Institute for Geological and Nuclear Sciences. (2014, May 15). Retrieved from http://www
.gns.cri.nz/

Intrusive

The term "intrusive" is used to describe igneous (magma-derived) rocks that form beneath the surface of the earth. In some cases these rocks form in the magma chamber beneath a volcano. Sometimes they form in the heart of a volcano itself, in the dikes and other features of its plumbing system. Still other intrusive igneous rocks are formed at great depth in the earth's crust, as magma is migrating upward from where it was formed in the earth's mantle.

The hallmark of intrusive igneous rocks is their large crystals which are visible to the naked eye. If a rock contains only crystals big enough to see without the aid of a microscope, then the rock most likely is intrusive in nature. Intrusive igneous rocks can have the same composition as basalt, andesite, dacite, or rhyolite. The extrusive rocks listed above have intrusive relatives. The only difference between these rocks and their intrusive cousins is the amount of time required to cool the rock from a liquid to a solid. Extrusive igneous rocks generally take anywhere from less than a second to a week to solidify. Intrusive rocks, however, form over years, decades, or even millennia. Because the magma stays liquid for so long during the cooling process, atoms have ample opportunity to arrange themselves into mineral crystals, which then grow large with time. Eventually, when the magma solidifies into a rock, virtually all space is filled with minerals. In many cases, those minerals have grown together and created an interlocking system of crystals. The intrusive equivalent of basalt is called "gabbro" and usually is black or dark gray in color. The intrusive equivalent of andesite is called "diorite." Dacite's equivalent is granodiorite. Rhyolite's equivalent is granite.

See Also: Andesite; Basalt; Dacite; Extrusive; Rhyolite.

Further Reading

Tarbuck, E. J., Lutgens, F. K., & Tasa, D. (2011). *Earth: An introduction to physical geology* (10th ed.). Upper Saddle River, NJ: Pearson Prentice Hall/Pearson Education, Inc.

J

Jaggar, Jr., Thomas Augustus

Thomas Augustus Jaggar, Jr., was a professor of geology at the Massachusetts Institute of Technology and founder of the Hawaiian Volcano Observatory. He was born in 1870 in Philadelphia, Pennsylvania; his father was a bishop in the Episcopal Church and his mother was Anna Louisa (Lawrence) Jaggar. As a boy, Jaggar was fascinated with nature, so it is not surprising that he chose to study geology when he enrolled in Harvard. He received three degrees in geology from Harvard (A.B., "artium baccalaureus"; A.M., "artium magister"; and Ph.D.), and also studied in Munich and Heidelberg, Germany. Jaggar spent much of his time as a graduate student and young researcher working to understand natural processes through laboratory experiments. He used a water flume packed with sand and gravel to understand stream erosion, and studied the properties of magmas by melting rocks in furnaces. Before long, however, Jaggar realized that true understanding of the natural world requires spending time in the field.

The year 1902 marked a major change in the trajectory of Jaggar's career. On May 8 of that year, two volcanoes erupted in the Caribbean. The volcano Soufrière on the island of Saint Vincent erupted, killing 1,500 people. Then a few hours later, Mont Pelée, a volcano on the island of Martinique, erupted with tremendous force. A pyroclastic flow swept into the city of Saint-Pierre, killing nearly all of its more than 28,000 residents. At that time, pyroclastic flows were completely unknown to science. It was unthinkable that a single event could kill all inhabitants of a city within a few minutes. Word of this tremendous disaster spread quickly, and many prominent geologists traveled to Martinique to investigate the aftermath of the eruption in an effort to understand what happened. Jaggar was one of five scientists sent by the United States to survey the damage and investigate the eruption. He was deeply upset by what he saw. As he walked through the ruined city, everywhere he looked he saw the bodies of men, women, and children—most shriveled from the intense heat of the eruption. Jaggar wrote of this experience: "The odor was a haunting one that returned in dreams—of foundry, steam, sulfur matches, and burnt stuff, and every now and then a whiff of roast, decayed flesh that was horrible. It was impossible to realize that this Pompeii had been a thriving French town two weeks before." (Jaggar, 1956).

After finishing his work in Saint-Pierre, he traveled around the Caribbean collecting volcanic ash and measuring its depth. During a stop in Barbados, he heard that two survivors of the disaster in Saint-Pierre were in the local hospital.

Rita Stokes, a 14-year-old girl, and her nurse, Clara King, had been on the ship *Roraima* in the harbor of Saint Pierre when Mont Pelée erupted. King had severe burns on her knees, arms, and hands. Stokes was burned on her head, hands, and arms. Rita's mother, brother, and baby sister were killed in the eruption. They all had been in the same cabin. King told Jaggar that they saw Pelée puffing "white smoke" in the distance, but that the crew reassured them that all was fine. Suddenly a steward rushed by them and shouted for them to close the door because the volcano was coming. Rita's mother slammed the door just as a terrible explosion nearly burst their eardrums. Scalding moist ash flooded into the cabin and they felt as if they were suffocating. She and Rita awoke in agonizing pain but had no trouble breathing. They could see Mrs. Stokes and her other children dying nearby.

Jaggar was deeply affected by Ms. King's story, as well as by the things he had witnessed on Martinique. He later wrote:

> As I look back on the Martinique expedition, I know what a crucial point in my life it was and that it was the human contacts, not field adventures, which inspired me. Gradually I realized that the killing of thousands of persons by subterranean machinery totally unknown to geologists and then unexplainable was worthy of a life of work (Jaggar, 1956).

By the time he returned to Harvard after his travels, Jaggar had decided to devote his career to the study of volcanoes. He considered it "a missionary field because people in it were being killed" (Dvorak, 2011).

Jaggar soon was appointed to assistant professor of geology at both Harvard and the Massachusetts Institute of Technology (MIT). He married Helen Kline but he was committed to his study of volcanoes as well, and it frequently caused problems in the couple's marriage. When Jaggar heard of the eruption of Vesuvius in 1906, he departed immediately for Italy so he could observe the eruption, despite the fact that his wife had given birth to their first child just a few months before. Unfortunately, Jaggar arrived just after the eruption ended. Although one can imagine that he was disappointed that he was unable to observe the volcano in eruption, Jaggar did not feel that his trip was in vain. He met fellow American Frank Perret on the slopes of Vesuvius.

Perret was an engineer who worked as an unpaid assistant at the Vesuvius observatory in the months leading up to the 1906 eruption. He designed the instruments such as seismographs and microphones used to record activity on the volcano. Jaggar was impressed with Perret's work, and was intrigued by the idea of having a permanent observatory on the slopes of a volcano. At that time, the observatory on Vesuvius was the only one of its type in the world. Jaggar instantly recognized the benefit of having a permanent site on a volcano where the mountain's activity could be constantly monitored, enabling repeated and consistent measurements. He knew that a great deal more could be learned about a volcano's behavior through this type of constant monitoring than by short expeditions to study the aftermath of eruptions. Jaggar thought this might be the way to learn enough to prevent cities from suffering the same fate as Saint-Pierre.

Jaggar traveled to Alaska on a four-month survey of the Aleutian Islands in 1907. The Aleutians comprise the longest chain of volcanoes on the planet, so there was no lack of material to study. He was, however, most fascinated by the volcano Bogoslof. The volcano had only recently emerged from the sea. Jaggar and his party spent six hours on the island. He was fascinated to note that there were beaches at several elevations above sea level, indicating that the island was still rising out of the sea, being pushed up from an unknown source under it. Three weeks later, the volcano erupted and the small island disappeared—but in its place was a steaming lagoon. Jaggar was fascinated by the speed at which the volcano changed its appearance. He knew that his idea of building a volcano observatory was indeed the only way to capture the subtle nuances of volcano appearance and behavior, and he thought that the Aleutians, with its great many volcanoes, would be an excellent place to build his permanent observatory.

Jaggar's first problem was that he had no source of funding to use to build an observatory. When his mother died in 1908, he received an inheritance and thought that his funding problem was solved. Jaggar had enough money to leave his job at MIT and work in Alaska for a few years. His wife, however, objected to the idea of him leaving his stable job and spending years in Alaska. She felt that they needed to use the money to purchase a house, because at that time they were living in a rented house that they shared with another couple. Jaggar reluctantly agreed to do as his wife wished, but he insisted that they use the remainder of the money to go on a trip. He gave public lectures in Boston throughout 1908 and early 1909 in which he described his vision for building "geonomic observatories" with seismographs and other instruments to observe the earth and to prevent disasters such as those that occurred in Martinique in 1902, San Francisco in 1906, and Messina, Italy, in December of 1908. He solicited donations from those in attendance. He received a donation of $10,000 for one of his geonomic observatories from Mrs. Caroline Whitney, with the stipulation that the seismic observatory be located near Boston. With funding for the observatory secured, Jaggar and his wife left in early 1909 for the Hawaiian Islands and Japan. That trip proved to be vitally important to his plans.

The couple arrived in Honolulu on April 1, 1909, and left the next day on a two-day ocean voyage to the city of Hilo on the island of Hawaii. A full day's trek took them to the summit of the volcano Kilauea, which had in its crater an active lava lake. The Jaggars spent three days at the Volcano House Hotel, and each day Jaggar hiked down into the massive crater to the edge of the pit that held the lava lake. He spent hours watching the lake. Suddenly, everything seemed to become clear to him. This place, not Alaska, was the perfect site for his observatory. It was located in the tropics, so the volcano was accessible year round. The eruptions from this volcano were fairly benign, so it would provide a relatively safe working environment. There were two major problems with his plan. One was that Kilauea was an incredibly remote site. The second was that he had no money to establish an observatory here; the money he had been promised by Mrs. Whitney had to be used at a site near Boston.

Following their stay at Kilauea, the couple went back to Honolulu to await a ship to take them to Japan. Dr. Jaggar was invited to give a presentation at the University Club on his last night in the city. He spoke eloquently about the destruction in Saint-Pierre, of his work in Alaska, and about the work Perret was doing at the Vesuvius Observatory. Jaggar ended his presentation by announcing that he would be starting work on a geonomic observatory near Boston as soon as he returned. When he finished, a reporter from a local newspaper approached him and asked if he felt Kilauea might be a better location for a research station than Boston. When Jaggar answered with a simple "Yes," the reporter asked if it was a matter of money that was to determine the location of the site. Jagger again said, "Yes," knowing that it would be difficult to persuade Mrs. Whitney to change the stipulations of her gift. The reporter invited Jaggar to speak with him further about the matter when he returned to Honolulu on his way home from Japan. The reporter was Lorrin Thurston, owner of the newspaper the *Pacific Commercial Advertiser*, and a member of a small group of extremely influential businessmen in Honolulu.

When the Jaggars returned to Honolulu, Thurston had arranged a meeting with the territorial governor. The governor told Jaggar that he would have support from the business and political communities of the islands should he choose to do any work on Kilauea. Jaggar felt buoyed by the governor's enthusiasm and returned home, determined to convince Mrs. Whitney that her funds would be put to better use in Hawaii. Jaggar and Thurston stayed in touch after Jaggar returned to Massachusetts. Thurston sent him personal accounts of the volcano's activity, keeping Jaggar's interest and enthusiasm in Kilauea high.

At home in Boston, Jaggar was met with a great deal of resistance on two fronts. The president of MIT did not approve of his plans, and Mrs. Whitney and the trustee of her estate balked at his request to redirect their donation to work in Hawaii. Mrs. Whitney was further offended when Jaggar made a personal appeal for her to increase her gift tenfold so he could build multiple observatories around the world. After some discussion with the president of MIT and the trustee of her husband's estate, however, Mrs. Whitney agreed to raise her donation to $25,000. The donation created an endowment, and Jaggar was allowed to use the interest accrued on the account to do his work in Hawaii.

Jaggar's first order of business was to hire Arthur Day of the Carnegie Institution to design a sensor that could be lowered into a lava lake to determine the temperature of the lava. He then asked Frank Perret to join him the following summer for field work at Kilauea. Jaggar could not personally take part in the field work because his wife was pregnant. Perret and Thurston carried out the work Jaggar planned. They measured the temperature of the lava in the lava lake, and Thurston published their results on the front page of his newspaper. Perret stayed for two months to keep the volcano under visual surveillance. When he left to study volcanoes elsewhere, Thurston requested that Jaggar return to Kilauea. A year later, Jaggar returned, with permission from the president of MIT to stay for a few months. He made daily measurements and observations, explored the slopes of Mauna Loa, and tried to find financial backing for his

How Do I Become a Volcanologist?

A volcanologist is a scientist who studies the behavior and characteristics of volcanoes. Students interested in a career in volcanology should take all the math and science courses offered in high school, and continue on to study at a university. Most volcanologists are geologists who have pursued specialized training on one aspect of volcano study, such as gas geochemistry, seismology, geodesy (ground deformation), or petrology (the study of igneous rocks). Some volcanologists, however, have an academic background in a field such as chemistry, and became interested in the chemistry of volcanic gases or the chemistry of igneous rocks. In most cases, volcanologists have advanced (master's or Ph.D.) degrees. The pursuit of an advanced degree involves specialized coursework in the area of interest, as well as performing at least one major research project in that area, directed by an academic mentor or adviser. After earning an advanced degree, a graduate is ready to become a professional, working volcanologist. Volcanologists most commonly work for the universities or government agencies responsible for monitoring volcanic activity. In the United States, the agency most directly responsible for monitoring volcanic activity is the United States Geological Survey. Some national parks and monuments, however, also employ staff volcanologists or geologists.

planned observatory. Soon his wife summoned him back home because both children were ill. After Jaggar returned home, Thurston sent a cable to the president of MIT offering to pay Jaggar's salary for five years if he would return and set up a volcano observatory on Kilauea. The president agreed to the arrangement, and Jaggar was granted a leave of absence. Jaggar officially began his new position on July 1, 1912. This is considered the "birth date" of the Hawaiian Volcano Observatory.

Jaggar spent the remainder of his life in Hawaii. His wife Helen brought their children to Hawaii in late 1912, but they left six weeks after their arrival. She took the children back to Boston and the couple divorced. In 1917, Jaggar married Isabel Maydwell. She was a widowed school teacher from California who worked with Jaggar at the observatory. She became a talented scientist in her own right.

The original site of the Hawaiian Volcano Observatory was on the north rim of Kilauea's summit caldera, on the site that is now occupied by the modern Volcano House Hotel. The observatory was a small wooden building with a basement in which Jaggar placed a Bosch-Omori seismograph. The seismograph also worked as a tilt meter, which was used to detect minute variations in the slope of the volcano. The combination of changes in tilt and an increase in earthquake activity under Mauna Loa allowed Jaggar to forecast his first eruption in November of 1914. He continued his work, refining his craft and training countless other scientists, until he retired in 1940. The volcano observatory was moved to a new site on the south rim of Kilauea's summit caldera. The basement of the original observatory has been preserved, and is known as the Whitney Vault in honor of the donation from Mrs. Caroline Whitney, the volcano observatory's first benefactor. Jaggar died in Honolulu on January 17, 1953, just one week shy of his 83rd birthday.

See Also: Hawaiian Islands; Hawaiian Volcano Observatory; Kilauea Volcano, Hawaii, United States; Mauna Loa, Hawaii, United States.

Further Reading

Apple, R. A. (1987). Thomas A. Jaggar, Jr., and the Hawaiian Volcano Observatory. In *Volcanism in Hawaii 2*. (U.S. Geological Survey Professional Paper 1350). Washington, DC: U.S. GPO.

Dvorak, J. (2011). The origin of the Hawaiian Volcano Observatory. *Physics Today 64*(5), 32–37.

Jaggar, T. A. (1956). *My experiments with volcanoes*. Honolulu: Hawaiian Volcano Research Association.

McNarie, A. D. (2012). The Watchmen. *Hana Hou: The Magazine of Hawaiian Airlines 15*(2).

Wright, T. L. (2014, January 15). *Thomas Jaggar, HVO's founder*. Retrieved from http://hvo.wr.usgs.gov/volcanowatch/archive/1997/97_03_21.html

Japan

Japan is located along the western margin of the Pacific Ocean. It extends from the Russian-administered Kuril Islands in the north to Taiwan in the south. Japan lies on the Eurasian Plate. The northern part of the island nation was created by volcanism from subduction of the Pacific Plate beneath Eurasia, and the southern part was formed by subduction of the Philippine Plate beneath Eurasia. Because of Japan's location on a major subduction zone, residents of the islands are accustomed to large earthquakes, tsunamis, and volcanic eruptions. Because of the long history of the Japanese civilization, and the fact that written records are so abundant, a great deal is known about natural disasters in Japan—even those that happened several hundred years ago. Japanese mythology even speaks of Namazu, a giant catfish buried in the mud. When he flops and squirms, the earth quakes.

Earthquakes are daily occurrences in the Japanese Islands, although most earthquakes are too small to be felt. Magnitude 6 earthquakes happen several times per year within the island chain. Magnitude 7 earthquakes can occur once a year or more, and magnitude 8 earthquakes strike every few years. On occasion, earthquakes as powerful as magnitude 9 have occurred within the islands. Because many of these earthquakes occur in coastal areas, tsunamis also are common occurrences.

Japan's shores are vulnerable not only to tsunamis generated close to home, but to tsunamis created throughout the Pacific as well. In 1960, for example 200 deaths were reported in Japan as a result of a tsunami created off the coast of Chile. In 1700, a tsunami was generated by a massive earthquake off the west coast of North America (likely in British Colombia) and caused many deaths in Japan. The largest earthquake to occur within Japan in the last 200 years happened on March

Minor eruption of Mount Meakandake on the island of Hokkaido, Japan. (Kyodo News/ Newscom)

11, 2011. The magnitude 9.0 earthquake struck off the east coast of Honshu. Not only were homes and businesses damaged by ground shaking, but a tsunami also was generated. Most of the 20,352 deaths from the earthquake were, in fact, due to the tsunami. The tsunami also critically damaged the nuclear power plant at Fukushima, causing an environmental disaster that is likely to persist for years.

Some earthquakes that have occurred within Japan did not create tsunamis but still had disastrous effects. In 1923, the Great Kanto Earthquake struck the Tokyo-Yokohama area. The earthquake itself was quite devastating, but it certainly was not the end of the destruction. Hundreds of small fires were started during and immediately after the earthquake, and no water was available to fight the fire due to water-main ruptures. The cities burned and were nearly totally destroyed. More than 140,000 people died in the earthquake and resulting fire. Since the end of World War II, deaths in earthquakes have been relatively uncommon. Most buildings are engineered to withstand severe ground shaking—a necessity of living in a tectonic setting such as that of Japan. In 1995, however, a magnitude 6.9 earthquake in the Kobe area claimed 5,502 lives and injured nearly 37,000 people. Nearly 200,000 buildings were damaged or destroyed, and fire again was a problem due to broken water mains.

The Japanese Islands owe their existence largely to volcanic activity. Japan has hundreds of individual volcanoes, many of which have been active in historic times. Every island within the Japanese archipelago has volcanoes on it, and many of the smaller islands are themselves the crests of single volcanoes. Japan also has a large number of known active submarine volcanoes, and eruptions at these submarine volcanoes have been monitored. Some eruptions produced pumice rafts, cloudy water, and other surface manifestations of their activity. Probably the most famous of Japan's volcanoes is Mount Fuji. The volcano is well-known for its symmetry and snow-capped beauty. It is, however, a volcano that is likely to erupt again. Its last eruption occurred in 1707. That eruption deposited ash on Tokyo, and a new crater formed on the eastern flank of the volcano. Fuji has geothermal areas that are popular tourist destinations, and has had a few earthquake swarms beneath the volcano. There clearly still is magma moving beneath the mountain.

Fourteen of Japan's volcanoes have been active since the year 2000. A minor eruption of Hokkaido-Komagatake occurred between September and November of 2000, sending a plume of ash into the atmosphere. The Toya volcano erupted in 2001. The Izu-Torishima ("Bird Island") volcano erupted in 2002. After Tokachidake erupted in 2004, there was a four-year gap in which no volcanoes erupted. In 2008, Akan erupted, sending ash 6,600 feet (2,000 meters) into the atmosphere. In 2008 and 2009, two separate short-lived eruptions of Asamayama occurred. In 2010 eruptions of both the submarine volcano Fukutoku-Oka-No-Ba and of Miyakejima occurred. Fukutoku-Oka-No-Ba turned the ocean yellow-green, and a plume of steam and ash rose to 330 feet (100 meters) above the ocean. Eruptions of Asosan and Kirishimayama occurred in 2011. An eruption just off the coast of Ioto Island caused discoloration of the ocean. Eruptions of Suwanosejima and Kikai began in 2013, and Aira erupted in 2014.

See Also: Eurasian Plate; Great Kanto Earthquake, Japan (1923); Kobe Earthquake, Japan (1995); Pacific Plate; Philippine Plate; Sendai Earthquake and Tsunami, Japan (2011); Subduction Zone.

Further Reading

Smithsonian Institution. National Museum of Natural History. Global Volcanism Program. (2014, June 16). Retrieved from http://www.volcano.si.edu/search_volcano_results .cfm#

U.S. Geological Survey. (2014, June 16). *Historic world earthquakes*. Retrieved from http://earthquake.usgs.gov/earthquakes/world/historical_country.php

Japan Meteorological Agency

Japan Meteorological Agency is a government agency responsible for monitoring weather, volcano activity, and earthquake activity throughout the Japanese Islands. Because tsunamis and the earthquakes that produce them are such an important part of life in the Japanese Islands, it is important to have as much warning as possible to evacuate low-lying coastal areas before tsunamis strike. The Japan Meteorological

Agency's function is just that—to watch the seas and monitor earthquake activity to issue alerts as soon as is practical to allow for timely evacuations. The agency also monitors volcanic activity and issues volcanic ash alerts. These alerts are important for individual citizens that have respiratory difficulties, but are even more critical for the aviation industry. Volcanic ash in the sky often looks like regular clouds, but it can cause significant damage to jet engines. Timely volcanic ash advisories are critical for saving lives and property in the event of a volcanic eruption. The Agency's website provides information about the most recent earthquakes, any volcanic activity within the country, and all weather advisories and warnings in effect.

See Also: Japan.

Further Reading

Japan Meteorological Agency. (June 16, 2014). Retrieved from http://www.jma.go.jp/jma/indexe.html

Jiji Earthquake, Taiwan (1999)

The Jiji earthquake—known in Taiwan as the 921 earthquake—was a major earthquake that struck central Taiwan on September 21, 1999. The quake registered a magnitude of 7.3 on the Richter scale, with its epicenter near the town of Jiji (sometimes spelled Chi-Chi) in central Taiwan. The earthquake and strong aftershocks caused significant damage to many structures, and 2,416 people were killed.

The earthquake struck central Taiwan at 1:47 a.m. on September 21, 1999, when most residents were sleeping. The quake was caused by a rupture of the Chelongpu fault, which runs roughly north-south across west-central Taiwan between the western lowlands and the central mountains. It is the location of the ongoing collision of two tectonic plates—the Philippine Sea Plate and the Eurasian Plate. Interestingly, Taiwan's Central Weather Bureau had installed a large system of seismic measurement instruments in the central part of the island, therefore much detailed information was collected about the movement and extent of the Jiji earthquake. Significant shaking was felt as far away as the capital city of Taipei, some 100 miles to the north. The hardest-hit places were in west-central Taiwan, however, especially the larger urban areas near the fault: Taichung and Nantou. Instruments detected 12,911 aftershocks in the month following the quake, including three with magnitudes greater than 6.8 within two weeks.

It long has been known that Taiwan is at a seismically active point on the earth's crust. Building codes were designed and implemented prior to the earthquake to ensure the safety of buildings in the event of a quake. Unfortunately, the peak ground acceleration—a measurement of how hard the surface actually shakes—was greater in some areas than that accounted for in the building codes.

A landslide covers a highway following the 1999 Jiji Earthquake in Taiwan. (JIM GENSHEIMER/KRT/ Newscom)

The Jiji earthquake therefore led to the collapse of some structures that were thought to be safe, as well as those that had identifiable design or construction flaws. Many buildings with "soft stories" (upper stories overhanging open spaces or walkways) and many older and historic structures in affected areas suffered collapses. In all, more than 100,000 buildings were damaged or destroyed; most of them small and midsized structures. Some buildings that were weakened by the initial quake collapsed due to the strong aftershocks.

Much of the damage occurred in cities and villages along the fault line. Surface rupture and slippage along the fault also destroyed some underground electric-, gas, and water-distribution systems as well as a dam on the Tachia River. Aboveground electric infrastructure sustained very heavy damage in some areas, especially near the epicenter. Landslides destroyed parts of mountain towns and covered vital roads connecting those towns with the lowland areas. Some highway bridges also were destroyed or damaged—some torn apart by the movement of the fault. Access to many hard-hit areas thus was restricted, which made recovery more difficult. A major landslide near the town of Caoling even created a lake by damming off water drainage.

The earthquake's human toll was significant, although it likely would have been much worse had the quake hit during the daylight hours—when far more people would have been driving on roads, and more commercial buildings would have been occupied. The official death count was 2,405, and 10,718 people were injured (about 1,000 of whom were very seriously hurt). Most of the casualties were in and around Taichung and Nantou, where the majority of building collapses occurred. A capable and fairly quick emergency response was essential to saving lives, and more than 5,000 people were rescued by emergency personnel. Some 100,000 people were displaced by the earthquake, either because their homes were destroyed or greatly weakened, or because they were afraid of the powerful periodic aftershocks. Shelters were set up at locations throughout the affected area to accommodate the great number of displaced people. The Taiwanese government declared a state of emergency on September 25. It lasted six months as investigations and initial repair and rebuilding were carried out.

The economic cost of the earthquake also was great, with direct rebuilding costs of more than US$8 billion and productivity losses of as much as US$30 billion. Monetary aid and rescue personnel flowed to Taiwan from around the world, although the country's longstanding sovereignty dispute with China was an obstacle. The United Nations was unable to assist immediately, as it does not recognize Taiwanese sovereignty and thus needed the approval of the Chinese government before helping Taiwan. Some countries, however, including Turkey—which recently had suffered the devastating Izmit earthquake (1999)—sent experienced relief personnel immediately.

Reconstruction legislation was passed by the Taiwanese government, which created an agency to plan and coordinate rebuilding efforts. Dissatisfaction with inadequate government enforcement of building regulations prior to the quake and poor emergency preparation in affected areas, however, led to political repercussions for the ruling Nationalist Party (Kuomintang). This, in turn, led to stricter adherence to laws and regulations in succeeding years. Repairing and rebuilding damaged structures and infrastructure damage eventually was accomplished, and reconstruction actually proved a net benefit for the Taiwanese economy, although better earthquake-readiness is perhaps the most important legacy of the destructive quake.

See Also: Earthquake; Earthquake Hazards; Eurasian Plate; Philippine Plate.

Further Reading

Edmonds, R. L., & Goldstein, S. M. (2001). *Taiwan in the Twentieth Century: A retrospective view*. Cambridge: Cambridge University Press.

Lee, W. H. K. (Ed.). (2003). *The international handbook of earthquake and engineering seismology*. London: Academic Press.

Schiff, A. J., & Tang, A. K. (Eds.). (2000). *Chi-Chi, Taiwan, earthquake of September 21, 1999: Lifeline performance*. Reston, VA: American Society of Civil Engineers.

Juan de Fuca Plate

The Juan de Fuca Plate is named for a Greek explorer who sailed under the Spanish flag and claimed to have been the first European to locate the strait between Washington's Olympic Peninsula and British Columbia's Vancouver Island in 1592. Although many scholars doubt these claims, de Fuca's name still is attached to the waterway between Vancouver Island and the mainland of Washington. The plate presumably gets its name from the Strait of Juan de Fuca.

The Juan de Fuca Plate is a small remnant of the much larger Farallon Plate that has been partially subducted beneath North America. The Farallon Plate once spanned the length of the entire west coast of North and South America. It was being consumed at a faster rate than it was being produced, however, so the plate began shrinking. Eventually, part of the plate's far boundary disappeared beneath North America, and the large Farallon Plate ceased to exist. The remnants include the Juan de Fuca Plate in the north, the Rivera Plate found off the coast of Mexico, the Cocos Plate off the west coast of Central America, and the Nazca Plate off the west coast of South America. All of these plates continue to be subducted beneath the land areas to the east, and eventually all will disappear beneath continents. That event will place the Pacific Plate in contact with the plates to the east, which will change the tectonic and geological dynamics of the entire eastern Pacific.

The Juan de Fuca Plate's southern margin is the Mendocino Fracture Zone located off the coast of northern California. Its northern boundary is located just off the coast of southern British Columbia. In between these boundaries, subduction of the Juan de Fuca Plate has led to large earthquakes and the creation of the Cascade Range—a chain of active volcanoes that runs from Lassen Peak in California to Mount Garibaldi in southern British Columbia. Other major volcanoes within this chain include Mount Shasta, Crater Lake, the Three Sisters, Mount Hood, Mount St. Helens, and Mount Rainier.

The subduction zone where the Juan de Fuca Plate sinks beneath the North American Plate is called the Cascadia Subduction Zone. Earthquakes there are relatively common, but large earthquakes are extremely rare. For many years scientists did not believe that the Cascadia Subduction Zone was capable of producing a great earthquake (a magnitude of more than 8). This was based partially on observations of a "creeping" plate boundary in which movement was occurring nearly aseismically, but partially on the fact that no earthquakes of this size had occurred in the approximately 200 years since Europeans first inhabited the area. Discoveries made in the 1990s by geologist Brian Atwater and his colleagues, however, indicate that the Cascadia Subduction Zone indeed was the site of a massive earthquake—likely a magnitude 9.0 event—in January of 1700. Native American legends had spoken of a catastrophic event in the past, and Atwater's work confirmed the existence of many areas of extreme subsidence along the coastline and large tsunami deposits that corresponded to the time of subsidence. Additionally, stories of an "orphan tsunami"—one without a known origin point— that struck Japan in January 1700 led the research team to investigate the origins of that tsunami. Atwater and a team of Japanese researchers concluded that the earthquake in the Pacific Northwest, along the Cascadia Subduction Zone, likely was the origin of the orphan tsunami. This discovery has huge implications for hazard mitigation experts in communities near the subduction zone. People in those communities now know that they must prepare for extremely large and damaging earthquakes, and the likelihood of locally generated tsunamis.

See Also: Cascadia Subduction Zone; Cocos Plate; Crater Lake, Oregon, United States; Farallon Plate; Hood, Mount, Oregon, United States; Lassen Peak, California, United States; Nazca Plate; Orphan Tsunami; Rainier, Mount, Washington, United States; Shasta,

Mount, California, United States; South Sister Volcano, Oregon, United States; St. Helens, Mount, Washington, United States.

Further Reading

Atwater, B. F., Satoko, M.-R., Kenji, S., Yoshinobu, T., Kazue, U., & Yamaguchi, D. K. (2005). *The orphan tsunami of 1700—Japanese clues to a parent earthquake in North America.* (U.S. Geological Survey Professional Paper 1707). Washington, DC: U.S. GPO.

Center for the Study of the Pacific Northwest. (2014, June 17). *1. Account of Juan de Fuca's Voyage.* Retrieved from http://www.washington.edu/uwired/outreach/cspn/Website/Classroom%20Materials/Reading%20the%20Region/Discovering%20the%20Region/Commentary/1.html

U.S. Geological Survey. (2014, June 17). *Historic earthquakes in the United States and its territories. Washington.* Retrieved from http://earthquake.usgs.gov/earthquakes/states/historical_state.php#washington

U.S. Geological Survey. (2014, June 17). *The Cascades.* Retrieved from http://volcanoes.usgs.gov/about/volcanoes/cascades/index.php

K

Kalapana Earthquake, Hawaii, United States (1975)

In the early morning hours of November 29, 1975, residents of the island of Hawaii were awakened by a major earthquake. The earthquake, a magnitude 7.2 event, was felt as far away as Oahu, more than 250 miles (400 kilometers) from the epicenter. People who were near the epicenter report being thrown off their feet due to severe ground shaking. Structural damage occurred in several locations on the island due to ground shaking, including the destruction of chimneys, water tanks, and a handful of homes. The earthquake also generated a tsunami that reached heights of up to 46.6 feet (14.2 meters) above sea level. Two people and four horses died in the tsunami, and additional damage occurred to coastal infrastructure. Boats were overturned, a pier in Hilo collapsed, and a few seaside buildings were destroyed. This was the largest earthquake to occur on the island of Hawaii in more than 100 years. It caused approximately $4.1 million in damage.

At approximately 3:36 a.m. on November 29, 1965, a magnitude 5.7 earthquake struck along the southeastern shore of the island of Hawaii. Several residents were awakened by the earthquake, but eventually they settled back down and returned to their beds. Only 72 minutes later, at 4:48 a.m., a much larger magnitude 7.2 earthquake struck very near the epicenter of the first earthquake. The ground shook for nearly a minute, which caused considerable damage to a number of structures across the southeastern quarter of the island. Cracks appeared in the roads within Hawaii Volcanoes National Park, and several small rockfalls and landslides occurred throughout the park. Portions of roads became impassable as asphalt buckled and bent, and as pieces of the road fell away into craters and the summit caldera. Rocks covered portions of the roads in other locations. At one viewing site, the entire viewing platform fell into the crater, leaving a guard rail projecting outward over the crater, anchored only by posts in the surviving portion of the parking area. At a military recreation facility located within the park, a chimney fell through the roof of the dining hall. Elsewhere on the island, 5 churches, 11 commercial buildings, and 80 homes sustained structural damage. Five old or poorly constructed homes and a handful of water tanks were destroyed.

The earthquake also generated a powerful tsunami. Damage was limited to the Hawaiian Islands; however, the tsunami was detected at tide gauges in California and several Pacific islands. The tsunami caused a great deal of damage, particularly along the southeast coast of Hawaii. A Boy Scout troop was camping at Halape, roughly 15.5 miles (25 kilometers) west of the earthquake's epicenter. At 3:36 a.m., the first earthquake awakened the boys and their troop leaders. Rock falls were occurring along the small cliff just inland from their campsite, so many boys moved their sleeping bags closer to the ocean to avoid the rocks. During the second earthquake, the boys were understandably frightened. They tried to run from the new rock slides, but were tossed off their feet unless they held tight to palm trees or boulders. Once the earthquake was over, a few of the campers knew to check for a tsunami. Within a minute or so, they noticed that the sea was rising visibly and began running inland. The water surged forward, knocking many of the boys off their feet. The wave receded and they continued moving inland. A second and more violent wave followed a short time later and carried everything—trees, rocks, people, and horses—325 feet (100 meters) inland. Some people washed into a large crack in the ground. One scout leader died after being battered by debris and drowned in the crack. Another leader was swept out to sea and is presumed dead. Four of the ten horses that the troop brought along died as well.

Although the Pacific Tsunami Warning System was in place and functioning at expected levels that morning, there was no time to warn those near the earthquake's epicenter. The first tsunami wave arrived 30 seconds after the ground shaking ended, and five successive waves struck the area. The largest wave occurred 10 minutes after the first hit—it destroyed 7 homes and 2 vehicles, and caused more than $1 million in damage. The southeast coast of Hawaii was hardest hit, but damage occurred to fishing boats and piers on the island's west coast as well. The most distant report of damage came from Catalina Island, which is off the coast of southern California.

In addition to the structural damage from the earthquake and the tragic effects of the tsunami, there were a number of other observed effects. Earthquake lights were seen during and immediately after the larger earthquake. These are often seen around the time of major earthquakes, and have been documented worldwide. They are described as intense flashes, bursts, or glows of blush or white light that last between a few seconds and a minute. Scientists still do not have an adequate explanation for what causes earthquake lights, but suspect they are caused by electrical perturbation of the atmosphere due to either pressure on the rocks, or vibrations of the earth.

The earthquake occurred on the south flank of Kilauea Volcano. Scientists who were called to the observatory after the earthquake noticed the appearance of harmonic tremor—a type of signal that appears on a seismogram when magma located at a shallow depth beneath the volcano is moving. At the summit of Kilauea, a 550-yard (500-meter) long fissure opened about half an hour after the earthquake occurred. Frothy, gas-rich lava began to jet as much as 165 feet (50 meters) into the air. The fountains died back to heights of 16 to 32 feet (5 to 10 meters) within about 15 minutes and stopped erupting completely by 7 a.m. The lava flow created by this event covered about 0.1 square miles (0.25 square kilometers) of the caldera floor. Today, the flow is marked clearly with a National Park Service sign, and can be seen on a driving or hiking tour of Kilauea's caldera.

On the south flank of Kilauea, new cracks opened at the base of several cliffs or slopes. These were cracks and landslide scars rather than faults. A new fault did appear, however, and scientists measured approximately 5 feet (1.5 meters) of displacement between the two sides of the fault. The south side of the fault moved down relative to the north side, which is consistent with the general movement of the larger fault measured by geologists. A thorough study of the large earthquakes and thousands of aftershocks defined a wedge of rock that was displaced along a sliding surface approximately 10 kilometers beneath the volcano's south flank, and tilted approximately 20° seaward, or toward the south.

The fault system involved in this earthquake, as well as in the last major earthquake that occurred on the island—an estimated magnitude 8.0 earthquake that occurred in 1868—is called the Hilina Fault System. The Hilina System is a series of faults that run east-west across the south flank of Kilauea Volcano. These faults have developed over millennia as magma has forcefully intruded into the rift zones of the volcano and shoved the south flank of the volcano southward. As this has happened, the un-buttressed south flank periodically has moved seaward along these faults, dropping huge segments of the volcano down and to the south. During the 1975 earthquake, it is estimated that this wedge of material moved approximately 11.5 feet (3.5 meters) downward. Evidence for this movement comes from measurements made of features at the shoreline. A grove of coconut palms at Halape (where the Boy Scouts were camped) once stood a few feet above sea level. Immediately after the earthquake, the palms were standing in the ocean. Detailed measurements indicate that the vast majority of subsidence occurred around the time of the major earthquake, but small adjustments also occurred during the next several months.

The earthquake came to be known as the "1975 Kalapana earthquake," named after the coastal town nearest the epicenter. The town of Kalapana and many of the other landmarks mentioned in contemporary reports of the earthquake no longer exist—not due to the 1975 earthquake and tsunami, but rather because of lava flows which occurred during the late 1980s and early 1990s covering the area.

See Also: Earthquake; Hawaiian Islands; Kilauea Volcano, Hawaii, United States; Tsunami.

Further Reading

Ando, M. (1979). The Hawaii earthquake of November 29, 1975: Low dip angle faulting due to forceful injection of magma. *Journal of Geophysical Research 84* (B13), 7616–7626.

Tilling, R. I., Koyanagi, R. Y., Lipman, P. W., Lockwood, J. P., Moore, J. G., & Swanson, D. A. (1976). *Earthquake and related catastrophic events, Island of Hawaii, November 29, 1975: A preliminary report.* (U.S. Geological Survey Circular 740).

U.S. Geological Survey. Hawaiian Volcano Observatory. (2014, May 19). *November 29, 1975 Kalapana earthquake.* Retrieved from http://hvo.wr.usgs.gov/earthquakes /destruct/1975Nov29/

Kamchatka Volcanic Eruption Response Team

The Kamchatka Volcanic Eruption Response Team (KVERT) is a governmental organization based in northeastern Russia. It was established in 1993 to monitor and respond to volcanic threats in the Kamchatka Peninsula of Russia and northern Kurile Islands (to its immediate south). KVERT works closely with the Kamchatkan Branch of Geophysical Surveys, the U.S. Geological Survey's Alaska Volcano Observatory, and the Geophysical Institute at the University of Alaska–Fairbanks. Because these areas are only very sparsely populated, the main focus of this agency is to provide information to the Federal Aviation Services of Russia and all major airlines about eruptions and air travel hazards within the region. When eruptions of volcanoes on the Kamchatka Peninsula or in the northern Kurile Islands occur, volcanic ash often drifts into high-traffic international air routes. Timely warnings are critical, as it is estimated that more than 700 planes transporting thousands of passengers fly through this region every day. This work is vitally important, particularly because volcanic ash has the potential to destroy airplane engines and even to bring down a plane. Communications from KVERT will become even more important as additional flights are added to handle global commerce between Asia and the United States.

KVERT continuously monitors 30 active volcanoes on the Kamchatka Peninsula, and 6 active volcanoes in the Northern Kuriles. Many of these volcanoes are highly active, and all have the potential to produce ash clouds that potentially could interfere with air traffic. The KVERT website maintains archival and current information about all active volcanoes on the peninsula, shows the webcams on several of the volcanoes, and provides excellent information about aviation hazards from volcanic eruptions. The website can be viewed in either English or Russian.

See Also: Russia; Volcanic Hazards.

Further Reading

Kamchatka Volcanic Eruption Response Team (KVERT). (KVERT). Retrieved October 16, 2014, from http://www.kscnet.ru/ivs/kvert/index_eng.php

Katmai Eruption, Alaska, United States (1912)

The June 1912 eruption of Katmai in southern Alaska was the largest of the Twentieth Century, and is categorized as a VEI 6.5. Over 3 days, more than 3.1 cubic miles (13 cubic kilometers) of magma erupted violently from vents 6.2 miles (10 kilometers) west of the summit of Katmai, at the head of a glacially carved valley between other volcanic peaks. Pyroclastic flows filled in the nearby valleys and left behind a steaming plain that one member of an early expedition dubbed

The Valley of 10,000 Smokes and neighboring Mount Griggs in Katmai National Park, Alaska, USA. (Hugh Rose / DanitaDelimont.com Danita Delimont Photography/Newscom)

"the Valley of Ten Thousand Smokes." Although the steaming ceased within a few years after the eruption, the valley retains its name to this day. It is located in the vast wilderness of Katmai National Park and Preserve.

In 1912, the area around Katmai was very sparsely populated. There were Eskimo populations living in the rugged and remote region, but there are no reports of settlements in the immediate vicinity of the eruption site in 1912. As a result, there are no records of any precursory activity prior to the eruption that began on June 6, 1912. The eruption began at about 1 p.m. local time with a violent explosion followed by approximately 60 hours of vigorous eruption. The eruption appears to have occurred in three stages. The eruption produced an impressive column of volcanic ash and enormously voluminous pyroclastic flows. The composition of materials erupted ranged from rhyolite to andesite, with the vast majority being dacitic in composition. There were multiple large explosions—heard up to a few hundred miles away. The ash in the eruption column was caught by the wind and transported eastward. By 5 p.m. on June 6, ash was falling in the town of Kodiak, which is located slightly more than 100 miles (170 kilometers) to the east. By June 9—the final day of the eruption—ash had accumulated in some places to a depth of six feet, with rare accumulations of 10 feet. Many people in Kodiak felt as if the world was ending. They had not seen the sun in three days. The ash cloud was creating its own eerie lightning. There were thunderous booms from the mountain. Water was contaminated with volcanic ash and therefore unfit to drink. Conditions were both dangerous and frightening.

When the eruption was over on June 9, the landscape around Katmai was vastly different than it had been only three days prior. The valley near where the eruption had begun had been filled by pyroclastic flows. In some areas, the valley had been more than 650 feet (200 meters) deep. After the eruption, the entire area was a wide, flat plain. A 1.2-mile (2-kilometer) wide crater stood where the eruption had begun, and pyroclastic flow layers draped back downward into the crater.

The summit of Katmai, 6.2 miles (10 kilometers) to the east, had become a broad circular caldera roughly 2,000 feet (600 meters) deep. This was a rather curious effect of the eruption, because there is absolutely no indication that any part of the eruption occurred at the summit of Katmai or in the vicinity of the caldera. The complex plumbing system of the volcano evidently ran laterally from beneath the summit of Katmai to the location of the eruption. The magma chamber beneath Katmai's summit was drained during the eruption, leaving the summit of the mountain unsupported. The caldera appears to have been created episodically throughout the eruption. A number of very large earthquakes were recorded at distant seismic stations, and are presumed to represent the collapse of sections of the caldera. Within the next several months, a volcanic dome composed of dacite formed in the eruption crater. This dome was named Novarupta.

The first scientific expedition to explore the eruption site was sponsored by the National Geographic Society in 1916. Upon seeing the valley filled with pyroclastic flows adjacent to Novarupta, scientist and expedition leader Robert Griggs stated "It was as though all the steam engines in the world, assembled together, had popped their safety valves at once, and were letting off steam in concert" (Francis & Oppenheimer, 2004). Griggs dubbed it "the Valley of Ten Thousand Smokes." The steam was generated by the stream in the valley being superheated by the pyroclastic deposits from the eruption. As could be expected, the steam jets stopped within a few years. The next serious study of the eruption and its deposits did not occur until the 1950s. Since that time, the Katmai eruption has been studied in great detail; it even was the subject of a centennial publication by the U.S. Geological Survey. Today, the area remains remote and largely uninhabited.

See Also: Andesite; Caldera; Crater; Dacite; Pyroclastic Materials; Rhyolite.

Further Reading

Francis, P., & Oppenheimer, C. (2004). *Volcanoes* (2nd ed.). Oxford: Oxford University Press.

U.S. Geological Survey. (1912). *The Novarupta-Katmai eruption of 1912—Largest eruption of the Twentieth Century.* (Centennial Perspectives: U.S. Geological Survey Professional Paper 1791). Washington, DC: U.S. GPO.

Kilauea Volcano, Hawaii, United States

Kilauea is the youngest of the five volcanoes that comprise the island of Hawaii. It also is the smallest of these volcanoes. Kilauea is bordered to the north by Mauna Loa—the most massive volcano on the planet—and to the south by a submarine volcano called Loihi. The summit of Loihi is still several thousand feet beneath the ocean surface; it will be thousands of years before it becomes an island. Kilauea is one of the most active volcanoes in the world. In fact, at this writing it has been in almost constant eruption since January 3, 1983. Only short periods of inactivity between eruptive phases has punctuated an otherwise continuous flow of lava. Kilauea is the site of the Hawaiian Volcano Observatory, founded in 1912 by Dr. Thomas Jaggar. The Hawaiian Volcano Observatory is the oldest volcano observatory in the United States. Today it is a part of the U.S. Geological Survey. Kilauea also holds a special place in Hawaiian mythology. Kilauea is believed by many to be the home of Pele, the goddess of the volcano and one of the most powerful gods in the Hawaiian pantheon.

Kilauea is structured like most other Hawaiian volcanoes; it has a large caldera that occupies its summit area. The summit caldera is an oval-shaped depression at the volcano's summit, 4.3 miles (7 kilometers) long and 3.1 miles (5 kilometers) wide at its widest points. It is oriented such that its long axis lies almost due east-west. The volcano has two major rift systems. The Southwest Rift Zone begins at the southwest edge of the summit caldera and continues southwestward toward the coastline of the island. The East Rift Zone begins at the southeast edge of the summit caldera and continues southeastward to a volcanic shield built during a 1968–1974 eruption, called "Mauna Ulu." At Mauna Ulu, the rift zone turns toward the northeast and continues to the easternmost point of the island, Cape Kumukahi, where it continues offshore for several additional miles. The vast majority of eruptions occur

Basalt lava flow from the volcano Kilauea dripping into the ocean on the island of Hawaii. (Stuart Westmorland Cultura/Newscom)

Volcano Art

Volcanoes evoke feelings of awe at the wondrous power of nature. They have served as inspiration for artists around the world. In addition to the many beautiful portraits that exist of volcanoes in their dormant state, active volcanoes have been the subject of artwork for hundreds of years. Mount Vesuvius in Italy is a famous subject of many artists. In 1760, Pietro Fabris painted a scene of a lava flow burying part of the countryside below the volcano. A painting entitled *The Eruption of Vesuvius* (1771) by Pierre-Jacques Volaire hangs in the Art Institute of Chicago. It depicts a fiery night-time eruption of Vesuvius. The scene includes rivers of lava and observers standing near the flow, taking in the awesome wonder of the sight. Volaire must have been quite inspired by this phenomenon, because he completed other paintings of this eruption. Joseph Wright depicted the same eruption in his painting *Vesuvius in Eruption, with a View over the Islands in the Bay of Naples*. Though he was not in Naples to witness the eruption himself, he had visited while the mountain sent up plumes of steam, so he clearly had a vision in his mind of what the volcano must have looked like in eruption. An eruption of Mount St. Helens was painted by Paul Kane in 1847. In his portrait, the symmetrical and snow-covered peak erupts from a vent on one of its flanks. Frederic Edwin Church, an American artist, painted a beautiful scene of Cotopaxi (Ecuador) erupting in 1862. This one of a series of paintings he completed while touring South America. He is perhaps one of the best known and most well-regarded landscape artists of the late 1800s, and his painting *Cotopaxi* is an excellent example of his work. The volcano Kilauea (Hawaii) is a constant source of inspiration for Hawaiian artists working in many media, and has been since the first westerners explored the volcano in the early 1800s.

either at the summit caldera or along one of these two rift zones. For the last hundred years, activity has been scarce on the Southwest Rift Zone. Almost all activity has been either at the summit area or along the East Rift Zone, except for a short-lived eruption occurring in 1974 on the upper Southwest Rift Zone near the caldera.

Rift zones are marked by a series of features, and can contain all or only some of the features. One feature is fissures, or ground cracks. The ground cracks trend parallel to the trace of the rift zone. Eruptions can occur from these cracks, or the cracks in the ground might be formed by the stresses in the area that tend to force rocks apart in this setting on the volcano.

A second feature that is common to see on Hawaiian rift zones is pit craters. Pit craters are small craters generally less than 0.25 miles (0.4 kilometers) in diameter. They seem to form when magma beneath an area of the rift zone erodes rock from below. When the roof of the cavity created on the rift zone is left thin and unsupported, the roof collapses and a small crater is left behind. Although eruptions certainly can occur at pit craters, they do not seem to form initially as a result of eruptions.

A third feature often seen on rift zones of Hawaiian volcanoes is a lava shield. Lava shields are broad, low hills formed by the sustained eruption of lava flows from a centralized vent. The feature "Mauna Ulu," located at the bend in Kilauea's

East Rift Zone, is a lava shield formed in recent times. A much larger lava shield called "Ailaau" formed hundreds of years ago during an eruption that likely lasted more than 60 years.

Yet another type of feature found along a rift zone is a cinder and spatter cone. As might be expected from the name, these cones are formed from a combination of material. Often they begin forming during a lava fountaining event when lava is shot into the air. Some lava cools while in the air and is solid when it strikes the ground. These particles are called cinder or scoria. Other lava is liquid when it hits the ground; this is called spatter. Cinder and spatter cones dot the rift zones of Hawaiian volcanoes, and are easily identified as sites of past eruptions.

Kilauea also has two prominent fault zones. The first, the Koae Fault Zone, is an east-west trending fault zone on the south flank of the volcano that drops large blocks of rock down toward the caldera. The second, the Hilina Fault System, is nearly parallel to the Koae Fault Zone but drops large sections of the volcano southward toward the ocean. The Hilina Fault System has been the location of the island's last two major earthquakes. In 1868, an estimated magnitude 8.0 earthquake struck just west of the old town of Kalapana. Nearly 30 people died in the earthquake and resulting tsunami. Many homes and businesses were destroyed, and island residents endured aftershocks for months afterward. A similar earthquake in 1975 occurred just a few miles away from the 1868 earthquake site. It also caused damage to buildings on the island and generated a tsunami. Two Boy Scout leaders were killed as they tried to escape the tsunami.

Kilauea is in the third stage of its expected life cycle. The typical life cycle for Hawaiian volcanoes begins with a deep submarine phase. During this stage the volcano begins forming on the ocean floor, and builds thousands of feet over tens of thousands of years. The second stage is the shallow submarine stage, which is when the volcano's summit approaches sea level. Phreatic eruptions are commonplace as the volcano builds into an island. The third stage—and the stage that Kilauea currently is experiencing—is the subaerial shield-building stage. Subaerial simply means exposed to the atmosphere. So, at this stage, Kilauea is part of an island and is erupting above the surface of the ocean. Subaerial shield-building volcanoes typically have a structure that includes a summit caldera and two well-developed rift zones.

The fourth stage is a post-caldera stage. During this phase the volcano's lava flows fill its summit caldera, and cinder cones dot the summit area. Kilauea's neighbor to the northeast, Mauna Kea, currently is in this stage. The fifth stage is an erosional stage, when the volcano no longer is erupting and instead is eroding. The volcano on the northern end of the island of Hawaii, called "Kohala," currently is in this stage. The sixth stage occurs when the island has been eroded so that only a small portion of it remains above sea level. This stage—called the stage of reef growth—is when coral reefs around the edges of the island become wide. The seventh stage is post-erosional eruptions, which might or might not occur. Oahu appears to have gone through such a stage, as there are late-stage cones and lava flows found on the island.

The final stage of Hawaiian volcanoes' life cycle is the atoll stage. Johnston Atoll is one example of a volcano in this final stage. At this point, the volcano has been eroded by wind, water, and waves to a point where its top is just below sea level and the only area above sea level is a coral atoll, the subaerial (above-ocean) portion of the massive coral reefs that surround the sunken island. Eventually even these reefs will be eroded, and the volcano once again becomes a seamount or submerged volcano.

Some of Kilauea's eruptions lasted for decades (as in the Ailaau shield mentioned above, as well as the current eruption) or were as short as a few hours. When an eruption begins it is impossible to estimate how long it will continue, whether it will continue at a specific site or move to another, or when the eruption will change character. Constant monitoring of Kilauea has enabled scientists to learn enough about the volcano's behavior to be able to forecast when and where an eruption will begin to within a few hours. It is likely, however, that scientists might never be able to forecast other parameters.

As noted, Kilauea has been continuously active since January 1983. For the first few years of the eruption activity occurred sporadically, roughly once every 20 to 30 days. At that time, spectacular lava fountains erupted at a spot on the middle East Rift Zone. As a cone built, it was named by island elders as "Puu Oo." "Puu" means "hill" in Hawaiian, and "Oo" is a type of bird that once lived in the area that is now extinct. Activity has been located at Puu Oo for most of the duration of the current eruption, with the exception of a few years in the late 1980s when activity shifted to a vent slightly more than 0.62 miles (1 kilometer) away, called Kupaianaha. Lava from Kupaianaha and Puu Oo were responsible for burying many homes and businesses in the late 1980s and early 1990s. The village of Kalapana on the southeast coast of the island, the Wahaula Visitor Center to Hawaii Volcanoes National Park, a lovely palm tree–lined black sand beach called Kaimu, and a subdivision called Royal Gardens (located upslope from Kalapana) all were destroyed.

Although lava began flowing from Kilauea in 1983, it did not reach the ocean until 1987. Many families were displaced, and those residents whose homes were not overrun by lava were cut off from all road access and modern services. Roads into and out of Kalapana were covered by lava, and all utilities became unavailable. A few hardy souls decided to continue living in their homes, but the last resident moved out in 2012 after much later lava flows from Puu Oo threatened his home. The house was destroyed on March 3, 2012. It was the last house standing in the Royal Gardens Subdivision. In 2008, a lava lake became active in Halemaumau—a pit crater found in Kilauea's summit caldera. It presently remains active. The current eruption of Kilauea built more than 500 acres of new land between 1983 and 2012.

See Also: Hawaiian Islands; Hawaiian Volcano Observatory; Jaggar, Jr., Thomas Augustus; Kalapana Earthquake, Hawaii, United States (1975); Mauna Kea, Hawaii, United States; Mauna Loa, Hawaii, United States.

Further Reading

McDonald, G. A., Abbott, A. T., & Peterson, F. L. (1983). *Volcanoes in the sea: The geology of Hawaii* (2nd ed.). Honolulu: University of Hawaii Press.

National Park Service. (2014, May 19). Hawaii Volcanoes National Park: Frequently Asked Questions. Retrieved from http://www.nps.gov/havo/faqs.htm

Sur, P. (2012, March 4). Lava claims final home. *Hawaii Tribune-Herald*.

U.S. Geological Survey. Hawaiian Volcano Observatory. (2014, May 19). *Kilauea's east rift zone (Puu Oo) eruption 1983 to present*. Retrieved from http://hvo.wr.usgs.gov /kilauea/summary/main.html

Kobe Earthquake, Japan (1995)

Early in the morning of January 17, 1995, Kobe, Japan, experienced the nation's most destructive earthquake since 1946. Its epicenter was at Awaji, offshore from Kobe, and 10 miles below the surface. Damage was extensive and there were many casualties. More than 5,400 people were killed, another 26,800 injured, and more than 300,000 people became homeless. Additionally, nearly 105,000 buildings were damaged beyond repair and numerous others suffered lesser forms of damage. The financial costs of the earthquake were in excess of $150 billion.

The Kobe area is dominated by the Philippine Tectonic Plate's subducting action as it moves beneath the Eurasian Plate at a rate of about two inches a year. Great subduction earthquakes arise from this action at average recurrence rates of 100 years. This part of Japan also has the most faults found anywhere in Japan and, like the main subducting action, these faults also have an average annual slippage rate, although it is much less than that of the main tectonic plate. As a result of these lesser fault movements, the Kyoto-Osaka corridor has experienced more intraplate earthquakes throughout history than any other region of Japan.

The quake devastated central Kobe, crushing buildings and homes and filling the narrow streets with debris. Train services—a vital part of Japan's transportation system—came to a sudden stop and all electricity and water provisions were cut off. The total and complete destruction of everything led to the birth of the term the "Great Hanshin Disaster," used to indicate an event similar to the "Great Kanto Disaster" of 1923. (The word "Hanshin" is another term for the Kobe Region.) The loss of all water supplies made it impossible to extinguish all the fires that broke out as electrical sparks and flammable materials were thrown together. Thus, a firestorm—like that which engulfed San Francisco in 1906 for the same reason— swept across Kobe. By late on January 17, there were 234 fires; before the middle of the next day, 500 conflagrations were consuming the large amounts of flammable materials that lay around.

The destruction that took place along Kobe's waterfront was another mirror image of the 1906 San Francisco earthquake—that of liquefaction. All along the waterfront zone of Kobe, extensive reclamation work had been performed for decades to provide space for shipping activities and warehouses. The widespread liquefaction that took place destroyed the roads leading to the waterfront installations, collapsed both housing and warehouses, and lowered the ground level across the whole area by several feet. A few buildings that had been erected on deeper geological formations remained intact. Liquefaction extended downward into the reclaimed areas as deep as 30 feet. In the wake of the thousands of aftershocks that followed the main quake, the wave movements in these deeper zones of liquefaction damaged several areas farther inland.

Minimum amounts of restoration took several months to complete. Gas and electrical supply lines had been so badly disrupted that even Japan's extremely efficient record system was incapable of determining which line belonged where. Officials had to interview individual family survivors, read mass media reports, and study a variety of telephone and printed records before reconnecting trunk lines. For the water lines, the available pressure initially was inadequate for identifying breaks in the system. When officials attempted to reach locations to examine conditions directly, they were held up by a total absence of roads—within the downtown part of Kobe, all the main streets were impassable. Before the water pipes could be reconnected, yet another hurdle had to be overcome; liquefied sand had to be removed from damaged pipes.

See Also: Great Kanto Earthquake, Japan (1923); Japan.

Further Reading

Gunn, A. M. (2014, 12 August). Kobe earthquake (1995). In *World geography: Understanding a changing world*. Santa Barbara, CA: ABC-CLIO.

Krafft, Katja (Katia), and Krafft, Maurice

Katja and Maurice Krafft arguably were the most active, experienced, and well-known volcanologists in the world throughout the 1970s and 1980s, and until the time of their death on June 3, 1991. Maurice Krafft was born March 26, 1946, in Mulhouse in the Alsace region of France. He became enamored with volcanoes during a family trip to Naples and Stromboli when he was seven years old. He became a member of the Geological Society of France at age 15, and chose to study geology first at the University of Besançon, then later at the University of Strasbourg. His wife Katja (née Conrad) was born April 17, 1942, in the nearby town of Guebwiller. Katja earned degrees in physics and chemistry at the University of Strasbourg. Maurice and Katja met on a bench at the university, and shared an instant connection. They married in 1970.

Maurice was known for his boisterous demeanor and his absolute dedication to his goals of documenting volcanic activity and educating the public about the hazards and beauty of volcanoes. Katja was soft-spoken but just as passionate about the study and documentation of volcanic behavior. They were a force of nature—with boundless energy and unlimited enthusiasm for their work. Together, the two became the world's first independent volcanologists. They held no university or government appointments. To fund their work, they wrote beautifully illustrated books and produced dramatic films of volcanic activity that were translated into multiple languages. During their careers, they became famous for being the first volcanologists on the scene of an eruption, no matter where in the world the eruption occurred. They structured their lives so they could drop everything and travel at a moment's notice. They often were notified by local scientists when a volcano began to show signs of an impending eruption. The Kraffts' body of work comprises 20 books, hundreds of thousands of still photographs, and hundreds of hours of film. Maurice in particular also spent a great deal of time lecturing.

The Kraffts often were called "daredevil" geologists because they frequently took greater risks to document eruptive phenomena than did other researchers. Although many people thought that the Kraffts were being irresponsible, Maurice and Katja were well aware of the risks they were taking. They weighed such risks against the potential benefit of learning something new about volcanic behavior, or capturing an event on film that they later could use to educate the public about volcanic hazards. One of the last film projects they finished was a pair of educational videos *Understanding Volcanic Hazards* and *Reducing Volcanic Risk*. The videos were designed to educate decision-making public officials about the scope of dangers communities face near active volcanoes and how to protect populations from volcanic risk. The project was sponsored by the International Association for Volcanology of the Chemistry of the Earth's Interior (IAVCEI) and the United Nations Educational, Scientific, and Cultural Organization (UNESCO).

In the spring of 1991, the Kraffts heard about relatively small eruptions taking place at Mount Unzen, Japan. The volcano was generating small pyroclastic flows. The Kraffts felt this situation was safe enough that they could approach the flows and obtain footage of this dangerous phenomenon. They knew the risks, and when asked about them, Maurice replied, "I am never afraid, because I have seen so much eruptions [sic] in 23 years that even if I die tomorrow, I don't care" (Auckland Museum, 2009). They filmed for several days from a vantage point well above the flows, then on June 3rd decided to change location. Unfortunately, the volcano produced a pyroclastic flow that was much larger than any of the preceding flows. The Kraffts, American volcanologist Harry Glicken, and the approximately 40 Japanese journalists that accompanied them were overcome by the pyroclastic flow and killed. Their bodies were recovered two days later.

Katja and Maurice Krafft were unique in the world of volcanology, and it is unlikely that any other scientists ever will approach their level of notoriety. IAVCEI established the Krafft Medal in their honor. It is awarded every four years to a volcanologist who has "shown altruism and dedication to the humanitarian and applied sides of volcanology and those who have made selfless contributions to the volcanological community" (IAVCEI, 2014). The University of Hawaii at Hilo established a fund in the Kraftt's name, which provides financial assistance to foreign students to attend the International Training Program in Volcano Monitoring Methods at the university's Center for the Study of Active Volcanoes.

See Also: Pyroclastic Materials; Unzen Eruption, Japan (1991–1995); Volcanic Hazards.

Further Reading

Auckland Museum. (2009, November 16). *Maurice and Katia Krafft.* [YouTube video]. Retrieved from https://www.youtube.com/watch?v=c5CAyaRIW8s

International Association of Volcanology and Chemistry of the Earth's Interior (IAVCEI). (2014, October 17). *Krafft Medal.* Retrieved from http://www.iavcei.org/IAVCEI _awards/kraft_IAVCEI.htm

Keller, J. (1992). Memorial for Katja and Maurice Krafft. *Bulletin of Volcanology 54*, 613–614.

University of Hawaii at Hilo. Center for the Study of Active Volcanoes. (2014, October 17). *Krafft Memorial Fund.* Retrieved from http://www.hilo.hawaii.edu/~csav/krafft/

Krakatau Eruption (also known as "Krakatoa" Eruption), Indonesia (1883)

Krakatau (or "Krakatoa," as it was known to Westerners until recently) is a volcano in the Sunda Strait between Java and Sumatra, the two largest islands of the Indonesian island chain. Prior to its infamous 1883 eruption, the volcano formed a single island with three major peaks. From north to south, these peaks were Perboewatan, Danan, and Rakata. Immediately following the 1883 eruption, only the dissected peak of Rakata remained. The eruption of Krakatau in August 1883 was one of the worst natural disasters of the Nineteenth Century. The eruption and accompanying events caused the deaths of more than 36,000 people, temporarily changed the global climate, and inspired people across the world to create classic works in both art and literature. This eruption was also one of the first well-documented disasters, due to a number of unique factors of time and place.

The eruption of Krakatau was incredibly well documented—perhaps better than any other volcanic eruption of the modern era up to that time, and for nearly two decades afterward. Of the many factors that enabled the rich and detailed descriptions of the eruption of 1883, the four most influential are the location of Krakatau in one of the world's busiest waterways; the existence of densely populated islands within sight of Krakatau; the presence of highly trained geologists and mining engineers in the vicinity of the eruption; and communications technology.

The Sunda Strait was then—and remains today—one of the world's busiest marine waterways. The Sunda Strait is the only passage between Java and Sumatra, the two largest islands in the densely populated nation of Indonesia. It also is the most commonly used shipping route between Europe and the Americas to the west

A plume of ash from Anak Krakatau, a volcanic island in the Sunda Straits between Java and Sumatra. (Alida Latham / DanitaDelimont.com Danita Delimont Photography/Newscom)

and Asia to the east. The Sunda Strait is 17 miles (27 kilometers) across at its narrowest. At the time of Krakatau's eruption, there were at least 10 ships within sight of Krakatau; giving each of these ships' captains an individual story based on his unique position and perspective of this eruption.

The population living within the influence of the direct effects of the eruption numbered in the hundreds of thousands. As a result, many people experienced the eruption and told their heartbreaking stories to the wider public through interviews with news media, official government reports, letters to friends and relatives, and personal diaries. Survivors told unbelievable stories of escape from terrifying and desperate situations.

Indonesia was a Dutch colony in 1883, and many Dutch government officials lived and worked in Indonesia. One of the most detailed land-based accounts of the eruption of 1883 comes from the diaries of Johanna Beyerinck, the wife of the Dutch Controller Willem Beyerinck. The Beyerinck family lived near the shore in Ketimbang, on the eastern tip of the island of Sumatra, at the time of the eruption. Those who lived in coastal areas of Sumatra nearest Krakatau experienced the worst of what the eruption delivered that awful day. Consequently, not only was Mrs. Beyerinck's account of the eruption articulate and heart-wrenching, she was also able to provide details of eruptive phenomena that others did not experience.

The Dutch long had recognized the potential for finding exploitable resources throughout Indonesia. As a result, several Dutch geologists and mining engineers lived and worked in Indonesia at the time of the Krakatau eruption. Mining engineer Dr. Rogier Verbeek had been living and working in the area since 1867, and knew both Krakatau and Sumatra quite well. He produced a map of Krakatau before the eruption that proved useful in making comparisons to the landscape of the island after the 1883 eruption. Dr. Verbeek wrote a detailed report of the eruption and its aftermath, which he published in 1885. His work included full-color chromolithographs of Krakatau before and after the eruption, black-and-white line drawings to illustrate the most dramatic effects of the eruption and its accompanying phenomena, detailed measurements of ash thicknesses, wave heights, particle sizes of volcanic debris, and areal extent of the destruction, estimates of death tolls, firsthand accounts of the events surrounding the eruption from survivors, chemical analyses of eruptive products (ash and rock), and comparisons with other known eruptions around the world. It was the most comprehensive study of its kind written at that time in history.

People living in today's world are accustomed to instant communication thanks to email, text messages, and the Internet. Communication before the mid-1800s, however, was quite a different matter. Newsworthy events often did not reach the public until days or weeks after they occurred because messengers on horseback were the most technologically advanced "communications networks" that existed. Telegraphs were put into service in the 1840s, however, and their ability to transmit information nearly instantaneously revolutionized the flow of information. Unfortunately, telegraph coverage at that time was limited, so very little of the world's population reaped the benefits of this ground-breaking technology. By 1865, however, telegraph wires traversed a significant enough portion of the world to be useful in intercontinental communication. Word of the 1883 eruption spread quickly to all corners of the globe thanks to the dedicated government telegraph operators in Indonesian ports such as Telok Betong, Ketimbang, Anjer, and Batavia.

Indonesia is a country that owes its entire existence to volcanoes. All of the more than 1,000 islands of Indonesia are, in fact, volcanoes; eruptions are a fact of life. As a result, the population of Indonesia acknowledges both the dangers and advantages of living in such an environment. Certainly some volcanic eruptions are dangerous and even deadly, but the volcanic ash they emit also provides fertile soil in which to grow crops including rice, fruit, vegetables, and spices. A swarm of earthquakes or a small ash eruption from one of the hundreds of known Indonesian volcanoes is not immediate cause for panic. The entire nation sits above an active subduction zone in which the Indian-Australian Plate is being forced beneath the Eurasian Plate. The whole region is prone to earthquakes and volcanic activity. That is why—in the early summer of 1883—most people who had spent any time at all in Indonesia were not at all alarmed when Krakatau began showing signs of activity.

The first activity recorded during the 1883 eruption cycle was noted in May of that year. Earthquakes were felt at First Point on the island of Java, 43 miles (70 kilometers) south-southwest of Krakatau, on May 9 and 10. Others were felt at Katimbang 25 miles (40 kilometers) north-northeast of Krakatau between May 15 and 20. The first small eruption occurred at 10:30 a.m. on May 20, 1883. It was observed by the crew of the German warship *Elisabeth*, and was documented by the ship's captain. According to Captain Hollmann, a white cloud rose vertically from the volcano for about half an hour, eventually reaching a height of about 36,000 feet (11,000 meters). Then the cloud began to spread horizontally, obscuring the otherwise clear blue sky. At about 4 p.m., the winds shifted and blew the ash cloud over the ship, dusting the ship with fine ash. The ash cloud followed the ship as it steamed onward, continuing through May 22. The captain also reported that the ash particles in the atmosphere gave the sun an azure blue color.

Throughout the late spring and into the summer of 1883, earthquakes shook homes and villages on either side of the Sunda Strait. Krakatau emitted small plumes of ash which often dusted towns and the decks of passing ships, and caused bothersome respiratory problems for both people and animals. The air smelled faintly like rotten eggs, a result of hydrogen sulfide (H_2S) emitted from Krakatau. Although most residents of the area paid little attention to Krakatau, Mrs. Johanna Beyerinck, a Dutch native and relative newcomer to Indonesia, was unsettled by the shaking of nearly constant earthquake activity. She was further disturbed by an incident in late May in which eight local fishermen came to visit her husband. They insisted, much to his surprise, that they had just come from Krakatau where the beach had split open at their feet, throwing up stones and ash. They fled as fast as they could. A short time later, their story was confirmed by two government officials who provided further information that the northernmost peak of Krakatau (Perboewatan) was also erupting "fire and smoke" (Simkin & Fiske, 1983). Through her journal writings, it is clear that Mrs. Beyerinck thought that she and her family were in danger.

The activity of Krakatau created a great deal of interest among the nearby population. On May 27, 1883, the steamship *Governor General Loudon* was chartered by the Netherlands-Indies Steamship Company to carry 86 passengers for a day trip to Krakatau. Among the tourists was a mining engineer, J. Schuurman. As the ship approached the island in the pre-dawn darkness, the passengers were treated to a view of a purple glow above the volcano, from which a "fire rain" fell. They noted as the sun came up that the island was devoid of vegetation, a rarity in this lush tropical environment. A layer of volcanic ash covered the island, giving it a somber and "angry" look. Adding to the angry look was a cloud of ash rising about 10,000 feet (3,000 meters) above the island. The captain of the ship allowed the passengers to go ashore for the day, where a number of brave souls, led by Mr. Schuurman, explored Perboewatan Crater. The ship returned to Batavia without incident. A short time later, Mr. Schuurman provided Dr. Rogier Verbeek with a description of the activity Schuurman witnessed, the rocks and volcanic ash he observed, and his measurements and observations of Perboewatan's crater. The only person to visit Krakatau after this was Captain H. J. G. Ferzenaar, Chief of the Surveying Brigade in Bantam. He went to the island on August 11 to determine whether a survey was feasible, and determined that conditions were too dangerous. Captain Ferzenaar, however, used his observations to create a sketch map of the island that provided the best topographic data available for making comparisons of the island's geography before and after the cataclysmic eruption of August 26–27.

Throughout August, Krakatau remained active. On August 26, activity increased dramatically, signaling the beginning of its paroxysmal eruption. A telegraph operator arrived on August 25 to take up his new position as telegraph-master in Anjer (Java) and reported a strong earthquake in the early afternoon of August 26. He met another telegraph operator that afternoon, and by 6:00 p.m. they noticed that the sky was unusually dark. They made contact with another individual near Batavia, who told them that the ground was shaking and asked if Krakatau was still in eruption. Shortly thereafter, the telegraph cable broke. The operator made arrangements for the cable to be repaired as soon as possible, and then he walked outside to investigate reports that a schooner had broken its mooring line. Much to his surprise, the telegraph master saw that the schooner and several small boats were being carried up the nearby river. The next day, as he visited people in town, he looked out to sea and saw an enormous wave in the distance, looking like a mountain rushing toward shore. He warned the other people in his presence, then turned and ran uphill as fast as he could go, finally collapsing as the wave retreated behind him. The tsunami destroyed many structures in town.

Another view of the same event came from a pilot that guided ships through the Sunda Strait, who emphasized the deafening explosions that shook the air and ground from Sunday, August 26, into Monday, August 27, as well as the dense ash cloud that drifted over his location. Although he was 25 miles (40 kilometers) from the mountain, also on the coast of Java, the pilot reported that the concussion and vibration from the constant shocks was terrifying. Ash from the eruption periodically blew toward his location, turning daylight into darkness. Even natives were panic-stricken. At night, a red glow was visible above the volcano, and the ground was shaking so severely people were afraid that their homes would collapse at any moment. On Monday morning some of the ash had cleared from the sky. To his surprise, at about 6 a.m. the pilot noticed a dark object traveling toward shore. He recognized it as a ridge of water and ran uphill. He saw houses being swept away and trees being overtaken by the wave. He was engulfed by the water and was saved only because he was swept within reach of a coconut palm tree, which he clung to for several minutes as he watched the water sweep away the city of Anjer. Thousands died in this part of the Java coast as a result of the tsunami.

Closest to the eruption were those aboard the British ship *Charles Bal*, which was under the command of Captain W. J. Watson. This ship was sailing through the strait en route to Hong Kong as the eruption began. The captain's log provides a detailed picture of the eruption's events from his vantage point to the east of Krakatau, in his log for August 26, 1883.

> At 2:30 p.m. noticed some agitation about the Point of Krakatoa; clouds or something being propelled with amazing velocity to the northeast. To us it looked like blinding rain, and had the appearance of a furious squall of ashen hue. At one shortened sail to topsails and foresail. At 5 p.m. the roaring noise continued and increased, darkness spread over the sky, and a hail of pumice stone fell on us, many pieces being of considerable size and quite warm. Had to cover up the skylights to save the glass, while feet and head had to be protected with boots and southwesters. About 6 p.m. the fall of larger stones ceased, but there continued a steady fall of a smaller kind, most blinding

to the eyes and covering the decks with 3 to 4 inches very speedily, while an intense blackness covered the sky and sea. Sailed on our course until we got what we thought was a sight of Fourth Point Light; then brought the ship to the wind, southwest, as we could not see any distance, and we knew not what might be in the straits, the night being a fearful one. . . . (Decker & Decker, 1998).

The log entry from August 27 contains even more frightful images.

From midnight to 4 a.m., the same impenetrable darkness continuing, the roaring of Krakatoa less continuous but more explosive in sound, the sky one second intense blackness and the next a blaze of fire; mastheads and yardarms studded with electrical glows and a peculiar pinky flame coming from clouds which seemed to touch the mastheads and yardarms. At 6 a.m., being able to make out the Java shore, set sail. Passed Anjer at 8:30 a.m., close enough in to make out the houses, but could see no movement of any kind. At 11:15 there was a fearful explosion in the direction of Krakatoa, now over 30 miles distant. We saw a wave rush right on to Button Island, apparently sweeping right over the south part and rising half way up the north and east sides. This we saw repeated twice, but the helmsman says he saw it once before we looked. The same waves seemed also to run right on to the Java shore. The sky rapidly covered in, by 11:30 a.m. we were inclosed in a darkness that might almost be felt. At the same time commenced a downpour of mud, sand, and I know not what. . . . At noon the darkness was so intense that we had to grope about the decks, and although speaking to each other on the poop, yet could not see each other. The horrible state and downpour of mud continued until 1:30 p.m., the roarings of the volcano and lightnings being something fearful. By 2 p.m. we could see the yards aloft, and the fall of mud ceased. Up to midnight the sky hung dark and heavy, a little sand falling at times, the roaring of the volcano very distinct although we were fully sixty-five or seventy miles northeast from it (Decker & Decker, 1998).

It is clear from Captain Watson's account that the ship's crew witnessed at least one set of tsunami waves as they washed ashore at Button Island and the Java shoreline. The captain, however, makes no mention of any effect of the tsunami on the ship; it was not tossed about or dragged ashore. This is common during the passage of tsunami underneath ships that are in deep water. The energy of a tsunami is distributed from the surface to the bottom of the ocean; therefore in deep water very little energy is contained in the upper parts of the water column. Consequently, those on a ship do not notice the tsunami passing beneath them. The *Charles Bal* also experienced heavy tephra fall and a strange phenomenon of volcanic eruptions in which static electricity within the ash cloud creates odd electrical effects such as sprites and ball lightning (which also is called "Saint Elmo's fire").

As frightening as events were on the coast of Java and shipboard within the strait, those living on the Sumatran shoreline experienced even more deadly and terrifying events. Sumatra is closer to Krakatau than is Java, and is located downwind of the volcano. The residents of Sumatra suffered not only the effects of the tsunami, but also heavy ash fall that caused collapse of roofs. Krakatau also unleashed immense pyroclastic flows that traveled unprecedented distances northeast across the Sunda Strait and reaching the island of Sumatra, where they killed and injured thousands of people. Mrs. Johanna Beyerinck, wife of the Dutch Controller, wrote a long and detailed account of what her family experienced during the eruption. She and her family were closer to Krakatau than were any other survivors who wrote accounts of their experiences, with the lone exception of Captain Watson of the ship *Charles Bal*. The Beyerinck family experienced the full range of horrors that Krakatau had to offer.

At the onset of the eruption, Mrs. Beyerinck was at home in Katimbang with her three children and the family's servants. Her husband was at work, but sent word that she and the children should have a good meal, dress warmly, and prepare for immediate flight from the coastal area. She was only too happy to comply. Pumice had been falling for hours, and the rumble of the mountain as it erupted was unnerving. Mrs. Beyerinck desperately wanted to escape. The servants prepared a meal for her and the children, but she was so worried she could not eat. During the meal, a servant came in and told her that the sea had gone far, far away. She did not understand how the sea could do such a thing, but his story was soon corroborated by several natives who came up to the house shortly thereafter. As the family waited in the house for Mr. Beyerinck to return, they heard a roaring sound approaching the house at lightning speed. Mrs. Beyerinck's hair stood on end and she immediately gathered the children and servants together, herding them upstairs and to the back of the house. The wave reached the house but went only as far as the backyard. Mr. Beyerinck and his clerk were only able to survive the wave by climbing a coconut tree. When the wave receded, Mr. Beyerinck returned to the house in a panic. The staircase in the house was gone, and everyone was upstairs. He called to them to jump so he could catch them. They turned the animals loose and began their journey to a house they owned in the hills, presumably away from the dangers of the erupting volcano. They were accompanied by about 3,000 terrified islanders as they began their journey around 8:30 p.m. on Sunday.

The usual route to the hill house began along a coastal road. Because of the dangers the volcano posed, however, they could not take the usual route. They walked through a rice paddy full of water, then through a forest where no path existed, and sank into knee-deep mud. At one point, Mrs. Beyerinck reached up and felt her neck and, much to her horror, found that it was covered in leeches. Her throat was dry and irritated, likely as a result of inhaling volcanic ash and gases. It was a miserable, exhausting trip. They reached the hill house shortly before dawn on Monday. About 16 people settled inside the house and the remaining 3,000 people lay on the ground outside.

Unfortunately for the people at the hill farm, there was little relief in sight. At 10:02 a.m., the loudest sound ever recorded issued from Krakatau. It was clearly heard in Singapore, nearly 3,000 miles (4,700 kilometers) away. The explosion ruptured ear drums and knocked people off their feet. The world went temporarily silent for those at the hill farm. Mrs. Beyerinck describes what happened next.

Someone burst in shouting "shut the doors, shut the doors." Suddenly it was pitch dark. The last thing I saw was the ash being pushed up through the cracks in the floorboards, like a fountain.

I turned to my husband and heard him say in despair "Where is the knife? The knife [is] on the table. I will cut all our wrists, then we shall be sooner released from our suffering." The knife could not be found.

I felt a heavy pressure, throwing me to the ground. Then it seemed as if all the air was being sucked away and I could not breathe. Large lumps clattered down on my head, my back and my arms. Each lump was larger than the others. I could not stand.

I don't think I lost consciousness for I heard the natives praying and crying "Allah il Allah."

I felt people rolling over me. I was kicked and I felt a foot on part of my body.

No sound came from my husband or children. Only part of my brain could have been working for I didn't realize I had been burnt and everything which came in contact with me was hot ash, mixed with moisture. I remember thinking, I want to get up and go outside. But I could not. My back was powerless.

After much effort I did finally manage to get to my feet but I could not straighten my back or neck. I felt as if a heavy iron chain was fastened around my neck and was pulling me downwards (Simkin and Fiske, 1983).

Mrs. Beyerinck stumbled outside and made it to the edge of the forest before her husband found her and carried her back to the hut. One third of the natives around the hut died of burns, and the skin of the survivors was blistered and burned. A servant brought Mrs. Beyerinck her youngest child—an infant—who died in her arms. The people in southeast Sumatra had experienced the outer edge of a massive pyroclastic flow that had traveled approximately 25 miles (40 kilometers) from Krakatau. It was the only site on land that experienced this horror during the eruption. The Beyerinck family was found and rescued by Captain Hoen, commander of the Kederie, on September 1. He described them as being in deplorable condition, covered with burns. He was not at all sure they would make it to the hospital alive but, miraculously, all four remaining Beyerincks recovered fully from their injuries.

By any measure available, the August 26–27, 1883, eruption of Krakatau was a horrific disaster. Approximately 36,000 people lost their lives, most of them in coastal areas of Sumatra and Java. The pyroclastic flows, which were contained to the southeast part of Sumatra closest to Krakatau, killed about 2,000 people. Miles of shoreline were swept clean of villages, fields, government buildings, and wildlife. The island of Krakatau was mostly gone. Only the southern half of Rakata peak remained after the eruption. The enormous volume of material—an estimated 4 cubic miles (17 cubic kilometers)—which erupted from the magma chamber beneath the volcano left the top of the mountain unsupported. Scientists believe that the last thunderous explosion at 10:02 a.m. on August 27 was the sound of

Krakatau breaking apart and the top of the mountain collapsing into the magma chamber below, creating a vast caldera.

Pumice rafts floated on the ocean and followed the currents for at least 21 months after the eruption. Pumice reached the coast of Africa in May 1885. Although mostly composed of small pieces, the rafts reached several acres in size and remained that large for months. Some larger pieces of pumice became home to crabs and sheltered small fish. Large volumes of ash and sulfuric acid aerosol were injected into the atmosphere. As a result, temperatures worldwide were cooler than normal for a full year after the eruption. Additionally, sunsets were eerily colored for months—and reports of extremely colorful sunsets came from Australia, Europe, Hawaii, North America, and Asia. Sunsets were so brilliantly red on the east coast of the United States that people feared there were large fires raging.

Krakatau remains today an active volcano. There was a period of quiescence at the site of the 1883 eruption from 1883 until 1927. In 1927, a new island breached the ocean surface roughly where the peak of Perboewatan once stood. It was christened Anak Krakatau, "Child of Krakatau." This small island has been growing in area and height since its first appearance, at times losing ground to the waves of the Sunda Strait. Krakatau is in a rebuilding phase and will likely not erupt with the violence of the 1883 eruption for thousands of years. But Anak Krakatau is a stark reminder that Krakatau remains a very active volcano.

See Also: Caldera; Indonesia; Pyroclastic Flow; Pyroclastic Materials; Tsunami.

Further Reading

Decker, R. W., & Decker, B. (1998). *Volcanoes* (3rd ed.). New York: W.H. Freeman and Company.

Simkin, T., & Fiske, R. S. (1983). *Krakatau 1883: The volcanic eruption and its effects.* Washington, DC: Smithsonian Institution Press.

U.S. Geological Survey. Cascades Volcano Observatory. *Description: 1883 eruption of Krakatau.* (United States Geological Survey, Krakatau, 2012). Retrieved August 20, 2012, from http://vulcan.wr.usgs.gov/Volcanoes/Indonesia/description_krakatau_1883 _eruption.html

Winchester, S. (2003). *Krakatoa.* New York: HarperCollins Publishers.

L

Lahar

Lahar is an Indonesian term that refers to a mixture of rock fragments and water flowing down the slopes of a volcano, often in river valleys. The lahar can be hot or cold, and it can occur before, during, or after an eruption at a volcano. Lahars are seen on composite volcanoes but rarely, if ever, are seen on other volcano types. This is because lahars require steep slopes and large quantities of water, which are much more likely to be present on composite volcanoes than on shield volcanoes or cinder cones. Lahars often resemble wet concrete. They can be dense enough to carry large boulders, trees, and homes, and can wipe out bridges and roads.

During a volcanic eruption, a lahar often is triggered by output of hot volcanic ash which melts a snow or ice cap at the summit of a tall, steep volcano. The volcanic ash mixes with water from the melting snow and ice, as well as with other debris such as pumice and rocks. The mass begins to move downhill and often invades a river valley. Additional water is incorporated into the lahar from the river, as is additional solid debris such as soil, old volcanic ash deposits, rocks, and trees. This results in the lahar growing larger as it flows downhill, occasionally up to ten times its initial size. As a lahar moves away from the summit of the volcano, however, it eventually loses energy and deposits sediment, thus becoming smaller. Lahars, however, can be swift and deadly even miles away from a volcano's summit. The Electron Mudflow (lahar) from Mount Rainier's last eruption, for example, traveled 60 miles (100 kilometers) downstream and into the Puget Sound lowlands. After 60 miles, it was still 98 feet (30 meters) deep. Lahars also can happen in the absence of an ongoing volcanic eruption. The area around Mount Pinatubo in the Philippines experienced lahars for more than 10 years after the eruption of that volcano in 1991. Whenever heavy rains would fall, streams would swell and erode the volcanic ash in their banks.

One of the most deadly lahars in history occurred in Colombia in 1985. The volcano Nevado del Ruiz erupted in November of that year. Although the eruption was rather small, it melted snow and ice near the vent. The melt water mixed with volcanic ash and formed a lahar. The lahar grew as it sped downhill and it eventually buried the town of Armero. Unfortunately, the townspeople had received no information about lahar hazards, and no evacuation order was given. That night more than 23,000 people died. The volcanology community galvanized after this tragedy. The U.S. Geological Survey started its Volcano Disaster Assistance

Program in an effort to help nations deal with volcanic crises before they turn into disasters. Maurice and Katia Krafft began work on a set of videos called "Understanding Volcanic Hazards," which were made to educate public officials and people at risk about the hazards they could be facing. Advances were made in volcano monitoring techniques, including the invention of lahar detection systems that could be installed in river valleys leading away from composite volcanoes. These lahar detection systems have been used successfully in many areas of the world, including the Philippines, where Mount Pinatubo caused similar chaos for a decade.

See Also: Composite Volcano; Krafft, Katja (Katia), and Krafft, Maurice; Nevado del Ruiz, Colombia; Pinatubo, Mount, Eruption, Philippines (1991); Pyroclastic Materials; Rainier, Mount, Washington, United States; Volcano Disaster Assistance Program.

Further Reading

U.S. Geological Survey. (2014, May 12). Lahars and their effects. Retrieved from http://volcanoes.usgs.gov/hazards/lahar/

U.S. Geological Survey. (2014, May 12). Significant lahars at Mount Rainier. Retrieved from http://volcanoes.usgs.gov/volcanoes/mount_rainier/mount_rainier_geo_hist_79.html

Lamington, Mount, Eruption, Papua New Guinea (1951)

The eruption of Mount Lamington in Papua New Guinea is notable because of its surprise factor. Prior to January of 1951, it was not properly understood that Mount Lamington was a volcano. There were no stories from indigenous people to indicate that they knew of the mountain's volcanic nature, and it had not been investigated properly by subsequent settlers. The mountain had a semicircle of peaks that surrounded the head of a valley opening to the north. On January 15, 1951, people who lived in the area noticed that there were fresh landslide scars on the inner faces of the semi-circle of peaks. Later that day, residents saw that the area just below the peaks was steaming. In the days that followed, the wispy clouds of steam turned into a vigorous plume of vapor accompanied by volcanic ash. The ash column rose at least 25,000 feet (7,600 meters) above the mountain's summit. Earthquakes occurred nearly constantly. People held onto ropes tied to the trees so the earthquakes would not knock them off their feet. At night, eerie lights were visible in the ash plumes. The smell of sulfur became overpowering. A few people became frightened and left the area, but the majority of people stayed.

On January 21, at 10:40 a.m., a great explosion occurred. A large vertical column of ash and gases burst vertically into the air. Unfortunately, either the velocity of the material was not great enough to allow it to rise buoyantly into the atmosphere or it was unusually dense. The result was that the plume collapsed and hugged the ground, racing downhill through the gap in the peaks. The pyroclastic flow destroyed everything within an area of 68 square miles (176 square kilometers), including the town of Higaturu and several small villages nearby. Approximately 3,000 people died in the eruption. The following day, Australian volcanologist G.A.M. Taylor arrived at Mount Lamington and carefully documented what he found. His report remains one of the classic studies of this type of eruption. Although there was a great deal of criticism of the local government for its lack of warning and evacuation orders, local officials who died in the eruption were on record saying they thought the town of Higaturu was in no danger because it was 8 miles (12.8 kilometers) from the volcano.

Mount Lamington went on to erupt for more than five additional years. During that time, it built a large and steep dacite lava dome over the vent. Periodically, material would break off the steep-sided dome and tumble downhill. This created minor pyroclastic flows throughout the dome-building phase of the eruption. The eruption was declared to be "over" in 1956.

See Also: Pyroclastic Materials; Volcanic Hazards.

Further Reading

Hawaiian Volcano Observatory. (2014, May 7). *A 1951 tragedy in Papua New Guinea provides an important reference in the volcanologic literature.* Retrieved from http://hvo.wr.usgs.gov/volcanowatch/archive/2008/08_09_25.html

Seach, J. (2014, May 7). *Mt Lamington Volcano.* Retrieved from http://www.volcanolive.com/lamington.html

Lassen Peak, California, United States

Lassen Peak is the southernmost volcanic area in the Cascade Range on the west coast of the United States. It is located in a remote area of northern California. The Lassen Volcanic Center includes Lassen Peak—a large volcanic dome—as well as a number of smaller volcanic domes, cinder cones, mud pots, and hot springs. Lassen Peak last erupted between 1914 and 1917. Prior to the eruption of Mount St. Helens in 1980, this was the most recent eruption in the Cascades.

The Lassen Volcanic Center has been active in various locations for 600,000 years. The first stage of volcanic activity occurred between 600,000 years ago and 400,000 years ago. This stage of activity built a cone which scientists call the "Brokeoff Volcano." The Brokeoff Volcano was extensively eroded by glaciers during multiple ice ages. What was left behind was a large central depression surrounded by four peaks: Brokeoff Mountain, Mount Diller, Mount Conard, and Diamond Peak. Near the time that activity ceased at Brokeoff Volcano, the character of volcanic activity changed. Brokeoff Volcano was a composite volcano that

Lassen Peak, a volcano composed of overlapping lava domes. Domes are visible in the photo as rocky patches on the volcano's slopes. (Custom Medical Stock Photo/Newscom)

erupted primarily basalt and andesite lavas. The more recent phase of volcanic activity was characterized by more explosive eruptions that produced dacite and rhyolite lava domes. This type of activity continues through the present time at Lassen Peak and in surrounding areas.

The most recent eruption of Lassen Peak began on May 30, 1914. Prior to the beginning of this eruption the peak had been dormant for approximately 27,000 years. The main mode of eruption between May 30, 1914, and early May of 1915, was steam explosions (phreatic eruption). As magma rose toward the surface beneath the volcano it heated groundwater. As the groundwater flashed to steam, it caused explosions. More than 180 relatively small phreatic eruptions occurred in the initial year-long phase of the eruption. The eruptions blasted out a 1,000-foot (305-meter) wide crater near the summit of Lassen Peak.

On May 14, 1915, people observed a change in the eruption. For the first time, glowing blocks of lava were seen bouncing down the side of the volcano. They were visible from up to 20 miles (32 kilometers) away. A dacite dome was growing within the volcano's new crater. Five days later, another phreatic eruption blew apart much of the new dome and created a second crater at the top of Lassen Peak. Hot rocks fell on the snow-covered summit. This generated an avalanche of snow and hot volcanic rock. As the rocks broke into smaller pieces and melted the snow, huge volumes of water were released and a lahar flooded the Hat Creek Valley, 7 miles (11 kilometers) downstream from the volcano. Additional flooding affected communities up to 31 miles (50 kilometers) downstream. Six vacation cabins were destroyed, and the few residents that were in the cabins at the time escaped with only minor injuries. That night, additional dacite lava was erupted and flowed 1,000 feet (305 meters) down the northeast and west flanks of the mountain.

The volcano's climactic eruption occurred on May 22, 1915, after two days of relative quiet. At that time, a powerful eruption sent a column of ash, pumice, and gases more than 30,000 feet (9,100 meters) into the atmosphere. The ash column was visible from the city of Eureka, California, located 150 miles (240 kilometers) to the west of Lassen Peak. Part of the column collapsed, sending pyroclastic flows down the northeast slope of the volcano. The area of destruction was the same vicinity that had been struck by the lahar less than three days earlier. Lahars flowed down several valleys leading away from the summit. Fine ash fell as far away as Winnemucca, Nevada, 200 miles (320 kilometers) to the east. The volcano continued to produce phreatic eruptions until 1917. Steam vents could be found in the crater until the 1950s, but are quiet today. Other geothermal features, however, still exist on and near the mountain. Active steam vents, hot springs, and boiling mud pots are still found within Lassen Volcanic National Park.

See Also: Andesite; Basalt; Dacite; Lahar; Lava Dome; Pyroclastic Flow; Rhyolite.

Further Reading

Clynne, M. A. (1992). Lassen, California. In Wood, C. A. & Kienle, J. (Eds.). *Volcanoes of North America, United States and Canada.* Cambridge: Cambridge University Press.

Clynne, M. A., Christiansen, R. L., Felger, T. J., Stuaffer, P. H., & Hendley II, J. W. (2014, October 18). *Eruptions of Lassen Peak, California, 1914–1917.* (U.S. Geological Survey Fact Sheet 173-98). Retrieved from http://pubs.usgs.gov/fs/1998/fs173-98/

Lava Dome

A lava dome is a rounded, steep-sided mound of lava formed over a volcanic vent. It is formed of thick, viscous lava such as rhyolite or dacite, which is unable to flow long distances from where it is erupted. Lava domes typically are formed on composite volcanoes, but occasionally can form independent of a large cone. Lava domes grow in two ways: exogenous growth and endogenous growth. Exogenous growth occurs when lava makes its way to the surface and then piles up on the outside of the dome. Endogenous growth occurs when a lava dome grows from the inside. Lava never makes it to the surface of the lava dome, and instead becomes trapped on the inside of the dome. Over time, endogenous growth makes the dome look as if it is inflating like a balloon.

Dome growth can happen at almost any stage of a volcanic eruption. It can occur prior to a major explosive eruption, when an old plug of magma is forced upward. This occurred prior to the catastrophic eruption of Mount Pinatubo in the Philippines in 1991. Typically, in this case the dome is blasted apart by a later eruption.

Domes also often grow after major explosive eruptions, when most of the gas pressure in the magma plumbing system has been relieved. Gas pressure can build again, and the dome could be destroyed by an explosive eruption, but then begin to rebuild again. This was the case during the 1980–1986 dome-building phase of the

Mount St. Helens eruption. Alternately, a continuously active volcano in its dome-building stage can produce deadly pyroclastic flows as parts of the lava dome break apart and tumble down steep volcanic slopes. Pyroclastic flows formed in this way at Unzen Volcano in Japan were responsible for the deaths of three respected volcanologists and 40 members of the press in 1991.

The third stage in which dome growth can occur is at the end of an eruption cycle. In this case, very little new magma is recharging the magma chamber below a volcano, but what little magma is present is pushed to the surface due to minor amounts of gas pressure. In this case, there is little danger of the volcano erupting violently enough to destroy the lava dome. Instead, dome growth simply slows and ceases with very little fanfare. The 2004–2009 dome-building eruption of Mount St. Helens was of this type. Other volcanoes with noteworthy dome-building eruptions include: Santiaguito Dome on Santa Maria Volcano in Guatemala; Novarupta at Katmai National Park and Preserve, Alaska; Lassen Peak, Mount Shasta, and Glacier Peak in the Cascade Range on the west coast of North America; Soufriere Hills on the Caribbean island of Montserrat; Mont Pelée on the Caribbean island of Martinique; and Unzen Volcano in Japan.

See Also: Dacite; Rhyolite; St. Helens, Mount, Washington, United States; Unzen Eruption, Japan (1991–1995).

Further Reading

U.S. Geological Survey. Volcano Hazards Program. (2014, May 6). *Photo glossary: Lava dome.* Retrieved from http://volcanoes.usgs.gov/images/pglossary/LavaDome.php

Lava Tube

A lava tube is a feature most often found in pahoehoe-type basalt lava flows. A lava tube is formed when a lava channel that is carrying lava away from a vent crusts over. It does this because the air is much cooler than the surface of the lava flow. A crust forms on the flowing lava, creating a solid outer crust with molten lava flowing just beneath the surface. A tube-shaped structure forms and lava continues to move downhill within the tube system.

Lava tubes can be quite long, depending on the terrain of the volcano and the temperature and viscosity of the lava. On the Hawaiian Islands, active lava tube systems more than 10 miles long are not uncommon. They form near the vent where a volcano is erupting. As lava channels form, they soon are roofed over and become lava tubes. This process continues as lava flows advance, eventually forming tubes several miles long and leading from vent to ocean.

The formation of lava tubes actually assists lava in traveling far from its source vent. Lava tubes are formed of hardened rock. Rock is an excellent thermal insulator. Therefore, anywhere lava is traveling in a lava tube, the molten lava is insulated so well it will not lose much heat to the air. It is a common occurrence

Ape Cave, a lava tube in Mount St. Helens National Volcanic Monument. (Kevin Schafer/ Minden Pictures/Newscom)

for a lava flow to lose only a few degrees of temperature along the entire length of a 10-mile long tube system, as long as new lava continues to erupt and there are few holes (or skylights) in the top of the lava tube. In addition to skylights, lava tubes have other interesting features. Where lava drips from a ceiling it is possible to have small stalactites. It even is possible to get stalagmites on the floor of a lava tube when lava leaks into the tube from above after the tube is clear of flowing lava. If lava flows at a constant level in the tube for any length of time, it is possible to get a line on the wall of the tube at that level. This is called a "bathtub ring."

Although lava tubes are formed in a very different way than typical caves such as Mammoth Caves in Kentucky or Carlsbad Caverns in New Mexico, old lava tubes are caves and are important recreational areas for spelunkers or cave explorers. In the past, lava tubes have been used as dwellings, animal dens, and burial chambers, as well as places to store food and collect water. Old lava tubes have served ceremonial purposes in some cultures as well. Lava tubes open to the public exist in many locations throughout the world. In the United States, they can be found in Hawaii Volcanoes National Park, Newberry National Volcanic Monument in Oregon, the Ape Caves at Mount St. Helens National Volcanic Monument in Washington, and Lava Beds National Monument in California. They also can be found in other areas that have pahoehoe lava fields.

See Also: Basalt; Pahoehoe.

Further Reading

U.S. Geological Survey. Volcano Hazards Program. (2014, May 6). *Description: Lava tubes and lava tube caves.* Retrieved from http://vulcan.wr.usgs.gov/Glossary/LavaTubes/framework.html

U.S. Geological Survey. Volcano Hazards Program. (2014, May 6). *Volcano Hazards Program Photo Glossary. Lava tube.* Retrieved from http://volcanoes.usgs.gov/images/pglossary/LavaTube.php

Lehmann, Inge

Inge Lehmann was born on May 13, 1888, in the Østerbro district of Copenhagen, Denmark. Her father, Alfred, was a professor of psychology at the University of Copenhagen where he was a pioneer in experimental psychology. Young Inge received an unconventional education for a girl of the late Nineteenth Century. Her parents enrolled her at a school run by Hannah Adler, who was an aunt of Neils Bohr. The school treated boys and girls equally in both work and play, which was rare at the time. Lehmann showed an aptitude at an early age for mathematics, and her teacher sometimes challenged Inge with special problems to solve. Although her parents were worried that she was not strong enough for this extra work, Inge later remarked that her parents must not have understood that she would have been stronger had she not been so bored with her school work.

Lehmann graduated from high school in 1906, and entered the University of Copenhagen in the fall of 1907, intending to study mathematics. She spent time studying abroad at Cambridge University in England despite undue restrictions she felt were "inflicted" on her simply because of her gender. She took time off from her studies between December 1911 and the fall of 1918. She graduated in the summer of 1920. Her work in seismology began in 1925, when she began working for a professor who was installing seismographs in Copenhagen and Greenland. She was largely self-educated in the field of seismology. Lehmann enjoyed it enough that she chose a seismological topic when she wrote her thesis for her graduate degree in geodesy. She graduated with her master's degree in 1928. Immediately after graduation, Lehmann was appointed chief of the seismological department in the Royal Danish Geodetic Institute. She held that position until her retirement from the Institute in 1953, at the age of 65.

Seismology was an uncommon career in Denmark, which is a country with few earthquakes. Nonetheless, Lehmann was responsible for keeping instruments running and well maintained, and for interpreting seismograms so she could compile station bulletins and forward them to the International Seismological Summary office in England for publication. Although research was neither expected nor encouraged, Lehmann found she had a talent for seismological research. In the early 1930s, Lehmann recognized anomalies in the expected travel times of seismic waves from an earthquake in New Zealand to her stations in Denmark and Greenland. At that time, scientists believed that the earth had a mantle and a homogeneous core. Through her research Lehmann found evidence for a differentiated core, which included a liquid outer core and a solid inner core. She published this information in 1936 and it was finally confirmed conclusively in 1970.

Lehmann enjoyed a long and distinguished career in seismology. She studied with scientists throughout Europe and North America during her years with the Royal Danish Geodetic Institute. Some of her most scientifically productive and collaborative years, however, came after her retirement. The advent of the Cold War led to unexpected research opportunities in seismology in the 1960s and beyond. A conference of seismological experts was convened in 1958 to determine the capacity of seismology to detect clandestine nuclear explosions. The conference report was dire primarily because of a lack of standardized equipment for recording seismic waves from such explosions. This finding led to an influx of funds for the Worldwide Standardized Seismographic Network. Copenhagen was the site of one station in this network. Data were freely communicated within the seismological community, therefore Lehmann and other seismologists had new and better-quality data than they had ever had for studying the interior of the earth. Lehmann found evidence for seismological boundaries within the earth at 137 miles (220 kilometers) and 249 miles (400 kilometers) in widespread areas of the planet, and published this information in the early 1960s.

Lehmann continued to work well into her seventies. She was honored by the American Geophysical Union for her discovery of the boundary between the outer core and inner core on the fiftieth anniversary of that revelation. The organization held a symposium in her honor. In 1988, on the occasion of her 100th birthday, Lehmann's friends and supporters officially proposed naming the boundary between the inner and outer core in her honor. It is now named the Lehmann Discontinuity. In 1996, the same organization established the Inge Lehmann Medal for outstanding contributions toward the understanding of the structure, composition, and/or dynamics of the earth's mantle and core. Inge Lehmann died on February 21, 1993, at age 104.

See Also: Earth Structure; Seismology.

Further Reading

American Museum of Natural History. (2014, May 6). *Inge Lehmann: Discoverer of the earth's inner core*. Retrieved from http://www.amnh.org/education/resources/rfl/web /essaybooks/earth/p_lehmann.html

Bolt, B. A. (2014, May 6). Inge Lehmann. Retrieved from http://www.physics.ucla .edu/~cwp/articles/bolt.html

Loma Prieta Earthquake, California, United States (1989)

The Loma Prieta earthquake rocked California's San Francisco Bay Area on October 17, 1989, killing 63 people, injuring 3,757 people, and leaving more than 12,000 people homeless. At the time it was the costliest natural disaster in U.S. history, causing more than $6 billion in damages. The magnitude 6.9 (on the Richter scale) quake struck at 5:04 p.m. and lasted 15 seconds—during which freeways collapsed and the entire city of San Francisco lost power. This was the first major earthquake in the area since the Great San Francisco Earthquake of 1906, which had a magnitude of 7.8.

The quake's epicenter was near Loma Prieta peak in the Santa Cruz Mountains, about 9 miles (14.5 kilometers) northeast of the city of Santa Cruz and 60 miles (96.5 kilometers) southeast of San Francisco. The earthquake resulted from a major slip between the Pacific and North American tectonic plates, which are two of the major plates that make up the earth's crust. The 1906 quake occurred along the same fault line—the San Andreas Fault—releasing the pressure created by the two plates constantly pushing against one another. Little seismic activity occurred during subsequent decades. Pressure again built up, however, and the plates finally slipped—causing the 1989 quake, which ruptured the fault line from a depth of 11 miles (18 kilometers) up to 22 miles (35 kilometers). A magnitude 5.2 aftershock struck in the same spot just 37 minutes after the initial quake.

The Loma Prieta quake was most intense in the mountains north of Santa Cruz and nearby areas. Near the epicenter, however, the densely populated urban areas of San Francisco and Oakland suffered about half of the total monetary damage and more than 70% of associated deaths. The deadliest incident was the collapse of part of the Cypress Freeway in Oakland, which killed 42 people—two-thirds of the earthquake's total death toll. The Marina District of San Francisco also was heavily damaged. Both the Cypress Freeway and the Marina District had been built on soft ground, composed mainly of sand or mud, which liquefied under the force of the quake and caused the land to buckle.

As the ground shook, water rushed out of Monterey Bay's north end and caused the sea level to drop three feet (1 meter) at Santa Cruz, only to form a four-foot (1.2 meter) tsunami that washed over the city of Monterey at the south end of the bay. The tsunami wave traveled from Santa Cruz to Monterey in 20 minutes. A section of the Bay Bridge connecting San Francisco and Oakland collapsed, Interstate 280 sustained major damage, and the Embarcadero Freeway along the waterfront was virtually destroyed. At least 27 fires broke out. The entire city of San Francisco went dark for the first time since the 1906 quake; power was not fully restored for three days. Emergency telephone service also was affected when a fire broke out in the city's 911 center. In the ensuing chaos, sporadic looting occurred.

The 1989 World Series of baseball between cross-bay rivals the San Francisco Giants and the Oakland Athletics also was affected by the disaster. The quake struck just four minutes into pre-game activities for Game 3 of the series at Candlestick Park in San Francisco. More than 60,000 spectators already had packed the stadium when the earth began to shake; but the building held up, and no one was injured. Officials quickly announced that the game would be postponed, and the following day Major League Baseball officials announced that the rest of the championship series would be delayed until October 27.

The Loma Prieta quake exposed the vulnerability of California's major urban areas to such natural disasters and prompted the U.S. Geological Survey (USGS) and local officials to review earthquake safety standards. In subsequent years, the USGS has focused more on the effects of earthquakes in urban areas, developing computer models to reassess when and where powerful quakes might occur. San Francisco and Oakland officials also reviewed and revised building codes for construction on soft or unstable land.

See Also: Northridge Earthquake, California, United States (1994); San Francisco Earthquake, California, United States (1906); United States of America.

Further Reading

Loma Prieta earthquake (1989). (2014, 12 August). In *World geography: Understanding a changing world*. Santa Barbara, CA: ABC-CLIO.

M

Magma

Magma is the molten rock found below the surface of the earth. Once magma reaches the surface of the earth, it is called lava. The two terms often are used interchangeably, but in the strictest of definitions the name depends on where the molten rock is located. Magma is formed when a small portion of the earth's upper mantle melts. Magma then rises through the remaining mantle and crust. In the crust, the magma can stop rising and cool in place, or it can rise to the surface and erupt as lava onto the surface of the earth through a volcanic vent.

Magma is formed at varying depths in the earth's mantle. The mantle is overwhelmingly solid, however, and there is no liquid layer in the mantle that all volcanoes tap into to feed their eruptions. Melting is not commonplace in the mantle. It occurs in small pockets due to one of three factors. One event that can cause magma to form is a localized increase in temperature. The earth gets hotter with increasing depth, and a corresponding increase in pressure keeps the earth's crust and mantle solid. If the temperature is increased in a small area by a hot spot, then small pockets of mantle can start melting. This melted mantle rises to the surface to form a volcano.

A second factor that can cause magma to be formed is a decrease in pressure. This happens in areas where two lithospheric plates are diverging, or moving away from each other. Divergent plates therefore are the only places where this pressure decrease occurs. Recall that the earth's temperature increases with depth. As long as there is a corresponding increase in pressure, then rocks remain solid. If pressure is removed through the thinning of overlying lithospheric plates, then the underlying mantle begins to melt and well up to fill the space between the two plates. In this way, large magma chambers are formed beneath mid-ocean ridges and continental rift zones. Volcanic eruptions are common, and new oceanic lithosphere is created.

The third condition which enables magma to be formed is when water is introduced into the mantle. This happens in the specific case of subduction of oceanic lithosphere. Oceanic lithosphere usually spends millions of years beneath the ocean where it becomes saturated with seawater. When subduction occurs, this slab of seawater-saturated rock is shoved into the mantle. Heat from the surrounding environment causes water to start migrating from the oceanic lithosphere into the surrounding mantle. The result is introduction of water into the mantle. Water has the ability to considerably reduce the melting temperature of a rock. Thus, the areas above subduction zones are favorable locations for formation of magma and thus formation of volcanic island or mountain chains.

Although at the surface lava comes in many varieties including basalt, andesite, dacite, and rhyolite, at its point of origin in the mantle all magma essentially is a low-silica form of basalt. Magma could change in composition due to the processes of assimilation of melt, magma differentiation, or magma mixing. As the magma rises through overlying mantle and crust, it can melt surrounding rocks and incorporate some of that melted rock into the magma. The rocks from the crust that are melted invariably are more silica-rich than the initial melt. The incorporation of the silica-rich material into the magma causes the magma to become more silica-rich as well, pushing the magma more toward andesitic composition. Magma differentiation, also known as crystal fractionation or fractional crystallization, is a means of changing magma composition through crystallization of minerals. Magma is composed of many elements. When the magma begins to cool as it sits in a chamber under the earth's surface, it triggers the formation of certain minerals. The minerals take specific elements out of the liquid melt and lock them into solid crystals. This process alters the composition of the liquid melt. The first minerals to form typically are those that are very low in silica. Thus, the minerals take elements other than silica out of the molten magma and leave silica behind. In this way, the magma becomes more silica-rich. Extreme cases of magma differentiation yield dacites and rhyolites.

The process of magma mixing happens when a magma body is sitting in a magma chamber, and fresh magma from below invades the chamber. This process tends to make magma less silica-rich, pushing it toward the basaltic end of the composition continuum. Disturbance of a magma chamber with fresh basalt from below is thought to be a contributor to many volcanic eruptions. At Mount Pinatubo in the Philippines, for instance, a major earthquake a year before the eruption signaled the beginning of volcanic unrest in the vicinity of Pinatubo. Scientists believe that a new influx of basaltic magma into the chamber unsettled the differentiating magma and caused it to become more volatile, eventually resulting in a large cataclysmic eruption.

When magma cools underground without ever erupting, the resulting rock is called an "intrusive igneous rock." (Igneous refers to the fact that the rock is magma-derived.) When magma cools aboveground after eruption from a volcano, it is called "extrusive igneous rock." This also is called volcanic rock.

See Also: Andesite; Basalt; Dacite; Rhyolite; Vent.

Further Reading

Tarbuck, E. J., Lutgens, F. K., & Tasa, D. (2011). *Earth: An introduction to physical geology* (10th ed.). Upper Saddle River, NJ: Pearson Prentice Hall/Pearson Education, Inc.
U.S. Geological Survey. (2014, May 15). *Magma, Lava, Lava Flows*. Retrieved from http://vulcan.wr.usgs.gov/Glossary/LavaFlows/description_lava_flows.html

Mariana Islands

The Mariana Islands comprise an island arc located adjacent to the Mariana Trench on the eastern margin of the Philippine Plate. Guam is considered a part of this island group, and is located at the arc's southern tip. The islands have been formed above the subduction zone on the eastern edge of the Philippine Plate where the Pacific Plate is subducting beneath it. The result is a chain of volcanoes and a great deal of earthquake activity. There are roughly 18 named volcanoes in the island chain, approximately half of which are submarine. Eleven of these have been active in the last 100 years, and five have erupted since the year 2000. The submarine volcano Ahyi erupted in 2001. Anathan began an explosive eruption in 2003, its first in historic times. Although the island was uninhabited at the time, volcanic ash from the eruption could have threatened aircraft, so it certainly was not without its hazards. Little was known about this volcano and no monitoring system was in place on the island, therefore when the eruption began the Commonwealth of the Northern Mariana Islands invited scientists from the U.S. Geological Survey to assist in monitoring and assessing volcanic hazards. American scientists stayed through the volcano's initial two months of activity, until the volcano returned largely to background levels. Anatahan erupted three more times between April 2004 and August 2008. Two submarine volcanoes, South Sarigan Seamount and Northwest Rota-1, erupted in 2010. Pagan erupted in 2012, and has showed signs of low-level unrest since that time.

Earthquakes are a major concern in the Mariana Islands. Because the islands lie on a subduction zone, large earthquakes are to be expected. Earthquakes of magnitude 5 and greater happen with great regularity in the island arc, and magnitude 7 to 8 earthquakes occur every few years. A magnitude 8.1 earthquake in 1993 caused more than $200 million in damage on Guam and generated a small tsunami that was detected throughout the Mariana Islands. Surprisingly, although large earthquakes are common in the islands, large and damaging tsunamis are not. Even during the 1993 earthquake and tsunami, the maximum wave heights were only 1 foot (0.3 meters). It is entirely likely that at some time the islands will be hit by a major Pacific-wide tsunami, most likely generated in nearby waters; but the islands largely have been immune to this point.

See Also: Pacific Plate; Philippine Plate; Subduction Zone; Tsunami.

Further Reading

Lander, J. F., Whiteside, L. S., Hattori, P. (2002). The tsunami history of Guam: 1849–1993. *International Journal of the Tsunami Society 20* (3), 158–173.

Smithsonian Institution. National Museum of Natural History. Global Volcanism Program. (2014, June 17). Retrieved from http://www.volcano.si.edu/

U.S. Geological Survey. (2014, June 17). *Guam/Northern Marianas earthquake information*. Retrieved from http://earthquake.usgs.gov/earthquakes/states/?region=Guam/Northern Marianas.

U.S. Geological Survey. Hawaiian Volcano Observatory. (2014, June 17). *Anatahan volcano*. Retrieved from http://hvo.wr.usgs.gov/cnmi/

U.S. Geological Survey. Volcano Hazards Program. (2014, June 17). *U.S. volcanoes and current activity alerts*. Retrieved from http://volcanoes.usgs.gov/.

Mariana Trench

The Mariana Trench (sometimes called the Marianas Trench) marks a subduction zone at the eastern extent of the Philippine Plate. It is located at the point where the Pacific Plate dives beneath the Philippine Plate. The trench is the deepest feature in the world's oceans. The deepest point within the trench is known as the Challenger Deep, which is in the southern part of the trench not far from Guam. The bottom of the Challenger Deep is 36,201 feet (11,034 meters) below sea level. As a comparison, Mount Everest, the tallest mountain on Earth, is 29,026 (8,848 meters) above sea level. If Mount Everest were placed in the trench, its summit would still be well over a mile beneath the ocean surface. The trench is about 1,580 miles (2,542 kilometers) long and 43 miles (69 kilometers) wide.

A great deal of speculation existed about conditions in the bottom of the trench until humans started exploring the area. The first visit to the base of the Challenger Deep happened in 1960. Two men, Lieutenant Don Walsh (United States Navy) and Swiss scientist Jacques Piccard, descended to the bottom of the trench in a bathyscaphe named "Trieste." When they touched down, they saw a rat-tailed fish and answered the question scientists had about whether life could exist in deep sea trenches. Since then, a great deal of life has been found in the trench, including one-celled foraminerans, small crustaceans called amphipods, and sea cucumber-like holothurians.

It took 35 years for another vessel to make the trek back into the abyss. In 1995, an unmanned Japanese submarine called Kaiko gathered samples and data from the trench. In 2009, the United States deployed a remotely operated vehicle, Nereus, which spent nearly 10 hours on the floor of the trench. In 2012, movie director James Cameron piloted the vessel DeepSea Challenger to the bottom of the trench. Unfortunately, hydraulic failures in his camera system meant he failed to capture any images from his voyage. In 2009, President George W. Bush created the Marianas Trench National Monument through presidential proclamation. The process allows for the protection and exploration of more than 95,000 square miles (246,000 square kilometers) of ocean and ocean floor.

See Also: Pacific Plate; Philippine Plate; Subduction Zone.

Further Reading

Dohrer, E. (2014, June 17). *Mariana Trench: The deepest depths*. Retrieved from http://www.livescience.com/23387-mariana-trench.html

National Geographic Society. (2014, June 17). *The Mariana Trench*. http://deepseachallenge
.com/the-expedition/mariana-trench/

Maui, Legend of

Maui is one of the best-known demigods of Hawaiian mythology. His home is the
island after which he is named. His reputation is that of a clever trickster and
sorcerer—even when he was a child. His mother is the goddess Hina, but his father
is unknown. Legend says that his mother wanted to gather seaweed, and as she
walked along the beach she found a man's loincloth. She put on the loincloth and
lay down to take a nap. This is how and when he was conceived. Maui is one of
many sons born to Hina. His brothers are not as clever as Maui, nor do they possess
the magical powers or strength that Maui is said to have. Several of his adventures
are popular myths, even today. The most popular of these were detailed in a song
about Maui entitled "Maui Hawaiian Sup'pa Man," recorded by Hawaiian musi-
cian Israel Kamakawiwo'ole for his 1993 album, "Facing Future."

In one story, Maui goes fishing with his brothers in the family canoe. His
brothers are excellent fishermen, but Maui, being younger than his brothers, does
not possess their skill. His brothers tease him and make fun of him when a fish
gets free from his hook, or when he lands fish that are much smaller than theirs.
Maui eventually grows tired of their teasing and decides to trick them. He casts his
line near one of theirs, and when the brother hooks a large fish Maui acts as if he
also has hooked a fish. Maui distracts his brother and then crosses the lines so it
appears that he, rather than his brother, has a taut line. As Maui taunts his brother
for allowing the fish to slip off his hook due to slack in his line, Maui flips the fish
on board the canoe and claims credit for catching it. Although his brothers at first
were confused by this trick, they later discovered what he was doing and refused
to take him fishing with them in their canoe. His mother became angry with him,
and his brothers made fun of him.

Maui's mother knew of his poor fishing skills and sent him to his father to
obtain a hook that had magic power. The hook was said to possess the power—
when it catches land—to bring the land together. With his new hook in hand, Maui
tried to climb in the canoe so he could go fishing with his brothers. They threw him
off the canoe and left him to swim back to shore. That day they returned with only
one fish, a shark. He told his brothers they would have caught better fish if they had
allowed him to come along with his new hook. They acquiesced and took him
along the next day. In the beginning, they caught only sharks again. Maui decided
to bait his magic hook with a bird called an "alae." Alae were sacred to his mother,
Hina. He threw his baited hook into the sea. Large waves started churning. Maui
had hooked a giant fish. The fish pulled the boys around for two days before it
tired. The line became slack, and Maui told his brothers it was time to pull the fish
in. To his surprise, as they pulled the fish, land began to rise out of the water. He
told his brothers not to look back, telling them that if they looked back, the fish

would be lost. One brother looked back anyway. The line snapped and left a chain of islands behind. This is the mythological explanation for how the Hawaiian Islands formed. Legends of the goddess Pele discuss volcanic activity in the island chain.

Another legend illustrates Maui's strength. Maui lived in an area where the sky had either fallen down, or never been separated from the earth. The sky was so heavy that it pressed all of the leaves on the plants so they were flat. As the plants grew slowly upward, they pushed up the sky just enough that people were able to move about. Maui came upon a woman and told her if he could drink from her gourd, he would push the heavens higher for her. A man nearby doubted Maui, and told him he did not believe he was strong enough to accomplish what he said he would do. Maui was very unhappy with him. After Maui had taken a long drink from the woman's gourd, he pushed the sky to the top of the trees. He continued pushing until the sky was at the tops of the mountains, then with one more push sent it to the place where we see it today. Then he turned to the man who had doubted him. The man ran to the other side of the island, near the town of Lahaina. There, the man was changed into a large rock.

Maui is also responsible for the length of day and night experienced today. Long ago, daytime was very short, and nighttime was very long. People struggled. Plants could not grow well. People could not complete all of their chores during daytime hours. Maui's mother was particularly frustrated because the bark she was wetting and beating into cloth called kapa would not dry. Everyone believed the sun was being very thoughtless. Maui decided to do something about this problem. He climbed to the top of a mountain to determine the course of the sun. When he determined that the sun rose over the mountain Haleakala, he devised a plan with his mother in which he would snare the sun, and then cut off its legs so it would be prevented from running so fast.

Maui was instructed to go near his grandmother's house and wait in a tree until he heard a rooster crow three times. His grandmother cooked bananas every morning for the sun when the roosters woke her up. Maui took away all of her bananas, so when the sun stopped by for his cooked bananas, there were none. His grandmother was nearly blind and could not see Maui. When he identified himself and told her why he was there, she gave him a stone axe and they waited for the sun to arrive. As the sun crept to the edge of the mountain, he saw there were no bananas and was furious. Maui used his rope to snare each of the sun's 16 legs as they came over the horizon. He tied the ropes to a strong tree. Maui began using the axe to wound the sun, but the sun begged him to stop. They struck a bargain. The sun would slow down and stay in the sky longer, but there would be longer days in the summer and shorter days in the winter.

One of Maui's great feats was bringing fire to the people. There had been no fire in a very long time. They used to get their fire from the lava of the volcano Haleakala, but the volcano had become extinct. Nobody knew how to create fire without lava, so people had to eat uncooked food. They grew tired of eating uncooked taro, fish, and shellfish and badly wanted to regain fire to cook their food.

Maui and his brothers went fishing early one morning. When they got to their fishing grounds far offshore, they noticed that there was a fire burning on the side of the mountain. They did not know whose fire they were seeing, but they were eager to return to land, find the fire, and cook their food before the fire died. When they got back to the beach, Maui took some fish and moved quickly to where he had seen the fire. What he found was a family of alae (mud hens) scratching the fire out. They flew away as he approached. This happened several times to the brothers, and before long they figured out that the alae knew the secret of making fire.

Maui devised a plan to catch the alae as they were making the fire so he could learn their secret. He fashioned some kapa (cloth made from bark) into a figure that from a distance looked like a man, and tied it to one end of the canoe so it looked like all of the brothers were together in the boat. He hid near where the alae had built their fires. The alae arrived, and the oldest hen started looking around for sticks for the fire. Rather than remaining hidden and watching them to learn how they made fire, Maui became impatient. He rushed toward the birds and grabbed the old hen. He demanded she tell him the secret of making fire. The alae would not give up the secret easily. She told him to try first one type of plant, then another. None of them produced fire. Finally, Maui grew tired of the hen's game and grabbed her around the throat. He twisted her neck until she could stand it no longer. The hen screamed out the name of the correct sticks to use, and Maui was finally able to make a fire. He was so angry with the bird that he rubbed the top of her head until it was red. Alae still have bald heads as a result.

See Also: Haleakala, Maui, Hawaii, United States; Hawaiian Islands; Pele, Legend of.

Further Reading

Beckwith, M. (1970). *Hawaiian mythology*. Honolulu: University of Hawaii Press.
Kamakawiwo'ole, I. (1993). *Facing future*. Honolulu: Mountain Apple Company.
Westervelt, W. D. (1987). *Myths and legends of Hawaii*. Honolulu: Mutual Publishing Company.

Mauna Kea, Hawaii, United States

Mauna Kea is one of five volcanoes that comprise the island of Hawaii. Measured from its base approximately 18,000 feet (5,500 meters) below sea level to its summit 13,796 feet (4,205 meters) above sea level, Mauna Kea is the tallest mountain on Earth. Mauna Kea is tall enough that the summit of the mountain can be covered in snow, particularly in the winter months. It was named "Mauna Kea," which means "white mountain," for this reason. Mauna Kea also is tall enough that it was covered in glaciers during at least three past ice ages. The last of the glaciers melted roughly 9,000 years ago. The most recent of Mauna Kea's lavas was erupted onto glacial deposits roughly 4,500 years ago.

A cinder cone near the summit of Mauna Kea on the island of Hawaii. The broad, snow-capped shield of Mauna Loa is in the background. (Peter French/Newscom)

Mauna Kea currently is in the post-caldera stage of its formation. This is the fourth of seven stages of formation of Hawaiian volcanoes. This stage is characterized by infilling of the caldera (if one exists) with lava, and the dotting of the volcano's surface with cinder cones. It also means that the volcano erupts very infrequently, and that it has different lava composition than it did when it was younger. Post-caldera volcanoes also have steeper slopes than younger volcanoes. Although it has been thousands of years since Mauna Kea's last eruption, this does not mean that the volcano is extinct. Mauna Kea is likely to erupt again in the future, but eruption could be many hundreds—or even thousands—of years in the future.

Mauna Kea occupies the northeast part of the island of Hawaii. Its lavas are interlayered with those of Mauna Loa to its south which means that, in the past, both volcanoes have been active at alternating times therefore their lavas overlap each other. Mauna Loa, however, is a much younger volcano that still is in its shield-building stage. Mauna Kea has been deeply eroded by rivers and hosts countless waterfalls. One of the most spectacular river valleys on the island of Hawaii is Waipio Valley. The valley is up to 2,000 feet (610 meters) deep with nearly vertical cliffs on the sides and back of the valley. Families live on and farm the valley floor.

The summit area of Mauna Kea has incredibly favorable conditions for telescope use and—beginning in the 1960s—some of the world's best telescopes have been placed there. Today, 13 telescopes owned by 11 different countries grace the summit of Mauna Kea. As natural as it might seem to further develop the summit of Mauna Kea to accommodate more telescopes, a moratorium is in place limiting the number of telescopes to 13. For any other telescope to be built on Mauna Kea, an existing telescope must be removed. This moratorium is in place because the summit of Mauna Kea is sacred to the Hawaiian people. Mauna Kea is said to be "the mountain of the god Wakea, from whom all things in Hawaii are descended" (Pihana, 2014). Mauna Kea also is home to Poliahu, the snow goddess of Mauna Kea and daughter of Wakea. Out of respect for Hawaiians and their native culture, the mountain now is administered jointly by a group of island elders and the U.S. National Park Service.

See Also: Hawaiian Islands; Mauna Loa, Hawaii, United States.

Further Reading

Kaahele Hawaii. (2014, May 19). *Poliahu, Goddess of Mauna Kea.* Retrieved from http://www.kaahelehawaii.com/pages/culture_Poliahu.htm

McDonald, G. A., Abbott, A. T., & Peterson, F. L. (1983). *Volcanoes in the sea: The geology of Hawaii* (2nd ed.). Honolulu: University of Hawaii Press.

Pihana, J. K. (2014, May 19). *The White Mountain.* Retrieved from http://www.ifa.hawaii.edu/info/vis/culture/the-white-mountain.html

U.S. Geological Survey. Hawaiian Volcano Observatory. (2014, May 19). Mauna Kea: Hawaii's tallest volcano. Retrieved from http://hvo.wr.usgs.gov/volcanoes/maunakea/

Mauna Loa, Hawaii, United States

Mauna Loa is the largest of the five volcanoes that comprise the island of Hawaii. It is not only the largest volcano on the island, but the largest volcano on the planet. Mauna Loa has a volume of approximately 19,000 cubic miles (80,000 cubic kilometers), and its summit is 13,680 feet (4,170 meters) above sea level. The name Mauna Loa translates to "Long Mountain." The name is quite fitting, as the part of the mountain that is above sea level is approximately 75 miles (120 kilometers) long, from the southern tip of Hawaii to Hilo on the island's northeast coast. The mountain's length is doubled if the areas offshore are included. It makes up fully one half of the island of Hawaii, and is as large as 85% of all of the other Hawaiian Islands combined. Mauna Loa is a relatively young volcano, although it is believed that it first rose above the surface of the ocean nearly 400,000 years ago. The volcano still is within the shield-building phase of its life cycle. Mauna Loa erupts frequently, with 33 well-documented eruptions since the first westerners observed an eruption in 1843. It is certain that Mauna Loa will erupt again, and the mountain is carefully monitored by the staff of the Hawaiian Volcano Observatory (an installation that the U.S. Geological Survey oversees).

Mauna Loa has a summit caldera named "Mokuaweoweo," which translates loosely to "Islet of the Aweoweo." "Aweoweo" is a red fish found in Hawaiian waters. The red fish is suggestive of lava as it moves and undulates through the landscape. The summit caldera is 2 miles by 3 miles (3 kilometers by 5 kilometers), with the long dimension oriented northeast-southwest. Mauna Loa has two major rift zones, the Southwest Rift Zone and the Northeast Rift Zone. Mauna Loa also has two minor rift zones; one extends to the north and the other to the northwest. Eruptions can occur along any of these rift zones or at the summit. Eruptions seem to be much more common along the major rift zones, however, than along the minor rift zones.

Mauna Loa also has a number of major faults that are believed to be locations of gravitational sliding. The Honuapo-Kaoiki Fault Zone is located just upslope of the border between Mauna Loa and the volcano Kilauea, which lies to the southeast. A curious feature lies to the west of this fault system near its southern extent. The Ninole Hills are a group of three towering plateaus. The hills contain some of the oldest rocks on the island. Some geologists think that the hills are formed as a result of movement along these faults—that the movement has brought a block of old Mauna Loa rocks to this high elevation, creating these hills. Other scientists think that the Ninole Hills are the only remnants of a large shield volcano that existed before Mauna Loa. In any case, the Ninole Hills are a prominent landmark on the southeast slope of Mauna Loa.

Another major fault is the Kahuku Fault, which lies parallel to the Southwest Rift Zone on the southern part of the island. Recent lava flows from Mauna Loa parallel the fault and reach the ocean near South Point, the southern tip of the island. One lava flow entered the ocean near South Point and created a beautiful littoral (coastal) cone. The cone has been eroded on the ocean side, and forms a cove with a beautiful green sand beach. The green of the sand is from the mineral olivine, which is a bright apple-green color. It was a component of the lava flow that fed the cone's eruption. As the hot lava hit the cold ocean, the lava exploded into small fragments that created the cone. As wind, waves, and rain erode the cone, these small crystals of olivine created the beach sand in that area. Approximately 60% of the sand is olivine, with remaining components composed of rock fragments and solid debris from the ocean, such as tiny shell fragments.

On the west side of the island, the Kealekekua-Kaholo Fault System is located near—and runs parallel to—the shoreline. The fault system, again related to gravitational sliding, is thought to be related to large landslides that have shaped the coastline in this area. Kealekekua Bay is a relatively small cove with a steep cliff at the rear of the bay. The bay is famous for excellent snorkeling, but also has historical significance. British Captain James Cook—the first western explorer to visit the Hawaiian Islands—made his first landfall here, and was killed in this location a few years later. A monument to Captain Cook stands in the water toward the northern end of the bay.

Scanning of the ocean floor of the west coast of Hawaii near Kealekekua Bay has led to an understanding that big landslides that involve gravitational sliding of immense blocks from the edges of the large Hawaiian volcanoes are a primary way that the islands have attained the shapes they have today. Volcanic activity is responsible for building the islands, but landslides and movement along faults alter the shape of the islands once the volcano creates them.

The most recent eruption of Mauna Loa occurred in March and April of 1984. The eruption began about 1:25 a.m. on March 25 in Mokuaweoweo, the volcano's summit caldera. Lava fountains erupted across the caldera floor and extended a short distance into the Southwest Rift Zone. A few hours later, the eruption migrated into the Northeast Rift Zone. Over the next several days, new cracks opened at progressively lower elevations along the Northeast Rift Zone. At one point, lava advanced to within 4 miles (6.5 kilometers) of the city of Hilo. Thankfully, the lava channels that were carrying lava rapidly toward Hilo degraded, starving the flow fronts near Hilo of their lava supply, so lava never entered the city. The eruption ended on April 15. The eruption caused quite a bit of distress within the city of Hilo, because people were understandably concerned about the possibility of lava reaching homes and businesses within the city limits. At some point in the future, this is a likely scenario. There is very little that can be done to prevent lava from reaching Hilo if an eruption of just the right duration in just the right location occurs on Mauna Loa.

See Also: Hawaiian Islands; Hawaiian Volcano Observatory; Kilauea Volcano, Hawaii, United States.

Further Reading

McDonald, G. A., Abbott, A. T., & Peterson, F. L. (1983). *Volcanoes in the sea: The geology of Hawaii* (2nd ed.). Honolulu: University of Hawaii Press.

U.S. Geological Survey. Hawaiian Volcano Observatory. (2014, May 20). *1984 eruption: March 25–April 15.* Retrieved from http://hvo.wr.usgs.gov/maunaloa/history/1984.html

U.S. Geological Survey. Hawaiian Volcano Observatory. (2014, May 20). *Mauna Loa, Earth's largest volcano.* Retrieved from http://hvo.wr.usgs.gov/maunaloa/

Megatsunami

"Megatsunami" is an informal term used by some researchers and the media to describe an unusually large tsunami. For many years, discoveries of massive slump blocks (related block units that moved downslope as a relatively coherent mass) on the ocean floor near the margins of the Hawaiian Islands led to the belief that these blocks slid into the ocean in one large event, causing giant tsunamis that towered more than 1,000 feet (330 meters) above the landscape. Other oceanic islands formed in the same way were viewed as equally dire threats. Another well-cited example, in addition to the Hawaiian Islands, is the Canary Islands in the Atlantic Ocean. Recent research from a group in Great Britain has cast some doubt on this characterization of landslides around volcanic islands such as Hawaii and the Canary Islands. Researchers found abundant evidence suggesting that landslides occurred incrementally, therefore no megatsunamis were created.

Although there now is some doubt about whether large sector collapses on oceanic islands could create megatsunamis, there was at least one tsunami of this magnitude that occurred in fairly recent history. A tsunami was created in Lituya Bay, Alaska, when a large block of material fell into one end of the bay. A tsunami more than 1,640 feet (500 meters) tall rushed across the bay, scouring the shoreline down to bare rock. The event is well documented, and there were survivors of the event who described their experience for researchers.

Another type of event that could have the potential to create an extremely large tsunami is a meteor or asteroid impact in a coastal area or in the ocean. Presently, this merely is an idea—and a remote possibility. The effects that this sort of impact has on creating a possible megatsunami cannot be known until such an event occurs.

See Also: Tsunami.

Further Reading

Bolt, B. A. (2004). *Earthquakes* (5th ed.). New York: W.H. Freeman and Company.

Decker, R. W., & Decker, B. (1998). *Volcanoes* (3rd ed.). New York: W.H. Freeman and Company.

National Oceanography Centre, Southampton (UK). (2014, May 21). New evidence for assessing tsunami risk from very large volcanic island landslides. *Science Daily.* Retrieved from http://www.sciencedaily.com/releases/2013/12/131211104242.htm

Mexico

The country of Mexico is the southernmost country on the continent of North America, and on the North American Plate. Mexico is bounded to the southwest by the Pacific Plate, and to the west are the Cocos Plate and Rivera Plate. The Cocos and Rivera plates are being subducted beneath North America in southern Mexico. Another plate boundary exists within the Gulf of California, between the Baja peninsula and mainland Mexico. It is a young divergent boundary, or spreading center, that is moving the Baja peninsula away from the mainland and toward the northwest. It is creating new oceanic lithosphere in the Gulf. Mexico therefore is a very tectonically active country.

Earthquakes abound in all types of plate boundary settings, and Mexico has two major earthquake zones. The northernmost of these is in the Gulf of California and surrounding areas. Although many earthquakes occur here, the vast majority are less than magnitude 6. On occasion, a more powerful earthquake occurs—along with more dire results. A magnitude 7.2 earthquake occurred in 2010 on the Baja peninsula and killed two people. The second large area of earthquake activity is along the southern coast of the country, roughly from Puerto Vallarta in the state of Jalisco to the border of Guatemala in the south. This is the beginning of the

Middle America Trench, where the Cocos Plate is being subducted beneath southern Mexico. The earthquake zone extends from just offshore to more than 100 miles (160 kilometers) inland. Within this area it is common for large earthquakes—of magnitude 6 or greater—to occur.

The structure of southern Mexico and the composition and thickness of the soil in places such as Mexico City, enable surface waves from earthquakes to travel very efficiently throughout the region. If a large earthquake occurs it is possible to have damage even far from the epicenter. This was the case in 1985, when a magnitude 8.0 earthquake occurred in the state of Michoacán. Significant damage occurred in Mexico City, more than 100 miles (160 kilometers) inland. More than 9,500 people lost their lives in that earthquake—most in Mexico City and most from building collapse caused by exaggerated ground shaking due to the soft material beneath the city. Mexico City is built on a dry lake bed, and surface waves are amplified in such material. Many public buildings, including hospitals, collapsed during the earthquake.

Volcanic eruptions also are part of life in southern Mexico. The volcano Popocatépetl is located near Mexico City. It is a tall and steep-sided cone that is capped with snow and glaciers. The summit of the volcano has a steep-walled crater that often emits light plumes of ash and steam. In fact, the volcano's name is Aztec for "smoking mountain." The Popocatépetl volcano has not had a major eruption in more than 1,000, years but that does not mean it is incapable of erupting. The last major eruption occurred around the year 800 CE and sent a large plinian column of ash and pumice skyward. It also generated pyroclastic flows and lahars that swept into basins at the volcano's base. If such an eruption happened today, it likely would displace tens of thousands of people. The volcano Colima is located in the state of Colima near Mexico's southern coast. The volcano consists of two peaks, one of which is located within a breached caldera and has been a source of multiple large debris avalanches. The volcano is capable of explosive eruptions that leave deep craters and produce both pyroclastic flows and lahars.

A third notable Mexican volcano is Parícutin, a cinder cone that was born in a farmer's cornfield in 1943. The world was transfixed by the volcano for nine years, watching as the new cinder cone grew from a meager hill to a tall cone, and then issued countless lava flows. This was the first time in history that scientists were able to observe, study, and carefully document the beginning, middle, and end of a volcano's life cycle. The volcano stopped erupting in 1952 and is not expected to erupt again. It is located in a volcanic field, however, in which dozens of cinder cones have been created over the last several thousand years. Even though Parícutin might not erupt again, the chances are good that another cinder cone will be born in the same area sometime in the foreseeable future.

See Also: Cinder Cone; Cocos Plate; Colima Volcano, Mexico; Divergent Boundary; Lahar; Mexico City Earthquake, Mexico (1985); North American Plate; Parícutin Volcano, Mexico; Popocatépetl Volcano, Mexico; Subduction Zone.

Further Reading

Smithsonian Institution. National Museum of Natural History. Global Volcanism Program. (2014, June 17). Retrieved from http://www.volcano.si.edu/

U.S. Geological Survey. (2014, June 17). *Historic world earthquakes. Mexico.* Retrieved from http://earthquake.usgs.gov/earthquakes/world/historical_country.php#mexico

Mexico City Earthquake, Mexico (1985)

On September 19, 1985, Mexico was hit with a magnitude 8 earthquake. Its epicenter was in a subduction zone in the western part of the country, near Michoacán. At least 9,500 people were killed, about 30,000 were injured, and more than 100,000 people were left homeless. Severe damage occurred in parts of Mexico City and in several states of central Mexico. It is estimated that the quake seriously affected an area of approximately 300,000 square miles, caused more than $3 billion in damage, and was felt by almost 20 million people.

This was one of the most devastating earthquakes in the history of the Americas, and it was followed by major aftershocks. In Mexico City, shaking from the quake lasted three to four minutes. The most damaged zones were those in the bed of historic Lake Texcoco, where the prevailing silt and volcanic clay sediments amplified the shaking. Building damage was worsened by occurrences of soil liquefaction, causing loss of foundation support and settlement of large buildings. Altogether 400 buildings collapsed and another 3,000 were seriously damaged. Extensive damage also occurred all across the country.

The earthquake generated a small tsunami, and the first aftershock that was a magnitude of 7.5 produced a small second tsunami. Both tsunamis spread across the Pacific and were recorded by several tide stations in Central America, Colombia, Ecuador, French Polynesia, Samoa, and Hawaii. No reports of damage were received from any of these stations and the only minor damage due to the first tsunami came from the source region. Seiches were observed in East Galveston Bay, Texas, and in swimming pools in Texas, New Mexico, Colorado, and Idaho. Water-well fluctuations were recorded at Ingleside, Texas; Santa Fe, New Mexico; Rolla, Missouri; Hillsborough County, Florida; and Smithsburg, Maryland.

As compared with California, which in the course of the Twentieth Century experienced five earthquakes of magnitudes greater than 7, Mexico had 42—most of them resulting in a high death toll. The September 1985 quake happened in a seismicity gap that had been identified by geologists as a risk area for the previous 10 years. Fortunately, the earthquake struck early in the morning of September 19, before schools and offices in Mexico City were occupied, because it was there that the greatest death toll occurred when buildings collapsed. The length of the intervening distance between the earthquake's source and Mexico City greatly reduced the amplitude of the seismic waves so that very few structures built on firm soil and rock suffered damage.

See Also: Mexico.

Further Reading

Gunn, A. M. (2014, August 12). Mexico earthquake (1985). *World geography: Understanding a changing world.* Santa Barbara, CA: ABC-CLIO.

Mitigation

Mitigation is the practice of working to reduce or eliminate risk to a population. Informing the public of the risk an event poses (should it occur in the future) is one simple form of mitigation. Using the example of a coastal community at risk from a future tsunami can illustrate a number of mitigation practices. The most basic thing that can be done to mitigate a community's risk is to warn the community members of their risk in the event of a tsunami. This informs the population that such a risk exists, and can take the form of stories in local and regional newspapers about tsunamis, or posting signs around the community warning people that they are in a tsunami hazard zone. Educating the public about what to do if a tsunami occurs is the next level of mitigation. Along with tsunami warning signs, it is simple to post signs showing tsunami evacuation routes. Evacuation also is a form of mitigation, if a disaster is forecast to occur. Many communities around the Pacific Rim hold evacuation drills to help prepare for tsunamis.

A higher level of mitigation can be employed when a community frequently is at risk from the same type of event. In such cases, the land can be altered, barriers erected, shelters identified or built, construction practices changed, or populations relocated. In areas that are prone to landslides or mudslides during rainy seasons, communities have stepped in to alter the slope of a hill or mountain to lessen the probability of a deadly landslide occurring. Many coastal Japanese cities have constructed 30-foot (10-meter) tall, pyramid-shaped walls with sturdy gates to mitigate the risk to the city's population from tsunamis. The harbor of Hilo, Hawaii, has a large breakwater constructed to slow the approach of incoming tsunamis and other large waves. Shelters can be built as temporary or permanent structures, and are used either to house those who have had to evacuate their homes due to a disastrous event, or to give people a place to go to avoid the effects of a natural event. Tornado shelters, for example, are places for people to go to avoid the effects of the tornado. These shelters typically are built below ground level. In other areas, such as the southern United States near the Gulf of Mexico, homes are raised on stilts to protect them from storm surges that rush ashore during hurricanes. In areas prone to earthquakes, permanent structures are built using best practices of earthquake engineering that are meant to minimize damage due to ground shaking. Relocation of a population is a more problematic mitigation program because of people's emotional attachment to homelands, legalities of land purchase or exchange, and a host of other reasons. It has been accomplished, however, in many areas when the risk of staying in a location has proven too great, or where land has disappeared due to coastal erosion or landslides.

Following the Chilean earthquake of 1960 and its resulting tsunami, the city of Hilo, Hawaii, redoubled tsunami mitigation efforts. The Pacific Tsunami Museum is a fixture on the Hilo bay front. The museum educates island school children and residents, as well as visitors, of the risk Hilo faces from tsunamis. Signs indicating tsunami evacuation routes now point visitors and residents to higher ground. Hilo also rezoned part of the city from residential to recreational land use. The city took this drastic step after tsunamis washed away many homes in the Shinmachi neighborhood in 1946 and 1960, and claimed many lives. The city agreed to rezone the area where the neighborhood had stood so that no permanent dwellings could be built there in the future. Most of the homes in the city of Hilo now are out of the typical tsunami inundation zone, and thus out of harm's way. Although parks, businesses, hotels, and restaurants still occupy parts of the inundation zone, very few people live there.

See Also: Earthquake Hazards; Hazard and Risk; Tsunami.

Further Reading

National Oceanic and Atmospheric Administration All Hazards Monitor. Retrieved from http://www.noaawatch.gov
Natural Hazard Mitigation Association. Retrieved from http://nhma.info
Pacific Tsunami Museum. Retrieved from http://www.tsunami.org
U.S. Geological Survey. (2014, October 21). *Natural hazards*. Retrieved from http://www.usgs.gov/natural_hazards

Modified Mercalli Intensity Scale

When an earthquake is reported on the news, there generally are two questions for which people want immediate answers: "Where was it?" and "How big was it?" Prior to the invention of modern seismographs, the only way to answer the first question was to look for the area that sustained the greatest damage and declare that to be the location of the earthquake. The question of earthquake size required considerably more information.

The first scientific study of earthquake size was undertaken in 1858, following a destructive earthquake in southern Italy in December 1857. British engineer Robert Mallet spent two months at the site of the earthquake making detailed scientific observations of the effects of the earthquake. Mallet devised a system in which he assigned numbers to severity of damage. The higher the number, the greater the amount of damage he observed in a specific location. He plotted the information on a map and drew lines connecting points of equal damage. In this way, Mallet drew a map showing the area affected by the earthquake, with zones of damage severity indicated clearly. Although it certainly was not quantitative in the sense of the mathematical formulas of the magnitude scales, Mallet's method nonetheless provided valuable information about where the greatest amounts of damage occurred. This categorization of damage caused by an earthquake is called "intensity."

In the decades that followed, two other intensity scales were devised and widely used. The first was developed in the 1880s by M.S. de Rossi of Italy and Francois Forel of Switzerland. The Rossi-Forel scale used Roman numerals from I to X to indicate severity of damage. The numeral "I" indicated that the earthquake was felt only by a few under especially favorable circumstances, and the numeral "X" indicated that damage was substantial.

Italian seismologist and volcanologist G. Mercalli refined and expanded the scale in 1902. His version used Roman numerals I to XII, in which increasing Roman numerals also indicated increasing amounts of damage. Both the Rossi-Forel Intensity Scale and a version of the Mercalli Intensity Scale (the abridged Modified Mercalli Intensity Scale) are used today. Of these, the Modified Mercalli Intensity Scale is much more widely used. The Abridged Modified Mercalli Intensity Scale is shown below (Table 1).

It might seem counterintuitive that anyone still uses an intensity scale today when there are several magnitude scales that can provide absolute information about the size and power of an earthquake. For many scientific purposes, the magnitude of an earthquake is completely adequate. Earthquake intensity studies, however, still have their place. Examples of businesses in which intensity studies can be useful include real estate, insurance, engineering, utilities, and construction. In each of these cases, it is important for the business to know where in an area to expect greater shaking and damage to occur. The amount of ground shaking could be greater in areas underlain by thick soil or loose material such as sand or mud. Ground shaking will be less in areas underlain by solid rock. Patterns of past earthquake damage that appear on intensity maps from previous earthquakes can help people to design more earthquake-resistant structures for specific areas, make intelligent real estate purchases, and place utility lines in areas that sustain less shaking than surrounding property. Intensity maps could enable insurance companies to set insurance premiums at appropriate prices for the level of risk they are undertaking by insuring a home or business that tends to experience more or less damage in an earthquake. Past intensity studies also can help first responders and aid workers to know where they are likely to be needed most in the event of a large earthquake.

Constructing an intensity map is a time-intensive process. After an earthquake occurs, those who experienced the earthquake, or later observers, must answer a series of questions about what happened during the earthquake, and must give the precise location of the observation. Each individual location is assigned a specific intensity number and that number is plotted on a map. After repeating this exercise several hundred times—or perhaps several thousand times—enough data are gathered to begin to draw lines connecting points of equal damage, called isoseismal lines, on the map. The end result is a map where damage can be estimated based

Table 1. Abridged Modified Mercalli Intensity Scale, with Corresponding Rossi-Forel Values (after Bolt, 2004)

Modified Mercalli	Description	Rossi-Forel
I	Not felt except by a very few under especially favorable circumstances.	I
II	Felt only by a few persons at best, especially on upper floors of buildings. Delicately suspended objects might swing.	I to II
III	Felt quite noticeably indoors, especially on upper floors of buildings, but many people do not recognize it as an earthquake. Standing automobiles could rock slightly. Vibration similar to the passing of a truck. Duration estimated.	III
IV	During the day felt indoors by many, outdoors by few. At night some people awakened. Dishes, windows, doors disturbed; walls make creaking sounds. Sensation similar to a heavy truck striking building. Standing automobiles rocked noticeably.	IV to V
V	Felt by nearly everyone, many people awakened. Some dishes, windows, and other items broken; cracked plaster in a few places; unstable objects overturned. Disturbances of trees, poles, and other tall objects sometimes noticed. Pendulum clocks might stop.	V to VI
VI	Felt by all, many people are frightened and run outdoors. Some heavy furniture is moved; a few instances of fallen plaster and damaged chimneys. Damage slight.	VI to VII
VII	Everyone runs outdoors. Damage negligible in buildings of good design and construction; slight to moderate in well-built ordinary structures; considerable damage to poorly built or badly designed structures; some chimneys broken. Noticed by people driving cars.	VIII
VIII	Damage slight in specially designed structures; considerable in ordinary substantial buildings with partial collapse; great in poorly built structures. Panel walls thrown out of frame structures. Fall of chimneys, factory stacks, columns, monuments, walls. Heavy furniture overturned. Sand and mud ejected in small amounts. Changes in well water. Persons driving cars are disturbed.	VIII+ to IX
IX	Damage considerable in specially designed structures; well-designed frame structures thrown out of plumb; damage is significant in substantial buildings, with partial collapse. Buildings shifted off of foundations. Ground cracked conspicuously. Underground pipes broken.	IX+
X	Some well-built wooden structures destroyed; most masonry and frame structures with foundations destroyed; ground badly cracked. Rails bent. Landslides considerable from river banks and steep slopes. Shifted sand and mud. Water splashed, slopped over river banks.	X
XI	Few, if any, (masonry) structures remain standing. Bridges destroyed. Broad fissures open in the ground. Underground pipelines put completely out of service. Earth slumps and land slips in soft ground. Rails bent greatly.	
XII	Damage total. Waves seen on ground surface. Lines of sight and level distorted. Objects are thrown into the air.	

on location. The U.S. Geological Survey (USGS) encourages those who experience earthquakes to fill out this information online. The USGS processes the information quickly and a computer draws and posts on the earthquake's website a "ShakeMap" that evolves through time as more people contribute information. Data is filled in as needed with additional observations and intensity maps are created for all earthquakes that were felt.

See Also: Earthquake; Earthquake Magnitude.

Further Reading

Bolt, B. A. (2004). *Earthquakes* (5th ed.). New York: W.H. Freeman and Company.
U.S. Geological Survey. (2014, May 13). Shake maps. Retrieved from http://earthquake
.usgs.gov/earthquakes/shakemap/

N

National Center for Prevention of Disasters

The official government agency responsible for natural hazard information and disaster preparedness in Mexico is the Centro Nacional de Prevencion de Desastres (CENAPRED) (National Center for Prevention of Disasters). CENAPRED scientists are responsible for monitoring all natural hazards in Mexico. This includes not only earthquakes and volcanoes, but also landslides, wildfires, severe weather, floods, tsunamis, and tropical cyclones (hurricanes). The agency's website (www .cenapred.unam.mx) hosts a wealth of information about geologic and meteorological hazards, how to prepare for weather events, volcano alerts, earthquake information, and news articles about training opportunities. Additionally, the website provides monitoring information about two active volcanoes near Mexico City: Popocatépetl and Colima. Both volcanoes have webcams stationed around their perimeters that can be accessed through the website. The website also includes historical information about these volcanoes and current reports about their activity.

See Also: Mexico.

Further Reading

Centro Nacional de Prevencion de Desastres (CENAPRED). http://www.cenapred.unam .mx/es/

Nazca Plate

The Nazca Plate is located in the eastern Pacific, adjacent to South America's west coast. The Nazca Plate is a remnant of the much larger Farallon Plate, much of which has been subducted beneath North America. More than 30 million years ago, the Farallon Plate was present in the eastern Pacific adjacent to the entire coasts of North America and South America. It was being subducted beneath both continents at a rate faster than the plate was being created at the East Pacific Rise. The result was complete subduction of a part of the plate. It was here that the Pacific Plate came into direct contact with the North American Plate. This created the San Andreas Fault, which grows slightly longer every year. Additionally, the Farallon Plate became known as its remnant parts. The Juan de Fuca Plate is located north of the San Andreas Fault. The Rivera Plate and Cocos Plate are located to the south of the San Andreas Fault and Gulf of California, along the Middle America Trench. The Nazca Plate is the largest and southernmost of the remnant plates. It extends from Colombia in the north to southern Chile in the south.

The Nazca Plate itself does not contain much land area. The small amount of land area it does contain is that of a few small and isolated islands. The best known of these is Easter Island, or Isla de Pascua, which is a possession of Chile. Easter Island is well-known for its "moai," which are giant statues found in various positions across the island. Earlier residents of the island carved these statues, likely in some sort of worship or competition. Easter Island was formed by a hot spot. The hot spot trace extends eastward from Easter Island, and then turns northeastward toward the Chilean coastline where it disappears in the Peru-Chile Trench. Easter Island is located at the "new" end of the hot spot trace, although there has been no activity there for at least 100,000 years. The hot spot likely died out soon after creating the island.

Subduction of the Nazca Plate beneath South America is responsible for a great deal of volcanic activity and major earthquakes. The Peru-Chile Trench marks the point of subduction. Some of the world's largest earthquakes have occurred in the vicinity of the trench. This includes the Arica Earthquake of 1868, which had an estimated magnitude of 9.0; the Chilean earthquake and tsunami of 1960, which was a magnitude 9.5 event; and the Maule (Chile) Earthquake of 2010, which was a magnitude 8.8 event. Great earthquakes at the Peru-Chile Trench tend to generate Pacific-wide tsunamis, and these three earthquakes were no exceptions. Although the most damage and greatest number of deaths occurred in the local area, tsunamis from all of these areas were observed across the entire Pacific. The 1960 earthquake took lives in places as far away as Japan. Other tragic earthquakes of note that occurred on this plate boundary include two large events in Peru in 1970 and 2007.

A great number of active volcanoes also exist on the South American continent. Those with notable eruptions include Chaitén (Chile), Galeras (Colombia), and Nevado del Ruiz (Colombia). The Chaitén eruption in 2008 disrupted air traffic for several days. Galeras erupted in 1993 with several geologists in its crater, killing a number of them. The eruption of Nevado del Ruiz in 1985 generated a lahar that buried the town of Armero and most of its 22,000 residents.

See Also: Arica Earthquake and Tsunami, Chile (1868); Chaitén Volcano, Chile; Chilean Earthquake and Tsunami (1960); Chimbote Earthquake, Peru (1970); Galeras Volcano, Colombia (1993); Nevado del Ruiz, Colombia (1985); South American Plate; Subduction Zone.

Further Reading

Smithsonian Institution. National Museum of Natural History. Global Volcanism Program. (2014, June 18). Retrieved from http://www.volcano.si.edu/

U.S. Geological Survey. (2014, June 18). *Historic world earthquakes.* Retrieved from http://earthquake.usgs.gov/earthquakes/world/historical_country.php

Vezzoli, L., & Acocella, V. (2009). Easter Island, SE Pacific: An end-member type of hot-spot volcanism. *Geological Society of America Bulletin 121* (5–6), 869–886.

Nevado del Ruiz, Colombia

Nevado del Ruiz is located within the Parque Nacional Natural de Los Nevados, approximately 60 miles (100 kilometers) west of Bogotá in the Andes of west-central Colombia. Its summit is slightly more than 17,000 feet (5,200 meters) above sea level. Volcán Ruiz is located just five degrees north of the equator, yet its summit is covered with glaciers and snow because of its high elevation.

In many ways, Ruiz is typical of Andean volcanoes. It is a composite volcano with a base of andesite lava that is between 600,000 and 1 million years old. During the past 10,000 years it has erupted on average every 160 to 400 years. The last major eruption at Ruiz occurred in 1595. Weak eruptions occurred in the early 1600s, in 1805, in 1826–1833, in 1845, and in 1985. What makes Nevado del Ruiz notable is not these minor eruptions, but the fact that even a minor eruption can have a devastating effect on communities several miles from the mountain. Its 1985 eruption also is a case study in failed emergency-management operations.

The latest eruption of Nevado del Ruiz began in November 1984. After approximately 130 years of quiet dormancy, residents of the area began noticing earthquakes in the vicinity of the mountain. Mountain climbers reported strong activity in fumaroles in the summit crater. On December 22, 1984, more than 65 earthquakes were felt on the mountain, occurring roughly every 15 minutes. The snow and ice at the summit of Ruiz was covered with a thin layer of ash and sulfur. Earthquakes and fumarole activity continued well into the new year. On January 6, 1985, a group of geologists from the hydroelectric company in the state of Caldas visited the summit crater and saw that a new, smaller crater had formed within it. They recommended to local authorities that a program for monitoring a probable eruption be implemented immediately. In response to this recommendation, a civic committee was formed in the city of Manizales near the mountain. Their task was to form and support a scientific commission to monitor the volcanic and seismic hazard.

Teams from various government and academic institutions visited the volcano to assess the situation. In late February, members of INGEOMINAS, Colombia's Geology and Mines Bureau, visited the summit of the volcano to investigate its activity. Unfortunately, nobody at INGEOMINAS appeared to have working knowledge of modern volcanology, therefore very little resulted from the visit. Seismologist Jeff Tomblin from the United Nations Office of the Disaster Relief Organization (UNDRO) in Geneva, Switzerland, was in Colombia on another mission in early March 1985. He and two Swiss seismologists investigated the volcano's activity. They witnessed a 325- to 500-foot (100- to 150-meter) column of vapor rising from the summit crater Arenas, and also heard accounts of continuing earthquakes from local residents. Tomblin communicated to INGEOMINAS that this type of behavior is typical for eruptions of magnitude, and recommended immediate installation of a portable seismograph on Ruiz. He also reminded INGEOMINAS that it had an obligation to conduct monitoring—using the expertise of international scientists as necessary. Additionally, Tomblin suggested that INGEOMINAS prepare hazard maps in anticipation of various types of possible eruptions. Colombian civil defense officials were alerted to their obligation to develop a plan for delivering alerts and evacuating at-risk populations.

As the spring progressed, additional international scientists visited Ruiz and offered further support to the pleas for the installation of seismographs on the volcano to monitor its activity, as well as for the creation of hazard maps. Progress was slow. The first seismographs became operational on July 20, 1985, but they were of little use for a variety of reasons, including: There were too few seismographs on the mountain to obtain reliable earthquake locations; the seismographs were analog systems using paper records that had to be retrieved daily, those records had to be mailed to the National University of Bogotá for interpretation; and the seismograph results were not reported for months. Data also were not shared willingly between groups in the states of Caldas and Tolima—even though they bordered each other and faced identical hazards should the volcano erupt. Some authors suggest that there was a lack of urgency to forge working relationships throughout the spring and summer of 1985 because the volcano did not show any increase in the intensity of its activity.

If there had been any doubt that the volcano indeed was building to a larger eruption, that doubt was erased on September 11, 1985. At 1:30 p.m. local time, a strong phreatic (steam-driven) eruption began, and it continued for at least six hours. Arenas Crater became deeper and its walls steeper. Large blocks were thrown more than half a mile (1 kilometer) from the crater. Ash fell on the cities of Manizales and Chinchiná, more than 15 miles (25 kilometers) from the volcano. National Park personnel left about 6 p.m. amid heavy ash fall, loud explosions, and lightning. Earthquakes associated with the eruption triggered an ice and rock avalanche on the northeast side of the volcano. The avalanche swept at least 17 miles (27 kilometers) down the Rio Azufrado Valley. Although there were no human casualties during this eruption, local and national officials suddenly understood that the volcano presented a real danger to communities around the volcano. Urgent requests for assistance were sent to various United Nations offices and the U.S. Geological Survey (USGS). Scientists from the United States, Ecuador, Switzerland, Costa Rica, and Italy were sent to help in monitoring efforts and preparation of hazard maps. A preliminary version of the hazard map was released on October 7, and the map was published on the front page of the nationally circulated Colombian newspaper *El Espectador* on October 9. The corresponding report warned of a 100% probability of damaging mudflows that would be generated by an eruption of the volcano, with the towns of Armero, Mariquita, Honda, Ambalema, and the lower part of the Rio Chinchiná being in the greatest danger. Probabilities also were estimated for occurrences of regional ash fall (67%), pyroclastic flows (21%), and lava flows (8%). A working hazard map finally was in circulation.

The hazard map indicated areas that were most likely to be affected by the expected mudflows. The certainty of damaging lahars during an eruption of Ruiz was based on historical accounts of past eruptions, and mapping work that had been completed in the early 1970s by USGS scientist, Darrell Herd. A Spanish priest, Pedro Simon, wrote an account in 1604 of the 1595 eruption of Nevado del Ruiz, which includes a vivid description of mudflows on the Guali and Lagunillas rivers. That eruption killed 656 people. Simon stated that mud overflowed channels of both rivers and left the land so devastated that, for several years afterward, nothing would grow except small weeds.

Colombian naturalist Joaquin Acosta presented his account of the 1845 eruption of Ruiz and resulting mudflows at a meeting of the Academy of Sciences in Paris. The 1845 eruption killed 1,000 people.

> Descending along the Lagunillas [River] from its sources in the Nevado del Ruiz, came an immense flood of thick mud which rapidly filled the bed of the river, covered or swept away the trees and houses, burying men and animals. The entire population perished in the upper part and narrower parts of the Lagunillas valley. In the lower part, several people were saved by fleeing sideways to the heights; less happily, others were stranded on the summits of small hills from which it was impossible to save them before they died. . . (Voight, 1990).

Both men described lahars originating from rather small eruptions of Ruiz. More significantly, Acosta's account describes the death of the majority of the population within parts of the Lagunillas River valley. By far, most of these fatalities occurred where the narrow valley of the Lagunillas River met the wider valley of the Magdalena River. It was on these lahar deposits at the confluence of these two rivers that the city of Armero was built. Scientist Jeff Tomblin noted in early October that "the area devastated in 1845 has a present-day population on the order of 20,000." He felt that the eruption of September 11had stimulated the reactions of scientists and public safety authorities, so he was hopeful that they would take the necessary measures to limit possible damage in the very near future.

Despite Tomblin's optimism, there was serious disagreement among public officials about how they viewed the dangers of the volcano and how they communicated those dangers to the public. The director of the Geophysical Institute of the Andes reported that he did not see anything happening at the volcano that threatened residents. The Chamber of Commerce in Manizales feared that irresponsible reporting of the volcano's activity and hazards would cause economic losses. The archbishop (also in Manizales) accused the media of "volcanic terrorism." There also was concern that publication of the long-awaited hazard map would cause devaluation of real estate. Regardless, officials from INGEOMINAS, the governor of Caldas, civil defense authorities, and the Minister of Mines insisted that this map was a useful tool that would enable the various civil defense organizations to prepare plans for evacuation. Civil defense authorities began the work of educating local and state officials and overseeing the drafting of evacuation plans. They were coordinating the placement of scouts with radios on the upper reaches of major river valleys who could warn of approaching lahars. Plans appeared to be moving forward. Yet the people in the communities at risk were confused about who was in charge, what interpretation of the volcano's activity was correct, how they would be notified it was time to evacuate, and who would pay for the evacuation if it needed to happen. The mayor of Armero in one interview said that many people in his town did not know whether they should stay or go. He felt that the local emergency committee "did not have the necessary information or financial resources to do anything in the event of a catastrophe. . . . For this reason, the people have lost confidence in the veracity of the information and have commended their fate to God" (Voight, 1990). Indeed, Armero had problems with its evacuation plans. A detailed map of the town indicated that there was no safe place for a shelter within the community, and that people would have to travel more than six tenths of a mile (1 kilometer) to safety. Any evacuation would be a major undertaking. Residents would require ample warning time, a clear order to evacuate, and clearly delineated evacuation routes. Sadly, none of these was forthcoming.

At approximately 3 p.m. on November 13, 1985, ranchers north of the volcano heard a deep rumbling and noticed a black plume rising from the summit of Ruiz. News of the eruption reached the director of civil defense of Tolima about an hour after the eruption began. He called the regional director of INGEOMINAS (Alberto Nuñez), who recommended that Armero and Honda be prepared for immediate evacuation. At 5 p.m. local time, the Emergency Committee of Tolima met. Referencing the volcanic hazard map, they discussed the evacuation of Armero, Mariquita, and Ambalema, and the need to post observers along the river valleys to warn of mudflow activity. At 7 p.m., the committee asked a police captain to step out of the meeting to alert police stations in Armero and its neighboring towns that the evacuation order was imminent. At 7:30 p.m., the Red Cross—at Nuñez's request—ordered the evacuation of Armero.

In the meantime, the eruption at Ruiz had subsided. The phreatic eruption of 3 p.m. had produced no long-reaching lahars. In Armero, residents heard messages from Radio Armero and the village priest reassuring them that the danger had passed.

At 9:08 p.m. a much stronger eruption began. Multiple pyroclastic flows were erupted and extended 3 miles (5 kilometers) down the Rio Azufrado. Eruption temperatures exceeded 1,600°F (900°C). The result of this eruption was melting of much of the snow pack. Torrents of meltwater and chunks of rock and ice poured into the headwaters of the Rio Azufrado and Rio Lagunillas. People living in the upper valleys of the Lagunillas, Molinas, and Guali reported hearing lahars as early as 9:15 p.m. By scraping soil and loose rocks from valley walls, the lahars grew in volume as they flowed down the river valleys. The mud flowed at speeds of 11 to 33 miles per hour (18 to 54 kilometers per hour), but moved in surges. Where the mud encountered a bridge, the flow was held back; as soon as the bridge was destroyed, the mud started moving again.

Lahars entered the Rio Chinchiná and struck the village of Chinchiná, 22 miles (35 kilometers) from the summit of Ruiz, at 10:30 p.m. Although some residents had evacuated, more than 1,100 people died.

The Rio Lagunillas is fed by the Rio Azufrado. When the two rivers converged, the peak flow (1.7 million cubic feet per second; 48,000 cubic meters per second) was equivalent to three times that of the average discharge of the Mississippi River. Between 9:45 p.m. and 10:00 p.m., officials in Ibagué attempted to order the evacuation of Armero. Shortly thereafter, civil defense officials using radios from the towns of Libano, Murillo, and Ambalema tried to warn Armero to evacuate. Armero experienced power outages, however, and the ash cloud from the erupting volcano disrupted radio and telephone communications, thus the order never reached authorities in Armero. Shortly after the lahar passed Libano, the initial lahar wave reached a dam on the Lagunillas. The dam broke and sent a cool water flood ahead of the lahar. Armero had run out of time.

A wave nearly 130-feet (40 meters) high emerged from the canyon just above Armero at about 11:30 p.m. Mud that was 6.5- to 16-feet (2- to 5-meters) deep flowed across central and southern Armero at a speed of 18 miles per hour (29 kilometers per hour). A second major pulse struck at 11:50 p.m., followed by several smaller surges. The last major pulse occurred just after 1 a.m. on November 14. Even though many people heard the commotion in the streets as the first wave struck, it was impossible to outrun the mud or to find shelter within the town. More than 22,000 people died as the mudflows moved through Armero. Several more people were partially buried in the mud and could not be rescued before they died from shock, exposure, or injuries. The few residents of Armero who escaped told of friends or relatives calling them and telling them to leave well in advance of the lahar. No official evacuation order was ever broadcast in Armero. One eyewitness, a geology student on a field trip who along with other students was staying in Armero that night, tells of the confusion and chaos of the event. When the students found that pea-sized particles were falling from the sky they woke their professor, who told them to pack because they were leaving, even though there was no alarm. The group turned on the radio and heard the mayor telling listeners not to worry. Then the radio went off the air and the power went out. The students began hearing noises that sounded like objects falling.

> We were running and about to reach the corner when a river of water came down the streets . . . we turned around screaming, toward the hotel, because the waters were dragging beds along, overturning cars, sweeping people away . . . [we] went back to the hotel, a three-story building with a terrace, built of cement and very sturdy . . . suddenly I felt blows, and looking towards the rear of the hotel I saw [something] like foam, coming down in the darkness . . . it was (a wall of) mud approaching the hotel, and sure enough it crashed against the rear of the hotel and started crushing walls . . . and then the ceiling slab fractured, and . . . the entire building was destroyed and broken into pieces. Since the building was made of cement, I thought that it would resist, but it [the bouldery mud] was coming in such an overwhelming way . . . the university bus

that was in a parking lot next to the hotel was higher than us [on a wave of mud], on fire, and it exploded, so I covered my face thinking, this is where I die a horrible death. . . . (Voight, 1990).

Perhaps the most heartbreaking moments of that night for that particular student came when he encountered a young girl stuck in the mud.

There was a little girl who I thought was decapitated, but what happened was that her head was buried in the mud. . . . A lady told me, "look that girl moved a leg." Then I moved toward her and my legs sank into the mud, which was hot but not burning, and I started to get the little girl out, but when I saw her hair was caught, that seemed to me the most unfair thing in the world. . . . And it started to be light, and that's when we lost control because we saw that horrible sea of mud, which was so gigantic . . . there were people buried, calling out, calling for help, and if one tried to go to them, one would sink into the mud . . . so now you must start counting time as before Armero and after Armero. . . . (Voight, 1990).

In his 1990 summary paper, geologist Barry Voight described the events leading up to and including what would become known as the Ruiz disaster. Voight concluded that the national and regional governments acted responsibly in their attempts to assemble appropriate experts to draw up a hazard map, monitor the volcano's activity, and determine evacuation routes and shelters for the population at risk. Scientists accurately determined the nature of the hazards facing the region's residents. Local authorities, however, were unwilling to bear the economic or political costs of early evacuation or a false alarm. This led to them taking a calculated risk that they could sound an alarm at the very last possible moment, when danger could be guaranteed, and could save populations at that time. Unfortunately, power failures, communications breakdowns, lack of properly funded and equipped local emergency officials, and conflicting messages to the populace made it impossible to save the people of Armero once danger was guaranteed and imminent. If city officials had demanded evacuation when the first alarm was sounded at 7:30 p.m., then the city would have been empty by the time the first wave of mud hit at 11:30 p.m. No lives had to be lost.

Voight's paper lists a number of valuable lessons learned at Armero. First and foremost, history had repeated itself. The 1985 tragedy was eerily similar to the 1845 disaster described by Acosta. Lahars covered nearly identical areas around the townsite of Armero, and killed about 70% of the population in that area in each eruption. Secondly, there were immense breakdowns in communication before and during the eruption. Communication devices and electricity failed during the eruption and no alternative plan or advanced technology was in place to bridge the gap created when traditional communications methods failed. There also were problems with communication between states, between regional officials and local officials, and between local officials and the general public. Risks had not been sufficiently explained to the public, and no evacuation instructions were distributed. Residents also were confused about who would order an evacuation should the need for one arise. There are isolated reports of firemen walking the streets of town at about 10:30 p.m. telling residents to leave. Several residents told the firefighters the evacuation order was a lie because the village priest earlier had told them that nothing had happened and they should not be alarmed. The third lesson to be learned from Ruiz is that even a small eruption can produce disastrous consequences under the right circumstances. Snow and ice capped volcanoes such as Ruiz are immensely dangerous when even small amounts of meltwater starts moving down steep river valleys.

After the eruption on November 13, 1985, the government of Colombia established a permanent, well-equipped volcano observatory in the town of Manizales. The United States also took action in cooperation with the U.S. Office of Foreign Disaster Assistance, forming a team of volcanologists within the USGS that would be ready to go at a moment's notice to assist with volcanic crises anywhere in the world. This became known as the Volcano Disaster Assistance Program (VDAP). At the request of a host country, and working through the U.S. Agency for International Development, VDAP has a three-fold mission. First, it directly assists in crisis response by bringing enough instruments to the site to create a fully functional volcano observatory, and leaves it in place permanently. The team provides data and support to the hosts, who are responsible for hazard communications. Its second task is to train the local scientists how to use their new instruments and interpret the data gathered. By doing these two important things, VDAP equips scientists with tools and knowledge to manage the volcanic crisis after the team returns home. The third part of the mission—and one equally important to the continuity of knowledge within the U.S. volcanology community—is to give the USGS scientists experience in working with an active, explosive volcano which they might otherwise have to wait decades to obtain if they worked only in the United States. Since 1986, the VDAP team has responded to crises at about 30 different volcanoes in nearly 20 countries.

See Also: Colombia; Composite Volcano; Lahar; Pyroclastic Flow; Volcano Disaster Assistance Program.

Further Reading

BBC News. (2013, May 22). *1985: Volcano kills thousands in Colombia.* Retrieved from http://news.bbc.co.uk/onthisday/hi/dates/stories/november/13/newsid_2539000 /2539731.stm

Decker, R., & Decker, B. (1998). *Volcanoes* (3rd ed.; Academic Version). New York: W.H. Freeman and Company.

Francis, P., & Oppenheimer, C. (2004). *Volcanoes* (2nd ed). Oxford: Oxford University Press.

Herd, D. G., & Comite de Estudios Vulcanologicos. (1986). The 1985 Ruiz Volcano disaster. *EOS, Transactions of the American Geophysical Union* 67 (19), 457–460.

U.S. Geological Survey. (2013, May 22). *Description: Nevado del Ruiz eruption and lahar, 1985.* Retrieved from http://vulcan.wr.usgs.gov/Volcanoes/Colombia/Ruiz/description _eruption_lahar_1985.html

U.S. Geological Survey. (2013, June 6). *Volcano disaster assistance program.* Retrieved from http://volcanoes.usgs.gov/vdap/

Voight, B. (1990). The 1985 Nevado del Ruiz volcano catastrophe: anatomy and retrospection. *Journal of Volcanology and Geothermal Research 44*, 349–386.

New Zealand

The country of New Zealand straddles the boundary between the Australian Plate and the Pacific Plate. North Island and the Kermadec Islands lie on the Australian Plate, and South Island lies on the Pacific Plate along with the southern island groups belonging to New Zealand. Beneath North Island and the northern tip of South Island, the Pacific Plate is subducting beneath the Australian Plate. The plate boundary abruptly shifts to a transform boundary called the Alpine Fault. It shears the western part of South Island, creating a mountainous terrain by means of faulting and folding rather than through volcanic activity. Because of the variation in the types of plate boundaries that exist in New Zealand, there is a great deal of variation in the terrain and geologic activity seen on the two islands, as well as within the smaller outlying islands.

The Kermadec Islands lie between North Island and Tonga. The subduction zone in this area is known for very large earthquakes, though they do not often produce tsunamis. The Kermadec Islands are volcanoes, although many of them are several thousand years old and most have not erupted in historic times. North Island has frequent earthquakes due to both the subduction zone and, more often, volcanic and geothermal activity. It is rare that an earthquake is large and damaging, but these types of earthquakes do occur. In 1931, a magnitude 7.9 earthquake occurred in Hawke's Bay and killed 256 people. A magnitude 6.6 earthquake off the east coast of North Island occurred in 2007, killing one person. South Island has more—and generally larger—earthquakes than North Island. A magnitude 7.8 earthquake occurred in 2009 off South Island's west coast. Another occurred in 2011 near Christchurch, killing 181 people—most in just two building collapses—and closing the downtown business district of the city for almost two years.

Volcanic activity is common throughout New Zealand, but most active volcanoes are located on or near North Island. White Island, just to the north of North Island, is a frequently active volcano. It has erupted three times since March of 2000. Tongariro on North Island is a volcanic complex comprised of nearly a dozen composite cones. Ngauruhoe is one of the peaks, and has been one of New Zealand's most active volcanoes during historical times. Ruapehu is Tongariro's neighbor to the south. Although its last eruption was in 2007, it is also one of New Zealand's most historically active volcanoes. One of New Zealand's largest and most dangerous volcanoes is Taupo. It has an immense 22 mile (35 kilometer) wide caldera, and is considered to be a super volcano. Its last eruption about 1,800 years ago was New Zealand's largest in the last 10,000 years. Raoul Island in the

Kermadecs erupted in 2006. Two seamounts in the Kermadec Islands also have erupted at some time since the year 2000.

See Also: Australian Plate; Pacific Plate; Ruapehu, Mount, New Zealand; Subduction Zone; Taupo Volcano, New Zealand.

Further Reading

Smithsonian Institution. National Museum of Natural History. Global Volcanism Program. (2014, June 18). Retrieved from http://www.volcano.si.edu/

U.S. Geological Survey. (2014, June 18). *Historic world earthquakes. New Zealand.* Retrieved from http://earthquake.usgs.gov/earthquakes/world/historical_country.php #new_zealand

New Zealand Earthquake (2011)

On February 22, 2011, Christchurch, New Zealand, experienced a magnitude 6.3 earthquake. The epicenter was located about 6.2 miles (10 kilometers) southeast of Christchurch's central business district, near the town of Lyttleton. The earthquake was an aftershock of a larger magnitude 7.1 earthquake that occurred in September of 2010. The main shock, often referred to as the Darville or Canterbury earthquake, was larger than the Christchurch earthquake. It occurred far enough from Christchurch that it did not cause any loss of life, however, and caused very little loss of property. In contrast, the earthquake that occurred in 2011 was close enough to Christchurch to cause tremendous amounts of damage, 1,500 injuries, and 185 deaths. Of the fatalities that occurred, more than 110 were due to collapse of two multistory office buildings in Christchurch's business district. Another 11 people were killed by falling bricks and masonry, 6 died in city buses crushed by crumbling walls, and 5 were killed by falling rocks in the Sumner and Redcliffs area.

Nearly 100,000 buildings were destroyed or severely damaged in the earthquake. Many buildings had been damaged in the 2010 main shock, and were damaged more severely or destroyed in this aftershock. Older masonry buildings were hardest hit. Several of Christchurch's historic buildings were extensively damaged, including Lyttleton's Timeball Station, the Provincial Council Chambers, the Anglican Christchurch Cathedral, and the Catholic Cathedral of the Blessed Sacrament. Christchurch's tallest building, the Hotel Grand Chancellor, also was a casualty of the earthquake. It was damaged so severely it had to be demolished.

Many homes in the eastern sections of the city were built on former swampland. When the seismic waves moved through the area, they were amplified in the soft material so ground shaking was very severe. Additionally, water-saturated sand and silt in the subsurface liquefied and bubbled upward through cracks in the ground. Homes and other buildings were partially buried in silt, and water and sewage from broken pipes flooded neighborhoods. Foundations cracked and buckled,

Earthquakes Don't Kill People—Buildings Do

It is an unfortunate reality that, for most earthquakes, the greatest percentage of the death toll is due to some element of a man-made structure collapsing on people that are inside or nearby. In 1755, a major earthquake occurring near Lisbon, Portugal, made hundreds of thousands of people question their faith because many of the people killed were inside churches that collapsed. A 1976 earthquake in China killed hundreds of thousands of people, most of whom lived in masonry buildings that collapsed in the quake. The significant death toll from an earthquake near Mexico City in 1985 largely was due to the collapse of buildings. The same is true of the horrific death toll caused by an earthquake in Haiti in 2010. There are, of course, notable exceptions. In the Chimbote, Peru, earthquake of 1970 most of the deaths were due to landslides. In 2004, the Indian Ocean earthquake centered near Banda Aceh, Indonesia, caused a tsunami which was responsible for most of the resulting deaths. In most major earthquakes, however, building collapse unfortunately is a common cause of death.

causing irreparable damage to most homes. Even though several thousand homes had to be demolished there were few serious injuries in these areas of the city.

Although the government immediately responded with well-rehearsed crisis management procedures, the fact remained that the city was hard hit by this earthquake. Electricity was restored to the majority of the city within three days, but Christchurch's central business district remained closed for more than two years. Approximately 70,000 people are believed to have left the city because their homes had been severely damaged or destroyed. Populations in neighboring cities swelled as a result. Many families were expected to return to Christchurch once adequate housing was built and neighborhoods could be reestablished. However, the eastern part of the city in the formerly swampy area probably never will be rebuilt.

The fault responsible for this earthquake is one that was previously unknown to scientists, although earthquake activity generally is related to the plate boundary between the Pacific and Australian plates. This particular fault did not break the surface. Scientists had to rely on maps of aftershocks to define the offending fault and dimensions of the rupture plane. The fault runs northeast to southwest for 8.7 miles (14 kilometers) across eastern and southern Christchurch. The maximum displacement along the fault was 8 feet (2.5 meters), measured diagonally in the direction of fault motion. The block to the northwest of the fault moved down and eastward relative to the land southeast of the fault. As much as 1.8 inches (4.5 centimeters) of uplift occurred on the southeast side of the fault, and 0.6 inches (1.5 centimeters) of subsidence occurred to the northwest.

See Also: Earthquake; Earthquake Hazards; New Zealand; Pacific Plate.

Further Reading

GNS Science. (2014, June 6). *The hidden fault that caused the February 2011 Christchurch earthquake*. Retrieved from http://www.gns.cri.nz/Home/Our-Science/Natural-Hazards /Recent-Events/Canterbury-quake/Hidden-fault

McSaveney, E. (2014, June 6). Historic earthquakes—The 2011 Christchurch earthquake and other recent earthquakes. In *Te Ara, The Encyclopedia of New Zealand*. Retrieved from http://www.teara.govt.nz/en/historic-earthquakes/page-13

U.S. Geological Survey. (2014, June 6). *Magnitude 6.1—South Island of New Zealand.* Retrieved from http://earthquake.usgs.gov/earthquakes/eqinthenews/2011/usb0001igm/#summary

Nicaragua

Nicaragua is located in Central America, between Honduras to the north and Costa Rica to the south. The country has more than 100 known volcanoes, seven of which have been active since Spanish settlement of the area in the early 1500s. The region also is prone to large and damaging earthquakes. Nicaragua's volcanoes and earthquakes are a result of the subduction of the Cocos Plate beneath the Caribbean Plate to the northeast. The subduction zone is marked by the Middle America Trench just off the country's Pacific coast. Nicaragua lies on the overriding Caribbean Plate.

The most recently active volcano in Nicaragua is San Cristóbal. It began its last eruptive cycle in June 2013, and its most recent report of activity was that of a small ash and gas cloud in April 2014. The volcano is the youngest of five cones in the San Cristóbal volcanic complex. It is Nicaragua's tallest volcano, and it has been active numerous times in the last 500 years. Concepción Volcano erupted between 2009 and 2011. It is a symmetrical cone that forms the northwest half of the island of Ometepe in Lake Nicaragua. It is connected to its inactive neighbor Madera by a narrow isthmus. The volcano Telica erupted in 2011 and 2012. The volcano has a geothermal area frequented by tourists, and geothermal exploration has occurred in nearby areas. Masaya is a large shield volcano with a steep-walled caldera that is up to 985 feet (300 meters) deep in places. An active lava lake existed in the caldera during the time of the Spanish Conquistadors. It last erupted in 2008.

Earthquakes are a part of life in Nicaragua. Because the country sits above an active subduction zone, the number of earthquakes that occurs within the country is predictably large. In the past 100 years, nearly 10,000 Nicaraguans have died as a result of earthquakes. The country's deadliest earthquake occurred in the capital city of Managua in 1972. The magnitude 6.2 earthquake occurred at a very shallow depth immediately beneath the city. The results were catastrophic. Nearly 5 square miles (13 square kilometers) in the heart of the city was utterly destroyed. Many buildings constructed in the local Taquezal style (wood frame covered with plaster) were completely demolished, shaken to the ground. Older buildings were more vulnerable than newer ones because of internal damage from termites and other erosive factors. Additionally, most of the city's multistory buildings were seriously damaged. Tens of thousands of homes were rendered unsafe, as were all four main hospitals and 53,000 units of low- and medium-income housing. More than

250,000 of Managua's 400,000 residents were displaced. Approximately 5,000 people lost their lives. The country's second most deadly earthquake occurred in 1931, when 2,500 people died in Managua in a magnitude 6.0 earthquake. A magnitude 5.8 earthquake killed 1,000 people in Cosiguina in 1951. A magnitude 7.6 earthquake killed 116 individuals in 1992. Major earthquakes also occurred in 2004 and 2005, but no fatalities were reported from those events.

See Also: Caribbean Plate; Cocos Plate; Subduction Zone.

Further Reading

Smithsonian Institution. National Museum of Natural History. Global Volcanism Program. (2014, June 13). Retrieved from http://www.volcano.si.edu/search_volcano_results.cfm

U.S. Geological Survey. (2014, June 13). *Historic world earthquakes. Nicaragua.* http://earthquake.usgs.gov/earthquakes/world/historical_country.php#nicaragua

North American Plate

The North American Plate contains the three countries of Canada, the United States of America, and Mexico, as well as the northernmost part of Guatemala. To its south lie the Cocos and Caribbean plates. Most of the western boundary of the North American Plate is in direct contact with the oceanic Pacific Plate, although there are two notable exceptions. In the far northwestern part of the North American Plate, to the west of the Aleutian Islands, it is bounded by the Eurasian Plate. Just off the west coast of the northwestern part of the United States is the Juan de Fuca Plate. The Juan de Fuca Plate's eastern boundary extends from near Cape Mendocino in northern California to southernmost British Columbia in southern Canada. The Juan de Fuca Plate is a small remnant of the much larger Farallon Plate that has completely subducted beneath most of the west coast of the United States.

The geology of the North American Plate is complex and variable, as might be expected due to its large size. Portions of the plate that are relevant to the context of this encyclopedia are located along the western edge of the plate. Beginning along the west coast of Mexico, the Cocos Plate subducts beneath the North American Plate. This results in large earthquakes and a chain of volcanoes known as the Trans-Mexican Volcanic Belt. In the Gulf of California, located between the Baja Peninsula and mainland Mexico, a small spreading center, is creating new lithosphere that is being added to both the North American and Pacific plates. Following this spreading center northward, it becomes a transform boundary known as the San Andreas Fault. Motion along this transform boundary involves the neighboring Pacific Plate moving northwestward relative to the North American Plate. The San Andreas Fault is responsible for many large and damaging earthquakes. The largest earthquake to occur on the fault in modern times was an estimated magnitude 8.0 earthquake that occurred just north of San Francisco in 1906.

That earthquake and subsequent fires destroyed much of the city. More recent earthquakes along the San Andreas Fault have included the 1989 Loma Prieta earthquake near San Francisco, California, and the 1994 Northridge Earthquake near Los Angeles, California.

North of the San Andreas Fault lies the Cascadia Subduction Zone. Here, the small Juan de Fuca Plate is subducting beneath the North American Plate. This subduction zone feeds volcanic activity in the Cascade Range, which is a volcanic mountain range that extends from northern California northward into southern British Columbia, Canada. The last volcano in that range to erupt was Mount St. Helens. It had a catastrophic eruption in May of 1980, with subsequent dome-building activity that continued to 1986. The mountain experienced a resurgence of dome-building activity from 2004 to 2009. Other volcanoes within the Cascades include Mount Rainier, Mount Hood, Mount Shasta, and Lassen Peak.

The coast of southwestern Alaska and the Aleutian Islands represent another major subduction zone, where the Pacific Plate is subducting beneath the North American Plate. This subduction zone extends thousands of miles and is marked both by a trench offshore, as well as a chain of volcanoes and volcanic islands that starts near Anchorage, Alaska, and extends westward thousands of miles toward the Kamchatka Peninsula of Russia. Several volcanoes within this chain frequently are active, including Augustine, Pavlof, Redoubt, and Shishaldin. The largest eruption of the Twentieth Century occurred at Katmai, which is found on the remote Alaskan Peninsula near the first of the Aleutian Islands. The eruption did not cause any loss of life or property because of its remote location, but it filled several valleys with pyroclastic material and created what early visitors called the "Valley of Ten Thousand Smokes." Even though the Aleutian Islands are remote, volcanoes there still pose a threat to life and property in that they have the potential to create large clouds of volcanic ash. Volcanic ash has the ability to damage aircraft engines, and thus cause airplanes to crash. Many resources go into monitoring of these volcanoes so that pilots can fly through the area with confidence, knowing that they will receive a volcanic ash advisory if a volcano erupts anywhere near their flight paths.

See Also: Aleutian Islands; Augustine Volcano, Alaska, United States; Caribbean Plate; Cascadia Subduction Zone; Eurasian Plate; Farallon Plate; Hood, Mount, Oregon, United States; Juan de Fuca Plate; Katmai Eruption, Alaska, United States (1912); Lassen Peak, California, United States; Loma Prieta Earthquake, California, United States (1989); Northridge Earthquake, California, United States (1994); Pacific Plate; Pavlof Volcano, Alaska, United States; Rainier, Mount, Washington, United States; Redoubt Volcano, Alaska, United States; San Andreas Fault; San Francisco Earthquake, California, United States (1906); Shasta, Mount, California, United States; Shishaldin Volcano, Alaska, United States; St. Helens, Mount, Washington, United States.

Further Reading

Tarbuck, E. J., Lutgens, F. K., & Tasa, D. (2011). *Earth: An introduction to physical geology* (10th ed.). Upper Saddle River, NJ: Pearson Prentice Hall/Pearson Education, Inc.

Northridge Earthquake, California, United States (1994)

The Northridge earthquake that struck the greater Los Angeles, California, area on January 17, 1994, killed 57 people, injured more than 9,000, and left more than 20,000 people homeless. It was felt over about 125,000 square miles in the United States and Mexico, and the quake caused the strongest ground movements ever recorded in an urban area in North America. Its epicenter was 20 miles west-northwest of Los Angeles and just one mile from the highly populated community of Northridge—part of the reason that it proved to be the costliest earthquake in U.S. history, The Northridge earthquake caused an estimated $20 billion in damages even though it measured a moderate 6.7 on the Richter scale.

The temblor struck at 4:30 a.m., waking Los Angeles-area residents with 10 to 20 seconds of strong vibrations that forced the earth's crust upward over an area of 2,500 square miles. The Northridge quake was the result of what is known as a blind thrust that occurred along the Oak Ridge fault system. The blind thrust caused a rupture of the fault plane from about 11 miles below the earth's surface up to about 3 miles below the surface. Thousands of buildings were destroyed, 7 freeway bridges collapsed, and another 170 bridges were damaged. Wood-frame buildings were most prone to be damaged severely. Vibrations also ruptured gas lines, causing fiery explosions. The greatest devastation occurred in the San Fernando Valley and Simi Valley, especially in the communities of Northridge, Santa Monica, and Sherman Oaks. The quake also triggered thousands of landslides that destroyed homes, roads, and utility lines.

This building was severely damaged in the 1994 Northridge, California earthquake. (Joe Sohm Visions of America/Newscom)

Several days later, 9,000 homes and businesses still had no electricity, 20,000 premises had no gas, and nearly 50,000 structures remained without water. Long-term clean-up and recovery efforts took the better part of two years, with more than $12 billion in public and private aid used for residential reconstruction alone. During the first 18 months of reconstruction, local authorities were able to recycle more than 80% of the earthquake debris—about 1.6 million tons of material.

Construction, building codes, and emergency response procedures all were tested by the Northridge quake—which revealed that even moderate-sized earthquakes could produce more intense ground motions than previously expected. After the 1971 San Fernando earthquake, local officials and engineers had launched building code revisions, freeway reinforcements, and retrofitting of buildings to sustain future strong quakes. The Northridge quake, however, which produced a stronger, more concentrated pulse of ground movement, revealed additional vulnerabilities in local construction. Although many well-engineered buildings near the epicenter survived with no structural damage, others unexpectedly sustained major damage, including fractured steel frames. As a result of such failures, local authorities and structural engineering associations developed a new set of construction requirements for steel-frame buildings. Freeway construction codes also were reevaluated.

See Also: Loma Prieta Earthquake, California, United States (1989); San Francisco Earthquake, California, United States (1906); United States of America.

Further Reading

Northridge earthquake (1994). (2014, August 12). In *World geography: Understanding a changing world.* Santa Barbara, CA: ABC-CLIO.

O

Okushiri Island Earthquake and Tsunami, Japan (1993)

On July 12, 1993, the island of Okushiri and neighboring west coast of Hokkaido experienced a large (magnitude 7.8) earthquake and a devastating tsunami. Very few deaths were attributed to the earthquake itself or from the fires that raged afterward, fueled by cooking and heating fuel. Most deaths occurred as a result of the tsunami. In all, 198 people lost their lives in the earthquake and resulting tsunami. Prior to the earthquake, the island of Okushiri was home to nearly 5,000 people. Most families earned their living from the ocean as fishing boat captains or in businesses that supported the fishing industry.

The earthquake struck at 10:17 p.m. local time. A tsunami immediately was generated, and it crashed ashore on Okushiri Island as soon as two minutes after the earthquake began. Wave heights—called runups—were highest on the west side of Okushiri, nearest the epicenter of the earthquake. Maximum wave height was measured near the town of Monai at 101 feet (31 meters). Throughout most of the west coast of the island, runups were 65 feet (20 meters) or more. Everywhere else along the coastline of Okushiri, runups reached 33 feet (10 meters) or more. The entire southern tip of the island—where the town of Aonae was located—was swept clean by the waves. No homes, businesses, or other structures were left standing. Waves struck the west coast of Hokkaido as soon as five minutes after the earthquake began. Several towns received heavy damage from waves that reached heights of up to 30 feet (9 meters). Waves also traveled west to the coast of Russia within 30 minutes, where runups as high as 14 feet (4 meters) were measured. Waves struck South Korea's coastline after 90 minutes with waves 6 feet (2 meters) high.

Following the tsunami, the Japanese government set about rebuilding devastated areas of Okushiri Island. Thirty-five-foot (11-meter) tall concrete seawalls were constructed along 8.7 miles (14 kilometers) of the island's 52-mile (84-kilometer) shoreline. Fishermen now reach the sea by passing through large, heavy steel gates in the seawall. A tsunami refuge was built in the town of Aonae. The refuge is a platform 21.5 feet (6.6 meters) tall which people can climb quickly to escape a tsunami in the nearly flat landscape of the island's southern coast. The refuge can hold 2,000 people. A tsunami memorial hall was also built to honor the dead. In all, more than US $1 billion was spent on rebuilding efforts in the first six years after the tsunami. Unfortunately, many residents think that the money was not well spent.

High-paying construction jobs available during the recovery efforts gave young people a taste for the higher salaries they could never earn as fishermen. Many people have moved away to neighboring Hokkaido or other places to find higher paying jobs that are less demanding on their bodies and time than the difficult life of a fisherman requires. Even before the earthquake, the population of Okushiri was declining because fish harvests were diminishing due to overfishing and global warming. The problem was exacerbated after the tsunami because it destroyed the shallow-water abalone beds which many people depended on for their living, and the beds did not recover. The number of fishermen dropped from 750 to less than 200 between 1993 and 2012.

Many island residents would have preferred that the government had given survivors lump-sum payments instead of spending so much money on infrastructure. Survivors could have used lump-sum payments to start new businesses or invest in tourism that would have rebuilt the island's economy. Instead, the numbers of available jobs is declining and only one modern hotel exists on the island. Perhaps this situation will serve as a lesson to the leaders of communities that are rebuilding after natural disasters. A realistic assessment of a community's needs must be made if aid money is to be spent wisely.

See Also: Japan.

Further Reading

Fackler, M. (2012, January 9). In Japan, a rebuilt island serves as a cautionary tale. *The New York Times*. Retrieved from http://www.nytimes.com/2012/01/10/world/asia/okushiri-japan-rebuilt-after-a-quake-is-a-cautionary-tale.html?_r=0

Hirata, Y., & Murakami, M. (2006, November 16). Island hit by 1993 killer tsunami remains vigilant. *Japan Times*. Retrieved from http://www.japantimes.co.jp/news/2006/11/16/national/island-hit-by-1993-killer-tsunami-remains-vigilant/

Hokkaido Tsunami Survey Group. National Oceanic and Atmospheric Association. (2014, May 7). *Tsunami devastates Japanese coastal region*. Retrieved from http://nctr.pmel.noaa.gov/okushiri_devastation.html

Orphan Tsunami

An orphan tsunami is one which reaches a shoreline, but the location of the tsunami's origin is unknown. In today's world—with its tsunami warning systems and other technologies—orphan tsunamis do not occur. Prior to the late 1800s (before rapid communication became the norm), however, it was not at all uncommon for tsunamis to appear at shorelines around the Pacific without warning, and without any indication of the location of the tsunami's origin. One of the best-known orphan tsunamis was documented in January 1700, in Japan. An orphan tsunami struck a nearly 600-mile (1,000-kilometer) long stretch of the shoreline of eastern

Japan. Wave heights reached nearly 13 feet (5 meters) in some areas, and many homes were washed away. An unknown (but probably relatively small) number of deaths occurred in Japan.

The "parent" earthquake that generated this orphan tsunami was unknown for nearly 300 years. In 1996, scientists in Japan and the United States were able to piece together clues that indicated a likely magnitude 9.0 earthquake occurring on the Cascadia Subduction Zone created the tsunami that struck Japan in 1700. Until that time, most scientists did not think that the Cascadia Subduction Zone could produce an earthquake with a magnitude any greater than 7.5. Scientist Brian Atwater, however, found a number of tsunami deposits in the wetlands and estuaries of Puget Sound that suggested otherwise. Atwater found evidence of drowned encampments and forests of dead trees partially submerged in seawater. These indicated that an earthquake of immense size had changed the landscape considerably. Carbon dating performed by both American and Japanese scientists confirmed that these trees died around the year 1700. The orphan tsunami now had a parent.

See Also: Cascadia Subduction Zone; Tsunami.

Further Reading

Atwater, B. F., Satoko, M.-R., Kenji, S., Yoshinobu, T., Kazue, U., & Yamaguchi, D. K. (2005). *The orphan tsunami of 1700—Japanese clues to a parent earthquake in North America*. (U.S. Geological Survey Professional Paper 1707). University of Washington Press.

P

Pacific Plate

The Pacific Plate is the largest of the earth's tectonic plates. It comprises a large part of the Pacific Ocean—the world's largest ocean. As such, the Pacific Plate does not contain an appreciable amount of land area, but does include the Hawaiian Islands, the Cook Islands, the Baja Peninsula of Mexico, and a portion of southwestern California west of the San Andreas Fault. The Pacific Plate is surrounded by six different tectonic plates. Beginning in the north and continuing clockwise, the plates are the: North American Plate; Juan de Fuca Plate; Cocos Plate; Nazca Plate; Antarctic Plate; Australian Plate; and Philippine Plate.

The majority of new lithosphere in the Pacific Plate is being generated at its southern and eastern boundaries. The southern boundary with Antarctica is a divergent boundary stitched together with long transform boundaries. The boundaries with the Nazca and Cocos plates also are divergent boundaries. The combined boundary between these three plates is called the East Pacific Rise. Small spreading centers also exist elsewhere, including on the western edge of the Juan de Fuca Plate adjacent to the Pacific Northwest of the United States, and in the Gulf of California between the Baja Peninsula of Mexico and mainland Mexico. The entire northern and western margin of the Pacific Plate is subduction zone where the Pacific plate is being consumed.

The northern boundary between the Pacific and Juan de Fuca plates is a subduction zone, as is the boundary between the Philippine Plate and the eastern boundary of the Australian Plate. In these areas, the Pacific Plate is being consumed. These also are places where strong earthquakes are commonplace, as is volcanic activity. In these areas, however, the volcanism and earthquake epicenters typically are in the overriding plates, so fewer are found in the Pacific Plate itself. Transform boundaries exist along the west coast of North America and in the vicinity of New Zealand in the southwestern Pacific. The North American transform boundary is the San Andreas Fault. In New Zealand, the transform boundary is called the Alpine Fault.

Another tectonic feature within the Pacific Plate is the Hawaiian Hot Spot. This feature is a long-lived mantle plume that produces a great deal of magma that feeds volcanism within the Hawaiian Islands. The entire Hawaiian Island-Emperor Seamount chain was produced by magma from this hot spot over the last 70 million years or so. The hot spot has been active at least that long, and probably longer. Any older features that were created by the hot spot, however, have been subducted beneath the Aleutian Islands at the Aleutian Trench.

See Also: Aleutian Islands; Australian Plate; Cocos Plate; Divergent Boundary; Hawaiian Islands; Hot Spot; Nazca Plate; New Zealand; Philippine Plate; San Andreas Fault; Subduction Zone; Transform Boundary.

Further Reading

Tarbuck, E. J., Lutgens, F. K., & Tasa, D. (2011). *Earth: An introduction to physical geology* (10th ed.). Upper Saddle River, NJ: Pearson Prentice Hall/Pearson Education, Inc.

Pahoehoe

"Pahoehoe" is a Hawaiian term for lava flow surface that is smooth, billowing, or ropy in appearance. Pahoehoe forms almost exclusively in basalt lava flows, because only basalt is fluid enough to allow lava to flow unabated and form relatively smooth surfaces. In places where basalt lava flows are common, the two textures that can result are pahoehoe and "aa" which has a jagged, clinker texture. One curiosity of basalt lava is that pahoehoe can turn into aa as it flows downhill; however, aa never can turn into pahoehoe.

Two factors seem to determine whether a flow is composed of pahoehoe or aa. One factor is the percentage of the lava that is composed of solid crystals. A more crystalline lava generally produces aa. The second factor is the speed of the lava flow. Lava flows that travel faster tend to be aa flows, and those that travel slower typically are pahoehoe flows. In addition to these factors, a lava flow that cools over the course of its path could transition from pahoehoe to aa.

Pahoehoe comes in a variety of forms, all of which have fitting descriptive names. "Ropy" pahoehoe looks like coils of rope laid on the ground. The "ropes" can be as small as an inch (2.5 centimeters) in diameter to more than 12 inches (30 centimeters) in diameter. Billowing, smooth pahoehoe typically looks like a large, even surface, similar to a sheet that is laid gently on a bed but still has a broad air pocket underneath. These billows often are broken by cracks. "Shelly" pahoehoe is a billowy pahoehoe flow that has air pockets underneath a thin crust. This often is seen near the eruptive vent and is quite dangerous to walk on. A person's body weight often is enough to break through the crust, and the resulting jagged-edged holes have been known to cause deep cuts to the ankle or lower leg, depending on the depth of the air pocket. "Entrail" pahoehoe looks oddly like the viscera of a large animal. "Slabby" pahoehoe is, as the name suggests, a pahoehoe flow in which slabs of crust form and are rafted along on the underlying flow. In some cases the slabs can be upended, creating an uncharacteristically sharp and jagged surface to the flow. The final form of pahoehoe is the "toe." Toes are often small, finger-like lobes that advance beyond the edge of the main flow. They typically are about 4 to 5 inches (10 to 13 centimeters) in diameter, and taper to a rounded point. Sometimes these toes even curl upward at the end.

Pahoehoe tends to creep across the surface of the ground. In the coastal areas of Kilauea Volcano, it is not uncommon to run across pahoehoe flowing at a rate of 3 feet (1 meter) per minute or slower. This makes lava flows on Kilauea——particularly within Hawaii Volcanoes National Park—spectacularly approachable. Millions of park visitors have come as close to these slow, beautiful flows as the heat allows. When it is hot and flowing the lava is red. It very quickly develops a thin, silvery crust composed of glass. As the flow continues to move around the edges, a slight tinkling sound occurs as the skin stretches and the glass breaks to accommodate the lava flowing behind it. Typically, the front of a creeping pahoehoe flow is no more than 8 to 10 inches (20 to 25 centimeters) tall. When the flow stops moving, dissolved gases in the lava begin to escape and form gas bubbles in the still-molten lava beneath the flow's crust. This causes the flow to "inflate," or grow in height over the next several hours.

See Also: Aa; Basalt; Kilauea Volcano, Hawaii, United States.

Further Reading

Cas, R. A. F., & Wright, J. V. (1988). *Volcanic successions, modern and ancient.* London: Chapman & Hall.
Francis, P., & Oppenheimer, C. (2004). *Volcanoes* (2nd ed.). Oxford: Oxford University Press.

Papua New Guinea

Papua New Guinea is located in the South Pacific just north of Australia, on the island of New Guinea. New Guinea is divided almost evenly between the country of Papua New Guinea on the eastern side of the island, and Indonesia, which controls the western side of the island. The smaller islands of New Britain, New Ireland, New Hanover, and Bougainville also are part of the country. Papua New Guinea lies on the northern boundary of the Australian Plate. Here, microplates interact with each other, with the end result appearing to be that the Australian Plate is subducting beneath the Pacific Plate. In reality, it is one of the microplates that is subducting. Subduction causes large and damaging earthquakes and produces magma that feeds volcanic activity. Papua New Guinea experiences both of these effects of subduction. Earthquakes are common occurrences throughout Papua New Guinea. The country experiences multiple magnitude 6 or greater earthquakes every year. The most deadly earthquake in recent history occurred in July 1998. A magnitude 7.0 earthquake struck the island but did not cause much serious damage. The earthquake unexpectedly produced a devastating tsunami, however, with wave heights of up to 49 feet (15 meters). The area that was hardest hit was an inhabited sand bar between the ocean and a lagoon. The waves washed completely over the sand bar and swept away many residents. More than 2,000 people died in the tsunami, and more than 9,000 people were left homeless.

Volcanic activity also is commonplace throughout Papua New Guinea, including on the smaller outlying islands. One of the best-known eruptions in Papua New Guinea happened in 1994 on the northeastern tip of New Guinea at the Rabaul caldera. The Rabaul caldera consists of a large depression that has a breach in its eastern wall which opens to the ocean. Both inside and outside the caldera's rim are a number of smaller vents. Two of these vents—the composite volcanoes Tarvurvur and Vulcan—erupted simultaneously for several weeks. Eventually, Vulcan became quiet. Tarvurvur continued its eruption, and has been active intermittently since then. Other volcanoes that have erupted since 2000 include: Bagana (2013–2014); Garbuna (2008); Karkar (2013); Langila (2012); Manam (2013); Pago (2012); Ritter Island (2007); and Ulawun (2013).

See Also: Australian Plate; Pacific Plate; Papua New Guinea Earthquake and Tsunami (1998); Rabaul, Papua New Guinea; Subduction Zone; Tsunami.

Further Reading

Smithsonian Institution. National Museum of Natural History. Global Volcanism Program. (2014, June 20). Retrieved from http://www.volcano.si.edu/

U.S. Geological Survey. (2014, June 20). *Historic world earthquakes. Papua New Guinea.* http://earthquake.usgs.gov/earthquakes/world/historical_country.php#papua _new_guinea

Papua New Guinea Earthquake and Tsunami (1998)

Approximately 6:49 p.m. on July 17, 1998, a magnitude 7.0 earthquake struck near the north shore of Papua New Guinea. The area borders a plate boundary where the Indian-Australian Plate is overriding the Pacific Plate, thus area residents are not strangers to earthquakes. Many earthquakes of magnitude 7 or greater had occurred near the island in the previous 100 years. This earthquake, however, proved to be incredibly deadly. The earthquake struck just offshore from the village of Aitape near the western extent of the West Sepik province—a remote and isolated area of the country. In 1907, an earthquake of similar magnitude hit the island and caused subsidence of a stretch of coastline, and created a large, shallow lagoon called Sissano Lagoon. The villages of Warapu and Arop were situated on the narrow strip of land between the ocean and Sissano Lagoon.

When the 1998 earthquake struck, a bulletin was dispatched from the Pacific Tsunami Warning Center stating that there was no threat of a destructive Pacific-wide tsunami from this particular earthquake. The earthquake, however, was unusual as compared to those typically occurring at subduction zones. This quake occurred on a nearly vertical fault—which happens only rarely in that tectonic setting. It was also a fairly shallow earthquake, meaning that a great deal of energy from the earthquake went toward the surface. A 25-mile (40-kilometer) length of fault broke in the earthquake, and displacement along the fault was approximately 6 feet (1.8 meters).

A tsunami was generated as a result of the fault motion, and rushed onshore with the sound of what villagers described as "fighter jets." Waves up to 49 feet (15 meters) tall rushed ashore. The communities of Sissano, Malol, Warapu, and Arop were hit the hardest. The tsunami swept over those villages entirely. Very little was left standing in some places, and in other places nothing at all remained. All traces of Warapu and Arop were wiped away by the tsunami. Bodies, pieces of huts, and debris washed either into Sissano Lagoon or out to the Pacific Ocean.

Approximately 3,000 people died in the tsunami, although the exact number of casualties probably never will be known. Sadly, the event occurred during the summer school break and children were home from boarding schools that were located further inland. Thus, the timing contributed to the death toll. When the waves hit people scrambled to try and escape, but there was no high ground nearby. All people could do was run inland or climb coconut palms—and hope that the wave energy dissipated before it reached them. Only the fairly young and fit could climb or run fast enough to outrun the waves, however. Disproportionate numbers of the very old and very young were caught by the wave. The tsunami killed nearly an entire generation of children.

Survivors flooded the 120-bed hospital in the town of Vanimo. The hospital treated more than 600 patients. Many people lay on cots or stretchers on the hospital's lawn waiting for treatment. Nearby Australia and New Zealand sent a portable field hospital and a team of doctors and nurses to help treat the injured. They later recounted that the majority of wounds they saw were lacerations, broken bones, and head and chest injuries. Lacerations had been filled with bacteria-laden sand and became infected quickly. Several survivors required amputation after gangrene set in. Disease also soon became a problem. Water became contaminated from decaying marine life and human bodies. Those who had been participating in search and recovery missions made the difficult decision to bury the dead where

Evolution of Sea Floor Mapping

Slightly more than 100 years ago, options for collecting data to determine something as simple as the depth of the ocean in a particular location were quite limited. Researchers aboard ships could lower an anchor to the ocean floor and measure how much rope or chain was required to reach the floor. This was a slow, laborious, and ultimately unreliable method. In the early 1900s, sonar (SOund Navigation And Ranging) was invented. This gave scientists and ships' crews the ability to use sound waves to determine the distance to an object, such as the ocean floor, by measuring the travel time of a sound wave from its point of origin on a ship down to the ocean floor and back. Velocity is equal to distance divided by travel time. The velocity of sound in water is known and the travel time of the sound wave can be measured, so the only unknown is distance. Later generations of sonar include multiple sensors to enable mapping of a swath of the sea floor, called side-scan sonar. Side-scan sonar can produce incredibly detailed maps of the ocean floor. It can also be used to search for objects on the ocean floor, such as shipwrecks.

they were found or to cremate them. This was unfortunate, as surviving family were denied the ability to take part in traditional funeral services. The danger of death from disease was very real, however, and recovery personnel thought that they had little choice. After a few days, bodies found both in the ocean and on land had been scavenged and were unidentifiable. In the hours and days following the tragedy, many world leaders expressed deep sympathy to the people of Papua New Guinea. Dozens of countries delivered supplies and personnel to the island. Because no disaster plan included provisions for distribution of relief supplies, however, the disbursement of food, water, medical supplies, and equipment did not go as smoothly as it should have.

After relief efforts were well underway and the immediate needs of survivors had been attended to, scientific teams moved in to investigate the tsunami and try to make sense of the event. What they determined was that the tsunami seemed to be much taller than would be expected from a magnitude 7.0 event. It fit better with what is expected from a larger earthquake with a magnitude of 7.5. Two groups of scientists, however, developed ideas related to the great height of the wave. A research vessel surveyed the offshore area and found what appeared to be a landslide scar approximately 25 miles (40 kilometers) long. Researchers suggested that it was not the earthquake that created the tsunami, but a landslide. Another scientist used computer modeling to determine that the unusual earthquake that occurred could have created a tsunami of the size observed because the ocean was extremely deep just offshore. He also correctly noted, however, that it is entirely likely that a combination of the earthquake and an earthquake-triggered undersea landslide could have combined to create the large tsunami that devastated the northwest shore of Papua New Guinea.

See Also: Subduction Zone; Tsunami; Tsunami Warning Centers.

Further Reading

Davies, H. L., Davies, J. M., Lus, W. Y., Perembo, R. C. B., Joku, N., Gedikile, H., & Nongkas, M. (2014, May 20). *Learning from the Aitape tsunami.* Retrieved from http://nctr.pmel.noaa.gov/PNG/Upng/Learned/

Dudley, W. C., & Lee, M. (1998). *Tsunami!* (2nd ed.). Honolulu: University of Hawaii Press.

Geist, E. L. (2000). Origin of the 17 July 1998 Papua New Guinea tsunami: Earthquake or landslide? *Seismological Research Letters 71* (3), 344–351.

Parícutin Volcano, Mexico

Parícutin is a cinder cone located in the Mexican state of Michoacán. Although relatively unremarkable as a volcano, it is famous because it was the first volcano that modern scientists were able to study from its birth in a cornfield to its eventual death nine years later. Parícutin is part of the Michoacán-Guanajuato Volcanic

Field, located west of Mexico City, Mexico. It is a subregion of the Trans-Mexican Volcanic Belt, which extends east to west across the entire country of Mexico—from the west coast near Colima, through Mexico City, to the east coast near Veracruz. The Michoacán-Guanajuato Volcanic Field contains more than a thousand individual volcanoes, most of which are cinder cones like Parícutin.

At the time of Parícutin's birth, the area around San Juan Parangaracutiro and Parícutin largely was agricultural. It consisted of small but fertile valleys between volcanic cones and ridges. The lowland areas were used for growing crops such as corn and wheat, as were the craters of many of the small volcanoes in the area. Slopes of the old volcanoes were covered in oak and pine forests, which were harvested for wood and turpentine. Parcels of land that contained both crop land and forested areas were considered particularly valuable. One such parcel, called Cuiyúsuru, was owned by Dionisio Pulido.

Although many families owned and farmed land, they lived in town rather than on their farms. Farmers traveled each day with their oxen and tools to their fields to work the land. The commercial center of the region was San Juan Parangaracutiro, a town with a population of approximately 4,000. San Juan also was home to a beautiful Eighteenth Century church that housed a figure of the venerated saint, Señor de los Milagros. Approximately 1.2 miles (2 kilometers) northeast of San Juan Parangaracutiro was the village of Parícutin, home to approximately 150 Tarascan families, the indigenous people of the area.

On February 5, 1943, the people of San Juan Parangaracutiro and Parícutin were shaken by a series of earthquakes. For two weeks the earthquakes increased both in number and magnitude. Further unnerving the population was the fact that the earthquakes were accompanied by loud underground noises. The earthquakes became so frequent and severe that people feared the church in San Juan Parangaracutiro would collapse. This prompted the priest to enlist parishioners to move the figure of El Señor de los Milagros from the church to the city plaza. On February 20, local officials sent a messenger to the regional government headquarters in the city of Uruapan asking for assistance, although it is unclear what sort of assistance—other than advice—was sought.

On the morning of February 20, Dionisio Pulido left his home in Parícutin with his wife Paula, his son, and their neighbor Demitrio Toral, who worked for Pulido as a field hand. Pulido and Toral spent the day preparing the field for planting while Paula and their son watched the family's sheep. At about 4 p.m., Demitrio Toral was plowing the field and Dionisio Pulido and his family were building a pile of brush to burn nearby. Just as Toral finished a row and turned around to begin a new one, the ground began to split open, almost exactly along the furrow he had just completed. This led some people to believe that Toral had "plowed up the volcano." What follows is Pulido's account of the afternoon's events.

> In the afternoon I joined my wife and son, who were watching the sheep, and inquired if anything new had occurred, since for 2 weeks we had felt strong tremors in the region. Paula replied, yes, that she had heard noise and thunder underground. Scarcely had she finished speaking when I, myself, heard a

noise, like thunder during a rainstorm, but I could not explain it, for the sky above was clear and the day was so peaceful, as it is in February.

I went to burn the branches when I noticed that a cueva [cave], which was situated on one of the knolls of my farm, had opened, and I noticed that this fissure, as I followed it with my eye, was long and passed from where I stood, through the hole, and continued in the direction of Cerro de Canicjuata, where Canicjuata joins Mesa de Cocjarao. Here is something new and strange, thought I, and I searched the ground for marks to see whether or not it had opened in the night, but could find none; and I saw that it was a kind of fissure that had only a depth of half a meter. I set about to ignite the branches again when I felt a thunder, the trees trembled, and I turned to speak to Paula; and it was then I saw how, in the hole, the ground swelled and raised itself 2 or 2½ meters high, and a kind of smoke or fine dust—gray, like ashes—began to rise up in a portion of the crack that I had not previously seen. . . . Immediately more smoke began to rise, with a hiss or whistle, loud and continuous; and there was a smell of sulfur . . . I ran to see if I could save my family and my companions and my oxen, but I did not see them and thought that they had taken the oxen to the spring for water. I saw that there was no longer any water in the spring, for it was near the fissure, and I thought the water was lost because of the fissure. Then, very frightened, I mounted my mare and galloped to Parícutin, where I found my wife and son and friends awaiting, fearing that I might be dead and that they would never see me again. On the road to Parícutin I thought of my little animals, the yoke oxen, that were going to die in that flame and smoke, but upon arriving at my house I was happy to see that they were there (Foshag & Gonzalez Reyna, 1956).

By 5 p.m., a column of smoke could be seen from the plaza in San Juan Parangaracutiro, and a group decided to investigate. They arrived on the scene and saw that "smoke" and red-hot stones were issuing from a 2 foot (0.5 meter) hole in the ground. The stones were being tossed up to 18 feet (5 meters) in the air. As they watched, the hole grew to six feet (2 meters) in diameter and the volume of "smoke" increased. As the evening wore on, the stones being hurled out of the ground became larger, in fact large enough to be seen from San Juan Parangaracutiro. Emission of volcanic ash increased, as did the noise from the new volcano. By midnight a thick ash column was producing lightning flashes, and this was accompanied by incandescent lava bombs being hurled into the air.

When Pulido returned the next morning at 8 a.m., he found a 30-foot (10-meter) cone. By early afternoon, the cone was 100 to 150 feet (30 to 50 meters) high. The first lava began to flow from the northeastern base of the cone that afternoon, covering Pulido's farm within hours. That lava flow continued for one month. By the end of the first week, the new cone was 475 feet (140 meters) high. Thunderous explosions could be heard as far away as Guanajuato, 220 miles (350 kilometers) to the northeast, and fine ash fell on Mexico City, 200 miles (320 kilometers) to the east. Every few seconds, lava was thrown 2,000 to 3,500 feet (600 to 1,000 meters) above the rim of the crater. According to Bullard (1984), "often the lava fragments shattered over the cone like a giant skyrocket, leaving a trail of fire as they cascaded down the sides. So abundant were these fragments that frequently the entire cone was covered with interlacing fiery trails."

Parícutin attracted a great deal of attention, not only from the scientific community, but also from the general public. Tourists flocked to the volcano to witness this spectacle of nature. The first geologist arrived on the scene when the volcano was just three days old, and scientists from the United States and Mexico kept the volcano under nearly constant surveillance during the entire duration of its nine-year eruption. Local residents set up food and drink stands for tourists. The National University of Mexico also built an observation cabin to house scientists studying the volcano. The cabin had to be abandoned when it was surrounded by lava, and it eventually was covered by lava.

The volcano put on amazing shows for its spectators. There were spectacular lava fountains in June 1943. In July and August of 1943, a lava lake existed in the cone's crater and was accompanied by explosive activity. That explosive activity was reduced significantly when a new lava flow broke out. In October 1943, a parasitic vent opened at the northeastern base of the cone. Scientists named this vent "Sapichu." As soon as Sapichu became active, activity within the crater of Parícutin ceased. In January of 1944, Sapichu stopped erupting and activity shifted back to the main crater of Parícutin. Sapichu was a prominent landmark at Parícutin until it was buried by lava flows in 1946.

Ash, bombs, and lava eruption persisted unabated through the first year and into the second. By February 1944, Parícutin was 1,000 feet (325 meters) tall. The volcano continued to grow but at a much slower rate. Pyroclastic material—used to build the cone—constituted the vast majority of the volcano's output during the first year of Parícutin's eruption. By the second year, however, it only accounted for slightly more than half of the eruptive material. Each year the volcano erupted fewer pyroclastics and more lava. By 1948 the amount of pyroclastic material was negligible. When the eruption ceased in 1952, Parícutin's summit was 1,345 feet (410 meters) above the original surface of Pulido's cornfield.

Parícutin's second year was its most destructive. Both the village of Parícutin, where the Pulido family lived, and the larger town of San Juan Parangaricutiro were engulfed by slow-moving lava flows from a long-lived cluster of vents at the southwest base of the volcano. This vent area was named "La Mesa de los Hornitos," which translates to "Table of the Little Ovens." The area's name was derived from a large number of small steep-sided cones, termed "hornitos." (The term "hornito" is the internationally accepted name for such features in the volcanological community.) Although there was no loss of life as a result of the lava flows that issued from La Mesa de Los Hornitos, all residents of the towns were displaced and had to be resettled elsewhere. Residents often waited until the last possible moment to evacuate, taking with them not only their possessions but also salvaging parts of their homes to use when they built new ones. Between 1945 and 1952, lava flows continued to cover additional land, but no towns or villages were buried during that time. The eruption ceased on March 4, 1952, after 9 years and 12 days of activity. Parícutin is not expected to erupt again in the future.

See Also: Cinder Cone; Pyroclastic Materials.

Further Reading

Bullard, F. M. (1984). *Volcanoes of the earth.* Austin: University of Texas Press.
Foshag, W., & Gonzalez Reyna, J. (1956). *Birth and development of Parícutin Volcano Mexico: Geologic investigations in the Parícutin area, Mexico.* (U.S. Geological Survey Bulletin 965-D).
Luhr, J. E., & Simkin, T. (Eds.). (1993). *Parícutin: The volcano born in a Mexican cornfield.* Phoenix, AZ: Geoscience Press.
Smithsonian Institution. National Museum of Natural History. (2013, June 27). *Parícutin: The birth of a volcano.* Retrieved from http://www.mnh.si.edu/onehundredyears/expeditions/Paricutin.html

Pavlof Volcano, Alaska, United States

Pavlof Volcano is located near the western tip of the Alaska Peninsula. It formed as a result of subduction of the Pacific Plate beneath the North American Plate. Pavlof is a composite volcano formed entirely within the last 10,000 years. Along with nearby Pavlof Sister, it forms a dramatic landscape of two symmetrical, glacier-covered mountains that tower above the bays below. Pavlof is one of the most consistently active volcanoes in the Aleutians, and has erupted more than 40 times in historical time. Eruptions vary between sporadic fountains of lava and explosions that produce ash plumes that can rise several thousand feet above the volcano.

Although the area around Pavlof is uninhabited, the Aleutian arc lies beneath one of the busiest air cargo routes in the world—the route between Asia, North America, and Europe. High-performance jet engines have a tendency to shut down when they encounter volcanic ash. This has occurred many times, with planes falling thousands of feet before pilots are able to restart the engines and land the planes safely. For this reason, volcanic-ash emission is regarded as the greatest hazard in the Aleutian region, and the area is monitored intensively for new plumes of volcanic ash.

Pavlof's latest eruptive episode occurred in 2014. In late May, the volcano began a low-level eruption that escalated over the next several days. During June 2, 3, and 4, the mountain erupted both fountains of lava and large columns of volcanic ash and steam. At least one ash plume reached an altitude of 30,000 feet (9,144 meters). Officials at the Alaskan Volcano Observatory issued a warning, and aircraft were directed away from the area. By June 6, the level of activity had decreased substantially. The alert level was increased again in November. Eruptive activity is likely to continue for weeks or months.

See Also: Aleutian Islands; North American Plate; Pacific Plate; Subduction Zone; Volcanic Hazards.

Further Reading

Alaska Volcano Observatory. (2014, June 9). *Pavlof volcano description and information.* Retrieved from http://www.avo.alaska.edu/volcanoes/volcinfo.php?volcname=Pavlof

Conners, D. (2014, June 9). Eruption subsides at Alaska's Pavlof volcano. *EarthSky.*

Smithsonian Institution. National Museum of Natural History. Global Volcanism Program. (2014, June 9). *Pavlof.* Retrieved from http://www.volcano.si.edu/volcano.cfm?vn =312030

Pele, Legend of

Pele is the Hawaiian goddess of volcanoes. Although Hawaiian mythology contains perhaps hundreds of individual gods and demigods considered more powerful, more important in the creation story, or who possess greater supernatural abilities, Pele is one of the best-known within the Hawaiian pantheon. The eerie sight of a lava lake in a crater, or of a lava flow snaking across the landscape at night, makes it easy to imagine the awe felt by newcomers to the islands. In a civilization which believed that every part of nature and of life was tied to the spirit world, it perhaps is no surprise that one of the most revered—and feared—of the gods was Pele. Her story is fascinating and complex, as is Hawaiian mythology in general.

Pele goes by a great many names. Her name "Pele-honua-mea" means "Pele of the sacred land," and her name "Pele-'ai-honua" translates to "Pele, eater of land." Her sacred spirit name is "Ka-'ula-o-ke-ahi," which means "the redness of the fire."

Pele was born in Tahiti and was one of several children in her family. Her older brother Ka-moho-ali'i was custodian of the Water of Life. He had the ability to use this Water of Life to bring someone back to life after death. Pele's sister, Na-Maka-o-Kaha'i, was the Goddess of the Sea. Pele was mortal, however, with a fiery temper and a lustful nature. She also always was plagued by wanderlust. Her parents made sure she had a canoe, attendants, and enough food and water to make the trip to Hawaii. They then asked her to carry with her an egg that contained her little sister Hi'iaka. Hi'iaka's egg hatched when they reached Hawaii, so Hi'iaka is the first truly Hawaiian goddess by birth. She is regarded today as a spirit of dance, and Pele's favorite sister.

Pele, like almost all Hawaiian gods, is a study in contrast. She is both a destroyer and a creator. She has the ability to destroy forests, homes, and beaches, but she creates new land. She is fickle in her love life, but battles fiercely with other goddesses and mortal women when she believes they have taken her lovers as their own. She is strong and independent, but always yields to the pig-god Kama-pua'a, who represents all things green and growing. Her lava flows always eventually are claimed by plants. Pele is impulsive but is capable of conceiving and carrying out intricate plans. She can be vengeful, but also is protective.

In another version of the legend that brings Pele to the Hawaiian Islands, Pele was expelled from Tahiti by her sister Na-Maka-o-Kaha'i after Pele seduced her husband. In this legend, her sister chased her all the way to Hawaii and tore her apart near Hana, Maui. A hill called Ka-iwi-o-Pele, which means "Bones of Pele," exists in that area. It was only after the death of her mortal body that her spirit was freed and elevated to the status of a god. In this way, Pele is a Hawaiian goddess because she was elevated to godly status in Hawaii.

Today, Pele is said to live in Halema'uma'u, a pit crater within the large summit caldera of the volcano Kilauea on the island of Hawaii, but she explored many other locations throughout the Hawaiian Islands before she made that her home. Pele's first stop was the island of Niihau, the northernmost of the islands. Today, it also is known to be the oldest of the islands. She enjoyed the company of those she knew on the island then moved on to the next island in the chain, Kauai. On Kauai, Pele met a powerful chief who took her as his wife. She left him soon after they were married, however, so that she could build a place where she and all of her family could live. She had a paoa, or magic digging stick, that she took with her. She tried digging near the shore on Kauai, but her fire was met with resistance by her sister, Na-Maka-o-Kaha'i. A great deal of "fire and sand" came out of her fire pit but, before long, the fires were drowned by the water. She moved from one island to the next, digging a fire pit near the shore; every time she moved, her sister saw the "smoke and fire" from her fire pit, and came to drown her fires. When Pele came to Maui, she decided to move uphill and dig in the crater of Haleakala. She threw great amounts of fire, smoke, and lava out of the crater, but that only attracted her vengeful sister to her again. But Pele had gained confidence and went down toward the shore to meet her sister and do battle. It is here that Na-Make-o-Kaha'i tore Pele apart, and Pele was elevated to goddess status.

Pele moved on to Hawaii, still in search of a permanent home. She found that, on this island, a god of fire already existed. Ai-laau ("one who devours forests") repeatedly destroyed communities in southern Hawaii with his fires. He lived for a very long time in Kilauea Iki (little Kilauea), a pit crater adjacent to Kilauea's summit caldera, and later moved to the summit caldera. Pele had been traveling a long time by the time she reached Hawaii. As she moved inland, she had a great desire to visit Ai-laau. She felt she might find a resting place with him in Kilauea, here at the end of her long voyage. When Pele reached the summit of Kilauea, however, Ai-laau was gone from his home. He had left because he'd seen her digging with her paoa as she approached. Ai-laau was terrified of Pele, and never returned. Pele found that Kilauea suited her, so she dug the foundations of her home in Halema'uma'u. She still resides there today.

It is very easy, in today's world, to discount these legends as pure myth; but many myths have some basis in reality. Pele's voyage through the Hawaiian Islands, for example, has some resemblance to the reality of timing of volcanic activity within the island chain. The oldest volcanoes are found in the northwestern part of the chain, and younger volcanoes are found toward the southeast. The island of Hawaii is the location of all of the volcanoes within the chain that are considered to be active today: Hualalai, Mauna Loa, and Kilauea. Of these three, Kilauea erupts most frequently. The legend of Ai-laau also might have a historical basis. A lava shield named Ai-laau exists near the summit of Kilauea. Ai-laau erupted for an estimated 60 years during the time the second wave of settlers came to the island.

It is possible that, at some point, eruptions at Ai-laau shield stopped and eruptions in other locations (such as near the shoreline, or within the summit of Kilauea) began, just as stated in the legend.

It also is easy to consider myths and the gods therein things of the past, but Pele still is very much alive to many on the island of Hawaii. Today, she is said to appear either as a beautiful young woman, or as an old, stately woman who is sometimes accompanied by a white dog. Many Hawaiians have reported encounters with a mysterious woman in one of these two forms. She appears most often to warn people of events to come. Occasionally, she has come with a warning to a specific person or family, and instructions for protecting their home from lava flows that will occur in the near future. In other cases, she simply appears during an eruption and shows herself to people in one of her two human forms. As with the Pele of legend, she has a temper and will not tolerate being ignored or treated with disrespect. If shown proper respect, however, she assumes a protective role. Author, historian, and ethnographer Herb Kane documents several modern encounters with Madame Pele, or Tūtū [Grandmother] Pele as she is sometimes known, in his book, *Pele: Goddess of Hawai'i's Volcanoes* (2000).

In one case from 1960, radio host Betty Curtiss was sitting with friends in Volcano House Hotel, which is located on the rim of Kilauea's summit caldera. She felt a sensation like a pinprick on the back of her neck, and turned around to find an elderly woman in a formal Hawaiian dress standing behind her. The woman asked if she was the radio host who broadcast from Kapoho, a town buried by lava earlier that year. She answered, respectfully, that she was, and asked how she could be of help. The woman told Betty that within 30 days, the island would be visited by either Hina (the goddess of the ocean) or Pele—with catastrophic effects. Then she walked away. People in the crowd let her pass, but did not seem to consciously pay her any mind. Betty returned to her friends and commented about the encounter. Her friends had not seen the elderly woman, nor had they heard what she said. Ms. Curtiss repeated the woman's prediction for five days on her radio show. Four weeks after her conversation with the woman, a tsunami generated by a massive earthquake in Chile hit the coast of Hawaii. Waves reached a height of 35 feet in the city of Hilo, killing 61 people and completely devastating one area of the city.

In another incident, a man who owned a ranch on the slopes of Mauna Loa found a stone resting on a mat within one of the caves on his property. He thought the stone was interesting, so he took it home and displayed it in his garden. The Hawaiians who worked for him on the ranch warned him that this stone was used in the worship of Pele, and begged him to take it back before Pele took her revenge. They told him that if he allowed them to take it back and appease Pele with a respectful observance, her wrath might be avoided. The ranch owner scoffed at their superstition. He was a devout Christian and did not believe in Pele. Shortly afterward, Mauna Loa erupted. Lava covered a corner of the ranch, then flows moved in a different direction. The Hawaiian cowboys again asked the owner for permission to take the rock back to its proper resting place, but the ranch owner refused. The flow returned to its earlier course, covering more and more of his land. It ultimately approached the house. Bible in hand, the ranch owner prayed through the night as the lava approached. Early the next day the flow stopped. The lava had split into two streams and bypassed the house. The owner told his workers that his prayers to his God had stopped the flow of lava. The workers confessed that, when they left work the evening before, they had taken the stone from the garden and returned it to its former resting place. They had made offerings and recited chants to Pele during the night. The man soon sold his ranch and moved to Honolulu.

How do Hawaiians feel about Madame Pele? They respect and revere her. There has been resurgence of traditional hula that in many cases honors the old religion, and on the island of Hawaii, dances and chants to Pele are common. Hawaiian families understand that Pele is a force they cannot fight. They recognize that if Pele decides she wants their land, she will take it and there is little protest to her doing so. There are many Hawaiians who still perform traditional ceremonies at Kilauea's summit, and when visiting the summit caldera of Kilauea it is not uncommon to find flower leis and offerings of fruit left for Pele. Hawaiians consider this to be in poor taste when done by non-Hawaiians.

Nobody knows the source of the belief, but visitors to the island are commonly told not to remove rocks from the island. Rocks are considered (according to many versions of the legend) to be either the body of Pele or sacred to her, so it is understandable that believers in the old religion would not want the rocks removed. Tourists, however, are told to leave the rocks because taking them home brings bad luck. Dismissive of this superstition, thousands of people take rocks from the island every year. And every year, thousands of rocks are returned to the island. They are sent to Hawaii Volcanoes National Park, to postmasters in various towns, to the scientists at the Hawaiian Volcano Observatory, and even to author Herb Kane (author of a popular book about Pele). Many rocks are accompanied by letters explaining the bad luck that has befallen the sender since taking the rock home. Perhaps Madame Pele's powers can influence matters even far from home.

See Also: Hawaiian Islands; Kilauea Volcano, Hawaii, United States; Maui, Legend of; Mauna Loa, Hawaii, United States.

Further Reading

Kane, H. K. (2000). *Pele: Goddess of Hawai'i's volcanoes* (Expanded ed.). Captain Cook, HI: Kawainui Press.
Westervelt, W. D. (1987). *Myths and legends of Hawaii.* Honolulu: Mutual Publishing Company.

Perret, Frank

Frank Alvord Perret was born in Hartford, Connecticut, in 1867. He attended Brooklyn Polytechnic Institute and studied physics. Perret was fascinated by electricity, and even before he would have graduated he went to work in Thomas

Edison's New York lighting company. There he demonstrated a propensity for invention of electrical gadgets. Perret left Edison's company to found his own company, Elektron Manufacturing Company, in partnership with one of his Edison coworkers. There, he made electric motors and other equipment that he designed. He was granted a patent in 1889 for a small electric motor suitable for powering electric fans, and manufactured a small number of them. In 1896, Perret left his company to work on electric automobiles. This business venture failed, however, and Perret suffered a nervous breakdown in 1902. In 1906, his company Elektron Manufacturing was bought out by Otis Elevator Company, and Perret decided to move to Italy for his health.

While living in Naples, Italy, Perret met Professor R.V. Matteucci who was serving as director of the Volcanological Laboratory of the Mount Vesuvius Observatory. Perret became fascinated with volcanoes through this association, and was permitted to design and test instruments as a visiting scientist at the volcano observatory. Perret was able to observe and record the 1906 eruption of Vesuvius in a comprehensive monograph. He continued to study the volcano for another 15 years. It was on the slopes of Vesuvius that he met Professor Thomas Jaggar (then of Harvard University). The two men shared a mutual interest in volcanology. Both saw the advantage of using a volcano as a natural laboratory to learn how to forecast eruptions. This was the beginning of many years of collaboration between the two scientists.

In 1909, Perret accompanied Jaggar (now at the Massachusetts Institute of Technology) to the island of Hawaii with the intent of scouting a site for a permanent volcano observatory on the volcano Kilauea. In 1911, plans were firm and the two established the first observation post on the rim of Halemaumau crater within Kilauea's summit caldera. A year later, a permanent volcano observatory was built on the rim of Kilauea caldera and the two were carrying out a wealth of observations, in many cases with instruments Perret designed. His expertise was noticed by Arthur Day, director of the Geophysical Laboratory at the Carnegie Institution of Washington. Perret became affiliated with the Carnegie Institution shortly after his arrival in Hawaii, and was named an official research associate in 1931. He remained as such until the time of his death. Perret published four books on volcanology through the Carnegie Institution of Washington.

Although Perret is well-known for his work on Vesuvius and Kilauea, he also produced an impressive study of the volcano Mount Pelée on the Caribbean island of Martinique. He was not present in the aftermath of its incredibly devastating 1902 eruption as was Jaggar, but he took it upon himself to study the 1929–1932 eruption of the volcano. Perret set up an observation post on a low hill just upslope from a valley through which pyroclastic flows moved in 1902. The pyroclastic flows had completely destroyed the city of Saint-Pierre and killed nearly 28,000 people. Knowing the danger of his position, he stayed in the observation post and made detailed observations of small pyroclastic flows that flowed on either side of him. Geologists today would consider the act one of lunacy. Perret published a volume entitled, *The Eruption of Mt. Pelée, 1929–1932,* describing the eruption in detail. He also opened the Musée Volcanologique on Martinique in 1932 as both a memorial to the victims of the 1902 eruption and a volcano education center. He studied other volcanoes and earthquakes around the world as well. Perret visited Stromboli and Etna in Italy, Sakurajima in Japan, and Tenerife in the Canary Islands, and studied the deadly 1908 earthquake at Messina on the island of Sicily.

Perret decided to leave the Caribbean and return to the United States in 1940, giving up his field studies of volcanoes. He became seriously ill but refused to retire. In 1943, he was working on a book using data from his notebooks when, at age 76, he succumbed to his illness. Other investigators finished the book and published it under the title *Volcanological Observations*.

See Also: Hawaiian Volcano Observatory; Jaggar, Jr., Thomas Augustus, Kilauea Volcano, Hawaii, United States.

Further Reading

Carnegie Institution of Washington Geophysical Laboratory. (2014, June 5). *Frank A. Perret.* Retrieved from https://library.gl.ciw.edu/GLHistory/perret.html

Durland, K. (1911, January 11). Perret of Vesuvius. *Boston Evening Transcript.*

Giblin, M. (1950). Frank A. Perret. *Bulletin Volcanologique 10* (1), 191–195.

Rondeau, R. (2014, June 5). *Antique phonograph, fan, and photography site.* Retrieved from http://www.edisontinfoil.com/fans/perret.htm

U.S. Geological Survey. (2014, June 5). *A pioneering volcanologist narrowly beats the reaper.* Retrieved from http://hvo.wr.usgs.gov/volcanowatch/archive/2005/05_08_25 .html

Peru

Peru is a country located on the west coast of South America. It sits on the South American Plate. To its west is the Pacific Ocean, which is underlain by the Nazca Plate. The Nazca Plate is subducting beneath the South American Plate in this area. The point of subduction is marked by the Peru-Chile Trench, which runs the entire length of the western coastline of South America. Subduction in this area has resulted in powerful earthquakes and a host of volcanoes. The largest and most deadly earthquake in Peru's history was a magnitude 7.9 event that struck in May 1970 near the city of Chimbote. More than 3,000 people died in coastal cities near the epicenter, most from building collapse. The worst death tolls, however, were in cities at the base of the Andes to the east, where large landslides from the tall, snow-covered mountains rushed downward into the valleys. Two cities were entirely buried by the landslides, and tens of thousands died. The ultimate death toll of that earthquake was more than 66,000 people. A 2007 earthquake near the city of Pisco resulted in more than 500 deaths and displaced nearly half a million people from their homes. Even several years later, many thousands of people still were living in makeshift shelters, awaiting government help to restore services to stricken areas and to rebuild homes.

Graves at the General Cemetery of Pisco, Peru, damaged in a 2007 earthquake in the region. (Ric Francis/ZUMA Press/Newscom)

Peru is a country of volcanic activity as well. Five volcanoes within the country have erupted during historic times. El Misti erupted last in 1985. Huaynaputina had a violent eruption in the year 1600 with a volcano explosivity index of 6. Snow-capped Sabancaya's last eruption was in 2013. Ubinas began erupting in 2013. Yucamane last erupted in 1902.

See Also: Chimbote Earthquake, Peru (1970); Nazca Plate; Pacific Plate; Subduction Zone.

Further Reading

Smithsonian Institution. National Museum of Natural History. Global Volcanism Program. (2014, June 19). Retrieved from http://www.volcano.si.edu/

U.S. Geological Survey. (2014, June 19). *Historic world earthquakes. Peru.* Retrieved from http://earthquake.usgs.gov/earthquakes/world/historical_country.php#peru

Philippine Institute of Volcanology and Seismology

The Philippine Institute of Volcanology and Seismology (PHIVOLCS) is the Philippines' government agency tasked with monitoring the nation's volcanic and seismic activity; mitigating volcanic, earthquake, and tsunami hazards; and

The Philippine Institute of Volcanology and Seismology (PHIVOLCS) monitors activity at Mayon volcano. (Pacific Press/Sipa USA/Newscom)

providing information about such hazards to the general public. The agency was formed in 1952 following the eruption of Hibok-hibok Volcano in 1951 which had illustrated the country's lack of preparedness for volcanic eruptions and related geologic disasters. Since 1952, the entity has existed under several different agencies and names, but it has been a service institute of the government's Department of Science and Technology since 1987.

PHIVOLCS has five official mandates: (1) Predict the occurrence of volcanic eruptions and earthquakes and their geotectonic phenomena; (2) Determine how eruptions and earthquakes will occur and also areas likely to be affected; (3) Exploit the positive aspects of volcanoes and volcanic terrain in furtherance of the socioeconomic development efforts of the government; (4) Generate sufficient data for forecasting volcanic eruptions and earthquakes; and (5) Formulate appropriate disaster-preparedness and mitigation plans. In other words, PHIVOLCS is tasked with monitoring the Philippines' volcanoes, earthquakes, tsunamis, and related phenomena; research related to these events; forecasting any forecastable geologic event; and preparing the public for disasters so loss of life can be minimized. The promotion of positive aspects of volcanoes and volcanic terrain likely includes the development of geothermal energy, invention and marketing of salable products from volcanic materials, encouragement of agricultural diversity in areas that have rich volcanic soil, development of resorts around hot springs and other geothermal features, and development of eco-tourism. This is a broad range of responsibilities for a single government agency.

The Philippines sit atop two active subduction zones. The result is a geologically active region that experiences large and damaging earthquakes, tsunamis from both local and distant earthquakes, and volcanic eruptions of all types, including large caldera-forming eruptions. In any given year, the Philippines experiences thousands of earthquakes. The islands are scarred with thousands of faults. Earthquakes often induce landslides and ground liquefaction. The islands of the Philippines also have hundreds of volcanoes known to have been active within the last 10,000 years. It is these volcanoes that are most likely to erupt in the foreseeable future. All types of volcanic hazards are possible.

PHIVOLCS has an excellent system for monitoring of volcanic activity but, in 1991, the agency faced an extraordinarily dire crisis. After recognizing that the volcano Pinatubo was reawakening after a dormancy that lasted hundreds of years, PHIVOLCS requested help from the United States government through international diplomatic channels. Working together, PHIVOLCS and U.S. Geological Survey personnel saved hundreds of thousands of lives by accurately forecasting the eruption of Pinatubo and giving local officials enough warning to order evacuations before the volcano's cataclysmic eruption. Two U.S. military installations were evacuated of personnel and equipment, and nearly 45,000 residents also were moved to safety. The eruption of Pinatubo in June 1991 was the second largest of the Twentieth Century (behind only Katmai, Alaska in 1912), yet through the work of PHIVOLCS, only 300 lives were lost.

The PHIVOLCS website (www.phivolcs.dost.gov.ph) includes much detailed information about individual faults and volcanoes, and hazards associated with both. Visitors can view the latest volcano bulletins and tsunami hazard maps, download directions for conducting a neighborhood earthquake drill, and learn the signs of an impending volcanic eruption (given in multiple languages).

See Also: Philippines; Pinatubo, Mount, Eruption, Philippines (1991).

Further Reading

Pappas, S. (2014, March 17). Pinatubo: Why the biggest volcanic eruption wasn't the deadliest. *LiveScience.com.* Retrieved from http://www.livescience.com/14603-pinatubo-eruption-20-anniversary.html

Philippine Plate

The Philippine Plate is one of about two dozen major lithospheric plates that comprise the outermost layer of the earth. It is located in the western Pacific, between the Eurasian Plate and the Pacific Plate in the general area of Southeast Asia. The Philippine Plate does not contain much in the way of land area. Other than the isolated island group of the Northern Mariana Islands and Guam, there is no other appreciable land area on the plate. The plate's eastern boundary is a subduction zone in which the Pacific Plate is subducting beneath it. It is at this subduction zone that the Northern Mariana Islands and Guam were formed. The Philippine

Plate is itself subducting beneath the Eurasian Plate at its western margin, resulting in the formation of the Philippines and the Japanese Islands. The eastern margin of the Philippine Plate is marked by the Mariana Trench, which holds the distinction of being the deepest trench on the earth. The trench is 36,201 feet (11,034 meters) deep at its lowest point within the Challenger Deep near Guam. If Mount Everest were placed in the trench, its summit still would be more than a mile beneath the ocean's surface.

See Also: Mariana Islands; Mariana Trench; Philippines; Subduction Zone.

Further Reading

Friedman, N. (2014, June 19). *The Mariana Trench: Earth's deepest place.* National Geographic Society. Retrieved from http://education.nationalgeographic.com/education /activity/mariana-trench-deepest-place-earth/?ar_a=1

Philippines

The Philippines is an island nation located, curiously enough, on the Eurasian Plate rather than on the adjacent Philippine Plate. The Philippine Plate, however, does influence the geology of the nation because subduction of the Philippine Plate

Lake Taal in the caldera of Taal Volcano on the island of Luzon, Philippines. (Christian Kober/ Robert Harding/Newscom)

beneath the Eurasian Plate is responsible for the earthquake activity and volcanism of the islands. Because it sits almost directly above the subduction zone marked by the Philippine Trench, the country does experience a great number of earthquakes of all magnitudes and at many depths. The most powerful earthquake to strike the Philippines in modern times was a magnitude 7.9 event in August 1976 that killed approximately 8,000 people, most on the island of Mindanao. Another major earthquake, a magnitude 7.7 event in July 1990, struck Luzon and killed 1,621 people. Many geologists believe that the changes in the stresses of the rocks at the plate boundary created by the 1990 earthquake might have led to eruptive activity at the volcano Pinatubo the following year. It was shortly after the magnitude 7.7 earthquake that local residents first started noticing changes on Pinatubo and in its behavior. A series of three major earthquakes occurred on July 23, 2010, in the area of Moro Gulf near Mindanao. The earthquakes had magnitudes of 7.3, 7.6, and 7.4.

Volcanic activity within the Philippines is commonplace. The volcano Mayon is one of the most active in the region and also has been quite deadly. It is a steep-sided volcano that is often restless. When it emits plumes of ash and steam, it is inevitable that some of the ash will fall back on the slopes of the volcano and form pyroclastic flows that rush downhill quickly because of the steep slope angle. These pyroclastic flows—and lahars—have flooded the more than 40 stream valleys that radiate from the summit. These events have devastated many of the lowland areas around the base of the volcano. An eruption in 1814 killed more than 1,200 people and destroyed several villages. Mayon's last eruption was in 2013. The volcano Bulusan was active between November 2010 and May 2011. Phreatic eruptions were the most common mode of eruption during this period. The volcano Kanlaon erupted in 2006.

The most well-known eruption in the Philippines in recent memory was that of Pinatubo in 1991. The volcano began showing some signs of unrest late in 1990, and by early 1991 it was clear that the volcano was becoming incredibly restless. The Philippine Institute for Volcanology (PHIVOLCS) requested help from the newly formed Volcano Disaster Assistance Program (part of the U.S. Geological Survey) to monitor the unrest at Pinatubo. The volcano had not been active in historic times, and a working geologic map of the volcano did not even exist before the American team arrived. Scientists from both countries worked side by side to install a thorough monitoring network around the volcano and to produce a volcano hazard map. The scientists immediately knew that this eruption had the potential to be devastating not just to the immediate area, but to the entire region as well. The volcano slowly increased its level of activity throughout the spring of 1991. In the first two weeks of June, the scientists knew that a major eruption was coming, and they advised evacuation of the area around Pinatubo. The mountain began its cataclysmic eruption on June 14. The eruption was so violent it drained a large portion of the magma chamber, which caused the summit to collapse. Lahars and pyroclastic flows swept down the volcano's flanks and into previously populated regions. Unfortunately, the eruption occurred during landfall of a typhoon, so those trying to escape the effects of the volcano had to deal not only with the typhoon, with its wind and heavy rainfall, but also with falling volcanic ash and constantly shaking ground. In the end, there were a few hundred deaths, which was a very tiny percentage of the millions of people at risk from the eruption. The eruption forced early closure of Clark Air Base and Subic Bay Naval Base, the two United States military installations in the Philippines. It also displaced hundreds of thousands of people from their homes. The country was also left vulnerable to lahars for years to come because of the amount of material that choked stream valleys leading away from the mountain. This was the second largest eruption of the Twentieth Century, second only to Katmai in Alaska.

See Also: Katmai Eruption Alaska, United States (1912); Pacific Plate; Philippine Plate; Pinatubo, Mount, Eruption, Philippines (1991); Subduction Zone.

Further Reading

Smithsonian Institution. National Museum of Natural History. Global Volcanism Program. (2014, June 19). Retrieved from http://www.volcano.si.edu/

U.S. Geological Survey. (2014, June 19). *Historic world earthquakes. Philippines.* Retrieved from http://earthquake.usgs.gov/earthquakes/world/historical_country .php#philippines

Phreatic Eruption

A phreatic eruption is a steam-driven eruption. Phreatic eruptions require that water—either below or above the surface of the ground—be heated by a volcano. Sources of heat include magma (beneath the ground surface), lava, hot rocks, or fresh volcanic deposits such as pyroclastic flows or ash fall. Water flashes to steam and generates an explosion that involves steam, water, ash, and lava bombs. These eruptions can be quite violent, and certainly can cause damage and loss of life.

Active volcanoes of all varieties are capable of having phreatic eruptions. Two documented explosive eruptions at the shield volcano Kilauea in Hawaii are known to be phreatic eruptions, generated when groundwater encountered hot rocks in the volcano's summit caldera. In 1790, a group of approximately 400 Hawaiian soldiers was killed in the summit area of Kilauea by a pyroclastic surge during a phreatic eruption. The eruption began shortly after the soldiers marched across the summit of Kilauea, the famed home of Pele (the volcano goddess). Many soldiers felt that the eruption was a result of her wrath, and they decided to concede the upcoming battle because they felt they did not have her favor. In that instance, a phreatic eruption had an influence on the course of Hawaiian history. A second phreatic eruption in 1924 claimed a single life. A photographer was struck by a large block hurled from the blast crater.

Mount St. Helens had innumerable phreatic eruptions during its period of activity in the 1980s. Even prior to its major eruption on May 18, 1980, hot volcanic material at the surface melted part of the snow and ice on top of the volcano. Meltwater seeped into cracks and pores in the volcano and percolated downward. The hot rocks inside the volcano caused the water to flash to steam, and phreatic blasts resulted. The same occurred occasionally even after the cataclysmic eruption. As the lava dome was building, rain and snowmelt caused phreatic eruptions. Periodically, these were large enough to destroy part of the building dome. At Katmai and Pinatubo, thick pyroclastic deposits stayed hot for many weeks after their emplacement. Rainfall or snowmelt would seep into the deposits and steam eruptions occurred. These eruptions were not in the newly created calderas, but in the actual pyroclastic flow deposits that surrounded the calderas.

See Also: Lava Dome; Pyroclastic Flow.

Further Reading

Israel, B. (2014, May 16). Kilauea Volcano's deadliest eruption revealed. *Livescience.com*. Retrieved from http://www.livescience.com/17338-hawaii-kilaeua-volcano-explosive.html

Moseley, M. (2014). Kilauea: The eruption of 1924. *Hawaii Tribune-Herald*.

U.S. Geological Survey. Volcano Hazards Program. (2014, May 16). *Phreatic eruption*. Retrieved from http://volcanoes.usgs.gov/images/pglossary/HydroVolcEruption.php

Pinatubo, Mount, Eruption, Philippines (1991)

Mount Pinatubo is a composite volcano located in the Philippines, in the west-central portion of the island of Luzon. In 1991, it was the site of the Twentieth Century's second largest volcanic eruption. This eruption was a landmark in the history of volcanology because it marked the first time an eruption of a composite volcano was accurately forecast by scientists. This feat was accomplished by a multi-agency team from the Philippine Institute for Volcanology and Seismology (PHIVOLCS), the United States Geological Survey (USGS), the University of the Philippines, and the University of Illinois at Chicago. Together, personnel from these entities comprised the Pinatubo Volcano Observatory Team. Accurate forecasting, along with open communication between the scientists and civil defense officials, saved countless thousands of lives. Despite the fact that more than 1 million people were at risk from Pinatubo's eruption, credible warnings and timely evacuations held casualties from this massive eruption to a few hundred people. Lessons learned at Pinatubo still are very much in use today throughout the volcanological community.

Precursors to Pinatubo's 1991–1992 eruption began as early as 10 months prior to its paroxysmal eruption on June 15, 1991. In late June 1990, a magnitude 7.8

Aerial view of Mount Pinatubo. A lake stands in the caldera created during the 1991 eruption of the volcano. (Cornelius Paas imageBROKER/Newscom)

earthquake occurred approximately 62 miles (100 kilometers) to the northeast of Pinatubo. Within two to three weeks of the earthquake, a landslide high on the upper northwest flank of Pinatubo, and related ground cracks, started emitting steam. Although Pinatubo had well-documented geothermal resources in the form of hot springs and abundant hot water in the subsurface, activity in this area was new. This might have marked the beginning of a disturbance of the magmatic system beneath Pinatubo. Members of the Aeta community, a group of indigenous people living on the slopes of Pinatubo, reported minor explosions in early 1991. Frequent earthquakes began to be felt on the slopes of Pinatubo in mid-March of 1991. It was at that point that officials in the area called on PHIVOLCS for an assessment of the situation. Because earthquake swarms are not in and of themselves indicative of impending volcanic activity, scientists were wary but not convinced that they had an awakening volcano on their hands. Phreatic (steam-driven) explosions on April 2 which opened three large steam vents high on the slopes of Pinatubo, and the smell of sulfur in the air, however, eliminated any doubt they'd had about the nature of activity at Pinatubo. Immediately after the explosions of early April, PHIVOLCS installed seismographs around the perimeter of the volcano. They recorded more than 200 small earthquakes during the first day of monitoring. Based on this information, the team recommended precautionary evacuations of those people living within 6 miles (10 kilometers) of Pinatubo's summit. The Philippine government soon asked for help from a relatively new organization within the U.S. Geological Survey, the Volcano Disaster Assistance Program (VDAP).

Geologists and geophysicists from the VDAP team arrived at Pinatubo in late April. They carried with them enough equipment to set up a fully functioning, portable volcano observatory. They installed seismic stations that radioed data back to a "home base" located at the United States' Clark Air Base, 15.5 miles (25 kilometers) to the east of Pinatubo, so that it could be instantly interpreted. The team established regular overflights of the volcano that were conducted with the assistance of U.S. Air Force personnel from Clark Air Base, installed tilt meters to determine whether the volcano was swelling with magma, and set up a system to monitor sulfur-dioxide emissions. They then set about the work of preparing a hazard assessment.

Prior to the onset of activity in March 1991, little was known about Pinatubo or its past eruptions. This put scientists at a disadvantage, because the best predictor of a volcano's future behavior is its past behavior. Scientists conducted a rapid field reconnaissance and found that the entire area—up to 18 miles (30 kilometers) from the volcano—was a maze of ridges carved from vast pyroclastic flow deposits. The team instantly realized that this volcano had the potential for enormous, deadly eruptions. Careful analysis of deposits and rapid carbon-14 dating of charcoals found in the volcanic debris told researchers that the most recent eruption of Pinatubo occurred 500 years prior, and previous eruptions occurred 3,000 and 5,500 years ago. That meant the volcano's typical cycle was to have a large, violent eruption followed by a period of several centuries to millennia of quiet. In general, the longer the period between eruptions, the more violent those eruptions tended to be. The scientists were extremely concerned.

Throughout late April and early May, thousands of earthquakes were recorded. The steam vents on Pinatubo became increasingly active. Sulfur dioxide emissions increased ten-fold in the final two weeks of May. Pinatubo slowly ramped up the severity of its activity. On June 3, a small explosion signaled the beginning of a new phase of the eruption. These signs included minor ash emissions, an increase in the number of earthquakes beneath the three steam vents, episodes of harmonic tremor (which typically indicates magma movement), and outward tilt indicating rising magma within the volcano. On June 5, scientists issued a higher-level alert to inform residents that a major pyroclastic eruption was likely to occur within two weeks. On June 7, the volcano had a steam and ash eruption that produced a column approximately 4 miles (7 kilometers) high. Scientists raised the alert level yet again, stating that an eruption was possible within 24 hours. Although not the eruption they clearly were waiting for, the first appearance of magma at the surface was on June 8, in the form of a small lava dome. Clouds obscured the summit area of Pinatubo much of the time, but the dome was seen, and was growing, at least through June 11.

Between June 8 and June 12, the volcano's ash emissions increased as did the number of earthquakes beneath the lava dome. On June 9, PHIVOLCS moved to the next level of alert—"eruption in progress." At that time, the evacuation zone was extended to a radius of 12 miles (20 kilometers) from the volcano's summit, and 25,000 additional people were told to evacuate. On June 10, approximately 14,500 Clark Air Base personnel and dependents received the evacuation order.

They traveled by motorcade to Subic Bay Naval Station, more than 24 miles (40 kilometers) from the volcano. Hundreds of planes, helicopters, and other equipment also were moved. The humble Pinatubo Volcano Observatory was moved to a more secure location at the far side of Clark Air Base, and only a skeleton crew of 1,500 soldiers remained on the base for security and maintenance.

On June 12, a series of several major vertical eruptions began. During the first eruption, which began at 8:51 a.m. on June 12, a column of ash and steam rose 12 miles (19 kilometers) above the mountain, according to weather radar from both Subic Bay Naval Station and Clark Air Base. The eruption lasted just under 40 minutes. The evacuation radius was enlarged to 18 miles (30 kilometers), encompassing 58,000 people. Slightly less than half of the remaining soldiers at Clark Air Base evacuated with local residents. Significant ash plumes were blown to the southwest, and small pyroclastic flows traveled down at least one river valley leading away from Pinatubo's summit. Four such vertical eruptions occurred throughout the next two days. Immediately following those was a series of 13 explosive eruptions, beginning on the afternoon of June 14. The weather was deteriorating, however, and only 1 of the 13 was observed directly. Typhoon Yunya, a weak hurricane, was moving in to the area. The remaining Clark Air Base personnel evacuated, as did the scientists. The scientists had second thoughts, however, and returned to their observatory at Clark Air Base shortly thereafter.

Early on June 15, winds and rain from Typhoon Yunya pelted Clark Air Base. Rather than blowing ash to the southwest, as prevailing winds usually did, the typhoon's winds blew a great deal of ash and debris directly over the base. Repeated eruptions brought total darkness for 30- to 40-minute intervals that morning.

The paroxysmal eruption of Pinatubo began at 1:42 p.m. on June 15. Seismometers became inactive one by one, presumably disabled by pyroclastic flows. The eruption cloud reached a height of 21 miles (34 kilometers) and expanded laterally. The scientists and very few remaining Clark Air Base personnel who had stayed behind to monitor the volcano finally left at about 3 p.m. that day. The eruption sent pyroclastic flows raging down all major river valleys around the volcano. Volcanic ash mixed with rainwater from the typhoon, and lahars moved further down the river valleys in advance of the pyroclastic flows. Within the last few hours of the eruption several moderate sized earthquakes were recorded. The summit of the volcano collapsed, creating a 1.5-mile (2.5-kilometer) wide caldera. The eruption ended around 10:30 p.m., 9 hours after its explosive start. Minor ash emissions and dome building continued throughout the remainder of 1991 and into 1992. The eruption was declared over in October 1992. This was not the last people would hear from Pinatubo, however. Even though the volcano was quiet, rainfall eroded ash from the landscape around the volcano and produced lahars during the next several years. The large quantity of ash and sulfur dioxide in the atmosphere following the eruption produced a 0.72° F (0.4° C) decrease in global temperatures. Temperatures did not return to normal until 1995.

See Also: Philippine Institute of Volcanology and Seismology; Philippines; Pyroclastic Materials; Volcanic Hazards; Volcano Disaster Assistance Program.

Further Reading

Decker, R., & Decker, B. (1998). *Volcanoes* (3rd ed.; Academic Version). New York: W.H. Freeman and Company.

Wolfe, E. W., & Hoblitt, R. P. (1995). Overview of the eruptions. In C. G. Newhall & R. S. Punongbayan (Eds.), *Fire and mud: Eruptions and lahars of Mount Pinatubo, Philippines.* Quezon City and Seattle: Philippine Institute of Volcanology and Seismology and University of Washington Press.

Pisco Earthquake (2007)

A magnitude 8.0 earthquake struck the Peruvian coast near the town of Chincha Alta at 6:40 p.m. local time on August 15, 2007. The earthquake produced widespread damage to homes, businesses, schools, and hospitals and destroyed many segments of the area's transportation and telecommunications infrastructure. More than 500 people died in the region, and more than 1,000 were injured. The highest concentration of deaths occurred in Pisco. Thousands were left homeless for years after the earthquake. A local tsunami was generated as well, with maximum runups of 33 feet (10 meters) in areas near the earthquake's epicenter.

This earthquake goes by two names—the "Ica Earthquake" and the "Pisco Earthquake." Both Ica and Pisco are cities in which the majority of buildings were destroyed. In Pisco, about 160 people died when the vault of the San Clemente church collapsed during a funeral. Across town, a portion of a hospital collapsed and killed 26 people, many of them patients. Still more people were killed due to the collapse of their homes.

A great many of the homes destroyed by the earthquake were at least partially constructed of adobe. Many older two-story homes were constructed of adobe on the first level, with a second story composed of wooden frames filled with crushed cane and covered with mud or gypsum. Roofs usually were flat features, consisting of wooden planks or crushed cane, often covered with straw mats and plastered with mud. This type of construction was possible because rain is a rare event in this region. Unreinforced adobe homes are weak structures that tend to crumble with severe ground shaking. Not only was ground shaking severe during the 2007 earthquake, it also was long lasting. Typical magnitude 8 earthquakes cause about 45 seconds of ground shaking. In this instance, the ground shook for approximately 100 seconds. This created ample opportunity for adobe structures and other unreinforced or poorly constructed masonry structures to be shaken to the ground. In Pisco, more than 80% of adobe homes collapsed or sustained enough damage that they had to be demolished.

Liquefaction was another major factor in damage that occurred as a result of the earthquake. Near the shoreline, many sand blows and ground cracks containing wet sand were noted by teams of earthquake engineers during the week after the earthquake. In several instances, liquefaction was responsible for settling and partial burial of structures. Liquefaction also was partially to blame for seaward movement of rocks and sediment along the coastline. In some areas, up to 9.8 feet (3 meters) of vertical offset and 3 feet (0.9 meters) of horizontal offset separated one side of the fault from the other. Liquefaction contributed to the landslides that covered highways, the rupturing of water and sewer lines, the disruption of port operations, and the toppling of power poles.

A local tsunami was generated as a consequence of the earthquake. Although the only tide gauge in the area was damaged by the earthquake and was unable to measure the tsunami's effects, runups are easily estimated by observing high-water lines. Three people were killed in the tsunami, all were members of the Lagunilla community, a tiny fishing village located on the south coast of the Paracas peninsula. Elsewhere, general knowledge that tsunamis often follow large earthquakes, coupled with prompt tsunami warnings delivered by Coast Guard officials, led to evacuations within 10 to 20 minutes of the earthquake. People in the village of Lagunilla, however, were not aware of the tsunami threat and did not evacuate. This tragic result underscores the need for education campaigns about the tsunami hazard in coastal areas.

Maximum runups were 33 feet (10 meters) just south of the Paracas peninsula, which is south of the epicenter of the earthquake. At Lagunilla, the runup was 16.5 to 19.5 feet (5 to 6 meters), and the land was exceedingly flat, so there were no nearby places of refuge for village residents. Runups elsewhere along the coastline were considerably less, but were still severe enough to cause damage. Boats were washed into the streets in the city of Pisco, and a prison was partially flooded in Chincha Alta. The prison had collapsed during the earthquake and most of the prisoners had escaped by the time the tsunami struck.

Immediately following the earthquake, the mayors of the stricken towns worked hard to get help for the cleanup of their cities and funding for rebuilding homes and businesses. The country's president at the time, Alan Garcia, spent a great deal of time touring the affected cities and offering advice to the cities' mayors regarding rebuilding plans. Aid, however, was slow to get to the cities. Four years later, many of those displaced by the earthquake were still living in temporary shelters and at that time only were receiving water and power service from the government.

See Also: Earthquake Hazards; Peru; Tsunami.

Further Reading

Chauvin, L. (2007, August 20). Recovering from the Peru earthquake. *Time Magazine*. Retrieved from http://content.time.com/time/world/article/0,8599,1654411,00.html

Earthquake Engineering Research Institute. (2014, May 27). The Pisco, Peru, earthquake of August 15, 2007. *EERI Special Earthquake Report*. Retrieved from https://www.eeri .org/lfe/pdf/peru_pisco_eeri_preliminary_reconnaissance.pdf

Long-Chavez, A. (2012, January 26). Pisco earthquake: Four years later, Peruvian refugees receive water and power. *Huffington Post*. Retrieved from http://www.huffingtonpost .com/2012/01/25/refugees-waited-four-years_n_1232611.html

Puertas, L., & Elsen, J. (2007, August 16). Earthquake in Peru kills hundreds. *The New York Times*. Retrieved from http://www.nytimes.com/2007/08/16/world/americas/16cnd-peru .html?_r=0

Plate Tectonics

Plate tectonics is one of the most revolutionary theories in the history of geology. Plate tectonic theory explains the formation of the world's oceans and mountain ranges, the occurrence of volcanic and seismic activity, and why ocean trenches exist. It is the result of decades of work by hundreds of scientists across the world, examining data from a variety of sources. Its importance cannot be overstated.

Plate tectonics has its roots in the concept of continental drift, published in the early 1900s by German meteorologist and geophysicist Alfred Wegener. Wegener spent a great deal of time looking at maps. He (as did many before him) noticed that the coastlines of South America and Africa appear to match. If a person were to cut out the shapes of the continents and moved them around, eastern South America would fit snugly into western Africa like a puzzle piece. Wegener also noted that North America, Europe, and Asia also fit neatly together in this way, as did Australia and the detached subcontinent of India. Unlike others who noted this apparent fit of coastlines, Wegener devoted a great deal of time and effort to perusing the scientific literature in an effort to determine if this could in fact have

A rare view of a divergent plate boundary. This rift, in the Lake Myvatn region of Iceland, is the boundary between the North American and Eurasian plates. (Geoff Renner/Robert Harding/Newscom)

been a feasible arrangement of continents at some time in the earth's past. He found a great deal of supporting evidence during his search.

The first piece of evidence Wegener assembled was paleontological evidence, or that of the occurrence of extinct plants and animals. Wegener found that a number of species of fossils could be found on multiple continents. Because of evolutionary pressures, isolation of one species on a separate continent (even if by some fluke it was able to raft or swim to another continent) results in evolution into a different species over time. Therefore, finding a set of plant and animal fossils on multiple continents makes no sense when put together with our understanding of evolutionary theory. If the continents were moved into the configuration he imagined by fitting coastlines together, however, Wegener found that the habitat ranges of these plant and animal fossils were continuous and consistent.

One animal, an extinct crocodile-like aquatic reptile called Mesosaurus, was found in both South America and Africa. The animal, like modern crocodiles, was capable of living in shallow water but could not swim across an entire ocean. If South America and Africa were joined, then the habitat area of Mesosaurus is continuous across the larger landmass. Thus, the conclusion is that South America and Africa were joined when Mesosaurus was alive. Fossils of a land reptile called Lystrosaurus were found throughout Africa, India, and Antarctica. Using the same line of logic as used for Mesosaurus, those continents must have been joined when Lystrosaurus was alive. A species of an extinct type of plant called a seed fern— Glossopteris—was found on South America, Africa, Antarctica, India, and Australia. It reproduced with heavy seeds that could neither float nor fly on the wind. The only way seeds could have spread to all of those locations was if the sites were part of a continuous land mass when the plant was living.

Wegener also looked at evidence of glacier activity. He found abundant evidence that widespread, thick glaciers existed in South America, Antarctica, Africa, southern India, and Australia. Given today's configuration of the continents, this made no sense to Wegener. Southern India is located in the tropics near the equator and at a low elevation, so there is no feasible way glaciers could exist there today, in its current location and climate zone. Glaciers also do not exist in Australia, or in non-alpine areas of South America or Africa. If these continental masses were joined in the configuration he suggested and located near the South Pole, however, then the areas showing clear glacial activity would have formed a continuous mass of ice. Indicators of the direction of ice movement also are consistent with movement away from a theoretical South Pole located in what today is southeastern Africa.

Another feature Wegener examined was the locations of mountain ranges on the continents. He found that if the continents were joined, then mountain ranges on separate continents lined up to form even longer, continuous mountain ranges. For example, the Appalachian Mountains in North America lined up with the Atlas Mountains in northern Africa, the British Isles, and the Caledonian Mountains of northern Europe so that they formed one continuous mountain range. Geological evidence also indicates that these four sets of mountains were formed at the same time. The logical conclusion therefore is that these mountains formed in response to the same geologic pressures—perhaps when these continents came together to form a larger continent that contained all of the world's land masses.

Wegener assembled his information and published a book titled, *Die Entstehung der Kontinente and Ozeane* (*The Origin of Continents and Oceans*) in 1915. His basic premise was that, at some point in the past, likely at the end of the Permian Period (about 200 million years ago), all of the earth's major landmasses were combined into a single supercontinent he named Pangaea. Pangaea is Latin for "all lands." Pangaea was surrounded by a large ocean Wegener called Panthalassa. The supercontinent broke apart and the individual continents drifted to their current locations over millions of years. He called his idea "Continental Drift." Wegener eventually wrote three more editions of the book, the last in 1929. When his book was translated in 1924 from the original German into several other languages, including English, French, Spanish, and Russian, he drew a firestorm of hostile criticism from the world's scientists. Despite the preponderance of evidence in support of continental drift, Wegener had a very difficult time getting his ideas accepted in the scientific community because he could not answer a host of basic questions about how and why a supercontinent could have broken apart, and how and why continents move.

Wegener died in Greenland in 1930. Even after his death, his ideas circulated widely in the scientific community and did garner some support. During his lifetime, however, evidence was painfully elusive. This was not because of his lack of talent as a scientist or any sloppiness in his work. Wegener's ideas, quite simply, were ahead of their time. Conclusive evidence that answered the nagging questions of how and why continents are able to seemingly drift about on the earth did not come until well after Wegener's death. Only after major advances in technology, and years of data collection and analysis, was Wegener's basic idea of Continental Drift proven correct. His published ideas about Pangaea and Panthalassa as well as the drifting of continents to their current positions, however, were only a small piece of a bigger picture. The earth's continents indeed had been joined into a single supercontinent at the end of the Permian Period, and the continents recognized today did derive from a breakup of the supercontinent, and movement into their current positions. The story is much more complex and interesting than that simple set of facts, however. Individual components of plate tectonic theory were published in a series of articles beginning in the late 1950s, and brought together into one coherent theory in the mid-1960s. The last pieces of tectonic theory were in place by the early 1970s, and it has been almost universally accepted by geologists since shortly after that time.

It is known today that the earth's lithosphere is broken into several pieces called "plates." There are approximately 16 major plates and dozens of smaller plates, including a number of small slivers of lithosphere termed microplates. These plates move around due to convection, or heat-driven circulation, of the rocks in the asthenosphere. The plates interact at their boundaries. It is at plate boundaries that the majority of geologic activity occurs. Earthquakes, formation of mountain ranges, volcanic activity, and formation of new oceanic lithosphere occur at the various types of plate boundaries.

During Wegener's time, very little was known about the interior of the earth. In the 1920s, great leaps were being made in the field of seismology and the study of the earth's interior. Seismologists were able to determine that the earth had a layered interior. The outermost layer, the lithosphere, is rigid and contains the crust and uppermost mantle. The asthenosphere contains the remainder of the upper mantle, and its base is the greatest depth at which earthquakes occur in the earth. The mesosphere is the solid lower mantle. The outer core is liquid, and the inner core is solid.

Before electronic technology was invented, anyone that needed to know the depth of a particular location in the ocean had to take a "sounding." The sounding consisted of dropping a weight attached to a rope or chain, and measuring the length of chain that had to be let out before the weight hit the ocean floor. It was terribly time-consuming and not very accurate in deep water. In the 1920s, the United States Coast and Geodetic Survey developed a method of determining the depth of the ocean by the use of sound waves. A sound was emitted into the water, and the length of time it took for the sound wave to travel to the ocean floor, reflect, and be detected back at the boat was used to calculate water depth. This method, known as SONAR (Sound NAvigation and Ranging), was refined in the early 1930s, and used in the mid- and late-1930s to map the ocean floor in great detail for military purposes.

Although the data collected prior to and during World War II were classified until the late 1950s, scientists who assisted in making the SONAR measurements knew that the data showed interesting features on the ocean floor. As expected, the shallowest parts of the oceans were found immediately next to the continents. At some shorelines, however, water depth increased dramatically immediately offshore. In these areas the water became incredibly deep parallel to the shoreline, creating something called a trench or deep ocean trench. The deepest of all trenches was found near the Mariana Islands, and is called the Mariana Trench. Here, the ocean is approximately 36,000 feet (11,000 meters) deep. These deep trenches are narrow. On the seaward side of the trenches the ocean floor rises to its typical depth, between 12,000 feet (3,650 meters) and 18,000 feet (5,500 meters).

In other areas, the ocean floor leading away from the shoreline has a very different profile. Off the Atlantic coast of North America, for example, the ocean floor has a slope of one-half degree to one degree. The ocean gets gradually deeper as one heads offshore. More than 100 miles (161 kilometers) offshore there is an abrupt change in slope, known as the continental slope. At the base of this slope, the ocean is between 8,000 feet (2,400 meters) and 15,000 feet (4,500 meters) deep. In the center of the Atlantic Ocean, however, there is an unexpected feature. The ocean floor builds to a massive mountain range that rises up to 10,000 feet (3,000 meters) above the surrounding landscape. It was discovered that this mountain range, called a mid-ocean ridge (the "Mid-Atlantic Ridge" in the specific case of the Atlantic Ocean), is volcanic in origin. At its summit are hydrothermal vents, very young lava flows, and other signs of recent volcanic activity.

By the mid-1950s, scientists routinely performed magnetic surveys of the world's oceans. This provided another valuable line of evidence crucial to the development of plate tectonic theory—a pattern of magnetic reversals. In the early 1900s, it was discovered that the earth's magnetic field has periodically switched polarity. In other words, compass needles presently point toward the magnetic north pole, which is located relatively close to the geographic north pole. At certain times in the earth's past, magnetic north has been located near the geographic south pole. These "magnetic reversals" are relatively easy to detect with instruments called magnetometers. Magnetometers can measure anomalies (or differences) in the magnetic field of the earth and its rocks very accurately. In surveys of the ocean floor, scientists recognized that it is a well-preserved record of magnetic anomalies. These anomalies show a very distinctive and interesting pattern; they look like stripes on the ocean floor, much like tire tread. Where a mid-ocean ridge existed, those stripes appear to be parallel to the ridge. Further study indicated that these magnetic anomalies are present in every ocean basin, and that the pattern always is the same—the stripes are parallel to any mid-ocean ridge that existed.

In the 1960s, scientists were able to determine a chronology of magnetic reversals for the last 80 million years. When they applied this chronology to what they found in the oceans, they determined three very interesting things. First, all of the very youngest parts of the ocean floor are found at the mid-ocean ridges. At these locations the rocks are so young they still have the magnetic signature of today's rocks. That means they have been formed in the last 780,000 years. For an earth that is 4.6 billion years old, these are very young rocks indeed. The second surprising discovery is that very little of the ocean floor is older than 140 million years, and none of it is more than about 180 million years old. Again, for an earth that is 4.6 billion years old, this means that the earth's entire ocean floor is extremely young. The third interesting discovery is that all of the oldest rocks have been found very near the continents.

Scientists now had an answer to one question that had plagued Wegener and those who thought seriously about his work: How can continents move across the earth? The answer opened the door to plate tectonics. The earth's lithosphere is pulled apart at the mid-ocean ridges. At these sites, a volcanic mountain range creates new oceanic lithosphere and the continental blocks on either side grow further apart. These areas are called spreading centers or divergent plate boundaries. A large part of Wegener's conundrum was solved, but many questions remained. For example, if the ocean floor is so young, where did more than 4 billion years of oceanic lithosphere go?

Common wisdom dictates that on a planet which remains the same size—as is thought that the earth has for the last 4.6 billion years—creation of new material must be balanced by destruction of an equal amount of material. Such is the case with plate tectonics. The process of destroying oceanic lithosphere occurs at places called "subduction zones." In these settings, oceanic lithosphere is pushed and pulled down into the earth's asthenosphere. The result is a violent collision of solid lithosphere and solid asthenosphere. Subduction zones are where the earth's most violent earthquakes occur, and are also places where a great deal of volcanic activity occurs. The location at a subduction zone where an oceanic plate dives beneath a neighboring plate is marked by the occurrence of a deep ocean trench. A number of active and deadly subduction zones exist in the western Pacific region. The location of the deadly 2004 Indian Ocean earthquake and tsunami that struck Indonesia and surrounding countries was on a subduction zone between the Pacific and Indian-Australian plates. The 2011 Tohoku (Japan) earthquake and tsunami occurred on the boundary between the Eurasian Plate and Pacific Plate. Both Japan and Indonesia are known for their widespread volcanic activity as well.

Another location where lithosphere might be destroyed is a setting known as a collision zone. Collision zones are places where two pieces of continental lithosphere collide. Rather than one plate descending beneath the other, these two thick, strong pieces of lithosphere are slowly but violently crumpled, deformed, and folded into mountains. It is this process of collision that formed the Appalachians, the Caledonians, the Alps, and the Himalayas. Collision does not result in volcanic activity, but it is a frequent cause of earthquakes. Many of those earthquakes are violent and deadly. India, for example, currently is colliding with mainland Asia. In the wide boundary between these two plates, deadly earthquakes occur with grim regularity in places such as India, Pakistan, Afghanistan, and even China.

In a careful examination of the earth, it becomes apparent that there are some areas of volcanic and earthquake activity that cannot be explained by the processes described above. For example, the Hawaiian Islands sit in the center of the Pacific Plate. According to the theory of plate tectonics as it existed in the late 1960s, there was no expectation that islands, volcanoes, or earthquakes should occur there; however, they obviously do. Some geologists used this fact to discard the entire theory of plate tectonics, but most realized there must be another piece to this puzzle.

After careful observation, it was discovered that a great amount of heat is escaping the earth's interior in the Hawaiian Islands, and in areas of volcanic and seismic activity around the world that occur away from plate boundaries. W. J. Morgan and his colleagues described convection plumes in the mantle that stayed stationary while plates moved over them. This explains why the Hawaiian Island chain exists, and why activity has ceased at all but the southeasternmost island of Hawaii. A mantle plume, or hot spot, exists in the center of the Pacific Ocean. As the Pacific plate moves over the hot spot, it melts part of the mantle and sends magma toward the surface, where it erupts to form volcanoes. These volcanoes build over time to become islands. As the plate moves on, volcanic activity slows and stops at one volcano but begins in a new place, which is now over the hot spot. Both physical and chemical evidence supported this hypothesis, so it was added to plate tectonic theory in the early 1970s. Today, we know of approximately 60 active hot spots.

See Also: Collision Zone; Divergent Boundary; Earth Structure; Hot Spot; Seismology; Subduction Zone.

Further Reading

Kearey, P., Klepeis, K. A., & Vine, F. J. (2009). *Global tectonics* (3rd ed.). Hoboken, NJ: Wiley-Blackwell.

Müller, R. D., Sdrolias, M., Gaina, C., & Roest, W. R. (2008). Age, spreading rates and spreading symmetry of the world's ocean crust. *Geochemistry. Geophysics. Geosystems.* 9 (Q04006), doi:10.1029/2007GC001743.

National Oceanic and Atmospheric Administration. (2014, April 30). *SONAR.* http://oceanexplorer.noaa.gov/technology/tools/sonar/sonar.html

Tarbuck, E. J., Lutgens, F. K., & Tasa, D. (2011). *Earth: An introduction to physical geology* (10th ed.). Upper Saddle River, NJ: Pearson Prentice Hall/Pearson Education, Inc.

Pliny the Elder

The given name of Pliny the Elder was "Gaius Plinius Cecilius Secundus." He was born in the year 23 CE to a wealthy Roman family in Novum Comum in Gallia Cisalpine (Como, Italy). He received a classical education in literature, oratory, and law, as well as military training. Pliny the Elder began his military career at age 23 and served in Germany, Gaul, Africa, and Spain. Despite that he remained an active military commander and served on the imperial council for multiple emperors, he was intensely curious about history, culture, and the natural world. Pliny the Elder wrote at least 75 published books and left behind 160 volumes of unpublished notebooks. His litany of works included books on cavalry tactics, history, grammar, rhetoric, and his most famous book, a 37-book encyclopedia called *Historia Naturalis* (*Natural History*).

Although Pliny the Elder certainly is remembered for his long and distinguished military career and prolific writings, his death also is noteworthy in the history of volcanology. Pliny the Elder was serving as an admiral in the Roman Navy, stationed at the port of Misenum near Naples, when Mount Vesuvius erupted. He wrote down his observations of the eruption that began at 1 p.m. on August 24 of the year 79 CE. He noticed that a vertical plume ascended many thousands of feet, and then spread out laterally similar to the shape of a Mediterranean pine tree that has a bare trunk and branches further up. Pliny the Elder was extremely curious about this phenomenon and wanted to sail closer for a better look, purely for the sake of satisfying his scientific curiosity, but he was soon summoned by those living nearer the volcano to perform a rescue mission. He did indeed sail closer to the volcano, although with more altruistic motives in mind. His ship was repelled from the shoreline at one port due to unfavorable winds, burning ash, and pumice fall. Pliny the Elder eventually made landfall at Stabiae (Castellammare, Italy).

When he met up with his friends they were in a state of panic. For several hours, Pliny the Elder attempted to calm those around him by acting completely unconcerned about the eruption raging nearby. He wrote down his observations of the eruption, took time to relax in the baths, and ate a large meal before going to

Death of Pliny lithograph depicting the death of Pliny the Elder in 79 A.D. (akg-images/Newscom)

sleep. The volcano was in full eruption. Fires had been started by falling pyroclastic materials, and those fires lit the terrifying black ash cloud above. He woke up a few hours later when his friends begged him to evacuate them from the area by ship. The winds had shifted, the eruption had become even more frightening, and they had no patience for Pliny's shows of bravery. The group made it to the vessel, but found that it was impossible to leave by ship at that time. Winds were blowing onshore and the water was extremely rough. As a result, they could not get away. The air was thick with ash and the smell of volcanic gases. Pliny the Elder became ill and lay down on a cloth on the ground; he asked for some water to drink. As the gases grew more bothersome, Pliny the Elder tried to rise and depart with his friends. He rose to his feet briefly and then fell to the ground, dead. Although contemporaries blamed the sulfurous fumes for his death, it is unlikely that he died from exposure to the gases but his friends survived. He likely died from a heart attack brought on by the stress of the situation and exacerbated by exposure to the volcanic gases.

Pliny the Elder is recognized today in volcanology as the first person to accurately and dispassionately describe the events witnessed during a major volcanic eruption. The shape of the volcanic plume he described, a long vertical column that spreads out at an altitude of several thousand feet above the volcano, is now called a plinian column. Volcanology now describes eruptions with such features as plinian eruptions. Pliny the Elder's descriptions and the story of his death were preserved as a result of the accounts of his friends, told to and retold by his nephew, Pliny the Younger. Pliny the Younger wrote a heroic story about the end of his uncle's life. It included a wonderful narrative of how he bravely fought against the forces of nature to save his dear friends, and paid the ultimate price for his bravery.

Pliny the Elder's Eruption

Pliny the Elder was a tremendous observer of the natural world. His name will always be linked with the eruption of Vesuvius in 79 CE, which contributed to his death in no small way. The eruption of Vesuvius, however, was much more complex than Pliny's observations. When Vesuvius began erupting, a plinian column rose thousands of feet above the volcano's summit. What goes up must come down; thus the areas downwind of the volcano—including the town of Pompeii—received heavy ash and pumice fall. Over the next several hours, Pompeii received enough ash and pumice fall to bury most of the town in more than 6 feet (1.8 meters) of debris. Many people who took refuge in buildings died of suffocation and were buried by pyroclastic materials. Later in the eruption, pyroclastic flows roared down the slopes of the volcano. The port town of Herculaneum was in the direct path of these pyroclastic flows. Hundreds of people waited for rescue by sea, but boats never came. A pyroclastic flow overtook Herculaneum and killed the people who were in the boat houses; the victims' skeletons were found in the 1980s.

Today, the ruins of Pompeii are a popular tourist attraction. The volcanic ash that buried the city preserved much of the city's architecture and art work, as well as the objects related to everyday life. Even the people who died in the eruption were preserved, in a way, as impressions in the hardened ash deposits. Excavators in the 1800s found that, by poking long rods into the deposits, they could locate cavities in the ash. By pouring plaster down holes and into the cavities, the researchers found many of the cavities were shaped like bodies. The corpses had decayed and disappeared, but their impressions were left in the soft, fine ash. In some cases, the plaster casts were so detailed that clothing and facial expressions could be seen. Frescoes and mosaics also were perfectly preserved, as were the buildings in which they were housed. Areas buried or destroyed by the eruption of Vesuvius in 79 CE comprise a UNESCO World Heritage Site due to their archaeological value.

See Also: Pyroclastic Materials.

Further Reading

Barran, M. (2014, May 15). *Pliny the Elder*. Retrieved from http://scienceworld.wolfram.com/biography/PlinytheElder.html

Francis, P., & Oppenheimer, C. (2004). *Volcanoes* (2nd ed.). Oxford: Oxford University Press.

Poás Volcano, Costa Rica

Poás is a large volcanic complex located in northern Costa Rica. The Poás volcano was created as a result of subduction of the Cocos Plate beneath the Caribbean Plate to the east. It is arguably the most active volcano in Costa Rica, producing frequent phreatic eruptions from within one of its crater lakes. Although eruptions are frequent, they also are quite small. This makes Poás an immensely popular

Poas Volcano, Costa Rica. (Weimann, P./picture alliance / Arco Images G/Newscom)

tourist destination. The volcano makes up the bulk of Poás Volcano National Park. It is difficult to discern the dates of the last eruption cycle because the volcano has been more active than dormant over the last 200 years. Periods of activity lasting from a single day to a few months are separated by no more than a year during most of that period. The last single eruption that attracted media attention occurred around noon on February 25, 2014. It was a phreatic eruption that sent material nearly 1,000 feet (300 meters) above the volcano's northern crater lake.

The volcanic complex consists of multiple features, including two peaks and two crater lakes. The southern lake is called "Botos" and its water is clear and cold. At the northern crater lake, Laguna Caliente, phreatic and phreatomagmatic eruptions are commonplace, and have been since its first historically recorded eruption in 1828. The lake is very warm, with an average temperature of 116° F (47° C). The temperature can fluctuate, however, depending on the volcano's level of activity. Phreatic eruptions often consist of relatively small columns of water erupting geyser-like from the surface of the lake. During periods when eruptions are common, columns rarely rise more than 100 feet (30 meters) from the surface of the lake. An eruption in 1910, however, sent a column of water more than 2.5 miles (4 kilometers) high.

Due to the high volume of sulfur dioxide that passes through the lake as it escapes the vent beneath the water, the lake is extremely acidic with a pH near zero. Sulfuric-acid droplets, as well as acid-laden steam, drift downwind and are extremely destructive to the lush forests growing there. Large swaths of tropical rainforest have been wiped out by the acidic emissions of the volcano. Occasionally, Poás exhibits another unusual feature within the northern crater. The crater contains a lake, therefore the temperature of the crater itself is somewhat moderated. This allows sulfur to accumulate rather than sublimate, as is much more common at almost all other volcanoes. The accumulations of sulfur in some cases can be liquid, forming pools of liquid sulfur that boil and bubble vigorously. These deposits are eerily green. If an eruption occurs when the sulfur pools are present, then liquid sulfur can be sprayed into the air as a pyroclastic material. Sulfur ejected in this way also can form stalactites and stalagmites on rocks where the droplets land.

See Also: Cocos Plate; Phreatic Eruption; Subduction Zone.

Further Reading

Arias, L. (2014, February 25). Poás Volcano spews material 300 meters high after explosion inside crater. *The Tico Times.*

Costa Rica National Parks. (2014, June 3). *Poás Volcano National Park.* Retrieved from http://www.costarica-nationalparks.com/Poásvolcanonationalpark.html

Smithsonian Institution. National Museum of Natural History. Global Volcanism Program. (2014, June 3). *Poás.* Retrieved from http://www.volcano.si.edu/volcano.cfm?vn=345040#February2014

Popocatépetl Volcano, Mexico

Popocatépetl is a composite volcano located about 43 miles (70 kilometers) southeast of Mexico City in the Trans-Mexican Volcanic Belt. Its summit elevation is 17,801 feet (5,426 meters), making it the second tallest volcano in North America. (The tallest is a dormant volcano called Pico de Orizaba, also located in Mexico.) The name Popocatépetl means "Hill that Smokes" in the native Nahuatl language. The volcano is known popularly as "El Popo," or at times as "Don Goyo." It is a steep-sided, glacier-covered mountain with a relatively small crater at its summit.

The current cone is approximately 23,000 years old, and consists of layered pyroclastic deposits and lava flows. At least three previous cones on the same site were destroyed by landslides and debris avalanches. A sharp-peaked feature on the northwest part of the cone, called "Ventorrillo," is a remnant of one of these earlier cones. Another previous cone, called "El Fraile," lies just to the north of the volcano's present cone. Frequent historical eruptions of Popocatépetl have occurred since pre-Columbian time. The earliest of these were recorded in Aztec codices. Nearly all of the volcano's historically recorded eruptions have been small, with VEI magnitudes of 2 or less. One slightly larger eruption, with a VEI

Geologists gather volcanic ash samples near Popocatépetl volcano, Mexico. (Alfonso Manzano/Notimex/Newscom)

of 3, however, occurred between 1519 and 1523. The most recent eruption of Popocatépetl began in 2005 and continues to the time of this writing. Minor emissions of ash, steam, and gases are frequent occurrences. At night, observers often are able to see incandescence in the crater, indicating the presence of fresh lava in the lava dome.

Popocatépetl is one of two large volcanoes near Mexico City. The other volcano, Iztaccihuatl ("White Woman" in Nahuatl), is the third tallest volcano in North America. Iztaccihuatl is mantled in white snow and ice, and in profile looks somewhat like a woman lying with her face turned upward toward the sky. Because of the proximity of these two volcanoes, there is a legend that pairs the volcanoes as two lovers. In the legend, Iztaccihuatl was a beautiful young princess of the Tlaxcaltecas people. The Tlaxcaltecas were bitter enemies of the Aztecs, who controlled the valley. The Aztecs levied a tax on the people of the valley, and the chief of the Tlaxcaltecas decided to fight for his people's freedom from this tax, and from the oppressive Aztecs. Iztaccihuatl and Popocatépetl, a young warrior, fell in love. Just before Popocatépetl was to leave for the war, he asked the Tlaxcaltecas chief for his daughter's hand in marriage. The chief agreed that when Popocatépetl returned from war, the chief would host a celebration and Iztaccihuatl and Popocatépetl would be married. Soon after Popocatépetl left, a love rival of his told Princess Iztaccihuatl that Popocatépetl had died in combat. The princess was overwhelmed by sadness and died. When Popocatépetl returned to his people, he received the tragic news of Iztaccihuatl's death. He ordered a tomb to be built for her, and ten hills were piled together to make a mountain. Popocatépetl took Iztaccihuatl to the summit and laid her on the mountain. He kissed her and held a smoking torch while he watched over her. Snow fell and covered their bodies. From then on, whenever Popocatépetl thinks of his beloved princess, his heart shakes and his torch smokes. Popocatépetl's rival, Tlaxcala, who lied to Iztaccihuatl, felt great remorse for what he had done and returned to his land in the distance. He watches the couple from afar as the mountain named "Pico de Orizaba."

See Also: Andesite; Dacite.

Further Reading

Orozco, C. (2014, June 4). *The legend of Popocatepetl and Iztaccihuatl.* Retrieved from http://www.inside-mexico.com/legends/volcanes.htm

Seach, J. (2014, June 4). *Popocatépetl Volcano.* Retrieved from http://www.volcanolive.com/popocatepetl.html

Smithsonian Institution. National Museum of Natural History. Global Volcanism Program. (2014, June 4). *Popocatépetl.* Retrieved from http://www.volcano.si.edu/volcano.cfm?vn=341090

Pyroclastic Flow

A pyroclastic flow is a current of pyroclastic materials, steam, volcanic gases, and other debris that flows down the slopes of a volcano during an eruption. It is one of the fastest-moving and most deadly phenomena that a volcano can produce. In French, pyroclastic flows are called "nuées ardentes" ("glowing clouds"). Pyroclastic flows are seen almost exclusively on composite volcanoes, although rare ash eruptions on shield volcanoes have been known to produce very small pyroclastic flows. There are a number of terms used for this type of event, depending on the makeup of the pyroclastic material, the proportion of ash to gas within the cloud, and even whether the flows occur as a single pulse or a sustained flow. The term "pyroclastic flow" is used in this context to describe the entire continuum of events of this nature that can occur during an eruption. At one end of the spectrum is a group of relatively small-volume, low-density flows that involve small amounts of solid material, such as volcanic ash, yet are propelled by proportionately larger volumes of steam and volcanic gases, such as might happen in a phreatic (steam-driven) eruption. At the other end of the spectrum is a very dense cloud of ash, rock fragments, and pumice that contains minor amounts of gas and steam and is propelled primarily by gravity. A cooled pyroclastic flow deposit often is called an "ignimbrite."

Regardless of the specific material involved, most pyroclastic flows involve a deadly combination of hot, fast-moving pyroclastic materials that are mixed with caustic and deadly volcanic gases, such as sulfur dioxide and hydrogen sulfide. Very few people trapped in pyroclastic flows have survived the experience. Those who have were either in sheltered conditions or were at the outer margins of the flows. Yet, even in those cases, people usually are burned very badly and can suffer respiratory problems for the rest of their lives. For those who do not survive, death is nearly instantaneous from the combination of heat, force of the fast-moving material, and poisonous gases.

Pyroclastic flows can be caused by three different mechanisms. The first is the collapse of all or part of an eruption column. This mechanism creates high-speed pyroclastic flows, because material first is blasted upward into the eruption column, and then falls back down to the slopes of the volcano before continuing its journey on the ground. A great deal of momentum is gained before the pyroclastic materials fall from the sky and begin their ground-hugging downhill journey. These pyroclastic flows can form sheets around the perimeter of the entire volcano, blanketing the landscape. Katmai in Alaska, Pinatubo in the Philippines, and Crater Lake in Oregon have produced this type of pyroclastic flow.

A second mechanism for forming pyroclastic flows is the partial collapse or explosion of a lava dome. If a partial collapse is responsible for the pyroclastic flow, then the flow begins at a very low velocity and gains speed as it moves downhill. In the case of an explosion-created pyroclastic flow, the initial velocity of the flow already is relatively high. In either case, the volume is fairly small and these types of pyroclastic flows often—but not always—are confined to valleys leading away from whatever crater contains the lava dome. This type of pyroclastic flow occurred with great regularity at Mount Unzen in Japan.

A third mechanism for forming pyroclastic flows is through a lateral blast of a volcano. In this case, a volcano erupts through a vent in one of its flanks rather than at the summit. The result is a sideways-directed blast. Instead of creating an initial

History's Deadliest Pyroclastic Flow

Pyroclastic flows are among the deadliest of volcanic phenomena. The most lethal occurrence of a pyroclastic flow to date was an event that occurred on the Caribbean island of Martinique in 1902. The volcano Mont Pelée gave clear signals throughout much of the spring that year that it was becoming increasingly restless. The air smelled faintly of sulfur and rotten eggs. Ash fell over Saint-Pierre, the city nearest the volcano. Small animals began to suffocate from the ashfall. The first deaths from the volcano's activity resulted from an overflow of hot water from the volcano's crater, which led to a lahar that destroyed a sugar mill and killed several of its workers. People were terrified. Many people fled the countryside for Saint-Pierre, but an equal number of people fled Saint-Pierre for areas of the island farther from the volcano. On the morning of May 8, Mont Pelée erupted. The eruption cloud poured over the crater rim and into the valley that led straight to Saint-Pierre. A pyroclastic flow rushed toward the city. Within two minutes, all of Saint-Pierre was incinerated along with nearly all of its residents. Not a single building was left intact, and approximately 28,000 people died.

vertical eruption column, as is typical for composite volcanoes, the eruption column comes out of the side of the volcano at very high velocity. The result is a lateral pyroclastic flow. Mount St. Helens' paroxysmal eruption in May 1980 produced this type of eruption when an earthquake-triggered landslide removed the confining pressure from the north-facing magma conduit. A lateral blast created an amphitheater-like scar on the volcano and directed pyroclastic flows to the north at a speed of 200 miles per hour (320 kilometers per hour).

See Also: Composite Volcano; Crater Lake, Oregon, United States; Katmai Eruption, Alaska, United States (1912); Pinatubo, Mount, Eruption, Philippines (1991); Pyroclastic Materials; Shield Volcano; St. Helens, Mount, Washington, United States; Unzen Eruption, Japan (1991–1995).

Further Reading

Francis, P., & Oppenheimer, C. (2004). *Volcanoes* (2nd ed.). Oxford: Oxford University Press.

Pyroclastic Materials

The term "pyroclastic" is derived from two Greek words, "pyro" meaning fire and "klastos" meaning broken. Thus, pyroclastic materials are "fire-broken" materials; they erupted explosively and were rendered airborne by a volcano. Many pyroclastic materials remain loose and unconsolidated and are not incorporated into solid rocks after eruption. In this case, the deposits of pyroclastic materials are referred to as "tephra." Pyroclastic materials that are incorporated into solid rocks go by different names specific to the type of rock they create. The most common of these is "tuff," a rock composed of "welded," or heat-fused volcanic ash.

Tephra, or pyroclastic materials, can be divided into different groups based on size, percent bubble content, or shape. Using size as the first discriminating factor, three categories of tephra exist. The smallest size, in which each particle is less than 0.08 inches (2 millimeters) in diameter, is called "ash." Ash can be formed when magma that is liquid in the throat of a volcano is blasted apart by expanding gases during the eruption. It also can be formed when cold rock is fragmented due to the force of the eruption. The next larger size, called "lapilli," is reserved for fragments of 0.08 inches to 2.5 inches (2 millimeters to 64 millimeters) in diameter. Lapilli can look like small cinders (which are tiny pieces of scoria). It can be small fragments of solid rock, or it can be composed of small spheres of ash, called "accretionary lapilli." The largest size, for particles greater than 2.5 inches (64 millimeters) in diameter, is split into two categories, "blocks" and "bombs." Blocks are larger particles that were solid when ejected by the volcano. They often are irregularly shaped, as they result from cold, pre-existing rocks that are blasted apart by the force of an eruption. Bombs are molten to semi-molten at the time of ejection. They tend to be somewhat aerodynamic in shape. One of the most common forms of bombs is called a "spindle bomb." Spindle bombs are elongated; they are thick in the center and taper to points on either end. This shape evolves as the bomb spins through the air. Another common type of bomb is a "bread crust bomb." This is a blocky bomb that has a cracked outer surface formed as gas bubbles expand in semi-molten rock.

Other types of pyroclastic materials exist as well, and are less defined by size than mode of formation. Lapilli-sized pieces of molten lava can be ejected from a volcano and cool as they move through the air. When they land they are black, teardrop-shaped glass forms. These are referred to as "Pele's Tears," after the Hawaiian goddess of volcanoes, Pele. These should not be confused with "Apache Tears," which are rounded pieces of obsidian that are dislodged from weathered obsidian flows or tuff deposits.

Another type of pyroclastic material is called "Pele's hair." This is a thin, delicate strand of glass formed in one of two ways. One way it can form is in conjunction with Pele's tears. As two small connected blobs of lava sail through the air, the lava joining the two blobs is stretched into a thin strand. This is common where cinder and spatter cones are formed, as well as in areas with lava lakes. The other method by which Pele's hair is formed is by stretching of lava into filaments at the edge of a lava channel. As lava moves through a channel, friction and cooling along the edges of the channel force small blobs of lava to become accreted to the channel's sides. The blob is stretched as the lava flows below it, turning it into a long hair-like filament.

The final category of pyroclastic material is one in which all members contain an appreciable amount of holes. The holes are caused by gas bubbles within molten lava. The pyroclastic material that contains (by percentage) the greatest number of holes is a type that is found almost exclusively on volcanoes erupting basalt. This is a type of tephra called "reticulite." Reticulite is a lacy, glass-constructed material that is brown in color. It is incredibly delicate and is usually produced in tall lava fountains that often mark the onset of eruptions of shield volcanoes or cinder cones. To form reticulite the lava must be incredibly gas-rich. The gases propel lava fountains high into the air and cause blobs of lava to expand. As the lava expands it cools, preserving the shape of the expanding gas bubbles.

A second form of tephra formed by gas-rich lava that cools to preserve bubbles in the rock is scoria. It usually is composed of basalt, but on occasion can be andesitic in composition. Scoria is considerably more solid than reticulite, and as a result is heavier and less delicate. Scoria often is called "cinder." It is a solid red or black rock that has both large and small holes. It often is used for landscaping rock, and can be crushed and used for roadbed material. A third type of tephra formed in this way is pumice. Pumice is lighter than scoria in both weight and color. Pumice is gray to white or pink in color and is so light that it floats on water. It looks like a more or less solid rock, but a microscopic view of the rock shows a network of tiny bubbles. Pumice most often is dacitic or rhyolitic in composition, but also can approach the composition of andesite.

See Also: Andesite; Basalt; Cinder Cone; Dacite; Rhyolite; Shield Volcano.

Further Reading

Cas, R. A. F., & Wright, J. V. (1988). *Volcanic successions, modern and ancient.* London: Chapman & Hall.

Francis, P., & Oppenheimer, C. (2004). *Volcanoes* (2nd ed.). Oxford: Oxford University Press.

San Diego State University. (2014, May 15). How volcanoes work: Tephra and pyroclastic rocks. Retrieved from http://www.geology.sdsu.edu/how_volcanoes_work/Tephra.html

R

Rabaul, Papua New Guinea

Rabaul is a large composite volcano located on the island of New Britain in the country of Papua New Guinea. The volcano is the result of subduction of the Australian Plate beneath the Pacific Plate. Rabaul has a large caldera that measures 5 miles by 8.7 miles (8 kilometers by 14 kilometers). The volcano sits on the tip of the Gazelle Peninsula in the northeast of New Britain. The caldera is breached in the east and is partially filled with seawater, forming Blanche Bay. On the west side of the bay is Rabaul City, which was the largest city on the island prior to a 1994 eruption. Rabaul City actually sits within the rim of the caldera—which, most geologists would agree, is not an ideal location for a major population center. The city's residents, however, are well aware of the risk and are fully prepared for the inevitability of eruptions.

The major caldera-forming eruption at Rabaul occurred about 7,100 years ago. The eruption probably originated offshore to the north, in the associated Tavui caldera. Further caldera collapse took place approximately 3,500 years ago. The breach in the caldera occurred during an eruption about 1,400 years ago. Three composite volcanoes are located outside the northern and northeastern caldera walls of Rabaul, and several smaller vents are located within the caldera.

In mid-1994, the caldera showed signs of unrest. There was uplift throughout the bay area. Mantupit Island rose about 6 feet (2 meters) between 1971 and 1985. Maximum uplift of the bay floor was about 18 feet (6 meters). The eruption began on September 19, 1994, at Tavurvur, which is one of the composite volcanoes located just outside the northern caldera rim. A dense plume of ash rose about 0.6 miles (1 kilometer) above the cone and drifted to the northwest. A short 71 minutes later, the composite cone Vulcan—located directly across the bay from Tavurvur—began erupting. Vulcan sent pyroclastic flows across the water. Eventually, the eruption column rose as high as 18 miles (30 kilometers) above the caldera. Ash fell over the city, and was carried west over much of New Guinea. In Rabaul City, the ash was up to two feet (75 centimeters) deep. Pumice was erupted along with the ash and formed pumice rafts in the sea. After the large explosive eruption, a small lava flow from near Tavurvur flowed for about 25 days. By October 2, 1994, Vulcan was quiet. Tavurvur continued to erupt until November 1994, and then began erupting again in early 1995. It has been in a state of near-constant unrest since the onset of the 1994 eruption. This was not the first

Rabaul volcano, Papua New Guinea. (Jones & Shimlock / Jaynes Gallery / DanitaDelimont.com Danita Delimont Photography/Newscom)

time that Tavurvur and Vulcan erupted simultaneously; this also happened in 1878 and 1937.

The 1994 eruption had the potential to create not only the destruction seen within Rabaul City, but also a great loss of life. More than 50,000 people lived in the area directly affected by the eruption. Thanks to vigilant monitoring of the volcanic unrest, scientists were able to forecast the eruption and many people were evacuated before the eruption started. The remainder of the city's residents left within a few days of the eruption's onset. Five people died in the eruption; four died because of roof collapse from the weight of the volcanic ash, and another resident was struck by lightning. The volcanoes, however, destroyed two-thirds of the city.

See Also: Australian Plate; Pacific Plate; Pyroclastic Flow; Subduction Zone.

Further Reading

Oregon State University. Volcano World. (2014, June 18). Rabaul caldera, Papua New Guinea. Retrieved from http://volcano.oregonstate.edu/oldroot/volcanoes/rabaul/rabaul.html

Smithsonian Institution. National Museum of Natural History. Global Volcanism Program. (2014, June 18). *Rabaul.* Retrieved from http://www.volcano.si.edu/volcano.cfm?vn=252140

Rainier, Mount, Washington, United States

Mount Rainier is a large composite volcano created by subduction of the Juan de Fuca Plate beneath the North American Plate. Its primary rock type is andesite. It is the tallest peak in the Cascade Mountain Range, at 14,410 feet (4,392 meters) above sea level, and the volcano is a prominent landmark in the State of Washington. Mount Rainier is located approximately 70 miles (112 kilometers) southeast of Seattle, Washington. On a clear day, it is visible from the Oregon border in the south to the Canadian border to the north. It rises 3 miles (4.8 kilometers) above the Puget Sound lowlands to the west. Because of Mount Rainier's size and high relief, it appears to be much closer to the cities of Seattle and Tacoma than it actually is.

Mount Rainier sits atop the eroded remains of an ancestral volcano formed one to two million years ago. The current edifice of Mount Rainier began to grow about 500,000 years ago. For the first 80,000 years of its history, the volcano grew quickly through a succession of high-volume eruptions. The volcano

Mount Rainier, a large composite volcano in the state of Washington, USA. (Mark Rightmire/MCT/Newscom)

produced pyroclastic flow deposits and thick lava flows. Isolated rock features on the mountain indicate that glaciers grew on top of the mountain in between eruptions, and steered lava so it flowed parallel to these glacial valleys. One particularly well-preserved feature near the road to the Sunrise visitor facilities within Mount Rainier National Park is an outcrop of ice-chilled lava columns that protrude from the tip of the lava flow. The columns are oriented horizontally, indicating that the lava flow cooled against the side of a glacier.

Between 420,000 years and 280,000 years ago, it appears that Mount Rainier's rate of eruption slowed. The only high-volume lava flow from this period is called the Rampart Ridge flow, and it is dated to about 380,000 years ago. Eruption rates jumped about 280,000 years ago, and the increased frequency and volume of eruptions lasted for approximately 100,000 years. Between 160,000 years ago and 40,000 years ago, the eruption rate again diminished. Erosion took over, and much of the upper north and south flanks of the volcano were removed as a result. A relatively large eruption occurred about 130,000 years ago and was chilled by glaciers filling the Carbon River valley. Between 40,000 and 15,000 years ago, the summit of the volcano was reconstructed with a number of lava flows. Within the last 11,000 years, lava flows have become less frequent. Debris flows, pyroclastic flows, and lahars are common deposits from this latest period of activity.

In the volcanology and disaster-planning communities, Mount Rainier is well-known for its lahar deposits. Within the last 11,000 years, Mount Rainier has had about five major periods in which lahars were produced and then flowed more than 40 miles (64 kilometers) away from the mountain. This is the hazard that most concerns civil defense officials and first responders. Many communities in the Puget Sound lowlands are built on old lahar deposits which flowed from Mount Rainier. The communities include many southern suburbs of Seattle, as well as the city of Tacoma. In fact, the Port of Tacoma is built on lahar deposits that helped to push the shoreline of Puget Sound 15.5 to 31 miles (25 to 50 kilometers) seaward roughly 5,000 years ago. What is even more worrying is that only a few of these immense lahars appear to have occurred during eruptions.

Mount Rainier has a great deal of hydrothermal activity near its summit. This activity weakens the rocks and alters them into water-saturated clays. It takes only a small phreatic eruption, a large earthquake, or even heavy rainfall to dislodge these materials from the summit area; they quickly can grow into a very large lahar. Lahar detection systems have been installed in the upper reaches of river valleys on Mount Rainier, and an alarm is sounded in the event that a lahar begins moving down a river valley. Lahars from Mount Rainier can reach Puget Sound in less than two hours, so evacuation must happen quickly to avoid loss of life.

The last confirmed eruption of Mount Rainier occurred approximately 1,000 years ago. About 500 years ago, a large lahar called the "Electron Mudflow" sent hydrothermally altered rock down the Puyallup River valley, but there is no evidence of an eruption occurring at that time. Reports describe small plumes of white steam and a single darker plume rising slowly from the summit of Rainier on December 24, 1894. A clear photograph taken five days later, however, shows no indication of any eruptive activity. No deposits of any type that could be related to a possible eruption in the late 1800s ever have been found.

See Also: Andesite; Lahar; Pyroclastic Flow.

Further Reading

Pringle, P. (1992). "Rainier, Washington." In C. A. Wood, & J. Kienle (Eds.), *Volcanoes of North America, United States and Canada*. Cambridge: Cambridge University Press.

U.S. Geological Survey. Cascades Volcano Observatory. (2014, May 22). *Mount Rainier.* Retrieved from http://volcanoes.usgs.gov/volcanoes/mount_rainier/

Redoubt Volcano, Alaska, United States

Redoubt Volcano is located on the west side of Cook Inlet on the mainland of southern Alaska. It is a large composite volcano, and its summit is 10,197 feet (3,108 meters) above sea level. The volcano is home to numerous alpine glaciers which are hard at work eroding the upper reaches of the volcano. Redoubt's

Mount Redoubt, Alaska, USA. (Ingo Arndt/ Minden Pictures/Newscom)

current edifice started forming approximately 200,000 years ago, with the eruption of basalt and basaltic andesite flows onto an ancestral cone and the 200-million-year-old intrusive igneous rocks of the Alaska Range Batholith. A later eruptive period capped the volcano with thick andesite flows and pyroclastic material that formed an apron around the volcano. Ash deposits around the Cook Inlet basin indicate that at least 30 eruptions of Redoubt have occurred within the last 10,000 years. The most recent eruption cycle was in 2008 and 2009.

Eruptions at Redoubt typically last several months and are characterized by periodic violent outbursts with ash emission. The volcanic activity typically melts large volumes of glacial ice, creating the potential for glacial floods, lahars, and outright destruction of glaciers. A massive lahar radiocarbon dated at 3,500 years old filled the Crescent River valley from the volcano southward to Cook Inlet, a distance of 15.5 miles (25 kilometers). Other lahar and debris flow deposits fill the Drift River basin to the north of the volcano. In 1966, an eruption produced towering ash clouds and caused the destruction of a glacier on the north side of the mountain. A "jokulhlaup" (Icelandic term for "glacier-burst flood") occurred when melting of the bottom of a glacier caused the ice to be lifted up enabling water to surge forward. Downstream flooding reached Cook Inlet. The glacier did not reconnect to the mountain until 10 years later. At that time, the glacier surged forward and nearly dammed the Drift River.

The next eruptive cycle (after that of the late 1960s) began on December 14, 1989, with a phreatomagmatic explosion. Throughout the next several months, ash-rich eruptions occurred which generated pyroclastic flows that followed Drift Glacier on the north side of the volcano. Lahars were generated and threatened the Drift River Oil Terminal 22 miles (35 kilometers) downstream. This scene was repeated in early January 1990 and mid-February 1990, as well. Scientists at the Alaskan Volcano Observatory kept employees and plant managers at the Drift River Oil Terminal apprised of the situation as it unfolded.

A new lava dome began to form within the summit crater. It often became over-steepened, however, and collapsed multiple times. Each dome collapse generated another pyroclastic flow and another lahar. Two powerful explosions accompanied other dome collapses and generated ash plumes that reached altitudes of more than 7.5 miles (12 kilometers). Ash in the air also was a major hazard. A Boeing 747 flew into an ash cloud from Redoubt in mid-December, 1989, and experienced complete engine failure. The plane's pilots were able to restart the engines and land safely in Anchorage. It is estimated that the 1989–1990 eruption of Redoubt cost approximately $160 million in lost revenue, damages to the oil terminal and airplane, and diverted air traffic.

Redoubt's last eruptive cycle occurred in 2009; the first eruption occurred in March. The volcano produced many ash-producing explosions, as well as andesite lava and other pyroclastic material. A lava dome grew in the summit crater. This was followed by a series of strong magmatic eruptions over the next three weeks, destroying the initial dome. Ash clouds reached altitudes of up to 62,000 feet (18.9 kilometers). Ash fall in Anchorage required that the international airport be shut down for nearly an entire day. The Drift River Oil Terminal was partially inundated with lahars on March 23 and April 4. Eventually, another lava dome grew in the summit crater, and the eruption ended in early July 2009. Redoubt is monitored by the Alaskan Volcano Observatory with seismometers and webcams.

See Also: Andesite; Basalt; Lahar; Pyroclastic Flow; Pyroclastic Materials.

Further Reading

Miller, T. P., McGimsey, R. G., Richter, D. H., Riehle, J. R., Nye, C. J., Yount, M. E., & Dumoulin, J. A. (1998). *Catalog of the historically active volcanoes of Alaska.* (United States Geological Survey Open-File Report OF 98-05282). Washington, DC: U.S. GPO.

U.S. Geological Survey. (2014, May 28). *Redoubt Volcano description and information.* Retrieved from http://www.avo.alaska.edu/volcanoes/volcinfo.php?volcname=Redoubt

Wood, C. A., & Kienle, J. (1992). *Volcanoes of North America, United States and Canada.* Cambridge: Cambridge University Press.

Rhyolite

Rhyolite is an extrusive igneous (magma-derived) rock that contains more than 70% SiO_2 (silicon dioxide) by weight. Rhyolite usually is white, light gray, pink, or orange in color and often contains visible crystals of minerals. Rhyolite is a very viscous material, and only extremely rarely is it erupted as a lava flow. In the rare cases it is erupted as a flow, it either sits directly over the vent in the form of a lava dome, or flows downhill only short distances. Rhyolite occasionally takes on the form of obsidian. Much more commonly, however, rhyolite is erupted explosively from a volcano and is found as the pyroclastic materials pumice or volcanic ash, as ignimbrite sheets, or as the rock tuff. Rhyolite is erupted exclusively from composite volcanoes.

The viscosity of rhyolite holds the key to the typical eruptive behavior of rhyolite volcanoes. The thick, sticky magma is extremely effective at trapping gases. Gas pressure therefore builds within the magma chamber until it exceeds the strength of the rocks above. At that point, the volcano's surface rocks break and gases expand violently. The rhyolite magma is blasted apart into fragments such as ash and pumice.

Some of the largest and most violent eruptions in history have involved rhyolite magma. Following an explosive eruption, enough gas pressure can be relieved to allow the formation of a lava flow or lava dome. These are erupted fairly quietly. If the volcano has depleted its magma supply at this stage, the flow or dome can represent the last stage of the eruption and remain intact until the volcano's next cycle of eruptive activity. Very commonly, however, gas pressure continues to build during or after lava-dome formation, and a series of domes can form and be blasted apart before the final stages of the eruption.

The intrusive equivalent of rhyolite is the rock granite. Granite is an extremely common rock in the earth's continental crust. In fact, the average composition of the lower continental crust is that of grano-diorite, a composition of about 70% silica that is between that of granite and diorite. Granite forms when rhyolitic magma sits underground and cools without reaching the earth's surface. Many of the United States' most recognizable landmarks are composed of granite. Half Dome in Yosemite National Park, California; Pike's Peak in Colorado Springs, Colorado; and Stone Mountain in Georgia are all composed of granite. Granite typically forms between 3.7 and 7.5 miles (6 and 12 kilometers) beneath the earth's surface. It comes to the surface only after millions of years of erosion strip miles of rock off the top of the granite body.

See Also: Dacite; Pyroclastic Materials.

Further Reading

Cas, R. A. F., & Wright, J. V. (1988). *Volcanic successions, modern and ancient.* London: Chapman & Hall.

Tarbuck, E. J., Lutgens, F. K., & Tasa, D. (2011). *Earth: An introduction to physical geology* (10th ed.). Upper Saddle River, NJ: Pearson Prentice Hall/Pearson Education, Inc.

Richter, Charles

Charles Francis Richter was born on April 26, 1900, near Hamilton, Ohio. His mother, Lillian, was a former school teacher. Richter's mother was divorced from his father (Frederick Kinsinger)—a rare situation in 1900. Lillian had resumed using her maiden name at or near the time of Charles' birth. According to Richter, he was never known by any other name. During his childhood, the Richter household consisted of young Charles, his older sister Margaret, his mother, and his grandfather (Charles Otto Richter). Richter's grandmother died when Charles was seven. In 1909, Charles' grandfather moved the family to Los Angeles. Charles attended public schools until age 12, when he was enrolled in a preparatory academy associated with the University of Southern California.

In his teenage years, Richter was an active amateur astronomer who regularly made detailed observations of variable stars and reported his results to the American Association of Variable Star Observers. He also became involved in the Lorquin Natural History Club (later the Lorquin Entomological Society), which consisted of roughly a dozen members who spent time hiking and backpacking in the mountains to view and collect plants. Richter's interests and abilities clearly were in the natural sciences.

Charles Richter graduated from high school at age 16, and then spent his freshman year of college at the University of Southern California as a chemistry student. Richter admits that he was "quite nervous and tended not to be neat, particularly with my hands, and this is fatal in a chemistry laboratory. So after some unfortunate experiences, I felt that this wasn't for me. . . " (Scheid, 1979). Richter had taken physics courses as a requirement for his chemistry degree, and found that he was much better suited to that field of study.

Charles' sister Margaret had just graduated from Stanford at the time he completed his first year of college. Margaret convinced Charles that he would enjoy the atmosphere of that school, so he transferred to Stanford and completed his bachelor's degree in physics there in 1920, at the age of 20. Soon after, Richter enrolled in graduate school at Stanford, intending to earn a Ph.D. in physics. Richter experienced what he later described as a "nervous breakdown," however, and he returned home to Los Angeles. At his mother's insistence, Charles spent the next year in a private sanitarium under the care of a psychiatrist.

After leaving the sanitarium, Charles found employment first as a messenger for the Los Angeles County Museum, then as a clerk for a hardware company. He saved money with the intention of someday returning to finish a graduate degree in physics. In 1923, the Throop Institute of Pasadena went through a transformation and became the California Institute of Technology, also known as Caltech. Physicist Robert Millikan was recruited to be head of the new school and teach. He was well-known for his pioneering work in discovering the charge of an electron. Richter occasionally traveled to the new university to hear Millikan lecture, and soon enrolled in graduate school there.

It was an exciting time for experimental and theoretical physics, and at Caltech. During his tenure as a graduate student, Richter had the opportunity to interact with many well-known and pioneering physicists, including Werner Heisenberg, Erwin Schrödinger, Hendrik Lorentz, and Max Born. Richter's major professor and thesis advisor was Paul Epstein. Charles' Ph.D. thesis was a study of the hydrogen atom with a spinning electron from both the classical mechanics and newly introduced quantum mechanics approaches. As he neared the end of his doctoral studies, Richter began looking for work at Caltech. He very much enjoyed the company of other academics and the stimulating environment of Caltech, and was reluctant to leave southern California. It was at this point that Charles Richter first was pulled into the science of seismology. Prominent seismologist Harry Wood was head of the Seismology Lab located in the hills overlooking Pasadena. Wood needed an assistant with a background in physics and recruited Charles Richter to fill that position. Richter began working for Wood in 1927, shortly before finishing his Ph.D.

Charles Richter received his Ph.D. in June 1928. He married Lillian Brand—a divorcee with a three-year-old son—in the same year. Although Richter did not speak much of his personal relationships, we do know that his sister Margaret earned a Ph.D. in English and was an accomplished poet—no small feat for a woman in the early part of the Twentieth Century. Margaret had two brief teaching appointments at universities but spent most of her career as a writer. Charles and Lillian tried to live in the Richter family home with his mother and sister for a short time after they got married, but unfortunately his sister and his wife could not get along. The situation proved too stressful for all involved, and Lillian and Charles moved to a home of their own in Pasadena.

Charles became an integral part of the Seismology Laboratory. In 1930, the lab recruited Beno Gutenberg, a German seismologist, to join its ranks. Gutenberg was well-known in the geophysics community, and Caltech felt quite fortunate to lure him away from his impressive-sounding position of Professor Extraordinarius at a university in Frankfurt. Gutenberg and Richter had a productive working relationship, although it was not always congenial. Of the two, Gutenberg is recognized as the more accomplished scientist. Richter, however, is better known. His name was attached to the magnitude scale he developed, making Richter a household name.

The magnitude scale, deemed the "Richter scale" by seismologist Perry Byerly, is an instrumentally based scale Richter formulated that allows for mathematical calculation of earthquake size. The journal article "An Instrumental Earthquake Magnitude Scale," describing the scale and how to calculate magnitudes, was published in 1935 in the *Bulletin of the Seismological Society of America*. The Richter scale is not a physical instrument. It is a set of calculations used to determine a single number that describes the size of an earthquake. To determine an earthquake's magnitude, waves recorded on a specific type of seismometer (the Wood-Anderson Torsion Seismometer) are read in millimeters. Next, correction for the distance from the earthquake's epicenter is performed. Ideally, no matter how far away an observer is located from the epicenter, the magnitude calculation for a single earthquake should yield the same result. Richter originally developed his equations for southern California, however, and the equations are accurate only for southern California. The equations had to be altered to make them more appropriate for general use. Gutenberg suggested these changes and worked with Richter to revise the magnitude scale. For this reason, the term "Richter scale" has fallen out of favor with seismologists and is rarely used, except in the context of Richter's own calculations from the early 1930s and in the news media.

Today, seismologists define several types of magnitudes based on the method used to compute them. Although a number of different magnitude designations and equations to calculate them are used today, all include similar measurements and distance corrections to those Richter published in his 1935 paper. This without a doubt was Richter's most profound and lasting contribution to the science of seismology. Although most of his contemporaries agree that Richter did most of the tedious work that led to the development of the magnitude scale, Richter acknowledged in interviews given later in life that the fact that his name alone was associated with the scale diminished Gutenberg's contributions. Many accused Richter of being a publicity hound, and Gutenberg's family was extremely offended that his work on the project went unacknowledged to the general public.

Despite their difficulties, Richter and Gutenberg teamed up to produce two additional important publications. The first is an article published in 1944 and entitled, *The Frequency of Earthquakes in California*, which describes the distribution of expected earthquake sizes. The article defined what still is referred to today as the "Gutenberg-Richter distribution." It is a relatively simple pattern that emerged from their catalog of southern California earthquakes—very large earthquakes occur infrequently, and smaller earthquakes occur with much greater frequency. Gutenberg and Richter also published a book in 1949 entitled, *Seismicity of the Earth and Associated Phenomena*.

Throughout his life, Richter could be described as socially awkward. He did not relate well to many of his colleagues, and he was quite famously unable to laugh at himself. Richter also rarely—if ever—opened up about his personal life or feelings. As a result, many of his colleagues considered him arrogant, unapproachable, and difficult. Several colleagues also recognized that Richter was disorganized about his work and seemed unable to publish scientific articles without a strong personality like Gutenberg's to keep him on task. Although Richter continued his research and became happily immersed in the field of observational seismology, his last important publication was a textbook, *Elementary Seismology*, in 1958. The book still is a valuable source of information and is a window into Richter's deep fundamental knowledge of the physics of earthquakes, as well as an encyclopedic knowledge of earthquakes that occurred prior to its publication.

Even though Richter found it difficult to relate to individuals, he was quite happy to speak to the press about earthquakes any time he was asked. He even had a seismometer installed in his home so he could give some details on an earthquake without having to leave home. (Richter also enjoyed showing the seismometer and records of earthquakes to neighbors and other visitors.) One colleague reported that when a large earthquake occurred, Richter would place the laboratory telephone in his lap so that he was the only person who could answer the phone. Again, some saw this as arrogance. One long-time acquaintance, however, viewed this as evidence of Richter's love of earthquakes—and for explaining them to the public.

What began as a temporary job at the Seismology Laboratory turned into a long and storied career with Caltech. With the exception of a single year spent in Japan on a Fulbright Scholarship, Richter spent his entire career, from 1927 to 1970, working as a seismologist at Caltech. Even after that, he maintained an office at the university and was a frequent visitor—especially after major earthquakes. He spent several years after his retirement consulting for the Department of Water and Power, speaking to the press about earthquakes, and advocating for stronger building codes in areas of seismic risk. Charles Richter died at the age of 85 of congestive heart failure. He is buried at the Mountain View Cemetery in Altadena, California.

See Also: Earthquake; Earthquake Magnitude; Gutenberg, Beno.

Further Reading

Hough, S. E. (2007). *Richter's scale: Measure of an earthquake, measure of a man.* Princeton, NJ: Princeton University Press.

Los Angeles Times. (1985, October 5). *Charles F. Richter dies; earthquake scale pioneer.* Retrieved from http://articles.latimes.com/1985-10-01/news/mn-19126_1 _richter-scale

Scheid, A. (1979). *Interview with Charles Richter.* Oral History Project. California Institute of Technology Archives. Retrieved from http://resolver.caltech.edu /CaltechOH:OH_Richter_C

Ruapehu, Mount, New Zealand

Ruapehu is a large composite volcano located on New Zealand's North Island. The name "Ruapehu" means "pit of noise" or "exploding pit" in the Maori language. The volcano was formed as a result of subduction of the Pacific Plate beneath the Australian Plate. Earthquakes and volcanic eruptions both are common events on North Island. Ruapehu is one of New Zealand's most active volcanoes, erupting dozens of times since the first written records were kept in the late 1860s. Major eruptions have occurred about every 50 years, in 1895, 1945, and 1995. More than 60 minor eruptions have happened since 1945. The mountain is about 200,000 years old and has formed four different cones during its lengthy history. Ruapehu is broad and quite tall, with a summit at 9,174 feet (2,797 meters) above sea level. The mountain is capped by snow and is a popular ski destination for the island's residents.

Ruapehu is composed primarily of andesite lavas and pyroclastic materials. The only vent that has been active in historic times is Crater Lake, located in the broad summit region of the volcano. In the last 10,000 years, however, at least five

Explosive eruption of Mount Ruapehu, New Zealand, in 1996. (Tui De Roy/ Minden Pictures/Newscom)

other vents have been active on the summit and flanks of Ruapehu. Eruptions from the Crater Lake vent typically do not produce pyroclastic flows, but are well-known for producing small to moderate-sized ash clouds. Lava flows and dome growth also have been witnessed by observers. Lahars also are extremely common on Ruapehu due to the lake in the volcano's crater. Lahars can occur as a result of hot volcanic ash mixing with snow and ice melt during an eruption; however, they can occur in volcanic areas in the absence of an eruption.

On December 24, 1953, a lahar of the second variety (no eruption occurring) struck with tragic consequences. Part of the wall of Crater Lake collapsed, sending nearly 71 million cubic feet (2 million cubic meters) of water and an unknown amount of silt, rock, and volcanic debris into the Whangaehu River. The result was a lahar that traveled 75 miles (120 kilometers) from the mountain to the ocean. The lahar was approximately 20 feet (6 meters) high, and flowed very quickly. Approximately 6 miles (10 kilometers) from the city of Waiouru, at Tangiwai, the lahar hit a rail bridge, damaging it. The Wellington-to-Auckland express train attempted to cross the bridge at 10:21 p.m. and the bridge collapsed. The engine and first five cars nearly hit the opposite bank of the river. Most people aboard died from impact or were drowned in the lahar. The sixth carriage teetered on the edge of the bridge, and two men warned the passengers to move to the car behind. Almost all passengers were able to move to the next car before it also fell into the river below. Most of the remaining passengers struggled from the train and made their way to shore, but some did fall into the river and were swept away. Of the 285 people on board the train that night, 151 died.

The last eruption of Ruapehu happened in September 2007, when an explosion of steam, ash, and rocks produced two lahars but no eruption column. The volcano is monitored by GNS Science, a scientific research company that is affiliated with the national government. There are 2 webcams, 10 seismometers, and 6 microphones stationed around the mountain, ready to alert scientists to any unusual behavior. Water and gas monitoring also is conducted, as is continuous monitoring of ground deformation using global positioning systems (GPS). State-of-the-art lahar detection systems also are stationed in multiple river systems headed on Ruapehu.

See Also: Australian Plate; Lahar; Pacific Plate; Pyroclastic Flow; Subduction Zone.

Further Reading

Christchurch City Libraries. (2014, June 5). New Zealand disasters, Tangiwai Railway disaster 1953. Retrieved from http://christchurchcitylibraries.com/kids/nzdisasters/tangiwai.asp

GeoNet. (2014, June 5). *Ruapehu volcanic alert levels.* Retrieved from http://www.geonet.org.nz/volcano/info/ruapehu

GNS Science. (2014, June 5). Ruapehu. Retrieved from http://www.gns.cri.nz/Home/Learning/Science-Topics/Volcanoes/New-Zealand-Volcanoes/Ruapehu

Smithsonian Institution. National Museum of Natural History. Global Volcanism Program. (2014, June 5). *Ruapehu.* Retrieved from http://www.volcano.si.edu/volcano.cfm?vn=241100

Russia

Tectonically speaking eastern Russia is a very active place. Three areas—the westernmost Aleutian Islands, the Kamchatka Peninsula, and the Kuril Islands—are both volcanically and seismically quite active. In this region, at least 17 volcanoes have been active since the year 2000, and strong earthquakes occur with surprising regularity. It is rare to examine a monthly earthquake report and not see a magnitude 5 or greater earthquake somewhere near Kamchatka or the Kuril Islands. The area is a subduction zone in which the Pacific Plate is subducting beneath the North American Plate. The result is violent earthquakes and a great deal of volcanic activity. Notable earthquakes within the region include a magnitude 8.3 earthquake in 2006 in the Kuril Islands, and a magnitude 8.1 earthquake east of the islands in 2007. A magnitude 7.8 earthquake occurred near the eastern coast of Kamchatka in 1997.

As common as major earthquakes are, it might be surprising to know that very few fatalities occur in connection with these events. A 1995 earthquake in which 1,989 people died on Sakhalin Island (west of the Kurils) was a rarity. Part of the reason for the low numbers of fatalities in major earthquakes is that the population density is quite low throughout much of the region. Low population translates into little risk for major loss of life. For those who do live in the region, however, experience and engineering have taught them to build homes that can withstand strong shaking. Island residents seem to have much more to fear of tsunamis than of the earthquakes themselves. Tsunami generation with magnitude 7 and above earthquakes is quite common in the Kuril Islands.

The area is quite active volcanically. One event of note is the 1955–1956 eruption of Bezymianny, in which the volcano behaved much like Mount St. Helens did in its catastrophic 1980 eruption. The volcano's summit collapsed into a large landslide and unleashed a significant lateral blast that flattened forests and left a large horseshoe-shaped crater. Subsequent eruptions mostly have filled in the crater. Bezymianny last erupted in 2013. Similar to the earthquake risk, the risk of loss of life in volcanic eruptions is fairly low because most of the region is very sparsely populated.

Two volcanoes that break this pattern are Acachinsky and Koryaksky. The city of Petropavlovsk—Kamchatka's largest city—lies just below Avachinsky. The city has a population of slightly more than 180,000 people, so there is some risk to the city's residents as a result. Avachinsky last erupted in October 2001. Although that eruption was minor and resulted only in small ash plumes, other historical eruptions in the 1820s, 1920s, and 1940s were more violent, resulting in larger ash columns, small pyroclastic flows, and lahars. Koryaksky also is located near Petropavlovsk, thus much of the same population also is at risk from this volcano. Its last eruption, in 2009, was a very low-level event, similar to most others of the last 10,000 years.

Other volcanoes that have erupted within the Kamchatka Peninsula since the year 2000 include Gorely (2010), Karymsky (2014), Kizimen (2013), Kliuchevskoi (2013), Mutnovsky (2000), Shiveluch (2014), and Tolbachik (2013). The Kuril Islands are even more sparsely populated than the Kamchatka Peninsula, thus few people are at risk from most eruptions of these volcanoes. Kuril Island volcanoes that have been active since 2000 include Alaid (2012), Chikurachki (2008), Chirinkotan (2013), Ebeko (2010), Ekarma (2010), Lomonosov (2008), and Sarychev Peak (2009).

See Also: North American Plate; Pacific Plate; St. Helens, Mount, Washington, United States; Subduction Zone.

Further Reading

Smithsonian Institution. National Museum of Natural History. Global Volcanism Program. (2014, June 17). Retrieved from http://www.volcano.si.edu/

U.S. Geological Survey. (2014, June 17). *Historic world earthquakes. Russia.* Retrieved from http://earthquake.usgs.gov/earthquakes/world/historical_country.php#russia

S

San Andreas Fault

The San Andreas Fault is located in western California. It is not just a major fault, it also forms the transform boundary between the North American Plate to the east and the Pacific Plate to the west. The San Andreas Fault was formed approximately 15 to 20 million years ago when the tectonic situation of the region changed. Prior to the formation of the San Andreas Fault, there was a plate between the Pacific Plate and the North American Plate called the Farallon Plate. The Farallon Plate was being formed at a spreading center on the western edge of the plate, and sub-ducted beneath North America to the east. The plate was being subducted faster than it was forming, however, meaning that the plate was shrinking in size. Between 15 and 20 million years ago, the spreading center on the western side of the Farallon Plate made contact with the North American Plate. This put a small corner of the Pacific Plate in contact with the North American Plate. It was at this point that the San Andreas Fault was born. As subduction of the Farallon Plate continued, a larger segment of the Pacific Plate came into contact with the North American Plate creating a longer plate boundary, and thus a longer San Andreas Fault. The San Andreas Fault has continued to grow in length since that time. Currently, the fault extends from the Mendocino Triple Junction off the coast of northern California to the Gulf of California. To the north of the Mendocino Triple Junction, a remnant of the Farallon Plate—the Juan de Fuca Plate—subducts beneath North America along the Cascadia Subduction Zone. To the south, the San Andreas Fault changes orientation and the plate boundary becomes a series of short spreading centers within the Gulf of California. Adjacent to southern Mexico, the plate boundary becomes a subduction zone. Here, the Cocos Plate and the Nazca Plate are subducting between Central and South America, respectively. The Cocos and Nazca plates also are remnants of the Farallon Plate.

Movement along the San Andreas Fault is described as dextral, or right-lateral strike-slip motion. This means that the two plates on either side of the boundary are moving laterally past each other. If an observer straddles the fault, then the right side is moving toward the observer. In some areas small bends in the fault change the sense of motion on the fault. Small amounts of compression across the fault have resulted in the formation of hills and mountains, such as the San Gabriel Mountains in southern California, the Santa Cruz Mountains south of San Francisco, and the famous hills within the city of San Francisco. Small amounts of extension across the fault result in depressions or basins. The Salton Sea near San

San Andreas Fault as it crosses the Carrizo Plain in southern California, USA. (Kevin Schafer/ NHPA/Photoshot/Newscom)

Diego is one location where this has occurred. Almost all earthquake activity within the San Andreas Fault zone is considered shallow, occurring at a depth of less than 12.5 miles (20 kilometers). This is fairly typical of transform boundaries elsewhere on the planet.

Large earthquakes occur on segments of the San Andreas Fault, but not along the entire length of the fault at one time. The northern segment of the San Andreas Fault includes the area that ruptured during the great 1906 San Francisco earthquake. The Loma Prieta earthquake of 1989 also occurred on the northern segment, although it was only a magnitude 7.1 event. The southern segment ruptured in the 1857 Great Fort Tejon Earthquake.

Both the northern and the southern segments of the San Andreas Fault have experienced large and damaging earthquakes more recently, but none that reached the estimated magnitude of the previous earthquakes noted above. There is a relatively high probability of powerful earthquakes hitting the northern and southern segments of the San Andreas Fault during the next 30 to 50 years. The center portion of the San Andreas—often referred to as the Parkfield segment—located near Parkfield, California, ruptured at regular intervals for more than 100 years. Moderate-sized earthquakes (between magnitude 5.5 and 6.0) occurred in 1857, 1881, 1901, 1922, 1934, and 1966. Earthquakes occurred so regularly in the Parkfield segment that scientists decided to set up an earthquake observatory to

Will California Fall into the Ocean?

People have been known to joke that the next big earthquake will cause California to "fall off into the ocean." This joke has no basis in reality. The western part of California—that portion which is west of the San Andreas Fault—is in absolutely no danger of separating from the rest of the state within the next several million years, and it will not move to the west, toward the Pacific Ocean. Even in the largest of earthquakes along the San Andreas Fault, the maximum amount of motion that can be expected is for the western side of the fault to move approximately 30 feet to the northwest, parallel to the fault. If it was possible to fast-forward tectonic movements, we would see that the land to the west of the San Andreas will continue to move northwestward, and eventually this area will become an island. The island will move northwestward through the Pacific, toward Alaska—however, it will take tens of millions of years for this to happen.

"capture" the earthquake that should have occurred in the late 1980s or early 1990s. The area around Parkfield was densely populated with instruments in anticipation of an earthquake during this time, but no earthquake occurred . . . until 2004. Prediction of an earthquake in Parkfield failed, despite constant surveillance and careful data analysis; but the earthquake that occurred in 2004 fit the model of the typical Parkfield earthquake in every other way. It was a magnitude 6.0 event that likely will be repeated within the next 30 to 60 years.

The San Andreas Fault is one of the most intensely monitored and studied faults in the world. Through a multi-billion-dollar initiative called "Earthscope" (Earthscope.org)—funded by the National Science Foundation—a research well was drilled into the San Andreas near Parkfield, California. The well was completed—including installation of the underground instruments—in 2008. This project is known as the "San Andreas Fault Observatory at Depth" or "SAFOD." Instruments measure strain along the plate boundary. The fault also is being monitored by the Plate Boundary Observatory, which is the geodetic component of the Earthscope project.

The San Andreas Fault is a source of many earthquakes in western California, but it is by no means the only major fault in the region. Many other active faults run parallel to the San Andreas or branch from it. The Hayward Fault runs parallel to the San Andreas, east of the San Francisco Bay. The Whittier Fault is parallel to the San Andreas Fault in southern California. The Garlock Fault branches northeastward from the San Andreas in southern California. There are countless others as well, both known and as yet undiscovered.

See Also: Cascadia Subduction Zone; Cocos Plate; Nazca Plate; North American Plate; Pacific Plate; Subduction Zone; Transform Boundary.

Further Reading

Bolt, B. A. (2004). *Earthquakes* (5th ed.). New York: W.H. Freeman and Company.

Earthscope.org. (2014, June 2). *San Andreas Fault Observatory at Depth*. Retrieved from http://www.earthscope.org/assets/uploads/pages/safod_five_years_hi.pdf

Kearey, P., Klepeis, K. A., & Vine, F. J. (2009). *Global tectonics* (3rd ed.). Hoboken, NJ: Wiley-Blackwell.

Schultz, S. S., & Wallace, R. E. (2014, June 2). *The San Andreas Fault*. Retrieved from http://pubs.usgs.gov/gip/earthq3/safaultgip.html

Tarbuck, E. J., Lutgens, F. K., & Tasa, D. (2011). *Earth: An introduction to physical geology* (10th ed.). Upper Saddle River, NJ: Pearson Prentice Hall/Pearson Education, Inc.

U.S. Geological Survey. (2014, June 2). *The Parkfield, California, earthquake experiment*. http://earthquake.usgs.gov/research/parkfield/

San Francisco Earthquake, California, United States (1906)

One of the most devastating earthquakes to occur on American soil occurred April 18, 1906, near the city of San Francisco, California. The earthquake struck at approximately 5:12 a.m. local time and shook the city for nearly two minutes. Nearly all observers noted an initial shock that lasted approximately 45 seconds, followed by a 10- to 12-second lull. A much larger shock occurred at 5:13 a.m., and the earth shook for nearly a full minute longer. Buildings lurched. Streets, sidewalks, and street car rails bent and buckled. Brick and stone facades of many homes and businesses fell onto the street. Chimneys crumbled. Eyewitnesses reported that they were unable to stay on their feet during the second, larger shock. It was immediately evident to all in the city that this was an extremely powerful earthquake, and there would be significant damage as a result. However, a greater danger loomed in the city.

Aftermath of the 1906 San Francisco (USA) earthquake. The earthquake was followed by several days of destructive fires that destroyed much of the city. (akg-images/Newscom)

In the early 1900s, much of the city's indoor and outdoor lighting was provided by gas lamps. Gas lines for lanterns and stoves were run directly into many homes. Electric lines had been strung somewhat haphazardly over the streets. Both electric lines and gas lines broke during the earthquake, creating a volatile environment. Gas jetted out of broken lines and was ignited by sparks from broken electric lines, and by flames from fireplaces, overturned candles, and small gas lanterns. This resulted in hundreds of small fires starting simultaneously. Although the fire-alarm system in the city's firehouses did not work following the earthquake, firefighters were well aware of what was happening. They knew they would be fighting a losing battle. They were understaffed, and the fire hydrant system throughout the city was inadequate. The main reservoir for water for fighting fires was a cistern system created in the Gold Rush days of the late 1840s and early 1850s. It was outdated and in extreme disrepair; in fact, it offered very little water in the best of circumstances for firefighting. Fire stations were not in optimal locations for fighting existing fires, or for enabling firefighters to control the spread of fires to other parts of the city. Fire insurance companies also were well aware of these problems, and had warned the city—in no uncertain terms just the year before—that the fire hazards created by these situations had to be addressed.

Despite the challenges they knew they faced, the firemen hurried to create a plan for fighting the fires. Firemen pulled their horse-drawn fire engines through streets—choked with debris and crowded with dazed people—to the sites of these fires. Unfortunately, what they found was that the water mains in the city had been broken during the earthquake. There was no water available for fighting the fires. The fires grew, coalesced, and raged for three days following the earthquake. The fires were stopped largely due to the (controversial) efforts of firefighters, and later military personnel, to create fire breaks by dynamiting buildings that survived the earthquake in an effort to starve the fire of fuel. It took those fighting the fire a full day or more of practice to learn how to correctly place the dynamite to achieve the desired effect. This use of dynamite by untrained but well-intentioned firefighters created many hard feelings but, in the end, the practice of creating fire breaks was the only thing that prevented even more of the city from being consumed in the fire. Fires burned an area of 4.7 square miles (12.2 square kilometers) and caused significantly more damage to the city than that of the earthquake alone. Very rough estimates of losses caused by the earthquake and fire total approximately $400 million. Between 3% and 10% of those losses likely were due solely to the earthquake. The fire was by far the worse of the two disasters.

This indeed was one of the largest earthquakes in known California history. This quake—together with the resulting fires—was responsible for the greatest number of deaths in a California earthquake to date. Although the number of people who perished in the earthquake and fires is unknown, several estimates have been published. Shortly after the earthquake, local newspapers reported that about 300 people had died. Subsequent reports provide a total of approximately 700 lives lost. A study completed in 1989, using reports from hospitals, city records, and out-of-town newspapers, suggests that the actual death toll was at least 3,000 (Hansen & Condon, 1989).

There are several reasons that the actual number of people who lost their lives in this disaster probably never will be known. City records collected prior to the earthquake do not list individual residents; even if they had, however, the building in which city records were housed was leveled by the earthquake and later burned. There are some reports that several bodies were buried hastily without proper investigation into their identities and without records of their burials. Many people who died in the earthquake had been crushed and buried beneath rubble. The fires spread so fast that there was little time to search the felled buildings. In a great number of cases, the bodies of those in the fallen buildings were incinerated in fires that ensued. Regardless of these factors, it is suspected that the number of deaths was never fully investigated, and in fact might have been "massaged downward" because business owners in the region were afraid that a high death toll would slow investment in the city's rebuilding efforts.

At the time of the earthquake, San Francisco was the largest city on the west coast with a population of approximately 410,000 people. The city had undergone rapid, uncontrolled growth in the 50 years between the late 1840s and the time of the earthquake in 1906. The time of fastest growth occurred in the late 1840s and early 1850s. This was a direct result of the Gold Rush that began with the discovery of gold in the Sierra Nevada in 1848. Men and women poured into California from across the United States by one of four major land routes. They traveled by horse and wagon because no railroad existed to connect cities in the eastern United States to the west coast. A few people also took the long sea route from the east coast, around the tip of South America, to San Francisco. Would-be miners flocked to California from across the Pacific as well. The influx of new residents caused San Francisco to grow incredibly quickly. Homes, businesses, and government buildings were built quickly and often were poorly constructed. Shoddy construction is one of many factors that led to the large number of casualties from building collapse in the 1906 earthquake.

Fire stations were clustered together in some areas of the city and were completely absent in others—and this had serious consequences. Significant portions of the city had burned multiple times before the 1906 earthquake, fueled by fierce winds, prodigious use of fuel and cooking oils, buildings sited in close proximity to one another, and the use of highly flammable building materials. Only after the 1906 earthquake and fire did city officials insist on redesigning the water-supply system and placing fire stations in locations that made sense for providing rapid and reliable service to the city's hundreds of thousands of residents.

Damage to many parts of San Francisco was nearly total. Fully half of the city's population was left homeless. Strong leadership was necessary to coordinate efforts across the city to control fires, restore order, care for the injured, and feed and shelter the homeless. Two men rose to the occasion. The first was Brigadier General Frederick Funston, the highest ranking soldier in San Francisco at that time. The earthquake shook him awake, and he immediately surveyed the situation and correctly determined that the well-trained soldiers in his command would be needed—in a great many capacities. Funston summoned all available troops and ordered them to make themselves available to the mayor and chief of police.

General Funston mobilized troops to protect federal buildings and assets. He sent requests to Washington for food, tents, and medicine. Soon, every tent the military owned was in San Francisco, and the largest hospital train in history left from Virginia. Within a few weeks, 10% of the United States Army was there as well. The navy sent several ships, including a fire boat. The navy and Revenue Cutter Service (later to become the Coast Guard) helped with evacuations.

When Mayor Eugene Schmitz was able to reach City Hall, he found that it had been utterly destroyed. Schmitz moved his command post to the Hall of Justice. He immediately sent some of General Funston's soldiers to City Hall to secure the treasury. The mayor then issued a proclamation stating that anyone seen looting or committing other crimes would be shot on sight, and then issued that command to the soldiers and policemen. Schmitz also ordered a curfew, closed saloons, prohibited the sale of liquor, and banned "naked candles." Additionally, Schmitz informed the public that both the electric and gas companies would remain closed and inoperative until he decided it was safe for them to resume operation. He sent telegrams to other officials in the state requesting food, medicine, fire engines, hoses, and dynamite.

A number of refugee camps were set up in the city using the tents sent by the military. Public feeding programs were established. The U.S. Post Office began delivering mail in the refugee camps within two days. The postmaster accepted mail from all refugees—whether stamped or not—so they could "tell their friends and loved ones of their condition and their needs." Mayor Schmitz made sure the camps had the basic necessities. Soon all camps had running water, sewers, and bath houses. Eventually, the tents were replaced with more comfortable small cottages, some of which were occupied for years after the earthquake. Within a very short time, San Francisco began to function again.

A number of celebrities and notable people were in the city on April 18. Italian opera star Enrico Caruso performed the evening before the earthquake at the Grand Opera House, and was staying at the Palace Hotel when the earthquake occurred. Although various accounts exist of his reaction to the earthquake, all indicate that he was thankful to leave the city as soon as the opportunity presented itself. Author Jack London also experienced the earthquake. He described the event in *Collier's Weekly* (magazine). Actor John Barrymore is known to have helped in cleanup efforts. Photographer Ansel Adams was four years old and living in west San Francisco in 1906. Adams later spoke about being ushered into the home's garden and waiting for aftershocks. One particularly violent aftershock struck as he was running to the table for breakfast. He fell against the garden wall and broke his nose.

The size of the earthquake that struck San Francisco still is a matter of great debate. No magnitude scale existed at the time of this earthquake, although several groups of scientists have used various methods to estimate the earthquake's magnitude. A local magnitude of 8.3 was determined in the 1950s. Local magnitude calculations, however, become incredibly unreliable at greater magnitudes. A surface wave magnitude of 7.7 was calculated using seismograms from the 1906 earthquake, and was recorded at several locations around the world. A moment magnitude of 7.9 was calculated using displacements along the San Andreas Fault.

For any earthquake, magnitude is expressed as a single number and indicates the total amount of energy released by the earthquake. To determine a reliable magnitude for an earthquake, scientists must have well-timed instrumental records of the earthquake and enough discernable information from them to perform calculations. In cases where this is not or was not possible, scientists use a subjective measure of earthquake size called "intensity." Intensity is based on damage done by the earthquake to man-made structures, as well as a few descriptions of effects on people and free-standing or hanging objects. Intensity, by its nature, is unique to the location at which it is observed. Not only is intensity dependent on location, it also is affected by the presence or lack of man-made structures, the perceptions of observers, the quality of a structure's construction, and the properties of the ground on which a structure is built.

In general, intensity usually is greatest near the fault responsible for the earthquake, and decreases as one moves away from the fault. There are exceptions to this general rule, however. In areas that lack observers or man-made structures, there is an absence of data. Poorly built structures tend to have more extensive damage than well-built structures if all other conditions are equal. Well-built buildings have structural ties between the foundation and walls, and between the walls and roof. Their walls are braced with diagonal or horizontal studs. They also are built of materials that flex as the earth moves beneath them. The best materials to use for structures in seismically active areas are steel and wood. Masonry and adobe are dangerously unstable because they do not flex. When the ground begins to shake, mortar between bricks begins to crumble. Because the mortar is the only material holding the bricks together, the bricks fall away and the building collapses. Adobe and mud bricks simply crumble.

Structures built on solid rock fare better than those built on loose materials like sand, mud, or gravel. "Made" land, such as valleys that have been filled to provide level building plots, or locations where debris is dumped into the ocean to create new land, are equally dangerous. Surface (seismic) waves are amplified in loose material, which means that such areas experience exaggerated shaking as compared with rocky areas nearby. Damage, therefore, also is exaggerated in structures built on this loose material.

The end result of a study to determine the intensity of an earthquake is a map that shows zones of damage severity. The intensity scale used at the time of the 1906 earthquake was the Rossi-Forel Intensity Scale. It is similar in many ways to the Modified Mercalli Intensity Scale, a form of which still is used today. At the low end of the Rossi-Forel scale, the Roman numeral I indicated almost imperceptible shaking and no damage. At the high end of the scale, the Roman numeral X indicated complete destruction. An elongated zone of high intensities extended throughout much of the city of San Francisco, as well as to areas well north and south of the city, parallel to the San Andreas Fault. The highest intensities—peaking at IX on the Rossi-Forel Scale—occurred on "made" land in the valleys leading down into the city, as well as along the waterfront. It is in these areas that the city dumped the burned remains of the city's buildings following destructive fires between 1849 and the early 1860s. Today, much of San Francisco's most coveted real estate is located in the Marina District. Much of the Marina District is composed of land created when the city dumped debris from the 1906 earthquake into the bay.

The San Andreas Fault is perhaps the best-known fault in the United States. Movement along this fault was responsible for the 1906 earthquake. The portion of the San Andreas Fault that ruptured in 1906 is 296 miles (477 kilometers) long. It extends from San Juan Batista in the south to Shelter Cove in the north, then extends several miles offshore to the west. The epicenter of the earthquake was in the northern offshore portion of the fault. Because the greatest amount of visible movement along the fault occurred near the town of Olema, however, it was misidentified as the epicenter for a number of years. It was in Olema, on what was known as the Skinner Farm, that a fence was broken and offset 20 feet (6.1 meters) by the earthquake.

See Also: Earthquake; Elastic Rebound Theory; Modified Mercalli Intensity Scale; Plate Tectonics; San Andreas Fault.

Further Reading

Bolt, B. A. (2004). *Earthquakes* (5th ed.). New York: W.H. Freeman and Company.

Hansen, G., & Condon, E. (1989). *Denial of disaster*. San Francisco: Cameron and Company.

Lawson, A. C., Gilbert, G. K., Reid, H. F., Branner, J. C., Leuschner, A. O., Davidson, G., Burckhalter, C., & Campbell, W. W. (Eds.). (1910). *The California earthquake of April 18, 1906: Report of the State Earthquake Investigation Commission in two volumes and atlas*. Washington, DC: Carnegie Institution of Washington.

Richter, C. F. (1958). *Elementary seismology*. San Francisco: W.H. Freeman and Company.

U.S. Geological Survey. Earthquake Hazards Program. (2014, October 29). *The Great 1906 San Francisco earthquake*. Retrieved from http://earthquake.usgs.gov/regional/nca/1906/18april/index.php

Virtual Museum of the City of San Francisco. (2014, October 29). *The Great 1906 earthquake and fire*. Retrieved from http://www.sfmuseum.org/1906/06.html

Winchester, S. (2005). *A crack in the edge of the world: America and the Great California earthquake of 1906*. New York: Harper Perennial.

Sanriku Earthquake and Tsunami, Japan (1896)

On June 15, 1896, a magnitude 8.5 earthquake struck the Sanriku coast on the northeast of Honshu, Japan, in the Iwate Prefecture. Its epicenter was 90 miles offshore, near an area of very deep water known as the "Japan Trench." The impact onshore was much weaker than normally is expected from such a powerful earthquake and there was little expectation of a tsunami, even though this part of the Japanese coast experiences earthquakes frequently. Thirty-five minutes after the earthquake, the most devastating tsunami in Japan's history reached the shore at the same time as high tide. The first wave receded back out to sea and returned in a second wave five minutes later. At times, the tsunami's wave reached a height of 125 feet. Everything in its path was totally devastated; 26,000 people were killed, and 9,000 homes were destroyed. The earthquake's epicenter on a reverse fault near the Japan Trench was the reason for the mild impact felt onshore. The earthquake lasted for five minutes and was accompanied by a slow shaking.

When the earthquake occurred, many villagers were at the beach celebrating two events: The return of soldiers from a successful war with China, the first Sino-Japanese War of 1894; and the annual Boys' Festival. Villagers observed minor shocks in the earlier part of the day, many hours before the earthquake. There also were reports of unusual phenomenon on that same day—low water levels in wells and large numbers of tunas every day. The violence of the tsunami was yet another unusual feature of the day. Victims of tsunami disasters typically die by drowning. In the Sanriku tsunami, however, the bodies of victims had suffered extensive damage, including fractured skulls and broken legs and arms. The impact of this tsunami carried across the Pacific. In Hawaii, wharves were demolished and several houses swept away. In California a 9.5 foot-high wave arrived. Unfortunately, in spite of the long history of tsunamis on this coast, very little beyond immediate humanitarian assistance was done by public authorities.

On June 16, 1896, the day following the tsunami disaster, a telegram reporting the disaster reached the Interior Ministry. After reporting to the Meiji emperor, the Interior Ministry contacted all the other ministries to deliver relief and rescue for the tsunami victims. The emperor delegated one person to visit the disaster site and cheer up the survivors with encouraging words. The governmental agencies dispatched inspectors and the army sent medical specialists. The military authorities also sent soldiers to secure public order, military engineers to recover bodies from the rubble, and the navy to search the water for bodies of the victims. The Japanese Red Cross Society and the Nurse Association sent doctors and nurses to treat the injured. It took 30 years more before action was taken on detailed preventive measures.

In 1937, another very strong tsunami hit the coast of Sanriku. This time the local authorities were better prepared. Authorities had installed tidal embankments, trees, and escape roads. They also prepared a booklet on precautions for preventing a disaster. This booklet included a warning about weak earthquake shocks, the type of event that was so misunderstood in 1896. At the same time, the booklet pointed out that a loud noise like thunder might indicate an approaching tsunami. The booklet also included information about avoiding the recession of the tsunami's first wave and being prepared to evacuate the coast quickly and move to higher ground.

See Also: Japan; Kobe Earthquake, Japan (1995); Sendai Earthquake and Tsunami, Japan (2011).

Further Reading

Gunn, A. M. (2014, August 12). Sanriku earthquake (1896). In *World geography: Understanding a changing world.* Santa Barbara, CA: ABC-CLIO.

Santa María, Guatemala

Santa María is a composite volcano located in southern Guatemala. Its summit is 12,375 feet (3,772 meters) above sea level. It is one of many volcanoes located in the southern half of the country. These volcanoes are there as a result of subduction of the Cocos Plate beneath the Caribbean and North American plates. The Santa Maria volcano primarily is composed of lower-silica andesite lavas and pyroclastic materíals. Santa María does not have a history of being a particularly deadly volcano, but it has been known to erupt quite violently—and a population of more than 1.2 million people live within 18.5 miles (30 kilometers) of its summit.

Prior to 1902, the volcano had a long period of dormancy that followed growth of its large symmetrical cone. When the volcano awoke in 1902, its eruption was one of the most violent of that century and left much of southwestern Guatemala buried in ash. A large, nearly 1-mile (1.5-kilometer) diameter crater was created during that eruption. Between 1903 and 1913, eruptions occurred within the 1902 crater. After 20 years, activity began in earnest on the southwest flank below the 1902 crater. Since that time, dome building has been the major mode of eruption. The volcano has built a subsidiary cone on its southwest flank called "Santiaguito." Eruptions from Santiaguito have yielded relatively minor ash fall, pyroclastic flows, and lahars. Early in the summer of 2014, a tropical storm dumped large amounts of rain on Guatemala, and the extra water triggered strong lahars on the rivers that emanate from that area. The Samala, San Isidro, Tambor, and Nima I rivers all were affected.

See Also: Andesite; Caribbean Plate; Cocos Plate; Lahar; Lava Dome; North American Plate; Pyroclastic Flow; Subduction Zone.

Further Reading

Smithsonian Institution. National Museum of Natural History. Global Volcanism Program. (2014, June 13). *Santa María.* Retrieved from http://www.volcano.si.edu/volcano.cfm?vn=342030

Volcano Discovery, "Volcano news: Santa Maria (Guatemala)," http://www.volcanodiscovery.com/guatemala/santiaguito/news.html. Cited June 13, 2014.

Volcano World. (2014, June 13). *Santa Maria.* Retrieved from http://volcano.oregonstate.edu/santa-maria

Seiche

A seiche is a rhythmic oscillation of a closed body of water. Seiches are different from tsunamis in that seiches can be caused by wind, tides, or surface waves of distant earthquakes. Tsunamis are caused by a vertical disturbance of an ocean floor, and are not caused by wind or the tides. Even the largest and most impressive seiches have much smaller amplitudes than the average ocean-wide tsunami. First described in 1890, these oscillatory waves are believed to be caused when low-frequency surface waves from earthquakes reach a body of water and start the water moving back and forth at the same frequency as the surface waves. Seiches have been described as an effect of earthquakes since the Lisbon earthquake of 1755, often occurring at surprisingly great distances from the epicenters of the causal earthquakes.

The Lisbon, Portugal, earthquake of 1755 was deadly and damaging. It was felt widely throughout the country, and generated a local tsunami. Because it was such a rare and destructive event in Europe, the earthquake's effects were meticulously documented and well-studied. Interestingly, virtually every water body between 500 miles (800 kilometers) and 1,500 miles (2,400 kilometers) from Lisbon was set in motion. Lakes in Switzerland, Finland, Norway, Scotland, Germany, and every country in between oscillated, as did canals and ports in England and the Netherlands. Lakes and ports closer than 500 miles (800 kilometers), however, were spared. It is believed that low-frequency waves alone cause seiches, and closer than 500 miles (800 kilometers) from Lisbon, the earthquake's seismic waves were of too high a frequency to create effective seiches. English physicist John Michell was fascinated by reports of oscillations in lakes and bays throughout western Europe in the hours following the earthquake, and used this information to devise the first scientifically derived theory of seismic waves and their transmission through the earth.

Seiches have been recorded in most large earthquakes. A 1955 earthquake in Assam, India, caused seiches in northern Europe that were recorded in both Norway and England. Following the Chilean earthquake and tsunami of 1960, lakes and bays more than 50 miles (80 kilometers) from the epicenter experienced seiches with amplitudes up to 3 feet (1 meter). When the Anchorage earthquake occurred in 1964, seiches were created not only in the Gulf of Mexico 2,500 miles (4,000 kilometers) away, but also in water wells in parts of the United States and swimming pools in Texas and Louisiana.

Although not nearly as deadly as tsunamis, seiches nonetheless can cause millions of dollars in property damage, and occasionally even cause death. Seiches sometimes are large enough to destroy boats by pulling them back and forth near docks, piers, or other boats. Water can be sloshed out of basins and cause flooding. In the most dangerous cases, seiches that occur in reservoirs with earthen dams can weaken those dams, posing significant risks to everything downstream.

See Also: Earthquake; Earthquake Hazard; Tsunami.

Further Reading

Myles, D. (1985). *The great waves.* New York: McGraw-Hill Book Company.
Richter, C. F. (1958). *Elementary seismology.* New York: W.H. Freeman and Company.
Tarbuck, E. J., Lutgens, F. K., & Tasa, D. (2011). *Earth: An introduction to physical geology* (10th ed.). Upper Saddle River, NJ: Pearson Prentice Hall/Pearson Education, Inc.

Seismology

Seismology is the science of earthquakes and related phenomena. Related phenomena include earthquake hazards, seismometers, plate tectonics, the process of fault rupture, earthquake location and size, seismic waves, the interior of the earth, and the use of seismology to detect non-earthquake events. People have studied seismology for as long as humans have experienced earthquakes. The first reliable instruments to record seismic waves, however, were invented and built between 1879 and 1890. The first known example of a distant earthquake being recorded by a seismometer was on April 18, 1889, when an instrument in Potsdam, Germany, recorded an earthquake in Japan. This momentous occasion ushered in the beginning of the modern science of seismology. Seismology today is highly dependent on the use of seismometers to detect seismic waves that move through the various parts of the earth's interior. Almost everything known about the interior of the earth comes from examining seismograms of distant earthquakes.

Seismic waves are composed of energy that radiates away from the source of an earthquake. Some seismic waves—called body waves—travel through the interior (or body) of the earth. One type of body wave is called a "P wave." "P" stands for "primary." Primary in this case means first; P waves are the first waves to arrive at a seismometer from an earthquake, because these waves move faster than any other type of seismic wave. P waves also are known as "compressional waves"

Staff members of the Japan Meteorological Agency monitor the country for earthquakes in their Tokyo office. As soon as an earthquake strikes, they can issue an alert that allows distant residents a few seconds of warning before strong ground motion begins. (CHINE NOUVELLE/SIPA/Newscom)

because of the way they travel. Imagine an extra-long spring lying on a table. When several coils of the spring are gathered together and then let go all at once, some coils are compressed together and others are extended away from each other. The area of compression travels from one end of the spring to the other. This is the type of motion experienced by matter as a P wave, or compressional wave, moves through it. Sound waves are another form of compressional wave. P waves can travel through any type of material, including solid, liquid, and gas.

The second type of body wave is called an "S wave." "S" stands for "secondary" or "shear." These typically are the second waves to arrive at a seismometer from an earthquake, because they are the second fastest type of seismic wave. These are also known as "shear waves" because of the way they travel. They cause particles to move perpendicular to the direction of motion. Imagine a length of rope tied to the wall on one end. If the other end is shaken up or down one time, a wave is created and travels to the end of the rope. This is an example of shear motion. The wave is traveling toward the wall but particle motion is up and down, perpendicular to the direction of motion. "S waves" only can travel through solid material. One indicator that the earth has a liquid outer core is that S waves stop abruptly at the core-mantle boundary. This creates a zone around the earth where direct S waves cannot be observed.

Although simple P waves and S waves follow the velocity relationships noted above (P waves travel faster than S waves), S waves are not always the second waves to arrive at a seismometer after an earthquake occurs. Both P waves and S waves can be reflected and refracted (bent). If a P wave is generated and bounces once on the boundary between the lithosphere and asthenosphere, it actually can arrive before an S wave. It therefore is possible to have a P wave and a reflected P wave detected before an S wave reaches the same location. This is a complicating factor that is ignored for the remainder of this discussion. It is important to know, however, that seismic waves—just like water or sound waves—have the ability to reflect and refract; and this can cause interesting patterns of seismic waves on a seismogram. If this is the case, how do seismologists know the difference between a reflected P wave and an S wave? The answer lies in travel-time studies.

During the time between the 1920s and 1960s, calculations were performed using the known velocities of P waves and S waves through the earth and the travel distances of these waves for every degree of distance from an epicenter—from 1 to 180 degrees. Refinements are being made even today for local anomalies in travel times of seismic waves. As an example, when an earthquake occurs a seismologist spends time with the seismogram locating "arrivals" of various seismic waves. These "arrivals" are marked by a change in the pattern of the incoming wave. After all visible arrivals are marked by time, they are compared to travel-time tables. By matching arrival times of all known waves with the travel-time tables, a seismologist can determine how far away an earthquake occurred located relative to the specific seismometer in use. Alternately, if a seismologist knows how far away an earthquake occurred, then by consulting the travel-time tables the seismologist can determine when various seismic waves should arrive at a seismometer.

A second type of seismic wave—called a surface wave—concentrates its energy in the earth's lithosphere, close to the surface of the earth. Surface waves do not travel through the earth's mantle or core as do body waves. Instead, surface waves travel around the outer perimeter of the earth. Because all of the energy of these waves is kept at a shallow level within the earth, surface waves often are the most energetic and damaging near the epicenter of an earthquake. Seismologists studying earthquake hazards therefore often are most concerned with surface waves. There are two types of surface waves, "Rayleigh waves" and "Love waves," and they are named after their discoverers. Love waves look much like S waves lying on their sides, and Rayleigh waves travel in retrograde elliptical motion. This means that the Rayleigh waves move in an elliptical motion, but the circulation occurs in a direction that looks like it is back toward the source instead of away from it, in the direction of wave movement. Rayleigh and Love waves travel at nearly the same speed, so when a person experiences an earthquake they might feel both side-to-side motion from the Love waves and elliptical motion from Rayleigh waves.

Most students of seismology have selected that field to learn more about the earth's interior, fault behavior, or the mechanics of earthquakes. Seismology, however, also can be used in non-traditional ways that are equally interesting. For example, seismology was used to determine that there were no explosives used in the World Trade Center buildings in New York City on September 11, 2001. Seismometers at Columbia University detected the impacts of the planes into the buildings, but did not detect any explosions immediately before the buildings collapsed. Similarly, seismology was used to determine what happened to the

How Do I Become a Seismologist?

Seismologists are scientific professionals. As students, potential future seismologists often enjoy taking math and science courses in high school, and then go on to study mathematics, physics, geology, or geophysics in college. Someone who has gained some experience in a seismological laboratory as a student can go to work as a seismic analyst after graduating with a four-year degree. Most people interested in becoming seismologists, however, pursue a higher level of education at a university that has at least one faculty member whose specialty is seismology. This faculty member—called a "mentor" or "adviser"—can guide the student toward appropriate coursework and research projects. These projects and courses often are completed by working with the mentor. After earning a master's degree or a doctorate (or Ph.D.) in an appropriate field, and gaining some seismology research experience, the scientist is prepared to become a working professional seismologist. There are two distinct paths for seismologists. One path leads to exploration seismology, which is used in the search for natural resources such as oil, natural gas, and mineral deposits. The other path leads to earthquake seismology. Most research seismologists in both exploration and earthquake seismology have doctoral degrees, but they often manage staffs of seismologists who hold master's degrees.

Russian submarine Kursk in August 2000. Experts looked at the seismic data and determined that two explosions hit the submarine, and the first was smaller than the second. Seismologists were able to determine this information because the blasts were recorded on ocean-bottom seismometers.

A third non-traditional way seismology is used is to discriminate between earthquakes and clandestine underground nuclear tests. As a result of the Comprehensive Nuclear Test Ban Treaty of 1996, all member nations pledged to cease all nuclear tests. A worldwide network of seismometers was put in place as one way to monitor for nuclear tests around the world. This network of seismometers has detected explosions in North Korea, India, and Pakistan.

See Also: Earth Structure; Earthquake; Earthquake Hazards; Plate Tectonics; Seismometer.

Further Reading

Bolt, B. A. (2004). *Earthquakes* (5th ed.). New York: W.H. Freeman and Company.
Richter, C. F. (1958). *Elementary seismology*. New York: W.H. Freeman and Company.
Savage, B., & Helmberger, D. V. (2001). Kursk explosion. *Bulletin of the Seismological Society of America 91* (4), 753–759.

Seismometer

Three different categories of instruments have been used to detect earthquakes. The most primitive of these, the seismoscope, is an instrument designed to alert users to the occurrence of an earthquake; it does not write or digitally record any data. The second category of instrument is a seismograph; this instrument writes permanent records of earth motion. These permanent records are called "seismograms." The third category of instrument is called a seismometer. Although the terms "seismometer" and "seismograph" often are used interchangeably, seismometers must satisfy the additional requirement that their physical constraints are known well enough to permit calibration, such that a scientist is able to calculate actual ground motion from its records. A seismograph does not have this requirement. Seismographs are used today on occasion at remote outposts, often in volcano monitoring. Almost all modern instruments used to record earth motion, however, technically are seismometers.

A seismometer is a combination of three units. The first unit consists of a device that senses ground motion. The basic seismometer design essentially is a mass on a spring or a type of pendulum. Pendulums in general are masses suspended on strings or wires. They swing back and forth with a natural frequency (number of swings per second). Therefore, each also has a natural period (seconds per swing). The natural period of a pendulum—including a pendulum in a seismometer—is an important characteristic. In seismometers, this natural period dictates how well a seismometer responds to earth shaking at various periods.

Different types of seismometers exist, and each has a characteristic period. A long-period seismometer has a design that includes a pendulum with a long natural period. The opposite is true for a short-period seismometer. Some seismometers—called "broadband seismometers"—are designed to record signals at both long and short periods. Others—known as "strong motion accelerometers"—are designed to only respond to the largest of ground motions. This is helpful in areas where large earthquakes are likely to happen. A typical seismometer would produce signals that go "off-scale." This means that the peaks and valleys of each oscillation are cut off because the range of the instrument is too restricted. Strong-motion accelerometers, however, are so well damped that they do not produce any appreciable movement unless ground shaking is very strong. Clever designs of many varieties have been used to enhance and damp the response of seismometers since the early days of seismometers, in the early 1900s. Most recently, pendulum devices often include a magnetic mass on a spring, in which the magnetic mass is surrounded by a coil of wire. This creates an electric current every time there is movement of the magnet within the coil. The electric current is the signal that gets recorded by the second part of the instrument, the data-recording device.

These seismometers (this name also is used for the pendulum device) usually are placed in wells, ideally about 100 feet (33 meters) deep. This is important because seismometers are extremely sensitive instruments. They can detect ground motion much too small to be felt by the human body. As a result, placing a seismometer on the surface would produce incredible amounts of unwanted signals, or "noise." Common sources of noise include the wind, storms, lightning, people or animals walking, traffic, and aircraft. Placing an instrument in a well minimizes noise.

The second component of the seismometer system is the data-recording device. Virtually all modern seismometers are digital. The seismometer itself (the pendulum device) is placed in a well but the recording device usually is located above ground level, where the electronics can be accessed for servicing and repair. The recording device in this case is a digitizer that converts electrical signals from the seismometer into voltages that then can be recorded digitally and sent to a computer base station at a researcher's lab. This typically is done via satellite or FM radio signal. Digital signals sent to the computer are plotted as the "squiggly lines" of a seismogram on a computer screen.

The third component of a seismometer system is a chronograph, or timekeeping instrument. Time is a critical variable in all seismology studies. Not only is it critical to keep absolutely precise time within a single instrument, it is also extremely important to make sure that each individual seismometer is in sync with all other seismometers. To accomplish this, modern seismometers include receivers that keep them synchronized via satellite or internet signals, typically with Global Positioning System (GPS) clocks. These timekeeping devices are part of the electronics package, often connected to the transmitting devices (FM radio antenna or satellite communication device).

See Also: Earthquake; Seismology.

Further Reading

Bolt, B. A. (2004). *Earthquakes* (5th ed.). New York: W.H. Freeman and Company.

Lay, T., & Wallace, T. C. (1995). *Modern global seismology*. San Diego, CA: Academic Press.

Richter, C. F. (1958). *Elementary seismology*. New York: W.H. Freeman and Company.

Sendai Earthquake and Tsunami, Japan (2011)

The Sendai earthquake and tsunami of 2011 was one of the largest seismic events in history, and one of the worst natural disasters to ever hit Japan. The earthquake occurred off the coast of northeastern Japan—its epicenter was located in the Pacific Ocean slightly more than 80 miles from the Oshika Peninsula, which juts from the island of Honshu. It was measured at a magnitude of 9.0, making it the most intense earthquake to occur near or on the Japanese islands in recorded history. The earthquake triggered a tsunami that inflicted great property damage and loss of life on the coastal cities of northeastern Honshu, most notably the large city of Sendai. More than 20,000 people were killed or remained missing two years after the event, and some 500,000 people were displaced, most by the effects of the tsunami.

The earthquake hit on March 11 at 2:46 p.m. local time, at a depth of 15.2 miles (24.5 kilometers). It was a megathrust quake, in which one tectonic plate

Debris swept inland during the 2011 Sendai earthquake and tsunami, Japan. (Pix Planete/ZUMAPRESS/Newscom)

moves under (subducts) another and the earth is pushed upward violently near the margin. (This type of earthquake is common in the Pacific region, and has been responsible for many of the largest earthquakes on record.) The event actually moved Honshu eastward by nearly 8 feet (2.4 meters), and the force produced by the subduction and upthrust displaced a significant amount of oceanic water, creating a tsunami. The seismic activity also might have triggered an eruption that occurred two days later at Shinmoedake, a volcano on the southern Japanese island of Kyushu.

Because the quake occurred rather close to the coast, there was very little time to warn and evacuate people living in coastal towns and cities before the tsunami waves arrived. The waves hit the nearest coastal land within 30 minutes of the earthquake, and the tsunami reached Sendai about 70 minutes after the quake. Many small coastal towns in the northeast were devastated; one such town, Minamisanriku, was virtually annihilated, and more than half of its more than 19,000 residents were unaccounted for in the wake of the tsunami. The coastal areas of Sendai—including the airport—experienced widespread property destruction. The city's power, water, transportation, and communications infrastructure was crippled. Fires erupted in some areas, including at oil refineries. The greatest destruction wrought by the tsunami was in southeastern Hokkaido and northeastern Honshu.

The tsunami moved throughout the Pacific from the earthquake's epicenter, but its power diminished as it traveled across the ocean. Tsunami warnings were issued across the region, but there was relatively little damage outside of Japan. Large waves hit the Hawaiian Islands, causing some damage to ships and harbors, and also were witnessed in other Pacific island countries. Large surges were reported along the west coasts of Canada, the United States, Mexico, Peru, and Chile, but they caused only minor damage.

Among the buildings damaged by the tsunami in Japan were several nuclear power plant complexes, most notably the Fukushima Daiichi plant in Okuma. The tsunami disrupted the primary electrical supply for running the nuclear reactors, and also disabled the backup generators designed to power reactor security and lockdown in the event of just such a natural disaster. The reactors shut down properly after the earthquake—before the systems failed—but the reactors required cooling for days afterward to prevent nuclear meltdown. With no power to the cooling systems, the reactors at the Fukushima complex quickly began to overheat, prompting fears of a meltdown at the plant. Two of the reactor buildings exploded, the first on March 12 (and again on March 15) and the second on March 14, and an explosion occurred inside another reactor building on March 15. The reactors were not destroyed but the explosions made it difficult to assess and control the situation. As of March 15, experts believed that all three reactors were in a state of partial meltdown, but the full extent of damage was unknown. A fourth reactor building on the site experienced a fire on March 15, which spread radioactive material into the atmosphere, leading officials to evacuate a 12-mile (19-kilometer) zone around the plant.

In the reactor buildings, pools of water housing spent nuclear fuel soon became a source of major concern, because the water was boiling off and potentially

Tsunami Debris

In March 2011, a magnitude 9.0 earthquake occurred off the coast of Honshu, Japan, and generated a powerful tsunami that killed many thousands of people. Although the victims were (as they should have been) the world's main focus in the days and months after the tsunami, a lesser-known story involved the millions of tons of debris washed out to sea when these large waves receded. Anything that could float was caught in currents and moved across the Pacific Ocean. About 15 months after the earthquake, in June 2012, a dock from the affected area washed ashore on Agate Beach, Oregon. It was encrusted with several species of marine creatures. This dock made people take notice of both the marine hazard of this debris field, and of the threat of invasive species traveling across the ocean attached to such structures.

The debris field is widely dispersed, therefore the west coast of the United States is not the only area expected to be impacted. By mid-2015, debris is expected to wash ashore in the Northwest Hawaiian Islands, the main Hawaiian Islands, and the west coast of North America from Alaska southward to at least Oregon. California's coastline might be somewhat protected by upwelling coastal waters that push the debris away from shore, but debris could show up there and in Mexico.

leaving the fuel uncovered. Most repair workers were evacuated from the compound, and water was dumped on the spent fuel pools from helicopters and was sprayed from fire trucks. Beginning on March 17, workers attempted to reconnect the power plant to the external electrical grid. Intermittent fires at the reactors prevented full-scale resumption of containment work, but electrical power was reconnected to all reactors on March 22. Seawater subsequently was pumped into the damaged reactors to cool them down, and on March 26 seawater injection ended and freshwater injection began. By that time, however, significant damage already had been done to the reactor containment vessels, and extremely high levels of radioactivity were observed around the plant and in nearby oceanic waters in the days following resumption of freshwater cooling.

In the days following the earthquake and tsunami, relief personnel worked to rescue victims, determine the extent of damage, and determine casualty numbers. The Japanese military, local police, and others worked to save people stranded or trapped in damaged buildings, and shelters were set up for the hundreds of thousands of people displaced by the disaster. The problems were compounded, however, when the danger from the Fukushima nuclear plant led officials to evacuate a large area of coastal Fukushima Prefecture. Governments and nongovernmental organizations around the world offered humanitarian relief funds to Japan to devote to the rescue and clean-up missions already underway. Rescue teams also were sent from Australia, Canada, China, Germany, Indonesia, Israel, Malaysia, Mexico, Mongolia, New Zealand, the Philippines, Russia, Singapore, South Korea, Sri Lanka, Taiwan, Thailand, the United Kingdom, and the United States.

See Also: Indian Ocean Earthquake and Tsunami (2004); Japan; Tsunami; Tsunami Warning Centers.

Further Reading

Sendai earthquake and tsunami (2011). (2014, August 12). In *World geography: Understanding a changing world.* Santa Barbara, CA: ABC-CLIO.

Shasta, Mount, California, United States

Mount Shasta is located in northern California, about 40 miles (65 kilometers) south of the Oregon-California border. It is the largest volcano in the Cascade Range, with an estimated volume of 84 cubic miles (350 cubic kilometers). Its summit is only about 300 feet (91 meters) lower than that of the second most voluminous volcano in the Cascades, Mount Rainier, which reaches 14,162 feet (4,316 meters). Mount Shasta is a compound composite volcano, or compound stratovolcano. It is a single volcanic center formed from four major cone-building episodes occurring at separate vents. Each cone is composed of andesite lava flows; pyroclastic flows; lahars; and, most recently, rhyolite domes and pyroclastic flows erupted from a central vent; plus cinder cones, domes, and lava flows coming from vents on the flanks of each cone. Its most recent eruption was documented somewhat ambiguously by explorer La Perouse in 1786 from his ship at sea. Subsequent investigations of Shasta revealed a crater in the summit dome, small groups of steam vents, acidic hot springs, and volcanic ash on the slopes of the volcano. Radiocarbon dates obtained from charcoals beneath this ash layer yield ages of approximately 200 years.

Mount Shasta's earliest eruptions probably occurred about 590,000 years ago. The volcano has grown more or less continuously since that time with periodic

Mount Shasta, California, USA. (Ingram Publishing/Newscom)

eruptions of lava and pyroclastic material. A large landslide about 300,000 years ago destroyed almost all of Mount Shasta's ancestral cone. Although the landslide occurred on a volcano, there is no evidence it occurred as a direct result of an eruption. It's more likely that weathered rocks on the volcano's slopes gave way following some triggering event, such as a large earthquake or massive rainfall. Evidence of this landslide is obvious around the northern base of the volcano. Hundreds of small hills called "hummocks" extend at least 27 miles (45 kilometers) northward across the floor of Shasta Valley. These hills are landslide blocks composed of pieces of lava flows, layers of pyroclastic flows and lahars, and other pyroclastic materials. Flat areas between hummocks consist of mixed volcanic products carried into the valley by the landslide. Some blocks are as tall as 238 feet (100 meters) above the surface of the landslide deposit.

Following the large debris avalanche, Shasta built new cones. Sargents Ridge cone is the oldest of the four cones that now comprises Mount Shasta. This cone was built between about 250,000 and 130,000 years ago. It has been eroded by two major episodes of glaciation and is found exposed on the south side of the mountain. The third oldest cone is Misery Hill. It was built between about 130,000 and 10,000 years ago. It also was eroded heavily by glaciers. This cone forms the majority of the upper part of Shasta. The final two cones, Hotlum Cone and Shastina, were formed during the last 10,000 years. Shastina likely formed first, between 9,700 and 9,400 years ago. Hotlum Cone deposits overlap those of Shastina, indicating that both were active within the same period. The latest Hotlum deposits, however, lie atop Shastina lavas, indicating that it probably is younger.

In the last 750 years, eruptions at Shasta have occurred on average about every 250 years. Future eruptions likely will come from either the Shastina or the Hotlum cone. Although Shasta certainly could break from its pattern and erupt more violently than its past several eruptive cycles, scientists expect that it will follow its pattern and erupt andesite or dacite lavas, creating a new volcanic dome and perhaps a short lava flow. The eruption likely will be accompanied by light ash fall, pyroclastic flows caused by dome collapse as the dome grows, and lahars. Prevailing winds blow from the west, therefore communities to the east will experience greatest ash accumulations. The more immediate threat, however, will be to the areas within 9 to 13 miles (15 to 20 kilometers) from any vent that feeds the eruption. Debris avalanches and lahars are likely to be the greatest hazards in the outer reaches of the hazard zone, and pyroclastic flows will be the greatest hazard closer to the vent.

See Also: Andesite; Dacite; Lahar; Pyroclastic Flow; Pyroclastic Materials.

Further Reading

U.S. Geological Survey. (2014, May 28). *Mount Shasta*. Retrieved from http://volcanoes .usgs.gov/volcanoes/mount_shasta/

Wood, C. A., & Kienle, J. (1992). *Volcanoes of North America, United States and Canada.* Cambridge: Cambridge University Press.

Shield Volcano

A shield volcano is a type of volcano composed of basalt. Although it could have minor amounts of pyroclastic material as part of the volcano's edifice, the primary material comprising a shield volcano is from lava flows. Shield volcanoes are found in a number of locations throughout the Pacific Rim. The Galapagos Islands and Hawaiian Islands are the two most common places to find them, though they do occur in French Polynesia and in isolated locations around the Pacific Rim, as well.

A typical shield volcano is a large mountain with fairly gentle slopes. The mountain has this shape primarily because of the properties of the basalt it erupts. Basalt is one of the most fluid types of lava that can be erupted by a volcano, so it has the potential to flow far from its source. This is even more likely if the volcano routinely erupts pahoehoe-type basalt that is able to form lava tubes. The lava tubes provide an insulated space for the lava to flow within, allowing it to stay hot and fluid much longer than surface flows can.

The Hawaiian volcanoes are typical—but extremely large—shield volcanoes. The volcano Mauna Loa is the most voluminous volcano on the planet, and its neighbor Mauna Kea is the tallest mountain (measured from its base on the ocean floor) in the world. All Hawaiian volcanoes have a large caldera—or a string of calderas—at their summits, and two zones of weakness that emanate from their calderas, called "rift zones." Eruptions occur at the summit or within one of the rift zones. Eruptions can be fissure eruptions that occur along cracks in the ground, or can occur via a central vent. The vent might build a small lava shield, a cinder cone, or a cinder and spatter cone. A spatter cone is a cinder cone held together by significant amounts of lava that was tossed in the air, but which still was molten when it came to rest on the ground.

Shield volcanoes can produce pyroclastic material in the form of scoria, which is the material that comprises cinder cones. Other pyroclastic materials can include a type of lacy pumice called reticulite, fine filaments of volcanic glass called Pele's hair, volcanic ash, and lapilli (which is composed of sand-to-gravel sized particles). By far, the most common type of material erupted at a shield volcano, however, is a basalt lava flow. These flows can be erupted as pahoehoe or aa, but pahoehoe has the ability to turn into aa if it flows down a steep slope and loses a great deal of its gas content. Thus, the surfaces of shield volcanoes are black patchworks of pahoehoe and aa lava fields.

The flanks of large shield volcanoes can become unstable and develop faults. Those faults are considered tectonic in nature if they are not linked to the plumbing system of the volcano. In some cases they are capable of producing quite powerful earthquakes (greater than magnitude 6). In the case of the Hawaiian Islands and other large shield volcanoes, the instability can lead to landslides. Evidence exists that some pieces of the Hawaiian Islands have slid into the ocean reducing the land area of the islands and possibly creating "mega-tsunamis." How often this happens is the subject of significant debate, and the risk of such an event occurring in the near future is exceedingly small. It has happened in the past, however, which means it could happen in the future. In general, shield volcanoes are fairly gentle giants.

See Also: Aa; Basalt; Caldera; Crater; Megatsunami; Pahoehoe.

Further Reading

Francis, P., & Oppenheimer, C. (2004). *Volcanoes* (2nd ed.). Oxford: Oxford University Press.
U.S. Geological Survey. Hawaiian Volcano Observatory. (2014, May 7). *Is Kilauea falling into the ocean?* Retrieved from http://hvo.wr.usgs.gov/volcanowatch/archive/other/landslide.html

Shishaldin Volcano, Alaska, United States

Shishaldin is a composite volcano located on Unimak Island, one of the eastern-most islands in the Aleutian chain located near the tip of the Alaska Peninsula. It is one of five volcanoes on the island, and the most active of the five. The Aleut name for the mountain is "Sisquk," which means "mountain which points the way when I am lost." The current cone of Shishaldin rises above the remnants of an older volcano that was eroded by glaciers and rivers then partially destroyed by a large debris avalanche. Shishaldin is a symmetrical cone that usually erupts basalt. Thus, the chemistry of Shishaldin is quite different from most Aleutian volcanoes that erupt andesite or dacite. It is located in a remote area that is very sparsely populated. Direct observation of the volcano is problematic as a result of its remote setting. It is located near the Arctic Circle, which means that the region spends much of the winter in perpetual twilight, and offers only fleeting glimpses of the mountain. Monitoring the volcano is important, however, because of its location beneath the very busy Pacific air routes. When eruptions of the Aleutian volcanoes occur, airborne volcanic ash poses a serious hazard for air traffic. Ash causes immense damage to airplanes and can cause jet engines to fail. Many documented cases of airplanes nearly being downed by volcanic ash exist. Thus, it is vital that—despite the remote location and unfavorable conditions—scientists know the state of activity for the Aleutian volcanoes, including Shishaldin.

The first ground-based monitoring network was put in place in 1997 by the Alaskan Volcano Observatory. It consists of six seismometers and one air-pressure sensor. The volcano also is monitored by three satellite systems: Advanced Very High-Resolution Radiometer (AVHRR), Geostationary Operational Environmental Satellite, and Geostationary Meteorological Satellite (GMS). The combination of ground- and space-based assets enable the monitoring of the volcano not only for seismic activity, but also for thermal anomalies that might indicate magma at or very close to the surface, and for volcanic ash plumes. Over the last 200 years, Shishaldin has erupted frequently, on average every 5 to 10 years. The last two eruptions of Shishaldin (beginning in 1999 and 2004) have been particularly well documented as a result of monitoring systems put in place in the late 1990s.

An eruption in 1999 was irregular in that scientists recognized the volcano was in an eruptive state several months after unrest began. The unrest began gradually, with sparse reports from the United States Coast Guard of "puffing" from Shishaldin's summit in late 1998. The volcano issues a nearly constant plume of steam from its summit, even in times of inactivity, so this alone did not seem unusual. In February 1999, scientists started to notice an increase in shallow earthquakes beneath the volcano. About a week afterward, the AVHRR satellite detected a thermal anomaly at the summit of the mountain, and detected then a steam plume rising several thousand feet above the vent. Clearly, the volcano had become active. When scientists went back and analyzed seismic records, they found a very weak seismic signal that indicated magma movement under the volcano that dated back to the beginning of January 1999. This type of gradual onset of an eruption rarely is seen. The volcano erupted somewhat violently on April 19, 1999. An eruption plume rose to 52,000 feet (16 kilometers), and then dissipated quickly. On April 21 and April 22, moderate lava fountaining was observed from a distance. Another vigorous eruption occurred late on April 22 into April 23. It generated a great deal of scoria and lahars that flowed partway down the cone. Activity decreased significantly in late April.

Other smaller episodes of volcanic activity have occurred since 1999. A minor eruption of Shishaldin occurred in 2004. A small amount of ash was deposited on the volcano's slopes, and vigorous steaming occurred at the summit. Another eruption occurred in February 2008. A small ash plume rose to an altitude of about 10,000 feet (3 kilometers), without additional reports of activity. Another eruption began in January 2009, detected by thermal anomalies in AVHRR satellite data. Thermal anomalies were detected throughout the spring and summer of 2009, and then ceased in August of that year. The latest eruptive cycle at Shishaldin began in January 2014. Elevated surface temperatures were detected by satellite in January. By February, there was likely at least one short-lived eruption that sent ash to an altitude of 25,000 feet (7.6 kilometers). Throughout the spring numerous brief explosions occurred and seismic activity indicated that the volcano was in a heightened state of activity.

See Also: Aleutian Islands; Andesite; Basalt; Dacite; Lahar.

Further Reading

Alaska Volcano Observatory. (2014, June 9). *Shishaldin activity*. Retrieved from http://www.avo.alaska.edu/activity/Shishaldin.php

Nye, C. J., Keith, T. E. C., Eichelberger, J. C., Miller, T. P., McNutt, S. R., Moran, S., Schneider, D. J., Dehn, J., & Schaefer, J. R. (2002). The 1999 eruption of Shishaldin Volcano, Alaska: Monitoring a distant eruption. *Bulletin of Volcanology 64* (8), 507–519.

Smithsonian Institution. National Museum of Natural History. Global Volcanism Program. (2014, June 9). *Shishaldin*. Retrieved from http://www.volcano.si.edu/volcano.cfm?vn=311360#February2008

South American Plate

The South American Plate contains the continent of South America as well as half of the southern Atlantic Ocean. The western margin of the plate is adjacent to the Nazca and Antarctic plates. Here, a subduction zone is marked by the Peru-Chile Trench. Both the Nazca and Antarctic plates are being subducted beneath South America. The result is a great deal of earthquake activity and the Andes—a chain of mountains that spans the entire length of the west coast of South America. To the north, the South American Plate is bounded by the Caribbean Plate. Throughout most of its extent this is a transform boundary, but in northwest Colombia, the Caribbean Plate is being subducted beneath South America. To the south, the small Scotia Plate forms a transform boundary with the South American Plate.

The South American Plate has a long and violent history of both volcanic eruptions and damaging earthquakes. The largest earthquake recorded to date occurred in 1960 near the coast of Temuco, Chile. The earthquake was a magnitude 9.5 event. It generated a Pacific-wide tsunami that devastated the local area and took lives in locations as far away as Japan. The earthquake caused more than US$550 million in damage in southern Chile, and killed 1,655 people. The quake also left more than 2 million people homeless.

Other earthquakes of note within the South American Plate include an 1868 earthquake in Arica, Chile, that killed 25,000 people during the earthquake and the tsunami that followed. An earthquake in Chimbote, Peru, in 1970 killed 66,000 people. Although there were a number of people killed in coastal cities from building collapses, most of the fatalities were due to the devastating landslides along the front ranges of the Andes.

The South American Plate contains hundreds of volcanoes that have been active in historic times. One of the most notorious is Nevado del Ruiz, which erupted in 1985. The eruption generated an ash cloud and melted part of the volcano's ice cap. Although it wasn't a large eruption, lahars formed and moved down the major river valleys around the mountain. One of these lahars traveled several miles from the volcano and buried the city of Armero, along with most of its 22,000 inhabitants. The people of Armero had not been warned the lahar was headed their way, nor had they been given instructions of what to do if a warning was sounded. This was a watershed moment in volcanology, when scientists redoubled their efforts to engage in public education of volcano hazards and find ways to educate public officials about the hazards their communities can face when a volcano becomes active. To date, there have not been any further volcanic disasters that resulted in such a great number of fatalities.

Another notorious South American volcano is Galeras in Colombia. In 1993, a group of scientists at a conference on Galeras were in the volcano's crater when the volcano had a short, minor eruption. Six volcanologists were killed and many more were injured. The event is controversial because there might have been warning signs that an eruption was imminent, and the warning signs possibly were disregarded by the person in charge of the group visiting the crater.

See Also: Caribbean Plate; Chile; Colombia; Ecuador; Galeras Volcano, Colombia (1993); Nazca Plate; Nevado del Ruiz, Colombia; Pacific Plate; Peru; Subduction Zone.

Further Reading

Smithsonian Institution. National Museum of Natural History. Global Volcanism Program. (2014, June 19). http://www.volcano.si.edu/

U.S. Geological Survey. (2014, June 19). *Historic world earthquakes.* Retrieved from http://earthquake.usgs.gov/earthquakes/region.php

South Sister Volcano, Oregon, United States

South Sister is one of a cluster of volcanoes located in central Oregon near the city of Bend. It is one of the three peaks that together are known as the "Three Sisters," and include North Sister, Middle Sister, and South Sister. There are at least 466 fairly young volcanoes in an arc that extends about 25 miles (40 kilometers) north and south of the Three Sisters. South Sister's earliest eruptions were between 45,000 and 50,000 years ago, and its last eruption was about 2,000 years ago.

South Sister is a composite volcano, composed primarily of andesite and rhyolite domes and flows, pyroclastic flow deposits, and debris avalanches. It has a summit cap of basaltic andesite lava and scoria that was erupted around

South Sister (left) and Broken Top (right) volcanoes in Oregon, USA. (imago stock&people/ Newscom)

22,000 years ago. The volcano then was quiet for approximately 20,000 years, until the most recent eruptive period began about 2,200 years ago. The first episode of eruption following this period of quiescence sent rhyolite ash at least 20 miles (30 kilometers) from the vent. Later lava flows produced a number of small rhyolite domes and the Rock Mesa coulee (elongated dome), a prominent landmark near the base of the southwest side of the mountain. A second period of eruptive activity occurred about 2,000 years ago. During that time, eruptions occurred along two linear trends on the southeast and north flanks of the volcano. "Devils Chain," a line of 20 domes and coulees was formed along the southeast arm, and a similar line of domes was formed to the north. A large amount of the lava erupted during this episode is in the Newberry flow, a prominent rhyolite and obsidian lava flow located on the southeast flank of South Sister.

South Sister gained a great deal of attention in 2001 when scientists using the volcano monitoring technique satellite interferometry found an area of deformation east of South Sister. In comparing elevations from satellite imagery collected during successive passes over the volcano between 1997 and 2001, scientists found that approximately 5.9 inches (15 centimeters) of uplift had occurred within a bull's-eye shaped area centered about 3.7 miles (6 kilometers) east of the volcano's summit. The researchers stepped-up monitoring efforts for the volcano and, in 2004, a swarm of earthquakes occurred near the center of the uplift area. Nothing happened as a result of the deformation or the earthquake swarm. The uplift likely represents either an intrusion of magma beneath the volcano, or the rise of hot groundwater and steam that caused overlying rocks to expand from the heat. In any case, uplift had slowed considerably by 2013. Without satellite interferometry, the uplift probably never would have been detected. Similar events have since been detected at other volcanoes. The volcano continues to be monitored by the Cascades Volcano Observatory.

See Also: Andesite; Basalt; Dacite; Pyroclastic Flow; Rhyolite; Volcano Monitoring Techniques.

Further Reading

U.S. Geological Survey. (2005). *Monitoring ground deformation from space.* (Fact Sheet 2005-3025).

U.S. Geological Survey. (2014, May 23). *Three Sisters.* Retrieved from http://volcanoes .usgs.gov/volcanoes/three_sisters/

St. Helens, Mount, Washington, United States

Mount St. Helens is a composite volcano located in southwestern Washington within the Cascade Range, near the west coast of the United States. It is the most active of the Cascade Range volcanoes, erupting more than 15 times during the

Aerial view of Mount St. Helens, Washington (USA). (Kevin Schafer/ Minden Pictures/ Newscom)

past 4,500 years. Mount St. Helens' composition is varied, and includes basalt, andesite, and dacite lavas as well as pyroclastic material, lahars, and debris flows. The last eruption at the volcano was from October 2004 to January 2008, but the volcano is more well-known for an explosive eruptive cycle that occurred between 1980 and 1986. The catastrophic May 18, 1980, eruption significantly altered the appearance of the mountain, and left 57 people dead.

Mount St. Helens has long been known to local inhabitants as an active volcano. Native Americans living in the area have two names for the mountain. One name, "Louwala-Clough," means "smoking mountain." A different Native American tribe called the volcano "Loowit." Legend says that Loowit was a beautiful maiden. Two sons of the Great Spirit, "Sahale," fell in love with her. Loowit was unable to choose between the two sons, Wyeast and Klickitat. The two braves fought for her affections, burying villages and forests during their great battles. The Great Spirit was furious and killed all three of them, and built a mountain peak where each fell. Loowit became Mount St. Helens, a beautiful, symmetrical cone blanketed in dazzling white snow and ice. Wyeast became Mount Hood, and Klickitat became Mount Adams. It is said that Wyeast stands with his head held high in pride, but Klickitat weeps to see Loowit wrapped in snow so he bends his head as he gazes on her.

Mount St. Helens received its modern name in 1792 from Captain George Vancouver, a British explorer. He saw the mountain for the first time on October 20, 1792, and proclaimed it Mount St. Helens in honor of the British diplomat

Alleyne Fitzherbert, whose title was Baron St. Helens. Lewis and Clark saw Mount St. Helens in April of 1806, near the end of their long journey to the Pacific Ocean. It was not erupting at the time, but authors relate accounts of eruptions in 1800–1801, 1831–1832, 1835, 1842, 1845–1847, and 1857. Much of what is known about the period before the early 1800s comes from detailed geologic mapping of the mountain that was undertaken by scientists from the U.S. Geological Survey in the 1960s and 1970s.

One of the best indicators of future activity at a specific volcano is its past behavior. United States Geological Survey scientists Dwight Crandell and Donal Mullineaux worked throughout their careers to map the most dangerous Cascade Range volcanoes and their deposits in great detail. Their goal was to determine how these volcanoes had behaved in the past so they would know what to expect during future eruptions. Crandell and Mullineaux headed a small field crew that worked for several years to complete a comprehensive hazard map of Mount St. Helens and the surrounding area. They published their completed map and an accompanying report in 1978, stating, "In the future, Mount St. Helens probably will erupt violently and intermittently just as it has done in the recent geologic past, and these future eruptions will affect human life and health, property, agriculture, and general economic welfare over a broad area" (Crandell and Mullineaux, 1978).

Crandell and Mullineaux specifically cited a number of hazards. Of greatest concern to them was that of dam breaks due to lahars on the Toutle, Kalama, and Lewis rivers, and damage to Swift Reservoir directly south of the volcano. Tephra fall was another serious concern, particularly in the area 180 degrees east of the volcano, due to westerly prevailing winds in the region. Tephra has the ability to injure people directly via inhalation and flying fragments. It can start fires; block roads; cause darkness during daylight hours; interrupt telephone, radio, and electrical services; cause roofs to collapse; smother crops and pasture land; damage machinery; and pollute water supplies. The report also listed gas emission, pyroclastic flows, floods, lava flows, dome growth, and explosive eruptions as hazards. Because the area nearest Mount St. Helens was not heavily inhabited, however, these were seen as lesser hazards to large population centers. They were not expected to directly affect areas more than a few miles from the mountain. Furthermore, Crandell and Mullineaux stated, "The volcano's behavior pattern suggests that the current quiet interval will not last as long as a thousand years; instead an eruption is more likely to occur within the next hundred years, and perhaps even before the end of this century" (Crandell and Mullineaux, 1978).

The release of the map and report initially caused a small panic among Washington State officials. When geologists explained that there were no signs an eruption was imminent but that it would be wise to prepare for a future eruption, however, the officials turned their attention to current threats. Very little was done prior to 1980 within the state government or the U.S. Geological Survey to prepare for the eventuality of an eruption within the Cascades.

The catastrophic eruption of Mount St. Helens in May 1980 was preceded by two months of precursory activity. Geologists monitoring seismic activity in the Cascades from a laboratory at the University of Washington noted a swarm of earthquakes at Mount St. Helens beginning March 16, 1980. Hundreds of earthquakes followed, becoming both more powerful and more frequent. On March 27, the volcano produced its first eruption, primarily composed of steam with minor amounts of volcanic ash. It also created a 200 foot (60 meter) wide crater at the volcano's summit, blasting through the mountain's thick ice cap and coating the southeast side of the mountain with a thin layer of volcanic ash. A week later, the crater had grown to about 1,300 feet (400 meters) in diameter and steam eruptions occurred at a rate of roughly one per hour throughout the rest of March. Eruptions slowed to one per day in the first few weeks of April, and there was a period between April 22 and May 7 in which no eruptive activity occurred. There was some hope among local officials that the volcano had settled down and would not produce a large-scale eruption; however, the volcano resumed small eruptions on May 7, and that behavior continued until May 17.

On March 27, 1980, as soon as it became clear that volcanic activity had begun, the U.S. Forest Service, local law-enforcement authorities, civil defense managers, the Federal Aviation Administration, and U.S. Geological Survey scientists went into crisis-management mode. The U.S. Forest Service took the lead in emergency management because it was used to managing information and evacuations from its experiences with forest fires. The Forest Service also had broad legal authority, a strict chain of command, and existing disaster plans in place. The Forest Service headquarters in Vancouver, Washington, became the command post for all scientists and authorities working on response to the activity at Mount St. Helens.

Other events that occurred in rapid succession included the closing of airspace around the mountain by the Federal Aviation Administration, and voluntary evacuation of residents within 15 miles of the mountain's summit. Within a few days, and with the help of U.S. Geological Survey scientists, authorities outlined exclusion zones around the volcano based largely on the hazard maps supplied by Crandell and Mullineaux. The Red Zone was oval in shape, with the long axis extending north-northeast and south-southwest. It extended approximately 3 miles (4.8 kilometers) from the east side and 4 miles (6.4 kilometers) from the west side of the volcano, and roughly 7 miles (11.3 kilometers) south and 8 miles (13 kilometers) north of the mountain. The Red Zone was off limits to everyone except administrative personnel of government agencies, scientists, law-enforcement personnel, and search-and-rescue personnel. The Blue Zone was much more irregular in shape because it followed major river valleys in anticipation of lahars. It extended from 0.1 mile (0.16 kilometer) to 5 miles (8 kilometers) outside the boundary of the Red Zone. It was closed to everyone except those with permission to enter to the Red Zone, but controlled access by landowners who had permits was allowed from 8 a.m. to 5 p.m.

During that same period, the scientists began the complex work of addressing the multiple questions they had about the volcano and its likely future behavior. The U.S. Geological Survey set up an observation post on Coldwater Ridge, about 6 miles (9.5 kilometers) north and across a valley from the summit of Mount St. Helens. The scientific outpost at Coldwater Ridge was manned 24 hours a day by volcano experts from various offices of the U.S. Geological Survey. Several scientists from the Hawaiian Volcano Observatory (HVO) soon were on site to assist in the monitoring efforts. The scientists from HVO had a great deal of experience working on active volcanoes and monitored the volcano using multiple methods that had been successful in predicting eruptions on the island of Hawaii. They installed multiple seismometers to monitor earthquake activity. An increase in earthquake activity, they believed, would warn them of an impending eruption. They used a correlation spectrometer (COSPEC) to monitor sulfur dioxide being emitted from the volcano. They routinely flew over the volcano in helicopters and fixed-wing aircraft to see inside of the crater. They also monitored the changing shape of the volcano.

As the magma chamber under a volcano fills with magma, it causes the mountain to inflate like a balloon. Normally, the entire volcano inflates at a rate that is imperceptible to the naked eye. At Mount St. Helens, however, the north flank of the volcano swelled ominously. Throughout April and May the volcano's north flank developed a bulge that grew at the astounding rate of 6.5 feet (2 meters) per day. By May 17, the bulge had grown 450 feet (140 meters) out from the side of the volcano and was clearly visible to the naked eye. Geologist Barry Voight, an expert on landslides from Pennsylvania State University, alarmed his fellow scientists by telling them the slope was so unstable that a large enough earthquake could dislodge the entire north flank, creating a massive landslide and releasing pressure within the volcano that would then trigger a violent eruption. This information was shared with cooperating agencies as part of the emergency-management reporting process. Following this alert, some scientists entertained the idea that if the volcano erupted in the way Voight suggested it might, the eruption could occur from the side of the volcano in a directed blast. Directed blasts are extremely rare, so the general consensus was that such an occurrence was only a remote possibility.

On the morning of May 18, 1980, David Johnston was the scientist on duty at Coldwater Ridge. He woke early and took his measurements. He spoke briefly with other scientists at the Vancouver field station, and reported that the situation was unchanged and unremarkable. The volcano was experiencing earthquakes at the same rate as it had been for weeks. The bulge was still growing at an alarming rate, but no faster or slower than it had been for the past several days. The scientists hoped that if the volcano was building to an eruption then the frequency and magnitudes of earthquakes would increase, and the north flank would show signs of more rapid movement.

Nothing was out of the ordinary that morning, but at 8:32 a.m. a magnitude 5 earthquake occurred beneath Mount St. Helens. Within a few seconds the north flank of the volcano dissolved into a massive debris avalanche that carried 0.5 cubic mile (2.3 cubic kilometers) of the mountain downward into Spirit Lake and the upper part of the North Fork Toutle River. The water from Spirit Lake was displaced, and debris from the landslide raised the lake bed by nearly 200 feet (60 meters) before the water came crashing back into place. This debris avalanche was one of the largest ever recorded. The landslide and subsequent eruption removed 1,314 feet (400 meters) from the summit of the volcano, and removed 0.67 cubic miles from the volcano. The resulting horseshoe-shaped crater is

2,084 feet (635 meters) deep, 1.2 miles (2 kilometers) wide from east to west, and 1.8 miles (2.9 kilometers) wide from north to south.

As the debris avalanche was still in motion, a faster-moving lateral blast broke through the landslide and moved at speeds of at least 220 miles per hour (100 meters per second). The area around Mount St. Helens had been heavily forested before the eruption, but this directed blast removed all trees to a distance of more than 6 miles (10 kilometers) from the summit of the volcano to the north, east, and west. Beyond that, to a distance of 12 miles (20 kilometers) to the north and 18 miles (30 kilometers) to the east and west, all trees were blown to the ground with their branches and twigs removed. The devastated area—230 square miles (600 square kilometers)—was covered with a deposit of hot debris carried by the lateral blast.

Within a few minutes, a vertical Plinian eruption began. The eruption column rose to a height of 12.5 miles (20 kilometers) and sustained that level of activity for nine hours. Ash from the eruption cloud was carried to the east by prevailing winds. Cities up to 125 miles (200 kilometers) away were plunged into total darkness as ash blotted out the sun. Significant amounts of ash fell as far eastward as central Montana, and visible ashfall was recorded as far east as the Great Plains, more than 1,000 miles (1,500 kilometers) away.

Closer to the volcano, the massive ash cloud produced lightning that started hundreds of small forest fires. Starting roughly 4 hours after the start of the Plinian phase of the eruption, and continuing until its conclusion 5 hours later, observers noted numerous small pyroclastic flows speeding down the slopes of the volcano. These flows extended up to 5 miles (8 kilometers) north to Spirit Lake and North Fork Toutle River. They covered an area of 6 square miles (15.5 square kilometers) to a maximum depth of 140 feet (40 meters). These deposits were extremely hot at the time they were emplaced. As they cooled over the next few months, they periodically produced steam explosions that created pits from 15 to 300 feet (5 to 100 meters) in diameter and 3 to 60 feet (1 to 20 meters) deep. The steam explosions made working within the area even more dangerous for search-and-rescue workers in the days after the eruption, and for scientists for weeks after that.

Lahars developed within minutes of the start of the eruption. The heat of the eruption melted snow and ice at the top of the mountain, and volcanic ash from the eruption cloud mixed with the meltwater to produce the earliest lahars. These mudflows swept up large blocks of ice and logs—both from the trees felled during the eruption and from commercial logging operations. The flows traveled at speeds of 100 miles per hour (161 kilometers per hour) in the upper reaches of the rivers, but decreased in velocity to as slow as 3.5 miles per hour (5.3 kilometers per hour) as they made their way to lower points in the valleys. The largest mudflow originated in the upper North Fork Toutle River valley in the debris avalanche deposits. It traveled more than 75 miles (120 kilometers) down the valley, eventually reaching the Cowlitz and Columbia rivers. The lahar in places was 13 feet (4 meters) above normal water levels. Roads, bridges, homes, businesses, and other structures were damaged or carried away.

Of the 57 fatalities that occurred during the May 18, 1980, eruption, only two were located within restricted zones. The first was U.S. Geological Survey scientist Dr. David Johnston. From his post on the north side of the mountain at Coldwater

Ridge, he certainly felt the magnitude 5 earthquake and turned his attention to the mountain. He did his best to convey this information to the incident command post in Vancouver, Washington. Dr. Johnston's message, "Vancouver, Vancouver! This is it!" was received by a local ham-radio operator, but it did not reach Vancouver. He tried a second time to reach headquarters saying "Vancouver! This is Johnston, over!" But, at that moment, the lateral blast began moving toward his position and overtook him. The second fatality within the restricted zone was Harry Truman, owner of Spirit Lake Lodge. Truman was a somewhat eccentric 80-year-old man who lived at the lodge with 28 cats. He became somewhat of a celebrity and folk hero by defying mandatory evacuation orders and granting a number of interviews with the press. He was repeatedly urged by law enforcement personnel as well as visiting reporters to leave the lodge, but he refused. Less than one minute after the start of the eruption, Harry Truman and his beloved lodge were buried under 200 feet (60 meters) of landslide debris.

The other fatalities directly attributable to the eruption occurred outside of restricted zones. They included families on camping trips, loggers working in the forests surrounding the mountain, a photographer for the Vancouver, Washington, *Columbian* newspaper, and scientists who had come to the area for a look at the mountain. Many of their bodies never were recovered. The sudden collapse of the northern flank of the mountain in the absence of precursors, and the lateral blast took both the scientists and the public by surprise. The size of the landslide on the north flank also was much larger than anticipated, and the unanticipated directed blast extended well beyond the boundaries of the Red Zone and the Blue Zone.

Prior to May 18, no new magma had been erupted from the volcano. The eruptions between March 27 and May 17 had produced steam and volcanic ash, but the volcanic ash was pulverized rock from the volcano's existing edifice. On May 18, the scientists had samples of the new batch of magma that had created the giant bulge on the volcano's flank and knew that it was dacitic in composition. That meant there was a high potential for continued violent explosive eruptions, and a continuing need to keep non-essential personnel out of areas affected by the May 18 eruption. Additional explosive eruptions occurred on May 25, June 12, July 22, August 7, and October 16–18 of 1980, although they were much smaller than that of May 18. The eruptions produced pyroclastic flows and relatively small volumes of volcanic ash, which fell on surrounding communities. The volcano also began to grow a lava dome in its crater. Various domes grew between 1980 and 1986, and several of these were destroyed by relatively minor explosive eruptions. By the time the eruption was declared over in 1986, however, a large dome was located in the vast crater of the volcano. It rose 876 feet (267 meters) above the crater floor, and had a diameter of about 3,500 feet (1 kilometer). The total volume is estimated to be about 97 million cubic yards (74 million cubic meters).

In the post-eruption analysis, U.S. Geological Survey scientists recognized both the successes and failures of their response to the volcanic crisis. They concluded that—although they correctly identified the products the volcano would produce (a large landslide, great volumes of volcanic ash, lahars, and pyroclastic flows) based on the monitoring work and the previous hazard assessment completed in

Harry Truman

Harry Truman became a folk hero of sorts during the precursory activity that led up to the May 1980 eruption of Mount St. Helens. Truman was owner of the Mount St. Helens Lodge, a fixture on the shores of Spirit Lake near the mountain. In 1980, Truman was in his early 80s and swore that he would never leave his home, despite the dangers scientists believed threatened him and his beloved lodge. To some, Truman became a symbol of the American spirit as he defied government authority and refused to comply with mandatory evacuation orders. To others, he was a cranky and stubborn old man who refused to listen to the voice of reason. Truman was a regular fixture on newscasts and in newspaper articles about the volcanic activity. His passion for the mountain and for his home of more than 50 years—as well as his profanity-laced monologues about his distrust of scientific predictions about the volcano's likely behavior—gained him a loyal following among the press and the general public. Truman received notes from school children begging him to leave, as well as letters of support urging him to keep up the fight. Although he occasionally expressed fear and trepidation to those closest to him, he acknowledged that he felt he would die if he were separated from his home. Truman decided that he would rather die at home than in unfamiliar surroundings. On May 18, 1980, Mr. Truman and the lodge were buried under a massive landslide that decapitated Mount St. Helens.

1978—there were a number of hazards for which they did not adequately prepare, because the hazards exceeded the magnitude of the volcano's past behavior. Scientists did not correctly predict the size of the debris slide on the north flank of the volcano, nor did they forecast a directed blast. They were also incorrect in their estimates of the volume of material contained within lahars or the distance the lahars would travel. There was a sober realization that the volcano created an emergency for which scientists and area public officials were unprepared.

The scientists had a general lack of knowledge concerning volcanic processes and hazards related to explosive composite volcanoes. They cited the need for volcanic-hazard coordinators who are familiar with the volcano, its history and hazards, as well as local infrastructure and community concerns. Also recognized was the need for a cadre of scientists to be trained to work on volcanoes of this type to the institutional knowledge necessary to adequately respond to the next volcanic crisis in the Cascades. This became a top priority in the Volcano Hazards Program of the U.S. Geological Survey. The Volcano Disaster Assistance Program eventually grew out of this identified need. The U.S. Geological Survey also established a permanent volcano observatory for the Cascades and named it the "David A. Johnston Cascades Volcano Observatory" in honor of the scientist who lost his life on May 18, 1980, while monitoring Mount St. Helens.

Between 1986 and 2004, there was very little surface activity at Mount St. Helens. The U.S. Forest Service opened the mountain's south flank to climbers in the late 1980s. In 1982, the U.S. government created the Mount St. Helens National Volcanic Monument, an 110,000-acre (445-square kilometer) site that was left untouched to be a natural laboratory for studying the recovery of a landscape after a major volcanic eruption. Numerous interpretive centers and visitors' centers were constructed around the mountain. Forests outside the Volcanic Monument were replanted, and the first trees replanted after the eruption now are being harvested. Life returned to normal, and the landscape that was so drastically changed in May 1980 began to lose its starkness as the forest regrew and animals returned to the area.

In 2004, Mount St. Helens surprised scientists and the public alike by reawakening with very little warning. With only two weeks of precursory activity, the volcano began a new phase of its eruption with a spectacular ash-emitting eruption on October 4. Scientists were surprised at this renewal in activity, because there were no signs in the four preceding years that the volcano was building toward an eruption. There was no increase in seismic activity, steam or gas emission, or in the shape of the volcano. In fact, the quietest period of seismic activity beneath the volcano since 1980 was the four years between 2000 and the onset of the 2004–2008 eruption. Although there were a few minor ash-emitting eruptions in the last few months of 2004, the vast majority of the 2004–2008 eruption consisted of quiet extrusion of lava that added volume to the previously existing dome in the crater. As large and impressive as the lava dome is at this time, the volcano has only rebuilt about 7% of the volume it lost in the 1980 eruption. There is no doubt that Mount St. Helens will erupt again, but when that will occur remains unknown.

See Also: Andesite; Basalt; Composite Volcano; Dacite; Lahar; Lava Dome; Pyroclastic Flow; United States Geological Survey; Volcano Disaster Assistance Program.

Further Reading

Columbian, The. (1980, May 19). *St. Helens spews death, destruction.* Retrieved from http://www.columbian.com/news/1980/may/19/st-helens-spews-death-destruction/

Crandell, D. R., & Mullineaux, D. R. (1978). *Potential hazards from future eruptions of Mount St. Helens Volcano, Washington* (USGS Bulletin 1383-C), 26.

Lipman, P. W., & Mullineaux, D. R. (1981). *The 1980 eruptions of Mount St. Helens, Washington* (United States Geological Survey Professional Paper 1250).

Thompson, D. (2000). *Volcano cowboys: The rocky evolution of a dangerous science.* New York: St Martin's Press.

U.S. Geological Survey. (2014, October 26). *Mount St. Helens—from the 1980 eruption to 2000* (Fact Sheet 036-00; Online Version 1.0). Retrieved from http://pubs.usgs.gov /fs/2000/fs036-00/

U.S. Geological Survey. Volcano Hazards Program. (2014, October 26). *Cascade Range volcanoes: Historical timeline.* Retrieved from http://vulcan.wr.usgs.gov/LivingWith /Historical/timeline.html

U.S. Geological Survey. Volcano Hazards Program. (2014, October 26). *Mount St. Helens: 1980 cataclysmic eruption.* Retrieved from http://volcanoes.usgs.gov/volcanoes/st _helens/st_helens_geo_hist_99.html

U.S. Geological Survey. Volcano Hazards Program. (2014, October 26). *Naming the Cascade Range volcanoes—Mount St. Helens, Washington.* Retrieved from http:// vulcan.wr.usgs.gov/LivingWith/Historical/naming_mount_st_helens.html

U.S. Geological Survey. Volcano Hazards Program. (2014, October 26). *The volcanoes of Lewis and Clark.* Retrieved from http://vulcan.wr.usgs.gov/LivingWith/Historical /LewisClark/volcanoes_lewis_clark.html

Vallance, J. W., Gardner, C., Scott, W. E., Iverson, R., & Pierson, T. (2010). Mount St. Helens: A 30-year legacy of volcanism. *Eos, Transactions of the American Geophysical Union 91* (19), 169–170. doi: 10.1029/2010EO190001

Subduction Zone

A subduction zone is a location where two tectonic plates, at least one of which must be oceanic, move toward each other. An oceanic plate yields and dives beneath the other plate. The downgoing (subducting) plate is driven deep into the asthenosphere beneath the overriding plate. Hallmarks of subduction zones include frequent earthquakes that can be extremely violent and deadly; the possibility of tsunamis generated by large earthquakes; and volcanic activity, usually in the form of explosive composite volcanoes.

The first study to suggest a structure such as a subduction zone was published by Hugo Benioff in 1949. Benioff gathered earthquake data from the vicinity of the Tona-Kermadec trench and plotted a cross-section, or profile, of the data. The earthquakes in that area varied in depth from very shallow to nearly 435 miles (700 kilometers) beneath the surface. Benioff noted the general pattern of earthquakes was such that the shallowest earthquakes occurred beneath or directly adjacent to the trench, and earthquakes got progressively deeper toward the shallower part of the ocean at an angle of approximately 45°. Similar cross-sections of earthquake locations beneath the west coast of South America showed the same pattern of earthquakes. They were shallowest at the trench and were progressively deeper toward the interior of the continent. Benioff proposed that deep-sea trenches were caused by massive faults in the earth's lithosphere. In a technical sense he was correct, but there certainly is a great deal more to the story.

In the 1960s, several other geologists investigated similar areas where island arcs were present. They found similar patterns of earthquakes in these areas, leading downward at varying angles from trenches. These regions were the only places on the planet where deep earthquakes (deeper than 62 miles, or 100 kilometers) occurred. Eventually a model was developed. Oceanic lithosphere is dragged into the mantle at these sites, called "subduction zones." Earthquakes occur in this brittle slab as it is subjected to increasing pressure from the surrounding rocks, and from the subduction process itself. Some of the earthquakes are powerful and damaging, and many have a significant component of vertical motion. This means that large, shallow earthquakes at the subduction zone have a fair probability of creating tsunamis.

As the slab descends, water in the oceanic lithosphere of the subducted plate is heated. It leaves the plate and invades the surrounding mantle. The introduction of water into the mantle lowers the melting point of mantle rocks, enabling magma to be created. Magma rises to the surface above these areas of melting, and volcanic activity occurs. Because magma must rise through the lithosphere, it melts rocks in its immediate vicinity. In many cases, the magma changes composition from basaltic to andesitic or dacitic. The result is a chain of composite volcanoes on the surface. If both plates involved in subduction are oceanic, then the chain of volcanoes becomes an oceanic island arc. If the overriding plate is continental, then it becomes a chain of volcanoes on the margin of the continent.

A number of prominent subduction zones are present on the earth. Virtually the entire western Pacific is a series of subduction zones—from the Aleutian Islands of Alaska west to the Kamchatka Peninsula of Russia, southward to Japan and the Philippines, then on to Indonesia, Tonga, Fiji, and New Zealand. The west coast of South America, Central America, and the west coast of the United States and Canada from just north of San Francisco, California, to British Columbia also are locations of subduction zones. The west coast of South America is a subduction zone, as is the west coast of Central America and the southern coast of Mexico. Together these subduction zones around the rim of the Pacific Ocean constitute the "Ring of Fire." All of these areas have been sites of immensely powerful earthquakes, source areas for tsunamis, and locations of powerful volcanic eruptions.

See Also: Basalt; Dacite; Plate Tectonics.

Further Reading

Benioff, H. (1949). Seismic evidence for the fault origin of oceanic deeps. *Geological Society of America Bulletin 60* (12), 1837–1856.

Kearey, P., Klepeis, K. A., & Vine, F. J. (2009). *Global tectonics* (3rd ed.). Hoboken, NJ: Wiley-Blackwell.

Oliver, J., & Isacks, B. (1967). Deep earthquake zones, anomalous structures in the upper mantle, and the lithosphere. *Journal of Geophysical Research 72* (16), 4259–4275.

Sykes, L. R. (1966). The seismicity and deep structure of island arcs. *Journal of Geophysical Research 71* (12), 2981–3006.

Tarbuck, E. J., Lutgens, F. K., & Tasa, D. (2011). *Earth: An introduction to physical geology* (10th ed.). Upper Saddle River, NJ: Pearson Prentice Hall/Pearson Education, Inc.

Supervolcano

The term "supervolcano," though not narrowly defined evokes images of a colossal and deadly eruption. Volcanoes that produce eruptions of magnitude 8 or higher on the Volcano Explosivity Index (VEI) could be considered supervolcanoes. This corresponds to an eruption volume of at least 240 cubic miles (1,000 cubic kilometers). The word "supervolcano" was not seen in geologic literature until fairly recently, although eruptions of this size have been noted for decades. In some part, the term was devised by the press, perhaps to emphasize the enormous potential of this type of eruption to create chaos. A number of supereruptions from this type of volcano have occurred in the past. None, however, have occurred in the last few thousand years, or in what is considered to be recorded history. The last supereruption to occur was likely that of Taupo, New Zealand, about 27,000 years ago. Prior to that, supereruptions

What Is a Recurrence Interval?

A recurrence interval very simply is the length of time between two events of the same type occurring in the same general area. For instance, along the stretch of the San Andreas Fault near Parkfield, California, moderately sized earthquakes occurred for nearly 150 years with surprising regularity—happening every 12 to 30 years. The recurrence interval for moderate earthquakes on this part of the San Andreas is about 22 years. A recurrence interval is average length of time between events, but nature rarely behaves perfectly according to schedules it is expected to follow. After withstanding regular earthquakes for many decades, the Parkfield segment of the San Andreas Fault was expected to experience its next moderate earthquake between 1985 and 1993. Defying its previous record of a predictable recurrence interval, however, the next moderate earthquake did not occur until 2004. Some events have not occurred often enough to enable an accurate estimate of recurrence interval. In 1811–1812, a series of major earthquakes occurred in the New Madrid area of Missouri. No earthquakes of that size have been recorded since, and there is no written history of when the last earthquake of that size occurred before the sequence in 1811–1812. Thus, we have no idea what the recurrence interval is for major earthquakes in this part of the United States.

likely occurred on every continent and throughout history. As with other abnormally large events, however, these events are rare. The next supereruption could occur at any time, but the odds of it occurring in the near future are negligible.

Supervolcanoes come in two varieties; one is a giant caldera-forming composite volcano. Yellowstone fits into this category as does Toba, Indonesia. The Yellowstone caldera complex is approximately 50 miles (80 kilometers) long by 30 miles (48 kilometers) wide. The magma volume beneath the caldera is immense, and is composed primarily of rhyolite. The rhyolite composition has the potential to create an incredibly explosive eruption that could generate millions of tons of volcanic ash per hour in an eruption that could last several days. In the event of that type of eruption, ash would blanket the entire center third of the contiguous United States.

A second type of supervolcano is difficult to identify or locate as a discrete volcano. In the past, there have been extremely large volumes of basalt erupted from volcanic centers, although no individual mountain ever has been identified as the source. More likely, eruptions broke out in a series of cracks (fissures) across the landscape. This occurred in Siberia and creates a region known as the "Siberian Traps"; it occurred in South Africa to create the Karoo Basalts; and it occurred in the United States and created the Columbia River Basalts. In each of these cases, the eruptions that created the vast basalt fields were extremely long-lived events. In most cases, it is thought that the eruptions went on for thousands—if not millions—of years, with small breaks in activity throughout. A miniature version of this type of eruption occurred in 1783 in Iceland. The result was a thick volcanic fog that blanketed most of Europe, a desperate famine, and loss of up to one third of Iceland's population and livestock. Clearly, both types of supereruption have the potential for devastation. Perhaps this is why a new category of eruption was created for such events.

See Also: Basalt; Rhyolite; Taupo Volcano, New Zealand; Toba Eruption, Indonesia; Volcanic Explosivity Index (VEI).

Further Reading

Decker, R., & Decker, B. (1998).*Volcanoes* (3rd ed.; Academic Version). New York: W.H. Freeman and Company.

Haslam, M., & Petraglia, M. D. Toba. (2009). *The Toba Super-eruption.* Retrieved from http://toba.arch.ox.ac.uk/edu.htm

U.S. Geological Survey. Yellowstone Volcano Observatory. (2014, May 15). Questions about supervolcanoes. http://volcanoes.usgs.gov/volcanoes/yellowstone/yellowstone_sub_page_49.html

T

Tambora Eruption, Indonesia (1815)

The largest eruption in recorded history occurred in April 1815, at Tambora, a volcano on the Indonesian island of Sumbawa. Although this fact alone would make the eruption noteworthy, Tambora's eruption of 1815 is important for two additional reasons. One is that this was the deadliest eruption in history; another is that the eruption caused such severe and far-reaching climate effects that people half a world away came to know 1816 as "the year without a summer."

Tambora is a large, caldera-forming composite volcano located on the Sanggar Peninsula on the eastern part of Sumbawa Island. Written records describing the eruption are sparse, but there is mention of precursory activity occurring at Tambora between 1812 and 1815. During this time, the volcano is described as being "mildly active." Ash and pebbles fell on the slopes of the volcano as a result of phreatic and phreatomagmatic eruptions. The character of the eruption changed on April 5, 1815, however. On that day a plinian eruption began, which deposited up to 2 feet (50 centimeters) of pumice fall on the slopes of the volcano. The eruption column reached a height of 108,000 feet (33 kilometers) for approximately 2 hours. Afterward, Tambora fell into a pattern of fairly quiet, low-volume ash eruptions. Five days later, the volcano's paroxysmal eruption began. The April 10 eruption lasted for two days, and kept downwind islands in the dark for up to four days. It sent an eruption cloud an impressive 144,000 feet (44 kilometers) skyward, well into the stratosphere. The eruption could be heard as far away as the village of Benkulen on Sumatra, 1,100 miles (1,775 kilometers) away. Earthquakes were felt on Java, 375 miles (600 kilometers) away.

At the climax of the April 10–11 eruption, pyroclastic flows swept down all sides of the volcano. The feudal kingdoms of Tambora on the north slope, and Sanggar on the east slope, were completely obliterated. More than 10,000 people were killed by these pyroclastic flows. The thick blanket of ash that fell on Sumbawa destroyed the island's crops, leading to a sudden and immediate famine. The island's climate also changed suddenly, becoming temporarily warmer and drier. As a result, additional crops would not grow. Crop and livestock losses were crushing. Almost all crops failed and more than 75% of livestock died. Approximately 38,000 people died as a result of starvation and disease in a second wave, and 36,000 people fled Sumbawa seeking to escape the ecological disaster on the island.

Tambora's eruption, however, did not just affect the island of Sumbawa. Ash fell primarily to the west of Sumbawa. On Lombok and Bali, ash fall collapsed roofs and again brought famine and disease from lack of clean water. On Lombok, an estimated 44,000 to 100,000 people died, and at least 25,000 died on Bali. As many as 100,000 people migrated to the island of Java, but the mass migration led to conflicts in the densely populated villages when the refugees reached their destinations. Even more deaths occurred as a result of violence. A conservative estimate of the death toll in Indonesia at minimum is 117,000 people.

Tambora is perhaps best known for its wide-reaching climatic effects. Sulfuric-acid aerosols and dust particles were carried into the stratosphere by the cataclysmic eruptions in April 1815. These particulates caused weather changes around the world as the eruption cloud spread. Major floods occurred in China during the summer of 1816. In India, the summer monsoons were delayed until September. Rice and other grains became scarce, and India, Bangladesh, and northwestern India (which today is Pakistan) suffered famine.

In Europe, a two- to three-year period of weather extremes followed the eruption. The summers of 1816 and 1817 were cooler and wetter than usual across the entire continent. Reddish or brownish snow, colored by volcanic dust in the atmosphere, fell as far south as southern Italy, but alpine areas in France, Switzerland, and Austria were hit the hardest. Growing seasons were shortened considerably, leading to crop failures and famine. Coming on the heels of the Napoleonic Wars, which already had taxed people to their limits—particularly in France and Germany—the effects of the Tambora eruption were catastrophic. Grain shortages claimed thousands of lives and caused the price of basic foods to skyrocket, especially in the cities. Harvests also failed in Ireland, and a typhus epidemic claimed many more lives. The number of people in Europe who died from the disaster is estimated to be 100,000.

Northeastern North America also was affected by these temporary climate changes. In New England 1816 was known as "the year without a summer." Unlike Europe, North America experienced dry conditions. As in Europe, temperatures were unusually cold, however, and killing frosts occurred throughout the summer. Growing seasons were shortened by 50% as far south as Massachusetts. Struggling farmers could do nothing but watch as their crops either froze or died from lack of rainfall. Many of these farmers gave up and moved westward where weather conditions were more stable.

It is important to note that in the early 1800s no one yet was able to correlate the eruption of a volcano in Indonesia to the climatic disruptions occurring elsewhere. It was not until decades later—after the eruption of Krakatau in 1883—that people realized an eruption in Indonesia could have such wide-reaching consequences. In the case of Krakatau, the effects were not nearly so severe or deadly as those from the eruption of Tambora. People in Europe and eastern North America noted brilliant sunsets—often including odd colors such as green and blue were seen. Although a very small drop in temperature occurred after the eruption of Krakatau, very few deaths outside of the immediate eruption area can be traced back to Krakatau, and those were almost entirely due to ash inhalation by people downwind of the volcano.

In addition to the deaths caused by starvation, hunger and malnutrition weakened affected populations, making them more susceptible to disease. Clean water became scarce, as it was contaminated by volcanic ash and acids from the eruption. A major outbreak of cholera occurred in India's Ganges River valley in 1816. The epidemic ravaged the Indian population and then spread to Nepal and Afghanistan, likely through British soldiers that were performing military operations in that area. Additionally, Muslim pilgrimages spread the epidemic farther west to the Arabian peninsula. The epidemic's spread slowed, but by 1823 cholera had reached the shores of the Caspian Sea. By 1830 it had reached Moscow, and in 1831 Cairo lost 12% of its population to cholera. Members of the Russian military spread the disease westward to Poland, and then the disease spread as far west as France. In 1832, immigrants leaving Europe carried the disease to North America and there were outbreaks in Montreal and New York City. Although it might be overreaching to attribute deaths from cholera in North America in 1832 to the eruption in Indonesia in 1815, the eruption no doubt caused hundreds of thousands of deaths from direct effects of the eruption as well as worldwide instances of crop failure, starvation, and disease.

If any good came of the eruption of Tambora, it came in the area of literature. During the summer of 1816, Percy Bysshe Shelley and his wife Mary rented a cottage on Lake Geneva in Switzerland. Lord Byron was staying nearby, and he and the Shelleys often spent time together during the summer. It was a wet, rainy summer and they were confined to the house for days on end. They found several volumes of ghost stories, which inspired a challenge for Percy Shelley, Mary Shelly, and Lord Byron to each write a ghost story of their own. From this summer exercise came Mary Shelley's classic novel, *Frankenstein*.

See Also: Indonesia; Pyroclastic Flow; Toba Eruption, Indonesia.

Further Reading

Francis, P., & Oppenheimer, C. (2004). *Volcanoes* (2nd ed.). Oxford: Oxford University Press.

Sigurdsson, H., Houghton, B., Rymer, H., Stix, J. & McNutt, S. (Eds.). (2000). *Encyclopedia of volcanoes*. San Diego, CA: Academic Press.

Zeilinga de Boer, J., & Sanders, D. T. (2002). *Volcanoes in human history*. Princeton, NJ: Princeton University Press.

Tangshan Earthquake, China (1976)

China's Tangshan earthquake of 1976 was the deadliest of the Twentieth Century. When the earthquake struck, the city of Tangshan was leveled, and more than 200,000 people died. It took more than a decade to rebuild, but today Tangshan's glass and concrete factories are thriving, and the population is larger than it was before the earthquake.

Odd things started happening in Tangshan on the day before the earthquake—the water level in wells rose and fell, animals acted strangely, and unusual lights and sounds were reported. On July 28, 1976, at 3:48 a.m., the earthquake struck. Measuring 7.8 on the Richter scale, the quake's epicenter was seven miles below the city, and the earthquake lasted between 14 and 16 seconds. The earthquake's timing increased its deadliness; most of the city's residents were asleep when the earthquake struck, therefore few people had a chance to protect themselves. Additionally, immediate rescue efforts were hampered by the early morning darkness and the loss of electricity, due to the earthquake.

That darkness also hid the scope of the earthquake's destruction. When daylight arrived, it revealed that 93% of residential structures and 78% of industrial buildings were destroyed. The majority of the city's water stations were damaged, as were many of its sewage pipes. Bridges collapsed, railroad lines were bent, and the roads were all cracked and buckled. Even if the hospitals hadn't been destroyed, it would have been nearly impossible to reach them. The one navigable road into Tangshan quickly was clogged by the relief workers' traffic.

The citizens of Tangshan quickly took charge of the situation. They set up areas to treat the wounded and searched for food, water, and medical supplies. People dug through the rubble to free any survivors and eventually rescued 80% of people who had been trapped. Those who had been killed were buried near where they had been found. This later caused problems when rain exposed the bodies, creating a health hazard. Workers had to find and exhume these victims before reburying them outside the city. That afternoon there was an aftershock that registered 7.1 on the Richter scale.

Left-wing leaders in China's government saw the earthquake as an opportunity to show their strength. They refused aid from international relief organizations and launched a campaign with the slogan "Resist the Earthquake, Rescue Ourselves." Doctors and soldiers traveled from all over the country to tend to the wounded. Many of the 150,000 people who were severely injured were evacuated to hospitals in other cities. Thousands of children who had been orphaned were sheltered by provincial governments.

The "official" death toll of the Tangshan earthquake is 250,000 people, although historians think that the number actually is closer to half a million people.

A Case of Earthquake Prediction: Haicheng, China

The one and only case in history in which an earthquake has been predicted and evacuation orders were issued is the earthquake that hit Haicheng, China, on February 4, 1975. In the previous several months, constant monitoring had revealed subtle ground deformation, as well as anomalies in water wells that included changes in water level, color, and chemistry. A series of foreshocks and strange animal behavior triggered a county-level evacuation order on the day of the earthquake. Evacuation of the city of Haicheng likely saved thousands of lives because the homes and businesses in the area were built of masonry and many of those buildings collapsed during the magnitude 7.3 earthquake that occurred.

It took more than a decade to rebuild the city, which has since been called a model of the Chinese people's resourcefulness. In Chinese tradition, disasters such as the Tangshan earthquake are believed to signal the end of a dynasty. In 1976, at the time of the earthquake, Mao Zedong—the leader of the People's Republic of China—was bedridden. Many citizens believed that the earthquake was a sign that Mao Zedong's days were numbered, although the communist regime scorned such superstitions. Mao died just six weeks after the earthquake.

See Also: Earthquake.

Further Reading

Chen, Yong. (1988). *The great Tangshan earthquake of 1976: An anatomy of disaster.* New York: Pergamon Press. Retrieved from TimeAsia. http://www.time.com/time/asia/index.html

Taupo Volcano, New Zealand

The Taupo Volcano is a super volcano located on New Zealand's North Island. It formed as a result of subduction of the Pacific Plate beneath the Australian Plate. The volcano has a poorly defined footprint, but is dominated by a 22-mile (35-kilometer) wide caldera that contains Lake Taupo, which is New Zealand's largest lake. The Taupo Volcano is approximately 300,000 years old. The most recent "super eruption" from the volcano occurred about 27,000 years ago, emptying a large portion of the magma chamber beneath the volcano and creating the large caldera. Many of the pyroclastic flows erupted during that eruption were hot enough to re-melt and become a rock called a "welded tuff," also known as a "welded ignimbrite." The dominant magma type erupted at Taupo is rhyolite.

The most recent eruption of Taupo occurred about 1,800 years ago and is counted among the most violent of eruptions within the last 5,000 years. The complex eruption produced a series of five pumice and ash fall deposits from an eruption column that rose to an altitude of 31 miles (50 kilometers) and covered all of New Zealand with at least 0.4 inches (1 centimeter) of ash. Taupo then erupted a high-energy pyroclastic flow that filled surrounding river valleys with pumice and ash. All areas near the lake were covered in pyroclastic flows 328 feet (100 meters) thick, which traveled up to 55 miles (90 kilometers) from the vent and covered all local features with the exception of the nearby mountain Ruapehu. Deposits from this eruption blocked the outlet of Lake Taupo, and caused the lake to rise more than 110 feet (34 meters). When the natural dam broke, a catastrophic flood moved down the Waikato River. Scientists speculate that the "red sunsets" described by people in China and Rome at that time were caused by the eruption of Taupo. Between the eruptions of 27,000 years ago and 1,800 years ago, at least 26 additional eruptions created lava domes and spread ash and pumice over the landscape.

Geothermal field in Taupo Volcanic Zone, New Zealand. (Westend61 / Valentin Weinhäupl/ Newscom)

One of the most prominent of these lava domes is Mount Tauhara, located near the shore of Lake Taupo.

The volcano is monitored using seven seismometers together with continuous monitoring of ground deformation by lake-level indicators and six global positioning system (GPS) stations. Scientists think that—before Taupo erupts again—the volcano will give ample warning in the form of increased earthquake activity, large-scale ground deformation, and increased activity of geothermal areas including likely phreatic eruptions. Although eruptions at rhyolitic calderas are violent, they also are relatively rare occurrences. The next violent eruption of Taupo is likely thousands of years away. It is much more likely that the next few eruptions will be the less dangerous dome-building eruptions.

See Also: Pyroclastic Flow; Rhyolite; Subduction Zone; Supervolcano.

Further Reading

GeoNet. (2014, June 5). *Taupo*. Retrieved from http://info.geonet.org.nz/display/volc /Taupo

GNS Science. (2014, June 5). *Taupo Volcano*. Retrieved from http://www.gns.cri.nz/Home /Learning/Science-Topics/Volcanoes/New-Zealand-Volcanoes/Taupo-Volcano

Smithsonian Institution. National Museum of Natural History. Global Volcanism Program. (2014, June 5). *Taupo*. Retrieved from http://www.volcano.si.edu/volcano.cfm?vn=241070

Toba Eruption, Indonesia

The largest volcanic eruption to occur during human history to date is that of Toba, a very large caldera located on the Indonesian island of Sumbawa. The eruption occurred roughly 74,000 years ago, ejecting approximately 670 cubic miles (2,800 cubic kilometers) of volcanic debris into the atmosphere and onto the surrounding landscape. The eruption site itself is fully re-vegetated, and much of the airborne debris ended up in the ocean. At sites where geologists have been able to investigate deposits, however, they find multiple thick layers of pyroclastic debris. This leads to the conclusion that the eruption occurred in multiple phases—perhaps over a series of hours, days, or weeks—with short breaks between the phases. When the volcano collapsed, it left a caldera 53 miles (85 kilometers) long and 15.5 miles (25 kilometers) wide, with cliffs more than 4,900 feet (1,200 meters) high. Today, the caldera houses the largest lake in Indonesia, Danau [Lake] Toba. In some places, the lake is more than 1,700 feet (530 meters) deep.

The eruption likely produced a column of pyroclastic material that reached altitudes of nearly 100,000 feet (30 kilometers), which is well into the stratosphere. The island of Sumbawa was blanketed with several meters of volcanic ash and other pyroclastic debris such as pumice, lapilli, and bombs. The eruptive cloud spread laterally and dropped significant quantities of ash over both the southern Indian Ocean and South China Sea. In a location 1,500 miles (2,400 kilometers) from Toba, in sediments on the bottom of the Indian Ocean, researchers have found a layer of ash from this eruption that is 12 inches (30 centimeters) thick.

In addition to millions of tons of solid debris, the volcano also produced many thousands of tons of gases. Sulfuric acid is well-known for becoming aerosolized. The aerosols from this eruption also were carried upward into the stratosphere, along with volcanic ash and dust. Together these materials were swept around the globe. The result was what scientists have dubbed a "volcanic winter." Aerosols and ash particles blocked sunlight and warming radiation from the earth's surface. Globally, temperatures dropped by an average of 18 degrees Fahrenheit (10 degrees Celsius). This volcanic winter could have lasted up to seven years, and would have had a devastating effect on vegetation, and thus on all life on earth. This amount of cooling slows or prevents pollen and flower formation in some plants, deactivates the process of photosynthesis in other plants, and inhibits the growth of most plants. Temperate to sub-Arctic evergreen forests would have been reduced by about half, and temperate vegetation would have fared even worse. Without these plants available for food, animal populations crashed. Humans appear to have fared no better. This was truly a global ecological disaster. The eruption also corresponds roughly with the onset of the last great cold period of the final ice age.

Genetic studies have been used to estimate the size of human populations throughout history. At some time prior to 60,000 years ago, there was a drastic reduction in the number of humans on the planet. The human population was reduced to perhaps 4,000 to 10,000 individuals, producing what researchers have termed a "bottleneck" in the human population that lasted for nearly 20,000 years. The timing is such that some researchers postulate that the Toba eruption and ensuing volcanic winter could have been to blame for reducing the population.

See Also: Indonesia; Pyroclastic Materials; Volcanic Hazards.

Further Reading

Rampino, M. R., & Ambrose, S. H. (2000). *Volcanic winter in the Garden of Eden: The Toba supereruption and the late Pleistocene human population crash.* Geological Society of America (Special Paper 345).

Sigurdsson, H., Houghton, B., Rymer, H., Stix, J., & McNutt, S. (Eds.). (2000). *Encyclopedia of volcanoes.* San Diego, CA: Academic Press.

Zeilinga de Boer, J., and Sanders, D.T. (2002). *Volcanoes in human history.* Princeton, NJ: Princeton University Press.

Tonga

The Tonga Islands lie on the eastern edge of the Australian Plate in the southern Pacific Ocean. Here, the Pacific Plate is subducting beneath the Australian Plate, generating many strong to severe earthquakes and producing a volcanic island arc that geologists call the "Tonga Arc." The subduction zone is marked by the Tonga Trench. There have been dozens of magnitude 7 or greater earthquakes in the vicinity of Tonga since the year 1900. Because the Tonga Islands lie very close to the actual subduction zone, earthquakes of all depths occur nearby. The shallowest earthquakes generally occur closest to the subduction zone, and those earthquakes get deeper farther west as the subducting slab angles downward below the Australian Plate. Most of the largest earthquakes in the region in the last 100 years have occurred at intermediate to deep depths within the earth—generally more than 93 miles (150 kilometers). Significant shallow earthquakes, however, are neither unheard of nor impossible. In 2009, for instance, a magnitude 7.6 earthquake occurred at a depth of 21.1 miles (34 kilometers); it did not cause any fatalities.

Tonga is an island nation that owes its existence to volcanism. Many of the nation's islands still have active volcanoes, as does much of the sea floor between the islands. Tonga's typical volcano is a composite volcano consisting of andesite or dacite. Several of the volcanoes are large and also have summit calderas. Since 2000, there have been three eruptions of note. The Tofua caldera began erupting in 2004 and continued into 2013. The eruption issued from a small crater inside the rim of the caldera, and plumes of ash and steam periodically rose several thousand feet above the island. In 2006, the submarine volcano "Home Reef" erupted, creating a large pumice raft that was encountered and documented by yachtsmen traversing the area. The pumice raft eventually washed ashore in Australia. The third eruption occurred at Hunga Tonga–Hunga Haapai, another submarine volcano that has its summit just above the surface of the ocean. The submarine caldera of the volcano was the location of the eruption, but the caldera's two islands, Hunga Tonga and Hunga Haapai, give the volcano its name. The eruption consisted of a large column of ash and steam that rose to an altitude of between 13,000 and 17,000 feet (4 to 5.2 kilometers) above the sea. The plume emanated from near the base of the island Hunga Haapai.

See Also: Australian Plate; Pacific Plate; Subduction Zone.

Further Reading

Smithsonian Institution. National Museum of Natural History. Global Volcanism Program. (2014, June 19). Retrieved from http://www.volcano.si.edu/

U.S. Geological Survey. (2014, June 19). *Historic World Earthquakes. New Zealand.* Retrieved from http://earthquake.usgs.gov/earthquakes/world/historical_country.php &new_zealand

Transform Boundary

A transform boundary is a tectonic feature defined as any place where two plates slide laterally past each other. Transform boundaries are incredibly common. They typically are found in association with divergent plate boundaries, where those boundaries are broken into discontinuous segments. They occasionally are present where subduction zones are broken into segments, but this is somewhat rare. Transform boundaries often experience shallow earthquakes, and some of these can be rather violent. They are not known for producing tsunamis, however, because they do not generally produce an appreciable amount of vertical motion. No volcanic activity typically is associated with transform boundaries, but this is not a hard-and-fast rule. If there is oblique (diagonal) motion, then the plate boundary could be stretching just enough to thin the crust and produce minor amounts of volcanism. In most cases, however, the diagonal motion simply produces hills (if it is convergent) or basins (if it is divergent). Death Valley, California, is an example of a landscape produced at a divergent transform boundary. A bend in the plate boundary has produced a situation in which the plates are moving away from each other diagonally, producing the basin that is Death Valley.

The Mid-Atlantic Ridge is a divergent boundary located in the center of the Atlantic Ocean. This is the boundary between the North American Plate and South American Plate to the west, and the African Plate and Eurasian Plate to the east. The earth is spherical, thus the plate boundary has broken into a number of parallel segments. The faults—or plate boundaries—that connect these segments are transform boundaries. These transform boundaries give the Mid-Atlantic Ridge an appearance similar to the stitching on a baseball. All other mid-ocean ridges also are divided into segments that are connected by transform boundaries, therefore all of the earth's spreading centers share this "stitch-like" appearance.

The best-known transform boundary in the western hemisphere is the San Andreas Fault. Not only is the San Andreas a fault, it also is a transform boundary between the Pacific Plate, to the west, and the North American Plate, to the east. The Pacific Plate is moving northwest relative to the North American Plate. The two plates slide laterally past each other. Although people commonly talk about part of California falling off into the ocean because of the San Andreas Fault, this is not California's future. Instead, the Pacific Plate will continue to move north-westward and carry the land areas to the west of the fault with it. In roughly 80 million years, Los Angeles will become a suburb of San Francisco. Then—as the land area that contains Los Angeles moves past San Francisco—the sliver of land that today is southwestern California will end up as a long, narrow island moving northwestward toward Alaska. Eventually, if plate motions continue as they are today, it will be subducted beneath the Aleutian Islands.

See Also: Divergent Boundary; Plate Tectonics; San Andreas Fault; Subduction Zone.

Further Reading

Kearey, P., Klepeis, K. A., & Vine, F. J. (2009). *Global tectonics* (3rd ed.). Hoboken, NJ: Wiley-Blackwell.

Tarbuck, E. J., Lutgens, F. K., & Tasa, D. (2011). *Earth: An introduction to physical geology* (10th ed.). Upper Saddle River, NJ: Pearson Prentice Hall/Pearson Education, Inc.

Tsunami

The word "tsunami" is Japanese in origin; "tsu" means harbor and "nami" means wave. This name is particularly fitting because tsunamis can become violent and deadly as they approach shallow water near the shoreline. They have the ability to reach terrifying heights and can rush inland for miles as they travel up river valleys. Tsunamis often are mistakenly referred to as "tidal waves." The term "tidal" refers to the daily movements of the earth's waters due to the gravitational effect of the sun and moon. Tsunamis are completely unaffected by the sun or moon, therefore they cannot correctly be called tidal waves. They are an altogether different phe-nomenon from the wind-driven waves seen at beaches and the twice-daily ebb and flow of the tides. Tsunamis are created by a severe disturbance of the ocean floor that causes displacement of a great volume of water. As the water tries to attain gravitational equilibrium, a tsunami can be generated.

Tsunamis have a number of interesting traits, some of which are surprising. They are markedly different from any other type of wave, current, or tidal motion that exists. One major attribute is that they have the ability to travel across an entire ocean. A tsunami generated on the west coast of South America, for example, has

A fisherman in the western Solomon Islands points to a scene where his mother-in-law and a baby were found following a 2007 earthquake and tsunami. (Kyodo News/Newscom)

the ability to impact coastal areas throughout the entire Pacific region. In the open ocean, tsunamis travel at speeds approaching that of a modern jet plane—in excess of 500 miles per hour (800 kilometers per hour). Another feature is that their energy is distributed throughout the entire depth of the ocean. In contrast, the energy associated with wind-driven waves is limited to the top 30 to 60 feet (10 to 20 meters) of the ocean, except in cases of high winds such as those occurring with hurricanes. Wave motion rarely occurs below a depth of 60 feet. Because the energy of a tsunami reaches from the surface to the ocean floor, on the open ocean tsunamis are imperceptible. Even the most energetic of tsunami waves can pass under a ship without those on board being aware of its existence. It is only when the wave approaches shore that the energy is compacted into a shorter column of water and causes water levels to rise.

Tsunamis are not necessarily large, damaging waves. A wave that is generated by an underwater disturbance and travels outward away from that disturbance with energy distributed throughout the entirety of the water column is a tsunami, regardless of how high the wave is when it reaches shore. It also is worth noting that tsunamis do not often come ashore as towering walls of water; they often come ashore like a rapidly rising tide. However, they also can first appear at a shoreline in the form of a quickly withdrawing wave. In many cases, witnesses describe the sea retreating several hundred yards, leaving the sea floor, coral, fish, and other organisms exposed. This can be a lure too difficult to resist for people unfamiliar with its meaning; there are many stories of people rushing out from the shore to retrieve fish, only to be drowned by the wave as it approaches too quickly for them to escape. Tsunamis routinely travel at speeds of 55 miles per hour (90 kilometers per hour) as they move onshore. Water overtakes everything in a tsunami's path.

Lastly, a single tsunami is an event that often lasts several hours. It is not a single wave that washes ashore and then retreats; rather, it is a series of waves. There is no way to know how many waves there will be in a series, nor which of the waves will be most damaging. If a tsunami warning has been issued, it is safest to remain on higher ground away from the coast for several hours, and until the all-clear is given. Returning to the coast after the first wave passes is extremely dangerous.

The most common cause of tsunamis is sea-floor earthquakes, particularly those that occur at shallow depths along subduction zones. Vertical disturbances—such as those occurring in subduction zone earthquakes—are most efficient at producing tsunamis; but not all shallow subduction zone earthquakes are capable of producing tsunamis. Scientists only become concerned about a possible tsunami when the magnitude of an earthquake approaches 7.0. Earthquakes that are less than a magnitude 7.0 generally do not produce sufficient movement along the fault to displace enough water to form a tsunami. In general, greater magnitude earthquakes are more likely to produce tsunamis than are lower magnitude earthquakes. The deadliest tsunami in recorded history occurred in 2004 as a result of a magnitude 9.1 earthquake that occurred off the west coast of Sumatra, Indonesia. Nearly 228,000 people died in 14 countries around the Indian Ocean.

Another well-known cause of tsunamis is landslides. The landslide can occur fully underwater, or could begin on land and send material into the water. The leading cause of underwater landslides is major earthquakes. For this reason, occasionally earthquakes that approach magnitude 7.0 can produce tsunamis because of the combined effect of minor displacement of the rocks of the ocean floor by the

How Do I Become a Tsunami Scientist?

Scientists that study tsunamis must be well-versed in mathematics and physics, and must have a strong working knowledge of the properties and behavior of the ocean. For those reasons, typical degrees sought by students who wish to study tsunamis include physics, mathematics, geophysics, marine geology, and oceanography. Following a four-year degree, most future tsunami scientists pursue an advanced degree (master's or Ph.D.). For something as specialized as tsunami studies at the graduate level, it is critical for a student to choose a university that has at least one faculty member who is an expert in some aspect of tsunamis. The student takes courses and conducts research with this faculty member to gain expertise in tsunamis. Upon graduation, the scientist is ready to pursue a career studying tsunamis professionally—either as a professor at a university or as a research scientist at a government agency responsible for monitoring the oceans for tsunamis, such as the National Oceanic and Atmospheric Association (NOAA), or the United States Geological Survey (USGS).

earthquake and a large volume of sediment moving downhill on the ocean floor during a landslide. A tsunami in Papua New Guinea in 1998 was generated in this manner. A magnitude 7.1 earthquake struck near the village of Aitape. Beginning approximately 13 minutes after the earthquake, a series of three waves inundated the shoreline with water that reached heights of up to 50 feet (15 meters). Approximately 2,200 people died and three villages were completely destroyed. This was a completely unexpected outcome of the earthquake, because magnitude 7 earthquakes do not usually produce such large and powerful tsunamis.

The largest known tsunamis have occurred as a result of landslides that began at least partially on land, and have sent material into the ocean. The 1958 Lituya Bay, Alaska, tsunami was generated immediately after a magnitude 8.0 earthquake occurred near the bay. The earthquake caused a massive landslide which created a tsunami that reached a height of 1,720 feet (425 meters). Large submarine landslides that have cleaved vast swaths of land from the Hawaiian Islands have yielded similar results. Although these tsunamis have been unbelievably large in the areas near where they were generated, the waves quickly lost momentum and were considerably smaller even relatively close to their sources.

A third cause of tsunamis is collapse of a volcano into the ocean during the course of an eruption. The most familiar case of this type of tsunami is that of the collapse of the volcano Krakatau into the Sunda Strait between the Indonesian islands of Java and Sumatra. As the volcano collapsed inward upon itself, seawater rushed to fill the area that had been occupied by the island. The waves created during this event obliterated all coastal villages on the shorelines facing the Strait, and killed an estimated 36,000 people. Prior to the 2004 Indian Ocean tsunami, this was the most deadly tsunami in recorded history. Although rare enough that it has not happened in the course of human history, a fourth cause of tsunamis is meteorite impact.

See Also: Hawaiian Islands; Indian Ocean Earthquake and Tsunami (2004); Krakatau Eruption (also known as "Krakatoa" Eruption), Indonesia (1883); Subduction Zone.

Further Reading

Davies, H. L., Davies, J. M., Lus, W. Y., Perembo, R. C. B., Joku, N., Gedikile, H., & Nongkas, M. (2014, November 3). *Learning from the Aitape tsunami.* Retrieved from http://nctr.pmel.noaa.gov/PNG/Upng/Learned/

Moore, J. G., Bryan, W. B., & Ludwig, K. R. (1994). Chaotic deposition by a giant wave, Molokai, Hawaii. *Geological Society of America Bulletin 106*, 962–967.

Tarbuck, E. J., Lutgens, F. K., & Tasa, D. (2011). *Earth: An introduction to physical geology* (10th ed.). Upper Saddle River, NJ: Pearson Prentice Hall/Pearson Education, Inc.

University of Southern California. Tsunami Research Group. (2014, November 3). *1958 Lituya Bay Tsunami.* Retrieved from http://www.usc.edu/dept/tsunamis/alaska/1958/webpages/

U.S. Geological Survey. Earthquake Hazards Program. (2004). *Magnitude 9.1—Off the west coast of northern Sumatra.* Retrieved from http://earthquake.usgs.gov/earthquakes/eqinthenews/2004/ us2004slav/#summary

Tsunami Warning Centers

The nature of tsunamis is such that a large earthquake can occur on one side of the Pacific Ocean and generate a tsunami that travels across the entire Pacific to create large and damaging waves thousands of miles from its site of origin. This situation has happened repeatedly throughout history, and has caused thousands of deaths from distant earthquake events. In an effort to prevent deaths from occurring on distant shores due to ocean-wide tsunamis, tsunami warning centers have been created. The first of these was the Pacific Tsunami Warning Center in Ewa Beach, Hawaii, on the island of Oahu. The Pacific Tsunami Warning Center was created by the United States government after the widespread destruction and dozens of deaths throughout the Hawaiian Islands caused by a 1946 earthquake and tsunami at Unimak Island in the Aleutians. This installation began issuing warnings in 1949. After unsuccessful warnings in Hawaii in 1960 following the Chilean earthquake and tsunami (1960), and as many as 200 deaths in Japan from the same event, the governments of the Pacific Rim began cooperating through the United Nations to contribute data to—and receive official warnings from—the Pacific Tsunami Warning Center. Today, multiple agencies have been established worldwide to issue official tsunami warnings in response to earthquakes that occur within their jurisdictions.

The first attempts at tsunami warnings came in the early 1900s from Dr. Thomas Jaggar. Founder of the Hawaiian Volcano Observatory, Jaggar was its director until his retirement in 1940. Dr. Jaggar had a handful of seismometers in his possession at the observatory, and these recorded large distant earthquakes in addition to the small volcanic earthquakes he was trying to detect on the volcano. Jaggar knew that seismic waves from large earthquakes could traverse the entire earth and show up on his seismograms within a few short minutes. A few brief calculations enabled him to estimate how long it might take a tsunami to travel to Hawaii, giving Dr. Jaggar not only information that a tsunami could be headed his direction, but also about when it might arrive. Dr. Jaggar gave his first warning to the harbormaster at Hilo, Hawaii, in 1923, following the devastating Great Kanto earthquake. He heard news reports of the level of devastation that occurred in and near Tokyo and knew that the earthquake was large enough to produce a Pacific-wide tsunami. Although Dr. Jaggar issued a warning, his method was untested and no official channel of communication or response plan had been devised or implemented. His warning went unheeded, and there was a great deal of damage done to fishing and cargo boats in the Hilo harbor. Coastal infrastructure including a rail line and wharves were damaged, and at least one person was killed. Dr. Jaggar's warning was ignored at the time, but it showed that it was possible to forecast the arrival of a tsunami on a distant shoreline.

Following this early failure of the warning system, there were a number of small successes. In one instance in 1933, Jaggar issued a warning and people in coastal areas prepared. Cargo was removed from docks, fishing vessels were anchored in deep water, and people moved away from the shorelines. As a result not a single life was lost when the tsunami came ashore. Damage to ships and cargo also was minimized. Why, then, were so many lives lost in the Hawaiian Islands in

1946 and 1960? In the early days of tsunami warnings, it was impossible to tell with any certainty whether a tsunami had been generated and, if so, how large it was. All warnings were based solely on seismic records. In short, tsunami warnings were issued for tsunamis that either never came or were so small that they were completely harmless. People grew complacent after so many false alarms. A new system had to be devised to minimize the false alarms.

System designers came up with a plan that included both more data and more steps to the process. When a large and damaging earthquake of magnitude 7.0 or greater was observed, a tsunami watch was issued immediately and automatically. Tide gauges and trained observers across the Pacific region were asked to report data to the Pacific Tsunami Warning Center. With additional data, information about the size of the tsunami—if one had indeed been generated—could be determined. This revised information then was used to issue a tsunami warning if appropriate, or to cancel the tsunami watch if necessary. Later, ocean-floor sensors were created that monitor sea level very precisely. Any data reflecting fluctuations of the sea level following a major earthquake are used to further refine tsunami warnings. The modern system of ocean-floor sensors and associated surface buoys is called the DART II system. DART stands for Deep-ocean Assessment and Reporting of Tsunamis. Sea-bottom sensors detect pressure changes that correlate to sea level changes. Data are radioed to a surface buoy, and the surface buoy communicates with the appropriate tsunami warning center via satellite communications. As soon as the data are recorded, they are available to the scientists at the warning center to be integrated into forecasts.

Today, several tsunami warning centers exist. The Pacific Tsunami Warning Center has responsibility for issuing warnings for Pacific-wide tsunamis as well as locally generated tsunamis in the Hawaii region and the South China Sea. The West Coast and Alaska Tsunami Warning Center is responsible for issuing tsunami warnings to California, Oregon, Washington, Canada, and Alaska for local tsunamis in those locations. Other tsunami warning centers exist for Australia, the Caribbean, Japan, the Mediterranean, the Northeastern Atlantic, and the Philippines.

See Also: Chilean Earthquake and Tsunami (1960); Earthquake Hazards; Earthquake Magnitude; Great Kanto Earthquake, Japan (1923); Hawaiian Islands; Tsunami; Unimak Island Earthquake and Tsunami, Alaska, United States (1946).

Further Reading

Dudley, W. C., & Lee, M. (1998). *Tsunami!* (2nd ed.). Honolulu: University of Hawaii Press.
National Oceanic and Atmospheric Association. Jet Stream—Online School for Weather. (2014, May 20). *Monitoring tsunamis*. Retrieved from http://www.srh.noaa.gov/jet-stream/tsunami/dart.htm
National Oceanic and Atmospheric Association. Pacific Tsunami Warning Center. (2014, May 20). *PTWC history*. Retrieved from http://ptwc.weather.gov/ptwc/history.php
Pararas-Carayannis, G. (1986). The Pacific Tsunami Warning System. *Earthquakes & Volcanoes 18* (3), 122–130.

U

Unimak Island Earthquake and Tsunami, Alaska, United States (1946)

Unimak Island is a remote outpost, the first island in the Aleutian chain which extends from the Alaska Peninsula, 1,800 miles (2,900 kilometers) westward toward the Kamchatka Peninsula of Russia. Unimak is one of the largest islands in the Aleutians and is home to five volcanoes—Roundtop, Isanotski, Shishaldin, Fisher, and Westdahl. The largest and most active of these volcanoes is Shishaldin, which was erupting at the time of this writing, in 2014. Unimak is one of hundreds of islands in the Aleutians, all of which were formed by a combination of volcanic activity and upwarping of the sea floor just north of the Aleutian Trench. Here, the Pacific Plate is subducting beneath the North American Plate at a rate of roughly 2.4 inches (6 centimeters) per year. Subduction leads to volcanic activity, intense compression and upwarping of existing sea floor rocks, and frequent earthquakes. As in other subduction zones around the world, the earthquakes here can be large and damaging.

Unimak Island today has one settlement, a town called "False Pass" located on the eastern tip of the island nearest the Alaska Peninsula. The Scotch Cap Lighthouse was located on the western tip of the island, standing guard at the dangerous approach to Unimak Pass. It had a crew of five Coast Guard members. The lighthouse was 98 feet (30 meters) tall, rising from a foundation that was 46 feet (14 meters) above sea level. The building was sturdy—built of reinforced concrete to withstand the harsh weather. Above the lighthouse on a bluff was another Coast Guard installation, a D/F (direction finding) station, also manned by a handful of Coast Guard personnel. At approximately 1:30 a.m. local time on April 1, 1946, both installations reported feeling a large earthquake that lasted 30 to 40 seconds. Those manning the structures were somewhat unnerved by the experience, but they spoke on the phone and confirmed that even though the shaking was severe, there was no damage to their respective buildings. Approximately 30 minutes later, another, larger earthquake struck. Again, phone conversations between staffers at the two buildings were full of assurances that the buildings were sound and undamaged. At that time, none of them knew that the second earthquake, a magnitude 8.1, had triggered an underwater landslide and a massive tsunami.

The Aleutian Trench—the location of the earthquake's epicenter—lay 90 miles (145 kilometers) to the south. In the open ocean, the tsunami traveled outward from its point of origin at several hundred miles per hour. As the wave approached shore, friction between the water and the ocean floor slowed the bottom of the wave as the top continued rapidly forward. Twenty-one minutes after the larger second earthquake, the crew of the D/F station at the top of the cliff heard a deafening roar. As it reached a volume many would later compare to that of a sonic boom, a wave hit the station with enormous force. This caused considerable damage to the building, and the station chief ordered his crew to evacuate to higher ground. As the crew was scrambling uphill, one of the men looked down and saw that the light from the lighthouse had been extinguished. The crew also realized that the foghorn was silent. The commanding officer of the D/F station was unable to make radio contact with the crew of Scotch Cap Lighthouse, and broadcast that he believed the lighthouse was lost; however, it was impossible to know with any certainty at that time, because it was night. Additional tsunami waves pounded the shoreline at regular intervals until a few hours later. At about 3 a.m., the D/F station's commanding officer ordered the crew to return to the station to rig emergency lights, get more clothing, and gather canned goods.

At dawn, the D/F station crew crept to the edge of the cliff and looked down. The lighthouse had been completely destroyed. Twisted steel girders and shattered concrete were all that remained. Debris was scattered for hundreds of yards along the shoreline, and it took the station crew members several days before they found the remains of two lighthouse crew members, far from the lighthouse's foundation. The other three men were presumably washed out to sea; their bodies were never found. The tsunami claimed its first five lives within twenty minutes of its formation, but those would not be its last victims.

The tsunami traveled outward in all directions, but the brunt of its energy traveled south at an average velocity of 490 miles (790 kilometers) per hour, arriving in the Hawaiian Islands just after sunrise. The first wave struck Kauai at 5:55 a.m. on April 1, 1946. There, several men had already started work at the McBryde Sugar Company. One suggested they go watch the tsunami come in from the top of a cliff. Thinking it was an April Fool's joke, the workers all went to see. The sea had retreated, leaving the ocean floor exposed. They stood and watched, mesmerized, as water flowed back into the bay and up the valley. When the water retreated again, the group climbed down to the floor of the bay to investigate. They kept an eye on the ocean, however, and were able to return to the top of the cliff before the water came back.

Waves reached Oahu just after 6:30 a.m. The pilot of a patrol plane radioed to Kaneohe Air Base that something was on the surface of the ocean. It looked like a line or a small wave. When he was asked to descend for a better look, the pilot informed the radio operator that the phenomenon had outrun his aircraft and was gone. The radio operator's friends assured him it was an April Fool's joke.

People on the north shore of Oahu experienced the wave as they were waking and preparing for the day. Dr. Francis Sheppard, a marine geologist with Scripps Institute of Oceanography, was staying in a beach cottage with his wife. They were awakened by a loud hissing sound, which he likened to dozens of locomotives blowing off steam directly outside the house. The doctor and his wife jumped out of bed and saw water boiling to the top of a 10-foot ridge between them and the ocean, then heading directly toward the house. Dr. Sheppard instantly recognized what was happening. As the wave subsided, he told his wife there were likely to be other waves. Not having experienced a tsunami before, however, the doctor erroneously told his wife that the later waves would not be as large as the one they had just observed. They were surprised to see the second wave advance and grow taller than the last. The wave passed through the house, picking up the refrigerator and depositing it in the cane field behind the cottage. The second wave subsided and the Sheppards decided to move to higher ground. A few more waves came and went. After the sixth wave, Mrs. Sheppard stayed on the elevated road behind the house, but Dr. Sheppard decided to go back to the house to see if anything could be salvaged. As he reached the back door, water again rushed through the house and he had to climb a tree to escape. Mrs. Sheppard chided her husband for a long time afterward about his supposed expertise in oceanography.

Maximum wave heights were 33 feet (10 meters) on Maui, 36 feet (11 meters) on Oahu, and 55 feet (17 meters) on the island of Hawaii. It therefore was the island of Hawaii that experienced the greatest amount of damage and most loss of life. Before the tsunami, businesses and homes ringed beautiful Hilo Bay. The bay had a significant breakwater, which protected the bayfront area from the worst of the tsunami's destruction. Several neighborhoods around the bay were flooded, however, as was the main business district downtown. Horrific waves overtook the docks at the main port in Hilo, sweeping away warehouse and dock workers as it did so. Prior to 1946, there was a coastal railroad that ran from the sugar cane plantations on the northeast coast of the island to the port in Hilo. The tsunami wrenched train cars from their tracks, and pulled the tracks from the ground. The railroad was never rebuilt.

Perhaps the most poignant stories of the tsunami come from the small community of Laupahoehoe, about 25 miles (40 kilometers) north of Hilo. Roughly 20 feet (6 meters) above sea level was a broad, flat area on which several small cottages and a school had been built. The children were arriving for school when the first wave hit. A few children who had arrived early were playing on the seawall, and they were intrigued when the sea retreated, leaving the ocean floor exposed and fish stranded. Some children rushed to catch fish, unaware of what was coming. Soon the water rushed ashore, and many of the children were caught up in the water as the first wave struck. The wave pushed inland and overtook the cottages, carrying several of them for a few seconds before they disintegrated and left debris swirling in the water. As the water retreated, numerous people were swept out to sea and never seen again. The water came back at an even higher level, and those residents who had retreated to the school building and beyond were caught in the wave. In all, 46 people died at Laupahoehoe. A memorial that bears the names and ages of the students, teachers, and family members who perished there was erected at the site.

In all, the 1946 earthquake and tsunami killed 159 people in the Hawaiian Islands, most on the island of Hawaii. In addition to the deaths of the five Coast Guard staff members at Scotch Cap Lighthouse on Unimak Island, there was one other death in Santa Cruz, California. The tsunami caused damage all along the west coast of North America, damaged fishing boats in Chile, and produced waves up to 30 feet (10 meters) high in French Polynesia. The Pacific-wide destruction ultimately was the impetus for creating what later became known as the Pacific Tsunami Warning Center at Ewa Beach on the island of Oahu.

See Also: Aleutian Islands; Hawaiian Islands; Subduction Zone; Tsunami.

Further Reading

Alaskan Volcano Observatory. (2014, March 7). *Shishaldin activity.* Retrieved from https://www.avo.alaska.edu/activity/Shishaldin.php

American Museum of Natural History. (2014, March 7). *The Aleutian subduction zone.* Retrieved from http://www.amnh.org/exhibitions/permanent-exhibitions/rose-center-for-earth-and-space/david-s.-and-ruth-l.-gottesman-hall-of-planet-earth/why-are-there-ocean-basins-continents-and-mountains/earthquakes/earthquakes-where-plates-collide/the-aleutian-subduction-zone

Dudley, W. C., & Lee, M. (1998). *Tsunami!* (2nd ed.). Honolulu: University of Hawaii Press.

Martinson, C. (2014, March 7). *Unimak Area.* Retrieved from http://unimak.us/index.shtml

Myles, D. (1985). *The great waves.* New York: McGraw-Hill Book Company.

University of Southern California. Tsunami Research Group. (2014, March 7). *1946 Aleutian tsunami.* Retrieved from http://www.usc.edu/dept/tsunamis/alaska/1946/webpages/

U.S. Geological Survey. Earthquake Hazards Program. (2014, March 7). *Unimak Island.* Retrieved from http://earthquake.usgs.gov/earthquakes/states/events/1946_04_01.php

United States Geological Survey

The United States Geological Survey (USGS) is the country's government agency responsible for monitoring of earthquake and volcano activity, as well as mineral resources, water quality, environmental health, and biological resources. The USGS has offices in nearly every state, and each office is dedicated to research the resources found in its specific region. In the context of the Pacific Rim, the most prominent divisions of the USGS are those which monitor volcanic hazards and earthquake activity (which can lead to tsunami generation). The USGS has multiple volcano observatories, located in Alaska, California, Hawaii, Washington, and near Yellowstone National Park. Staff members at these observatories carry out research related to volcano hazards, and also are responsible for monitoring the activity of volcanoes within their jurisdictions. The first volcano observatory in the United States was the Hawaiian Volcano Observatory. It was founded in 1912 by Thomas A. Jaggar who, at the time, was a faculty member at the Massachusetts Institute of Technology.

Earthquakes are monitored nationwide using a network of seismometers both in locations prone to earthquakes and locations that are not. Although it might seem unnecessary to place seismometers in areas that do not experience earthquakes, in actuality these often are excellent places to establish seismometer networks because they are not in danger of "going offline" during a major earthquake. The instruments are sensitive enough to record earthquakes from a distance, but are far enough away so as not to be damaged or jostled, rendering their data meaningless. The western United States is the place that most people expect earthquakes to occur but, in reality, earthquakes can happen in any state. Aside from California, all states west of the Rocky Mountains experience frequent—though usually small—earthquakes. The four-state area that contains Missouri, Kentucky, Tennessee, and Illinois is another seismically active region. Known as the "New Madrid" area, this region was struck by four extremely powerful earthquakes in the years 1811 and 1812. Today, earthquakes in this region are very common, but they also usually are quite small. This earthquake activity is known largely due to the monitoring conducted by the U.S. Geological Survey. The nation's seismometers also supply data to the tsunami warning centers around the rim of the Pacific Ocean. Most tsunamis are generated by large earthquakes; it therefore is critical that the USGS seismometers provide data to the warning centers. This collaboration is seamless and results in very timely tsunami watches and warnings after major earthquakes.

See Also: Hawaiian Volcano Observatory; Jaggar, Jr., Thomas Augustus; Seismometer; Tsunami Warning Centers.

Further Reading

U.S. Geological Survey. http://www.usgs.gov

United States of America

The United States of America occupies the center of the North American continent, but also includes Alaska and Hawaii as well as territories in both the Caribbean Sea and the Pacific Ocean. Thus, four different plates include parts of the United States: the North American Plate, the Pacific Plate, the Caribbean Plate, and the Philippine Plate. Guam and the Mariana Islands are located on the Philippine Plate. Puerto Rico and the U.S. Virgin Islands are on the Caribbean Plate. The Pacific Plate includes Hawaii and American Samoa as well as portions of southern California. The North American Plate contains the balance of the United States, including the 48 contiguous states and Alaska.

The territories in the western Pacific are associated with the boundary between the Philippine and Pacific plates. Here, the Pacific Plate is subducting beneath the Philippine Plate. The resulting Mariana Island arc is composed of volcanic islands. Volcanoes Pagan and Anatahan both have erupted since the year 2000. The area also is prone to extremely large earthquakes, although tsunamis are not commonly generated in this region. This plate boundary is marked by the Mariana Trench, which is the deepest trench in all of the world's oceans. The deepest part of the trench is called the Challenger Deep and is located near Guam. It has only been visited a few times by both humans and remotely operated vehicles. These expeditions, however, have proven that life in many forms exists within the depths of the trench.

In the central Pacific lie the Hawaiian Islands. This island group was formed by the Hawaiian Hot Spot, a long-lived stationary plume of hot material in the mantle. The hot spot generates immense amounts of magma that feed volcanism. The hot spot has been active for at least 70 million years. This is known because a continuous chain of volcanoes exists, starting from the current site of the hot spot near the southeast coast of the island of Hawaii, extending northwestward and then northward to the Aleutian Trench. It is entirely possible that other, older volcanoes have been subducted at the trench so the hot spot could be older than 70 million years.

The eight main islands within the state of Hawaii are—from oldest to youngest—Niihau; Kauai; Oahu; the grouping of Molokai, Lanai, Maui, and Kahoolawe; and the island of Hawaii. Most of the active volcanoes within the chain are located on the island of Hawaii, or just off the southeastern coast. The volcano Kilauea, at the time of this writing, has been in nearly constant eruption since January 1983. It shows no signs of slowing down or stopping. Mauna Loa, the next most active volcano on the island, last erupted in 1984. It tends to erupt once every decade or two. The third volcano on the island is Hualalai which sits above the Kona coast, the resort area of the island. It last erupted in 1801. The other two volcanoes on the island, Kohala and Mauna Kea, have not erupted in thousands of years. Minor eruptive activity likely occurred on the volcano Haleakala, on Maui, sometime in the 1700s, although the exact date is not known. The only other volcanic activity within the Hawaiian islands occurs offshore, at a seamount (submerged volcano) called "Loihi." Loihi will likely be the sixth volcano on the island of Hawaii when it emerges from the ocean in about 30,000 years.

The mainland of the United States is a very big place, and not surprisingly it has a great deal of geologic features that influence its geography. The east coast of the continent is a passive margin, meaning no tectonic activity currently is underway there. The eastern edge of the North American Plate is the Mid-Atlantic Ridge, which is in the center of the Atlantic Ocean. The Mid-Atlantic Ridge is nearly as far from the east coast of the United States as the east coast of the United States is from the west coast of the country. Thus there is no significant geologic influence on the east coast of the United States from the Mid-Atlantic Ridge. In the western United States, the Rocky Mountains have been formed along an ancient plate boundary. Sparse volcanism throughout the American West has shaped landscapes and provided mineral deposits that have been exploited. The west coast of the United States, however, has a unique geology caused by interactions of other plates with the North American Plate.

In the Pacific Northwest the Juan de Fuca Plate is located just offshore. It is subducting beneath North America at the Cascadia Subduction Zone, and the result is earthquake activity and a chain of volcanoes known as the Cascade Range. The volcanoes in the Cascades are active, as evidenced by two eruptions in the Twentieth

Century—one at Lassen Peak in northern California and the other at Mount St. Helens in southern Washington. Lassen Peak is a volcanic dome complex with geothermal features nearby, so its eruption in 1912–1914 produced new volcanic domes. The eruption of Mount St. Helens began in March of 1980 and culminated in a catastrophic eruption in May of that year. The volcano continued dome-building processes for several years thereafter before it appeared to become dormant. It awoke again in 2004, and continued building its crater dome until early 2009, when the eruption ceased. Earthquakes continue to occur beneath the volcano's crater, so additional activity from Mount St. Helens in this eruptive cycle is possible.

The southern end of the Cascadia Subduction Zone marks the northern extent of the San Andreas Fault, which also serves as the transform plate boundary between the North American Plate and Pacific Plate. These two plates are moving laterally past each other in a dextral motion—meaning that if a person were to straddle the plate boundary, then the right side would be moving toward that person. The Pacific Plate is moving to the northwest relative to the North American Plate, so everything to the west of the San Andreas Fault, including Los Angeles and points south, are moving northward. At some point in the distant future, Los Angeles will become a suburb of San Francisco as the Pacific Plate carries parts of what today is southern California past northern California. Although California to the west of the San Andreas Fault never will "fall into the ocean," it will become a long, thin island that moves northwestward out into the Pacific Ocean. The creation of the island, however, will not occur for tens of millions of years.

The San Andreas Fault has been the site of many large and damaging earthquakes. The most severe of these earthquakes was one that occurred north of San Francisco in April 1906. The earthquake destroyed many of the buildings in the city, broke gas and water mains, and upset open flames (causing many fires and explosions). Broken water lines left firemen without water to fight fires that started in the earthquake. The fires raged for days and caused a great deal more damage and loss of property than did the earthquake itself. Other major earthquakes that have occurred on the San Andreas Fault include the Loma Prieta earthquake near San Francisco in 1989, and the 1994 Northridge Earthquake in the suburbs of Los Angeles.

See Also: Caribbean Plate; Cascadia Subduction Zone; Haleakala, Maui, United States; Hawaiian Islands; Hot Spot; Hualalai, Hawaii, United States; Juan de Fuca Plate; Kilauea Volcano, Hawaii, United States; Lassen Peak, California, United States; Loma Prieta Earthquake, California, United States (1989); Mariana Islands; Mariana Trench; Mauna Kea, Hawaii, United States; Mauna Loa, Hawaii, United States; Northridge Earthquake, California, United States (1994); Pacific Plate; San Andreas Fault; San Francisco Earthquake, California, United States (1906); St. Helens, Mount, Washington, United States; Subduction Zone; Transform Boundary.

Further Reading

Smithsonian Institution. National Museum of Natural History. Global Volcanism Program. (2014, June 19). Retrieved from http://www.volcano.si.edu/search_volcano_results.cfm

U.S. Geological Survey. Earthquake Hazards Program. (2014, June 19). *Information by country/region/state/territory*. http://earthquake.usgs.gov/earthquakes/region.php

Unzen Eruption, Japan (1991–1995)

Unzen Volcano (also known as Mount Fugen) is located on the Shimabara Peninsula of western Kyushu Island, Japan. It is a composite volcano known for its multitude of lava domes that cover much of the Shimabara Peninsula. Unzen is located in the southwest Japan arc, formed near where the Philippine Plate is subducting beneath the Eurasian Plate. Historically, Unzen has not been a particularly active volcano, erupting only eight times since the year 860. One of its most notable eruptions occurred in the year 1792. Following an earthquake, a large portion of a volcanic dome detached from the volcano. A relatively small (0.07 cubic mile, or 0.3 cubic kilometer) debris avalanche traveled 4 miles (6.4 kilometers) from the volcano to the sea. The landslide generated a tsunami when it hit the ocean. The resulting tsunami drowned 9,528 people on the Shimabara Peninsula, and then swept across the Ariake Sea to kill 4,996 people in the Higo and Amasuka provinces.

Unzen erupted for the first time in its most recent cycle of activity in November 1990. This eruption—a phreatic, or steam-driven eruption—occurred after several months of precursory activity. Volcanologists first became aware of a potential

Family members of those who lost their lives in a 1991 eruption visit Mount Unzen, Japan. (Kyodo News/Newscom)

hazard at Unzen following a series of earthquakes that occurred under Tachibana Bay to the west of the volcano in November 1989. Earthquakes continued in the region but migrated eastward toward the cone of Unzen. Harmonic tremor—which indicates magma movement—began in earnest in July 1990 and continued sporadically until the phreatic eruption in November of that year.

Unzen is a complex volcano, composed of multiple volcanic dome systems that exist within various craters on the mountain. Often multiple domes occupy the same crater. Phreatic eruptions occurred at several craters on the volcano for several months. The first eruption that involved magma occurred in May 1991. At that time, a new lava dome began forming at two of the craters. A dacite dome began forming on May 20 in one crater, and soon pyroclastic flows began emanating from the crater as pieces of the growing dome fell away. These pyroclastic flows were relatively small and followed predictable courses. Although the flows were predictable and small, they still were dangerous. The government evacuated the town of Kamikoba, which was located 2.5 miles (4 kilometers) from the volcano's summit, to prevent loss of life.

These small pyroclastic flows caught the attention of French volcanologists Katia (Katja) and Maurice Krafft, and their American colleague Harry Glicken. The Kraffts were in the process of creating a film entitled, *Understanding Volcanic Hazards*. Their aim was to gather footage of volcanic phenomena and compile it into a short film that could be shown to public officials, in an effort to explain to them how dangerous volcanic hazards could be. They were intrigued by stories of these small pyroclastic flows at Unzen and thought this could be their chance to film these usually large and deadly phenomena in a relatively safe environment. Glicken was studying debris avalanches, so his interest was piqued as well. The trio met up on Kyushu and began filming these pyroclastic flows. After a few days, the news media heard about their work and several reporters accompanied them.

Late on the afternoon of June 3, 1991, an unusually large piece of the lava dome broke free, creating a pyroclastic flow that was much larger than previous flows. The pyroclastic flow, moving at more than 60 miles per hour (100 kilometers per hour), engulfed the group. The Kraffts and Glicken died, as did 40 reporters who were with them that day. Throughout the whole of the five-year eruption of Unzen, only one other person died. All 44 who perished on Unzen were within restricted zones. In most cases, scientists would count the low death toll and lack of deaths outside the restricted zone as a major victory in eruption forecasting and civil defense planning. Those in the small community of volcanologists, however, felt the loss of these three scientists very deeply. The Kraffts were the world's best-known and most experienced volcanologists, and Glicken was a respected veteran of the Mount St. Helens eruption of 1980.

The lava domes on Unzen continued to grow at variable rates between 1991 and 1995, when the eruption stopped. The lava domes grew both internally through eruption beneath existing dome material, and externally via lava flows that broke through the dome. Pyroclastic flows continued throughout most of the remainder of the five-year eruption.

See Also: Dacite; Japan; Krafft, Katja (Katia) and Krafft, Maurice; Lava Dome; Subduction Zone.

Further Reading

Bardintzeff, J.-M., & McBirney, A. R. (2000). *Volcanology* (2nd ed.). Sudbury, MA: Jones and Bartlett Publishers.

Decker, R. W., & Decker, B. (1998). *Volcanoes* (3rd ed., Academic Version). New York: W.H. Freeman and Company.

Francis, P., & Oppenheimer, C. (2004). *Volcanoes* (2nd ed.). Oxford: Oxford University Press.

Nakada, S., Shimizu, H., & Ohta, K. (1999). Overview of the 1990–1995 eruption at Unzen Volcano. *Journal of Volcanology and Geothermal Research 89*, 1–22.

Sato, H., Fujii, T., & Nakada, S. (1992). Crumbling of dacite dome lava and generation of pyroclastic flows at Unzen volcano. *Nature 360* (6405), 664–666.

V

Vanuatu

The island nation of Vanuatu is a seismically and volcanically active area. The islands are located on the eastern edge of the Australian Plate, where the Pacific Plate subducts beneath it. The islands of Vanuatu also are referred to as the "New Hebrides arc." Vanuatu experiences multiple magnitude 6 and greater earthquakes each year. Deaths due directly to earthquakes, however, are rare. The few instances of loss of life due to seismic activity have been a result of tsunamis.

Vanuatu also has a number of active volcanoes. Many volcanoes have erupted in historic times, and six have erupted since the year 2000. The volcano "Epi," an offshore caldera, erupted briefly in 2004. The summit of its cone is approximately 112 feet (34 meters) below sea level, according to a 2001 survey. "Lopevi"—a composite volcano composed of basalt and andesite—produced a minor eruption in 2007. In 2010, the volcano "Gaua" erupted minor ash and steam plumes. The shield volcano "Aoba" erupted in 2011 from one of its two crater lakes, Lake Manaro Ngoru. The volcano "Ambrym" erupted in 2013.

"Yasur" is one of the most active and most visited volcanoes on the islands. It has been erupting more or less continuously at least since Captain Cook landed on the island in the late 1700s, and additional evidence suggests that it has been erupting for at least 800 years. The volcano typically is not dangerous, although it certainly has the potential to be perilous, as does any volcano. Yasur's typical mode of eruption, however, is one of low explosivity and minor ash and steam plumes. Its summit largely is unvegetated because of the nearly constant volcano activity and ash fall. The volcano also is in a tectonic zone. Together, Yasur and the tectonic movement have raised the elevation of Port Revolution harbor on Tanna Island by more than 66 feet (20 meters) in the last 100 years.

See Also: Australian Plate; Pacific Plate; Subduction Zone.

Further Reading

Smithsonian Institution. National Museum of Natural History. Global Volcanism Program. (2014, June 16). Database search. Retrieved from http://www.volcano.si.edu/search _volcano_results.cfm

U.S. Geological Survey. (2014, June 16). *Historic world earthquakes. Vanuatu.* http:// earthquake.usgs.gov/earthquakes/world/historical_country.php#vanuatu

Vent

A vent is an opening in the earth's surface through which magma is erupted. The term vent also sometimes is used to describe not just the opening where magma reaches the surface, but the structure a volcano builds around that opening. A single volcano can have a single vent or multiple vents. It is not uncommon for multiple vents on a volcano to erupt at the same time. Single vents can erupt for decades or centuries on end, or can erupt just a single brief time.

In the case of many shield volcanoes and cinder cones, a new vent often assumes the form of a crack in the ground, called a "fissure." An eruption through a crack in the ground is called a "fissure eruption." A fissure eruption produces a "curtain of fire," or wall of lava. Over time, as magma erupted through the fissure begins to cool and harden, in many places the crack is filled. The eruption then narrows down to a single opening—which is a more stable and longer-lived vent.

In composite volcanoes, vents vary according to type of eruption. An explosive eruption can open a new vent. That vent can be quite wide, torn open by the force of expanding gases in the magma. As the eruption wanes, a large vent can begin to be filled by the material that collapses back into it. The actual opening through which magma was erupted can be obscured by debris. In a less explosive eruption—such as one that produces a lava flow or a lava dome—the vent can be completely covered by the lava erupted from the opening. Especially in the case of a lava dome, this is a situation in which the vent is identified largely as the feature (the dome) created by eruptions from that site.

See Also: Lava Dome; Magma.

Further Reading

Tarbuck, E. J., Lutgens, F. K., & Tasa, D. (2011). *Earth: An introduction to physical geology* (10th ed.). Upper Saddle River, NJ: Pearson Prentice Hall/Pearson Education, Inc.

Volcanic Explosivity Index (VEI)

The Volcanic Explosivity Index (VEI) is a scale used to describe the size of volcanic eruptions. It was proposed by volcanologists Christopher G. Newhall and Stephen Self in 1982 to address the scientific community's need for a systematic way to describe the relative size of explosive volcanic eruptions. Much like the magnitude scale in seismology, the VEI was structured so that every increase of 1 on the VEI corresponds to roughly a ten-fold increase in volume of erupted material. This logarithmic arrangement enables the VEI to describe eruptions that span a wide range of severity.

It is difficult not to draw parallels between the earthquake magnitude scale and the Volcanic Explosivity Index. This is intentional, as scientists and the general public are used to the magnitude scale and intuitively understand that a smaller number means a smaller event. In both the magnitude scale and VEI, smaller magnitude events are much more common than large magnitude events. Unlike the magnitude scale which permits negative values and is open-ended, however, the VEI is a scale from zero to eight in which zero represents the smallest of eruptions, and eight indicates the most powerful eruptions. Newhall and Self did not believe that they could distinguish more than eight levels of eruption severity based on the historic or geologic record.

Many scientists had attempted to measure different aspects of volcanic eruptions to arrive at a quantitative scale and objectively compare eruptions prior to the proposal of the Volcanic Explosivity Index. Previous attempts were based on factors such as temperature records, the amount of material injected into the atmosphere, thermal and kinetic energy involved in the eruption, eruption column heights, and the combined volume of lava and pyroclastic materials. Although each of these is an important factor in eruption studies, most of these values are unavailable for prehistoric eruptions, as well as for most historical eruptions occurring before the 1970s. On the VEI scale, magnitude is assigned based on the volume of pyroclastic material erupted. This scale is imperfect and has limitations, particularly on how accurately past eruptions can be assessed. It often is difficult to estimate a total volume of pyroclastic material an eruption produces, even today. The VEI, however, is the most widely accepted method for describing eruption size.

VEI values of notable historic eruptions include the following.

Location	(Date)	VEI Value
Tambora, Indonesia	(1815)	7
Krakatau, Indonesia	(1883)	6
Pelée, Martinique	(1902)	4
Novarupta (Katmai), Alaska	(1911)	6
Paricutin, Mexico	(1943–1952)	4
Bezymianny, Kamchatka	(1956)	5
St. Helens, Mount, Washington	(1980)	5
El Chichón, Mexico	(1982)	4
Kilauea, Hawaii	(1983 to Present)	0
Nevado del Ruiz, Colombia	(1985)	3
Pinatubo, Philippines	(1991)	6
Galeras, Colombia	(1993)	2

It should be noted that George P. L. Walker suggested an alternate scale for eruption size. He refers to this as a "magnitude scale," and the magnitude of an eruption is based on the mass of erupted material. The equation for eruption magnitude is shown below.

$$M = \log_{10}m - 7$$

Where "M" is magnitude and "m" is mass of erupted material in kilograms.

The magnitude scale for eruptions theoretically is open-ended, although the largest of known eruptions—that of the La Garita caldera in the United States—is a magnitude 9. Using this scale, the Pinatubo eruption of 1991 was a magnitude 7.1 event, Krakatau's 1883 eruption was a magnitude 6.5 event, and Mount St. Helens' 1980 eruption had a magnitude of 4.9.

See Also: Pyroclastic Materials.

Further Reading

Decker, R., & Decker, B. (1998). *Volcanoes* (3rd ed., Academic Version). New York: W.H. Freeman Press.

Francis, P., & Oppenheimer, C. (2004). *Volcanoes* (2nd ed.). Oxford: Oxford University Press.

Newhall, C. G., & Self, S. (1982). The Volcanic Explosivity Index (VEI): An estimate of explosive magnitude for historical volcanism. *Journal of Geophysical Research 87* (C2), 1231–1238.

Smithsonian Institution. National Museum of Natural History. Global Volcanism Program. (2014, June 18). http://www.volcano.si.edu/index.cfm

U.S. Geological Survey. Volcano Hazards Program. (2013, June 18). *VHP photo glossary: VEI.* Retrieved from http://volcanoes.usgs.gov/images/pglossary/vei.php

Volcanic Hazards

Numerous hazards are associated with active volcanoes. These hazards can vary significantly depending on the type of volcano, the volcano's eruptive style, and the shape of the landscape around the volcano. In general, shield volcanoes and cinder cones pose less dramatic threats to nearby populations than do composite volcanoes. Even normally quiescent shield volcanoes have the capability to produce devastating effects, however, and composite volcanoes can behave in a quite docile manner.

One hazard that exists around every volcano is noxious gases. All volcanoes produce some mixture of water vapor, carbon dioxide, sulfur dioxide, hydrogen sulfide, chlorine, and fluorine. Volcanoes are difficult to approach and study because of this mixture of toxic and caustic gases. Water vapor (steam) has a great deal of potential energy. When released quickly, this can lead to phreatic—or steam-driven—eruptions. Although phreatic eruptions typically are less violent than magma-driven eruptions, they still can cause death for any person in close proximity to the vent.

Carbon dioxide is heavier than air. If it seeps from a vent and settles in a populated valley then it causes death by suffocation. In 1986, a large cloud of carbon dioxide emerged from Lake Nyos in Cameroon. Within just a few minutes it suffocated 1,746 people including those who lived up to 15 miles away from its shores. Even greater numbers of the area's livestock and wildlife also were killed.

When mixed with water vapor, sulfur dioxide becomes sulfuric acid. Minute droplets of sulfuric acid get caught in local wind patterns and can cause respiratory problems and eye irritation to people who are miles downwind, and metals experience rusting and corrosion. Hydrogen sulfide—which smells like rotten eggs—can cause both gastric and respiratory distress. When mixed with water vapor, chlorine becomes hydrogen chloride or hydrochloric acid. Like sulfuric acid, it can cause irritation of the eyes and respiratory system. Significant amounts of fluorine in volcanic ash can lead to fluorosis, or fluorine poisoning. Fluorine in high enough concentrations can irritate skin and eyes, and destroy bones and teeth. It takes only one millimeter of high-fluorine ash spread on a pasture to induce fluorosis in livestock grazing there.

In addition to the direct problems coming from gas emissions, gases can cause a number of other negative effects. Gases are emitted through cracks in the ground and the rock around these cracks is chemically altered by the gases. These rocks often are turned into soft clays. When wet, the clay can become a major landslide hazard if slopes are steep enough. In significant amounts—such as those reached during a large explosive eruption—sulfur dioxide aerosols can enter the lower stratosphere and circulate worldwide. These aerosol droplets block sunlight from reaching the earth's surface and have a cooling effect on the earth's temperatures. Sulfur-dioxide emissions from the 1815 eruption of Tambora (Indonesia) created a global decrease in temperatures of up to 5.4° F (3° C). The year 1816 is frequently referred to as "the year without a summer." The United States, Canada, and western Europe saw killing summer frosts which led to crop failure.

A second hazard that is present at all volcanoes is the possibility of an explosive eruption. One cause of explosive eruption is gas pressure. All magma contains gases, and as magma rises toward the earth's surface the gases expand. If magma is fluid, as is the case with basalt and some andesite, then it is likely that the gases will vent to the surface and there will be little danger of explosive activity. If magma is thick and pasty, as with dacite and rhyolite, however, then there is no escape route for the gases. Gas pressure rises as the gases expand. When the pressure of the gases within the volcano exceeds the strength of the rocks keeping the gases contained, the volcano erupts violently. Another cause of explosive eruption is water flashing to steam. A phreatic eruption often is triggered by groundwater being heated by a magma source below. The water flashes to steam and expands to several times its original volume, causing gas pressure to rise instantly. This often causes rocks to break and the energy to be released in a minor explosive eruption.

Yet another hazard present at all volcanoes is lava. Lava flows most commonly come from cinder cones and shield volcanoes, but are frequent features at composite volcanoes as well. Although lava flows rarely are fatal to humans or animals that can move out of the way, flows can be immensely destructive to man-made structures and vegetation. Throughout history, many attempts have been made to divert or stop lava flows. In the 1930s, lava flows from Mauna Loa were bombed in an effort to break levees and send lava flowing away from the city of Hilo, Hawaii. This approach only was minimally successful in accomplishing its main mission. In the 1970s, residents of the fishing port of Heimaey, Iceland, attempted to stop a lava flow that threatened to close the entrance to the city's harbor by spraying the lava flow front with seawater. Fortunately, the eruption stopped before the harbor was completely cut off from the open ocean. Had the eruption continued, the constant deluge of seawater would have done little to stop the inevitable advance of lava.

Earthquakes always are a component of volcanic unrest. Although most earthquakes are small—too small to be felt, in fact—occasionally volcanically active areas experience larger earthquakes associated with magma movement, readjustment of the volcanic edifice, or tectonics that contribute to volcanic activity. Scientists suspect that, in some instances, tectonic earthquakes in subduction zone settings might shift rocks just enough to allow magma to rise under volcanoes during subsequent months or years. As an example, the June 1991 eruption of Mount Pinatubo (Philippines) followed a magnitude 7.8 earthquake that occurred on July 16, 1990. The earthquake killed 1,621 people. It became clear in March and April of 1991 that magma had risen beneath Pinatubo, as small earthquakes, phreatic eruptions, and gas emissions signaled the beginning of an eruptive cycle. The eruption itself killed about 300 people.

Volcanic ash is a major volcanic hazard. Any type of volcano can produce volcanic ash, but the greatest volumes of ash are produced by composite volcanoes. Volcanic ash is pulverized rock or magma that has been torn apart by rapid expansion of gases during eruption. Through microscopic analysis of volcanic ash scientists can determine whether an eruption is the result of "juvenile magma"—which is fresh magma being erupted from a magma chamber below—or if the ash simply is the result of steam and gases breaking apart cooled existing rocks. Volcanic ash created from magma is full of microscopic gas bubbles and has jagged edges where gas bubbles have broken apart during rapid expansion. Ash created from pulverized cool rock simply looks like microscopic pieces of solid rock.

Ash can become a hazard in many settings and situations, both close to the volcano and many thousands of miles away. Ash that is blasted upward into the air can linger there for several minutes to several hours (or even longer). Ash clouds are a major hazard to aviation. Many cases exist in which airplanes have lost engine power after pilots unwittingly flew through ash clouds. It might seem a simple matter to distinguish an ash cloud from a regular cloud, however the contrary is true more often. It is nearly impossible for radar to distinguish between the two types of clouds. Ash clouds can drift downwind several hundred miles, and can be encountered when the airplane is not even within sight of the offending volcano. At night, ash clouds are invisible to pilots. In 1982, a British Airways flight carrying 247 passengers en route from Kuala Lumpur, Malaysia, to Perth, Australia, lost power to all four engines as it flew over Indonesia at an altitude of 37,000 feet (11,300 meters). The plane dropped to an altitude of 12,000 feet (3,660 meters) before the pilots were able to get the engines restarted.

The flight landed safely in Jakarta, Indonesia. It was clear they had flown through something unusual, because the aircraft was heavily abraded. The source of the ash cloud in short order was confirmed to be Mount Galunggung, a volcano in the Indonesian archipelago.

Volcanic ash is a respiratory hazard, causing irritation of the eyes and respiratory system in the short term, and—if too much is inhaled—eventually causing death by suffocation. Many of those who died in the eruption of Vesuvius (Italy) in 79 CE died of suffocation from ashfall. Livestock are particularly susceptible to suffocation and poisoning from ash because they spend a great deal of time grazing on grass which can be covered with volcanic ash. As for chickens, ducks, and other fowl, their small lungs do not need exposure to a great deal of volcanic ash before they are overwhelmed. In 1902, people noted birds dropping from the sky in Saint-Pierre, Martinique even though only a minimal amount of volcanic ash was falling in the city.

British Airways Flight Endangered by a Volcano

In June 1982, during what should have been a routine flight from Kuala Lampur, Malaysia, to Perth, Australia, a British Airways flight experienced an unusual sequence of events. After climbing to a cruising altitude at 37,000 feet, the pilots noticed that there was smoke and a strange, almost electrical smell coming from the air vents. Soon afterward, they noticed that the atmosphere seemed to glow with electricity. Much to their alarm, the engines also were glowing as if they were lit by a fire within. The flight engineer soon reported that one after another of the plane's engines failed. Although clearly the engineer was correct, the pilots were in disbelief. No plane loses power to all four engines at once. Electrical power within the plane failed as well, and one of the flight attendants later noted that the only light entering the cabin was from the lightning dancing on the plane's wings. Oxygen masks deployed as the plane glided past 26,000 feet, but many of the masks did not work properly. The pilots quickly descended to about 14,000 feet so the passengers would have enough oxygen.

When the plane reached an altitude of 12,000 feet—over Indonesia—the pilots were able to restart the engines one by one. The crew tried to get the plane to ascend to avoid the mountainous terrain of the islands, but the same problems started again when the plane reached about 15,000 feet. The pilots gained permission to make an emergency landing in Jakarta. Landing the plane also proved to be tricky, however, because the wind screens were abraded, giving the glass a "frosted" appearance. The pilots had to look out of the small side windows to be able to see well enough to safely land the plane.

Why had this flight been disrupted so severely? The plane flew through a cloud of volcanic ash from Mount Galunggung, an Indonesian volcano. The ash cloud was not visible on the plane's radar system, so the pilots had no idea the ash plume was in front of the plane. This was one of the most harrowing occurrences of an encounter between aircraft and a plume of volcanic ash. Following this incident, scientists and aviation professionals were determined to prevent loss of life from aircraft encounters with volcanic ash. Today, special radar and satellite monitoring helps to detect volcanic ash plumes so that aircraft can be warned away from regions in which volcanoes are emitting large amounts of volcanic ash high into the atmosphere.

Volcanic ash becomes much more hazardous when it is mixed with water. Many composite volcanoes are tall and steep-sided mountains. Multiple rivers flow down their slopes, and often volcanoes are capped with snow and ice. During an eruption, large volumes of volcanic ash fall on the slopes of a volcano. When that ash mixes with meltwater from snow and ice and finds its way into rivers, it becomes a mass of mud that has the consistency of wet cement. The technical term for this mud flow is "lahar." Lahars can reach a height of 50 feet (15 meters) or more, and can travel down steep inclines at 55 miles per hour (90 kilometers per hour). Lahars can travel as far as 50 miles (80 kilometers) away from a volcano, and they follow stream valleys. Often, the people in danger cannot even see the volcano generating the lahar. People living in river valleys that lead away from volcanoes therefore must be aware of the hazards they face, and must have a well-publicized and rehearsed evacuation plan in place to keep themselves safe. One of the most tragic cases of a modern lahar occurred in 1985 at the volcano Nevado del Ruiz in Colombia. A relatively minor eruption of the volcano melted snow and ice from its summit and sent a lahar roaring down a river valley toward the city of Armero. The town's residents had no warning or evacuation instructions, and that night more than 23,000 people were buried by the fast-moving wall of mud.

Although lahars most commonly are formed during an active eruption, they also can plague communities for decades after an eruption. When Pinatubo erupted in the Philippines, many feet of ash were deposited on the slopes of the volcano. People were warned to expect lahars to remobilize this volcanic ash for at least 15 years after the eruption ended. Indeed, for several years after the 1991 eruption, whenever heavy rains fell on the island of Luzon the communities experienced not only flooding but also lahars.

Perhaps the most deadly of volcanic hazards is the pyroclastic flow, also known as a "nuée ardente," which is French for "glowing cloud." A pyroclastic flow is a hot, fast-moving, ground-hugging cloud of ash, gases, pumice, rocks, and other debris that rushes down the slopes of a volcano. It can form in one of several ways. It can form when part of an eruption column loses upward momentum, falls back to earth, and then rushes downhill. It also can form when material in a crater erupts or falls over the rim, again causing material to rush downhill. It also can occur when a lava dome collapses. In each case the result is the same. Temperatures within pyroclastic flows are known to exceed 1,000° F (700° C). Flows move at speeds of 100 miles per hour (160 kilometers per hour) or more. Pyroclastic flows contain toxic gases. Flows also can pick up nearly anything in their paths, including trees, boulders, trucks, bridges, and buildings. The city of Saint-Pierre on the island of Martinique was hit by a pyroclastic flow in May 1902. Nearly all inhabitants of the city were killed, and not a single building was left intact. Roofs, walls, windows, and fences were broken, bent, and twisted into grotesque shapes. In many cases bodies were not just burned, but were carbonized so nothing was left but a human-shaped lump of charcoal. Pyroclastic flows are known almost exclusively from composite volcanoes.

See Also: Andesite; Basalt; Dacite; Indonesia; Nevado del Ruiz, Colombia; Philippines; Pinatubo, Mount, Eruption, Philippines (1991); Pyroclastic Materials; Rhyolite.

Further Reading

BBC News Magazine. (2014, March 12). When volcanic ash stopped a Jumbo at 37,000ft. Retrieved from http://news.bbc.co.uk/2/hi/uk_news/magazine/8622099.stm

Decker, R., & Decker, B. (1998). *Volcanoes* (3rd ed., Academic Version). New York: W.H. Freeman and Company.

Newhall, C., Hendley, J. W., & Stauffer, P. H. (1997). *The cataclysmic 1991 eruption of Mount Pinatubo, Philippines* (U.S. Geological Survey Fact Sheet 113–97).

Slate.com. (2013). Lake Nyos suffocated over 1,746 people in a single night [Atlas Obscura Blog]. Retrieved from http://www.slate.com/blogs/atlas_obscura/2013/07/26/lake _nyos_killed_1746_when_it_released_a_huge_pocket_of_co2.html

U.S. Geological Survey. Earthquake Hazards Program. (2014, March 12). *Deaths from earthquakes in 1990.* Retrieved from http://earthquake.usgs.gov/earthquakes /eqarchives/year/1990/1990_deaths.php

U.S. Geological Survey. Volcano Hazards Program. (2014, March 11). *Volcanic gases and their effects.* Retrieved from http://volcanoes.usgs.gov/hazards/gas/

U.S. Geological Survey. Volcano Hazards Program. (2014, March 11). *Volcanoes and global cooling.* Retrieved from http://vulcan.wr.usgs.gov/Glossary/VolcWeather /description_volcanoes_and_weather.html

Volcano Disaster Assistance Program

The Volcano Disaster Assistance Program (VDAP) was founded in response to the tragedy at Nevado del Ruiz Volcano in Colombia in 1985. That eruption resulted in the deaths of more than 23,000 people, largely due to confusion about the nature of the hazards faced by communities; the lack of modern monitoring equipment; and poor communication between scientists, public officials, and the general public. VDAP teams were deployed to more than 30 volcanoes during the program's first 25 years. Those volcanoes were located across the globe, in Central America, South America, the Caribbean, Africa, Indonesia, the Philippines, and Papua New Guinea.

The VDAP program is under the purview of the U.S. Geological Survey Volcano Hazards Program. When a nation faces volcanic unrest, the government of that country can request assistance from the VDAP program through the United States Agency for International Development (USAID). When the request is granted, VDAP scientists respond quickly with satellite data, assistance with forecasting, and—if necessary—a portable volcano observatory, complete with seismometers and equipment to radio seismic data back to a base station for instant analysis. The VDAP scientists serve in an advisory role to the host institution, therefore the local scientists are in charge of communications with public officials. Members of the VDAP team also have ongoing research projects at some volcanoes and provide training to scientists located around the world so that the scientists have a greater capacity to deal with volcanic crises in their home countries.

Since the founding of the VDAP program, the team has had a number of successes. The team was present at Mount Pinatubo (Philippines) in 1991 during that volcano's cataclysmic eruption. Team members, along with Philippine scientists from the Philippine Institute for Volcanology and Seismology (PHIVOLCS), monitored the volcano closely and were able to forecast its eruptions accurately. The forecasts led to timely evacuations, and saved untold thousands of lives. Likewise, when Nevado del Huila, Colombia, became active in 2007, VDAP members worked with Colombian scientists at the Instituto Colombiano de Geologìa y Minerìa (INGEOMINAS) to improve monitoring capabilities at the volcano and develop effective alert systems to enable quick evacuation. INGEOMINAS scientists then were able to respond effectively to an eruption that occurred in November 2008. Four thousand people were evacuated from the town of Belalcázar within half an hour of the eruption's onset. The town was inundated with a lahar only 15 minutes after the evacuation was complete but, due to rapid response by INGEOMINAS, there were no deaths.

See Also: Nevado del Ruiz, Colombia; Pinatubo, Mount, Eruption, Philippines (1991).

Further Reading

U.S. Geological Survey. (2014, May 12). *Volcano Disaster Assistance Program.* http://volcanoes.usgs.gov/vdap/index.php

Volcano Monitoring Techniques

Volcanoes are complex systems, therefore a number of techniques and methods are employed in monitoring them for evidence of unrest or an impending eruption. Some techniques—such as monitoring tilt—are based on relatively simple principles and are fairly easy to interpret. Other methods—such as satellite interferometry—require intricate data-collection and processing protocols to produce results. Rarely is only a single technique used to monitor volcanoes. Volcano observatories usually employ a host of methods to obtain the most detailed picture possible of the volcano's current status.

There are six major categories of monitoring techniques used in the study of active volcanoes. The first category is ground deformation, or the study of geodesy. Volcanoes often change their shape, and those changes in shape can be detected in a number of different ways. One method scientists use to determine whether a volcano is changing shape is to measure the tilt of a volcano's slopes. This can be done digitally using an electronic tilt meter, or manually using a water-tube tilt meter. The water-tube tilt meter is an extremely simple instrument. Two reservoirs are filled with water almost completely. A tube is placed between them, connecting the

Scientists install monitoring equipment on an active volcano in Mexico. (Carlos Pacheco/Notimex/Newscom)

two reservoirs. If the slope of the volcano begins to tilt, the level of water in one reservoir will be higher than the level in the other reservoir. This difference in water height can be measured and the data can be converted to an angle of tilt. This angle can be monitored at several different locations on a volcano to determine where the center of elevation change is located. This can provide information about the volcano's likely behavior. Electronic tilt meters have a similar design, except that the dual water reservoirs and tube are replaced by a small container filled with conducting fluid and a bubble that moves with tilt. Electrodes placed in the fluid determine the location of the bubble, which is converted to angle of tilt. In either case, the standard unit of tilt is the microradian, which is equal to 0.00006°. A typical range of tilt measured on an active volcano is between 100 and 10,000 microradians.

Surveying is another method of determining the change in shape of a volcano and its slopes. A number of instruments have been used over the last several decades to help scientists determine the changes in shape. The oldest method of surveying is called leveling. This is a slow and arduous task that requires traversing the area of measurement multiple times. For that reason, it rarely is used for monitoring of volcanoes that are nearing the eruption state.

A more widely used technique is electronic distance measurement (EDM). This technique uses a laser to measure the distance between the instrument and a pair of reflectors placed on the volcano. This method can be accurate to within 0.2 inches (5 millimeters). Another method for measuring ground deformation is the use of global positioning systems (GPS). Scientific GPS systems often enable users to obtain positions of GPS receivers to an accuracy of less than 0.4 inches (1 centimeter). This type of measurement requires collecting data for between 8 and 24 hours at each individual station, and carefully processing the information. Scientists typically install permanent (or semi-permanent) stations and revisit the same sites to determine whether deformation has occurred.

Satellite interferometry is the final type of ground-deformation monitoring technique. In this method, satellites collect radar images of the earth's surface. Two images taken at different times are electronically processed so it appears that they overlay each other. The two images then are compared and the differences appear as bands of color, similar to a rainbow. The amount and shape of ground deformation can be determined by examining the patterns of the color bands. This is an excellent method for mapping deformation in large areas. An entire volcano can be imaged in a single pair of images, and just a few centimeters of deformation over a square that is perhaps 30 to 60 miles (50 to 100 kilometers) in size is easily detected.

The second category of methods used to monitor volcanoes is remote sensing. Remote sensing involves monitoring activities that are performed by satellite. This certainly can include satellite interferometry, but it also can include monitoring of thermal activity from space, and using weather satellites to monitor the eruption of major ash clouds into the atmosphere. This is especially important in areas with composite volcanoes that lie near major air-traffic routes. Volcanic ash in the atmosphere is extremely hazardous to aircraft. In several cases, planes have been damaged and partially disabled as a result of encounters with volcanic ash clouds. In 1984, a British Airways jet flew through a volcanic ash plume from Galunggung Volcano (Indonesia). The plane lost power to all four engines and fell a harrowing 24,000 feet (7 kilometers) before the pilots could restart the engines and land in Jakarta. Since that time, detection of volcanic ash in the atmosphere has become a major international priority for the aviation industry, and several satellites monitor the earth for that hazard.

The third category of monitoring techniques is gas geochemistry. All volcanoes emit gases. The primary gases emitted from volcanoes include steam, sulfur dioxide (SO_2), hydrogen, hydrogen chloride (HCl), hydrogen fluoride (HF), hydrogen sulfide (H_2S), carbon dioxide (CO_2), and carbon monoxide (CO). Although it is certainly possible to monitor all of these gases given the right equipment and time and a safe collection location, geologists typically prefer not to spend a significant amount of time on top of a volcano making measurements or collecting samples. In some cases, geologists will approach fumaroles, or gas vents, and collect gases in vacuum bottles. They then bring the gases back to the laboratory for analysis. Continuous on-site gas monitoring can be done remotely and in real time using carefully placed sensors; the data is radioed back to a base station. This obviously is helpful where it is practical, but many active volcanoes do not provide a practical location for this type of study. Even for cases that provide an appropriate location, there are ways to measure gases from a distance. An instrument called a "correlation spectrometer" (COSPEC) is designed to measure the amount of sulfur dioxide in the atmosphere—from a safe distance. Scientists point the correlation spectrometer toward the gas plume issuing from a volcano, and make measurements over a specific time interval. This enables researchers to calculate the volume of sulfur-dioxide emissions per day—which can be valuable information in the interpretation of a volcano's behavior.

A fourth category of monitoring techniques is to use earthquake activity information. When an active volcano is being instrumented, seismometers typically are the first instruments placed on the mountain. The number, locations, magnitudes, and types of earthquakes are noted and can indicate the level of activity and thus warn geologists before many eruptions occur. Earthquakes on volcanoes come in many varieties. Volcano-tectonic earthquakes occur when magma breaks rocks as it moves underground. Harmonic tremor is a continuous oscillation that indicates magma movement near the surface. Eruptions often are accompanied by harmonic tremor, as are intrusions of magma into a shallow dike system. Still other volcanic signals indicate rock falls in a volcano's crater, or gases being released at a crack in a lava dome. In general, the number of earthquakes increases as a volcano nears eruption, as does the energy released by those earthquakes. Rapid and accurate location of earthquakes can provide vital information about the likely location of a new vent, or of the depth of magma beneath a volcano.

A fifth category is the use of non-seismic geophysical measurements. These can include monitoring the electrical, magnetic, or gravity fields of the volcano for indications of changes. A sixth category is the monitoring of river valleys for lahars. This is accomplished using special seismometers that are "tuned" to listen for the signal of thick fluids descending into valleys around the mountain at high speed.

Volcano monitoring is accomplished most effectively by a team of scientists that includes specialists in all of these areas. If budgets are small or time is short, then gas measurements, seismology (including monitoring for lahars), and ground deformation are considered the most critical measurements for rapid determination of a volcano's state of unrest. Valuable information can be gained, however, from all six categories of monitoring techniques mentioned above.

See Also: Geodesy; Lahar; Seismology.

Further Reading

U.S. Geological Survey. (2014, May 13). *Monitoring ground deformation from space* (Fact Sheet 2005-3025). Retrieved from http://volcanoes.usgs.gov/activity/methods/insar/public_files/InSAR_Fact_Sheet/2005-3025.pdf

U.S. Geological Survey. Volcano Hazards Program. (2014, May 13). *How we monitor volcanoes*. Retrieved from http://volcanoes.usgs.gov/activity/methods/

Volcanoes and Earthquakes, Mythology of

Man always strives to provide an explanation for things that happen in the natural world. Occurrences of volcanic eruptions and earthquakes were—and in many ways still are—some of the most mysterious events in nature. As a result, most cultures that experience these events have some form of mythology that surrounds them. In some cases, the myths are general explanations of phenomena, such as why earthquakes occur, or why islands have risen out of the sea. In other cases, the myths are specific to certain events or locations, such as how a specific mountain came into being. In the latter case, these myths actually might be a form of eyewitness account of an event.

In Japan, a group of creatures called the "yo-kai" were said to be the harbingers and bringers of disaster and misfortune. The giant catfish "Namazu" was one such creature. He was buried deep in the earth, and the god Kashima immobilized him with a heavy stone on top of his body. If Kashima lost focus and was distracted from his duty, however, then Namazu became free enough to wiggle, causing an earthquake as his movement shook the foundations of the earth. Several versions of this myth exist, and in some the catfish is either a dragon or a giant eel. In other versions the catfish is attacked by the good people of a village and those secretly hoping to profit from a disaster work against them, trying to free Namazu from his restraints.

In New Zealand, the Maori god of earthquakes and volcanoes is Ruaumoku (also known as Ruamoku). Ruaumoku was the son of the earth (Papatuanuku) and the sky (Ranginui). The earth and sky had been separated from each other, and Ranginui's tears flooded the land. The other sons of Papatuanuku and Ranginui decided to turn their mother to face downward, so that she and her husband no longer could see each other's sorrow, thus deepening their grief. Ruaumoko, however, still was nursing at his mother's breast when his brothers turned their mother over. He was carried to the world below, and given a fire to keep himself warm. The earthquakes now experienced in New Zealand are said by the Maori to be caused by him as he walks about.

In western North America, Native Americans have stories about many of the individual mountains within the Cascade Range. Mount St. Helens was known as "Loowit," a beautiful maiden. Two sons of the Great Spirit ("Sahale"), "Wyeast" and "Klickitat," fell in love with Loowit and fought for her affections. Loowit could not choose between them. When Sahale found out that his two sons were hurling rocks at each other—and burying villages and forests in the process—he became furious. He killed all three of the young people and constructed mountains where they fell. Loowit became the beautiful, symmetrical, snow-capped peak of Mount St. Helens. Wyeast held his head up proudly, and became the sharp peak of Mount Hood. Klickitat hung his head in sorrow, and he became Mount Adams.

Another story, from the Klamath people of Oregon, tells of a giant battle that ended poorly for one chief. "Skell," the chief of Above World, for many days battled fiercely with "Llao," the chief of Below World. The chiefs hurled rocks and flames at each other, and their fight caused darkness to fall across the land. Llao climbed the tallest mountain he could find to see Skell better. When Llao reached the top of this peak (called Mount Mazama) the peak collapsed, crushing and burying him under the debris. The remnants of Mount Mazama today are called Crater Lake.

Hawaiians also have complex and fascinating stories of the formation of the islands, as well as the volcanic activity that frequently rages. Maui, one of many demigods within the Hawaiian pantheon, is said to have been fishing one day with a magic hook. He caught his hook on the ocean floor and pulled up the islands. After the islands were formed, the goddess Pele was born. She was a beautiful young woman with a lusty spirit and a terrible temper. She frequently offended her sisters and battled fiercely with them over insults and misdeeds. The sister she clashed most often and most violently with was the goddess of the ocean. Pele was chased from one island to another. She started in the northwest part of the island chain and used her fire stick to dig a fire pit in the mountain. Her sister followed her and drenched the flame. She was chased to the next island down the chain and the same thing happened, time and time again. Eventually, Pele made it to the island of Hawaii and was able to establish a safe and secure fire pit on the volcano Kilauea. She still resides there today with a host of other gods and demigods.

It should be noted that different cultures view these legends in vastly different ways. In some cases, these are seen as amusing stories meant to pass the time and give a fanciful explanation for very serious natural phenomena. Most cultures see them as a part of their past. In some cases, however, these gods and goddesses are very much alive to the cultures that created them. In Hawaii, Pele is seen as very much alive and well—still making mischief on the island of Hawaii in the form of a beautiful young woman or a stately old woman, often accompanied by a white dog.

See Also: Crater Lake, Oregon, United States; Maui, Legend of; Pele, Legend of; St. Helens, Mount, Washington, United States.

Further Reading

Bressan, D. (2014, June 18). Namazu the earthshaker. Retrieved from http://blogs .scientificamerican.com/history-of-geology/2012/03/10/namazu-the-earthshaker/

Bressan, D. (2014, June 18). The mythical fire-mountains of the Cascades. Retrieved from http://blogs.scientificamerican.com/history-of-geology/2014/05/18/the-mythical-fire -mountains-of-the-cascades/

McSaveney, E. (2014, June 18). Historic earthquakes—earthquakes in Maori tradition. Retrieved from http://www.teara.govt.nz/en/historic-earthquakes/page-1

Vitaliano, D. B. (2007). Geomythology: Geological origins of myths and legends. *Geological Society of London Special Publications* 273, 1–7.

W

Williams, Howel

Howel Williams was born in Liverpool, England, on October 8, 1898. He had a twin named David, who also became a noted geologist, and had six other siblings. Howel's parents noticed his talents when he was young, and encouraged his academic pursuits. He earned a scholarship to the University of Liverpool and graduated with a bachelor's degree in geography before he was 20. His interests drifted toward archaeology so he participated in excavations as he pursued a master's degree in geography, also from the University of Liverpool. While excavating baths at a Roman camp site in Wales, however, Williams took an interest in fossils in the slate that paved the bath floors. He sought information from one of the university's geology professors, and soon after began taking geology courses and working toward a master's degree in that. He received his master's degree in 1924. Williams earned a scholarship to study at Imperial College toward attaining a D.Sc. in geology. Study of ancient volcanic rocks in northern Wales led him to investigate classic European volcanic fields in the Eifel district of Germany and the Auvergne in France. Williams had stumbled upon the field that would become his primary research interest for the remainder of his life—volcanic geology.

Williams received a fellowship from the Commonwealth Fund that allowed him to spend two years at the University of California at Berkeley. He spent his time conducting field work on Sutter Buttes in the Sacramento Valley and Lassen Peak, and visited Tahiti and Hawaii. After his two years, he returned to England and received his D.Sc. in geology at the University of Liverpool. Williams then spent two years at Imperial College before he was asked to return to Berkeley as an associate professor, in 1930. He rose to the rank of full professor in just seven years, and served as chairman of the geology department between 1945 and 1949. Professor Williams was elected to the National Academy of Sciences in 1950. In 1952 he was named William Smith Lecturer of the Geological Society of London.

Williams' most important contribution to the science of volcanology was a series of works on Crater Lake and on the formation of calderas in general. He also published numerous papers on volcanic domes, classification of pyroclastic rocks, volcanic centers in the Navajo-Hopi region of the southwestern United States, and several volcanic centers in the Cascades. Later in his career, Williams turned back to archaeology and assisted in the study of monoliths in Mexico, as well as studying ancient human footprints near Managua, Nicaragua. He then began studies of several volcanoes within Central America, including those in

Nicaragua, central Costa Rica, El Salvador, Guatemala, and Honduras. He wrote a popular textbook on microscopic study of igneous rocks, published in 1954. His last textbook was *Volcanology*, published just two months before his death on January 12, 1980.

See Also: Crater Lake, Oregon, United States; Lassen Peak, California, United States.

Further Reading

McBirney, A. R. (1991). *Howel Williams, 1898–1980*. National Academy of Sciences. Retrieved from http://www.nasonline.org/publications/biographical-memoirs/memoir-pdfs/williams-howel.pdf
Pabst, A., Carmichael, I. S. E., Constance, L., & Curtis, G. H. (2014, June 9). *Howel Williams (1898–1980)*. Retrieved from http://eps.berkeley.edu/content/howel-williams

World Organization of Volcano Observatories

The World Organization of Volcano Observatories (WOVO) is a commission of the International Association of Volcanology and Chemistry of the Earth's Interior (IAVCEI). It serves volcano observatories worldwide and has roughly 80 member institutions. Although the IAVCEI is a professional organization that admits both individual scientists and organizations as members, WOVO members are organizations, and the vast majority of organizations are government affiliated. Member organizations are actively engaged in volcano monitoring and are responsible for warning the public and appropriate authorities about volcanic activity.

WOVO provides a number of valuable services for several constituents. For the scientists in its member observatories, WOVO maintains a directory of member observatories, information about staff scientists and monitoring networks at each observatory, a library of volcano monitoring reference materials, and a virtual location to facilitate communication and collaboration between observatories. For the general public, there is a list of individual member observatories with links to their websites and a list of news articles. For public officials who must make decisions that impact public safety, there is information regarding volcanic alert levels and aviation color codes that can help guide them toward appropriate decisions. The list of volcano observatories with websites also is available to assist officials in finding the appropriate scientists and organizations to help them understand hazards specific to their situations.

See Also: Volcanic Hazards.

Further Reading

World Organization of Volcano Observatories. http://www.wovo.org/homepage-wovo.org/

Bibliography

Academy of Achievement, a Museum of Living History. (2010). *Robert D. Ballard, Ph.D.* Retrieved August 7, 2012, from http://www.achievement.org/autodoc/page/bal0bio-1

Alaska Earthquake Information Center. *The great Alaska earthquake of 1964.* Retrieved August 1, 2012, from http://www.aeic.alaska.edu/quakes/Alaska_1964_earthquake .html

Alaska Volcano Observatory. *Augustine volcano description and information.* Retrieved August 5, 2012, from http://www.avo.alaska.edu/volcanoes/volcinfo.php?volcname =Augustine

Alaska Volcano Observatory. *Pavlof volcano description and information.* Retrieved June 9, 2014, from http://www.avo.alaska.edu/volcanoes/volcinfo.php?volcname=Pavlof

Alaska Volcano Observatory. *Shishaldin activity.* Retrieved June 9, 2014, from http://www .avo.alaska.edu/activity/Shishaldin.php

Aleuts, The. (1998). In *Red book of the peoples of the Russian Empire.* Retrieved June 9, 2014, from http://www.eki.ee/books/redbook/aleuts.shtml

American Geophysical Union. *Beno Gutenberg (1889–1960).* Retrieved May 9, 2014, from http://honors.agu.org/bowie-lectures/beno-gutenberg-1889-1960/

American Geophysical Union. *Welcome to the Geodesy Section of the American Geophysical Union.* Retrieved June 13, 2013, from http://www.agu.org/sections /geodesy/

American Museum of Natural History. (2000). *Inge Lehmann: Discoverer of the earth's inner core.* Retrieved May 6, 2014, from http://www.amnh.org/education/resources/rfl /web/essaybooks/earth/p_lehmann.html

American Museum of Natural History. *The Aleutian Subduction Zone.* Retrieved March 7, 2014, from http://www.amnh.org/exhibitions/permanent-exhibitions/rose-center-for -earth-and-space/david-s.-and-ruth-l.-gottesman-hall-of-planet-earth/why-are-there -ocean-basins-continents-and-mountains/earthquakes/earthquakes-where-plates -collide/the-aleutian-subduction-zone

Ando, M. (1979). The Hawaii earthquake of November 29, 1975: Low dip angle faulting due to forceful injection of magma. *Journal of Geophysical Research 84* (B13), 7616–7626.

Apple, R. A. (1987). Thomas A. Jaggar, Jr., and the Hawaiian Volcano Observatory. In R. W. Decker, T. L. Wright, & P. H. Stauffer (Eds.), *Volcanism in Hawaii.* (USGS Professional Paper 1350).

Arenal.net. (2011). *Arenal Volcano overview.* Retrieved June 3, 2014, from http://www .arenal.net/arenal-volcano-overview.htm

Arias, L. (2014, February 25). Poás Volcano spews material 300 meters high after explosion inside crater. *The Tico Times.*

Arlington National Cemetery. (2006, December 10). *Harry Hammond Hess, Rear Admiral, United States Navy.* Retrieved May 12, 2014, from http://www.arlingtoncemetery.net/hhhess.htm

Atwater, B. F., Satoko, M.-R., Kenji, S., Yoshinobu, T., Kazue, U., & Yamaguchi, D. K. (2005). *The orphan tsunami of 1700—Japanese clues to a parent earthquake in North America.* (USGS Professional Paper 1707).

Atwater, B. F., & Yamaguchi, D. K. (1991). Sudden, probably coseismic submergence of Holocene trees and grass in coastal Washington State. *Geology 19* (7), 706–709.

Auckland Museum. (November 16, 2009). *Maurice and Katia Krafft.* [video] Retrieved November 4, 2014, from https://www.youtube.com/watch?v=c5CAyaRIW8s

Bardintzeff, J. M., & McBirney, A. R. (2000). *Volcanology* (2nd ed.). Sudbury, MA: Jones and Bartlett.

Barran, M. (2007). *Pliny the Elder.* Retrieved May 15, 2014, from http://scienceworld.wolfram.com/biography/PlinytheElder.html

Basaltic Volcanism Study Project (1981). *Basaltic volcanism of the terrestrial planets.* New York: Pergamon Press.

BBC News. *1985: Volcano kills thousands in Colombia.* Retrieved May 22, 2013, from http://news.bbc.co.uk/onthisday/hi/dates/stories/november/13/newsid_2539000/2539731.stm

BBC News. (December 26, 2003). *Iran earthquake kills thousands.* Retrieved November 4, 2014, from http://news.bbc.co.uk/2/hi/3348613.stm

BBC News Magazine. (2010). *When volcanic ash stopped a jumbo at 37,000ft.* Retrieved March 12, 2014, from http://news.bbc.co.uk/2/hi/uk_news/magazine/8622099.stm

Beget, J. E., & Kowalik, Z. (2006). Confirmation and calibration of computer modeling of tsunamis produced by Augustine Volcano, Alaska. *Science of Tsunami Hazards 24* (4), 257–266.

Benioff, H. (1949). Seismic evidence for the fault origin of oceanic deeps. *Geological Society of America Bulletin 60* (12), 1837–1856.

Bolt, B. A. (1997). Inge Lehmann. *Biographical Memoirs of Fellows of the Royal Society.* Retrieved May 6, 2014, from http://www.physics.ucla.edu/~cwp/articles/bolt.html

Bolt, B. A. (2004). *Earthquakes* (5th ed.). New York: W.H. Freeman and Company.

Bommer, J. J., Benito, B., Ciudad-Real, M., Lemoine, A., Lopez-Menjivar, M., Madariaga, R., Mankelow, J., Mendez de Hasbun, P., Murphy, W., Nieto-Lovo, M., Rodriguez-Pineda, C. & Rosa, H. (2002). The El Salvador earthquakes of January and February 2001: Context, characteristics and implications for seismic risk. *Soil Dynamics and Earthquake Engineering 22* (5), 389–418.

Bressan, D. (2011, September 16). Large igneous provinces and mass extinctions [Scientific American Blog]. Retrieved from http://blogs.scientificamerican.com/history-of-geology/2011/09/16/large-igneous-provinces-and-mass-extinctions/

Bressan, D. (2014, June 18). Namazu the earthshaker [Scientific American Blog]. Retrieved from http://blogs.scientificamerican.com/history-of-geology/2012/03/10/namazu-the-earthshaker/

Bressan, D. (2014, June 18). The mythical fire-mountains of the Cascades [Scientific American Blog]. Retrieved from http://blogs.scientificamerican.com/history-of-geology/2014/05/18/the-mythical-fire-mountains-of-the-cascades/

Bruce, V. (2001). *No apparent danger: The true story of volcanic disaster at Galeras and Nevado Del Ruiz*. New York: HarperCollins Publishers.

Bullard, E. C. (1980). *William Maurice Ewing, 1906–1974*. National Academy of Sciences. Retrieved June 9, 2014, from http://www.nasonline.org/publications/biographical-memoirs/memoir-pdfs/ewing-william.pdf

Bullard, F. M. (1984). *Volcanoes of the Earth*. Austin: University of Texas Press.

Carn, S. A., Pallister, J. S., Lara, L., Ewert, J. W., Watt, S., Prata, A. J., Thomas, R. J., & Villarosa, G. (2009). The unexpected awakening of Chaitén Volcano, Chile. *EOS Transactions of the American Geophysical Union 90* (24), 205–212.

Carnegie Institution of Washington. Geophysical Laboratory. (2005). *Frank A. Perret*. Retrieved June 5, 2014, from https://library.gl.ciw.edu/GLHistory/perret.html

Carrigan, C. R. (2000). Plumbing systems. In H. Sigurdsson, B. Houghton, H. Rymer, J. Stix, & S. McNutt (Eds.), *Encyclopedia of volcanoes*. San Diego, CA: Academic Press.

Cas, R. A. F., & Wright, J.V. (1992). *Volcanic successions, modern and ancient*. London: Chapman & Hall.

Casadevall, T. J. (1993). *Discussions and recommendations from the Workshop on the Impacts of Volcanic Ash on Airport Facilities, Seattle, Washington, April 26–28, 1993*. (USGS Open-File Report 93-518).

Center for the Study of the Pacific Northwest. *Account of Juan de Fuca's voyage*. Retrieved June 17, 2014, from http://www.washington.edu/uwired/outreach/cspn/Website/ClassroomMaterials/ReadingtheRegion/DiscoveringtheRegion/Commentary/1.html

Centro Nacional de Prevencion de Desastres (CENAPRED) (National Center for Prevention of Disasters). Retrieved November 21, 2014, from http://www.cenapred.unam.mx/es/

Chauvin, L. (2007). Recovering from the Peru earthquake. *Time Magazine*. Retrieved May 27, 2014, from http://content.time.com/time/world/article/0,8599,1654411,00.html

Christchurch City Libraries. *New Zealand Disasters, Tangiwai Railway Disaster 1953*. Retrieved June 5, 2014, from http://christchurchcitylibraries.com/kids/nzdisasters/tangiwai.asp

Clague, J. J. (1997). Evidence for large earthquakes at the Cascadia Subduction Zone. *Reviews of Geophysics 35* (4), 439–460.

Cloud, W. K., & Scott, N. H. (1969). Distribution of intensity, Prince William Sound earthquake of 1964. In L. E. Liepold (Ed.), *The Prince William Sound, Alaska, earthquake of 1964 and aftershocks, volume IIB and C* (pp. 5–48). United States Coast and Geodetic Survey. Washington, DC: Government Printing Office.

Clynne, M. A. (1992). Lassen, California. In C. A. Wood, & J. Kienle (Eds.), *Volcanoes of North America, United States and Canada*. Cambridge: Cambridge University Press.

Clynne, M. A., Christiansen, R. L., Felger, T. J., Stuaffer, P. H., & Hendley II, J. W. (2005, April 28). *Eruptions of Lassen Peak, California, 1914–1917*. (USGS Fact Sheet 173-98). Retrieved from http://pubs.usgs.gov/fs/1998/fs173-98/

CNN. *Canada quake triggers Hawaii tsunami scare*. Retrieved October 29, 2012, from http://www.cnn.com/2012/10/28/world/americas/canada-earthquake/index.html?iref=allsearch

Conners, D. (2014, June 9). Eruption subsides at Alaska's Pavlof volcano. *EarthSky*.

Corliss, J. B., & Ballard, R. D. (1977). Oases of life in the cold abyss. *National Geographic 152* (4), 441–453.

Corliss, J. B., Dymond, J., Gordon, L. I., Edmond, J. M., von Herzen, R. P., Ballard, R. D., Green, K., Williams, D., Bainbridge, A., Crane, K., & van Andel, T. H. (1979). Submarine thermal springs on the Galapagos rift. *Science 203* (4385), 1073–1083.

Cornell University. (1997). *Galapagos geology on the Web*. Retrieved June 13, 2014, from http://www.geo.cornell.edu/geology/GalapagosWWW/GalapagosGeology.html

Costa Rica National Parks. *Poás Volcano National Park*. Retrieved June 3, 2014, from http://www.costarica-nationalparks.com/Poásvolcanonationalpark.html

Crandell, D. R., & Mullineaux, D. R. (1978). *Potential hazards from future eruptions of Mount St. Helens Volcano, Washington*. USGS Bulletin 1383-C. Washington, DC: Government Printing Office.

Darwin, C. (1839). *Journal of researches into the geology and natural history of the various countries visited by the HMS Beagle under the command of Captain Fitzroy, RN, from 1832 to 1836*. London: Henry Colburn.

Davies, H. L., Davies, J. M., Lus, W. Y., Perembo, R. C. B., Joku, N., Gedikile, H., & Nongkas, M. *Learning from the Aitape tsunami*. Retrieved May 20, 2014, from http://nctr.pmel.noaa.gov/PNG/Upng/Learned/

Decker, R., & Decker, B. (1998). *Volcanoes* (3rd ed., Academic Version). New York: W.H. Freeman and Company.

Diggins, J. E., & Bell, C. (1965). *String, straightedge, and shadow: The story of geometry*. New York: Viking Press Juvenile.

Dohrer, E. *Mariana Trench: The deepest depths*. Retrieved June 17, 2014, from http://www.livescience.com/23387-mariana-trench.html

Dudley, W. C., & Lee, M. (1998). *Tsunami!* (2nd ed.). Honolulu: University of Hawaii Press.

Dunn, D. A. (2014). *William Maurice Ewing (1906–1974)*. American Geophysical Union. Honors Program. Retrieved June 9, 2014, from http://honors.agu.org/william-maurice-ewing-1906%e2%80%931974/

Durland, K. (1911, January 11). Perret of Vesuvius. *Boston Evening Transcript*.

Dvorak, J. (2011). The origin of the Hawaiian Volcano Observatory. *Physics Today 64* (5), 32–37.

Earthquake Engineering Research Institute. (2007). *The Pisco, Peru, earthquake of August 15, 2007: EERI special earthquake report*. Retrieved May 27, 2014, from https://www.eeri.org/lfe/pdf/peru_pisco_eeri_preliminary_reconnaissance.pdf

Earthscope.org. *San Andreas Fault Observatory at depth*. Retrieved June 2, 2014, from http://www.earthscope.org/assets/uploads/pages/safod_five_years_hi.pdf

Erickson, G. E., Plafker, G., & Concha, J. F. (1970). *Preliminary report on the geologic events associated with the May 31, 1970, Peru earthquake*. (USGS Circular 639).

Espinosa, A. F. (Ed.). (1976). *The Guatemalan earthquake of February 4, 1976, a preliminary report*. (USGS Professional Paper 1002).

Fackler, M. (2012, January 9). In Japan, a rebuilt island serves as a cautionary tale. *New York Times*.

Fisher, R. V., Heiken, G., & Hulen, J. B. (1997). *Volcanoes, crucibles of change*. Princeton, NJ: Princeton University Press.

Foshag, W., & Gonzalez Reyna, J. (1956). *Birth and development of Parícutin volcano Mexico: Geologic investigations in the Parícutin area, Mexico*. (USGS Bulletin 965-D).

Francis, P., & Oppenheimer, C. (2004). *Volcanoes* (2nd ed.). Oxford: Oxford University Press.

Fransson, F. (2006). *Fredrik and crew on Maiken*. Retrieved June 16, 2014, from http://yacht-maiken.blogspot.com/2006/08/stone-sea-and-volcano.html

Geist, E. L. (2000). Origin of the 17 July 1998 Papua New Guinea tsunami: Earthquake or landslide. *Seismological Research Letters 71* (3), 344–351. doi: 10.1785/gssrl.71.3.344

Geology.com. *Plate tectonics and the Hawaiian Hot Spot.* Retrieved November 4, 2014, from http://geology.com/usgs/hawaiian-hot-spot/

GeoNet. *About GeoNet.* Retrieved November 4, 2014, from http://info.geonet.org.nz /display/geonet/About+GeoNet

GeoNet. *Ruapehu Volcanic Alert Levels.* Retrieved June 5, 2014, from http://www.geonet .org.nz/volcano/info/ruapehu

GeoNet. *Taupo.* Retrieved June 5, 2014, from http://info.geonet.org.nz/display/volc/Taupo

Giblin, M. (1950). Frank A. Perret. *Bulletin Volcanologique 10* (1), 191–195.

GNS Science. *Ruapehu.* Retrieved June 5, 2014, from http://www.gns.cri.nz/Home /Learning/Science-Topics/Volcanoes/New-Zealand-Volcanoes/Ruapehu

GNS Science. *Taupo Volcano.* Retrieved June 5, 2014, from http://www.gns.cri.nz/Home /Learning/Science-Topics/Volcanoes/New-Zealand-Volcanoes/Taupo-Volcano

GNS Science. *The hidden fault that caused the February 2011 Christchurch earthquake.* Retrieved June 6, 2014, from http://www.gns.cri.nz/Home/Our-Science/Natural -Hazards/Recent-Events/Canterbury-quake/Hidden-fault

GPS.gov. *Official U.S. Government information about the global positioning system (GPS) and related topics.* Retrieved June 14, 2013, from http://www.gps.gov/

Grambling, C. (2010, April 15). Tracking volcanic ash: Helping airplanes avoid catastrophe. *Earth Magazine* [digital edition]. Retrieved from http://www.earthmagazine.org /tags/april-2010

Gutenberg, B., & Richter, C. F. (1956). Earthquake magnitude, intensity, energy, and acceleration. *Bulletin of the Seismological Society of America 46* (2), 105–145.

Hanks, T. C., & Kanamori, H. A. (1979). Moment magnitude scale. *Journal of Geophysical Research 84* (B5), 2348–2350.

Hansen, G., & Condon, E. (1989). *Denial of disaster.* San Francisco: Cameron and Company.

Hansen, W. R., Eckel, E. B., Schaem, W. E., Lyle, R. E., George, W., & Chance, G. (1966). *The Alaska earthquake March 27, 1964: Field investigations and reconstruction effort.* (USGS Professional Paper 541). Washington, DC: Government Printing Office.

Haslam, M., & Petraglia, M. D. (2009). *Toba, the Toba super-eruption.* University of Oxford. Retrieved November 4, 2014, from http://toba.arch.ox.ac.uk/edu.htm

Helz, R. L. (2005, July). *Monitoring ground deformation from space.* (USGS Fact Sheet on InSAR). Retrieved June 14, 2013, from http://volcanoes.usgs.gov/activity/methods /insar//public_files/InSAR_Fact_Sheet/2005-3025.pdf

Herd, D. G., & Comite de Estudios Vulcanologicos. (1986). The 1985 Ruiz volcano disaster. *EOS, Transactions of the American Geophysical Union 67* (19), 457–460.

Hess, H. H. (1962). History of ocean basins. *Petrologic Studies 4,* 599–620.

Hirata, Y., & Murakami, M. (2006, November 16). Island hit by 1993 killer tsunami remains vigilant. *Japan Times.*

Hokkaido Tsunami Survey Group. National Oceanic and Atmospheric Association (NOAA). (May 7, 2014). *Tsunami devastates Japanese coastal region.* Retrieved from http://nctr.pmel.noaa.gov/okushiri_devastation.html

Hough, S. E. (2007). *Richter's scale: Measure of an earthquake, measure of a man.* Princeton, NJ: Princeton University Press.

Hutchinson, I., & McMillan, A. D. (1997). Archaeological evidence for village abandonment associated with Late Holocene earthquakes at the Northern Cascadia Subduction Zone. *Quaternary Research 48*, 79–87.

Institute for Geological and Nuclear Sciences. Retrieved May 15, 2014, from http://www.gns.cri.nz/

International Association of Volcanology and Chemistry of the Earth's Interior [website]. (2014, August 10). Retrieved from www.iavcei.org

International Volcanic Health Hazard Network. *The health hazards of volcanic ash: A guide for the public*. Retrieved August 5, 2012, from http://www.ivhhn.org/images/pamphlets/Health_Guidelines_English_WEB.pdf

Israel, B. (2014, May 16). Kilauea volcano's deadliest eruption revealed. *Livescience.com*. Retrieved from http://www.livescience.com/17338-hawaii-kilaeua-volcano-explosive.html

Jaggar, T. A. (1956). *My experiments with volcanoes*. Honolulu: Hawaiian Volcano Research Association.

Japan Meteorological Agency. Retrieved June 16, 2014, from http://www.jma.go.jp/jma/indexe.html

Kaahele Hawaii. (2014, May 19). *Poliahu, Goddess of Mauna Kea*. Retrieved from http://www.kaahelehawaii.com/pages/culture_Poliahu.htm

Kamchatka Volcanic Eruption Response Team (KVERT) [website]. Retrieved November 5, 2014, from http://www.kscnet.ru/ivs/kvert/index_eng.php

Kanamori, H. (1970). The Alaska earthquake of 1964: Radiation of long-period surface waves and source mechanism. *Journal of Geophysical Research 27* (26), 5029–5040.

Kanamori, H. (1977). The energy release in great earthquakes. *Journal of Geophysical Research 82* (20), 2981–2987.

Kanamori, K. (1978). Quantification of earthquakes. *Nature 271* (5644), 411–414.

Kane, H. K. (2000). *Pele: Goddess of Hawai'i's Volcanoes, Expanded Edition*. Captain Cook, HI: Kawainui Press.

Kearey, P., Klepeis, K. A., & Vine, F. J. (2009). *Global tectonics* (3rd ed.). Hoboken, NJ: Wiley-Blackwell.

Keller, J. (1992). Memorial for Katja and Maurice Krafft. *Bulletin of Volcanology 54*, 613–614.

Lander, J. F., Whiteside, L. S., Hattori, P. (2002). The tsunami history of Guam: 1849–1993. *The International Journal of the Tsunami Society 20* (3), 158–173.

Lara, L. E. (2009). The 2008 eruption of the Chaitén Volcano, Chile: A preliminary report. *Andean Geology 36* (1), 125–129.

Lawson, A. C., Gilbert, G. K., Reid, H. F., Branner, J. C., Leuschner, A. O., Davidson, G., Burckhalter, C., & Campbell, W.W. (Eds.). (1910). *The California earthquake of April 18, 1906: Report of the State Earthquake Investigation Commission in two volumes and atlas*. Washington, DC: Carnegie Institution of Washington.

Lay, T., & Wallace, T. C. (1995). *Modern global seismology*. San Diego, CA: Academic Press.

Lee, R. V. (2010). Darwin's earthquake. *Revista Médica de Chile 138* (7), 897–901.

Lipman, P. W. (2000). Calderas. In H. Sigurdsson, B. Houghton, H. Rymer, J. Stix, & S. McNutt (Eds.), *Encyclopedia of volcanoes*. San Diego, CA: Academic Press.

Lipman, P. W., & Mullineaux, D. R. (1981). *The 1980 eruptions of Mount St. Helens*. (USGS Professional Paper 1250). Washington, DC: Government Printing Office.

Livescience.com. (2012). *30 years later: Eruption of Mexico's El Chichón.* Retrieved March 24, 2014, from http://www.livescience.com/31299-el-chichon-eruption-anniversary.html

Long-Chavez, A. (2012, January 26). Pisco earthquake: Four years later, Peruvian refugees receive water and power. *Huffington Post.* Retrieved May 27, 2014, from http://www.huffingtonpost.com/2012/01/25/refugees-waited-four-years_n_1232611.html

Los Angeles Times. (1985, October 1). *Charles F. Richter dies; earthquake scale pioneer.* Retrieved from http://articles.latimes.com/1985-10-01/news/mn-19126_1_richter-scale

Ludwin, R. S., Dennis, R., Carver, D., McMillan, A. D., Losey, R., Clague, J., Jonientz-Trisler, C., Bowechop, J., Wray, J., & James, K. (2005). Dating the 1700 Cascadia earthquake: Great coastal earthquakes in native stories. *Seismological Research Letters 76* (2).

Luhr, J. E., & Simkin, T. (Eds.). (1993). *Parícutin: The volcano born in a Mexican cornfield.* Phoenix, AZ: Geoscience Press.

Major, J. J., & Lara, L. E. (2013). Overview of the Chaitén volcano, Chile, and its 2008–2009 eruption. *Andean Geology 40* (2), 196–215.

Malloy, R. J., & Merrill, G. F. (1969). Vertical crustal movement of the sea floor associated with the Prince William Sound, Alaska, earthquake. In L. E. Liepold (Ed.), *The Prince William Sound, Alaska, earthquake of 1964 and aftershocks, volume IIB and C* (pp. 327–338). United States Coast and Geodetic Survey. Washington, DC: Government Printing Office.

Martinson, C. (2014, March 7). *Unimak Area.* Retrieved from http://unimak.us/index.shtml

McBirney, A. R. (1991). *Howel Williams, 1898–1980.* National Academy of Sciences. Retrieved November 5, 2014, from http://www.nasonline.org/publications/biographical-memoirs/memoir-pdfs/williams-howel.pdf

McDonald, G. A., Abbott, A. T., & Peterson, F. L. (1983). *Volcanoes in the sea: The geology of Hawaii* (2nd ed.). University of Hawaii Press.

McNarie, A. D. (2012). The watchmen. *Hana Hou: The Magazine of Hawaiian Airlines 15* (2).

McSaveney, E. (October 14, 2014). Historic earthquakes—earthquakes in Maori tradition. *Te Ara, the encyclopedia of New Zealand.* Retrieved June 18, 2014, from http://www.teara.govt.nz/en/historic-earthquakes/page-1

McSaveney, E. (October 14, 2014). Historic earthquakes—the 2011 Christchurch earthquake and other recent earthquakes. *Te Ara, the encyclopedia of New Zealand.* Retrieved June 6, 2014, from http://www.teara.govt.nz/en/historic-earthquakes/page-13

Miller, T. P., McGimsey, R. G., Richter, D. H., Riehle, J. R., Nye, C. J., Yount, M. E., and Dumoulin, J. A. (1998). *Catalog of the historically active volcanoes of Alaska.* (USGS Open-File Report OF 98-05282). Washington, DC: Government Printing Office.

Moore, J. G., Bryan, W. B., & Ludwig, K. R. (1994). Chaotic deposition by a giant wave, Molokai, Hawaii. *Geological Society of America Bulletin, 106*, 962–967.

Moseley, M. (2014). Kilauea: The eruption of 1924. *Hawaii Tribune-Herald.*

Müller, R. D., Sdrolias, M., Gaina, C., & Roest, W. R. (2008). Age, spreading rates and spreading symmetry of the world's ocean crust. *Geochemistry. Geophysics. Geosystems. 9*, Q04006.

Myles, D. (1985). *The great waves.* New York: McGraw-Hill Book Company.

Nakada, S., Shimizu, H., & Ohta, K. (1999). Overview of the 1990–1995 eruption at Unzen Volcano. *Journal of Volcanology and Geothermal Research 89*, 1–22.

National Geographic Society. *The Mariana Trench*. Retrieved June 17, 2014, from http://deepseachallenge.com/the-expedition/mariana-trench/

National Geographic Society. *The Mariana Trench: Earth's deepest place*. Retrieved June 19, 2014, from http://education.nationalgeographic.com/education/activity/mariana-trench-deepest-place-earth/?ar_a=1

National Information Service for Earthquake Engineering (NISEE). Earthquake Engineering Research Center (EERC), University of California, Berkeley. The Earthquake Engineering online archive. Retrieved August 1, 2012, from http://nisee.berkeley.edu/elibrary/

National Oceanic and Atmospheric Association (NOAA). Jet Stream—Online School for Weather. *Monitoring tsunamis*. Retrieved May 20, 2014, from http://www.srh.noaa.gov/jetstream/tsunami/dart.htm

National Oceanic and Atmospheric Administration (NOAA). National Geophysical Data Center. *Arica, Chile, earthquake*. Retrieved August 5, 2012, from http://www.ngdc.noaa.gov/nndc/struts/results?EQ_0=983&t=101650&s=8&d=22,26,13,12&nd=display

National Oceanic and Atmospheric Administration (NOAA). NOAA Watch. NOAA's all hazards monitor [website]. Retrieved November 5, 2014, from http://www.noaawatch.gov

National Oceanic and Atmospheric Administration (NOAA). (2013, April 16). Ocean Explorer. SONAR. Retrieved April 30, 2014, from http://oceanexplorer.noaa.gov/technology/tools/sonar/sonar.html

National Oceanic and Atmospheric Association (NOAA). Pacific Tsunami Warning Center (PTWC). *PTWC history*. Retrieved May 20, 2014, from http://ptwc.weather.gov/ptwc/history.php

National Oceanic and Atmospheric Administration (NOAA). (2014, June 03). *What is LIDAR?* ("LIDAR—light detection and ranging—is a remote sensing method used to examine the surface of the Earth.") Retrieved June 13, 2013, from http://oceanservice.noaa.gov/facts/lidar.html

National Park Service. *Crater Lake National Park, Oregon*. Retrieved May 12, 2014, from http://www.nps.gov/crla/index.htm

National Park Service. Hawaii Volcanoes National Park. *Frequently asked questions*. Retrieved May 19, 2014, from http://www.nps.gov/havo/faqs.htm

Natural Hazard Mitigation Association (NHMA) [website]. Retrieved November 5, 2014, from http://nhma.info

Neal, C. T., Casadevall, T. J., Miller, T. P., Hendley II, J. W., & Stauffer, P. H. (1997). *Volcanic ash—danger to aircraft in the North Pacific*. (USGS Fact Sheet 030-97, Online Version 1.0). Retrieved August 5, 2012, from http://pubs.usgs.gov/fs/fs030-97/

New Mexico Bureau of Geology and Mineral Resources. *The Ship Rock landform*. Retrieved June 17, 2013, from http://geoinfo.nmt.edu/tour/landmarks/shiprock/

Newhall, C., Hendley, J. W., & Stauffer, P. H. (1997). *The cataclysmic 1991 eruption of Mount Pinatubo, Philippines*. (USGS Fact Sheet 113-97). Washington, DC: Government Printing Office.

Newhall, C. G., & Self, S. (1982). The Volcanic Explosivity Index (VEI): An estimate of explosive magnitude for historical volcanism. *Journal of Geophysical Research 87* (C2), 1231–1238.

Nye, C. J., Keith, T. E. C., Eichelberger, J. C., Miller, T. P., McNutt, S. R., Moran, S., Schneider, D. J., Dehn, J., & Schaefer, J. R. (2002). The 1999 eruption of Shishaldin

Volcano, Alaska: Monitoring a distant eruption. *Bulletin of Volcanology 64* (8), 507–519.

Office of the Home Secretary & National Academy of Sciences. (1999). *Biographical Memoirs.* Vol. 76. National Academies Press.

Oliver, J., & Isacks, B. (1967). Deep earthquake zones, anomalous structures in the upper mantle, and the lithosphere. *Journal of Geophysical Research 72* (16), 4259–4275.

Orozco, C. (2012). *The Legend of Popocatepetl and Iztaccihuatl.* Retrieved June 4, 2014, from http://www.inside-mexico.com/legends/volcanes.htm

Pabst, A., Carmichael, I. S. E., Constance, L., & Curtis, G. H. (2031). *Howel Williams (1898–1980).* Retrieved June 9, 2014, from http://eps.berkeley.edu/content/howel-williams

Pacific Northwest Seismic Network. *Plate tectonics.* Retrieved June 12, 2014, from http://www.pnsn.org/outreach/about-earthquakes/plate-tectonics

Pacific Tsunami Museum [website]. Retrieved from http://www.tsunami.org

Papahānaumokuākea Marine National Monument [website]. Retrieved June 16, 2014, from http://www.papahanaumokuakea.gov/about/

Pappas, S. Pinatubo: Why the biggest volcanic eruption wasn't the deadliest. *LiveScience .com.* Retrieved March 17, 2014, from http://www.livescience.com/14603-pinatubo -eruption-20-anniversary.html

Pararas-Carayannis, G. (1986). The Pacific tsunami warning system. *Earthquakes & Volcanoes 18* (3), 122–130.

Philippine Institute of Volcanology and Seismology (PHIVOLCS) [website]. Retrieved November 5, 2014, from www.phivolcs.dost.gov.ph

Pihana, J. K. The white mountain. *Mauna Kea Visitor Information Station.* Retrieved May 19, 2014, from http://www.ifa.hawaii.edu/info/vis/culture/the-white-mountain.html

Plafker, G. (1965). Tectonic deformation associated with the 1964 Alaska earthquake. *Science 148* (3678), 1675–1687.

Plafker, G. (1976). Tectonic aspects of the Guatemala earthquake of 4 February 1976. *Science 193* (4259), 1201–1208.

Premiere Motivational Speakers Bureau. *Robert Ballard, oceanic researcher who discovered the wreckage of the Titanic.* Retrieved August 7, 2012, from http://premierespeakers .com/robert_ballard/bio

Pringle, P. (1992). Rainier, Washington. In C. A. Wood, & J. Kienle (Eds.), *Volcanoes of North America, United States and Canada.* Cambridge: Cambridge University Press.

Public Broadcasting System (PBS). A Science Odyssey: People and Discoveries. *Harry Hess 1906–1969.* Retrieved May 12, 2014, from http://www.pbs.org/wgbh/aso/databank /entries/bohess.html

Puertas, L., & Elsen, J. (2007, August 16). Earthquake in Peru kills hundreds. *The New York Times.* Retrieved May 27, 2014, from http://www.nytimes.com/2007/08/16/world /americas/16cnd-peru.html?_r=0

Rampino, M. R., & Ambrose, S. H. (2000). *Volcanic winter in the Garden of Eden: The Toba supereruption and the late Pleistocene human population crash.* Geological Society of America (Special Paper 345).

Reid, H. F. (1910). *The California earthquake of April 18, 1906: Report of the State Earthquake Investigation Commission in two volumes and atlas. Volume II: The mechanics of the earthquake.* Washington, DC: Carnegie Institution of Washington.

Richter, C. F. (1935). An instrumental earthquake magnitude scale. *Bulletin of the Seismological Society of America 25* (1), 1–32.

Richter, C. F. (1958). *Elementary seismology*. San Francisco: W.H. Freeman and Company.

Romero, F. (2010, January 13). Top 10 deadliest earthquakes. *Time Magazine.* Retrieved November 5, 2014, from http://content.time.com/time/specials/packages/article/0,28804,1953425_1953424_1953359,00.html

Rondeau, R. (2014, June 5). "Elektron" Perret patent bi-polar battery fan 1889–1890. *Antique Phonograph, Fan, and Photography Site.* Retrieved November 5, 2014, from http://www.edisontinfoil.com/fans/perret.htm

San Diego State University. *How volcanoes work: Tephra and pyroclastic rocks.* Retrieved May 15, 2014, from http://www.geology.sdsu.edu/how_volcanoes_work/Tephra.html

Sato, H., Fujii, T. & Nakada, S. (1992). Crumbling of dacite dome lava and generation of pyroclastic flows at Unzen volcano. *Nature 360*, (6405), 664–666.

Savage, B., & Helmberger, D. V. (2001). Kursk explosion. *Bulletin of the Seismological Society of America 91* (4), 753–759.

Scheid, A. (1979). Interview with Charles Richter. *Oral History Project.* California Institute of Technology Archives. Retrieved from http://resolver.caltech.edu/CaltechOH:OH_Richter_C

Schultz, S. S., & Wallace, R. E. *The San Andreas Fault.* United States Geologic Survey. Retrieved June 2, 2014, from http://pubs.usgs.gov/gip/earthq3/safaultgip.html

Science Daily. *New evidence for assessing tsunami risk from very large volcanic island landslides.* Retrieved May 21, 2014, from http://www.sciencedaily.com/releases/2013/12/131211104242.htm

Seach, J. Mt Lamington Volcano. *Volcano Live.* Retrieved May 7, 2014, from http://www.volcanolive.com/lamington.html

Seach, J. (2013). Popocatépetl Volcano. *Volcano Live.* Retrieved November 23, 2014, from http://www.volcanolive.com/popocatepetl.html

Sherrod, D. R. (1992). Hood, Mount, Oregon. In C. A. Wood, & J. Kienle, *Volcanoes of North America, United States and Canada.* Cambridge: Cambridge University Press.

Sigurdsson, H., Houghton, B., Rymer, H., Stix, J., & McNutt, S. (Eds.). (2000). *Encyclopedia of volcanoes.* San Diego, CA: Academic Press.

Simkin, T., & Fiske, R. S. 1983. *Krakatau 1883: The volcanic eruption and its effects.* Smithsonian Institution Press.

Slate.com. (2013). *Lake Nyos suffocated over 1,746 people in a single night.* [Atlas Obscura Blog]. Retrieved November 5, 2014, from http://www.slate.com/blogs/atlas_obscura/2013/07/26/lake_nyos_killed_1746_when_it_released_a_huge_pocket_of_co2.html

Smithsonian Institution. National Museum of Natural History. Global Volcanism Program. (2014). *Chaitén summary.* Retrieved November 5, 2014, from http://www.volcano.si.edu/volcano.cfm?vnum=1508-041

Smithsonian Institution. National Museum of Natural History. Global Volcanism Program. (2014). *Welcome to the Global Volcanism Program.* Retrieved November 5, 2014, from http://www.volcano.si.edu/

Smithsonian Institution. National Museum of Natural History. (2013). *Parícutin: The birth of a volcano.* Retrieved June 27, 2013, from http://www.mnh.si.edu/onehundredyears/expeditions/Paricutin.html

Spaeth, M. G., & Berkman, S. C. (1965). *The tsunami of March 28, 1964, as recorded at tide stations.* United States Coast and Geodetic Survey. Washington, DC: United States Government Printing Office.

Squier, E. G. (1869). The great South American earthquakes of 1868. *Harper's New Monthly Magazine 38* (227), 603–623.

Steinbrugge, K. V. (1985). *Catalog of earthquake related sounds, 1985 update, record 1.* Retrieved July 27, 2012, from http://webshaker.ucsd.edu/soundRecords.html

Steinbrugge, K. V. (1967). Introduction to the earthquake engineering of the Prince William Sound, Alaska, earthquake. In F. J. Wood (Ed.), *The Prince William Sound, Alaska, earthquake of 1964 and aftershocks, volume IIA* (pp. 1–6). United States Coast and Geodetic Survey. Washington, DC: Government Printing Office.

Steinbrugge, K. V., Manning, J. H., & Degenkolb, H. J. (1967). Building damage in Anchorage. In F. J. Wood (Ed.), *The Prince William Sound, Alaska, earthquake of 1964 and aftershocks, volume IIA* (pp. 7–217). United States Coast and Geodetic Survey. Washington, DC: Government Printing Office.

Sur, P. (2012, March 4). Lava claims final home. *Hawaii Tribune-Herald.*

Swanson, E. R., & McDowell, F. W. (1984). *Calderas of the Sierra Madre occidental volcanic field Western Mexico (abstract).* Retrieved August 20, 2012, from http://www.agu.org/pubs/crossref/1984/JB089iB10p08787.shtml

Sykes, L. R. (1966). The seismicity and deep structure of island arcs. *Journal of Geophysical Research 71* (12), 2981–3006.

Tarbuck, E. J., Lutgens, F. K., & Tasa, D. 2011. *Earth: An introduction to physical geology* (10th ed.). Upper Saddle River, NJ: Pearson Prentice Hall/Pearson Education, Inc.

Terra Daily. *Costa Rica volcano erupts, national park evacuated.* Retrieved May 24, 2010, from http://www.terradaily.com/reports/Costa_Rica_volcano_erupts_national_park_evacuated_999.html

The Columbian. (1980, May 19). *St. Helens spews death, destruction.* Retrieved November 5, 2014, from http://www.columbian.com/news/1980/may/19/st-helens-spews-death-destruction/

Thompson, D. (2000). *Volcano cowboys: The rocky evolution of a dangerous science.* New York: St. Martin's Press.

Tilgner, E. E., & Peterson, J. R. (1969). The Alaska tsunami warning system. In L. E. Liepold (Ed.), *The Prince William Sound, Alaska, earthquake of 1964 and aftershocks, volume IIB and C* (pp. 309–324). United States Coast and Geodetic Survey. Washington, DC: Government Printing Office.

Tilling, R. I., Koyanagi, R. Y., Lipman, P. W., Lockwood, J. P., Moore, J. G., & Swanson, D. A. (1976). *Earthquake and related catastrophic events, Island of Hawaii, November 29, 1975: A preliminary report.* (USGS Circular 740).

University of California Berkeley. Seismological Laboratory. (2008). *Today in earthquake history: Mexico City 1985.* Retrieved from http://seismo.berkeley.edu/blog/seismoblog.php/2008/09/19/title

University of Hawaii at Hilo Center for the Study of Active Volcanoes [website]. http://www.hilo.hawaii.edu/~csav/krafft/

University of Southern California. Tsunami Research Group. *1946 Aleutian tsunami.* Retrieved March 7, 2014, from http://www.usc.edu/dept/tsunamis/alaska/1946/webpages/

University of Southern California. Tsunami Research Group. *1958 Lituya Bay Tsunami.* Retrieved November 5, 2014, from http://www.usc.edu/dept/tsunamis/alaska/1958/webpages/

U.S. Geological Survey. (2005). *A pioneering volcanologist narrowly beats the Reaper.* Retrieved June 5, 2014, from http://hvo.wr.usgs.gov/volcanowatch/archive/2005/05_08_25.html

U.S. Geological Survey. (2012, May 10). *The Novarupta-Katmai eruption of 1912—largest eruption of the Twentieth Century: Centennial perspectives.* (USGS Professional Paper 1791).

U.S. Geological Survey. (2013, September 11). *Natural hazards* [website]. Retrieved November 5, 2014, from http://www.usgs.gov/natural_hazards

U.S. Geological Survey. Alaska Volcano Observatory. *Redoubt Volcano description and information.* Retrieved May 28, 2014, from http://www.avo.alaska.edu/volcanoes/volcinfo.php?volcname=Redoubt

U.S. Geological Survey. *Canada volcanoes and volcanics.* Retrieved May 23, 2013, from http://vulcan.wr.usgs.gov/Volcanoes/Canada/description_canadian_volcanics.html (Canada volcanoes).

U.S. Geological Survey. *Cleveland activity.* Retrieved May 28, 2014, from http://www.avo.alaska.edu/activity/Cleveland.php

U.S. Geological Survey. *Description: Lava tubes and lava tube caves.* Retrieved May 6, 2014, from http://vulcan.wr.usgs.gov/Glossary/LavaTubes/framework.html

U.S. Geological Survey. *Description: Nevado del Ruiz eruption and lahar, 1985.* Retrieved May 22, 2013, from http://vulcan.wr.usgs.gov/Volcanoes/Colombia/Ruiz/description_eruption_lahar_1985.html

U.S. Geological Survey. *Harry Hammond Hess: Spreading the seafloor.* Retrieved May 12, 2014, from http://pubs.usgs.gov/gip/dynamic/HHH.html

U.S. Geological Survey. *M7.7—139 km S of Masset, Canada.* Retrieved October 29, 2012, from http://earthquake.usgs.gov/earthquakes/eventpage/usb000df7n#summary

U.S. Geological Survey. *Magnitude 6.1—South Island of New Zealand.* Retrieved June 6, 2014, from http://earthquake.usgs.gov/earthquakes/eqinthenews/2011/usb0001igm/#summary

U.S. Geological Survey. *Monitoring ground deformation from space: Fact sheet 2005–3025.* Retrieved May 13, 2014, from http://volcanoes.usgs.gov/activity/methods/insar/public_files/InSAR_Fact_Sheet/2005-3025.pdf

U.S. Geological Survey. *Mount St. Helens—From the 1980 eruption to 2000.* (Fact Sheet 036-00. Online Version 1.0). Retrieved from http://pubs.usgs.gov/fs/2000/fs036-00/

U.S. Geological Survey. (1999). *Shrinking Farallon Plate.* Retrieved June 12, 2014, from http://pubs.usgs.gov/gip/dynamic/Farallon.html

U.S. Geological Survey. *The orphan tsunami of 1700—Japanese clues to a parent earthquake in North America* (Professional Paper 1707). Retrieved May 23, 2013, from http://pubs.usgs.gov/pp/pp1707/pp1707.pdf

U.S. Geological Survey. Earthquake Hazards Program. *Canada earthquake information.* Retrieved June 4, 2014, from http://earthquake.usgs.gov/earthquakes/world/?region=Canada

U.S. Geological Survey. Earthquake Hazards Program. *Deaths from earthquakes in 1990.* Retrieved March 12, 2014 from http://earthquake.usgs.gov/earthquakes/eqarchives/year/1990/1990_deaths.php

U.S. Geological Survey. Earthquake Hazards Program. *Earthquake glossary—earthquake.* Retrieved June 17, 2013, from http://earthquake.usgs.gov/learn/glossary/?term=earthquake

U.S. Geological Survey. Earthquake Hazards Program. *Historic earthquakes.* Retrieved August 5, 2012, from http://earthquake.usgs.gov/earthquakes/world/events/1868 _08_13.php

U.S. Geological Survey. Earthquake Hazards Program. *Historic earthquakes. Magnitude 6.8 WASHINGTON. 2001 February 28.* Retrieved October 29, 2012, from http:// earthquake.usgs.gov/earthquakes/eqarchives/year/2001/2001_02_28.php

U.S. Geological Survey. Earthquake Hazards Program. *Historic earthquakes in the United States and its territories.* Retrieved June 17, 2014, from http://earthquake.usgs.gov /earthquakes/states/historical_state.php#washington

U.S. Geological Survey. Earthquake Hazards Program. *Historic world earthquakes. By Country/region & date.* Retrieved June 16, 2014, from http://earthquake.usgs.gov /earthquakes/world/historical_country.php

U.S. Geological Survey. Earthquake Hazards Program. *Historic world earthquakes. By Country/region & date. Columbia.* Retrieved June 5, 2014, from http://earthquake.usgs .gov/earthquakes/world/historical_country.php#colombia

U.S. Geological Survey. Earthquake Hazards Program. *Historic world earthquakes. By Country/region/state/territory.* Retrieved June 16, 2014, from http://earthquake.usgs .gov/earthquakes/region.php

U.S. Geological Survey. Earthquake Hazards Program. *Magnitude 5.8—VIRGINIA.* Retrieved June 17, 2013, from http://earthquake.usgs.gov/earthquakes/eqinthenews /2011/se082311a/#summary

U.S. Geological Survey. Earthquake Hazards Program. (2004). *Magnitude 9.1—off the west coast of northern Sumatra.* Retrieved from http://earthquake.usgs.gov/earthquakes /eqinthenews/2004/us2004slav/#summary.

U.S. Geological Survey. Earthquake Hazards Program. *ShakeMaps.* Retrieved May 13, 2014, from http://earthquake.usgs.gov/earthquakes/shakemap/

U.S. Geological Survey. Earthquake Hazards Program. *The Parkfield, California, earthquake experiment.* Retrieved June 2, 2014, from http://earthquake.usgs.gov/research /parkfield/

U.S. Geological Survey. Earthquake Hazards Program. *Unimak Island.* Retrieved March 7, 2014, from http://earthquake.usgs.gov/earthquakes/states/events/1946_04_01.php

U.S. Geological Survey. *Guam/Northern Marianas earthquake information.* Retrieved June 17, 2014, from http://earthquake.usgs.gov/earthquakes/states/?region=Guam /Northern Marianas

U.S. Geological Survey. Hawaiian Volcano Observatory. (1998, December 7). *November 29, 1975, Kalapana earthquake.* Retrieved May 19, 2014, from http://hvo.wr.usgs.gov /earthquakes/destruct/1975Nov29/

U.S. Geological Survey. Hawaiian Volcano Observatory. (2006, October 12). Devil's Throat has evolved into a shadow of its former self. *Volcano Watch.* Retrieved August 20, 2012, from http://hvo.wr.usgs.gov/volcanowatch/archive/2006/06_10_12.html

U.S. Geological Survey. Hawaiian Volcano Observatory. (2008, September 25). *A 1951 tragedy in Papua New Guinea provides an important reference in the volcanologic literature.* Retrieved May 7, 2014, from http://hvo.wr.usgs.gov/volcanowatch/archive /2008/08_09_25.html

U.S. Geological Survey. Hawaiian Volcano Observatory. *Anatahan volcano.* Retrieved June 17, 2014, from http://hvo.wr.usgs.gov/cnmi/

U.S. Geological Survey. Hawaiian Volcano Observatory. *East Maui, or Haleakala—a potentially hazardous volcano.* Retrieved May 20, 2014, from http://hvo.wr.usgs.gov /volcanoes/haleakala/main.html

U.S. Geological Survey. Hawaiian Volcano Observatory. *Hualalai, Hawaii's third active volcano.* Retrieved May 19, 2014, from http://hvo.wr.usgs.gov/volcanoes/hualalai /main.html

U.S. Geological Survey. Hawaiian Volcano Observatory. *Is Kilauea falling into the ocean?* Retrieved May 7, 2014, from http://hvo.wr.usgs.gov/volcanowatch/archive/other /landslide.html

U.S. Geological Survey. Hawaiian Volcano Observatory. *Kilauea—perhaps the world's most active volcano.* Retrieved August 20, 2012, from http://hvo.wr.usgs.gov/kilauea/

U.S. Geological Survey. Hawaiian Volcano Observatory. *Kilauea's East rift zone (Puu Oo) eruption 1983 to present.* Retrieved May 19, 2014, from http://hvo.wr.usgs.gov/kilauea /summary/main.html

U.S. Geological Survey. Hawaiian Volcano Observatory. *Lava-flow hazard zones, Island of Hawai'i.* Retrieved March 24, 2014, from http://hvo.wr.usgs.gov/hazards/FAQ _LavaFlowHazardZone/P2.html

U.S. Geological Survey. Hawaiian Volcano Observatory. *Mauna Kea: Hawaii's Tallest Volcano.* Retrieved May 19, 2014, from http://hvo.wr.usgs.gov/volcanoes/maunakea/

U.S. Geological Survey. Hawaiian Volcano Observatory. *Mauna Loa, Earth's largest volcano.* Retrieved May 20, 2014, from http://hvo.wr.usgs.gov/maunaloa/

U.S. Geological Survey. Hawaiian Volcano Observatory. *Mauna Loa 1984 eruption: March 25–April 15.* Retrieved May 20, 2014, from http://hvo.wr.usgs.gov/maunaloa/history /1984.html

U.S. Geological Survey. Hawaiian Volcano Observatory. *On the trail of hotspots: The Galapagos and Hawaiian islands.* Retrieved June 11, 2014, from http://hvo.wr.usgs .gov/volcanowatch/archive/2006/06_03_30.html

U.S. Geological Survey. Hawaiian Volcano Observatory. *Youngest lava flows on East Maui probably older than A.D. 1790.* Retrieved May 20, 2014, from http://hvo.wr.usgs.gov /volcanowatch/archive/1999/99_09_09.html

U.S. Geological Survey. Volcano Disaster Assistance Program. Retrieved June 6, 2013, from http://volcanoes.usgs.gov/vdap/

U.S. Geological Survey. Volcano Disaster Assistance Program. Retrieved May 12, 2014, from http://volcanoes.usgs.gov/vdap/index.php

U.S. Geological Survey. Volcano Disaster Assistance Program. *VDAP responses at Chaitén in Chile.* Retrieved November 5, 2014, from http://volcanoes.usgs.gov/vdap/activities /responses/chaiten.php

U.S. Geological Survey. Volcano Hazards Program. (2008, August 13). *How we monitor volcanoes.* Retrieved May 13, 2014, from http://volcanoes.usgs.gov/activity/methods/

U.S. Geological Survey. Volcano Hazards Program. *Lahars and their effects.* Retrieved May 12, 2014, from http://volcanoes.usgs.gov/hazards/lahar/

U.S. Geological Survey. Volcano Hazards Program. *Lava, lava flows, lava lakes, magma.* Retrieved May 15, 2014, from http://vulcan.wr.usgs.gov/Glossary/LavaFlows/description _lava_flows.html

U.S. Geological Survey. Volcano Hazards Program. Cascades Volcano Observatory. *Cascade Range volcanoes: Historical timeline.* Retrieved from http://vulcan.wr.usgs .gov/LivingWith/Historical/timeline.html

U.S. Geological Survey. Volcano Hazards Program. Cascades Volcano Observatory. *Description: 1883 eruption of Krakatau.* (U.S. Geological Survey, Krakatau, 2012). Retrieved August 20, 2012, from http://vulcan.wr.usgs.gov/Volcanoes/Indonesia /description_krakatau_1883_eruption.html

U.S. Geological Survey. Volcano Hazards Program. Cascades Volcano Observatory. *Mount Hood.* Retrieved May 23, 2014, from http://volcanoes.usgs.gov/volcanoes/mount _hood/

U.S. Geological Survey. Volcano Hazards Program. Cascades Volcano Observatory. *Mount Rainier.* Retrieved May 22, 2014, from http://volcanoes.usgs.gov/volcanoes/mount _rainier/

U.S. Geological Survey. Volcano Hazards Program. Cascades Volcano Observatory. *Naming the Cascade Range Volcanoes—Mount St. Helens, Washington.* Retrieved from http://vulcan.wr.usgs.gov/LivingWith/Historical/naming_mount_st_helens.html

U.S. Geological Survey. Volcano Hazards Program. Cascades Volcano Observatory. *Report: Eruptive history of Mount Mazama and Crater Lake Caldera, Cascade Range, U.S.A.* Retrieved August 20, 2012, from http://vulcan.wr.usgs.gov/Volcanoes /CraterLake/Publications/BaconJVGR83/abstract.html

U.S. Geological Survey. Volcano Hazards Program. Cascades Volcano Observatory. *The Volcanoes of Lewis and Clark.* Retrieved November 5, 2014, from http://vulcan.wr.usgs .gov/LivingWith/Historical/LewisClark/volcanoes_lewis_clark.html

U.S. Geological Survey. Volcano Hazards Program. *Mount Shasta.* Retrieved May 28, 2014, from http://volcanoes.usgs.gov/volcanoes/mount_shasta/

U.S. Geological Survey. Volcano Hazards Program. *Mount St. Helens: 1980 cataclysmic eruption.* Retrieved from http://volcanoes.usgs.gov/volcanoes/st_helens/st_helens _geo_hist_99.html

U.S. Geological Survey. Volcano Hazards Program. *Photo glossary: Aa.* Retrieved July 26, 2012, from http://volcanoes.usgs.gov/images/pglossary/aa.php

U.S. Geological Survey. Volcano Hazards Program. *Photo glossary: Andesite.* Retrieved August 3, 2012, from http://volcanoes.usgs.gov/images/pglossary/andesite.php

U.S. Geological Survey. Volcano Hazards Program. *Photo glossary: Basalt.* Retrieved August 17, 2012, from http://volcanoes.usgs.gov/images/pglossary/basalt.php

U.S. Geological Survey. Volcano Hazards Program. *Photo glossary: Lava dome.* Retrieved May 6, 2014, from http://volcanoes.usgs.gov/images/pglossary/LavaDome.php

U.S. Geological Survey. Volcano Hazards Program. *Photo glossary: Lava tube.* Retrieved May 6, 2014, from http://volcanoes.usgs.gov/images/pglossary/LavaTube.php

U.S. Geological Survey. Volcano Hazards Program. *Photo glossary: Phreatic eruption.* Retrieved May 16, 2014, from http://volcanoes.usgs.gov/images/pglossary /HydroVolcEruption.php

U.S. Geological Survey. Volcano Hazards Program. *Photo glossary: VEI.* Retrieved June 18, 2013, from http://volcanoes.usgs.gov/images/pglossary/vei.php

U.S. Geological Survey. Volcano Hazards Program. *Significant lahars at Mount Rainier.* Retrieved May 12, 2014, from http://volcanoes.usgs.gov/volcanoes/mount_rainier /mount_rainier_geo_hist_79.html

U.S. Geological Survey. Volcano Hazards Program. *The Cascades.* Retrieved June 17, 2014, from http://volcanoes.usgs.gov/about/volcanoes/cascades/index.php

U.S. Geological Survey. Volcano Hazards Program. *Three Sisters.* Retrieved May 23, 2014, from http://volcanoes.usgs.gov/volcanoes/three_sisters/

U.S. Geological Survey. Volcano Hazards Program. *U.S. volcanoes and current activity alerts.* Retrieved June 17, 2014, from http://volcanoes.usgs.gov/

U.S. Geological Survey. Volcano Hazards Program. *Volcanic gases and their effects.* Retrieved March 11, 2014, from http://volcanoes.usgs.gov/hazards/gas/

U.S. Geological Survey. Volcano Hazards Program. (2005). *Volcanoes and global cooling.* Retrieved March 11, 2014, from http://vulcan.wr.usgs.gov/Glossary/VolcWeather /description_volcanoes_and_weather.html

U.S. Geological Survey. Volcano Hazards Program. Yellowstone Volcano Observatory. *Questions about supervolcanoes.* Retrieved May 15, 2014, from http://volcanoes.usgs .gov/volcanoes/yellowstone/yellowstone_sub_page_49.html

U.S. Navy Museum. *Biography: Dr. Robert Ballard 1942–.* Retrieved August 7, 2012, from http://www.history.navy.mil/branches/teach/ends/ballard.htm

Vallance, J. W., Gardner, C., Scott, W. E., Iverson, R., & Pierson, T. (2010). Mount St. Helens: A 30-year legacy of volcanism. *EOS, Transactions of the American Geophysical Union 91,* 169–170.

Vespermann, D., & Schmincke, H.-U. (2000). Scoria cones and tuff rings. In H. Sigurdsson, B. Houghton, H. Rymer, J. Stix, & S. McNutt (Eds.), *Encyclopedia of volcanoes.* San Diego, CA: Academic Press.

Vezzoli, L., & Acocella, V. (2009). Easter Island, SE Pacific: An end-member type of hotspot volcanism. *Geological Society of America Bulletin 121* (5–6), 869–886.

Vitaliano, D. B. (2007). Geomythology: Geological origins of myths and legends. In L. Piccardi, & W. B. Masse (Eds.), *Myth and geology, Special Publications* (v. 273, pp. 1–7). London: Geological Society of London.

Voight, B. (1990). The 1985 Nevado del Ruiz volcano catastrophe: Anatomy and retrospection. *Journal of Volcanology and Geothermal Research 44,* 349–386.

Volcano Discovery. *Guagua Pichincha Volcano.* Retrieved June 4, 2014, from http://www .volcanodiscovery.com/guagua_pichincha.html

Volcano Discovery. *Llullaillaco volcano.* Retrieved June 11, 2014, from http://www .volcanodiscovery.com/llullaillaco.html

Volcano Discovery. *Volcano news: Colima Volcano (Mexico).* Retrieved June 4, 2014, from http://www.volcanodiscovery.com/colima/news.html

Volcano Discovery. *Volcano news: Santa Maria (Guatemala).* Retrieved June 13, 2014, from http://www.volcanodiscovery.com/guatemala/santiaguito/news.html

Volcano Discovery. *Which is the world's highest volcano?* Retrieved June 11, 2014, from http://www.volcanodiscovery.com/volcanology/worlds-highest-volcano.html

Volcano World. *Colima.* Retrieved June 4, 2014, from http://volcano.oregonstate.edu /colima

Volcano World. *Rabaul Caldera, Papua New Guinea.* Retrieved June 18, 2014, from http:// volcano.oregonstate.edu/oldroot/volcanoes/rabaul/rabaul.html

Volcano World. *Santa Maria.* Retrieved June 13, 2014, from http://volcano.oregonstate .edu/santa-maria

Vrijenhoek, R. C. (2009). Hydrothermal vents. In R. G. Gillespie, & D. A. Clague (Eds.), *Encyclopedia of islands.* University of California Press.

Wallace, P., & Anderson, Jr., A. T. (2000). Volatiles in magmas. In H. Sigurdsson, B. Houghton, H. Rymer, J. Stix, & S. McNutt (Eds.), *Encyclopedia of volcanoes.* San Diego, CA: Academic Press.

Wang, K., Chen, Q.-F., Sun, S., & Wang, A. (2006). Predicting the 1975 Haicheng earthquake. *Bulletin of the Seismological Society of America 96* (3), 757–795.

Weintraub, B. (1982). Fire and ash, darkness at Noon. *National Geographic Magazine 162* (5), 660–678.

Welch, W. M. (2006, October 16). Buildings shake, power fails in Hawaii earthquake. *USA Today.*

Westervelt, W. D. (1987). *Myths and legends of Hawaii.* Honolulu: Mutual Publishing Company.

White, P. (2012). Darwin, Concepción, and the geological sublime. *Science in Context 25* (1), 49–71.

Williams, H. (1976). *The ancient volcanoes of Oregon.* Eugene, OR: University of Oregon Press.

Williams, S., & Montaigne, F. (2001). *Surviving Galeras.* Boston: Houghton Mifflin Company.

Wilson, S. D. (1967). Landslides in the City of Anchorage. In F. J. Wood (Ed.), *The Prince William Sound, Alaska, earthquake of 1964 and aftershocks, volume IIA* (pp. 253–297). United States Coast and Geodetic Survey. Washington, DC: Government Printing Office.

Winchester, S. (2003). *Krakatoa.* New York: HarperCollins Publishers.

Wolfe, E. W., & Hoblitt, R. P. (1995). Overview of the eruptions. In C. G. Newhall, & R. S. Punongbayan (Eds.), *Fire and mud: Eruptions and lahars of Mount Pinatubo, Philippines.* Quezon City and Seattle: Philippine Institute of Volcanology and Seismology and University of Washington Press.

Wood, C. A., & Kienle, J. (1992). *Volcanoes of North America, United States and Canada.* Cambridge: Cambridge University Press.

World Organization of Volcano Observatories [website]. Retrieved November 5, 2014, from http://www.wovo.org/homepage-wovo.org/

Wright, T. L. (1997, March 21). Hawaiian Volcano Observatory. Volcano Watch. *Thomas Jaggar, HVO's founder.* Retrieved January 15, 2014, from http://hvo.wr.usgs.gov /volcanowatch/archive/1997/97_03_21.html

Yousafzai, G. (2013). Iran earthquake news: Tehran lowers death toll, Pakistan bears brunt. *Huffington Post.* Retrieved November 5, 2014, from http://www.huffingtonpost .com/2013/04/16/iran-earthquake-news-pakistan-death-toll_n_3092563.html

Zeilinga de Boer, J., & Sanders, D. T. (2005). *Earthquakes in human history.* Princeton, NJ: Princeton University Press.

Index

Note: **Bold** page numbers indicate the location of main entries.

About the Author

Bethany D. Rinard Hinga, Ph.D., is Associate Dean for Academic Affairs at Morningside College in Sioux City, Iowa. Prior to this appointment, Dr. Hinga was Director of Assessment at the University of Nebraska at Kearney, and Associate Professor of Geosciences at Tarleton State University in Stephenville, Texas. Dr. Hinga holds a Ph.D. in geophysics from Southern Methodist University.